Individual Behavior

Under the Editorship of GARDNER MURPHY

Individual Behavior

A PERCEPTUAL APPROACH TO BEHAVIOR

REVISED EDITION

ARTHUR W. COMBS
University of Florida
Gainesville, Florida

DONALD SNYGG
State University of New York
Teachers College
Oswego, New York

HARPER & ROW, PUBLISHERS

New York, Evanston, and London

For information address Harper & Row, Publishers, Incorporated
49 East 33rd Street, New York 16, N. Y.

M-P

The Library of Congress catalog entry for this book appears at the end of the text.

CONTENTS

FOREWORD

THE perceptual approach to behavior described in this book was first stated by Donald Snygg and the present author in an earlier edition published in 1949. The point of view expressed in that volume seemed so novel at the time that it was felt appropriate to title the book, *Individual Behavior: A New Frame of Reference for Psychology.* Time, however, does not stand still and what was new but a few years ago has become widely accepted and practiced today. Now, ten years later, there still seems little reason to change the basic outline of the perceptual point of view stated earlier, but it can hardly be called "new" any longer. The point of view just emerging at the time of the first edition has come of age as one of the most virile and exciting movements in current psychology.

The foreword to the first edition stated the purpose of the book as one of giving expression to what looked like the beginning of an inevitable trend in understanding human behavior. Subsequent events seem to have amply corroborated that observation. In the last few years new developments in perceptual psychology have occurred with such rapidity that, like Alice in Wonderland, one must run as fast as he can just to keep up. Almost every psychological journal reports new and intriguing studies bearing upon some aspect of the personal frame of reference. Much of this research has supported the perceptual approach and that, of course, has been gratifying. Some errors and inconsistencies have been uncovered, and that has been challenging and helpful. Old concepts have been refined and expanded and some new concepts have been developed. All this activity has proved so fruitful as to make necessary the extension and development of the perceptual approach to behavior presented in this new edition.

The close collaboration Dr. Snygg and I enjoyed in writing the first edition when we lived but a few miles from each other was an intensely exciting and rewarding experience for each of us. We had hoped to repeat this team arrangement when a new edition was called for, but, unhappily, this was not to be. The great distance between us occasioned by my move to Florida and the pressure of other duties upon Dr. Snygg made it necessary for him to withdraw from this project. As a consequence I have written this volume alone. Dr. Snygg's influence, however, will still be discerned in this volume in much of the material carried over from the previous book. His influence may be observed too, in many of my own contributions, I am sure, for the stimulation and growth afforded by the intensive collaboration with such a man, I find, is a continuous, developing thing. I count that period of our former partnership as one of the most truly creative experiences of my life. I am also indebted to him for his critical reading of several of the early chapters of this edition. Although I have worked alone this time, therefore, I believe it is fitting that this edition of *Individual Behavior* should carry the names of both its original authors since the basic development of the perceptual frame of reference was, and still is, our joint contribution. As the author of this edition, however, the responsibility for whatever errors it contains must be laid at my door.

I have often been asked by students, "Where did these ideas come from?" This is always a difficult question, for who can ever be sure of the origins of thought? It is even probable that there can be no "new" ideas in human behavior; only new ways of looking at what has always been. While the first edition was still in press, I remember discovering other authors whom I had never read before and finding they had written many of the same ideas, sometimes even in identical words! There seem to be great trends in human thought and when the time is ripe "new" ideas occur to numbers of people in widely separated places by a kind of psychological osmosis from the very times in which they live. I believe many of the ideas in this book are of this character. Others can be more specifically traced to particular authors or experiments in clear figure in my perceptual field. No matter how carefully he tries, however, the developer of a frame of reference, will seldom be aware of all the influences acting upon him to determine his ways of thinking and no bibliography can ever include more than a small fraction of those who have contributed to the formation of the ideas contained within it.

Since a frame of reference is a way of looking at events it can be applied to the interpretation of all research within its scope including that which may have been originally designed from a different point of view. Many of the studies I have included in the documentation of this volume were first designed in the more traditional frame of reference of objective psychology. I am especially grateful, however, to those writers and researchers who have honored this point of view by studies designed to test its basic premises. It is largely because of their productivity that this book has been made necessary. Indeed, the number of authors who should be recognized as contributing to these views is so great that in order to avoid filling these pages with too many distracting footnotes and hundreds of names, I have included a separate Reference Index for documentation. In this index the reader will find listed, page by page, reference to those authors whose work is relevant to the topics under discussion.

For their special contributions to the preparation of this manuscript my particular thanks and appreciation are extended to the following:

To Mrs. Marion Maines and Mrs. Virginia Brannan, my successive secretaries, for cheerful and efficient secretarial service far beyond the call of duty,

To my very good friends, Ted Landsman and Daniel Soper, for critical reading of the entire manuscript and innumerable helpful suggestions,

To my wife, Mildred, and my daughter, Carol, for hours of labor on the difficult task of checking the manuscript, the bibliography, and the production of the figures.

To the hundreds of students who have explored these concepts with me in the past ten years I owe a deeper debt than I can say. Their enthusiastic response to this frame of reference has been a continual inspiration, while their doubts, frustrations and criticisms have been challenging and stimulating beyond measure. In a very real sense, this book is as much their contribution as mine.

A book, no matter how disciplined and objective its author, can never escape being an intensely human and personal document. So it is with this one. This edition of *Individual Behavior* represents the most inclusive, consistent, and useful way of understanding behavior of which I am currently capable. As psychologist, teacher, counselor, researcher, and human being, both professionally and personally, I have been engaged for as long as I can remember in a search for more adequate understandings of the nature of man and his behavior. This book is the product of that quest. It is offered here in the hope that it may prove equally helpful to others engaged in a similar search.

ARTHUR W. COMBS

June 14, 1958

PART I

The Perceptual Frame of Reference

CHAPTER 1

The Challenge to Psychology

WITH the explosion of the first atomic bomb at Alamogordo in 1945 man embarked upon a new era—the era of the social sciences. The magnificent achievement of our physical scientists in setting free the sources of energy in the atom has given man, for the first time in his long struggle to wrest a living from his environment, the promise of almost unlimited control over his physical world. At long last he has at his command sufficient power and know-how to feed, clothe, and house the entire world. Despite this knowledge, however, millions of people are starving and millions more are ill clothed and ill housed. The greatest problems of our time are no longer the problems of production and control of "things" but of communication and coöperation among people. Having won control over our physical world, we find ourselves confronted with a new problem, the problem of how to control ourselves!

It is not, after all, atomic bombs we fear, but the people who might use them. We have achieved control of "things" only to find ourselves faced with the equally vital problem of learning to live with one another. The explosion of the atomic bomb gave dramatic emphasis to problems that have existed for centuries but became critical in our time because of two great trends: (1) the ever-increasing interdependence of people in modern society, and (2) the tremendous increase of power in the hands of individuals.

We are often impressed with the competitive features of our society and like to think of ourselves as essentially a competitive people. Yet the fact of the matter is that we live in the most coöperative, interdependent society the world has ever known! We are thoroughly and completely dependent upon the good will and coöperation of millions of our fellow men, from the engineer who keeps the electric turbines running through the night to the modern missile expert on whom we depend to defend us in time of war. We are equally dependent upon the less romantic occupations. We need garbage men to keep our cities livable, laborers to dig our pipelines, and stevedores to load and unload our ships. There is perhaps no better example of this interdependence than the modern supermarket. Behind the gleaming displays stand veritable armies of people who have coöperated in one form or another to bring the displayed products together for our use.

Our society is so complex and interrelated that few of us could live more than a very short time apart from his fellows. Whether we like it or not, we are thoroughly dependent upon the good will of others. Even our great industries, often referred to as examples of free competition, on closer analysis turn out to be monuments of human coöperation. We are likely to forget that the great contribution of Henry Ford to modern industry was the development of the assembly line, a highly organized method of getting people to work together in the manufacture of a product. Our great "competitive" industries are, themselves, remarkable examples of coöperative endeavor.

Accompanying this growth of interdependence has been a vast increase in the power available to each of us. The great industrial and scientific advances of the last century have contributed to make individuals more important than ever. The power of the "common" man for good or evil has been immensely increased. Any citizen in our society has hundreds of horsepower at his disposal at the nearest light switch. He can purchase firearms at his hardware store. When he sits behind the wheel of his car he has a fearful projectile at his command—more than a ton of metal capable of propulsion at speeds exceeding a mile a minute. Properly handled, his car is a "pleasure car" for himself and his friends. Improperly handled, it becomes a juggernaut wreaking terrible death and destruction. We would not dare to drive a car, if we could not count on others to stay on their own side of the road and obey the rules of the highway. The welfare and safety of each of us rest upon the coöperation and understanding of our fellow citizens. In an interdependent society there can be no unimportant people!

Our society has become so complex and its people so interdependent that the failure of one individual among thousands can disrupt the delicate balance of organization to such an extent that millions may suffer. The behavior of an individual is no longer the concern only of his own little group. It concerns all of us. To deal adequately with the problems of human relationships we need to understand, as never before, the whys and wherefores of human behavior. Time presses upon us and we need to seek ever more adequate ways of viewing behavior if we are to meet the challenge of human destiny. To live effectively in our modern world we need to gain the very best understandings we can achieve concerning the nature of man and of his behavior.

People can behave only in terms of what seems to them to be so. How we attempt to solve the great human problems of our time depends upon the ideas we hold about what people are like and why they behave as they do. If I believe a man is honest, I will trust him. If I believe he is dishonest, I will take steps to protect myself against him. How I behave toward him and how he behaves toward me will be a direct result of what each of us believes the other is like. In a broader sense, how we deal with our great human problems in industrial relations, in our homes, in our schools, in our communities, even in our diplomatic negotiations with other countries, will depend upon the ideas we hold about the nature of man and why he behaves as he does. Our success or failure in dealing with the problems before us will depend upon the adequacy of our understanding. It is the knowledge to make our understanding adequate which the modern science of psychology attempts to provide.

Psychology—The Science of Behavior

People have always been interested in the problems of human behavior. In a sense, all of us deal with human behavior every day of our lives. The salesman, the teacher, and the business administrator are constantly observing the activities of other people and adjusting their own behavior accordingly. A science, however, cannot be built upon this kind of casual observation. What makes a science is the careful, disciplined approach taken to the solving of problems—whether it be the behavior of airplane wings under stress, of chemicals in solution, of atoms in an atomic pile, of winds in a hurricane, or of people behaving, and misbehaving, with each other. Careful, controlled observation is the essence of all science—whether it concerns the physical sciences like physics, chemistry, and mathematics, or the social sciences like sociology, anthropology, and psychology.

Science is not static and unchanging, however. Like everything else we know, science is continually growing and progressing. Things are seen one way today, and tomorrow someone discovers a new and better way to look at the same problem. In the eternal search for knowledge science must continually explore and test its concepts. It does this in two major ways: (1) the accumulation of data through observation, and (2) the organization of data into frames of reference, theories, or systems which make understanding useful and meaningful.

It is through the development of theories and frames of reference that psychology seeks to provide adequate understanding of people and their behavior as the basis for the solution of the great human problems of our time. This book is but one attempt to organize the data of psychology into a useful and effective frame of reference. Before this point of view is more closely investigated, however, it will pay us to examine more closely some facets of the relationship between observation and theory.

THE ACCUMULATION OF DATA FROM OBSERVATIONS

Every science is based upon the careful accumulation of data from observations about the behavior of its subject matter. In the 70-odd years of its existence as a scientific discipline psychology has amassed thousands upon thousands of observations about people and their behavior. People have been observed in all kinds of situations and with varying degrees of exactness. We have compiled a vast literature including observations of children and adults, of males and females; of people at work and at play, in the home, at school, in industry, or in the community. Nothing has been too private or too sacred to be left out in this search. Psychologists have invaded every aspect of life to observe human behavior and thus further our understanding of people. Some observers have even penetrated the delivery room to observe the behavior of babies at the moment of birth. Others have made observations of persons under torture in the concentration camps of the last war. We have recorded observations of the sick and the well, the successful and the failures, the rich and the poor. Psychological journals are bulging with observations of human behavior.

Psychologists' observations of people and the ways in which they behave, have been made with every degree of control, ranging from informal observations of a group of children in a playground to precise measurements of the conditioned eye blink. The majority of data about behavior are of a normative or objective character. That is, they are observations made from the point of view of an outsider, someone other than the behaver himself. These observations permit us to state that, given a particular situation, "the chances are" that people will act thus or so. Such observations are helpful to us when we are dealing with masses of people. They make it possible for us to predict the probable number of persons who will do some particular thing we have in mind. By means of certain kinds of tests (which are simply devices for making controlled observations), for example, we can predict the probable number of college freshmen who will make it through to graduation, or the probability that a particular soldier may become a good pilot.

Other psychologists have attempted to make more personal observations of people. They are not content with knowing what a group of people *may* do. They hope to understand what a particular individual *will* do. As a consequence they have directed their observations to the behavior of individuals in an attempt to discover the nature of personality and the sources and forms of human uniqueness. Whatever the purpose behind the observations, however, psychology is forever seeking to accumulate new observations about human behavior, wherever it occurs. Indeed, we have almost more data than we know what to do with. Our problem now is to discover what it all means. For this we need the second great function of science: the organization of data into meaningful frames of reference.

THEORIES AND FRAMES OF REFERENCE

A frame of reference, or a theory, is nothing more than an organization of data, or a way of looking at data, to make them meaningful. Facts, by themselves, have little meaning or value. It is only when facts are combined into some sort of framework, that they become useful to understand or deal with problems. The temperatures, wind directions, and barometric pressures reported by observers all over the country to a weather bureau have little meaning as isolated facts. They do not have much more meaning even when we see them all together plotted on a large map of the United States. It is only when we bring all these data into a meaningful relationship to one another by a theory of weather changes, that they come alive for us, i.e., that they serve as a basis to predict the weather conditions for the next 24 hours. All science is continually engaged in the search for new and more adequate frames of reference, or theories, by which accumulated data make the most effective and efficient sense.

A fact is not an independent thing that we can memorize, depend upon, and know will always be true. When we feel our railroad coach moving it may be because we are leaving the station, but it may be because we are watching a moving train on the next track. What one believes to be true will depend upon the way in which observations are organized and upon the point from which the observer makes them. In the same way ". . . a bomb dropped from an airplane over a European city is seen by the aviator to fall in a straight line, by an anti-aircraft gunner to describe a parabola, by a North Polar observer to rush counterclockwise, by a Martian to perform a spiral movement about the sun, while to an observer on Sirius it would seem to follow a curved path through the heavens . . ." (Diehl). What seems to us to be true or a fact depends upon the frame of reference from which we make our observations. Theories are attempts to bring order and meaning to observation by providing a frame of reference for making observations; they give to facts the meanings which make them useful.

Theories vary with the purpose of the observer. There are almost unlimited numbers of ways in which facts can be organized or looked at. What is more, each of these ways may be quite useful and acceptable, depending upon the needs for understanding we have at a given time. The same data looked at in different ways lend themselves to quite different kinds of orientations. One might look at the data concerning the number and age of automobiles in the state of Montana, for example, from a number of different points of view. One could interpret these data in terms of the problem of safety on the highway, the probable replacements the auto companies need to turn out next year, the kind and numbers of roads needed in a particular area, the number of quarts of oil required for the following year, or the probable number of seat covers to be sold in the state within the next six months.

As Angyal suggests: "The utility of a theory consists essentially in that it serves as a guide, as a point of reference, for empirical studies, which otherwise are likely to result in an utterly chaotic and incoherent mass of data. The utility of a good theory is twofold: it allows us to question nature intelligently and offers a background for the interpretation of empirical data." Theories provide an interpretation of what is. This makes it possible for us to ask new questions leading to further extension of our knowledge. No theory is, of course, ever "right." Good theory is only the best approximation of meaning we can make in our time. Every theorist must recognize the tenuousness of his conceptions and look forward to the certainty that his theory will one day be superseded by some new and more inclusive, or more satisfying explanation of events.

Theories vary also as to the amount of data they attempt to include. Some theories refer to fairly minute aspects of a major problem, others attempt to include great masses of data covering a broad field of understanding. Generally speaking, the more inclusive the frame of reference, the more useful the theory becomes. Whatever problem we face, the most useful frame of reference will be one that most adequately helps us understand and use all of the facts before us.

Let us investigate this principle by examining Fig. 1. As man reached a point in his development where it became necessary for him to deal with numbers of things, represented in Fig. 1 by the marks between *A* and *B*, he developed a number system, represented by the triangle *ABC*. The development of this number system made it possible for him to deal with his environment more effectively than he could before and to understand many new concepts. In time, however, this number system became inadequate as new facts were discovered and new needs arose, represented in Fig. 1 by the marks between *B* and *D*. New facts could not be dealt with in the old number system and out of this need a new frame of reference called algebra was developed, represented by the triangle *ADE*. The new frame of reference did not deny what had gone before but made it possible to deal with matters never before approachable. But even this frame of reference could not suffice forever and soon man's insatiable striving made it necessary to deal with still more new facts and problems, represented in Fig. 1 by the marks between *D* and *F*. This, in turn, led to the development of still another frame of reference, known to mathematicians as calculus, represented by the triangle *AFG*. This relationship of facts and frames of reference is characteristic of the progress of science. Through the continual search for facts and for frames of reference in which these facts can be comprehended the frontiers of knowledge are pushed forward.

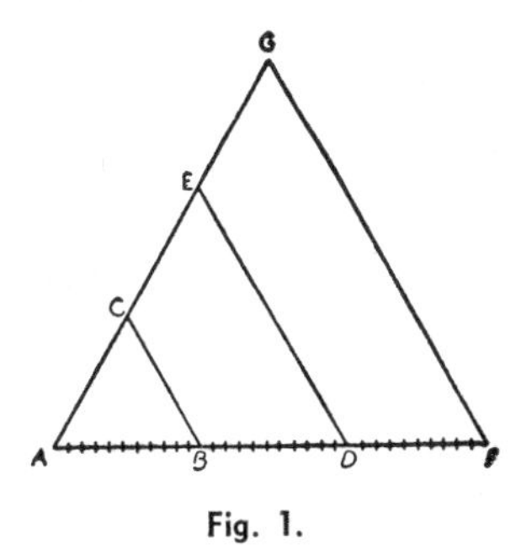

Fig. 1.

All sciences are constantly engaged in this never ending search for better explanations of the largest possible number of facts. Often the best explanations are the simplest as well. This is often called the principle of parsimony. Indeed, one might well say that the goal of science is the reduction of the largest possible amounts of data to the simplest possible explanations. Perhaps the best example of this search for ultimate simplicity in our time is to be found in Einstein's comprehensive theory of matter expressed in the simple formula $E = mc^2$. Here a vast subject is reduced to an ultimate of simplicity.

Frames of Reference of Psychology

Psychology, too, has its frames of reference and its theories of behavior. Observations about human behavior made over the years have been organized in a multitude of ways, depending upon the problems the psychologists were trying to understand. These attempts at understanding range from two broad general approaches, called frames of reference, to a great number of smaller theories developed for dealing with more limited aspects of behavior.

The older of the two great frames of reference in psychology we might call the "external," or "objective," approach. In this frame of reference, behavior is examined from an outside observer's point of view. The psychologist observes his subjects through tests, laboratory experiments, and many other means in order to determine just what they will be likely to do in a given situation. As he places his subjects in one situation or another and observes their behavior change, he seeks to explain their behavior in terms of the situations to which they react. In this way the causes of behavior are assigned, with one modification or another, primarily to the environments in which the subjects are reacting. It has been observed, for example, that delinquents very frequently come from broken homes, from association with bad companions, from poverty-stricken homes, or from homes with immoral parents. These factors are, therefore, regarded as environmental influences producing delinquent behavior. Making their observations in this frame of reference, psychologists describe behavior in terms of the environmental stimuli which seem, to an outside observer, to be acting upon and producing the behavior of the individual. This has sometimes been called *S-R* psychology because it attempts to explain behavior, or the response (*R*) of the subject, in terms of the stimulus (S) to which he appears to be reacting.

This frame of reference has aided psychology tremendously, and during the three-quarters of a century of psychology as an experimental science, psychologists have amassed a huge amount of data about the circumstances under which different types of behavior occur. As a result of these studies progress has been made in the prediction of normative behavior, i.e., of what the "average," "normal," or "typical" individual, or even the "typical 10-year-old," may do under a given set of circumstances.

Such predictions are useful in fields like advertising, politics, or business administration, all of which are concerned with behavior of masses, and in which the prediction of what particular individuals will do is seldom necessary. However, in the great majority of situations this understanding of normative behavior is not enough. Most of us must deal with individuals; thus, it is usually necessary to understand the behavior of individuals with greater accuracy than normative methods allow.

To deal with the problems of individual behavior another frame of reference has emerged more recently, called the "personal," or the "perceptual," or the "phenomenological" approach to psychology. This approach seeks to understand the behavior of the individual from *his own* point of view. It attempts to observe people, not as they seem to outsiders, but as they seem to themselves. People do not behave solely because of the external forces to which they are exposed. People behave as they do in consequence of how things seem to them. We run very hard from the danger we *think* is there and ignore the danger we do not know exists. Behavior in this frame of reference is seen as a problem of human perception. *This perceptual view of behavior is the frame of reference of this book.*

Within these two great frames of reference for psychology, the external and the perceptual, are many more specific theories. Some of these are devised in the external frame of reference and some have been developed in the perceptual view. Some of them are restricted to a very small segment of the whole problem of behavior. Others are general attempts to organize large accumulations of data into meaningful explanations of problems of human relationships. Like any other science, psychology can be explored in many ways and on many different levels.

Theory Level and Application

There is nothing sacred about theory. Theory in any field of endeavor is nothing more than a systematic explanation of events useful to the purposes one has in view. Theory which holds for one frame of reference or one problem may be totally inadequate, even misleading, in another. Theory can be constructed on many levels and for many different purposes, but its maximum efficiency is reached only on the levels and purposes for which it is designed. To examine this question of theory level let us draw an analogy with physical science as illustrated in the left side of Fig. 2.

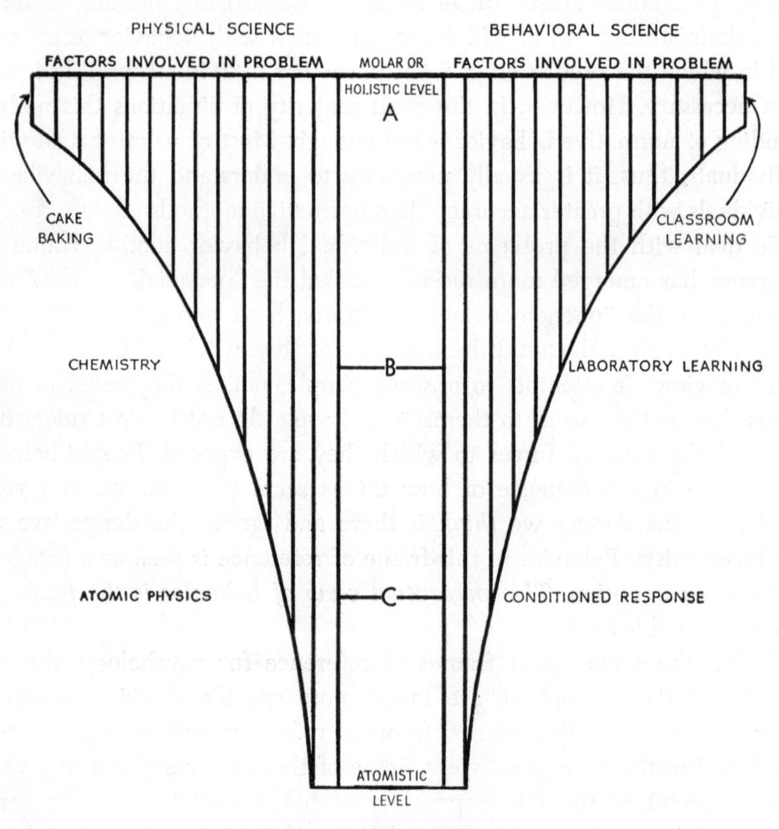

Fig. 2. Levels of Theory Construction.

We might think of all data about any subject as spread along a continuum from the molar or holistic level, where we are concerned with the totality of a problem, to the atomic level, where we are primarily concerned with minute aspects of events (the vertical axis of Fig. 2). On any level along this continuum we may construct theory which will be helpful in explaining the matters we need to deal with at that level. Beginning at the bottom of Fig. 2, atomic theory, for example, is useful in dealing with problems of the atom. At that level (*C*) and for those purposes, it is relevant and essential. On another level (*B*) theories of organic and inorganic chemistry are useful and pertinent for the pharmacist when he makes up a doctor's prescription. He may know little or nothing about atomic theory, however, and he is able to carry on his job quite effectively without this knowledge. This is not to imply that atomic theory does not hold for the chemicals with which he deals. Indeed, it does, but the pharmacist does not need to know atomic theory to carry on his profession adequately. On still another level, the molar level, colleges of home economics have developed theories of cake baking sometimes quite without reference to chemical or atomic physics. Cakes can be baked with flour, water, sugar, and other ingredients by people who know nothing at all of the chemical composition of the ingredients. While it is true that chemical and atomic theory is at work in the batter along with the hands of the cook, the cook does not need to guide her behavior by them, or even to know chemical and atomic theory exist. This is as it should be. Society needs its atomic physicists to control the atom, but most of us would prefer that our cakes be baked by cooks!

This relationship of utility to level is also true of behavioral theory. The theory of behavior most useful for one's purposes depends upon the number of variables one attempts to control in studying a process. Looking at the right hand side of Fig. 2, for example, theory may be constructed in order to understand what happens to children as they are learning in a classroom (the molar level). To do this it is necessary to deal with people as they are and with a large number of factors affecting behavior left quite uncontrolled. Nevertheless, it is possible to construct effective theories which are extremely helpful for our purposes. This is the kind of study many educators carry on in the classroom to discover better methods to induce learning. These educators seek to understand people just as they are in the situations in which they must deal with them.

Such studies, however, make some people very uncomfortable. Too many variables remain uncontrolled! Accordingly, one may seek to study learning on a level wherein more of the variables are controlled. One can, for instance, study learning in the laboratory instead of in the classroom, where theories of learning can be developed from experiments using tachistoscopic exposures (level *B*). In the laboratory one can go further and control the material being learned by removing meaning from it, as in the use of nonsense syllables. Other factors, too, can be controlled, e.g., the circumstances and the time the subject is exposed to the material, or the surroundings in which the experiments take place. In this way one can find new theories of learning applicable to the more "pure" situations constructed under such laboratory conditions. It is possible to go even further in the elimination of variables and to study a single stimulus-response unit, as Pavlov did in his experiments with dogs (level *C*). Here, too, it will be feasible to construct learning theories applicable to the kind of situations studied. Unfortunately, when learning is examined under these restricted conditions the subject of study is no longer people but an isolated process. Molar approaches cannot answer atomic questions and atomic approaches are far too narrow to provide practical solutions to molar problems.

Theory on any level is true and helpful for its purposes, but it hardly suffices at other levels. Any theory of behavior may be devastatingly criticized by the simple expedient of examining it at a level different from the level at which it was devised. Failure to realize this relationship of theory to level sometimes causes serious breakdowns of communication among scientists. To the laboratory psychologist, for example, the failure of the applied psychologist to control all the variables in his study of problems may seem like a shocking disregard for the rigorous discipline of science. In turn, the applied psychologist may regard his laboratory colleague's narrower interests with impatience and irritation over what seems a callous disregard for "the really important matters." Theories are not "right" or "wrong"; they are merely more or less adequate for the problems they were designed to deal with.

The great human problems of our time press upon us and we need the best possible understanding we can acquire about the nature of man and his behavior. In adopting any frame of reference or any theory of human behavior, however, we need to be keenly aware that all such theories are always only an approximation of the true nature of events. Sooner or later, the best of theories is likely to be superseded by something a little better, a little more accurate, a little more comprehensive, or simpler, or more useful for accomplishing our major purposes. This should not dismay us. Rather, it should give us courage to make the very best attempt we can to achieve the best approximations to the truth of which we are capable in our generation.

The remainder of this book represents an attempt to set forth a broad and inclusive personal frame of reference for the understanding of human behavior. This frame of reference may be applied to any level of psychological exploration, but in this book it has been applied with special reference to the aspects of individual behavior which are most essential for the solution of the immediate problems of our time. It includes the thinking and work of thousands of psychologists and social scientists interpreted in the frame of reference I have found most adequate to bring order and organization to the great quantity of data psychology has collected about human nature. It is presented here in the hope it may prove as useful and helpful to others as it has to me.

CHAPTER 2

The Perceptual View of Behavior

HUMAN behavior may be observed from at least two very broad frames of reference: from the point of view of an outsider, or from the point of view of the behaver himself. Looking at behavior in the first way we can observe the behavior of others and the situations in which such behavior occurs. It is then possible to attempt the explanation of behavior in terms of the interaction of the individual and the situations in which we have seen him operating. This is the "objective," or "external," frame of reference. The second approach seeks to understand behavior by making its observations from the point of view of the behaver himself. It attempts to understand the behavior of the individual in terms of how things "seem" to him. This frame of reference has been called the "perceptual," "personal," or "phenomenological" frame of reference and is the point of view of this book.

The Perceptual View of Behavior

In the personal, or perceptual, frame of reference we attempt to observe behavior from the point of view of the individual himself. As a matter of fact, that is what almost all people, professional psychologists or laymen, do as soon as they are confronted with the task of dealing with the behavior of an individual. "What does he want?"—"What is he thinking?"—"How does he feel about this?" are some of the questions they ask as they try to put themselves in his place to understand and anticipate his behavior. The clinical psychologist may have carried out research concerning the relation between juvenile delinquency and objective factors such as family income, the parents' age, the number of brothers and sisters, and the percentage of home ownership in the district; but when he is actually dealing with a delinquent boy, he is almost certain to ask "What does he think of himself?" and

"What does he think of his parents?" and otherwise attempt to see the situation from the point of view of the boy. Even the psychologist in the animal laboratory finds himself thinking "That rat is hungry" or "This rat is afraid." We take it as a matter of course that people's ideas, emotions, and opinions have an effect upon their behavior, and we are consequently alert and sensitive to them.

People do not behave according to the facts as *others* see them. They behave according to the facts as *they* see them. What governs behavior from the point of view of the individual himself are his unique perceptions of himself and the world in which he lives, the meanings things have for him. Recently, I heard a kindergarten child try to tell his teacher how pretty a little girl looked in her brand-new party dress. "She was pretty as . . . , pretty as . . . , pretty as a mother!" said the little fellow searching his mind for the prettiest thing he could think of. Now the fact of the matter is, from the outside observer's point of view, this child's mother could only be described as a very homely woman! To this little boy, however, his mother is the epitome of beauty and the criterion by which loveliness is to be judged. How this mother looks to other people is largely irrelevant information in trying to understand this child and his relationship to his mother.

Disregarding, for the moment, the objective facts about behavior some of us have learned, let each one of us look at his own behavior as we actually see it at the moment we are behaving. At once, we find lawfulness and determinism. From the point of view of the behaver himself behavior is caused. It is purposeful. It always has a reason. Sometimes the reasons are vague and confused, in which case his behavior is equally vague and uncertain; sometimes the meanings are extremely clear and definite. But everything we do seems reasonable and necessary at the time we are doing it. When we look at other people from an external, objective point of view, their behavior may seem irrational because we do not experience things as they do. Even our own behavior may, in retrospect, seem to have been silly or ineffective. But at the instant of behaving, each person's actions seem to him to be the best and most effective acts he can perform under the circumstances. If, at that instant, he knew how to behave more effectively, he would do so.

From the point of view of an observer who knows the location of an exit, the behavior of a fire victim rushing back again and again to a jammed door is completely unreasonable. From the point of view of the victim in those circumstances, it is the most reasonable thing he can do because the door is the closest approximation to an exit he can find. However capricious, irrelevant, and irrational his behavior may appear to an outsider, from his point of view *at that instant*, his behavior is purposeful, relevant, and pertinent to the situation *as he understands it.* How it appears to others has no bearing upon the causes of his behavior. The important thing is how it seems to the person himself. These personal meanings which govern behavior the psychologist calls perceptions. It is the fundamental thesis of this book that all behavior is a function of the individual's perceptions. In the remainder of this chapter, let us examine the fundamental premises upon which this point of view depends.

All Behavior Is Lawful

It is a necessary assumption of any science that its subject matter is regular and lawful. If this assumption could not be made, there could, of course, be no science. It is the purpose of science to discover the laws of events, but if the events with which the science deals are totally capricious and without meaning, there can obviously be no science at all. Like all science, then, we begin our study of behavior with the assumption that it is lawful and meaningful. Beginning with this assumption psychology may hope to discover the laws of behavior through careful observation and interpretation.

The Perceptual Field Determines Behavior

Behavior, we have assumed above, is lawful. To the behaver himself behavior always seems relevant, purposeful, and caused. But, if the behavior is caused, where are the causes? To the individual the causes of his behavior appear to be in the world around him and in his relation to it. As he experiences it, he eats, not because of stomach contractions, or a lowering of the sugar content of his blood, or because of habit, but because he is hungry, or because he does not wish to disappoint his wife, or just because he *feels* like eating. In any case, it seems to him that his behavior is a reasonable and necessary result of his present situation.

This situation is, of course, not the physical situation or the objective situation but the *perceived* situation, the situation as it appears to the behaver. An "hereditary" Democrat (or Republican) may believe that Republicans (or Democrats) are customarily wrong-headed, misguided, and—to some degree—enemies of society. If he believes so, he will act and vote accordingly. He will not doubt the validity of his own views and he will think that he is basing his behavior upon objective facts. It should be clear, however, to other people that his behavior is determined, not by the objective field, but by a personal, individual way of perceiving which is not identical to that of any other individual.

THE "FIELD" CONCEPT

Modern science has long since discovered that many matters cannot be understood solely in terms of the "things" with which it deals. Many of the complex events we hope to understand and predict can only be dealt with through an understanding of *interrelationships*. Even when the precise nature of these interrelationships is not known, it may still be possible to use them effectively. To deal with such interrelationships modern science has invented the very useful concept of a "field." When something occurs at one point in space apparently because something else happened at another point with no visible means by which the "cause" can be related to the "effect," the scientist often says the two events are connected in a field. This field serves as a kind of bridge between cause and effect by which the scientist can deal with a problem even though he may not be clearly aware of all intervening aspects. No one has ever seen electricity, for example, nor are we entirely certain just what it is or exactly how it works. In spite of this lack of exact knowledge, however, we are able to deal with the phenomenon by assuming the existence of an electric field. Using this field, scientists and engineers have been able to predict and control electric currents and to build devices using its properties.

A field, it should be recognized, is an inference. Whether or not it really exists in any tangible fashion, we do not know. Although no one knows exactly how this field is composed, or what it is that makes it operate, nevertheless, the concept is useful as it makes it possible to deal with events that behave predictably even though we may be ignorant of the reasons why or how. That an event can be utilized in a predictable way is sufficient to make it useful for the scientist's purposes. Thus, the field concept has proved tremendously useful to modern science; it has made it possible to by-pass some unsolved problems and to deal effectively with matters about which we do not know all we should like to know. The astronomer uses the concept to predict the orbits of the stars. The atomic physicist finds it helpful in understanding the structure of matter. The embryologist explains the determination of function by referring to the location of cells in a growth field. Psychologists, too, have found the field concept useful for the understanding and predicting of human behavior.

THE PERCEPTUAL FIELD

In this book we shall use the field concept to refer to that more or less fluid organization of meanings existing for every individual at any instant. We call it the perceptual or phenomenal field. *By the perceptual field, we mean the entire universe, including himself, as it is experienced by the individual at the instant of action.* It is each individual's personal and unique field of awareness, the field of perception responsible for his every behavior.

Several years ago a friend of mine was driving a car at dusk along a Western road. A globular mass, about two feet in diameter, suddenly appeared directly in the path of the car. A passenger screamed and grasped the wheel attempting to steer the car around the object. The driver, however, tightened his grip on the wheel and drove directly into the object. The behavior of both the driver and the passenger was determined by his own phenomenal field. The passenger, an Easterner, saw the object in the highway as a boulder and fought desperately to steer the car around it. The driver, a native Westerner, saw it as a tumbleweed and devoted his efforts to keeping his passenger from overturning the car.

In understanding this behavior it is not necessary to know what the object "really" was. Each individual in the car behaved toward it according to its nature in his own perceptual field. What a botanist or a geologist might have known about the object had no effect on the behavior of these travelers as they struggled to get the wheel. The behavior of each was determined, not by the objective facts, but by his own perceptual field. In other words, the factors effective in determining the behavior of an individual are those, and only those, which are experienced by the individual at the time of his behavior. These experiences we call perceptions and the entire field of these perceptions we call the perceptual field.

The concept of complete determination of behavior by the perceptual field is our basic postulate. It may be stated as follows: *All behavior, without exception, is completely determined by, and pertinent to, the perceptual field of the behaving organism.* The perceptual field has also been called the personal field, the private world, the behavioral field, the psychological field, the individual's life space, and the phenomenal field. The last term is derived from a school of philosophy known as phenomenology which holds that reality lies not in the event but in the phenomenon, that is to say, in the individual's experience of the event. It will be recognized that this is essentially the position we have taken—that behavior is a function, not of the external event but of the individual's perception of it. Because it is similar to the early view of the phenomenologists, perceptual psychology is sometimes called phenomenological psychology, and the perceptual field is sometimes referred to as the phenomenal field. In this book we will not use the term "phenomenological" but we shall occasionally use the term "phenomenal field" synonymously with the term "perceptual field,"only because this synonym will serve to avoid repetition.

The Perceptual Field as "Reality"

The perceptual field is the universe of naive experience in which each individual lives, the everyday situation of the self and its surroundings which each person takes to be reality. To each of us the perceptual field of another person contains much error and illusion; it seems an interpretation of reality rather than reality itself; but to each individual, his phenomenal field *is* reality; it is the only reality he can know. This perceptual field is far richer and more meaningful than that of the objective, physical world. We do not live in a world of objects without meaning. On the contrary, we invest the things about us with all sorts of meanings; these meanings are for each of us the reality to which we respond.

The restriction of "reality" to the attenuated field of physics means a complete abandonment of everything that we ordinarily recognize as real. A friend of mine owns a desk at which he writes and on which his friends sit and spill cigarette ashes. An inquiry about the real nature of the desk had the following results:

"It is really cellulose."
"What is that?"
"A molecular combination of carbon, hydrogen, and oxygen."
"What are they?"
"They are made up of protons and electrons."
"What are they?"
"They are really charges of electricity."
"What are they?"

"They are not matter, just waves."
"What are they?"
"Not waves in anything, just waves."
"What are they?"
"All right, waves of nothing!"

In other words, what the desk *really* is depends upon the professional perceptual field of the person who answers the question. From the point of view of chemistry, my friend owns some rather refractory and unusable cellulose; from the standpoint of subatomic physics he owns no matter at all. Neither science says that he has a desk because neither science deals with desks.

No matter what we are told, our own perceptual field will always seem real, substantial, and solid to us. It is the only field and the only reality we can directly experience. It includes all the universe of which we are aware—including not only the physical entities which exist for us but such other entities as justice, injustice, and public opinion. It also includes experiences of love and hate, of fear, anger, and human compassion which do not exist outside the experience of people. So strong is our feeling of reality with respect to our perceptual field that we seldom question it. We accept that how it seems to us must truly be so. When others do not see things as we do, we are quite likely to jump to the conclusion that they must be either stupid or perverse; for what is right and proper seems to us so clear with respect to our own observation that no other conclusion seems warranted.

Our perceptions always have the feeling of reality at the instant of behaving. This may not be true in prospect, or in retrospect. Looking back at what we thought was so last week, we may feel now that our observations at that time were in error. But these are observations after the fact. At the time we acted, it seemed to us that the things we did, the thoughts we had, and the feelings we felt were reasonable, correct, and real. Even the murderer, at the moment he commits his crime, may feel that he is solving his problems in the only way he can under the circumstances. Later, reviewing his action, he may regret his decision and doubt the "reality" of his past thinking. On the other hand, looking forward today to the situation we will be in next week, we may plan very carefully what will be right and proper to do. When the time comes, however, we may behave quite differently because it may "seem" different at that moment. We behave in terms of the immediate meanings existing in our perceptual fields on both occasions.

Characteristics of the Phenomenal Field

A field, as it is understood in modern science, always has at least four properties: stability, fluidity, intensity, and direction. The reader may recall his experiments in his physics or science classes with iron filings and a magnet. When iron filings are scattered upon a piece of paper over a magnet they can be observed to line up in patterns of force about the magnet. That is, the iron filings placed in the electromagnetic field around the magnet respond to the force of the field and fall into patterns that reveal something of the character of the field. From the behavior of these filings it can be observed that the electromagnetic field is stable, that is, it tends to retain its character until some event causes it to change. At the same time, the field is also fluid. It can be changed, for instance, by the introduction of other magnets to the field. The intensity and direction characteristic of the field are revealed by the patterns taken by the iron filings. These same four properties are also characteristic of the phenomenal field although they are expressed in somewhat different fashion.

THE PERCEPTUAL FIELD IS FLUID. The phenomenal field is continually changing, and thus it is sometimes difficult to study. Like the Irishman's pig which ran around so fast that he could not count it, the phenomenal field is sometimes difficult to observe because, even as we attempt to look at it, it changes. It is this fluidity of the field, however, which makes change in behavior possible. Without a degree of fluidity, the individual would be unable to adjust to the changing circumstances in which he must live his life and find need-satisfaction. The capacity for change in the perceptual field also makes learning, reasoning, remembering, forgetting, and creativity possible.

THE PERCEPTUAL FIELD HAS STABILITY. Although the perceptual field is highly fluid it is by no means unorganized; the organization of the field necessarily gives it a degree of stability. To live successfully each of us needs an organized, stable, predictable field. Without some stability of the field we could not live at all. The nature of the organization producing this stability is the major concern of this book.

THE PERCEPTUAL FIELD HAS DIRECTION. In the same physical situation, or in objectively identical situations, the perceptual fields of different individuals will differ. Furthermore, during successive presentations of the same physical situation the perceptual field of even the same person changes. However, although the content and form of organization vary from individual to individual and from time to time, the perceptual field always has direction, i.e., it is always organized and meaningful. Our perceptions are never masses of meaningless and unrelated stimuli.

This organized characteristic of the perceptual field was first studied by the Gestalt psychologists who objected to the orthodox, stimulus-response psychology of their day and pointed out that, surely, human understanding is much more than an addition of unrelated stimuli. When we look at a picture we see much more than spots of paint; our response to a musical composition is much more than hearing a series of notes. The Gestalt psychologists pointed out that perception is always organized into what they termed a "Gestalt," or configuration. What is perceived, they said, is always a "total" and never an isolated event.

The perceptual field of any individual is both much more and much less than the field which is potentially available in the immediate physical environment. It is much more in that it includes many things not physically present. The most detailed perceptual field, however, includes only a very few of the vast (practically infinite) number of objects, details, and meanings which are present, or which might be present, in the fields of other individuals in the same physical situation. For instance, if any of us began to make a close study of the room in which we are at this moment, it is probable that we could spend months, years, or even a lifetime making a series of discoveries about it, even though we may think we are already very familiar with the room. Fig. 3 actually contains all the three-letter words in the English language, but it is extremely unlikely that anyone not actively seeking new details and aspects in Fig. 3 would ever discover even one of them. Having studied Fig. 3 the reader may discover for himself how the entire alphabet is contained in the figure by turning to Fig. 5 on p. 26.

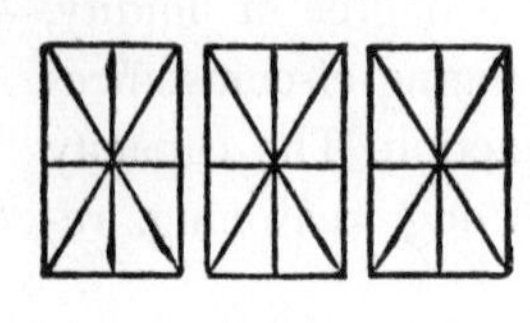

Fig. 3.

At any given time, the field of a given individual is organized with reference to his need and the activity by which he is trying to satisfy his need at the time. The field of a professor playing golf, for instance, is very different from the field of the same professor engaged in teaching a class or in conversation with his wife. In each case, the field is organized around the activity of the moment and the perceptions occur which have bearing upon the professor's immediate problem. If thoughts of the lecture intrude into his golf game or if thoughts of his wife intrude into his lecture, it is only because: (1) the intruding activity has not been brought to a conclusion and, from his point of view, is still in progress; or (2) the intruding activity is more important to the satisfaction of the individual's need than the activity in which he is formally engaged. What is perceived is always a function of the individual's need operating in an organized field.

THE FIGURE-GROUND CHARACTER OF ORGANIZATION. The Gestalt psychologists observed that the meaning of any event was always a result of the relationship of any item to the totality observed. This relationship of the part to the whole they called the figure-ground relationship. The figure-ground relationship is familiar to all psychologists but the accompanying illustration, Fig. 4, will show some of its salient points. If the whole illustration is seen as a candlestick there is relatively little detail. As soon, however, as the observer looks for details in the base of the candlestick, the details in the top fade into ground. To illustrate the above point, the observer will note that the figure always is something. As long as any part of it is figure, it is meaningful. It is either a vase, a candlestick, two faces, or, at least, an undifferentiated object. When the illustration is seen as two faces there is a striking change in the character of the area between the faces as it fades down into ground. When the illustration is seen as a vase or a candlestick the same area emerges into figure, and a previously nonexistent solidity emerges that is striking. Objectively there has been no change, but the perceptual change can have a marked effect on the behavior of the observer. This process of emergence of figure from ground is known as *differentiation* and makes possible change in our perception of events.

Fig. 4.

An example of the figure-ground relationship and its effect upon behavior may be seen in the difference between the field and the behavior of a motorist who is testing his brakes, and between the field and the behavior of another motorist who is stopping his car to avoid an imminent accident. In the first case the figure is rather diffuse and includes some awareness of his tires; consequently, he brings his car to a stop in a way that will not damage the tires. It is almost impossible for a responsible driver to bring his car to the required, abrupt stop under those conditions since, as soon as he feels the wheels slide, he eases

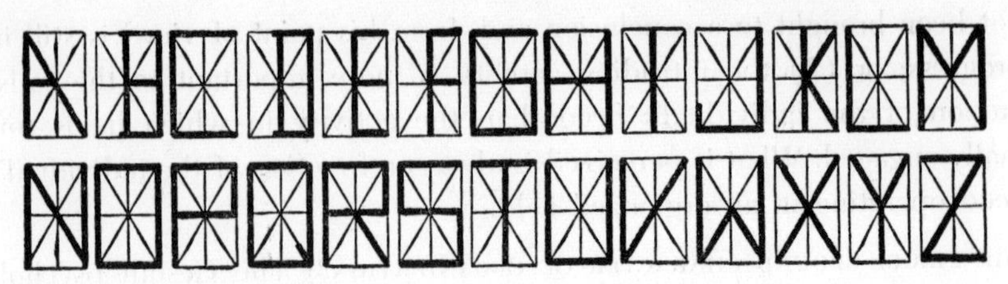

Fig. 5.

up on the brake pedal. In a real emergency, however, the object to be avoided and the need for stopping stand out so sharply that his concern for tires drops into the ground, and the brakes are applied with violence and decision.

The effect of such a narrowing of the figure upon behavior was amusingly illustrated in the case of a young man so intent upon chasing a jack rabbit down the road with his car that he suddenly discovered he had followed the rabbit through a barbed-wire fence and into a pasture. Similar, although perhaps less dangerous, samples of intent response to figure are common in almost everyone's experiences. Perhaps one of the best examples is to be seen in our experience at a movie. Entering the theater we perceive the screen and its content as ground, the aisle and seats as figure. Having found a seat we perceive the screen somewhat more precisely as we make ourselves comfortable. At this stage, we are still aware of our surroundings, of the edge of the screen, even of the screen as a screen. Shortly, however (if the picture is a good one), the images on the screen move into exclusive figure so that we lose practically all awareness of the ground surrounding us, to the extent that we feel so "alone" with the images on the screen that we may cry unabashedly in a manner which we certainly would not had all the strangers around us been clearly in figure.

The use of these illustrations should not mislead the reader into thinking that figure exists only in the visual aspects of the field. It may occur in any sense field or in any combinations of sense fields. In taste perception, for example, the figure-ground relationship can be observed when we attempt to bring into clearer awareness some particular component of a tasty dish whose recipe we are seeking to guess. In connection with the sense of hearing, the relationship may be observed when, lying in bed, we suddenly become aware of a dripping faucet or a rattling window which only a moment ago caused no annoyance to us at all when it existed as part of the ground of our perceptual field.

Anything in the field can become figure, including bodily fatigue, pain, and abstract ideas. As the Gestaltists have pointed out, however, two events may not appear in figure simultaneously. We may perceive Fig. 4 as a candlestick or as faces but not as both at once. How an individual behaves at any moment, however, is always a function of the total perceptual field in existence at that time. The meaning of any event perceived is always a product of the relationship of that figure to the total ground of which it is a part.

The intensity with which events are experienced in the phenomenal field will be a function of differentiation and levels of awareness. Although the perceptual field includes all the universe of which we are aware, we are not aware of all parts with the same degree of clarity at any moment. For instance, we walk through the living room without paying specific attention to the exact location of the lamps and the chairs, but our behavior indicates that we are aware of them. We do not bump into them. We know they are there even though we may be intent upon other matters. Awareness of these objects is at a low level of clarity adequate for the purposes of the moment. If our needs change, however, the same chairs we were only vaguely aware of a moment ago may emerge into very clear figure; for example, if our wives suggest redecorating. Until this moment the reader, if he is sitting down, has probably been aware at only a very low level of his point of contact with whatever it is he is sitting on. Were he not aware that he is firmly in contact with something he would not behave as he does; he would be busily trying to keep himself from falling. The reader may also discover that now that we have drawn his attention to his point of contact, the perception may be in very clear figure. Other low-level-awareness phenomena like breathing, the feel of the tongue in the mouth, or of the toes inside our shoes can also be brought into clearer figure when necessary. This process by which aspects of the perceptual field are brought into clear figure is called differentiation. At any moment perceptions in the field may exist at any and all levels of differentiation from the vaguest to the sharpest.

We have said that behavior is always determined by the nature of the perceptual field at the instant of behaving. It follows that at whatever level of awareness perceptions exist in the field, they will have their effects upon the individual's behavior. When we perceive clearly and sharply, behavior is correspondingly direct and efficient. When we perceive only vaguely, then behavior, too, is likely to be fuzzy and inaccurate. Perceptions at low levels of awareness, it is true, will affect behavior with less precision than perceptions more clearly in figure, but as long as they exist at all in the perceptual field, they must have their expression in behavior. The mass activity elicited by a fly buzzing around the face of an uneasy sleeper is an example. In the sleeper's field the fly functions as a vague, relatively undifferentiated annoyance and his response is made accordingly. When the level of awareness is sharpened and the fly, as source of annoyance, has been clearly perceived, behavior similarly becomes more precise and direct.

It should not be supposed that all meanings existing in the phenomenal field at low levels of awareness can always be called readily into clear figure, or reported to other people. Not at all! Many aspects of experience are destined to remain in ground all our lives. Consequently it may never be possible to bring them into sufficiently clear figure to relate them to others. However, reportable or not, since behavior is always the product of the total field, even vague awarenesses play their part in our behavior. Early in this century Freud noted this effect upon behavior and based a great deal of his theory of psychoanalysis upon what he called the "unconscious." Much of people's behavior, he observed, was motivated by events discernible by him but denied by his patients. He concluded, therefore, that behavior was often controlled by unconscious impulses. This is a point of view similar to the one we have been expressing.

Freud's description of behavior produced from low-level awareness as "unconscious," however, has turned out to be most unfortunate. The terms "conscious" and "unconscious" leave the impression of a clear-cut dichotomy instead of a continuous gradation of awareness from sharp and precise perceptions to vague and indistinct perceptions. The term "unconscious" has also been used by some people as though there were perceptions of which the individual is unaware. They have described the "unconscious" as a kind of "place" (even sometimes, as a kind of dark closet) where one could hide away things one does not want to look at. These are unfortunate aberrations of the perfectly useful idea that behavior may be significantly affected even by perceptions at low levels of awareness. In this book, we shall avoid the use of the terms "conscious" and "unconscious" because of the unfortunate connotations these terms have gathered about them.

DIFFERENTIATION, THE PROCESS OF FIELD CHANGE. Each of us is constantly searching his field for details and meanings which will better enable him to satisfy need. This process involves a continual change in the perceptual field by the constant rise of new characters into figure and the consequent lapse of other characters into ground, in the manner described above. This process, from the point of view of the behaver, is one of increased awareness of details and is, therefore, called differentiation. It is through differentiation that change in the perceptual field and, hence, change in behavior occurs.

An example of differentiation, or change in the field, may be seen in the process of becoming aware of an object. When persons are shown a figure or group of figures for varying lengths of time and asked to reproduce what they see, the first awareness is ordinarily of a vague, relatively undifferentiated whole, which then differentiates in more or less orderly fashion into more detailed parts. Since the properties of a newly emerging object are determined by its relationship to the rest of the field, at this stage it can easily be, and frequently is, distorted and misinterpreted. Illusions, hallucinations, and many cases of mistaken identity, as well as the common errors of proof reading, result. Who has not made errors like the traveler expecting a bridge, who mistakes a billboard for the anticipated span? Who has not been surprised to discover that a sign he thought said one thing on closer examination actually said something quite different?

The factors which appear to determine the nature and extent to which an event is differentiated are the need of the behaver and the opportunities for differentiation that are available. Since the figure is the only aspect of the field of which we are clearly aware, change in the field means change in the figure. The figure may become more precise, more detailed, and more intense, or it may become larger, more vague, and more diffused. On the other hand, the figure may become so large, so vague, and so diffused that it practically merges into ground. This probably does not happen except in deep sleep or unconsciousness, as under ordinary circumstances of daily life the individual is engaged in a continual search for the means of satisfying his needs; this requires a continual emergence of new characters into figure.

In the same way the figure is constantly shifting in size it is also changing in character as new characteristics and entities arise and differentiate from the ground. Since precision of behavior can only result from precision of figure, it is this emergence into figure which is the basic cause of more effective behavior. Change in behavior occurs with differentiation in the perceptual field. Thus, learning, problem solving, remembering, forgetting, and the like are all aspects of the process of differentiation occurring in the individual's phenomenal field.

SYNTHESIS, GENERALIZATION, AND PERCEPTION OF ABSTRACT EVENTS. It is the differentiations an individual is able to make in his perceptual field that determine the nature of his perceptions—both the direct perceptions of concrete events apprehended through our sense organs and the perceptions of complex events understood only through the medium of abstract thought. This broad use of the word "perception" is somewhat of a departure from traditional practice in laboratory psychology and a word of explanation seems in order. Historically, psychologists have used the word perception to refer only to, "a single, unified meaning obtained from sensory processes while a stimulus is present." To describe acts of knowing, understanding, or forming ideas, they have used the words "cognition" or "conception." In this book, however, the word "perception" is used to refer to *any* differentiations the individual is capable of making in his perceptual field whether an objectively observable stimulus is present or not. There seems little need for more than one process to explain these events. Differentiations in the phenomenal field resulting in perceptions of seeing, hearing, smelling, or feeling are precisely the same as those made in conceiving, knowing, or understanding. Although the subject matter varies, the process is the same. The differentiation of an idea or a concept is not basically different from the differentiation of a scent, a sound, or the printed words on a page.

Differentiation, as we have been describing it, seems to correspond to a process of analysis. But, it may be asked, do we not synthesize as well? Do we not also see examples of generalization? Are not synthesis and generalization the opposites of differentiation? To answer these questions, it is necessary to remind ourselves that the perceptual approach to understanding behavior is concerned solely with the problem of how events are experienced by the behaver. What seems like integration, synthesis, or generalization observed from an objective point of view, becomes—observed from the behaver's own frame of reference, simply another form of differentiation. When an individual, for example, perceives that "all these things have this aspect in common," what is occurring is not an "adding up" of separate and discrete perceptions. Rather, the observer has differentiated from his field of perceptions the unifying principle that "all these things have this aspect in common." Thus, what appears on the surface to be integration or synthesis, is—from the behaver's own point of reference—a differentiation of the relationship of events to each other.

Common Perceptions Make Communication Possible

Since the perceptual field cannot be observed directly by any other individual it may appear to the reader that in this frame of reference the causes of behavior are so secret that actual prediction of behavior must be beyond any outsider's power. Indeed, if the perceptual fields of different individuals were completely private, there would be no way of knowing another person's field and the prediction and control of behavior would, of course, be impossible. When I whistle to a dog, call to a friend, or lecture to a class, however, the dog, my friend, and the students, in a large percentage of cases, behave as if the sounds I make in my perceptual field are also present in theirs. In other words, changes in my own field are often accompanied by behavior on the part of others which indicates that a change has also taken place in their phenomenal fields.

It is probable that this relationship arises in the following way: each of us is born into a situation in which certain common characters and objects exist. For example, both the Eskimo and the South African tribesman are born into a world where things will fall if they are dropped, where there is ground under their feet, where there are people around them, where there are forms of precipitation, where there are colors and sounds to be experienced. Even among people as remote from one another as these, there is considerable agreement about the things they experience. There is even more among people in the same culture, who have many more common aspects as potential characters of their perceptual fields and of their individual "realities." Thus communication is possible through that part of the phenomenal field that is common to two persons. For instance, among most members of western society there are common gestures which make some communication possible although the spoken languages are different. However, they can do so only when the physical gesture has the same phenomenal significance. An American, to whom the nod means assent, will be unable to communicate by this means with a Greek, to whom it means negation, until he discovers the meaning of the gesture in the other's field. It is not the physical nature but the perceived character of the action that is important in determining behavior.

Communication is essentially the process of acquiring greater understanding of another's perceptual field and it can take place only when some common characters already exist. In speech, for instance, communication is possible only to the extent that the objective physical sounds or characters have the same meanings in the two fields. An American cattle fancier found his ability to communicate with a Scottish dealer much enhanced as soon as he discovered that "coo" meant not cow, as he had inferred, but calf. The same words often have very different meanings in the perceptual fields of different individuals. Even strangers of the same general culture often have difficulty communicating, but old friends who have shared many experiences can understand one another's fields so well that they can communicate and anticipate one another's behavior without using words at all.

The well-known phenomenon by which twins communicate with each other in a private language is possible because of the mutual nature of so much of their experience, so that there is an unusual correspondence between their perceptual fields. People who have common experiences tend to have common characteristics in their phenomenal fields and, as a result, show common tendencies in their behavior. Consequently, one finds at a social gathering the skiers, the bridge players, the teachers, the businessmen, or those who have been to Europe forming into groups despite the best efforts of a hostess to "mix them up." We feel more comfortable with persons whose phenomenal fields have much in common with our own. Because we see alike we also behave similarly and we can thus predict more easily what the other will do and how he will be likely to react to our own behavior. It is through the area of overlap in our respective fields that communication becomes feasible.

COMMON MEANING AS A FUNCTION OF DIFFERENTIATION. Whatever meanings the individual possesses are the direct outgrowth of the kinds of differentiations he has been able to make. Since no two people ever have identical perceptual fields, no two people can ever have identical meanings. All human beings, however, have their humanity in common. In addition, large numbers of us live in common cultures. Consequently, many of us will, in the course of our experience, acquire many differentiations held by other people. The fact of our similar kinds of experience makes it likely that what one person has differentiated from a given situation is some assurance that others may do likewise.

Some differentiations are so common to the experience of all people that they are made almost automatically. In their early studies of perception the Gestalt psychologists were intrigued by a number of these common ways in which people order their perceptions. As a result of their studies they isolated a number of principles of figure-ground relationships which seemed to them so universal that they were first ascribed to structural differences. There seems good reason now to believe that these common ways of differentiating are not so much matters of structure as learned ways of responding. Some of the common differentiations explored by the early Gestaltists are as follows:

1. Other things being equal, perceptions are differentiated in terms of the *nearness* of the events experienced. For example, in the line below it will be noted that those letters appearing together seem to stand out from the rest of the printed line.

a bc d e fg h i jk

2. Other things being equal, perceptions are likely to be ordered by the differentiation of *similarity* in the events experienced. In Fig. 6, for example, the circles and dots are not seen as a helter-skelter, unordered series of events. Rather, one's perceptions are ordered in terms of the similar aspects of the field and circles and dots are seen as alternate rows.

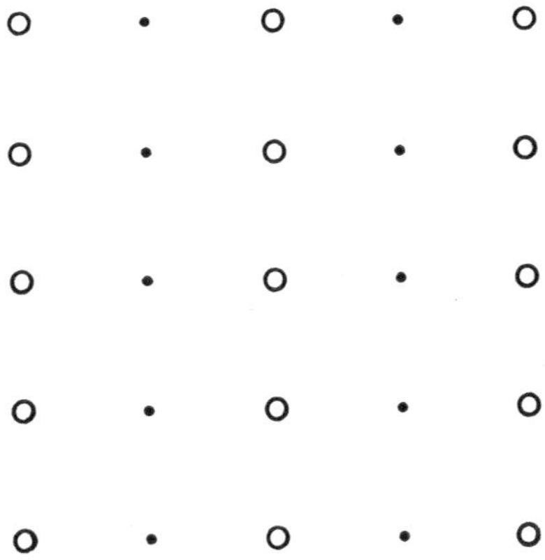

Fig. 6.

3. Other things being equal, perceptions are likely to be differentiated in terms of the **intensity** of the event experienced. In the sentence you are **now** reading, the **words** printed in **bold face type** seem to stand **out** from the rest of the **words** in the **sentence** as a consequence of their greater **intensity** (in this case, blackness) compared to the other words of the sentence.

4. Other things being equal, perceptions are likely to be differentiated in terms of their *common fate*. That is, events which seem to share a common direction, continuity, or characteristic are likely to be seen in figure. In Fig. 7, for example, the dots are perceived as two lines perpendicular to each other with the line with the dots from A to B seeming to belong together, and the dots

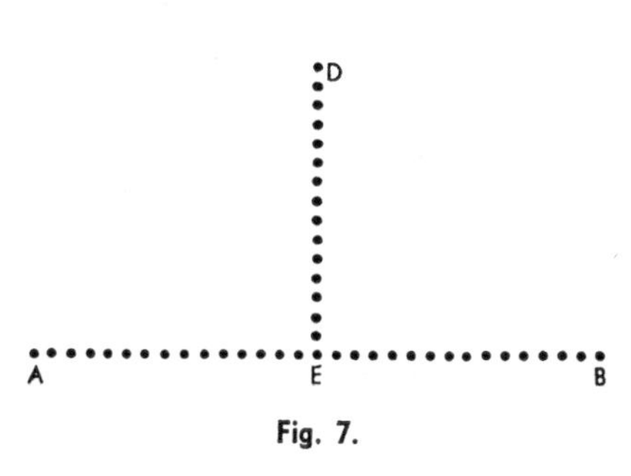

Fig. 7.

from D to E also seeming to belong together—but in a different category than the dots from A to B.

5. Other things being equal, perceptions are likely to be differentiated in terms of their *novelty* or *contrast.* That is to say, in a series of similar events what is new or contrasting is more likely to appear in figure in the perceptual field. In any classroom the appearance of a Hindu student in a sari will invariably capture everyone's attention. Newness or difference is a well known attention gainer.

6. Other things being equal, events sharing a *common movement* or *direction* are more likely to be differentiated. Events which appear to be moving in an otherwise still setting are more likely to appear in figure than the surroundings. When the rabbit "freezes" it is much more difficult to see him; the hunter who moves is much more likely to be shot for a deer than the hunter who stands still.

These fairly common ways in which figure-ground relationships may occur in the perceptual fields of different people take place not only in the field of visual perception. They may also be found in our perceptions as a consequence of our other sense modalities. The notes which are heard together seem to us to belong together. The taste of a food is heightened by contrast with another food of different character. Although we quickly become adapted to given odors, a newly introduced odor is almost invariably perceived quickly. The above figure-ground principles of differentiation apply to comparatively simple cases of perception.

Perceptions in daily life, however, are almost never simple. Rather, they are likely to involve vast areas of the perceptual field. Items within the field are interacting and interdependent, and any new thing in the field derives its properties from its relationship to the field as a whole. For instance, yawning by one person in a group will have a varying effect on the others since it will have varying functions in their individual perceptual fields. It may appear as a cue for the awareness of our own throat sensations, as a vaguely recognized sign of boredom, as a deliberate act of discourtesy, or it may not appear in the field at all. In any case, the character of the perception is affected by the observer's concept of the relationship between himself and the person yawning and his general concept of the total current situation in which he is involved. While the simple principles stated above are examples of differentiation, such common kinds of experiences will almost never occur as pure cases in ordinary life. What is perceived will always be a function of the individual's need and the antecedent field which he possesses at the moment.

The Understanding and Prediction of Behavior

The presence of common meanings in the perceptual fields of different persons makes communication possible. It also makes possible the understanding and prediction of the behavior of other people. The relation between one's own perceptual field and one's own behavior is relatively simple and well known to each of us because of our lifelong experiences in which we have been able to observe the relationship between our own perceptions and behavior. Because of this experience, the process of reconstructing another individual's perceptual field by observing his behavior is a relatively simple and easy task, which can often be done with little training. Since behavior is always determined by the individual's perceptual field, we need only to learn to read behavior backwards in order to understand the perceptions of another person. That is, we can infer from another's behavior the nature of the perceptions which probably produced it.

As a usual thing, when we see a man scratch, we can infer that he itched. When we see him yawn, we often share his field so vividly that we are impelled to duplicate his behavior. By this kind of inference from what we are able to observe, we can understand the perceptions lying behind a great deal of human behavior. We can accomplish this by asking ourselves "Now why did he do that?" or "Under what circumstances would I have done that?" To ask such questions effectively, moreover, we do not need to learn to do something entirely new. Everyone has been making observations of this sort all his life, so that the problem is one of learning to do more accurately, effectively, and explicitly what one already has learned to do albeit implicitly and unsystematically. When important people with whom we are conversing begin to fiddle with their watches or stand and walk to the door, all but the most eager and obtuse people can infer that they are impatient for us to leave. As a consequence, we are likely to take our departure without waiting to obtain an electroencephalogram reading or measures of our subject's heartbeat, blood sugar, or breathing rate.

The social scientist, attempting to understand and predict human behavior approaches the problem of prediction in exactly the same manner, that is, by inference from observed behavior. What the rest of us do, often haphazardly and implicitly, however, the professional worker seeks to accomplish more explicitly, more precisely, and with greater discipline and care. In Chapter 20 we will look much more closely at some methods of observation and inference commonly used by psychologists.

The Variables of Perception

In this chapter we have postulated that all behavior, without exception, is determined by the perceptual field at the moment of action. To produce change in behavior, then, it will be necessary to produce some change in the individual's perceptual field. To understand other people and to use ourselves effectively as instruments for human welfare, our own welfare as well as the welfare of others, we will need to understand, as clearly as possible, the factors controlling and limiting the processes of perceiving and the function of the perceptual field. Some of the factors controlling perception have been known and studied for generations by several disciplines. The importance of other factors bearing upon perceptual processes have been only more recently appreciated and subjected to experimental scrutiny. In the next seven chapters, we shall examine seven of these known variables of perception.

It should not be supposed that these seven factors are in any sense definitive. Indeed, it could be argued that several of these factors could be consolidated thus reducing the list of variables. On the other hand, it is conceivable that in the years to come still other variables may be differentiated as having important effects upon the perceptual process. The factors discussed in the remaining chapters have been classified in this way solely because it is convenient to discuss and present them so. The reader, of course, is free to interpret and order them in any way that seems most helpful for his own purposes.

Because the effect of human need upon perception is so fundamental and all-pervasive a factor we shall begin our exploration of the variables of perception with the problem of human need in the following chapter.

CHAPTER 3

What Do People Need?

ANY understanding of human behavior must be based upon some knowledge of what people are trying to accomplish when they behave or misbehave. The teachers in a certain school who conceived the notion of cutting down misbehavior by granting a banner to the classroom showing the best deportment each week were completely unprepared for the results. Deportment improved in the lower grades but the upper grades went on a rampage. The lower grades worked for the banner while the upper grades felt disgraced if they won it! To deal effectively with others it is necessary to have the most accurate possible conception of what it is people are trying to do, for whatever we believe about their motives will inevitably affect our behavior toward them.

What, then, is it that people are characteristically trying to do? A glance at the behavior of people about us would seem to indicate that people are motivated by a vast number of needs, people have need for love, clothing, prestige, food, drink, automobiles, hate, revenge, exercise, lipstick, cigarettes, crossing streets, or even, sometimes, death. Behavior seems characterized by an almost unlimited number of motives, some of which may be quite antagonistic to one another. The opposing desires for living and for dying, for having money and for spending it, for being slim and for eating heartily, for example, are motives difficult, if not impossible, for most people to carry out at the same time. A conception of human motives based upon so large and conflicting a picture of what it is that people are striving for leaves us hopelessly confused when we try to understand human behavior. We need a simpler, more accurate understanding of motives in order to understand ourselves and to serve as an effective guide in our dealings with others.

Is there a simpler, more fundamental view of what it is the man is seeking that avoids this confusion? I believe there is. Indeed, I believe it is possible to reduce all these seemingly diverse and confusing goals toward which people seem to strive to a single, all inclusive human need which motivates all human behavior at all times and in all places. In this chapter we shall examine this concept from three points of view: (1) the origins of need in the nature of man himself, (2) the fundamental need defined, and (3) the effects of need upon perception.

The Origins of Need in the Nature of Man and the Universe

MAN IS CONTINUOUS WITH HIS UNIVERSE

To the best of our knowledge about the evolution of life on earth, man, like all living creatures, has developed from a long and continuous line of animal life. Man is composed of chemical elements found in the soil, the rivers, and the mountains of his world. He is part of the universe, part of a vast and magnificent organization. Like rocks, rivers, plants, animals, planets, and suns, as a part of this great organization, man participates in its processes. Like everything else in the universe, man is affected by the organization of which he is part.

Man is himself an organization within the larger organization of the universe in which he exists. Indeed, he is an organization within a whole series of organizations leading outward from himself to the larger structure of the universe. This is familiar to school children who sometimes make a game of addressing themselves as "John Smith, 105 Main St., Santa Barbara, California, U.S.A., North America, the World, the Solar System, the Universe." These are some of the larger organizations in which man participates. Every one of these organizations of which man is a part has, in turn, its effect upon man and his behavior.

The man illustrated in Fig. 8, facing in one direction, for example, can look out from himself to a series of ever larger organizations of which he is part, ending in the universe itself. But this is not the only way man participates in organization. Like the universe itself, he, too, is an organization of smaller organizations. His physical being, for example, is composed of a large number of other smaller organizations such as the skeletal, respiratory, digestive, excretory, and reproductive systems, among others. These organizations are diagramed on the oppo-

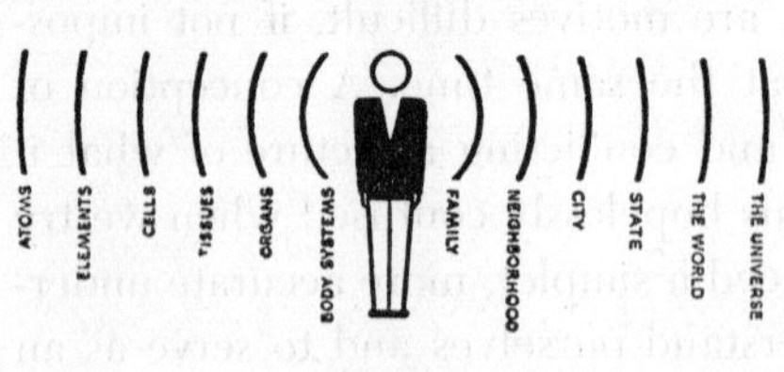

Fig. 8.

site side of Fig. 8; they are composed, in turn, of organizations of cells, which are organizations of chemical elements, which are organizations of atoms and so on, ad infinitum. Man thus appears to be an organization in a long chain of organizations extending within and without himself as far as we have learned to see.

THE DYNAMICS OF ORGANIZATION

In this continuity of organization, the more intimately related the organizations, the more direct and specific is the effect of a larger organization upon a smaller. Let us take, as an example, the case of John Smith whom we mentioned before. John's family organization, the Smiths, will more intimately and directly affect young John's life and behavior than his neighborhood group which is represented by his street address. John's neighborhood, in turn, will probably affect his behavior more intimately than his city, state, or nation. Each one of these larger organizations, however, will have its effect upon John and will govern, less specifically but no less surely, his behavior. In the same manner, John's own organization will affect the organizations of which he is composed. What John eats will affect directly the organization of his digestive system and, less directly but no less surely, the cellular organizations of which that system is composed. As an organization within a larger organization, thus it seems clear that man is affected by the larger organizations of which he is a part.

The reverse effect seems also true. An organization made up of many parts is affected by the parts of which it is composed. The introduction of a new element, or a change in an old element necessarily affects the total organization of which it is a part. The birth of a child into a family certainly changes the organization of the family in many ways. Less directly but no less certainly, change in the family organization affects the community, city, state, and nation of which the family is a part. In this sense, man as an organization is both affected by and affects the organizations in which he participates. By his participation, indeed by his very existence, man produces change in the universe of which he is a member.

The action and interaction of man and his world which we have been discussing, is by no means limited to physical events alone. Similar effects may be observed in the realm of ideas, values, attitudes, and human thought. Here too, the world in which man lives both affects and is affected by the organization of human thought. People from the North think differently about Negroes than do people from the South. Russians think like Russians, and Americans think like Americans. The organization of man's ideas and understanding even produces changes in the environment in which he lives. One need only point out the way our entire world has been changed because of our new knowledge about atomic energy. Our ideas and values affect the culture in which we live and, in turn, are affected by it.

As a participating member of the universe, man must necessarily be affected by the organization of which he is a part. The characteristics of that larger organization will be characteristic of man as well, although with different expression and magnitude. Is there any universal characteristic of organization which we can select for examination which seems to have this relationship? There seems to be.

THE MAINTENANCE OF ORGANIZATION

Perhaps the most outstanding characteristic of our universe is the very fact of its organization. Our universe, above all things, seems characterized by the maintenance of its organization. Whatever else may occur, the universe maintains an order. This maintenance of its organization has been the subject of awe and thanksgiving for generations of philosophers, scientists, poets, and theologians. Various explanations of the existence of this organization have found favor with different groups of students. Each may choose the explanation that satisfies him. We shall not be concerned here with the explanation for this maintenance of organization. For our purposes it is sufficient that the phenomenon seems to exist.

The maintenance of organization by our universe seems also characteristic of the organizations of which that universe is composed. According to all our observations, it seems inherent in the nature of an organization itself. Wherever we turn for illustration organizations show this same enduring quality. To maintain their organizations is the dominant characteristic of all things. It appears true of living and non-living things, and of the universe itself. The simplest atoms tenaciously resist disruption, and heavenly bodies maintain their established orbits.

The universe maintains its organization, our world maintains its spheroid character, rocks remain rocks and water remains water until some influence forces a change in its organization. Even then, although one organization may be destroyed, its component organizations continue. Water may be broken into hydrogen and oxygen; these elements, in turn, maintain their organizations. Thus, the outstanding attribute of an organization seems to be its perpetual tendency to self-maintenance.

BIOLOGIC OPERATION OF MAINTENANCE OF ORGANIZATION

This characteristic maintenance of organization is not confined to inanimate objects alone. It is more true of the living than of the dead. Schrodinger, for example, has pointed out that living organisms actively create organization by concentrating energy and organizing matter. In spite of its fluid condition, the lowly amoeba hangs together and resists destruction. It actively seeks and stores food. When its environment dries up completely the amoeba may still encyst and protect itself from such disturbing forces. Plants, too, display this characteristic, for grasses bent by the lawn roller regain their upright state, and the notched tree soon adjusts itself to the damage and maintains its organization. Among higher animals, wounds cover with scar tissue, and the entire body becomes a battleground as the organism adjusts to infection. In fact, as Dashiell expressed it, "Through all animal life an outstanding characteristic runs—the tendency of the organism to maintain its normality against internal or external disrupting agencies."

It is this tendency of the organism to maintain its organization, or equilibrium, that Cannon described in his concept of "homeostasis," meaning the tendency of the organism to maintain its stability. This general law of constancy of the internal environment has become a basic tenet of biology. Richter, for example, has reported a series of experiments with rats to investigate this tendency of the organism to maintain internal balance or consistency. In these experiments, when the "need" for water, constant temperature, sodium, calcium, phosphorus, and carbohydrates was surgically created, the organism responded vigorously to maintain its internal organization by actively seeking such materials in its environment. When extraordinary requirements for salt were produced in rats by the removal of the adrenal glands, they became able to distinguish between water and a salt solution in concentrations of one part of salt in 33,000 parts of water. Normal rats made this distinction only when concentrations were as strong as one part of salt per 2000 parts of water. Richter concludes from his experiments that: "These forces have their origin in the deep biological urge of mammals to maintain a constant internal environment. The activities may be diverse, and there may be different goals, but the underlying biological drives remain the same." Experiments with other animals have demonstrated similar effects. There could be no life without the maintenance of organization, for life is dependent upon the relationship of parts to other parts. Without the stability of these relationships life could not continue.

As a result of his intensive studies of brain damage Kurt Goldstein was led to base his theory of the organism upon the homeostatic tendency of living beings. Even in cases of severe damage to the brain, he found his subjects maintaining organization by avoiding any situation which would place a strain upon impaired capacities. There seems little doubt that a major characteristic of life is a tendency to maintain organization or wholeness.

MAINTENANCE OF ORGANIZATION IN MAN

Turning to human beings, the art and science of medicine has been predicated upon this fundamental characteristic. The task of the physician is to remove, destroy, or immobilize the causative agent of disease and to help build up the organism to the point where the body can readjust itself. The physician or surgeon helps this process along, but it is the organism itself which brings about the cure through its own return to effective organization. This action has often been referred to as the "healing power of nature." Psychology has long overlooked this important principle, and it is only recently that we have come to recognize its operation in psychological as well as physical functions. Mental patients, for example, often get well despite lack of treatment and even, sometimes, in spite of treatment.

It has been commonly observed that even under the most severe psychological shocks most people manage to make adjustments. Certainly, it is true that most people do so without the help of psychoanalysis, psychiatry, psychotherapy, or other formalized treatment. As Fletcher said discussing this principle: "Rationalization of one's behavior is no less an act of organic defense against ego disturbance than is a change of blood count against infectious disease. The rise of temper against an insult is not essentially different from the rise of temperature against infection."

If this struggle to maintain the organization of the organism is seen in a purely physiological sense, the only possible conclusion is that the fundamental motive of human behavior is the preservation of the physical organism. But, this conclusion is inadequate because many things men do are not directed toward their physical survival. One needs only look around to observe that man does not seek to maintain only his physical self. If that were his only concern, we would have no suicides, nor would anyone ever join the army, fly a plane, or climb a mountain. If maintenance of the physical self alone were the goal of human beings, we would not eat too much, drink too much, or stay up late. We would even avoid such dangers to our bodily health as shaking hands, appearing in public places, or kissing beautiful girls. We would, indeed, live a sterile existence in more ways than one.

Man does not live in a physical world alone. The universe in which he lives and maintains his organization is a universe of ideas, values, societies, and people. Man, furthermore, is as much a part of these aspects of his universe as he is of its physical aspects. Like the larger organization of which he is part and the smaller organization of which he is product, he maintains the organization he is. The self man seeks to maintain is not just his physical body but the self of which he is aware, the self he has come to consider his personality, that unique being known as John Jones or Sally Smith. This self is called the perceived, or phenomenal, self.

The Basic Human Need

By the phenomenal self we mean those aspects of the perceptual field to which we refer when we say "I" or "me." In common with the rest of the perceptual field it has the feeling of complete reality. Its physical boundaries are roughly the skin or clothing surfaces. Man can extend these boundaries; for example, when he uses a cane, or when he drives a familiar vehicle. It is a common observation that many a man reacts to a crumpled fender as though it were violence to his own person.

Sometimes the perceived self may be experienced as if a portion of the body were excluded. When circulation in one's foot or one's fingers is cut off we have the feeling that these limbs are not there; we have no feeling of them and, thus, they are not part of us. This definition of the self in such a way as to exclude a portion of the body is illustrated by the case of a young woman who applied to the author for graduate work in psychology. Noting that she was very badly crippled, he asked if she had considered the degree to which her handicap might make things difficult for her. "I don't have a handicap!" she snapped. Clearly, she so defined her "self" as to ignore her crippled legs.

THE PHENOMENAL SELF DEFINED

The perceived, or phenomenal, self includes far more than the physical aspects of self. Perceptions of the self as strong, honest, good-humored, sophisticated, just, guilty, and a thousand other qualities may be a part of the phenomenal self of a particular individual. We shall even discover later that the phenomenal self may include, by identification, persons and objects entirely outside our physical selves. For instance, we are quite likely to react to attacks upon our sons, daughters, wives, husbands, or parents, as though these were attacks upon ourselves. Indeed, for all practical purposes they are. In short, the phenomenal self includes not only a person's physical self but everything he experiences as "me" at that instant.

It will be recalled that we have defined the perceptual field as the universe, including himself, as it appears to the individual at the moment. Although behavior is always determined by the total field, that portion which the individual regards as part or characteristic of himself influences almost all of his behavior. Since it is always the self which is perceived as behaving, behavior must always be appropriate to the phenomenal self. Aspects of the perceptual field having a specific reference to the self will, therefore, be of paramount importance in understanding the individual's field and, hence, his behavior.

Each of us has literally thousands of more or less discrete perceptions of himself in all kinds of situations. Among them are such perceptions of his physical self as being blue-eyed or brown-eyed, tall or short, fat or thin, blond or brunette. One will also have concepts of himself in social or judgmental terms when he sees himself as being afraid or unafraid, acceptable or unacceptable, liked or unliked, able or unable. The number of self perceptions a person may possess will be almost unlimited, but for each person they are unique to himself. They are his experiences of himself. All perceptions of the self a person has at a particular instant we call the phenomenal self, or the perceived self. It is the phenomenal self which each human being is forever seeking to maintain.

The phenomenal self, it should be understood, is not a physical entity, that is, it does not exist someplace in our bodies. To the individual himself the phenomenal self is real. It *is* himself. To the outsider observing the individual, the phenomenal self is pure abstraction inferred from the observed behavior and representing only an approximation of the self experienced by the behaver. Such a concept is useful in helping us to understand and deal with problems of human behavior. It helps us to focus attention upon those aspects of the perceptual field of particular importance in understanding behavior, and at the same time makes it possible to exclude many aspects of minor importance.

THE STRIVING FOR ADEQUACY: THE BASIC NEED OF HUMAN BEINGS

From birth to death the maintenance of the phenomenal self is the most pressing, the most crucial, if not the only task of existence. To maintain this personal organization of the self in the universe in which he lives, however, requires of a human being much more than mere survival. Man lives in a changing world, a world in which the organizations of which he is composed and of which he is part are continuously changing. A changing world requires changes in the organization of the self if it is to be maintained. Each of us needs to do more than merely change with the flow of events. Because we are aware of the future and must maintain ourselves, in the future as well as in the present, it is necessary to enhance the self against the exigencies of tomorrow. The self, therefore, "has to be maintained in the future, built up and enhanced so that the individual feels secure for tomorrow. And since the future is uncertain and unknown, no enhancement of the individual's experience of personal value, no degree of self-actualization, is ever enough. Human beings are, by nature, insatiable."

Thus, man seeks not merely the maintenance of *a* self but the development of an *adequate* self—a self capable of dealing effectively and efficiently with the exigencies of life, both now and in the future. To achieve this self-adequacy requires of man that he seek, not only to maintain his existing organization, but also that he build up and make more adequate the self of which he is aware. Man seeks both to maintain and enhance his perceived self.

Though the maintenance and enhancement of the self are two different words, this does not mean that man has two different needs. We express maintenance and enhancement as two different words, but both relate to exactly the same function—the production of a more adequate self. Both refer to man's striving to accomplish, like the rest of his universe, an adequate organization. I may shore up the timbers of my house to keep it from collapsing or I may plant trees to improve its looks. One activity maintains the structure, the other enhances the property. Both activities have a common result—a more adequate, better functioning dwelling for me and those important to me. In the same manner, I seek to become the most adequate person I can become in every situation in which I may find myself. I may do this by seeing my dentist to have my cavities filled, by reading a new book in my professional field, or, I may seek to enhance myself by buying a new suit of clothes or by making a speech at a national convention. Whether I seek to maintain myself as I am or enhance myself against the exigencies of the future, I am always seeking to be the most adequate personality I can be.

In the previous pages we have seen: (1) that man, like the universe of which he is a part, characteristically seeks the maintenance of organization; (2) that the organization man seeks to maintain is the organization of which he is aware, namely, his phenomenal self; and (3) that, because man lives in a changing world and is aware of the future as well as of the present, maintenance of the self requires, not simply maintenance of the status quo, but an active seeking for personal adequacy.

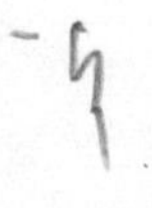

We can define man's basic need, then, as a need for adequacy. It represents in man the expression of a universal tendency of all things. It is expressed in man's every behavior at every instant of his existence. Asleep or awake, each of us is engaged in an insatiable quest for personal adequacy. This quest may find its expression in a wide variety of behavior aimed, in one form or another, at the maintenance or enhancement of our perceptions of personal worth and value. Other authors have spoken of this need as a need for self-actualization, or self-realization. In the field of psychotherapy this need has been described as a need for growth. In this book, whenever we refer to man's basic need, we mean that *great driving, striving force in each of us by which we are continually seeking to make ourselves ever more adequate to cope with life.*

NEED AND THE PREDICTION OF BEHAVIOR

Seen in this light it is possible to understand much of human behavior which would otherwise seem unreasonable. Even odd behavior such as wearing gaudy clothing, speeding, arguing with the police, or going over Niagara Falls in a barrel can not only be understood, but, if enough information is available, it can become completely and accurately predictable. If each act is seen as an attempt to preserve or to fortify the individual's perception of personal adequacy, behavior becomes meaningful. Rather than appearing inconsistent, behavior then becomes more predictable. Note how this point of view helps to clarify behavior in the following summary of a "typical" clinic case.

Eight-year-old Jimmy Allen, an only child, is brought to the psychological clinic by his parents at the insistence of his teachers. The parents are much incensed and regard all of this as a direct insult to the family and a threat to their feelings of adequacy. They raise a thousand complaints against the school and are completely at a loss to understand why the teachers should have suggested this consultation. Jimmy, they tell the psychologists, is a delightful child at home. He has his "moments" now and then, but on the whole, he is his Mother's and Daddy's darling, the center of a comfortable suburban home. Jimmy plays with a group of younger children whom he completely dominates much to the delight of his father. Jimmy's slightest wish is his parents' command. His manners are delightful with adults and he speaks like a polished young gentleman. With the adults at the clinic, he is calm, poised, and helpful. To the psychologist he seems too helpful for a child of eight. The parents feel that the school must be a terrible place because, as they point out, Jimmy just hates to go, and he cries and begs to be allowed to stay home. He has even made himself sick over it and had to stay home because he got so upset.

The school's report about Jimmy presents a vastly different picture. His teachers complain that he is "not bright," stubborn, and a "very nasty child." He does not get along well with the other children; he beats up those younger and smaller than he, and he attempts to "buy" those older and stronger with lollipops and licorice shoe-strings. In class he is constantly talking and showing off. He must always be the center of attention. He likes art work and this is the only thing he does well. Whenever his work is displayed, he brags insufferably. He has been known to cheat on exams. When he lost the leading part in the school play recently, he skipped school for three days in a row. With forty children in her class the teacher is at her wits' end and does not know what to do with Jimmy.

Jimmy joined the local Y, went four times, and never returned again. The boys' work director of the Y reports that Jimmy never got along with any of the boys, stuck to the director "like molasses" and wanted to do nothing but swim. Jimmy refused to participate in the gym classes and stayed out of the various Y clubs entirely. He was an excellent swimmer and enjoyed this sport immensely until one day he was sent home for holding two younger boys under water. Jimmy hasn't been back to the Y since that incident.

When we can see this child as he sees himself, his behavior becomes much more understandable. While we might analyze his behavior in terms of many specific needs, all these needs become a function of the one dominant aspect and that is the boy's need to protect and to enhance his own phenomenal self and to become the most adequate person he can.

Thus Jimmy has developed at home a concept of himself as being very important, as indeed he is, to his parents. At home he is able to achieve a feeling of adequacy by controlling his indulgent parents and adopting the accepted modes of behavior in an adult world. When he moves from this sheltered atmosphere, however, to the wider world of school and community, his associates do not react to him in the same way. They are unwilling to accept him at his own evaluation of himself. They are not even aware of the values he places on himself, but react to Jimmy only in terms of his behavior. All this must be very puzzling to Jimmy. Since his concept of himself is not accepted by his associates he is forced to defend himself, and he does so by means interpreted by others as "stubbornness," being "nasty," and cheating on exams. In his attempts to gain what he feels is his rightful due, he buys off the older boys and beats up the younger ones, he sticks close to the director of the Y and, of course, brags of his accomplishments and enjoys doing what he can do well.

A delight at home to his parents, a nuisance away in the community; his need for self-esteem surfeited at home and opposed in the community—seen in this way, Jimmy's behavior becomes consistent. Indeed, given enough information about a new situation, his behavior can be accurately predicted.

ONLY ONE NEED

Even such apparently conflicting tendencies in the individual as the desire for self preservation and the desire for death, seem conflicting only because they have been observed from a frame of reference inadequate to encompass such behavior under a single heading. From the point of view of the outsider, behavior often seems motivated by conflicting or antithetic goals. From the individual's own point of view, however, the goals are quite harmonious. This is well illustrated in the following excerpt from a counseling record concerning a young man in the depth of despair:

YOUNG MAN: I don't know what I would do. I've thought about hanging myself, sometimes. It's an awful thing. It's entered my mind several times.
COUNSELOR: That scared you pretty much.
YOUNG MAN: I often wonder what people would think if I did.
COUNSELOR: You find this not satisfactory either.
YOUNG MAN: It doesn't accomplish anything. I suppose if a fellow got low enough, he'd have the guts.
COUNSELOR: It scares you a bit that you've thought of that kind of out.
YOUNG MAN: To the point, sometimes, where I couldn't read a book on sociology. Sometimes I've thought, too, of going away—*but that's a kind of quitting, too. I don't like to be a quitter.*

In this example from counseling, it is clear that the thought of suicide is not the result of a death wish. If it were, this man would have committed suicide, because certainly, at that moment, the rest of his picture looked deeply depressing. Note, however, that the client rejected this possible solution, not because of a desire for self preservation, but because of his concern with "what people would think" if he committed suicide. Even suicide does not remove the individual from the necessity of maintaining and enhancing the self.

The soldier in wartime is not torn between a desire for self destruction and a desire for self preservation as he faces the coming battle. On the contrary, he is concerned solely with the adequacy of his phenomenal self. Although the situation will vary from individual to individual, it might roughly be described as follows: He may risk death on the one hand to *preserve* himself from becoming the kind of person who "lets his buddies down," and on the other hand, to *enhance* his self concept by being the kind of person who is "one of the gang," or as brave as the others. Many of us place our physical selves in jeopardy to achieve a more adequate concept of ourselves.

Students of human behavior have in the past postulated a number of basic human needs. Murray, for example, has described 28 needs which seem to him basic to human personality. In an article, published several years ago, I suggested a list of 40 such basic needs. Freud, the first of the psychologists to look at behavior from the point of view of the behaver, felt there were two basic needs: the desire for life and the desire for death. One might well ask, "What does it matter, after all, whether one conceives of human beings as having one need or many?"

THE EFFECT OF THEORIES OF NEED ON BEHAVIOR

We have already seen that each of us behaves according to his own conception of things. How we behave in dealing with the people and the things around us will be the direct outgrowth of our perceptions about them. Hence, the concepts we hold about what people are trying to do, must inevitably affect the way in which we attempt to deal with them. Inaccurate or conflicting concepts of human need will, of necessity, result in inaccurate and inconsistent behavior on our part toward others. It is important for anyone required to cope with the behavior of others to have the simplest, most accurate understanding of human need of which we are capable. Numerous and overlapping concepts of human needs are confusing and difficult to work with. We must have a broad and accurate concept of human need for the simple reason that we will behave according to what we believe to be true.

Perhaps an even more important reason for finding the simplest possible definition of human need, is in the very nature of the concept of need. When the psychologist speaks of need, he usually means some very basic, fundamental, even incontrovertible goal of human behavior. Needs for many psychologists arise from the basic physiology of the organism itself; there are, for example, "needs" for water, food, warmth, or sexual gratification. Thus the concept of need denotes an absolute necessity to human welfare, so that satisfaction of a need cannot be denied without the most dire results. This seems to me an unfortunate and even highly dangerous concept in many practical situations. For example, if one conceives a very homely girl as suffering from a "need" to be attractive, what shall one do to help her adjust? If this need is truly basic, therapy must be directed toward the attempt to improve her appearance; but this may be a task defying all the skill of a Hollywood make-up artist. Similarly, if homosexuality is regarded as a "need," what hope is there for treatment? What we believe to be true about people's need will directly control our own effectiveness in dealing with human problems. Too narrow or inaccurate a view of what people are striving for may even make it impossible for us to deal effectively with human problems.

Years ago, Adam Smith, an economist, postulated that people were motivated by a need for food, clothing, and shelter. Accordingly, a whole generation based its economic planning upon his assumption. The idea was partly true but completely failed to enable us to deal with many of our pressing economic problems just because it was only partly true. Adam Smith, in this assumption, overlooked entirely the psychological aspects of man's striving. His theory could not offer an explanation, for example, why Germany should twice go to war despite the fact that it had the highest standard of living of any country in Europe, or why General Motors workers should remain on strike for nineteen weeks ostensibly because of a difference with management over a salary increase of half a cent an hour.

Since 1914 the Children's Bureau of the U. S. Department of Labor has been publishing a pamphlet entitled "Infant Care" which is intended to guide parents in the care of young children. As these pamphlets have been revised in the course of the years, they represent an interesting mirror of the beliefs held by experts about the needs of children. They illustrate, too, how conceptions of need are translated directly into patterns of behavior. In 1914, for example, needs were conceived almost exclusively in terms of physical well being. Mothers were advised to pay attention to their infants only when the child really *needed* attention. They were warned not to succumb to the baby's demands to be picked up, carried, or played with. Babies were regarded as delicate beings who needed rest and quiet; but babies also needed to be guarded against lest they control the adults around them. The mother of 1914 was told, for example: "The rule that parents should not play with the baby may seem hard, but it is without doubt a safe one. A young, delicate, and nervous baby needs rest and quiet, and however robust the child, much of the play that is indulged in is more or less harmful. It is a great pleasure to hear the baby laugh and crow in apparent delight, but often the means used to produce the laughter, such as tickling, punching, or tossing, makes him irritable and restless. It is a regrettable fact that the few minutes' play that the father has when he gets home at night . . . may result in nervous disturbance of the baby and upset his regular habits."

In 1945, however, concepts of a baby's need had changed and mothers were then told: "A baby sometimes cries because he wants a little more attention. He probably needs a little extra attention under some circumstances just as he sometimes needs a little extra food and water. Babies want attention; they probably need plenty of it." Whatever beliefs we hold about what people need have an inevitable effect upon the way we consider appropriate to deal with them.

In the field of education, ideas about children's needs have produced similar wide swings in our methods of dealing with youngsters in the public schools. Our early school philosophies were based upon the idea that children's needs were largely perverse and animalistic and that the task of the school was essentially the task of civilizing them. Children were seen as having natural needs for self gratification, play, and amusement which had to be curbed or trained in more acceptable adult patterns. At a later period, the so-called Progressive Movement saw children's basic needs as essentially good, and it was considered the task of the school to encourage the expression of these basic needs. With such a view of children's needs, some schools swung as far toward giving children freedom of expression as previous schools had in repressing them.

THE CONCEPT OF NEED IN INDUSTRIAL PRACTICE

Perhaps one of the most interesting demonstrations of the importance of our concepts of human need may be observed in the famous Hawthorne Studies. These studies were carried out in the Hawthorne plant of the Western Electric Company. In setting up the experiments, the researchers were interested in finding out what would happen if the "needs" of workers were systematically varied. To accomplish this purpose, a small group of workers assembling telephone relays was isolated in a room where working conditions could be varied and where the workers' behavior could be studied carefully and systematically. The researchers believed that to achieve high productivity workers need improved work conditions. Accordingly, they gave employees rest periods of varying lengths and at one or more times during the day. In other experiments production changes were measured when the work day and the work week were shortened or lengthened, when lunches were prepared at company expense or provided by the worker. The experimenters found that employee productivity steadily increased with each variation in working conditions, even when workers had no rest periods at all, when they had to supply their own lunches, and when they had to work a longer week and longer hours per day! In reporting their results, the experimenters stated: "In many respects these results were puzzling to the investigators for they were not what they had expected. The general upward trend in output independent of any particular change in rest pauses or shorter working hours was astonishing. The improvement in mental attitude throughout the first two years of the experiment was also perplexing. Neither one of these developments could be related to the kind of working day in any simple one-one correlation."

Like thousands of industrial supervisors and foremen before them, the investigators in these experiments believed that employee productivity was a direct result of the working conditions and they designed their experiments accordingly. They were misled by their own beliefs about the nature of human behavior. What seems to have happened in these experiments was that the workers, feeling themselves to be set apart as a special group, became highly identified with the company and experienced a great lift in their morale. They felt like important people doing an important job and their production records mirrored their feelings. As a result of these experiments, management was impressed with "the stores of latent energy and productive coöperation which clearly could be obtained from its working force under the right conditions. And among the factors making for these conditions the attitudes of the employees stood out as being of predominant importance." Looking at the problem of productivity in this new way, the management of Western Electric Company started a research program in employee morale which, in turn, led to important changes in personnel policies and procedures which have become models for many other industries. With a more accurate conception of human behavior, they were able to deal with the human-relations aspects of industrial management with greater effectiveness than ever before.

In the modern world, and particularly as members of our society, we have to deal with people of all ages and all cultures. A theory of human motivation adequate for that purpose must be broad enough to include all human behavior in all cultures, at all times, and at any age. It must make all behavior from the founding of empires to the winking of an eye accountable in the simplest possible terms.

IS PERSONAL ADEQUACY A "SELFISH" NEED?

At first glance it may seem a very depressing and sordid picture of man as being perpetually concerned with the search for a more adequate self. It seems to make him a very selfish creature indeed. This picture will be true, however, only if we conceive of man as an isolated organization. We have seen that organizations are affected by the organizations of which they are part and that they are affected by the organizations of which they are the product. Man does not live as an isolated self but as the product of organizations present and past, and as part of organizations present and future. As part of larger organizations of which he is a unit, the achievement of personal adequacy requires the adequacy of the larger organization as well. The change or destruction of the larger organization changes or destroys the smaller as well. Thus, to maintain adequately and enhance his own organization requires of man that he seek ever greater adequacy of the organizations of which he is part. The juvenile delinquent seeks the maintenance and enhancement of his gang of which he feels he is a part but the destruction of any segment of society in which he feels he has no place or which threatens his existence. The well-adjusted man has a broadly encompassing self which is by no means restricted to his personal being but which is also concerned with the welfare of others. What he does to achieve personal adequacy contributes also to the adequacy of society. In later chapters of this book we shall want to examine this proposition much further.

The Effects of Need on Perception

Man, we have seen, is an insatiably striving organism forever seeking the maintenance and enhancement of the self. From birth to death he is continually engaged in the search for greater feelings of adequacy. Whether or not he is successful in this quest will be determined by the perceptions he is able to make in the course of his lifetime. If he could not see or know about himself and his world, he could not behave effectively toward his environment, and he would be unable to exist at all. His perceptions enable him to be aware and to behave in ways which lead to the satisfaction of his fundamental need. We would expect, then, that an individual's need would have profound effects on his perceptions, and this is exactly what proves to be so.

Out of all the things we *might* perceive, we perceive what is meaningful to us and what helps us to maintain the organization of our phenomenal field and, thus, to satisfy our fundamental need. Each of us can observe the effect of need on his perception when he gives just a little thought to his own behavior. Though we look at the newspaper every day, it is not until we feel a need for a new suit that we spend much time reading advertisements for clothes. We do not even see the bicycle shop we pass every day until our youngster's bike needs fixing. It doesn't seem important to us to study until the week before an exam. The passenger in an automobile does not know the unfamiliar road home because he was not watching the road on the way out; it was not a part of his need. We see what we need to see.

Many psychologists have been intrigued with this problem of the effects of need on perceiving and have amassed a veritable mountain of research demonstrating the effect in a wide variety of settings from food selections to politics. One of the earliest of these experiments was the "cafeteria feeding" study of Davis in 1930. She permitted newly weaned children to select their own foods from an assortment of items in any quantity they pleased and she found the children could and did select what, for them, was an adequate and well balanced diet. Children with special dietary needs, moreover, seemed to choose the "right" foods to satisfy their particular deficiencies! Experiments on food deprivation in which subjects were systematically starved have repeatedly demonstrated that, as starvation levels are reached, subjects find it difficult to keep their minds off the topic of food. They find themselves thinking about food continually. Osgood describes such an experience as follows: "An office that I pass each day is numbered 400D; inevitably, when the hour is near mealtime, I perceive this as FOOD. The car I used to drive had the euphemistic label SILVER STREAK on its dashboard; inevitably, when the hour was near mealtime, I would read this as SILVER STEAK."

Other research studies have shown that college students, asked to judge their college aptitude test scores, respond in ways that protect their feelings of adequacy. Children from wealthy homes, it has been demonstrated, perceive half a dollar to be smaller than children from poorer homes. When words are presented for very short periods of time in a tachistoscope, people tend to see the words they value most more quickly than those words having less value. Even the learning of pro-Communist and anti-Communist material seems affected by the political leanings of the learner, for Communist material is learned more readily and retained more tenaciously by persons with Communist leanings, while anti-Communists behave similarly regarding anti-Communist materials. I have found in my own classes that some of my most rabidly anti-Communist students sometimes describe passages from the U.S. Constitution as Communist-inspired!

It has been demonstrated that persons tend to associate favorable characteristics with members of Congress from their own party. It seems apparent that the effect of need on perception is to be found in every aspect of human endeavor. It is the custom on the campus of the University of Florida for all roads to be closed while students change classes; the campus police place signs in the road reading CLASS CHANGE. One hot day, as I approached my classroom I thought, "I'd better get a drink before I go to class as I probably won't have another opportunity to get one for two hours." As I entered the building I sought the drinking fountain and bent over to slake my thirst. As I did so, I glanced outside at the sign in the middle of the road which said just as clear as could be, LAST CHANCE. Even psychologists who should know about these things are not immune to the effect of need on perceiving. In a study of the evaluations of other people by clinical psychologists, Weingarten found that clinicians saw more problems in their clients in those areas in which the clinicians themselves had problems. Even when it was brought to their attention what the experiment was designed to show, they, nevertheless, continued to see in the cases they examined the problems they wrestled with themselves!

We have been able to mention here only a few of the research studies demonstrating the effects of need on perception. There are many more studies in the psychological literature exploring every facet of this fascinating problem. We shall want to look at further studies in later chapters when we examine the satisfaction of need more specifically through the individual's goals and values, the development of the self and its protection from threat. Whatever the behavior of the individual, it is always directed at the satisfaction of need. The search for adequacy is the central factor controlling the organization of the phenomenal field and the perceptions of which we are capable.

Need and the Problem of Motivation

A great deal of the time and energy of teachers, advertisers, administrators, social workers, and others concerned with human relations has been devoted to the problem of motivation; how to get others to do the things they "should" do. It should be clear from our discussion in this chapter, however, that from the point of view of the behaver himself, he is never *un*motivated. We have stated the fundamental human need as a continuous search for personal adequacy. In this sense each of us is always motivated. We are forever seeking the maintenance and enhancement of our perceived selves. People are never unmotivated from their own points of view, even though it may seem so from an outsider's point of view.

When people seem to us to be unmotivated, it is not because they are really so, but because we don't understand their goals. Thus, a child's resistance to learning arithmetic or spelling may cause the teacher to think the child is unmotivated and has no desire for self improvement. To the child, however, learning arithmetic or spelling may seem to have nothing whatever to do with his quest for self enhancement, at the moment, and, thus, he remains uninterested in the subject matter until the teacher threatens him with failure. When that happens, he may perceive the matter differently and seek to maintain his concept of self by getting by—but only just! People are never unmotivated although they may sometimes seem to the outside observer to be unaffected by the values the observer holds dear.

From the outsider's point of view it may seem highly doubtful that other people are always motivated to seek their most adequate selves. Yet this is exactly what proves true the moment we look at the situations with which people are confronted through their own eyes. The delinquent taunting the police, sassing his teachers, and walking about with a chip on his shoulder seems to the outsider hardly pursuing personal adequacy. Rather, he seems to be perversely seeking his own destruction. When one gets to know delinquents better, however, it becomes clear that such swaggering behavior is an outgrowth of deep feelings of inadequacy. Seen from his own frame of reference, the delinquent's behavior may be compared to whistling in the dark while passing a graveyard. It is a pathetic attempt to convince himself and the world about him of an adequacy he does not feel.

If it is true that each human being is always doing the best he can to be adequate according to his perception of events at the moment of his behavior, or misbehavior, it becomes obvious that a great deal of "blaming" people for their behavior, is misdirected and futile. People are always trying as best they can to be adequate. Thus, the problem of changing behavior is not one of motivating people but of helping them to perceive differently. In our experience working with parents over the years, we have rarely seen a parent who viciously set out to destroy his child. Time after time we have discovered that even parents who did terrible things to their children often did so "because I want Jimmy to be a good boy!" The problem was not motivation. The problem was how to help parents to develop better and more effective ways of perceiving themselves and their relationship with others. When this was accomplished the individual's own need for adequacy could be counted on to supply the necessary power for change.

The task of teachers, parents, writers, and anyone else whose task is affecting the behavior of others is a problem of perception. To change behavior it is necessary to help people change the way they see themselves and the world they live in. When people see differently they will behave differently. The need of the individual for adequacy, for the maintenance and enhancement of the self, will permit nothing less. The need for adequacy provides the direction, the drive, and the organization for every behavior. How it is expressed in a particular personality will be dependent upon the scope, the richness, and the availability of an individual's personal meanings. We need now to know more specifically and precisely what affects perceiving and the nature and organization of the individual's perceptual field. In the next six chapters I have attempted to set forth what I believe to be the most important factors, other than need itself, which determines each person's perceptual field.

CHAPTER 4

The Physical Organism: Vehicle of Perception

THE most self-evident factor affecting perception is the organism in which the process of perceiving occurs. The physical body in which each of us is more or less tenuously housed makes perceiving possible. We must have eyes to see, ears to hear, taste buds to taste, and olfactory end organs to enable us to distinguish odors. Even these organs, however, would not be sufficient without the marvels of our brain and nervous system. What limits the functioning of these organs must inevitably limit our perceptions as well.

We can, after all, perceive only those things which we have the equipment to perceive. Dogs and birds can hear high-frequency sounds which most human beings cannot. We are limited by our human auditory equipment to the sounds we, as human beings, can hear. We cannot perceive like honey bees, navigate in the dark like bats, or find our way home like pigeons. Our physical equipment sets broad limits to the kinds of things we can perceive directly. Within these broad limitations, however, we find that human perceptions can be extremely varied and extensive.

Physical Limitations on Perceiving

Human perceptions extend far beyond our experiences of sight, hearing, smell, taste, and touch. We have ideas, values, concepts, perceptions of relationships, and meanings that far transcend the limitations of our sense organs. It is possible for Helen Keller to live an extraordinarily rich and meaningful life though she is totally blind and deaf. Though it is, of course, necessary for us to have sense organs to perceive, our physical bodies impose fewer restrictions upon our perceptions than we are, at first glance, likely to assume.

An automobile is roughly limited by its structure. It will not run successfully under water, nor will it normally fly through the air. Within the broad limits of its structure as a vehicle for operation on land, however, it has tremendous potentialities. From a study of its mechanics and condition we can tell whether it will operate or not. But no matter how detailed our study of its carburetor, pistons, or tires, we cannot tell from such data where the automobile has gone, where it will go next, or even where it is now! In the same way the behavior of a human being cannot be understood through a study of the structure of the organism alone. We must, of course, have eyes to see and ears to hear. But given the necessary equipment for seeing and hearing, *what* we see and *what* we hear is affected little by the structure of our eyes and ears. The structure of the eye tells us *whether* one can see. It tells us nothing about what is seen. Our bodies provide the vehicle of behavior; they do not explain it. We are broadly limited by our fundamental physiology, but the variety, the richness, and the almost limitless patterns of human behavior can never be fully understood exclusively in terms of the physical organism.

Our physical bodies are only one of a number of factors affecting human behavior. Man's whole history has been one of escaping from the bonds of his physical limitations to understand, predict, and control the forces of the world about him. He has learned to move loads far beyond his personal strength, to hear and to talk with people at the opposite ends of the earth, to fly through the air and travel under the sea. If human behavior could be understood by a study of the physical organism alone, we should not need psychologists, sociologists, political scientists, or theologians. We could get all the advice and help we need from the physiologists alone. The vast development of the physical sciences has been perhaps the most outstanding achievement in man's development in the past hundred years. We are impressed by these achievements and inclined to carry over the principles applying to the physical sciences in all other aspects of living. Our physical selves, of course, have important effects upon our abilities to perceive; and to understand human behavior we need to have as keen an awareness of these limitations as modern science can give us. We need, however, to see such limitations in their proper perspective, without overvaluing or underestimating them. What effects does the physical organism have on perceiving? In the remainder of this chapter, we will explore something of the relationship of the physical organism to the perceptual field.

The Biological Origins of Awareness

Perhaps the most outstanding characteristic of all living things is their ability to react. The biologist calls this characteristic "irritability" by which he means the ability of the organism to respond to its environment. If one places a drop of acid in a solution containing one-celled amoebae, the amoebae move away from the acid. Conversely, amoebae move toward food particles. This ability of living things to react to physical events is true of all living things from the simplest to the most complex organisms. If animals did not have this characteristic they could not exist. Amoebae unable to move away from danger or toward food would very quickly disappear from the earth.

The peculiar organization of matter which makes this responsiveness to stimuli possible in animal life is unknown. Though we can isolate the chemical elements in a living organism, the peculiar organization of these elements which produce life still eludes us. Scientists seem to agree that irritability is a function of the particular *organization* of elements that make up a living organism. It is a property of protoplasm but not of the elements of which protoplasm is made. Whatever its nature, however, we can observe that every animal possesses some kind of awareness whether it be a primitive sort of irritability as in one-celled life or the highly developed ability to perceive in higher forms of life. All animals, regardless of complexity, seem able to perceive, that is, to give meaning to experience.

The Development of Spatial Awareness

The survival of any organism depends upon its ability to deal with those parts of the physical environment with which it comes in contact. From the environment it touches, it secures the energy and materials for maintenance. From the environment, too, it may receive injury and destruction. However, before either happens the source and the organism must come into physical contact. Food which remains an inch away is not food. As for danger, "a miss is as good as a mile."

As we trace the development of animal life from its most primitive beginnings in the single cell through more complicated organizations of cells in the sponges, worms, fishes, amphibians, to the mammalian forms of life, we find life characterized by an ever-increasing organization of structure for special functions. In the course of this evolution some cells become modified for special processes of digestion while others become organized into special functions for breathing, excretion, reproduction, and for awareness. As we trace the phylogenetic scale of animal life from its simplest beginnings to the complex being, called man, we find an ever-increasing development of specialized structures for increased irritability, or awareness. In human beings these structures seem to have reached their highest levels of development in our tremendously complex brain and nervous system. One of the outstanding characteristics of this development is the continual improvement of these organs, particularly the organs of vision and hearing, which make it possible for the animal to be aware of events at a distance from him.

Organisms without distance receptors can use, to maintain their organization, only materials which they happen to bump into or with which they blindly come into contact. They are unable to seek out and secure such materials with precision or efficiency. At the same time they are unable to anticipate and avoid the disruptive forces in their neighborhood and they are at the mercy of any they happen to encounter. By developing distance receptors and motility any organism may considerably expand its field of action and increase its ability to maintain its organization. By enlarging the area of the physical field of which it is aware at any given moment, the organism gains access to a greatly augmented supply of the energy and materials it requires; it has thus acquired the means of detecting danger at a distance. It has also gained a wider field into which it can escape from danger. Any increase in awareness of its surroundings is valuable in aiding the organism to achieve effective maintenance.

A significant factor in the rise of man to his present degree of control over his environment has been the development of erect posture which has given him a wider range of vision than that of his four-footed competitors and, because he can keep his hands free for precise manipulation of the environment, he has been enabled to achieve and profit from a visual and tactual precision far greater than that of other animals. The value of any physical function to the organism is determined and limited by the other qualities of that organism. Vision is of no value to a tree. Because their short stature limits their field of vision, a high level of visual acuity would be equally useless to most breeds of dogs. The long-legged sight hounds, who can make use of visual acuity, are the only dogs who have good eyesight. The primates, living in trees, are high enough above the ground and also have the manual equipment to be able to utilize a higher degree of visual acuity. Because of their upright posture, this superior eyesight was still useful when our ancestors came down to the ground. Having a highly differentiated visual field gives man a tremendous advantage over the rest of the animal world.

The Awareness of Time

The extension of the organism's phenomenal field by the development of distance receptors involves much more than an expansion of space. The possession of distance receptors gives the organism a perceptual field of which time, as well as distance, is an aspect. Distance receptors cannot be effective unless some sort of time awareness develops along with them. In turn, the possession of distance receptors makes a sense of time possible. Objects at a distance are not immediately available or immediately disruptive. In relation to the organism itself such objects are in the future or in the past but not in the present. As a result, the awareness of objects at a distance brings with it an awareness of temporal distance and relations, i.e., of past and future. The animal whose total experience is a matter of events immediately impinging upon him has no need of a sense of time. It is only when events are perceived at a distance that such awareness becomes possible. The bridge I see in the road ahead is not here now, but I know that if I keep going I shall reach it. The ability to perceive remote events, thus, makes awareness of time possible.

An organism having achieved such a perceptual field lives in and commands the resources of a behavioral field vastly greater, in size and potentialities, for the satisfaction of need than an organism, mobile or immobile, whose behavioral fields are limited to the aspects of environment which touch their body surface. And this is not all. Through a complementary process of physical evolution and social invention it is now possible for a human being, by the use of symbols, to enlarge his phenomenal field to include events and objects which are far distant in time and space, to include ideas, principles, and concepts far beyond the range of his senses. Language, for example, makes it possible for us to experience events long past. When we read of dinosaurs we can grasp something of an era before man existed, and when we read science fiction we can plunge light years ahead of our time. Through the medium of words we can deal with honor, justice, and other abstract concepts unavailable to us through our sense organs alone.

From this point of view the perceptual field is an essential aspect of the organism's equipment for dealing with its environment. Until now, the development of the perceptual field has been primarily a product of evolution. Recently, however, we have taken an important part in expanding and enriching the phenomenal field. Evolution is too slow; we can now expand our individual potentialities with radar, Geiger counters, electronics, new systems of mathematics and other types of symbols, which can still further enlarge and enrich perceptions.

From the simple irritability of the single cell to the specialized functions of the sense organs, the brain, and the nervous system in man, there has been throughout the evolution of animal life an increasing refinement of the organism's capacity for awareness. The ability of man to perceive broadly and richly seems fundamental to man's superiority over the rest of the animal world. Though man is endowed with the physical machinery which makes such perceiving possible, we still need to know much more than we do now about how the richness and breadth of the perceptual field of the adequate personality come about. What limits does our physical structure place upon our perceptual fields?

The Growth of Awareness

We cannot observe the growth of awareness in human beings in the same manner in which we can observe physical growth. We can be sure that sensitivity to its environment exists in the embryo, for we can observe the reactions of the developing fetus from the fertilization of the egg to the birth of a new human being. It is impossible for us to know, however, exactly what the embryo's experience of his environment is like. The precise nature of the development of awareness we can only infer. It seems reasonable, however, to assume that awareness progresses by a process of differentiation and organization concomitant with the development of the nervous system as other functions of our anatomy become differentiated with their developing organs. The simple interchange of oxygen and carbon dioxide of the single cell becomes organized during prenatal development into the highly specialized organs of the respiratory and circulatory systems of the new-born child. The primitive elimination of waste products by a process of diffusion in the single cell becomes the special function of specialized kidneys in the mature human being. Similarly, the organization of the organism for more effective awareness is brought about by the development of the sense organs, the nervous system, and the brain. How this process is experienced by the fetus we cannot know, of course, but by the time of birth the physical organism has developed a highly complex and efficient system of structures which makes awareness possible, and has already had some months of experience in perceiving.

Our experience of awareness is not something which occurs all at once. It does not arise full blown, nonexistent at one moment, and complete and functioning in the next. It begins as a characteristic of animal life, and with the development of our highly specialized sense organs, our nervous systems, and our brains, we become increasingly able to perceive more and more sharply and clearly. The human organism's perceptions probably begin as vague awareness which becomes clearly and sharply differentiated only with the development of the sense organs and the passage of time.

AWARENESS OF THE PHYSICAL SELF. The perceptual field contains many perceptions of our physical selves which make it possible to be aware of what is going on within us and to move our physical bodies from place to place. Some of these perceptions, like the feeling of pain experienced as a result of a pin prick, are sharp and clear. Many other perceptions will be so vague that we cannot describe them to others. We may, indeed, not even be able to feel them very clearly ourselves. An example of such vague perception is an awareness that we are off balance and falling when walking. We perceive almost at once when we are off balance and we adjust our body posture automatically, although we could not put into words precisely what we felt that led us to make the necessary movements returning us to an upright position.

It should not be supposed that because perceptions exist they are necessarily reportable. Most of the perceptions we have about physical beings we can report only vaguely, if at all. There are at least three reasons why this should be.

1. The first reason has to do with the relationships of larger and smaller organizations discussed in Chapter 3. We spoke of the nature of our physical selves as a series of organizations ranging from single cells, to tissues, to organs, to systems, to the body proper. Any change in a suborganization affects its immediate parent organization most directly with an intensity diminishing as it becomes more remote in the chain of organizations. The same seems true of our awareness of the physical self.

We are most keenly aware of the larger or more immediate organizations, and we are less keenly aware of the minute or remote ones.

Our awareness of body functioning is somewhat like the perceptions of the general manager of a large industry about his organization. He is most keenly aware of the departments directly within his purview, or of problems reported to him by his department heads. He may be almost totally unaware of things going on in a far corner of one of his factory buildings. Of other matters on a higher level or organization he may have a vague awareness as, for example, he may have a feeling that something is wrong in the receiving department, but be unable to state exactly what bothers him. This problem may not come clearly into focus, however, until the day when the strained relationships in the receiving department cause it to fail in providing necessary production materials. At this point the manager becomes clearly and sharply aware of the problem. Other things being equal, we are aware of those aspects of our physical selves which are most immediately in our purview or which have an immediate and precise effect upon our overall functioning. A freezing hunter does not know his fingers are numb until he has to reload his gun. Athletes keyed up to the excitement of the game have often been known to finish the game before becoming aware of injuries. Farther down the scale of organization it is increasingly difficult to be able to call perceptions of body states into clear figure. It is notoriously impossible, for example, to perceive the precise location of abdominal pains. The best we can do is to ascribe them to general areas.

2. A second factor making for the vague character of many of bodily perceptions has to do with need. A great many of our perceptions about our bodily processes are vague because there is no real need to bring them into clear figure. Many of these perceptions could be so clearly perceived as to be reportable if we wished to turn our attention to them. Many of us have had the experience, perhaps in church, of having our stomach rumble in an embarrassing way. Following such obstreperous behavior of our digestive system we may become keenly aware of a great many more vague rumblings and movements going on within us as we turn our attention from the sermon to our bodily selves. We can perceive our heart beat quite clearly if we listen for it. Though we are always aware of our muscle tensions (otherwise we could not move), we do not ordinarily maintain these perceptions sufficiently clearly to be able to report them to others. Nevertheless, we can bring many of these into clear focus simply by concentrating upon them. If it

were sufficiently important to us to spend our time on it, we could undoubtedly bring many more aspects of our physical selves into clear perception. This seems to be what the hypochondriac does when he fears he is sick. He becomes sharply aware of body functions that most of us ignore. We do not perceive them because there does not seem to be any need to do so in our peculiar economies.

Finally, many perceptions about our physical beings are not reportable because we lack the necessary symbols by which we can communicate what we feel to others. We do not have words adequate to convey some perceptions. We cannot report any definite place "where it hurts" for our doctor when he asks us. Indeed, we may not be sure what it is that hurts or even whether it hurts at all! Sometimes our awarenesses are extremely vague as when we complain of being "kind of sick," "nauseated," or "blue."

3. Many other perceptions we react to so quickly that we are unable to describe them, for their experience is so fleeting that it is impossible for us to grasp them. Who can describe, for example, what he feels when he corrects his stride to regain his balance while he is walking. We just do not have the language to enable us to report such perceptions to others. Indeed, the experience may be so vague to us that we cannot grasp its meaning even for ourselves, much less to be able to report it to others.

In the previous chapter we have seen that human beings are continuously engaged in a never-ending attempt to achieve a more adequate self. This self, moreover, is not the physical self, but the phenomenal self of which the physical organism is but a part. Though the phenomenal self includes the physical self, it extends far beyond to include the vast area of our perceptions of interactions with other people and the world about us. In Chapter 3, we have also seen that organizations both affect and are affected by the organizations of which they are part. If this is so, we would expect that our physical selves should both affect our perceptual fields and be affected by them. This is exactly what seems to be true.

Some Effects of the Physical Organism on the Perceptual Field

There can be no doubt that the physical endowment of the individual has important effects upon his perceptual field. We have already mentioned that to perceive one must have the equipment with which to do so. Other factors having to do with the physical organism will play an important part although these may vary considerably from individual to individual. Some of the factors in the physical organism affecting the perceptual field will be open to manipulation. Others will lie outside our control, or, at least, they will be beyond our control by any means of which we are now aware.

THE POSSESSION OF ADEQUATE SENSORY EQUIPMENT

Most obvious of the factors affecting perception will be the effective operation of the sensory equipment which makes perception possible. The adequate functioning of eyes and ears is an essential for visual and auditory experience, for example. One does not expect a blind man to see nor a deaf one to hear. Possession of the necessary equipment for taste, smell, and touch will also be important for perceptions to occur in these areas of experience. People lacking such essential physical equipment for perceiving live in a world different from the rest of us. Let us not make the mistake of supposing they have fewer perceptions than we. Though their perceptual fields may be limited in respect to visual or auditory perceptions, their perceptual fields may be far richer than ours in other respects. Interesting experiments with the blind and the deaf, for example, have demonstrated how such persons may develop certain common perceptual abilities to a degree of proficiency much higher than that of the sighted and those who can hear.

The functioning or nonfunctioning of essential sensory equipment for perception is usually dramatic and easily recognized. Perhaps more common, and certainly less simple to recognize, are instances in which there is impairment of function rather than outright loss. What each of us perceives seems to him to be so. The near-sighted child who cannot see as far as the blackboard but only as far as his book is missing important perceptions available to other children, but his difficulty may be overlooked by his teachers and his parents. Indeed, he may not even be aware of his problem himself since he has always seen this way. If he thinks about it at all, he may assume that this is the way other people see things. Persons with impaired vision and hearing are often quite unaware of their own disabilities.

The sense organs we possess provide us with the means by which we may perceive the world about us. They make possible our contact with the world of reality. We assume that what we see and hear is what is there to be seen and heard. Our perceptions are our own personal "realities." We are rarely led to question them. The child who has never seen or heard well assumes his experience is all there is until he sees or hears differently or is made aware that the experience of others is different.

The writer is "red-green blind." This is a form of color blindness in which a person is unable to see red and green quite as vividly as other people. I did not know of this defect until my senior year in college when one of my teachers gave a test of color vision to the class. I can recall painful instances during my childhood on family expeditions to pick wild strawberries. It always seemed that others could fill their pails much more quickly than I could fill mine and I became the object of much annoyance to the other members of my family who shoved me aside with such comments as, "For heavens sake, move over, you big lummox. You're standing right on 'em!" I remember, too, how irritated adults were if they sent me to the store to match a spool of thread. I could never do it right! Neither I nor my parents knew that I was color blind and, thus, we all behaved as though I could see normally.

Even today, it is somewhat difficult for my friends to understand that my perceptions are different from theirs. When people hear that I am red-green blind, they may pick up a red object and ask, "What color is this?" When I answer, "Red," they are crestfallen and say, "But I thought you said you are color blind!" When I assure them I am color blind, they want to know, "Well, how do you know it is red if you are color blind?" To this I always reply, "Just as you do. I have always heard this color you are pointing at called 'red' so that is the name I call it too. However, the fact that I call it red does not mean that I see the same as you." Suppose I ask you, "How do *you* know this is red?" For each of us, our own experience is real. We cannot know our senses are impaired without some standard of comparison. The healthy functioning of our sense organs has vital effects upon our perceptual fields.

LIMITATIONS OF THE CENTRAL NERVOUS SYSTEM

The existence of a normally functioning sensory apparatus is an obvious requirement for effective perception. Our sense organs make it possible for us to perceive our environment. Less obvious, but no less essential to the process of perceiving, is the existence of an adequate nervous system behind these receptors which makes possible the communication and interpretation of stimuli. Just how this happens in the nervous system is still a mystery. We know a good deal about the physiology and growth of the nervous system and we know something of the transmission of nerve impulses. However, the process of converting these simple impulses into the complex meanings of our perceptions is a mystery that still eludes us.

Just as a person may be born with certain weaknesses or impairments of his sensory equipment, so too, he may be born with deficiencies in his nerve structure. We know something about a few of these anomalies but much still remains to be discovered. There may be impairments of which we are still completely unaware. We know, for example, that children are sometimes born with serious handicaps directly related to malfunctioning of the nervous system. These include such disorders as Mongolism, and microcephaly or macrocephaly which seem to be the result of maldevelopment during the uterine period. Persons afflicted with such disorders seem unable to perceive as effectively and efficiently as other people. Even when given many opportunities, they are apparently less able to profit by their experience or to modify their perceptions in the light of what has happened about them.

Other disturbances affecting the central nervous system are certain types of glandular dysfunction. Best known among these is cretinism. Children suffering from severe thyroid deficiencies in early childhood may develop a malfunctioning body which seriously impedes their efficiency in perceiving. Such children are often classed as mentally deficient because of their failure to learn as well as normal children. We know very little about how or why this reduction of perceptual efficiency occurs, but apparently a lack of normal secretions from the thyroid glands impairs the functioning of the nervous system and this, in turn, has restricting effects upon the child's ability to perceive.

Impairment may also be caused by a mechanical injury to the brain or the spinal cord. Injuries of this sort may occur in the process of entering the world at birth or may be the result of accident or illness later in life. Whatever their origin, however, they may markedly affect the individual's ability to perceive efficiently. Children with severe brain damage, for example, are apt to be extremely distractible. They often seem unable to control their perceptions and attention jumps rapidly from point to point so that they never seem to alight long enough to catch up with themselves. The exact nature of the mechanics producing this unfortunate impairment of perceptive functioning is still unknown.

Other types of damage which we know produce serious limits upon perceiving may result if the organism has been deprived of oxygen for any reason (anoxia). This sometimes happens to deep sea divers who dive too deep or remain down too long. It occurs, too, to persons overcome by gas. Lack of oxygen apparently causes destruction of brain cells, giving typical symptoms of brain damage.

A further limitation of the nervous system upon perceiving may be observed in cases of cerebral palsy. In this and similar disorders, damage to the nervous system may more or less seriously impair normal body functioning. Thus, in cerebral palsy, a malfunctioning nervous system may cause muscles to work in opposition to each other causing a spastic kind of movement, instead of the smooth operation of muscle groups characteristic of most of us. The ability of such persons to perceive effectively and clearly may be quite unaffected. Any impairment of bodily functioning, however, has effects upon perceiving as a result of the restrictions it places upon mobility. People who do not get about as well as others do not perceive the same things in the same ways. As the vehicle of our perceiving, our bodies provide the platform from which we make our observations, and important changes in this platform inevitably affect our perception. The victim of cerebral palsy sees the world differently from the unafflicted, although he does not necessarily see it less richly or less completely. Similarly, the epileptic may be quite able to perceive effectively and efficiently, but he inevitably perceives himself and the world around him differently because of his handicap.

In recent years we have come to understand that certain diseases like *encephalitis lethargica* can have effects upon perceiving such that marked behavior changes may occur following an attack of this disease. Personalities have been known to change with dramatic suddenness following encephalitis so that patients appear to be quite different people. Such behavior changes must be the result of different ways of perceiving themselves and the world around them, but the details of how and why these changes occur we do not know. Similarly, we now know that any disease accompanied by high fever, especially in early childhood, may be followed by a more or less serious impairment of intellectual functioning.

Anyone who has had the misfortune to be seriously ill at some time in his life may have experienced the distortion of perception characteristic of delirium. This, too, is a physical effect upon perception; it occasionally happens when a person has a high fever. He may have wild delusions or hallucinations of weird happenings to himself or to the world around him. These seem to be concomitant effects of temporary impairment of the normal functioning of the nervous systems.

Fortunately, most of us have relatively intact and functioning nervous systems which make it possible for us to perceive with ease and accuracy. Indeed, it is remarkable that despite its complexity the human nervous system manages to function as perfectly as it does.

LIMITATIONS OF GENERAL HEALTH

Most of the above effects of our physical structure upon perceiving are obvious and dramatic. They are effects we are not likely to miss. Perhaps even more important, because they are so much more likely to be missed, are the less readily observable effects upon perception resulting from debilitating, but not disabling, physical impairments. Any physical disturbance which seriously reduces energy reserves of the organism has its effects upon the scope of perception. When an individual is sick enough to be confined to his bed, it is easy for us to understand how his abilities to perceive may be restricted by his inability to get around. Listlessness or lack of interest may have similar effects. Whatever decreases alertness has inevitable effects upon perceptive efficiency.

Lesser degrees of illness, in which the individual is handicapped, but not incapacitated, may also have their effects upon perceiving, for whatever depletes our abilities to get around and become involved with life must necessarily affect our perception. We know, for example, that the physical and mental development of children is closely related. Even intelligence, which is, in a sense, the ability to perceive effectively and efficiently seems closely related to the general physical well being of the individual. "Studies of Genius" has shown us that children with high I.Q.'s are also generally taller, heavier, healthier, and in every way superior to average children. Intelligence has even been known to improve with improved nutrition. Whatever affects the general level of efficient bodily functioning may also affect the individual's perceptual field. Limitations of general health such as malnutrition, chronic focal infections, or long-continued fatigue may affect perception in at least three general ways:

1. *By reducing mobility.* When energy levels are depleted, we do not move around as much as when we are well. We prefer to hoard our limited supplies and to avoid activity. It is quite possible for people to perceive richly and broadly although confined for a lifetime to a small space but, other things being equal, most of us perceive more richly and

more effectively when our freedom of movement is unhampered. A person confined to his bed by illness may find his perceptions confined to tracing the patterns of the wallpaper. When we are fatigued, malnourished, or suffering from disease or chronic focal infections, we do not feel like exerting ourselves. It is an effort to move about, and we prefer to take it easy. Such inactivity saves energy, but also has restricting effects upon our perceptual fields.

2. *By reducing interest.* Interests are a vital factor in controlling the richness and variety of the perceptions we make. Any physiological condition which affects the degree or intensity of interest, whether directly or indirectly, must have its concomitant effects upon the ability to perceive. Thus, when energy levels are depleted by disease, malnutrition, focal infections, fatigue, or any other debilitating factor, interest levels will be sharply lowered and perception restricted. The man who is ill and tired finds it difficult to work up much enthusiasm for active participation in events. He is not interested in going to a meeting, attending a lecture, or getting involved in an activity, and so loses an opportunity for perceiving. Indeed, if he is very ill or in great pain, he may find it almost impossible to perceive more than his own unhappy state.

3. *By focusing attention under deprivation.* In the preceding chapter the nature of the organism's fundamental need for the maintenance and enhancement of the self was discussed. One of the prime requirements for the satisfaction of this need is the healthy condition of the physical organism which does the perceiving. This need has an organizing or limiting effect upon our perceptions. We would expect, then, that when the operations of our bodies are seriously impaired, there should be an organization of our perceptions with respect to such threats. This is exactly what seems to occur. We may go for long periods unaware of some portion of our bodies as long as it is operating smoothly or effectively. However, the moment some part of our physical self is injured or begins to function badly, we immediately become aware of that part, and our attentions are directed to it. All of us have had experiences of this sort in which our perceptions become focused more or less intensely on some portion of our physical bodies momentarily out of order, such as when we have injured a finger. Before the injury, we took our fingers for granted and accepted their functioning without question. But when we have smashed a finger in the car door, or hit it with the hammer, our perceptions become suddenly concentrated on the injured member of our organization. Indeed, we may momentarily be incapable of perceiv-

ing anything else. Even long after the first shock of injury has passed, we are keenly aware of our hurt finger during the period of convalescence.

Similarly our perceptions become organized whenever our physical selves suffer deprivation. When we are hungry our perceptions become focused on food, and when we are thirsty, our perceptions are concerned with drinking fountains, the kitchen sink, or mountain streams. Several psychologists have carried out interesting experiments by systematically depriving subjects of food or drink for long periods and examining the effects of such deprivation on perception. Subjects report an increasing concern for food or drink as the degree of deprivation increases until consciousness itself begins to be affected. They report spending many hours daydreaming about delicious food, memorizing recipes, or imagining sumptuous banquets. They became disinterested in other people and protested their places in the food line. On shopping trips they bought cooking utensils for which they had no real need.

THE EFFECT OF DRUGS UPON PERCEPTION. Alcohol and drugs, which are often used as a means of escape from the crueler facts of life, have interesting effects upon the perceptions of the individual. Such narcotics seem to create a feeling of well-being by reducing the clarity and sharpness of perception, or by temporarily providing a feeling of strength and freedom of action. These effects can be clearly observed in the use of alcohol. It is a common observation that light "social drinking" at a party helps to loosen the tongues of the guests and make them more at ease, especially when they are strangers to one another. As people become less able to perceive the reactions of others and experience a lessening of awareness of their own tensions or inadequacies, their inhibitions are relaxed and feeling tone is enhanced. With a deadening of awareness of self, individuals do not have to face so sharply the distasteful fact of not being what they would like to be. They are relieved of normal burdens of self consciousness and can behave in a less inhibited fashion. When an individual is in complete stupor, unpleasantness can be escaped entirely.

One of the effects of fear and anxiety is to restrict the individual's perceptual field. Anything, therefore, which tends to eliminate anxiety thus seems to leave the individual free to perceive both himself and the world about him. Drugs which tend to eliminate anxious feelings have even been known to result in changes in intelligence test scores.

Some narcotics seem to produce this effect of well-being not by the dampening of perception alone, but by temporarily giving the individual additional reserves of energy which, in turn, add to the person's feeling of well-being and adequacy. Alcohol, for example, is quickly converted to energy in the body, and this is experienced as an increase in strength or power so that the individual may feel more capable. The feeling of strength may also be augmented as the drug counteracts the effects of fatigue. Narcotics which are accompanied by dreaming may produce an added sense of well-being through fantasy which permits the individual to be, for a while, almost anything he pleases.

Such effects are not limited to narcotics. Actually, the same effects, to a lesser degree, may be produced by food or fatigue. Anyone who has ever worked with young children must surely have observed how quickly active youngsters react to food. A child who has been whining and irritable may, in a few moments, be transformed into a fairly pleasant human being by giving him a meal or a between-meal snack of milk and cookies. Apparently the sense of well-being induced by the restoration of energy gives the child an entirely different perception of himself and his world. Beyond a certain point the chemical products of fatigue seem to produce a deadening of awareness similar to the narcotic effects mentioned above so that the behavior has a spurious feeling of capacity which can sometimes prove highly dangerous. Automobile drivers, for example, after long hours at the wheel seem to become less aware of the need to stop. They feel, instead, quite capable of going on when they had much better not.

EFFECTS OF BODY STRUCTURE. The general body structure with which we are endowed may not affect our perceptions directly, but it has important indirect effects upon the nature of our perceptions. Our bodies provide the vehicle or platform from which perceptions are made and we have already seen that what is observed is in large measure a function of the point from which the observations are made. The tall man sees things quite differently from the short man for the simple reason that his eyes are higher above the ground. Some years ago on a trip to New York, I got so engrossed in a mystery thriller that I did not notice the people who got on the train and took seats around me during the last hundred miles of the trip. When the train pulled into Grand Central Station, of course, everyone stood up. When I stood up with the rest of the passengers I was struck with a moment of panic, for everywhere I looked I was looking at belt buckles! When I boarded the train I had been a man of average height. Now, suddenly, I was a pigmy among giants. For a moment I had a very strange feeling that my whole world had lost its stability until I noticed that all the men standing around me carried bags marked "New York Knickerbockers," the name of a famous professional basketball team!

Almost any aspect of our general body structure or condition can have its indirect effects upon our perceptions. Children see differently from adults by the mere fact of being of different height. But perceptions may also be affected by our weight, skin color, strength, sex, and appearance. These effects will be particularly marked if our society has developed expectancies about them. Thus, the perceptions of the self held by stout women in Russia, where stoutness is acceptable, are quite different from that of the stout young American woman who must live in a world which values the slim, svelte figure.

Everyone's perceptions are deeply affected by his sex. Men and women do not perceive alike. From the moment of his birth our society begins to impress upon the child the fact of his maleness or femaleness, what is expected of boys and girls, of men or women in our culture. Similarly the values we place upon appearance have their inevitable effects upon the individual's perceptions. We call some people ugly and some beautiful. Some kinds of skin blemishes we regard with horror or disgust. The structure and appearance of our physical beings is the platform of perception and has its vital effects upon ways of perceiving.

HANDICAPS AFFECT PERCEPTION. Any kind of physical handicap may have its effect upon the perceptive field. Speech defects or various forms of physical abnormalities may deeply modify the perceptions of the individual afflicted with them. The perceptions of self and of the world about him are inexorably affected by the mere presence of such handicaps. For some the handicap may even become one of the most central aspects of living. Our folklore is replete with tales of persons who have spent their lives compensating for the existence of a personal inadequacy.

EFFECT OF BODY CONDITION ON THE PHENOMENAL SELF

We have previously pointed out that the phenomenal self is more or less roughly defined by the body surfaces of the individual. Thus, the body and its condition as a part of the field of the organism must affect behavior. It is probable that for most of us every field state includes more or less of this body condition as an integral part of the total field. Furthermore, in the course of our development we learn to differentiate more or less strongly the particular aspects of body condition which are more or less important in the definition of the phenomenal field. Which aspect we differentiate most strongly is likely to be a function of the phenomenal self. Thus, in our culture, men are more likely to be concerned with physical vigor, while for women the particular figure in vogue or facial beauty is likely to be most strongly differentiated. Frequently children are far more concerned with physical size and strength than with other aspects of the body, while adolescents are mainly interested in those aspects which make for successful competition for the attention of the opposite sex.

Since the physical body is the most constant aspect of our experience, it is not surprising that it should play a very large part in defining the phenomenal self. For most people the smooth-running body in good condition is likely to give a feeling of enhancement of the self, as it makes its owner feel adequate, competent, and in control of situations. Poor physical condition, on the other hand, may result in the definition of the phenomenal self as in some fashion humiliated. This is a frequent symptom of people with a physical handicap. I once worked with a young girl who was frightfully conscious of the size of her nose. In my estimation her nose was not in the least unusual, but she regarded it as a constant badge of shame and humiliation. She finally had plastic surgery which, in her opinion, helped her a great deal by reducing her nose, although no change was apparent to me. It is clear that she was attending to an aspect of her body dictated by her concept of herself. Furthermore, a slight change in this bodily characteristic apparently resulted in considerable change in her phenomenal self.

EFFECT OF THE PHENOMENAL SELF ON BODY CONDITION

It seems evident that the effect of the body on the phenomenal self is not the only direction in which this body-self relationship can operate. The reverse situation is also very frequent with the phenomenal self profoundly affecting the bodily condition of the individual. This is particularly evident in the new field of psychosomatics where bodily disturbances appear as the result of psychological problems. Physicians have discovered an increasingly long list of human diseases and ailments which seem to have their origin in the affective, emotional, or psychological life of the individual. The study of the interrelationship between behavior and the physical organism in which behavior occurs is called psychosomatics, and it is destined to play an increasing part in the practice of medicine. Fascinating as the topic of psychosomatics is, we shall not stop to deal with the problem here. That is subject matter for several books.

One of the most interesting examples in my experience of the effect of the self on the physical condition was the case of a young woman who had been overprotected all her life by a very domineering mother. At college she had stuck closely to another girl very much like herself. Immediately after graduation her friend left to be married but this young woman remained at home. Within a few days of graduation she developed eczema on one hand which rapidly spread to cover her entire body and particularly her face. Obviously, in such a condition it was impossible for her to seek a position. She traveled about from doctor to doctor and from clinic to clinic without success. When she went to a camp her eczema disappeared completely, but as soon as she returned to the city it returned in full force. During psychotherapy I observed that this skin condition became less and less pronounced while we talked. However, the slightest reference to her condition or any attack upon her organization would bring it back. Eventually this client came to achieve some insight into her condition but found it difficult to admit its nature even to herself. To admit any such shenanigans would be a threat to her concept of herself as a brilliant student of psychology. The fact, that others in whom she had faith thought her condition to be psychological was, however, disturbing. It was necessary for her to rid herself of the condition without accepting the cause as psychological. This she did by adopting a diet she heard about from someone she met on the street. Within a week her skin cleared up. Since then she has found a job and moved on to a better adjustment in other ways as well. It is significant that, in spite of discontinuing her absurd diet, her condition has not returned. From many examples of this type, it would seem possible that in certain types of physical disturbances, real changes in the bodily condition of an individual may be brought about by changes in the phenomenal self.

It is the thesis of this book that behavior is the product of the perceptual field. Perception makes possible such behavior as feeding, drinking, or sheltering one's self against the elements. Without perception reproduction would be impossible. Where the body goes, what it eats, drinks, enjoys, or avoids is the product of its perceptions. The perceptions available to the organism even determine whether it lives or dies. This entire book is, in a sense, devoted to the question of the effect of perception upon the physical organism since we attempt to understand behavior from a perceptual point of view.

CHAPTER 5

Time and Opportunity Affect Perception

THE physical body provides the vehicle which makes perceiving possible. The fundamental need for adequacy provides us with motive and direction. These factors impose important limits upon individual perception and behavior. But these alone are insufficient to explain the richness and diversity of human perception, or the variety of behavior produced by the perceptual field. It is a commonplace observation that people behave differently depending upon the time and place in which they are involved.

These determinants of behavior, observed from an external point of view, are also important in order to understand behavior from a perceptual frame of reference. Both time and environment are important variables in controlling the nature and extent of the perceptual field.

Perceiving Takes Time

Other things being equal, what an individual is able to perceive in any situation will depend upon the length of time he has been exposed to the event. This principle is familiar to anyone who has ever studied a painting. The longer one looks, the more he is able to perceive. The reader may test this now for himself by looking intently at the floor, the ceiling, or the walls of his room. He first sees the grosser aspects of the object. Very quickly, however, he will find he is noting more detail. Looking at a wall, for example, one may first perceive its general shape and color. Looking longer one may become conscious of the texture, of parts of the wall, of relationships, cracks, inequalities in the paint, and so forth. The same effects may be noted in our other senses. The more often one hears a piece of music, for example, the more he perceives. With each hearing, different nuances, not heard before, may come into figure. This process of discerning increasing detail out of the total field of awareness is called differentiation. We shall want to examine this phenomenon much more closely in a later section of this book.

Considering the effect of time upon perceiving, we must keep in mind that we are speaking of the duration of the individual's experience with an event rather than the observer's. Thus, while it may appear to an outside observer that a person is confronted by an experience, from that person's own point of view he may have no contact with the experience whatever. A child may sit in school all day, apparently exposed to the curriculum, but may actually experience and perceive quite different aspects of the situation. While the teacher labors under the delusion that a child is being exposed to arithmetic, he may actually be admiring the pretty girl across the aisle, examining the names of former students carved on his desk, or he may even, in fantasy, be hunting bears in Alaska. Perception is an internal, individual phenomenon and the perceptual field of one individual may be quite different from that of another, even in what seems to be the same situation. In considering the time of exposure to an event, therefore, we must see the problem from the point of view of the behaver.

The time required for perception to occur varies tremendously from a minute fraction of a second to generations. Tachistoscopic studies, for example, have shown that it is possible for a person to differentiate single words exposed in such machines at speeds of as little as one hundredth of a second. Subjects shown an object for very short periods of exposure report only seeing "something there." As the time of exposure is increased they may be able to perceive the object vaguely, and when exposure has been increased to a full second or more, quite complicated perceptions can be made. The perceptions we make of many events in the external world around us can be made with great speed. On the other hand, human beings lived with gravity for thousands of years before it was perceived and stated as a principle of physics. People had been looking at the sun for a long time before Copernicus helped us to perceive that the earth went around the sun instead of vice versa.

The purely mechanical aspects of perceiving are extremely rapid. Given something the individual "knows" and is "set" to perceive, he can perceive at incredible speed. Events new to the individual or buried in a larger, more complicated field take considerably longer to be perceived.

A second factor affecting the time required for perception has to do with the fact that most perceptions the individual makes are functions of previous perceptions. Before one can perceive the mechanics of multiplication, for example, he must have perceived addition. The child cannot perceive the need for the sand dome on the locomotive until he has first perceived that sometimes locomotive wheels slip. Many of our perceptions are based upon long series of previous discriminations extending back to our earliest beginnings. It seems axiomatic that to make differentiations a person must have lived long enough to do so, a fact we recognize in the construction of intelligence tests calibrated for various age levels and which teachers recognize in the concept of readiness or maturation.

A great many of our difficulties in communication seem to stem from our failure to recognize the importance of time in perceiving. The speaker who moves too fast loses his audience and makes himself ineffective. Communication may fail because the audience has not had sufficient previous experience to perceive the new aspects conveyed by the speaker. Since new perceptions derive their meaning in large part from already existing perceptions in the field, the time required to perceive a given event will be affected by the existing field. Listening to a lecture in advanced mathematics, would leave most of us hopelessly unable to comprehend for lack of the proper differentiations at earlier periods in our lives.

Opportunity Affects Perceiving

For perception to occur, there must be an opportunity for perception. We are accustomed to believing that what we perceive is so. Our perceptions seem to us to be an accurate picture of what exists. When we perceive a chair, we believe the chair exists; so much so, that we are willing to sit down on it. We can see for ourselves that the chair holds us up. What is more, other people in whom we have confidence also believe the chair exists. We can confirm our experience of the chair by testing our perception with our other senses; we can feel the chair with our hands, we can hear it when we move it, we can even smell it and taste it, if necessary. Best of all, we can corroborate our impressions from the reports of other people whom we trust and who agree that what we perceive is true.

Now, whether there is anything *really* there when we perceive is a problem philosophers have been arguing about for generations. To understand behavior, however, it is not necessary for us to settle that argument. Since behavior is a function of perception, it is the perceptions of people with which we must be concerned, and these perceptions can be studied whether or not they have any counterpart in reality.

To understand an individual's behavior the only reality we need to be concerned with is what *seems real to him.* If people believe an event is so, then for them it is so. As students of human behavior this is the reality with which we must deal. In the following pages, when it is necessary for us to discuss external events, objects, or opportunities we shall refer to the generally accepted beliefs people have about the world in which they live, leaving the question of whether these beliefs or perceptions have any counterpart in an objective world to the philosophers and logicians.

There is a vast world of people, things, and abstract ideas which we can see, hear, feel, measure, or perhaps only think about, which seems to us real and objective. This is the environment in which we live; it provides much of the raw material of our experience. This environment, furthermore, provides many opportunities for perception, which may be more or less concrete, or physical, contacts of the individual with his world, or which may be vicarious experiences.

CONCRETE OPPORTUNITIES FOR PERCEPTION. In the first place, the perceptions possible to any individual will be limited, in part, by the individual's own direct experience of the environmental factors to which he has been exposed. Eskimos ordinarily do not comprehend bananas, nor African bushmen snow, since neither has had the opportunity to experience them in his environment. In a similar way, each of us has come to perceive many aspects of the physical environments in which we have lived. The major sources of concrete experiences are:

1. The natural scene—the geographic and geologic features about us such as rocks, rivers, seas, mountains, and plains, as well as the recurring tides and our experience of night and day.

2. The constructions of man—the highways, harbors, buildings, machinery, furniture, signboards, papers, autos, and a million other items.

3. The world of living things—animals, insects, plants, microörganisms.

4. The experience of the self—one's own physical, emotional, and thinking being.

5. The interaction with others—the social existence of man and the impact of other people upon him.

VICARIOUS OPPORTUNITIES FOR PERCEPTION. Perceptions may also occur in the individual's field as a consequence of exposure to the experience of others, through reading, conversation, movies, and other means of communication. The development of language makes possible vast opportunities for perceiving on a symbolic level what we could not ordinarily hope to experience. Although I cannot directly perceive that it is dangerous to expose myself to rays from an atomic pile, for example, I can differentiate this notion through what others whom I respect have told me. Many of our perceptions are acquired through this kind of symbolic exposure. Certainly most of our formal schooling falls in this category, which may explain, in part, why so little of it is effective in changing behavior. Ideas which we have not differentiated ourselves from the broad background of our perceptual field are apt to remain isolated from the rest of the field and to have little effect on behavior.

What people perceive is necessarily limited by the opportunities to which they have been exposed in the course of their growth and development. This fact is nowhere better demonstrated than in the now famous Ames demonstrations in perception. These startling phenomena demonstrate with great clarity several important basic principles concerning perception:

1. *What is perceived is not what exists, but what one believes exists.* This principle is illustrated in the chair demonstration. This demonstration consists of a large wooden box into which one can look from several holes in the front. Looking into the box through one of these peep holes, one sees a chair as shown in Fig. 9. When, however, one goes around behind the box to look down inside it, there is no chair at all, only a series of white strings suspended in the otherwise empty space of the box, as shown in Fig. 10. What we have seen looking through the peep holes is not what is actually there, but only what the observer believes to be there. As Ames said,

> Everybody believes that when we use our eyes, we look at "something out there" in our environment from which light rays come to our eyes and bring about images on our retinas. Everybody believes that "what is out there" contributes to what is in our visual awareness. But not everybody believes that we ourselves also contribute to what is in our visual awareness, although this is the case.
>
> While modern physics has disclosed a great deal about certain aspects of the something "out there," and while modern physiology has disclosed a great deal about our stimulus patterns and bodily processes, relatively little has been learned about the nature of what we ourselves "subjectively" contribute to our perceptions of the "something out there."
>
> You have, it would seem, sufficient evidence that what is in your visual

Fig. 9. Chair Demonstration (Seen from the Front). (From W. H. Ittelson, *The Ames Demonstrations in Perception,* Princeton University Press, Princeton, N.J. Reprinted by permission of the publisher.)

Fig. 10. Chair Demonstration (Seen from the Rear). (From W. H. Ittelson, *The Ames Demonstrations in Perception,* Princeton University Press, Princeton, N.J. Reprinted by permission of the publisher.)

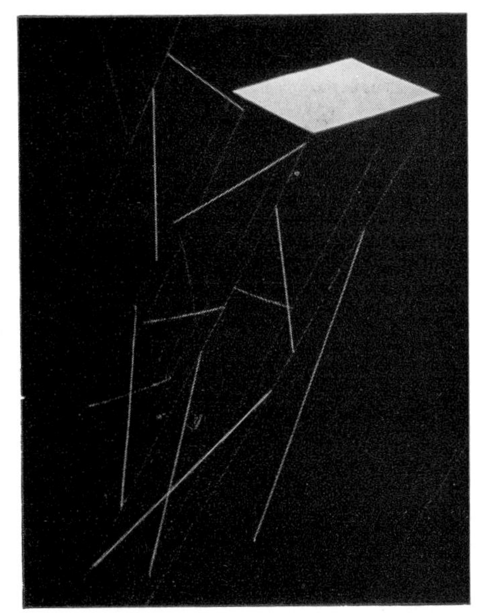

awareness was neither in your stimulus patterns nor in the environment, but was your own contribution to the perceptual event.

Stated in terms of field dynamics, objects and events impinging upon our perceptual fields are perceived in the way which best "fits" the field of that instant. In Ames' demonstration it is significant that a "chair" requires less differentiation. It takes less time to perceive a chair than to carry the process of differentiating further and to break the experience down into a number of strings. We could equally well draw illustrations of this principle from many experiences of daily life wherein we hear or see what we consider reasonable to perceive. Because we are hungry and it is near lunch time, the call from the kitchen is heard as a call to come to lunch. Vague impressions of another person may be put together so that we believe we see a friend only to discover, after we have hailed him, that he is a total stranger. We often jump to apparently reasonable conclusions even though these conclusions may later prove to be wrong. This characteristic of people to perceive what fits into their mental picture rather than what exists, constantly creates problems for our courts in determining the credibility of witnesses. It is often difficult to recognize whether a witness is reporting what actually happened or what he believes "must have happened."

Since the perceptual field is always organized, what is perceived must be the product of this organization. If perception occurs at all, it must occur with meaning. Meaning is given to events by the relationships in the perceptual field in which they occur. The words read by each reader of this page have different meanings. Even the same reader rereading the page will perceive differently. Reading is not so much a matter of taking meaning *from* a book as bringing meaning *to* the printed page. This is not to suggest that the ideas set down by an author are unnecessary or without value. Not at all. Experience is, of course, essential to perceiving, but what is perceived is determined by the unique perceptual field of each person which includes much more than the direct experience of our senses.

2. *What is perceived is what we have learned to perceive as a result of our past opportunities or experiences.* To illustrate this principle, Ames has developed several distorted rooms, one of which is diagramed in Fig. 11. This room is obviously distorted with a tilting floor and ceiling when one looks at it from a distance. Coming close, however, and looking into the room without extraneous cues to guide him, the observer

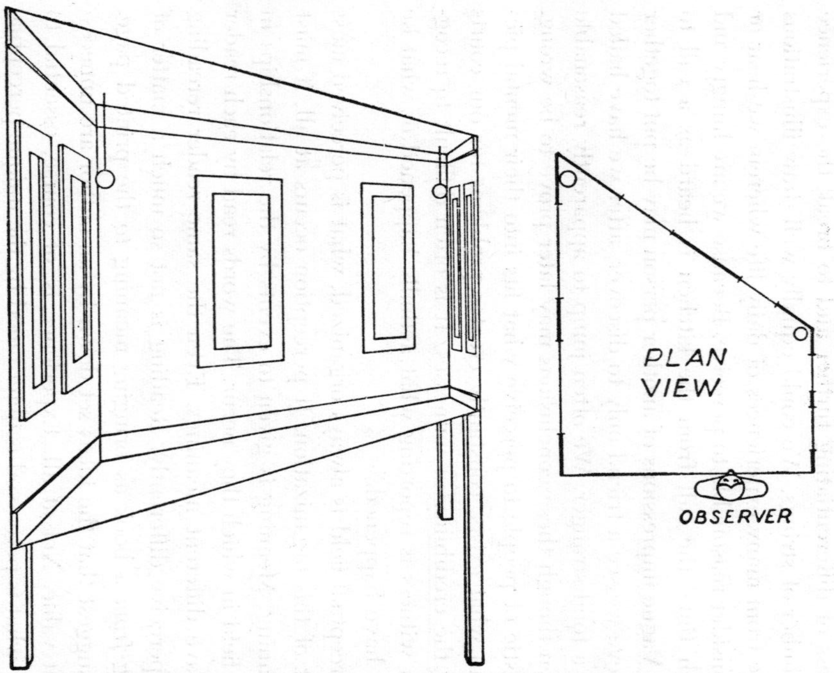

Fig. 11. This Is a Drawing of the Distorted Room. It does not show the distortion fully, because the back left corner does not appear to be far enough away from us. The reason for this is that there are so many things built into the room which violate the usual rules of perspective. For example, consider the two back windows. If they were the same size, the left one should look smaller than the right one, because it is farther away. It is actually larger, and when drawn larger, the left corner refuses to go back where it belongs. In order to realize how far away the back left corner is, we have to have the plan view, which is a horizontal cross section of the room. For the experiment, the observer is placed nearer the right wall than the left one. (From Earl C. Kelley, *Education for What Is Real*, New York, Harper, 1947.)

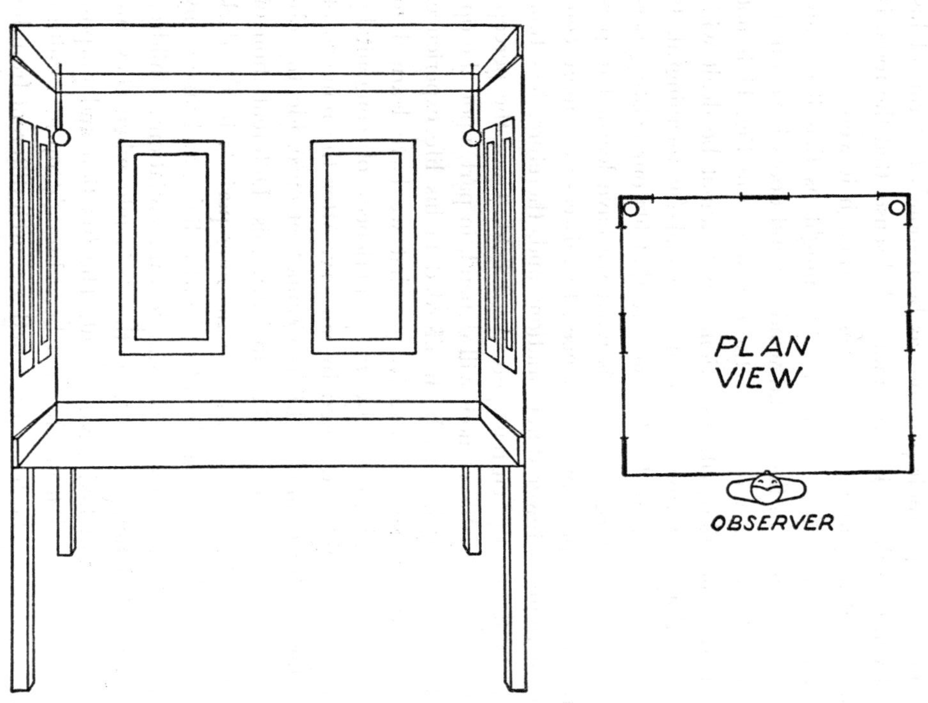

Fig 12. This Is the Distorted Room as It Appears to the Observer. Note that the back left corner appears to be the same distance away as the back right one. The back windows appear to be the same size. In the plan view, note that while the observer is actually to the right of the center (see Fig. 11), he seems to be in the center. (From Earl C. Kelley, ***Education for What Is Real***, New York, Harper, 1947.)

discovers that the room looks perfectly normal with level floor and ceiling, windows of equal size and properly squared corners, as shown in Fig. 12. Even though the observer has seen the distortion of the room a few moments before, he now sees it like a normal room. Moreover, when he is given a pointer and asked to touch various points in the room, he badly misjudges their positions as he responds in terms of his perceptions. Even though he "knows," in a verbal sense, that the room is distorted, he sees it as normal and behaves as though it were.

Our experience since our earliest days has taught us that floors are level, ceilings are parallel to floors, and windows and doors have square corners and parallel sides. A room like the one shown in Fig. 11 is not meaningful. It does not jibe with experience and cannot be dealt with without the additional information required to make it meaningful. It is seen, therefore, not as it is, but in the way that fits our existing perceptions of reality. What is perceived is what we have learned to perceive as a result of our previous experiences. In this case the more conventional room requires fewer differentiations and, therefore, less time and effort, to fit it into the current perceptual field. Thus, the perceptions an individual is capable of now will depend, in part, upon the opportunities for perceiving he has been afforded in his life experience.

This principle that what we perceive is what we have learned to perceive is effectively illustrated by the experiences of congenitally blind persons whose sight is restored by surgery. After the removal of congenital cataracts, for example, children cannot, at once, identify objects by size and shape. It takes time to learn this. Differentiation of color is even slower. Chimpanzees raised for long periods in the dark are extremely incompetent when first placed in the light, and take many months to be able to perceive fairly simple differentiations. Children raised in extreme isolation demonstrate this principle when they are placed in a new and enriched environment. The function and purpose of bath tubs is not obvious if one has not been brought up in a culture that uses them. Anyone who has ever visited a church different from his own may recall his own struggles to comprehend what was going on in the service and the way in which it became clear when he learned to interpret the symbolism correctly.

When we are faced with incongruous events, we tend to perceive them in the way that is most familiar or meaningful to us at that moment. This is the basic principle upon which projective tests are constructed; namely, that, when an individual is asked to respond to an ambiguous situation, he will invest it with the meanings important to him. Even simple forms or diagrams may be interpreted and named in this fashion. Ink blots, for example, may be seen as all sorts of things by subjects taking the Rorschach test. The meanings we have learned, moreover, are often highly stable and difficult to change. Experiments of changing child attitudes toward people of other nationalities by showing the child movies, for example, demonstrate that, though new information may temporarily change child values, when the pressure to change has passed, perceptions gradually revert to earlier forms.

Apparently the proverb "seeing is believing" is not as sure-fire an indication of what is so as we are led to believe. Indeed, the existence of the principle that perceptions are largely learned calls for a reexamination of some of our most cherished and time-honored beliefs and practices in human relationships.

The Concept of Constancies

The physical world in which we live, of course, provides us with important opportunities for perception. In fact, just to exist in any situation makes demands on an individual's perceptual field. If I am immersed in water in the middle of a lake, this predicament imposes upon me perceptions that enable me to keep afloat. When the temperature gets low in my living room, it affects my perceptions and I become aware that I must keep warm. When my car is going too fast, I soon perceive that I must slow down before I have an accident. All situations in which people are involved have some effect upon their perceptions. Some of our experiences are so frequent, stable, or important, moreover, that they serve us as frames of reference for judgment.

Because of this interaction with the physical world around him, the individual learns to perceive when he is right side up or upside down, in warm places or cold. He also learns to orient himself in space by perceiving himself in relationship to objects in the environment. These perceptions become the individual's "anchors to reality" and provide a stable base for his behavior. Psychologists have called these perceptions "anchorages." They provide the individual with standards for judgment and meaning. Most of us, for example, have come to rely upon the horizon as a fixed point of reference for many of our perceptions. Similarly, we judge distance, weight, time, and appropriateness of behavior with reference to important or stable aspects of our own experience which can serve as bases of comparison.

We do not, however, rely only upon our experience of the external world to provide us with standards of judgment. We actively invest some objects, events, or concepts with stability. We build up "constancies" and, thereafter, depend upon them as platforms or frames of reference to comprehend the world about us. Cantril says of these constancies, "We create these constancies by attributing certain *consistent* and *repeatable* characteristics to what they refer to, so that we can guess with a fair degree of accuracy what the significances and meanings are of the various sensory cues that impinge upon us. We do this so that we will not have to make fresh guesses at every turn. These significances we build up about objects, people, symbols, and events, or about ideas all orchestrate together to give us what we might call our own unique "reality world."

The use of personal experience as frames of reference is done so smoothly and naturally that we often do not even perceive that we are doing it. When, however, we must behave without the use of such guides, we become keenly aware of their importance. This is well illustrated in the autokinetic phenomenon which concerns the apparent behavior of a fixed spot of light in a completely dark room. Without a reference point to which the spot of light can be referred, it is seen by most subjects as drifting about in space. It is difficult to localize or pin down an experience when we do not have access to our usual points of reference. When such anchorages are lost or when they become too variable to be depended upon, sane people become quite ill. This seems to occur in sea sickness, when many of one's normal anchors to reality become unpredictable and even the horizon seems to leave its moorings. An amusing illustration of this relationship is to be found in the experiences of the test pilot who wanted to determine if there was any truth to the idea that pilots fly "by the seat of their pants." Before take off the pilot had several shots of novocaine injected into his posterior to deaden his perception of contact with his seat. As a result he became nauseated and ill after turning and diving maneuvers which were no more than routine in the ordinary course of his duties!

Our perceptions of the physical world generally are adequate because inadequate perceptions of the physical world tend to be self correcting. I may be unhappy because I arrived at my friend's party just as the party was breaking up because I missed the proper turn and lost my way. But when I go there again I shall still have to make the same turn and I shall be able to differentiate clearly and rely upon my differentiation. Physical factors have a high degree of predictability. The same stability often cannot be found in people and, consequently, adequate frames of reference are harder to discover. Thus, a child finds it easier to adjust his perceptions about the streets he must cross on his way to school than to discover what his teachers or relatives expect of him. Streets stay where they belong but people, sometimes, refuse to sit still long enough to know what they are about.

There is evidence to suggest that some forms of maladjustment have their roots in the individual's inability to cope with events because he does not clearly understand the "expectancies." Experimental neurosis can be produced, for example, by forcing animals to deal with capricious events. Rats or goats, for instance, which have been trained to escape severe punishment by making a particular choice of behavior, may become quite desperate when such choices are no longer possible because they are continuously shifting and changing. Need satisfaction is impossible in an unpredictable world. The development of dependable constancies and anchorages is essential to the individual's very existence.

Despite its difficulties establishing anchorages with respect to people is essential to successful living in an interdependent and social world like ours. Because we are so dependent on other people for need satisfaction, we must work out effective relationships with them. To do this, it is necessary to invest other people with elements of consistency and predictability. As a consequence, we attempt to classify people, to give them roles, status, prestige, authority, and the like, to provide handy reference tags to help us deal with them. The particular social anchorages or constancies differentiated by a particular person are the product of his experience with the important people in his world while he grew up. From those around him he learns about authority figures and what to expect of men and women. He develops expectancies about Negro people and white people, about labor and management, and so on; in time these expectancies may become so firm as to serve him as predictable guides. Some of these frames of reference about people will be quite unique, sometimes even bizarre. When this happens individuals have difficulty dealing with each other. Effective interaction must be based upon stable, accurate concepts of what other people are like. Fortunately, many of our expectancies about people are shared with others, because we have grown up in a common culture.

The Individual's Culture and Opportunities for Perceiving

It is not physical situations alone that force perceptions upon us. For most of us social demands are far more frequent and pressing in daily life. Demands are imposed upon the individual by his family, his friends, his community, and his nation; in short, by every life situation with which he is faced. Much of any person's behavior is the observable expression of his unceasing attempt to achieve need satisfaction when he is confronted with the necessities imposed upon him by the cultures in which he moves. Consequently, a very large portion of the perceptions we are able to make are a direct result of the particular cultures in which we have been brought up. Indeed, the social setting in which we live is so all-pervasive that even the inanimate aspects of our worlds are given meaning by the culture.

The experience of the individual in meeting the demands of life in his particular culture plays a large part in determining the richness and variety of perceptions in his phenomenal field. Many of these perceptions will be similar to the perceptions of his fellows in the same society. This is important, because it is only on the basis of common meanings that it is possible for one person to communicate with another. If similar meanings did not exist for members of a common culture, communication with his fellows would be extremely difficult and need satisfaction would be impossible. When one's house is on fire, to confuse the letter box with the fire alarm box does not contribute to the maintenance of self. Knowledge of the meanings of objects existing in the culture is essential to need satisfaction of the individual. Such meanings in the culture will therefore come to have counterparts in his perceptual field. It will be equally true of the concepts, values, ideas, and other abstractions existing in the particular culture in which he is brought up.

As W. Kohler expressed it, "The world *looks* today what our forefathers learned to say about it; we act and speak accordingly." What were once new ideas and concepts are matter-of-fact perceptions of people today. The matters the students of one generation learned to perceive with difficulty and painstaking effort are calmly accepted by the next. The germ theory of disease, the concept of evolution, or the controversy over nature-nurture, all difficult concepts for workers in former times, are used as the accepted basis for new explorations in our time. The culture we live in has vital effects upon the discrimination, conceptualization, and evaluations we learn to make of things we see about us.

THE FAMILY AS CULTURE TRANSMITTER

The human infant is born into an existing society—a structured, more or less organized society in which all individuals are bent upon maintaining their own integrations. The search of these individuals for need satisfaction produces a society which is not only responsive to the demands of its members, but also enforces upon its new members its own peculiar framework. From the moment of birth, if not before, this social pressure begins its work. From the very start socially acceptable differentiations are imposed upon the infant—for example, we present blue booties to a newborn boy, pink booties to a girl. Even the physical behavior of the child is subject, almost at once, to social control. Babies may be fed on schedule, subjected to hospital routine, and very shortly are taught "proper" habits of elimination, eating, and sleeping by their parents who, as products of their society, are guardians of its values.

From them we learn to define the world about us in terms of the culture into which we are born. We come to accept as our own "reality" the differentiations we acquire as a result of our experience with those who most closely affect us. We apply the labels of our culture to things and people around us. We accept also the values, taboos, and moral concepts of our culture and subcultures. The meanings of these things become part of our own "reality." A child can only see himself in terms of his experience and the treatment he receives from those responsible for his development. He is likely, therefore, to be strongly affected by the labels which are applied to events by other people. As his experience with them contributes to need satisfaction or frustrates such satisfaction he is likely to perceive things as good or bad, desirable or undesirable, friendly or hostile, etc. Once such perceptions have become part of his perceptual field they may persist as important determinants of behavior for the rest of his life. Such values, in turn, affect his perceptions so that even the things he sees and hears may become functions of his cultural experience. Autistic children, for example, who have learned to perceive adults as deeply threatening, dangerous, or untrustworthy, behave as though people did not exist. They have nothing to do with people and prefer to spend their time with things; they even treat people as "things" when it becomes necessary to use them for need satisfaction.

Persons with whom we are strongly identified provide us with anchorages or constancies in terms of which we make judgments about the world about us. In some instances this identification may be so strong that even the ordinarily stable world of things may be perceived awry by contrast. The following, for example, is a description of such an occurrence reported by Cantril in connection with the distorted room we discussed on page 85:

> Since the room is seen as square, persons or objects within the room or people looking through the windows become distorted. I had shown this room to hundreds of individuals and among other phenomena had demonstrated that when two people look through the back windows, the head of one individual appeared to be very large, the head of the other to be very small. When the individuals reversed the windows they were looking through, the size of their heads appeared to the observer to change. But on this Sunday morning when my friend's wife was observing him and me, she said, "Well, Louis, your head is the same size as ever, but Hadley, your head is very small." Then we changed the windows we were looking through and she said, "Louis, you're still the same, but Hadley, you've become awfully large." Needless to say this remark made a shiver go up my spine and I asked her how she saw the room. It turned out that for her—unlike any other observer until then—the room had become somewhat distorted. In other words, she was using her husband—to whom she was particularly devoted—as her standard. She would not let him go. His nickname for her was "Honi" and we have dubbed this the "Honi phenomenon."
>
> This observation was followed systematically in a series of experiments on married couples by Dr. Warren Wittreich. He found that if couples had been married less than a year there was a very definite tendency not to let the new marital partner distort as quickly or as much as was allowed by people who had been married for a considerable time. But, again, I hasten to add that it is not a simple matter of how long one has been married that determines how willing one is to distort the size or shape of one's marital partner! The original observation was made on a couple who were already grandparents. Preliminary investigation also seems to show that parents of young children will not allow their children to distort as readily as will parents of older children.

Examples of this use of our experience as yard stick for judgments are also common in daily life. We are familiar with the child who believes his father is right and the world is wrong or the mother who believes "they were all out of step but Jim!" Many of us have experienced, too, how our concept of a decent standard of living increases with our income.

The ways the individual learns to differentiate people will differ widely from culture to culture. What we call *man,* is *hombre* to the Spanish, *homme* to the French, or *inuk* to the Eskimo. The same is true of other objects. What they are called, what they are described as, and even their meanings may differ in different cultures. Certainly the American ideal of a "man" is far different from that of the Frenchman, the

Spaniard, or the Eskimo. Even what is included in the definition of self may vary from culture to culture. The Wintu Indians, for example, have a much more holistic concept of the self than we. They do not make the kinds of distinctions we do between the self and the body. The Wintu Indian is so much more anchored to his environment than we are that when he is bitten on the arm by a mosquito he does not speak of his right or his left arm; he scratches his "East" arm going downstream and, later in the day, coming upstream he scratches his "West" arm!

Even the same objective events may be perceived with varying degrees of differentiation in different cultures. Though we have only one word to describe snow the Eskimo has several words to designate varying conditions and properties. The precise character of snow is of far more import to the Eskimo than it is to us. Similarly, the Masai, an African tribe whose economy is based on cattle, have 17 words referring to different conditions of a cow. In such a society a cow carrying a calf is not to be lightly confused with a cow which is not.

A student from India at an American school had never seen snow except at a great distance on mountain peaks. During the fall months she asked many questions about it and looked forward with increasing excitement to the first snowfall. At last, one December day a snow flurry filled the air but the student from India did not recognize what she had been looking for for several months. Much to everyone's surprise she asked "What kind of insects are these?" In our own country, experience with the testing of children in various parts of the nation has shown that perceptions are highly limited by the environmental conditions surrounding the individual. Mountain children, for example, often give bizarre responses on intelligence tests.

There are differences between the perceptions of rural and urban children, children from the North and children from the South, from mountain and valley, from seaboard and the plains. Nor are such differences confined only to children. Adults, too, are limited in their perceptions by environmental factors. During the war, I worked in an induction station receiving men from the mountains of Kentucky, West Virginia, and southern Ohio. An intelligence test in use at this station was composed of a series of five pictures with instructions to cross out the picture in each series that did not belong with the others. One set of five pictures showed a trumpet and four stringed instruments, a guitar, a harp, a violin, and a bass fiddle. Many of the men crossed out the harp because they had never seen one or because, as they explained, "all the others are things in our band." On the basis of these tests we cannot assume that these men were less able to make differentiations or had perceptive fields less rich than their examiner. We can only suggest that their perceptions were formulated in a culture different from those who made up the test. Presumably, had the mountain men made a test and administered it to the psychologist, the psychologist would have appeared rather dull!

No one is ever free from the effect of culture upon perceiving. We are continuously sensitive to those around us and to the meanings of events for them. These meanings become a vital part of our own reality. The individual's perceptions tend to become more and more like the perceptions of the important people in his world. Acting on other premises, basing his behavior on perceptions unacceptable to them would make him and his behavior unacceptable to these important people and thus frustrate his search for adequacy. Perceptions unacceptable to people we value are essentially disorganizing and are, therefore, unacceptable to us. We can observe this in the ways in which people defend their points of view and the groups they belong to. Americans defend the perceptions of Americans even when subsequently they may discover them to be wrong. For some people, it is inconceivable that Americans could *ever* be wrong.

These effects have also been demonstrated in a number of researches on group influences on perceiving. Schein, for example, had a number of subjects judge the weights of a series of objects, first alone and later in the presence of other people making similar judgments. He found his test subjects were influenced to a marked degree by the judgments of the other people they heard responding. Hearing other people make judgments different from their own even influenced Schein's subjects to change their judgments when they were more correct than those of their fellows. In other experiments Negro children were found to have become aware of their social status very early in life. Their perception of the lower esteem granted the Negro in our culture even led a majority of young children to describe brown as a "bad" and white as a "nice" color.

CULTURAL DIFFERENCES AND INTERNATIONAL UNDERSTANDING. The effects of culture upon the beliefs, values, and self concepts of people create serious problems for human relationships and international understanding. The experience of people always seems real to them so that whatever has been differentiated as a result of a particular culture always seems right, proper, and natural. It is easy, therefore, for people raised in one culture to fail miserably to understand those raised in another.

When Queen Elizabeth and Prince Philip of Great Britain visited America in October, 1957, the royal party attended a football game between Maryland and North Carolina. The following is a United Press report of the British difficulties in understanding our game:

BRITISH PRESS PUZZLED BY ANTICS ON GRIDIRON

London, Oct. 20 (UP)– American football threw the British press for a loss today.

Every newspaper played up the visit of Queen Elizabeth and Prince Philip to the Maryland-North Carolina game at College Park, Md., yesterday. But they found it frightfully hard to follow.

The newspapers generally followed the lead of Arthur Helliwell in The People, who wrote: "Don't ask me to describe the match. It baffled me as completely as it baffled the Duke. Every few seconds play was held up while the players went into head-down huddles and bands and prancing cheer-leaders went into action."

The Sunday Express in apparent desperation fell back on cricket terms.

"The Queen and Prince Philip sat swaddled in yellow and blue two yards from the pitch (field)," it said.

The Sunday Observer tried hard.

The players were "padded and armored like stag-beetles," it said. "They worked up and down the field, tunneling through the uproar of music and shouting, jerking from one scrimmage to another, obeying some intricate and secret pattern of play."

But not one of the newspapers reported the score (Maryland 21, North Carolina 7), or even which team won.

(Jacksonville, Florida, *Times Union,* Oct. 21, 1957)

Minor misunderstandings like this one can sometimes prove amusing, but more serious misunderstandings have been known to result in the tragedy of war.

The problem of intercultural communication is perhaps nowhere better illustrated than in the difficulties encountered when new techniques are introduced into old, established cultures. With the best of intentions, attempts to "help" people of foreign cultures have failed miserably primarily because the helping agencies failed to appreciate and adjust to the unique values and beliefs of the people they wanted to help. To further understanding of these matters and to help innovators behave more effectively, UNESCO published a book entitled *Cultural Patterns and Technical Change.* The book describes a number of instances in which good intentions fell awry because of failure to understand that things are perceived differently in different cultures. The following are some of the more amusing of these incidents:

The British, who regarded the hill tribes of Burma filthy for taking almost no baths were, in turn, considered dirty by the Indonesians because they bathe only once a day!

The Western handkerchief for pocketing mucous is considered revolting by a number of other societies!

Among the Zuni it is customary to go to bed only when one is ready to die. Imagine, then, the consternation of the Zuni tribesman with a cold who is ordered to bed by the white man's physician!

In one community the proposal to install a village pump as a labor saving device for the women was met with unexpected opposition until it was understood that in *that* village water carrying was a time-honored mark of womanhood.

In an attempt to increase the food supply the British Government once supplied veterinary service to certain cattle-raising tribes. Unhappily, this only contributed to soil erosion and made the people poorer because the cattle increased and ate up all the ground cover, for the people loved their cattle and only killed them on ceremonial occasion!

The Permanence of Perceptions

Behavior, we have said, is the product of the total field of perceptions open to the individual at the moment of his behaving. How he behaves will be a function of the state of his awareness at the moment he is called upon to act. The perceptual field is continuously being organized and reorganized in the light of the new perceptions or differentiations as long as the individual lives. Once made, differentiations in the field probably remain forever. Awareness is an irreversible process.

This statement may prove a bit startling to the reader who knows that he has "forgotten" things. Nevertheless, there is evidence that this statement is true. Once an event has been experienced, this experience cannot be reversed. Perceptions once experienced form the groundwork for all later perceptions. A number of experiments on forgetting have demonstrated this point. One of the most interesting was that of Burtt, who read his infant son long passages of Greek poetry. In later years, Dr. Burtt had his son learn a number of passages of Greek poetry by heart. Among the passages the child learned at ages 8, 12, and 16, were some passages which he had heard as a baby. He learned the passages he had heard as a baby more quickly than the passages he had never heard before! Forgetting, it would seem, is not so much a fading out of what we have learned as it is a matter of organization of the perceptual field in which some perceptions became less capable than others of being called into clear figure on demand.

Although it seems true that the effect of perceptions is permanent, it should not be supposed that we mean they are solid and unchangeable or lie fallow in the perceptual field until called upon. The perceptual field is an organization continuously changed and modified by the perceptions occurring within it. As the total field changes, moreover, changes are produced in the perceptions within the field as well. Thus, an individual's experiences exert an irreversible effect on the field. It should not be assumed, however, that the original event can always be recalled just as it happened. Isolated perceptions like the Greek passages of Burtt's experiment may remain unchanged for long periods. Had these been brought frequently into figure over the years, they would undoubtedly have changed considerably. I recently visited my childhood neighborhood which I had not seen since I was ten years old. I found it extremely difficult to recognize and was particularly shocked to discover that what I remembered as a bright, sunny, spacious neighborhood with considerable distances between houses was now a neighborhood of narrow streets, dark and overgrown with trees, and houses practically on top of each other. My perceptions, originally made when the neighborhood was new, when trees had just been planted, and when distances seemed greater because my legs were shorter, had changed but little in the years that passed. Had I returned more often to the old neighborhood in the years between, the likelihood is that my perceptions would probably have changed and I might have been less shocked.

The Effect of Past Opportunities on Future Perceptions

The perceptual field as it exists at any moment has a controlling and determining effect upon other perceptions which the individual can experience. We have already seen that many perceptions are dependent upon previous perceptions. This means that the opportunities for perceiving which the individual has had in the past must have a vital bearing upon possible further perceptions. This is nicely demonstrated in another of Ames' demonstrations in perception which illustrate that new events are perceived in ways consistent with what we have previously learned to perceive.

The need for adequacy cannot be fulfilled without a degree of stability in the world in which the individual lives. When, therefore, events are perceived at odds with long established experience, these events must somehow be brought into consistency with other more basic perceptions. This phenomenon is illustrated in the trapezoidal window demonstration. The demonstration consists of a trapezoidal piece of sheet metal with holes cut out to resemble window panes and with shadows painted on to resemble thickness, mounted on a shaft which is slowly turned by a small electric motor as shown in Fig. 14. All our past experience has taught us that, as an object moves away from us, it appears to grow smaller and, as it approaches, it appears to grow larger. Looking at this window as it rotates, the long edge always appears to us to be closest, and we see the window slowly oscillate back and forth instead of turning round and round. Even though we "know" the window is going round in a circle, we still "see" it waving back and forth, the long edge always near us and the short edge always away. Apparently, our past experience has taught us so thoroughly the nature of perspective, that we cannot controvert this evidence. So strong is this learned way of perceiving that even when a small box is hung on the corner of the window, it appears to break loose from the oscillating window and take off into space on an orbit all its own, as shown in Fig. 14.

Aniseikonic lenses are specially designed to distort the visual image delivered to the retina of the eye. Nevertheless, persons wearing such lenses often experience no distortion of vision whatever when they wear them in familiar surroundings. The image delivered to the eye is "seen" as quite normal despite the physical damage to the stimulus. Away from familiar cues, persons wearing aniseikonic lenses usually see other people somewhat distorted. Even this distortion, however, seems to be related to the strength of the constancies developed by the individual. In one experiment, for example, navy recruits saw petty officers less distorted than recruits like themselves!

The effect of past experience can also be demonstrated in the use of the old time stereoscope. When different pictures are exposed to the left and right eye in the stereoscope under controlled conditions, individuals tend to see what their past experience "sets" them to see. Thus, when a group of teachers from North and South of the border looked at a picture of a bull fighter with one eye and a baseball player with the other, the Mexican school teachers "saw" the bull fighter, while the American teachers "saw" the ball player!

Fig. 13. Monocular Distorted Room. (From W. H. Ittelson, *The Ames Demonstrations in Perception*, Princeton University Press, Princeton, N.J. Reprinted by permission of the publisher.)

Fig. 14. The Rotating Trapezoid Demonstration. (From W. H. Ittelson, *The Ames Demonstrations in Perception*, Princeton University Press, Princeton, N.J. Reprinted by permission of the publisher.)

The state of the perceptual field at any moment sets limits upon what new events may be perceived. New perceptions are dependent upon antecedent experiences. If this seems somewhat depressing that we are able to perceive only what our previous experience has made it possible for us to perceive, we need to remind ourselves that our previous experience has also made it possible to perceive events we might not have been able to perceive without that experience. Our previous perceptions both limit the new events we can perceive and open vast new possibilities for further perceiving. The fact that I have been a psychologist for twenty years probably means that I shall never become famous as a dress designer. My perceptions of the past do not permit me to grasp the fine points of that profession. I must be content with admiring the product of others. On the other hand, the experiences I have had which have made me a psychologist have opened a vast horizon of possible new perceptions not open to people without that experience. Because of my previous experience I perceive events differently than my colleagues in engineering, business, or homemaking. For them and for me perceptions narrow possibilities in some directions and open new vistas in others.

In this chapter we have seen that what an individual perceives will to a great extent be dependent upon the kinds of opportunities to perceive he has been afforded in the past. It will be recognized at once, however, that exposure to events in no sense completely determines the perceptions an individual will make. The opportunity to perceive does not guarantee that a particular perception will occur. Even with equivalent exposure the perceptions of different people are not alike. Exposure to events is only one of the factors involved in determining whether or not an event will be differentiated.

We have now explored four of these factors, namely, the physical organism, need, time, and opportunity. In the following chapter we shall examine still another factor affecting perceiving, the effect of goals, techniques, and values.

CHAPTER 6

Goals, Values, and Techniques

ALTHOUGH each of us is motivated at all times and in all places by the same basic need for adequacy, the expression of this need in different people is as varied as human beings themselves. Some people seek the maintenance and enhancement of the self in possessions and, thus, spend much of their lives collecting things like money, houses, shells, old automobiles, or human heads. Others find adequacy in the ideas and concepts of religion, law, science, literature, art, or music. Still others find adequacy in various sorts of activities like running, driving, eating, farming, swimming, building houses, taking dope, or sleeping. These ways in which individuals seek to achieve the maintenance and enhancement of self we call goals, techniques, and values. They are the differentiations people make to achieve need satisfaction. The character of these differentiations in an individual determines in very large measure his personality structure and behavior.

THE DIFFERENTIATION OF GOALS

In the course of an individual's growth and development and as a product of his experience with the world around him, certain aspects of the perceptual field become more or less clearly differentiated from the remainder of the field because they satisfy need. These differentiations are called goals. Thus, certain objects, feelings, or events become differentiated as more or less related to the satisfaction of the basic need for a more adequate self. The newborn infant has few if any goals beyond the extremely undifferentiated one of maintaining organization. In time, however, with the differentiation of certain objects, persons, and sounds, which accompany the satisfaction of his basic need, his goals become more clearly defined. In time, the goals differentiated by a particular individual may become permanent and characteristic parts of his personality and are evident in so much of his behavior that other people are able to predict with great accuracy what he is likely to do in a given situation.

This goal differentiation is interestingly illustrated in the use of the word "Daddy" by a friend's young son. The child's first use of this word was greeted in his family with much pride in his accomplishment until it was discovered that thunder arriving at mealtime was also "Daddy" to him! Apparently he had differentiated the word from the speech matrix as meaning a loud noise of which his father was but one producer. Similarly, a child's other goals become differentiated in the course of time with developing satisfaction from food, water, persons, toys, and the like. Even the concept of "mother" is not exempt from this process of gradual differentiation from the remainder of the field. Many a heartbroken mother has had the distressing experience of leaving her infant for a week or two and returning to find the child "does not even recognize his own mother!" Specific persons such as father, mother, sister, aunt, or grandmother, with the special meanings which our society attaches to them, take considerable time to differentiate.

In the course of differentiation of the child's goals from the remainder of the perceptual field, it is apparent that not all children will develop the same patterns. In fact, the opportunities and circumstances of growth present so vast a number of possibilities for differentiation that it is unlikely that any two individuals ever have identical goals. Thus, a very young child may differentiate a goal of "bed" as a source of security; while another may come to differentiate the same object as a place to play, to have a bowel movement, to be fed, or as a place of punishment.

Even where two children appear to have the same goals, it will probably be discovered on further examination that wide differences exist. In similar situations there cannot be like goals for different children because each one sees his situation from his own unique point of vantage. Even for identical twins in apparently identical situations this is true, for a moment's reflection will make it clear that each twin is a part of the other's environment so that twin A's environment contains twin B, but twin B's environment instead contains twin A.

Living in the midst of a particular family group the child will adopt the goals of those who are important in satisfying his need and, thus, he may become a Republican, a Methodist, an outdoorsman, or a gypsy, depending upon what is important to the people who surround him. This process of differentiating goals similar to (but not completely like) those of the group in which the individual moves gives a certain degree of continuity and similarity of goals among the various representatives of the same culture.

THE DIFFERENTIATION OF TECHNIQUES

It is probable that very little human behavior is the result of direct movement toward goals; rather it moves through a series of subgoals to reach its major goal of need satisfaction. If crossing the street to a friend's house is our goal, we cannot reach it without achieving certain subgoals in the process. For example, it may be necessary for us to descend the stairs, open the door, reach the curb, avoid a car, and so forth. Such chains of goals which provide the means of achieving adequacy we call techniques. During his growth, the child develops many techniques which make it possible for him to reach the goals he has previously differentiated. Techniques are methods of reaching goals and thus satisfying need. Like goals they are fundamentally designed to maintain or enhance the self. Everyone develops highly characteristic techniques. One person may characteristically placate people and win their good will by flattery; another may seek to attain self assurance by dominating and criticizing others. Our friends can usually recognize and identify the particular techniques that we are most apt to use—this is signified by the slang phrase, "He would!" Since behavior is usually best described in terms of its path, techniques are usually described in terms of the goals or the subgoals which they involve. For instance, reading, drinking, or movie going are typical techniques of escape from feelings of inadequacy, and the people who use them have as goals the acquisition of certain types of books, of liquor, or attendance at movies.

Techniques become differentiated in the perceptual field of the individual in the same manner as that described for the differentiation of goals. At first such techniques may be extremely generalized but with the passage of time they tend to become more and more refined. In any case, techniques are always the result of the individual's striving for need satisfaction. Thus, the young child who feels frustrated by someone and desires revenge or mastery over the object of his frustration, may at first be openly aggressive—fighting, kicking, and laying about him generally. In time, as he discovers that this technique does not bring real satisfaction of his need because of the violent reaction of others, he may come to differentiate a modified technique of attack upon a verbal level expressed, perhaps, in tattling, or verbally abusing the object of his aggression. Since even this behavior is likely to bring censure upon him as he grows older and, therefore, result in less satisfaction of his need, he may learn to modify his technique still further, as he discovers that he can reach the same end through gossip or undercover slander of his tormentor. Eventually he may even be able subtly to get others to do what he wishes while he remains in the background.

THE DIFFERENTIATION OF VALUES

We have seen that the process of differentiation of goals and techniques within the perceptual field is always related to need satisfaction. Some goals and techniques are differentiated as positive or satisfying and, hence, to be sought. Others may be differentiated as negative, destructive, or humiliating to the self and, therefore, to be avoided. In the experience of the young child these differentiations are made with a high degree of specificity, but before very long he begins to differentiate that some goals and techniques are more or less alike in their abilities to yield or inhibit need satisfaction. He perceives that some objects, goals, or techniques have similar properties; this differentiation of common value serves as a kind of frame of reference for making further differentiations. We call these frames of reference, which are more or less clearly differentiated in the perceptual field and serve as guides for seeking or avoiding values.

Whereas goals and techniques apply to specific aspects of behavior, values are differentiations of a generic rather than a specific character and, thus, affect a much wider field of behavior. For psychologists, social workers, teachers, and other students of behavior a person's values are, therefore, of great importance in understanding the behavior of others. When a person's values are known it often becomes possible to predict with great accuracy how he may behave in given situations. This use of people's values as important clues to their behavior, however, is not confined to psychologists or professional people. All of us become highly sensitive to the values of those around us in the course of our development. Very early we recognize the crucial character of values affecting a person's behavior. This provides us with guide lines to the behavior of others and makes possible a degree of prediction of what they will do. Even young children discover that "Uncle Joe does like kids" or that "mother doesn't want me to grow up" and are, thereafter, able to adjust their behavior in terms of these inferences.

It should not be supposed that all of an individual's values can be clearly and precisely stated by the individual. Values differ greatly in the degree of clarity with which they are perceived. Some values will be quite definite and precise in the individual's perceptual organization so that he may be able to express them aptly and succinctly in the symbolism of words. Others will be so vaguely differentiated that the individual may be quite unable to report the nature of the value determining his selection of perceptions. This latter state of affairs is illustrated in instances where outsiders may be able to perceive a value affecting our perceptions which we, ourselves, may be quite unable to identify clearly. It may also happen that an individual will lay claim to the symbol of a value acceptable to his social group but be so vague in his differentiation of its meaning that the value has little effect upon his behavior. It is a common thing, for example, to hear people claim to value democracy while behaving in most undemocratic ways.

Values will affect the perceptions of particular individuals depending upon the extent of applicability they seem to have to the behaver. Some values, for example, may be differentiated as applying only to a limited number of situations or goals. Such values might be a dislike of pickles, a disapproval of people who "scratch off" at traffic lights, or an appreciation of double camellias. Values may also be so extensive as to affect almost every area of one's life, such as a value which calls for respecting the dignity and integrity of people, or a concern for justice and fair play. There may also be any degree of applicability between these two extremes; for example, when a general value espousing the dignity and integrity of man is carefully circumscribed to apply only to one's own religious or national group, or when a specific value is extended to generalities and we assume "they must be nice people because they support the boy scouts."

THE PERMANENCE OF GOALS AND VALUES

When goals have been differentiated and have served to aid the individual to the satisfaction of need they tend to persist as a part of the field organization of that individual. The degree of this persistence is likely to be a function of the degree of differentiation from the remainder of the field. Generally the more the achievement of the goal serves to bring the organism to the satisfaction of basic need, the greater will be its differentiation from the remainder of the field, and the more likely it is to appear as a goal on future occasions. Almost any parent is familiar with the changes in an infant's behavior when he has been left with his grandmother for a week. On the child's return to his family he may have acquired new goals or techniques which he has learned brought satisfaction when used with "grandma." When he returns to his own home, these persist or disappear, depending upon whether or not they get results at home.

The more strongly goals lead to satisfaction of the fundamental need, the greater is the differentiation from the remainder of the field, and the greater is the likelihood of persistence. This is particularly well illustrated in connection with negative goals. Negative goals, which become differentiated in the field as objects to avoid, threaten the organization of the individual. His need, however, is to maintain his phenomenal self. Hence, such threats are likely to be very strongly differentiated—so strongly, in fact, that often a frightening object may be experienced only once to be avoided ever after. This may frequently be observed in childhood fears which persist far into adult life and may continue for the entire life span. Goals which seem to the individual less strongly related to need satisfaction are less clearly differentiated and easily displaced. I will give up the idea of going to the movies tonight when friends drop in to see me, since going to the movies was only mildly related to making me feel adequate anyhow. Ask me to give up my job, my wife, or other goals of vital importance to me and my reaction will be very different.

A second major factor contributing to the permanence of goals and values has to do with the selective effect such differentiations have upon perception. The emergence in the perceptual field of any goal or value determines to a great extent what related matters are likely to be differentiated thereafter. The possession of any goal or value has both a narrowing and expanding effect upon capacities for differentiation. The person who has differentiated "country music" as desirable and valuable, and "long-hair" music as boring and unpleasant has made a differentiation which cannot help but affect his behavior and further experience. Having these values he will avoid concert music and listen to hillbilly songs. This effectively closes him off from some kinds of experience while at the same time it opens up new possibilities in the area he has learned to value. The decision to become a school teacher probably shuts the door to the possibility of becoming a great physician but it opens up vast new areas of exploration unknown to the physician. By controlling the opportunities we have for further perceiving, the differentiation of goals and values tends to perpetuate itself in our perceptual fields.

The Effects of Goals and Values on Perceiving

Once established, goals and values have intimate effects upon perceiving. Indeed, the peculiar patterns imposed upon perception by goals and values produces much of the uniqueness of behavior we have come to describe as the individual's personality. The goals, values, and techniques we have differentiated as leading to need satisfaction serve us thereafter as reference points to the achievement of adequacy. Once clearly differentiated, they consequently exert a selective effect on later perception, and thus, they markedly affect behavior. As a consequence of this crucial relationship, many psychologists have been led to experiment with the effects of goals and values upon perception, and a vast literature has accumulated on this topic.

Perhaps the most striking and commonplace examples of the effects of values upon perception are to be found in the differing perceptions of men and women. The two sexes in our culture often have widely differing values which, in turn, have selective effects upon the perception of the two groups. Men brought up to value machinery are often appalled at the lack of care and respect given mechanical equipment by women. Similarly, women raised to be deeply sensitive to social and interpersonal matters are sometimes shocked at what seems like unthinking, unfeeling attitudes of men. Many a hostess has been distressed by the tendency of her guests to drift into male and female groups where similar values make communication easier. Several interesting researches have demonstrated that women seem to depend more on visual frames of reference in orienting themselves to the world around them, while men rely more heavily upon kinesthetic and tactual experience.

The effect of values on perceiving may also be observed in hypnosis wherein subjects may, for the sake of controlled experimentation, be given values they have not previously held. Subjects fond of fruit juices, for example, may be told they detest such things and, thereafter, under hypnosis may be observed to react with disgust at the sight of fruit juices. It is even possible to reverse the subject's normal aversions; for example, a subject who dislikes dogs can be instructed that he is quite fond of them. We have already observed in an earlier chapter how food deprivation affects the kinds of perceptions people have under semi-starvation conditions.

Much of modern psychological diagnosis relies heavily on the use of various types of projective tests. All of these tests provide more or less structured materials or situations to which the subject responds. The assumption is that whatever meaning he puts into such materials must be related to his own perceptual field. In the Thematic Apperception Test, for example, he is asked to tell a story about a picture, the details of which are purposely quite vague and ambiguous. Therefore, whatever story the subject tells, he is projecting into the picture from his own personality or experience; the skilled interpreter is thus provided a sample of some of the subject's meanings. In perceptual terms such tests make it possible to explore the individual's perceptual field with particular reference to the goals, values, and techniques important in his unique economy. These tests have been subjected to a great deal of experimentation, so there seems little doubt that they can provide us with important data about perception. What concerns us at the moment, however, is only the fact that the tests demonstrate so effectively the selective effect of the individual's goals and values on perception.

In an experiment in which subjects thought they were about to see words related to animals, they read sael as seal, and wharl as whale. The same subjects expecting to see words related to boats saw sael as sail and wharl as wharf. Several experiments have demonstrated that people perceive words of greater personal value more quickly than those of less importance to them. In our society certain four- and five-letter Anglo-Saxon words are strictly taboo, and experimenters have demonstrated that the reaction time to such words is considerably greater than the reaction time to less value-laden words. Even skin color may be seen as darker or lighter depending upon individual values. In one experiment, for example, Negro students saw the skin color of popular school principals most nearly like that they personally preferred, while the skin color of unpopular principals was seen as close to what the students disliked. There seem to be no aspects of perceiving unaffected by values. Study after study has demonstrated this intimate relationship.

The effect of values upon perception has important implications in all types of social problems. It has been shown, for example, that persons whose values favor a certain event or outcome tend to expect such desired outcomes. Thus the same poorly clad man may be seen by pro-labor observers as a "forgotten man" and an object of sympathy, while anti-labor observers see in him a "wastrel getting just what he deserved." Prejudice, group conflict, and break-downs of moral judgment and communication are frequently the unhappy societal products of unfortunate, personal values. Persons with strong values tend to perceive events in terms of their values, and therefore, they are more likely to see things as black or white than neutral observers.

We have already seen in the previous chapter how goals and values are affected by the culture in which the individual is raised. Once established such values continue to affect the perception of people throughout their lives. The great social problem we face in the desegregation of our public schools is vastly complicated because people raised in different cultures have differentiated different goals and values. These goals and values, in turn, affect the ways people are able to perceive the very same data. The dynamics of value development and change lie at the very heart of our great social problems and are the primary data of sociologists, social psychologists, political scientists and others interested in social change. More adequate understanding of human values is essential to the solution of our great human problems.

GOALS AND VALUES AFFECT REASONING AND LEARNING

Goals and values have important effects upon reasoning and learning. I remember the Kentucky moonshiner to whom I once administered the Wechsler-Bellevue intelligence test, who could not tell me how many pints there are in a quart although he had certainly been taught this fact in his early schooling. Knowing that my client did a considerable business in bootleg liquor, I framed the question differently asking, "Well, how do you sell your liquor?" He smiled tolerantly and replied, "Oh, boss, I just sell it by the jugful!" In his community to have done otherwise would have been to risk bankruptcy. In a culture where a jug is the standard container for spirits, there is no need to know about quarts.

In a fascinating series of studies on human reasoning, Maier demonstrated how the values people hold may interfere with their ability to solve problems. Given two sticks and a clamp and instructed to make a hat rack some subjects were unable to solve the problem, apparently because they could not differentiate the clamp as a hook. Others, used to seeing pliers as a tool, were unable to solve problems which required the use of the pliers as a pendulum weight. Deep-seated cultural values have a considerable effect on learning. College students from Southern states, for instance, show more distortion in reasoning where ethnocentricism, or racial attitudes, are involved than students from Northern states who do not have such strong values. Another experimenter has demonstrated that positive and negative values affect students' learning of psychology.

Students who have values similar to the values of their instructors seem to get higher class marks than students whose values differ from the values of their instructors although their marks are based on objective tests derived solely from textbooks.

GOALS AND THE LEVEL OF ASPIRATION AND INTERESTS

There seems almost no limit to the variety of ways in which goals and values affect behavior. Even the hopes, aspirations, interests, and objectives toward which persons strive will be determined by the goals they have differentiated in the perceptual field and the strength of the values which individuals attach to them. For example, I have for several weeks been working hard on this manuscript and resented almost every intrusion to the extent, on occasion, of resenting the very work which is the source of my livelihood. Other goals have arisen at times, but almost all of them have had to give way before the impelling force of finishing this book. And this would be expected since I am aware that one's prestige in psychological work is very largely dependent upon one's publications. To suggest the possibility of spending the afternoon at an exhibition of Ming china vases would be unlikely of any response, because it would not be consistent with the way in which I regard myself at this time, nor would it seem related to my most pressing current goals. The things toward which people aspire will, in the final analysis, depend upon the degree to which they perceive goals as contributing to the maintenance and the enhancement of the self.

The kinds of interests people hold are also a function of the goals and values that seem important to them. We are interested in what serves to satisfy need. As long as goals and values lead to need satisfaction they remain important to us and we are interested in the objects or events they represent. When, however, such goals and values no longer provide us with feelings of adequacy, new interests arise as expressions of shifting patterns of goals and values. A good example of this may be seen in the child learning to roller skate. Other children like him skate, and to maintain and enhance his phenomenal self he, too, wants to roller skate. When he puts on his new skates, however, he finds skating much harder than he had expected and, probably, Mother Earth less comforting than he had been led to believe. But the reactions of those about him are encouraging, and he is told that he is doing well. This evaluation is at variance with what he feels, but it results in further efforts and more commendation while he is developing his skill. He is interested in learning to skate. Eventually the time comes when he has developed some degree of skill and regards himself as able to skate or, even, as a good skater. Now, however, the commendation and plaudits of others are likely to be far less strong or frequent and his ability to skate is taken for granted. Much of the satisfactions involved are lost. Unless others have taken their place, it is likely that his interest and desire to skate will disappear.

Observations of this sort of behavior have caused people to think that we are interested in the things that are problems to us, and that we are likely to lose interest when they are no longer problems. This seems partly true and there is good reason for it. The feeling of personal adequacy derived from any accomplishment is always enhanced if there is a possibility of failure. The things we know we can do are less challenging than those we have yet to try. The adolescent who can't dance when this is expected in his group feels learning to dance is a problem; the adult who desires to keep up with his neighbors finds figuring out how to get a new car an interesting problem.

It sometimes happens that people set goals for themselves which are far above their capacities. This is characteristic of some college students. College students must have been fairly successful at school—otherwise they would not have reached college. Having been successful and having differentiated goals and values in these terms by comparison with less brilliant contemporaries in the grade- and high-school years, many come to college expecting to operate on the same level. College students, however, are usually more highly selected, and the competition for grades is much keener than the student has ever experienced before. His level of aspiration being higher than the conditions of his new environment warrant, he sets goals in terms of what was previously normal for him. This may bring him lower grades than he is accustomed to receiving. Not to reach his goals is a threat to his organization. He may insist on them all the more strongly because they are under attack. He may even raise them. Until he can readjust his level of aspiration according to his new environment or call upon new reserves of energy and application, he is likely to suffer severe feelings of failure and inadequacy. Fortunately, most college students are able to make this adjustment in a reasonable period of time. Occasionally, however, people with unrealistic goals are unable to accept their own limitations and continue to strive for impossible objectives for most of their lives.

The Effects of Techniques on Behavior

Like goals and values, when techniques are differentiated they become an integral part of the organization of the individual's perceptual field and are subject to the primary forces in its operation. We have already seen how this organization tends to persist and how techniques, as a part of the field, also persist depending on the degree to which they contribute to the satisfaction of the basic need of the individual. Furthermore, once differentiated, techniques tend to remain as a part of the fundamental organization. Thus, certain techniques of reaching goals may become characteristic ways of behaving for the individual depending upon his unique concept of himself. For instance, the child who regards himself as a "tough guy" is likely to act in accord with this concept and is likely to meet many situations in an aggressive manner even though this may lead to less ultimate satisfaction for him. It becomes what he considers the appropriate method of arrival at his goals for the sort of person he considers himself. Often the "radical" adopts certain kinds of behavior as appropriate for himself and shuns conformity in any form. The amusements of more conventional people are inconsistent with his conception of himself and are rejected for behavior he considers more sophisticated. In time, the techniques we differentiate as appropriate for reaching our goals may become so characteristic of us as to be integral parts of our personalities. Other people expect us to behave in a certain way. Indeed, others may be able to predict with great accuracy how we will behave in a given situation.

NEGATIVE TECHNIQUES

In the course of his development, everyone comes to differentiate both positive and negative techniques and to utilize or avoid such techniques, depending upon whether or not they lead to the satisfaction of his basic need. Thus, the child who has been subjected to extremely severe punishment administered consistently over a period of time may differentiate techniques for reaching his goals by meekness or fawning as attention-getting devices while, at the same time, he differentiates aggressive tactics as techniques to be avoided at all cost because they result in behavior on the part of others which threatens the self. Such techniques may, furthermore, become an integral part of the individual's field organization with, or without, repetition. While the majority of techniques probably become differentiated with repeated behavior, they are not a direct result of repetition. Indeed, they may become effectively differentiated with no repetition whatever. In traumatic or highly emotional situations, for example, a single incident may result in a relatively fixed differentiation.

CONSISTENCY OF TECHNIQUES

In everyday life many people utilize the same techniques to arrive at many different goals. The go-getter may find aggressive techniques so useful in satisfying his needs that he applies them almost indiscriminately to every activity. He runs down his business rivals, dashes from place to place, hangs a DO IT NOW sign in his office, bids wildly in his bridge game, and may even apply such techniques to courtship as he attempts to sweep a girl off her feet. Still another person may find a technique of suppression best leads to the satisfaction of need; he may literally swallow his pride, even when he is seething within. The opposite aspect of the relationship of goals and techniques may also be possible wherein an individual may utilize differing techniques to arrive at the same goals. A woman seeking to build up her self-esteem may try to accomplish this by gossiping about her neighbor, buying herself a new dress, powdering her nose, striving for a career, or raising ten children. For both goals and techniques the determining factor of persistence lies in the degree to which it is differentiated, either positively or negatively, with respect to need satisfaction in the total field. Techniques or goals most clearly differentiated in the individual's field organization will tend to persist.

CLASSIFICATION OF TECHNIQUES

Attempting to maintain and enhance the self, a person differentiates many techniques in the course of his experience which lead more or less adequately to achieving this end. For the most part these techniques are concerned with what the layman calls boosting self-esteem which is another way of saying the enhancement of the self. For practical purposes it is convenient to classify such behavior in a number of categories. It should be recalled in any such classification, however, that there are probably no pure cases of the use of any of these techniques. Techniques can be roughly divided into three major categories: (1) mastery over people or things, (2) identification with a powerful individual or membership in a potent group, and (3) physical change in the body organization.

Need Satisfaction by Mastery over People

THE USE OF FORCE

Techniques for achieving mastery may be found in many devices, ranging from the completely obvious to some so subtle as to pass unnoticed by the ordinary observer. Among the most primitive of such techniques is, of course, the use of physical force. Beating people with a club to gain mastery is by no means obsolete in our society and, although our methods are often more refined, the essential principle still exists. Direct aggression or the wielding of superior force is still a major means of achieving mastery for many individuals. Although physical size is no longer as important for mastery as it once was in adult society, the clenched fist is still a favorite technique even of many adults for achieving their fundamental goals. The technique may be disguised as legal action, social position, employer-employee relationship, or presumed superiority of knowledge as in a teacher-pupil relationship, but the principle is the same. The force compels although the club has given place to more genteel devices. Coercion is used to achieve the end even though this coercion may appear in verbal or other symbolic dress. Almost anyone, after failing to achieve his ends by more subtle means, may explode in anger. This is true of nations as well as of individuals, so that force of arms is necessary to achieve the goals which diplomatic pressure has failed to gain.

From the social point of view the use of direct aggression is a particularly bad technique because it sets up a whole chain of aggressive reactions in which each victim attempts to forget his own humiliation by using his power to humiliate others. A man who has been humiliated at work may come home to bully his family; his wife, to regain her lost self esteem may nag at him and the children, who, in turn, seek self enhancement by aggressive behavior in the neighborhood.

SYMBOLIC TECHNIQUES OF FORCE

In order to maintain its own organization, our society frowns upon the use of direct physical aggression by its members. Therefore, in the course of his growth, the child may acquire symbolic techniques which are quite as effective as the more primitive techniques. Symbolic aggression is frequent in clinical practice. For example, a little girl brought up by her mother to be a "little lady," was referred to a clinic because she persisted in wetting her bed. The child had talked the matter over with her mother and agreed that one of the things she might do would be to refrain from drinking water after four in the afternoon. The following highly revealing conversation with the family cook took place that same evening:

CHILD: (*coming into the kitchen*) Elsie, what do you suppose would happen if I were to drink four glasses of water after supper?
ELSIE: Oh My! Why, I suppose you'd wet your bed.
CHILD: (*vainly trying to suppress her delight*) Oh dear! That's just what I did!

Apparently the child had learned to utilize bed wetting as an aggressive technique against her mother. It is a common observation that such aggressions are often expressed in play. A large part of a child's time in play therapy may be spent in such symbolic activities as breaking balloons, playing "accident," knocking down block houses, or making clay figures of mother and father to be smashed to bits.

While adult symbolic aggressions are less obvious than those of the child, they are, nevertheless, often effective. Veiled techniques, such as gossiping, whispering campaigns, excessive blame, or even "constructive" criticism may fool the average observer but should not deceive the psychologist. If people cannot satisfy their needs by one technique they must turn to more successful techniques. There are a great many ways to enjoy mastery over others that may be more or less disguised, and they are often not only accepted in society, but encouraged. Games of all kinds are primarily played to give the participants and their supporters an opportunity to enhance the phenomenal self by defeating worthy opponents. Ordinary polite conversation may be used by the speaker to build up his self concept by dominating the listener, while the listener is waiting for his opportunity to act as an authority. The humorist, Strickland Gilliland, once said "If you see one man talking to another on the street, it is not a conversation. The other fellow is just waiting to tell about his operation." As a rule, large informal gatherings break up into small conversational groups where people do not have to wait so long for an opportunity to talk.

DEMONSTRATIONS OF SUPERIORITY

Kidding, ribbing, hazing, and practical joking are further methods by which the individual may take advantage of a social situation to feel superior to a victim. Since it is essential that either the victim or the audience be important, ribbing, like gossip, is often a kind of flattery, and many young girls are well aware that the insults of preadolescent boys are really compliments of a rare character.

Ostentatious spending and making of gifts are other ways in which people find a sense of superiority or worth. Among the Indians of British Columbia, the most important way of acquiring such superiority was the public presentation of gifts which the humiliated recipients were unable to repay. Families lived in destitution for years and individuals sold themselves into slavery to secure the means of recovering their prestige by outdoing their enemies. This potlatch custom eventually became such a menace to the community that it had to be forbidden by the Canadian government, probably to the relief of all concerned.

Another interesting variation of the use of subtle aggression is often seen in clinical experience with the negative or dawdling child. This is a form of aggression put to effective use on a larger scale by Gandhi and his followers in India and has been used in our own country by labor in strikes and slowdowns in industrial disputes. In all of these cases the technique is useful to gain a feeling of power over those who would force one action or another on the individual or the group. The adoption of a negative "you can't make me do it" attitude is a potent means of regaining feelings of competence and independence.

Perhaps the most subtle and least recognized function of mastery in operation is to be observed in a certain type of leadership dependent upon the skillful manipulation of people. This kind of leader is able by means of subtle techniques to gain mastery over the group, and to sway individuals to his way of thinking without their being aware of the techniques in use upon them. He may thus be able to obtain mastery by planting ideas in fertile ground, by selectively praising his fellows' ideas and, if he is a good leader, he may even succeed in doing so while he remains completely in the background.

Need Satisfaction Through Mastery of Things

Fortunately for the human race, domination of others is not the only way in which people may build up and reinforce their phenomenal selves. Another way of achieving adequacy lies in the mastery of things. To achieve this end it is necessary that the individual have a feeling that he is able to do something that gives him power over his surroundings. At all ages, but especially in childhood, the control may be destructive, as when young children enjoy themselves by banging on the kitchen pans or tearing up the family magazines. Much of the pleasure in building with blocks comes from the pleasure in knocking them down. Among adults, too, such destructive attempts at mastery are not uncommon. Building contractors report that their men enjoy wrecking a building more than building one, probably because the destruction is faster and more spectacular thus providing greater awareness of personal power. Many an adult remains a fire-engine chaser long after childhood, and crockery-breaking booths are always popular at carnivals.

For most adults, however, it is probable that the greatest amount of mastery over things is gained from constructive behavior. The engineer takes pride in his bridge, the architect in his building, the small home owner takes pride in garden walls built with his own hands. It is probable that the inexorable breakdown of jobs to more and more minute details in assembly-line production has destroyed for many workers their opportunity for mastery over things as it was possible in the production of a complete article. As a consequence some industries have attempted to reverse this trend by giving workers opportunities to work with larger units of the product involving a number of processes, or some industries have turned to assigning a group to produce a unit leaving workers free to rotate the tasks within the group as they please. It is probably true that handling of giant machines in modern industry contributes to the feeling of power for some people. Many a man has probably not yet lost his secret desires to command the monstrous huffing-and-puffing railroad engine, which so impressed him in his youth.

Need Satisfaction by Identification with Others

The second group of techniques to maintain and enhance the phenomenal self is so universally used and is so different from the dominating techniques we have been discussing that some writers contend that it must be due to a completely independent motive, which they have called the need for social approval. For a number of years, during infancy and childhood, we are almost completely dependent upon adults for the satisfaction of our physical and psychological welfare. Children who win the good will and attention of adults are fed, clothed, and comforted. Children who incur ill will are punished, ignored, or humiliated. As a consequence, the sympathy and good will of other people are vitally necessary to every child, and much of this feeling of need for others survives into adult life. From a practical point of view, the adults in our present highly specialized economy are almost as dependent upon other people as children. Even if this were not true, it is not likely that any adult having had the normal experiences of childhood could fail to gain a feeling of security and self assurance from the approval of people he respects.

If the technique of seeking the approval of others were motivated, as many suppose, by an independent drive for social approval, then the approval of one person or group should be as satisfying as the approval of another. If, on the other hand, it is simply an alternative method to secure a consciousness of self worth, then we should prefer the approval of the individual or membership in the group which seems important to us. There is evidence that this is the case. People often travel long distances to see famous personages and, thus, identify themselves with success. The politician who said "If you can't lick 'em, join 'em" was simply expressing a common type of behavior. Even in times of peace, the less powerful members of a group tend to seek security by identifying themselves with a powerful group or a dominant leader. Large numbers of Canadian mental patients identify themselves in one way or another with the United States and claimed to be American secret agents, relatives of the President, or to be receiving messages from the "hearts of the American people." No similar preoccupation with Canada is apparent among patients in American hospitals. In the United States such attempts at identification with a strong group or leader are by no means uncommon; advertisers find that it pays to have their products endorsed by public figures. Many people like to use the soap their movie idol uses or smoke the cigarette approved by an All-American fullback.

Individuals tend to seek self esteem through winning the approval of groups or individuals they believe to be important but they tend also to withdraw from groups which no longer contribute to their feelings of importance. It is a common observation that, when an individual has achieved the highest office in an organization, his ardor for the work of that group often disintegrates rapidly and he may soon have broken his relations completely.

Need Satisfaction Through Body Change

A third major group of techniques seems to be that in which the individual seeks some form of bodily change which contributes to redefining his phenomenal self in a more favorable, or less humiliating, light. Often the excitement attendant upon thrills results in increased body tonus which is exhilarating to the individual and is likely to give a feeling of increased power and effectiveness. Such boosts to the self esteem are often consciously sought and paid for in amusement parks. Indeed, in some people this feeling becomes almost a permanent goal in life and much of their time is spent in a search for thrills. Gambling is a familiar example of this device. In the excitement and anticipation of winning or losing the gambler is able, for the moment, to forget his feelings of inadequacy and incompetence and gets a feeling of heightened tonus which is exhilarating and gives him a feeling of power. Lotteries and policy games are most popular in the poorest sections of cities, apparently because to many people they furnish the only hope of achieving property or power. Economically these people cannot afford to gamble, but psychologically they cannot afford not to gamble.

TECHNIQUES, ROLES, AND TRAITS

The techniques people differentiate in the search for need satisfaction, we have seen, often have a high degree of stability and provide a measure of predictability for behavior. The roles people play in life are to a great extent the product of the particular techniques an individual has differentiated as appropriate for a person like himself. Thus, seeing myself as a teacher, I have differentiated certain kinds of behaviors as proper expressions of that self. In a similar manner, I have differentiated certain kinds of behavior as appropriate to my conception of myself as an automobile driver, a father, a husband, an American, a friend, a Floridian, etc. The techniques which each of us differentiate are always an expression of our fundamental need to maintain and enhance the self. As a consequence of this close connection, techniques are often valuable clues to the self structure of the individual. When we know enough about his techniques it is often possible to make remarkably good inferences of the nature of the self to which an individual's techniques are related.

From the point of view of the outside observer the characteristic behavior produced by the individual's pattern of techniques, goals, and values provide the basic clues to understanding his personality. When we wish to describe another person we usually do so by describing his traits. We describe people, for example, as a devoted father, a fine swimmer, a hard drinker, or a person of great sensitivity and feeling, depending upon what we have observed about him. These traits are the manifestations of the individual's techniques of achieving need satisfaction as they can be observed by the outsider in overt activity of one sort and another. They are the means most of us use in daily life to describe other people.

Psychologists often find it useful to describe human personality in terms of traits. For many purposes it is enough to know that individuals are likely to behave in a particular fashion under given circumstances. Industrial psychologists, for example, may use observations of the ways in which people typically behave to develop more efficient production techniques or decrease fatigue and tension on the job. For more precise understanding of human beings, however, the trait approach to personality has more often than not proven disappointing. Traits describe what is characteristic of an individual's behavior but they are by no means an accurate indication of what a particular individual will do in a particular situation. The same techniques may have quite different expressions in behavior on different occasions. The teacher who knows she can help children by communicating her affection for them soon discovers that this communication must be quite different for little boys and for little girls, and even for individual little boys and girls.

Behavior is always related to the purposes of the behaver. Thus, a trait appearing at one time may not appear on another occasion even in what seems an identical situation. The teacher who today conveys her appreciation and interest in a child by praise and commendation may the next day keep him after school for punishment, not because she loves him less, but because her immediate goals have changed. Traits though they are often useful in describing behavior are likely to break down as criteria for prediction. Of much more value for the understanding and predicting of behavior are the individual's purposes expressed in his goals, values, and techniques of behavior.

Behavior we observe in others, like the symptoms of disease or the rumble of thunder in a storm, are but the external manifestations of dynamic processes within the system we are observing. Sometimes, it will be enough to deal with such surface indications. For deeper and more precise understanding, however, it will be necessary for us to penetrate behind the behavior trait to more dynamic factors in the unique character of the individual's personal self and the goals, techniques, and values through which this self is expressed.

CHAPTER 7

The Development of the Phenomenal Self

THE most important complex of differentiations in the individual's perceptual field is his phenomenal self. What a person thinks and how he behaves are largely determined by the concepts he holds about himself and his abilities. If a man believes he is Napoleon, he will act like Napoleon or, at least, like his concept of Napoleon. How we act in any given situation will be dependent upon (1) how we perceive ourselves, and (2) how we perceive the situations in which we are involved. The self is the most stable portion of the individual's phenomenal field and is the point of reference for everything he does.

As discussed in Chapter 3, human beings are continually and insatiably engaged in a never-ending attempt to achieve an adequate self. In view of this fundamental need, the self perceptions we possess have a tremendous role in determining every behavior. Indeed, the phenomenal self is so important in the economy of each human being that it gives continuity and consistency to his personality. It provides the central core around which all other perceptions are organized. When the individual's phenomenal self is understood, the various and diverse behaviors of people become consistent and predictable. The very perceptions we are able to make at a particular time are dependent upon the concepts we hold about ourselves and our abilities. Self is a basic variable affecting and controlling perception.

Human beings have, of course, always behaved in terms of some kind of understanding of the self. The use of the concept of self in the behavioral sciences is, however, comparatively recent. William James devoted a chapter to the self in his *Psychology,* published in 1890, and Freud developed his concept of the ego at about the time of World War I. Although these men pointed the way to fascinating possibilities for the understanding of human beings, a considerable period elapsed before the concept came into its own. It is only within the last twenty years that the self has been given serious attention as a basic tool of the behavioral sciences. Today, many psychologists have adopted the concept and it is currently the subject of a vast body of theory and experimentation.

What Is the Self?

The word self, in its dictionary sense, is a word we use to describe, or refer to, a particular individual, i.e., some unique personality we wish to single out from the rest of mankind. It is a term referring to a specific person and has been indispensable in the historical development of man as a conscious and thinking entity. When we wish to go further and describe the characteristics and attributes of a particular, given self, however, the job becomes a more complex and difficult one, for a self can be observed from innumerable frames of reference. A self may be described from the point of view of any number of people, including the individual himself.

What the particular qualities of a "real self" are, of course, we can never know, for the self can only be understood through somebody's perceptions. These perceptions may be more or less close approximations to the real self but surely they will never be entirely accurate. Unless it is more precisely defined the self is not very useful as a scientific construct. In fact, the question of whether a real self exists or does not exist is primarily an academic or philosophical question. It is probable that no one can observe a self—his own or anyone else's—directly. To understand human behavior, however, it does not seem necessary to do so. The ways in which the self is perceived can be studied, and that is all that is necessary for us to deal effectively with it.

Concepts of Self

The ways in which the self may be described are practically limitless. Individuals may see themselves as men or women, children or adults, Republicans or Democrats. More specifically, a particular individual may see himself as George Jackson, owner of a 20-foot sailboat, who lives at 627 Blackmoor Street, Alleghany, Missouri. These are descriptions which serve to differentiate the self from all other selves. They make it possible to distinguish a unique individual out of the mass of humanity. Each of us is possessed of a large number of such ways of describing and distinguishing ourselves as unique among other people.

These are descriptions of the self which the individual shares with others. People also have many other ways of seeing themselves, which are of little importance to outsiders but are the particular property of the individual himself. There may even be concepts of the self in a particular person which would be highly surprising to others. It is possible for a person to have concepts of himself completely at variance from the ways in which he is regarded by other people. George Jackson, whom we have mentioned above, may see himself also as a ukulele player, a great wit, a neat dresser, or a young man. Outsiders might be quite surprised to know of these concepts George has of himself, if indeed, they were interested at all. They might even find it funny that George considers himself a great wit, recalling the times they have been bored with his long-winded stories. Concepts of the self may be held in common by the individual and by outsiders or they may be the peculiar perceptions of the individual's own private world of experience.

The perceptions people have of themselves do not stop with description alone. Much more important, people perceive themselves in terms of values. We do not see ourselves simply as fathers or mothers, students or cab drivers. We see ourselves as good fathers or mothers or as bad fathers or mothers. We see ourselves as A, B, or C students, and as successful or unsuccessful cab drivers. People regard themselves as attractive or ugly, as pleasant or unpleasant, as fat or thin, as adequate or inadequate, or in terms of a thousand other descriptions of greater or lesser degree of value or importance.

Whatever his way of describing himself, each individual has developed a large number of such perceptions. These more or less separate perceptions are called concepts of self. By concepts of self we mean those more or less discrete perceptions of self which the individual regards as part, or characteristic, of his being. They include all perceptions the individual has differentiated as descriptive of the self he calls *I* or *me*.

The varied ways in which an individual perceives himself are by no means of equal importance in the peculiar economy of a particular human being. The particular concepts of the self held by a person seem to vary in at least the two following important respects:

1. Some self perceptions appear to be much more central, or basically part of us than others. If only because our society expects very different conduct from men and women we are reminded of our sex dozens of times a day. As a result, our concepts of ourselves as man or woman are usually related to the very core of being. They seem to the individual as

basic and fundamental truths. What is more, because they do seem so basic he resists with great vigor and determination any attempt to change them. Other concepts of the self may not be so strongly defended because they do not seem quite so important in our particular organizations. A man may regard himself, for example, as a man, as a Presbyterian, as a teacher, smoker, and as a driver of a 1956 Dodge. He may also regard himself as an American citizen, as younger-looking than his age, as a good tennis player, and as the life of the party. Each of these perceptions will seem to the individual to be more or less true of his personality and he will energetically resist attempts by an outsider to change such concepts, depending upon how basic the concept seems to him. Thus, it may be quite easy to change the above person's concept of himself as the driver of a 1956 Dodge. We could, for instance, buy him a 1957 Cadillac. If he does not particularly value his concept of himself as a good tennis player we might change it fairly easily if we could manage to get him thoroughly trounced a few times. Changing his concepts of himself as an American, as a teacher, or as younger-looking than his age, would be more difficult depending upon the value these concepts hold for him. Trying to change his concept of himself as a man would probably be next to impossible. Concepts of the self vary in the degree of importance or centrality they have in the person's peculiar economy.

2. Concepts of the self vary in sharpness or clarity. Perceptions about the self may range all the way from concepts which are vague and barely discernible to concepts which are clear and sharply in focus. This is a figure-ground relationship. The mother in the psychological clinic, for example, may be quite certain that she is Jimmy's mother. This is a perception of herself in clear figure. However, whether she is a "good mother" may be far less clear to her. Indeed, it may be this very lack of a clear concept of self that causes her difficulty. The adolescent moving through his teens is at first highly doubtful of his status as an adult and only slowly he comes to see himself in that role clearly and sharply. In his early adolescence he is not quite sure whether he is a man or a boy, and thus he behaves in terms of his confusion. Little by little as he grows closer to his twenties his concept of himself as an adult comes more and more sharply into figure and his behavior as an adult becomes more precise and predictable too.

The self is differentiated with greater and greater clarity throughout life. We are continually discovering who and what we are. Consequently,

at any moment, we will find the concepts of the self held by a particular person to vary widely from concepts in clear, sharp figure to concepts so vague and fuzzy as to be inexpressible by the person himself.

The Phenomenal Self and Self Concept

Each individual has had literally hundreds of thousands of more or less discrete perceptions of self. This myriad of self perceptions does not exist in the perceptual field as a mere enumeration of ways of seeing one's self. Rather, the concepts of self which each individual possesses is an organization which is the individual's own private conception of himself in all his complexity. This organization of all the ways an individual has of seeing himself we call the phenomenal self. We might also call it the perceived self.

By the phenomenal self is meant the individual's own unique organization of ways of regarding self; it is the Gestalt of his concepts of self. Whereas the concepts of self about which we have been speaking describe isolated aspects of the person, the phenomenal self is the organization or pattern of all those which the individual refers to as "I" or "me." It is himself from his own point of view. The phenomenal self is not a mere conglomeration or addition of isolated concepts of self, but a patterned interrelationship or Gestalt of all these. It is the individual as he seems from his own vantage point.

In Fig. 15 we have diagramed the perceptual field representing all of an individual's perceptions by the circle ABC. The perceptual field, as we have seen, includes all of a person's perceptions, including those about himself and those about things quite outside himself, the not self. Within the total perceptual field we may think of a second and smaller circle *B*, including all those perceptions which an individual has about himself irrespective of their importance to him. This circle encompasses all those perceptions of self in a particular situation which we have called the phenomenal self. It will be recalled that the perceptions of self vary widely in their importance or centrality in the personality. Many of our concepts of self have little or no immediate value to us at a particular moment. Thus,

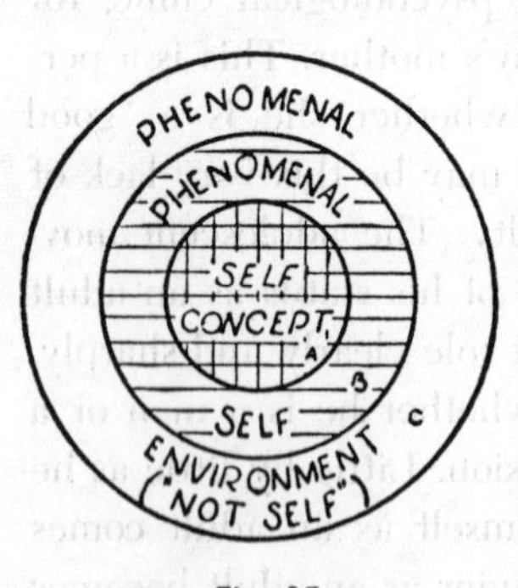

Fig. 15.

if one turns his attention to his little toe, he can become quite keenly aware of that member of his body and regard it as a distinct part of himself. This perception may have little real value, however, in understanding any very large or characteristic aspects of a person's behavior. The phenomenal self is the self in a given situation.

To describe the organization of those very important or central perceptions of self involved in a great deal of the individual's behavior, it is sometimes helpful further to differentiate the perceptual field to include only those perceptions about self which seem most vital or important to the individual himself (diagramed in our figure as circle *A*). We call this organization the self concept. In this way he may extract from the phenomenal field those particular concepts of self which are such fundamental aspects of his phenomenal self that they seem to the individual to be "he" in all times and at all places. This is the very essence of "me" whose loss is regarded as personal destruction. The Indian brave who conceived of himself so completely as a man that he maintained those perceptions even when dying at the stake is an example. Whatever these concepts are for any individual they are the very core of personality. The self concept is the self "no matter what."

Raimy, who first defined the self concept in 1943, said of it: "The Self concept is the more or less organized perceptual object resulting from present and past self observation . . . [it is] what a person believes about himself. The self concept is the map which each person consults in order to understand himself, especially during moments of crisis or choice." The self concept serves as a kind of shorthand approach by which the individual may symbolize and reduce his own vast complexity to workable and usable terms. The self concept represents for the individual his generalized self, just as the fifth grade teacher may describe "fifth grade children" in terms of her experience of them. In using such terms she recognizes that the children she refers to are quite different individuals, but to talk about the group as a whole it is necessary to symbolize them in some fashion. Just so the individual uses the self concept as the symbol or generalization of self which aids in perceiving and dealing with self. It is his attempt to reduce his self organization to its essence so that he may be able to perceive and manipulate it effectively.

THE PHENOMENAL SELF AS INFERENCE

This shorthand description of a complex self is helpful to outsiders, too. Psychologists, for example, frequently find the self concept a useful construct for studying individuals, because it represents the most stable, important, and characteristic self perceptions of the individual. The self concept can be used as a convenient approximation of the personality of his subject. In this way the psychologist is able to achieve an amazingly accurate prediction of an individual's behavior in a wide variety of settings. Though we may sometimes use the self concept as a convenient device for understanding the individual, it should never be forgotten that people always behave in terms of the *total* phenomenal field, never in terms of an isolated part. The self concept is a useful approximation of a larger organization; it is not synonymous with it. The self concept is never a sufficient explanation of behavior by itself. The phenomenal self as a discrete *physical* entity does not exist. Like the concept of the atom or the concept of electricity in the physical sciences, the phenomenal self is an inference which makes it possible for us to deal with a complex function not directly observable. The physicist infers from the behavior of the atomic pile the existence and relationships of the atoms within, or infers from the behavior of his voltmeters or ammeters introduced in the electrical circuit the nature and functions of electricity. In the same fashion the individual himself infers from his experiences who he is and what he is. He perceives of himself as tall or short, man or woman, liked or unliked, acceptable or unacceptable, able or unable, depending upon his experiences with the world about him, but most particularly from how people who inhabit that world treat him. All these perceptions contribute to his perception of himself, to his phenomenal self. To the individual himself the phenomenal self is always real; in origin it is an inference from his experience. The outside observer using the perceptual approach may also infer the nature of the phenomenal self or of the self concept from the nature of the individual's behavior.

From an objective point of view, the widely diverse behavior of any individual is likely to cause the external observer to feel that there is little or no consistency in the behavior he observes. It is the thesis of this book that this is only true when we observe behavior as an outsider. When we understand behavior from the point of view of the behaver it becomes clear that he is not acting inconsistently. Far from it. Although the phenomenal self is complex, it is by no means disorganized. Rather, it is a highly organized function which operates in consistent and predictable fashion. The activities which result from a given phenomenal self may represent varied and puzzling behaviors, but do so only when we fail to see the person in terms of his own perceptions of himself.

Characteristics of the Phenomenal Self

CLARITY AND CENTRALITY OF SELF PERCEPTIONS

Like all other perceptions the phenomenal self has the feeling of reality to the individual. His perceived self seems to him to be truly himself. However, it is probably not possible for the individual ever to perceive the total organization of his self perceptions clearly at any one moment. Rather, he perceives those aspects or concepts of self which emerge into figure from time to time as he goes about the daily business of satisfying his fundamental need.

CONSISTENCY OF THE PHENOMENAL SELF

Although the perceived self may include numerous concepts of self, it should not be supposed that the phenomenal self is a mere collection of self perceptions existing without relationship to each other. Quite the contrary is true. An organization, we have seen, is a relationship of things or events to one another. This is true of the phenomenal self as well. The concepts which make up the perceived self have a definite relationship to each other. The fact that the phenomenal field is organized requires a high degree of consistency in the perceived aspects of self.

This characteristic consistency of the self seemed so important to Prescott Lecky that he postulated a need for self consistency as the one basic need of the organism. He describes this characteristic as follows: "Immersed in an environment which he does not and cannot understand, the individual is forced to create a substitute world which he can understand and in which he puts his faith. He acts in consistency with the conception, derives his standards of value from it, and undertakes to alter it only when convinced by further experience that it fails to serve the goal of unity. Since this self-made scheme of life is his only guarantee of security, its preservation soon becomes a goal in itself. He seeks the type of experience which confirms and supports the unified attitude." For Lecky, "The goal for which the individual strives is the maintenance of a unified organization." This, he calls "self consistency."

It will be recognized that Lecky's position is similar to the one we have taken in this book. We have described the fundamental need of the organism as the search for adequacy. To achieve the adequate self, however, will require of the individual that he develop a high degree of consistency within his phenomenal self. An organized self must necessarily be a self-consistent one. It would be hard to conceive of a stable, effective, integrated personality characterized by inconsistency. Other things being equal, the degree of internal consistency in the phenomenal self will control in large part the degree of adequacy a particular personality may be able to achieve. The search for adequacy, then, must necessarily involve the individual in a search for self consistency as well.

One of the characteristics of organizations is that they resist change. The phenomenal self, as an organization, is also characterized by this effect. Casual observation of the behavior of the same individual in various situations would lead one to believe that the self undergoes wild and fluctuating changes in differing situations. What seem like wild and fluctuating changes in the phenomenal self, however, are in reality artifacts of the frame of reference from which they are observed. For example, the overbearing foreman who browbeats, threatens, and curses his men may become a fawning, obsequious lackey the moment the plant supervisor appears on the scene. At first glance it would certainly appear that his self has undergone a very decided shift in character. This appears true, however, only if we regard the matter externally. From the point of view of the foreman, his phenomenal self may have undergone no change whatever. Regarding himself as being of a level of competence, authority, ability, etc., greater than that of his workers but less than the plant supervisor, his behavior in the two situations can be observed to be a natural and expected outgrowth of such a concept in either case. There remains no necessity to infer any change in his phenomenal self in the two situations. If the self were newly structured by every momentary situation, any degree of consistency of behavior would become an impossibility.

STABILITY OF THE PHENOMENAL SELF

Once established in a given personality, the perceived self has a high degree of stability. The phenomenal self with the self concept as its core represents our fundamental frame of reference, our anchor to reality; and even an unsatisfactory self organization is likely to prove highly stable and resistant to change. This stability has been repeatedly demonstrated in modern research.

A rapidly changing self would not provide the kind of stable frame of reference the individual needs in order to deal with life effectively and efficiently. To be able to deal with life at all, he needs a firm basis from which to operate and the maintenance of his phenomenal self is essential. The very operation of his fundamental need leads to a high degree of stability in the perceived self. Anyone who has ever attempted to rebuild a child's feeling of competence once he has developed a concept of himself as incompetent and inadequate, can testify to the difficulty of bringing about such changes. Ordinarily it is only upon repetition of many experiences of adequacy and with much praise and encouragement that such a shift in the self concept becomes possible. Even in the traumatic situation of the man who has lost a leg in an accident or in battle, the redefinition of the self to exclude that lost member often requires an extended period and in some cases may never occur at all.

It is interesting that even a phenomenal self in which the individual regards himself as very inadequate, stupid, or inept will often be defended to the last ditch. Almost anyone knows how difficult it is to convince the person with severe inferiority feelings of his true level of worth. He is likely to be pleased by praise, even highly embarrassed, but continues to act in the same old ways. Any college counselor is familiar with such people who when told of a high score on a test, for example, profess that "there must be some mistake. That couldn't be me. Are you sure?" To accept such statements about themselves would require that they do things they do not feel able to do.

The very existence of the individual's need to maintain self imposes a selective effect upon his perceptions. Once the phenomenal self has become established, experience thereafter can only be interpreted in terms of that self. Thus all perceptions which are meaningful to the individual derive their meaning from their relation to the phenomenal self already in existence. Obviously this selective effect contributes to making the phenomenal self less likely to change. The woman who sees herself as misused and interprets all her experience in the light of that fact is not likely to change her position with any degree of readiness. So far as she is concerned, everything that happens to her is further proof of how right she was in the first place. In the same way, the child who feels rejected may interpret his parents' mildest rebuke as further evidence to prove what he already thinks—his parents don't love him. His resulting behavior may even cause his belief to come true.

The phenomenal self is an extremely stable organization which provides the core of human personality. Its existence gives stability and consistency to the individual and his behavior. To say that it is a stable function, however, does not mean that it is incapable of change. In a later chapter we shall want to examine more closely how such changes are brought about.

The Origins of the Phenomenal Self

In a previous chapter we have suggested that some kind of perceptual field exists for every individual even before birth. The precise character of this prenatal field must of necessity be closed to our understanding. We can do little more than speculate about what it must be like as the organism's awareness develops from the primitive "irritability" of the single cell to the awareness made possible by the highly specialized sensory equipment of the human fetus. Even with a highly developed nervous system, during the months the developing child spends in its mother's uterus its perceptions of the world outside its own skin must be extremely limited. Whatever the exact nature of this field, it seems probable that it is vague and undifferentiated, restricted for the most part to perceptions of pressure.

The major development of the phenomenal self begins with the birth of the child into the world of which he is going to become a part. It seems likely that James's description of the child at birth as existing in a "blooming, buzzing confusion" is a highly realistic description of the field of the newborn infant. As the infant is plunged suddenly into a world of sight, sound, taste, smell, and feeling, perception must be, at first, a hazy matter. We have some indication of what this may be like from the reports of persons who have been surgically cured of blindness. Suddenly plunged from a world of darkness into sight, such people tell us that at first they perceive only a blurr, a kind of light-colored fog. Following this, they become increasingly able to differentiate items in their surroundings with greater and greater sharpness and detail. The experience of the newborn child is probably similar, although he begins, of course, with far less than adults recovering from surgery, for he does not have their highly developed senses of touch, taste, smell, and hearing or their vast stores of previous experience.

For the newborn only the most intense stimuli elicit responses. As time passes, more precise differentiations become possible and in the first few hours after birth the amount of stimulation necessary to bring forth a response may be observed to decrease rapidly. With sharper differentiation within the field behavior also becomes increasingly well defined.

It is a fascinating experience to watch a young child throughout the months after birth as bit by bit he organizes and orders his movements with greater and greater accuracy and precision. Research in child development, whether investigating sucking, locomotion, the Babinski reflex, or the ultimate development of language, illustrates this trend from generalized behavior to precise operation. Once his equipment for sensing taste, smell, sight, and hearing begin to function at birth, vast new potentialities for differentiation become available and the child launches upon a voyage of exploration destined never to cease throughout his entire life span.

This process of exploration and differentiation of himself and the world about him is the most outstanding characteristic of child behavior. Young children are notoriously "into everything." Everything must be examined, felt, and tasted with little or no regard for adult standards of safety or hygiene. Harassed adults attempting to keep up with a young child as he goes about this business develop a keen respect for the unceasing energy with which this process of exploration is carried on. Even when the child seems most quiet he may be deeply engrossed in some new and intriguing discovery not always approved of by adults, but fascinating and compelling to the young explorer. Nothing is exempt from the continuous process of differentiating, testing, and perceiving.

Among the earliest of differentiations made by the infant are those concerned with the discovery of self. This is not an easy or simple process, but rather a long and involved matter of exploration and discovery probably beginning with the differentiation of the distinctions between "me" and "not me." The earliest differentiations of self from the rest of the world are of a tactual, kinesthetic sort made as the child explores his physical being and its contact with his surroundings. As a result of such explorations he discovers such things as: These fingers are "me," but those blocks are not; all this within the confines of my skin is "me," but what lies outside my skin is "not me." Bit by bit as experience increases, the self becomes more and more clearly differentiated from the remainder of the phenomenal field.

While these differentiations are at first made slowly and with much difficulty, with the development of language the process of self differentiation is vastly accelerated. The development of language and the ability to communicate by means of words open new frontiers of experience. Language makes it possible to experience vicariously what would otherwise have to be experienced slowly and painfully. It even makes possible experiences one could never otherwise have. Few of us have the problems of queens or presidents, but we can differentiate and understand them through the spoken or written word. Language provides a "shorthand" by which experience can be symbolized, manipulated, and understood with tremendous efficiency. Above all, the possession of language vastly facilitates the differentiation of self and the world about.

The Development of the Phenomenal Self

We have already seen in a previous chapter how the physical body affects perception. As the child grows and explores himself, he discovers that he is male or female, tall or short, fat or thin, blond or brunette. Some of these perceptions he arrives at through his own explorations of self. Other concepts, particularly those which have to do with values, he acquires from his interactions with people about him. He discovers not only what he is, but also what he is not and attaches values to these discriminations. He perceives himself as "good" or "bad," adequate or inadequate, handsome or ugly, acceptable or unacceptable, depending upon the ways he is treated by those who surround him in the growing-up years. He learns about himself not just from his own explorations, but through the mirror of himself represented by the actions of those about him.

The self is essentially a social product arising out of experience with people. Although some of the individual's experience of self may be achieved in isolation from other people, by far the greater portion of his self arises out of his relationships with others. Human personality is primarily a product of social interaction. We learn the most significant and fundamental facts about ourselves from what Sullivan called "reflected appraisals," inferences about ourselves made as a consequence of the ways we perceive others behaving toward us. We learn who we are and what we are from the way we are treated by those who surround us; in our earliest years by our families, and in later years by all those people with whom we come in contact. People are continually discovering and rediscovering themselves from birth to death.

THE EFFECT OF THE FAMILY ON THE DEVELOPMENT OF SELF

No experience in the development of the child's concepts of self is quite so important or far-reaching as his earliest experiences in his family. It is the family which introduces a child to life, which provides him with his earliest and most permanent self definitions. Here it is that he first discovers those basic concepts of self which will guide his behavior for the rest of his life. In examining these effects of the family on the individual's self definitions we are likely to be particularly struck by the traumatic events in his family life: births, deaths, family upheavals or great periods of happiness or unhappiness. These are, of course, vital experiences in the life of the individual and have important bearings upon his perception of self. Of even greater significance, however, are the everyday interactions among the members of a family which often seem too prosaic and commonplace to notice. Yet it is these very commonplace experiences which probably have the deepest and most profound effects upon the development of the self.

Traumatic events in the lives of people are, of course, important, but we have often overvalued them. Far more important for most of us have been those events so commonplace that we do not even think to report them in describing ourselves. They may have been so trivial that we cannot even remember them when asked to recall them at a later date. Indeed, it may even be true that the traumatic events in our lives were only traumatic because of their relationship to the more fundamental and basic feelings about self acquired in the prosaic humdrum of daily life in a family setting. Thus, the death of a grandfather might be accepted with little or no trauma by the child who felt adequate and accepted in his family, but would seem an irreparable loss to the child for whom such a grandfather represented the only love and acceptance in a family setting where such treatment was lacking from mother and father.

The reverse may also be true. Events which sometimes seem to an outside observer as deeply traumatic and shocking may actually appear to the child who experiences them as only momentarily distressing if he has had much experience of adequacy in the everyday interactions of his family life. Fundamentally well-adjusted youngsters show a surprising ability to take even the most shocking experiences in stride with an aplomb that seems almost callous to adults. Some years ago the author worked with a 12-year-old girl brought to our psychological clinic for examination following a sordid attack by an elderly man in her home community. The parents of the child were fearful that she had suffered some irreparable psychological damage as a result of this experience and brought her to the clinic for study. To the amazement of everyone, after complete psychological study and a number of play-therapy sessions we could only conclude that the child had suffered no major permanent damage. She was a thoroughly normal 12-year-old, poised and charming as she could be. When asked, she discussed her unhappy encounter simply and matter-of-factly with the staff. She expressed a wish that it had never happened, described her assailant as "that nasty old man," then turned her attention to the more interesting business of present projects and events. Her experiences in her family had apparently provided her with so basic a feeling of adequacy and worth that she was able to accept even this shocking experience without being crippled by it.

THE FAMILY PROVIDES EARLY EXPERIENCE OF ADEQUACY OR INADEQUACY. The child's family provides the earliest experience of the individual's adequacy. As the child is successful or unsuccessful in making his way in his family, as he is loved and cherished or rebuffed and rejected, the infant experiences his first perceptions of adequacy or inadequacy. This is strikingly illustrated in some research with very young children. Even in the first few weeks after birth, deeply rejected children become listless, refuse to eat, and seem to "pine away." They behave as though they felt completely inadequate to deal with life, as though the struggle to live were just too much. Spitz, who studied hospitalized children, found similar striking examples of deep feelings of inadequacy and despair even in very young infants neglected by parents for long periods of time.

In his interaction with father, mother, and siblings, the young child begins his differentiations of self as liked or unliked, wanted or unwanted, acceptable or unacceptable, able or unable, worthy or unworthy, adequate or inadequate. These are the kind of perceptions through which the individual is able to symbolize his own degree of self actualization. The more positive self definitions he acquires, the greater is the feeling of adequacy and need satisfaction; and, conversely, the more negative self definitions he acquires, the more frustrated and unhappy he becomes. Experience later in life may change the concepts developed as a product of family living but never easily or quickly. The most basic of such self concepts may be so deeply rooted in the individual's organization that they cannot easily be changed even by the most drastic of later experiences.

It is seldom that families consciously and purposefully set about the business of creating feelings of adequacy or inadequacy in a child. Rather, these feelings arise as a product of the interactions of the various members of the family often motivated by quite opposite ends than those produced in the child. Ordinarily the self concepts differentiated by the child are acquired quite without regard to parental motives. It sometimes happens, for example, that parents with the best of intentions set such high goals for children as to give the child a feeling of incapacity and unacceptability because, try as he may, he can never seem to achieve the goals his parents set for him. If too long continued, the child may eventually reject his family and their values completely. Such feelings may persist to adult life where they produce behavior which causes other people to describe him as "lacking confidence," "having an inferiority complex," "lacking ambition," or "afraid to take a chance." The concepts of self differentiated by the child are the product of his personal experience of events and may have little relationship to the motives and intentions of those who surround him.

THE FAMILY PROVIDES EXPERIENCE OF ACCEPTANCE. The feeling of adequacy provided the child as a result of his early experience in his family contributes as well to his capacities for acceptance of self and of others. One can, after all, only deal with those aspects of self of which he is aware. Facts about self which the individual is unable to accept into awareness cannot be assimilated in the perceptual field; and if not part of the field, they do not affect behavior. It is only the self which the individual can accept which provides the basis for his behavior. The person unable to accept the fact that he does not know cannot listen to advice. The entertainer beginning to slip from public acclaim may be unable to accept this fact and so behave in ways quite inappropriate to the facts of the matter as perceived by other people. The accurate and realistic acceptance of self is essential to effective living. People unable to accept themselves are under serious handicaps, because they must necessarily deal with life from false or inadequate premises.

The capacity for acceptance is closely related to the individual's experience of adequacy. Generally speaking, the greater the feeling of adequacy, the greater the capacity for acceptance of self and of others. The origins of this capacity, like the child's earliest experiences of adequacy and inadequacy, lie first in the kinds of treatment he has been accorded in his early family life. Here it is that children first experience whether or not they are acceptable or unacceptable human beings. The very young child is so completely dependent upon his family and so exclusively confined to their company that the kind of acceptance or lack of acceptance he experiences from them is likely to have long-lasting effects. Children can accept what is acceptable to those they feel are important and must reject what seems unacceptable to those with whom they are highly identified.

This early learning of acceptance is illustrated in the case of "Edith Moore," a young woman with whom the author worked some years ago. Miss Moore had a shriveled hand, but so carefully had she kept it hidden that until she came for counseling help I was quite unaware of her handicap, despite the fact that she had been in one of my classes for a year. She was almost totally unable to accept her hand as part of herself. For years she had never been able to order food in a restaurant which would have required bringing her hand into view above the table. She had never owned an evening dress or gone to a formal party because evening dresses do not have pockets. Though she was confronted many times a day with the fact that her hand existed, she attempted to live her life as though it did not. This lack of acceptance was no accident. She learned not to accept her hand from the way in which she was treated by her family in the years of her growing up. Here are some of her own statements in the process of counseling, illustrating how this lack of acceptance was learned:

COUNSELOR: (Summing up what has gone before) So this has been kind of a secret that everybody knew, but nobody talked about.

CLIENT: Sometimes they tried to keep it even from me. I remember one day I overheard a telephone conversation from my aunt and they were talking about my hand. It made me feel terrible. I know my mother never told me, but I always thought that each child in the family, when he reached a certain age, was told not to speak of Edith's hand. They have never even spoken of it. It seems queer to me.

COUNSELOR: This makes you feel like a special case.

CLIENT: That's why I like to come up here to school. At home, we never speak of it. Sometimes I wish they would.

COUNSELOR: You think that if this thing had been brought out in the open as a young child that you wouldn't feel so badly about it.

CLIENT: Keeping it secret just makes me feel more uncomfortable about it. Another problem: I know that my family knows about it, but when I meet old family friends I always wonder—do they know or don't they? Will it be a shock to them, or do they already know? I don't know how to act.

COUNSELOR: Keeping this thing a secret has really seemed to make it more obvious to you.

CLIENT: I think so. I think that keeping it a secret in the family just brought more attention to it. I have gotten to feeling, from my family and the way I have been treated, that this thing has to be kept a secret. If my family thinks so, for heaven's sake, what will strangers think? It has to be hushed up and hidden. The way they acted, I don't know what to think.

COUNSELOR: Sometimes your family's attitude made you feel somewhat guilty.

CLIENT: Yes, it made me feel so much so that I have never even spoken of the matter. I guess that maybe I thought that because of my family's attitude of their never even speaking of it that maybe nobody is supposed to see it—like as if it was something bad in the family. I felt I was to blame.

THE FAMILY PROVIDES EARLY EXPERIENCE OF IDENTIFICATION. It is from his family, too, that the child first experiences feelings of self expansion and identification with others. In addition to his most personal self he differentiates also what is *my* mother, *my* father, *my* brothers and sisters, aunts or uncles, family or friends. These are more than mere differentiations of others; they are experienced more or less fully as real parts of the self, so that when they are lost by separation or death the individual often has the feeling that part of himself has been lost as well.

While at first such identifications occur through the individual's intimate experiences with his family, as he grows older his capacities for identification normally become much broader. As he becomes emancipated from his family and moves into the wider and wider world of adult life he may develop many other identifications. In this way he comes to feel that other people or institutions are also part of self and he accordingly behaves toward wife, country, church, fraternity, plant, or neighborhood as though these too must be maintained and enhanced. Such feelings of identification are extremely important for the existence of a coöperative and interdependent society. A society made up of persons who felt no identification with others would be an impossibility.

Though feelings of identification usually begin to develop in the family circle, this does not always occur. It is fortunate that most children grow up in families wherein they learn to identify with friendly adults, but some children are not so lucky and may be forced to make their way in their early years with little opportunity to form positive identifications. In later years they may in turn find great difficulty in developing strong feelings or identification with other people. Whether or not the capacity for identification develops depends upon the individual's success in finding need satisfaction in his interactions with those most closely associated with him. Families, friends, institutions, even nations are likely to become strongly identified with self when they contribute to feelings of adequacy, or may be rejected when they result in humiliation and failure.

THE FAMILY ESTABLISHES EARLY EXPECTANCIES. The family provides the individual with his earliest contacts with the society of which he is going to become a part. Families, as part of the culture, are the unconscious conveyors of culture to the new generations. It is from his family that the child first differentiates those goals, values, techniques, and ways of behaving acceptable to his society. From the way in which he is treated by his parents and early guardians he develops expectancies, concepts of what is appropriate behavior. He learns what is expected of boys, or girls, of children and adults, of *our* family, *our* church, *our* country, as distinguished from others. From those about him he learns, too, what is worth working for and what not, what one *should, ought, must* do to be acceptable to the world about him.

In addition to these fairly general kinds of expectancies, the individual also acquires expectancies of a much more precise character having to do with what is expected uniquely and more or less exclusively of him. He thus learns that "Sister is expected to do well in school but I am not." Or, "Joe can go around with anybody, but I have to go with the *right* people." Many of these kinds of expectancies are established very early in life and have vital effects upon behavior for years afterward. The closer they become associated with the individual's concepts of self, the more stable they become and the more difficult to change with the passage of time.

In later life these expectancies form the individual's level of aspiration. Depending upon the concept of self possessed by the individual, he will choose this goal or that as appropriate for such a person as he regards himself to be. The man who regards himself as a pretty good bookkeeper probably does not set a goal for himself to be President of the United States, nor does the successful physician adopt as a goal for himself retirement to a comfortable job as garbage collector. Whatever goals are considered worthy of the individual's consideration are dependent upon the way in which he regards himself and the kinds of self expectancies he has acquired in the course of his experience.

SOME EFFECTS OF THE CULTURE ON THE DEVELOPMENT OF THE PHENOMENAL SELF

To this point we have spoken of the development of the self for the most part as a product of the individual's experience with his family. The family itself, however, is a product and conveyor of the culture which produced it. Even the world of physical objects into which a child is born are subject to the particular interpretations of the culture, so that the phenomenal self becomes overwhelmingly the product of the culture.

Human beings are born into a culture and live in some sort of one the greater part, if not all, of their lives. Of course, it would be theoretically possible for one to develop a phenomenal self even if he existed entirely alone on a desert island. For practical purposes, however, the culture in which we move is so completely and inextricably a part of our experience as to overshadow almost all else in determining the nature of the concepts of self developed by each of its members. Even our definitions and values with respect to the purely physical aspects of our environment are left not entirely to our own experience but are colored, interpreted, and valued one way or another by the culture into which we are born, as they are interpreted to us by the acts of the people who surround us. Even the so-called "objective facts" which surround us are likely to be no more than the interpretations of the culture in which we are raised. Rain is seen quite differently in the farm community, where it tips the balance between success and failure of crops, and by the city dweller who regards it only as an interference with a planned picnic. Automobiles are seen quite differently by adolescent boys and their middle-aged fathers.

The inclusion by the individual of the meanings of his culture applies not only to things and events but to himself as well. The self concept of most people will be found to have many elements of similarity with what other people think of them. The child who is surrounded by parents, teachers, and friends who regard him as adequate and capable comes in time to adopt as his own much of their definitions of him. To regard himself as anything else would lead him into behavior unacceptable to his circle and would be unlikely to reach his maximum need satisfaction. The conceptual self is the product of the individual's experience, and since his experience almost always occurs in some cultural setting, it should not surprise us if the self has many elements in common with the individual's culture.

At first glance this would lead one to believe that the individual must always conform to his culture, but the concepts of self people possess are not always what one might expect from the culture they live in. Sometimes they may be quite different from what we would expect. We need but look about us to observe that many persons have developed meanings about themselves quite different from those we might expect from the cultures in which they move. Such differences in meanings may be the result of (1) a change in the culture or (2) a change in the self concept, or both of these.

CHANGE IN THE CULTURE

It must be remembered that the individual lives not in a single culture but in a whole series of cultures, at any moment. We might describe these as subcultures within a larger culture. At any moment a person may be living in a family, a school, a community, a church, a state, a nation, or a world subculture. What is more, the demands made on the individual by these various subcultures may differ very widely. Since the individual may be raised in a subculture, his self concept develops as a function of that subculture. When he moves from it into the larger group at some later date, his self concept may no longer be consistent with the demands of the new group. His actions may continue to be appropriate to the self concept he derived from the previous group and may appear to him to be completely adequate. To the new society his actions may appear to be "queer," "unusual," or even "quite daft," depending on how far they deviate from the expectations of the new social group.

The author remembers how impressed he was as a child by the old gentleman who was invited to the family Thanksgiving dinner. For years he had lived almost as a hermit. To the children he was an object of curiosity in his fancy dress suit, but the old gentleman was quite unconscious of his odd appearance. When the gravy boat was passed he disregarded the ladle and poured the gravy out, much to the astonishment of this young child. Obviously he was doing what he considered in his day to have been both "right" and "proper." He was completely consistent with himself and the culture he had known, but out of place in the one he had entered. Other examples of this sort may be observed in the adjustments of immigrants to a new country.

This inconsistency between the phenomenal self and the expectations of others offers an explanation for the increasing conservatism and rigidity to change observable in the later years of life. Having formed his self concepts in earlier life, the individual tends to maintain them. As life continues, the culture in the midst of which he lives undergoes changes. Thus its demands become different, while the self concept may remain more or less static. This has the effect of separating behavior from the cultural demand, and the individual is likely to feel threatened by the new factors in his culture. Under threat the need of the organism is to protect its organization, and its concepts become more strongly defended than ever. The likelihood of any momentous changes in the perceived self while under such attack must be extremely remote. It is not surprising therefore that age brings greater rigidity, since the very passage of time is likely to place the self under threat.

CHANGE IN THE SELF CONCEPT

The self concept may also change without any change in the culture. For instance, the teacher who has come to expect a particular behavior of a child may sometimes be quite bewildered by a sudden change in his behavior. Although the classroom situation may not have changed, the child's behavior becomes quite different because his concept of himself has changed. In a certain school Peter had always been a very shy and retiring child who never raised problems for the teacher. He was quiet, orderly, and gentlemanly at all times. In fact, the child seemed to be repressed and almost fearful of those around him. From Peter's own point of view, he regarded himself as being unimportant and pretty much incapable of dealing with his fellows in class. As a result he took a back seat and showed very little "push." Peter had been subjected to a great deal of bullying by a group of neighborhood boys of whom he was in mortal terror. He was unused to combat and did not know how to defend himself. Whenever he could he scurried off home through back streets to avoid his tormenters. One day, however, the gang caught him. They pushed him around. They called him names till Peter was wailing in tears. Finally, the leader of the gang knocked him down and sat on his chest while the rest of the boys stood around and jeered. Peter was terrified. When the leader threatened to kill him, however, it was too much and Peter lashed out in desperation. In a frenzy of fear he threw the leader from his chest and sailed into him. Much to his surprise he discovered himself beating up his tormenter, while the gang that had been jeering at him a moment before was now yelling encouragement. Having knocked the leader down in the first rush of his terror, he now pounced upon him, grabbed him by the hair, and beat his head on the ground. In a few moments the leader of the gang was sobbing with pain and begging to be let off. Peter let him go and was led from the field of battle as a hero. For months afterward the gang, impressed with his ferocity, treated him with respect. Peter's impression of himself changed too. He gained confidence in himself; he was looked up to and was no longer afraid. He became more active, got into more mischief, and even went so far as to defy his teacher in front of his new-found friends. All of this was puzzling to the teacher, who was unaware of Peter's new status. Peter's concept of himself had changed, while the school situations had not.

CHAPTER 8

The Effect of Self on Perceiving

The Individual's Frame of Reference

The phenomenal self is the individual's basic frame of reference. It is the only self he knows. Whether other persons would agree with his self definitions or not, the phenomenal self has the feeling of complete reality to the individual. It is himself from his own point of view. Wherever he is, whatever he does, the maintenance and enhancement of this self is the prime objective of his existence.

Gardner Murphy has described this feeling as follows: "To most men in most societies, the self may be full of blemishes, of sin, of incompetence, but it is the one beloved self, the lawgiver. In a fundamental sense, the self is right. My nation is right, my class is right, my family is right, and I am right. The altercation that follows an automobile collision and the account the driver gives later to his friends are hardly the primitive 'rage' that Watson traces to obstructed movements. They are portraits of the artist as the right kind of person; he has been insulted by the carelessness or incompetence of another driver who did not see what the traffic situation really was. The first postulate is that I saw the situation as it was; the accident was due to the fact that the other driver did not see it as I did." As the central point of the perceptual field, the phenomenal self is the point of orientation for the individual's every behavior. It is the frame of reference in terms of which all other perceptions gain their meaning. It is involved in greater or lesser degree in all perceptions. It provides meaning to what would otherwise be meaningless.

The self provides the frame of reference from which all else is observed. People are not really fat unless they are fatter than we. Negroes asked to judge skin color of other Negroes use their own color as reference. Even in regression under deep hypnosis the self "core" persists and individuals behave, not as a child, but rather as "self pretending to be a child." It has even been demonstrated that we discriminate our own forms of expression from those of others even when there is no "conscious" awareness that they are ours. Experiments which manipulate environmental cues in such a fashion that the relationship between the self and the external world is difficult to maintain are often so distressing to the subject that he may experience nausea. It is this separation of self from normal anchors in the environment which seems responsible for some of the nausea people experience in "sea sickness."

PERCEPTIONS ARE ORGANIZED AROUND THE SELF CONCEPT

Since the purpose of an individual's behavior is the satisfaction of his own need, the perceptual field is usually organized with reference to the behaver's own phenomenal self. The meaning of an object or event is thus his definition of the relationship between the object and himself. We have already seen in an earlier chapter that perceptions have a bearing upon the individual's behavior in the degree to which they seem to him to be related to the self. We are much more concerned about our own children than about others, about our school, our country, or our front lawn than we are about those relating to other people. The self is the individual's basic frame of reference, the central core, around which the remainder of the perceptual field is organized. In this sense, the phenomenal self is both product of the individual's experience and producer of whatever new experience he is capable of. Even when we are concerned with matters that have to do with other people, the degree of this concern will be roughly proportional to the degree to which we are able to identify with others. This is another way of saying the degree to which we feel they are also ourselves. When we feel identified with other people, it becomes possible for us to empathize with them and we can also experience the situation from their point of view. A situation then which is not dangerous to us may seem so because we recognize that it is dangerous to another. It seems fairly certain that this seeing the situation from another's point of view is not possible, however, unless some degree of identification exists. The different attitudes toward new weapons of people on opposing sides in a war is a case in point. Effective weapons introduced by the enemy are cruel and inhuman because they threaten us or our friends, similar ones introduced by ourselves are clever and humanitarian because they protect us and our friends.

All perceptions existing in the perceptual field acquire their meaning through their relationship to the existing self. It is only when events are perceived as having some important relationship to self that they are likely to produce much change in the individual's behavior. Thus most of us know all of the good reasons why we ought not to be prejudiced, yet most of us continue to be prejudiced in more or less degree. Most of us, similarly, have pretty fair notions of the kinds of things we should eat and the kind of care we should take of our physical beings to maintain the best of health. Yet this knowledge is likely to have little effect upon our behavior until such time as we discover the personal meaning of those ideas for ourselves.

THE PHENOMENAL SELF AND THE INTENSITY OF BEHAVIOR

Only when some relationship to self is perceived in any new event is it likely to have any marked effect upon behavior. The very meaning and importance of events is determined by the relationship perceived between them and the phenomenal self. Imagine for a moment all possible experiences as being arranged along a line, as in Fig. 16, from those which have a very close relationship to self at one end to those having little or no relationship to self (as perceived by the behaver, not an outsider, of course) at the other end. Now, keeping this diagram in mind, let us suppose that I am driving my car to work on any morning. It is a pleasant morning and I am in no hurry. I am driving at a moderate speed along the highway, listening with half an ear to my radio. What is coming to my ears from the radio has very little relationship to me and has little or no effect on my behavior. I hear, for instance, the morning livestock quotations from the local stockyard. Since I am not a farmer, meatpacker, or buyer of meats, this information has little or no relation to me. It is information at point *E* on our diagram. Having no perceived relationship to me this information passes through my awareness with little or no effect upon my behavior. "It goes in one ear and out the other," as we sometimes say, and it does this precisely because I do not see that it has anything to do with me.

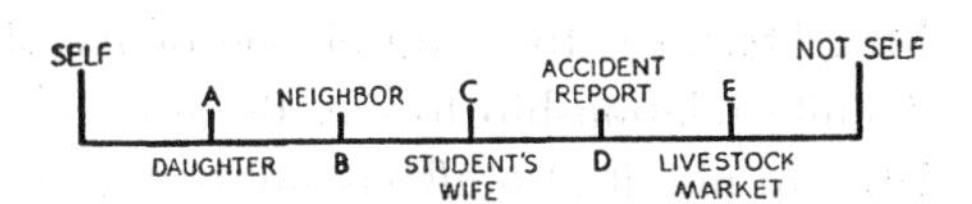

Fig. 16. Behavior and the Degree of Personal Meaning.

Now let us suppose that the next item of information which comes over the radio has a relationship to me approximately that of point *D* on our diagram. As I drive along, the news report comes on and I hear the announcer tell of a very bad automobile accident which has just been reported at the corner of Fifth and Oak Streets. He goes on to say that a Mrs. Ethel Martin, who was driving one of the cars, has been taken to the hospital in very serious condition. I hear this information, and because I am a driver myself at the moment, it has somewhat more bearing upon me than the previous information about livestock prices. I perceive in this event a mild sort of relationship to self and I react mildly to it. I may say to myself, "Another serious accident. How awful!" I may even look about me uneasily for a moment or slow down the speed of my car temporarily. Because I do not perceive any very important relationship to myself, however, this item of information has comparatively little effect on my behavior.

Let us suppose, however, that this same item of information is perceived as having the relationship to me roughly indicated by point *C* on our diagram. Let us suppose, for example, that I know Mrs. Martin. I met her once at a tea last year. She is the wife of one of the graduate students in our department. Now the information which previously had little or no relationship to me is seen to have some definite relationship. Mrs. Martin is the wife of one of *my* students. She has a more or less definite relationship to me. Because this information is perceived as related to me, it also affects my behavior more markedly. I am distressed and unhappy at this news. It starts a whole chain of thoughts about Bill Martin, his family, his relations with the staff, his ambitions, background, and a thousand other details. The news occupies my thoughts for most of the rest of the way to the office and continues to affect my behavior even after I arrive there, for I talk to others about the matter. I may call the hospital. I ask questions about whether Bill knows about the accident or not and what we might do to be helpful. I inquire a bit among the rest of the staff as to Bill's financial condition with an idea that he may need special help in this emergency.

If Mrs. Martin were even closer to me, let us say, at point *B* on our diagram, it is possible that my behavior would be even more markedly affected. If, for example, Mrs. Martin were my next-door neighbor with whom our whole family had been on good terms for many years, the information about her accident would be perceived as much closer to self and the resulting behavior it set in motion would be much more extensive and personal. My very good friends are in a sense a part of me, and what happens to them is of vital concern to me. So, on hearing what has happened to Mrs. Martin I may be deeply shocked. I call my wife to discuss what we can do to help. I find it difficult to stop thinking about Ethel Martin all day long. I make plans with my wife and neighbors to take care of the Martin children, or to lend Ed Martin a car. When I get home I take in the wash Mrs. Martin left on the line, pick up the tools Ed left in his driveway, and congregate with my neighbors to discuss the details all over again.

Finally, let us suppose the information I hear over the radio has a relationship to me indicated by point *A* on our diagram. Let us suppose, for example, that Mrs. Ethel Martin is the married name of my daughter! Now the relationship of this simple piece of information has a vital and direct relationship to myself, and the behavior I exhibit as a result may verge on the violent as I forget about everything else and drive directly to the hospital!

Events acquire their meaning from the relations we perceive between them and our phenomenal selves. The perceptions we hold about self determine the meaning of our experiences. Generally speaking, *the more closely related an experience is perceived to the phenomenal self, the greater will be its effect upon behavior.*

This is an extremely important principle with wide implications for every aspect of human behavior. It is the fundamental problem of learning and explains why it is that so much of our schooling has had so little effect upon us. In a very real sense we might even define learning as the discovery of one's personal relationship to events or ideas. Most of us learned at one time the principal exports of Venezuela, but most of us have long since forgotten what these are, along with thousands of other similar bits of information whose relationship to ourselves was never made quite clear to us. Indeed, it is in this principle that we find the greatest single problem of education. Education has been highly successful in gathering information and making information available to people, but has been far less successful in helping people to make information so much a part of themselves that they would behave differently as a result. To be effective, education must find ways of helping people discover the personal meaning of events for them. Events which do not seem to have any relationship to self are likely to be ignored if, indeed, they are perceived at all. It is only when events are perceived as having some relationship to self that behavior is changed as a result of perceiving.

The Selection of Perceptions

Anyone comparing the ways in which he perceives with the perceptions of someone of the opposite sex can very quickly discover that men do not perceive in all things as women do. Nor do children perceive like adults, Americans like Russians, or schoolteachers like engineers. The self concepts we hold have a vital effect upon the ways we perceive. They determine the ways it is necessary and appropriate for us to behave and, as a result, the things we see, the ideas we note, and the objects we accept or reject.

At any instant, the things possible for us to perceive in any situation are almost limitless. Yet we do not perceive in any such chaotic fashion. What we perceive is always organized and has meaning, and that meaning derives from the phenomenal self. Men see what seems appropriate for men to see while women see what seems appropriate for them. In our society the use of taboo words is regarded a more serious offense for women than for men and this difference shows up when men and women are asked to report such words after they have seen them. Under these conditions men report more taboo words than women. People with low opinions of themselves underestimate their performance more than people with higher self concepts.

We need but to look about us to see thousands of examples of this selective effect of the phenomenal self upon perception. The same political candidate is seen quite differently by the Republican and the Democrat, and segregation is not the same seen by the Northerner or the Southerner. Professors do not see college-student behavior in the same way in which parents do, students do, or the city police do. Mr. and Mrs. Brown on the way home from the party discuss the people who were there. When Mrs. Brown asks her husband if he noticed "the dress that Helen was wearing," she may be quite annoyed to discover that her spouse did not notice Helen's dress at all. Being a man, there may have been other things about Helen more appropriate for men to perceive, however, which Mr. Brown did notice, but about which his wife does not think to ask him.

Little boys in our society are raised quite differently from little girls and come to see themselves quite differently as a result. When boys fall down and bump their noses, we are inclined to say, "Here, now! Little boys don't cry!" So little boys learn that it is not proper for boys to display their emotions. When little girls fall down and bump their noses, however, it is a very different matter! We rush to their assistance, pick them up, and comfort them as best we can. So little girls discover that crying is acceptable female behavior. In later life the results of these self concepts may make it difficult for the young wife to understand why her husband is "such an unfeeling brute" or may make it hard for a husband to understand why his wife "gets so upset over little things." The ways we see ourselves, once established, continue to select our perceptions throughout our lives.

The self even affects the relationships between the individual and other people through this selective effect upon perceptions. Harry Stack Sullivan, for example, pointed out: "If there is a valid and real attitude toward the self, that attitude will be manifest as valid and real toward others. It is not as ye judge that ye shall be judged, but as you judge yourself so shall you judge others." The principle that self acceptance is related to capacity to accept others has also been demonstrated in studies of counseling improvement. Even the individual's levels of aspiration are a function of the kinds of self concepts he holds.

We are only beginning to discover the tremendous importance of this fact in dealing with human problems. Every day brings to light some new and intriguing consequence of individual self perceptions. People behave in terms of the self concepts they possess, and this fact is tremendously important to anyone who must work with people in any capacity whatever. We are even beginning to discover that many, if not most, problems which persons bring to the psychological clinic are primarily problems brought about by unfortunate concepts of self.

In working with children who were poor spellers, for example, Lecky noted that otherwise normal children who were unable to spell seemed to make about the same number of errors per page in their written work *irrespective of the difficulty of the material!* When spelling tests were cut in half there were about the same number of mistakes on each half, again irrespective of the difficulty of the material. Lecky observed, furthermore, that such children did not make such mistakes in spelling when they were dealing with a foreign language. He concluded that these children must be spelling in terms of the concepts they held about their capacities as spellers. They were spelling in a manner consistent with the beliefs they held about their spelling abilities!

What is more, when methods were employed to help these children change their concepts of themselves, they learned to spell with little or no difficulty. Here is Lecky's own report of what can be done in this vein:

> If we are able to change the self-conception which underlies this viewpoint, however, his attitude toward the material will change accordingly. With the resistance eliminated, he learns so rapidly that tutoring is often unnecessary.
>
> Such a change in the pupil's attitude often results in improvement which is quite astonishing. A high school student who misspelled 55 words out of a hundred, and who failed so many subjects that he lost credit for a full year, became one of the best spellers in the school during the next year, and made a general average of 91. A student who was dropped from another college and was later admitted to Columbia was graduated with more than 70 points of "A" credits. A boy failing in English, who had been diagnosed by a testing bureau as lacking aptitude for this subject, won honorable mention a year later for the literary prize at a large preparatory school. A girl who had failed four times in Latin, with marks between 20 and 50, after three talks with the school counselor made a mark of 92 on the next test and finished with a grade of 84. She is now taking advanced Latin with grades above 80.
>
> Two of the poorest spellers in the High School of Clifton, New Jersey, were used to demonstrate this method before a university class in psychology. Given twenty words to spell, one missed all twenty and the other nineteen. The school counselor, continuing the use of the method, reports that both are now excellent spellers and have taken up spelling as a sort of hobby. The results reported are taken from the work of three different counselors, showing that the method lends itself to general use in the school system.

Similar examples of the profound effects of the phenomenal self upon the individual's abilities to perceive accurately and effectively may be seen in any reading clinic. It is becoming increasingly rare in these days of periodic eye examinations and continuous checkups on child health to find youngsters unable to read because of faulty vision. Most of the cases coming to the reading clinic are poor readers who have nothing whatever wrong with their eyes. They are not unable to read in a physical sense, but are children who for one reason or another have come to *believe* they cannot read. What is more, because they see themselves as nonreaders, they approach reading expecting to do badly, and a fine vicious circle gets established which goes something like this:

Jimmy has been poorly taught to read and develops the feeling that he is not very good at reading. Because he *feels* he is a poor reader, he avoids reading as much as possible and thus avoids the very experience and practice which might make it possible for him to learn to read better. When asked to read, he does so, hesitatingly, without confidence, expecting to make mistakes, and he does. These mistakes are noted both by those around him and by himself and corroborate his impressions. His teacher, seeing him read so badly, may make the mistake of saying, "My goodness, Jimmy, you really don't read very well!" and send him home with a low grade on his report card—which proves what Jimmy has been thinking all along: "I don't read very well!" A very large part of remedial reading instruction is directed at helping children or adults to perceive more accurately and effectively not only the words on the printed page, but even more important, new and more adequate concepts of themselves!

THE CIRCULAR EFFECT OF THE PHENOMENAL SELF

This effect of the perceived self upon human behavior, it should be understood, is not limited to children who are unable to read and spell. A great many of us are the unwitting victims of our concepts of self in just the same way as the poor readers and spellers we have mentioned above. It is even possible that some of the readers of this book may be laboring under unfortunate concepts of themselves as unable to make a speech, do mathematics, drive a car, swim, or remember people's names. Indeed, this limiting effect of our phenomenal self upon perception sometimes produces great tragedies.

As Lecky has pointed out, we perceive in ways that are consistent with our concepts of self. A given phenomenal self perpetuates itself by permitting only such perceptions as are consistent with its already existing structure. People limited by their self perceptions behave in ways that seem to corroborate the self concepts they already hold. They seem almost to be "asking for" proof of what they feel about themselves, and indeed, they often get just what they ask for. The individual who, for example, feels that he is incapable of successfully making a speech perceives so many flaws in everything he does and turns his attention so intensely upon himself, expecting himself to fail, that he may stumble and falter or become tongue-tied with stage fright, which of course simply serves to demonstrate how right he was in the first place!

Perceptions are selected which are consistent with the perceived self of the behaver. Such selection occurs, furthermore, without regard to whether such perceptions seem to be complimentary or self-damaging in the eyes of an outside observer. It will be recalled that we have stated the fundamental need of all human beings is the maintenance and enhancement of the phenomenal self. Since the first need of the individual is to maintain his perceived self, perceptions inconsistent with what he believes are unlikely to occur because they would not fit his self structure. The girl who has a deep feeling of her own unattractiveness may feel we are cruelly baiting her when we tell her how pretty she looks. It seems inconceivable to her that we mean what we say. She may believe quite genuinely that we are "just trying to make her feel good."

There are literally millions of people in this world who are the prisoners of their own perceptions of self. Vast numbers of people believe they are able to do far less than they really can. As a result, they remain chained to unhappy, unproductive, and unsatisfying ways of life. Studies with various self concept scales at Vanderbilt University show that (1) patients are differentiated from nonpatients; (2) failures in paratroop training, from passers; (3) alcoholics, from nonalcoholics; (4) delinquents, from nondelinquents; (5) drop-outs, from stay-ins in school—all on the basis of self-concept. Can one conceive the kind of world we might achieve could we but find the means to release ourselves from the slavery of inadequate concepts of self? Here is a waste of human resources compared with which our losses in warfare or automobile accidents seem small indeed.

DISTORTION OF PERCEPTION

When individuals are confronted with events inconsistent with their self structure they may seek consistency of perception by doing violence to the facts. They may perceive a particular event in so distorted a fashion as to be almost unrecognizable to a disinterested outside observer. Thus, the senator who sees himself as a professional Communist hunter and savior of the nation may begin seeing Communists behind every bush or discover conspiracies where none actually exist. Labor and management in the midst of a strike often see events in a manner distorted beyond recognition by the onlooking public. Rationalizations, in which people may be found giving *good* reasons instead of *real* reasons for their behavior, are a form of seeking for better organization by which inconsistent events can be brought into closer harmony with existing self concepts. This is a form of self deception to which all of us succumb on occasion.

When it is unflattering to admit the truth, it is sometimes much easier to distort the perception enough to make it appear in a more flattering light. In our society the term "laboring" class carries distasteful connotations, so most people prefer to class themselves as "workers" rather than as "laborers." We can avoid the consequences of our mistakes by seeing them as none of our doing. We failed to make the meeting, not because we failed to start on time, but because the train was late, the streets were too crowded, or the clock did not go off. What is more, we may even believe this story! We would certainly object with vigor if anyone suggested it were not true!

Inconsistent or threatening events may also be dealt with by denying their existence entirely. A person confronted with a situation highly derogatory or destructive to his concepts of self may find it possible to maintain or enhance his integrity by the simple expedient of relegating the perception to someone else or denying its existence entirely. Thus, he may really not see what he would rather not see. The scientist who has spent his life proving the truth of a particular notion may be unable to accept the possibility of another solution and protects his phenomenal self by simply denying the new fact exists. Threatening derogatory comments about self can often be effectively dealt with by assuming they really refer to others. The teacher who asked the class to keep quiet was really directing her remarks "at Jane, not me!" In the next chapter we shall want to give more detailed attention to these kinds of distortions.

THE PHENOMENAL SELF AND ROLE

The concepts of self held by the individual determine the perceptions he will have of any particular event. Out of all the perceptions possible at any moment only those which are appropriate and consistent with the phenomenal self are available to him. This selective process determines the roles people play in any life situation.

The particular roles we feel called upon to play in life are the result of the goals and techniques we have differentiated as appropriate for us in those circumstances. Such roles will be appropriate to the phenomenal self existing for the individual at the moment. The professor and student act quite differently in the classroom. The behavior of each depends upon the concepts he has of himself and of the situation. The same person in the same situation at different times might feel called upon to make a speech, keep scrupulously clean, faint, tell a story, start a fight, or powder his nose (in preparation for a TV appearance, of course).

Though we speak here of "playing a role," we are not using the term in the theatrical sense of putting on a mask or playing a part not natural or appropriate to one's self. We use the term to mean simply the selection by the individual from his perceptual field of those goals, techniques, or ways of behaving that seem to him appropriate for the kind of person he feels himself to be in the situation he sees himself in. These roles will be the kinds of behavior that seem to him appropriate to or consistent with his phenomenal self in the situation.

Whatever roles we feel called upon to play will always be a function of need satisfaction. Whenever it becomes clear to us that our roles are inconsistent with our way of regarding ourselves, we will change them to others more likely to produce results and more consistent with our perceived selves. Changes of this sort may occur as follows:

The culture in which one moves can tolerate some differences in behavior from the expected. How much latitude it can tolerate will vary widely from situation to situation. When the individual's behavior passes this point of tolerance, it can no longer be accepted. The people about him begin to behave in unfriendly ways. At this point he may perceive that people do not act as he expects them to. His need satisfaction is frustrated. This results in feelings within him that "something is wrong." He feels unhappy and dissatisfied. In his subsequent search for need satisfaction he may differentiate new goals and techniques which bring him better results. This may or may not involve major changes in the phenomenal self.

Let us take as an illustration the case of the man who considers himself to be a skillful driver. With such a concept of himself the situation demands that he have no accidents. However, our driver may have differentiated his role as one of demonstrating that he is a skillful driver by an air of nonchalance, by taking chances, by coming close but not too close, and the like. One day he has an accident. This is terrible! An accident is not at all consistent with his concept of himself, and he does everything he can to place the blame elsewhere. What is more, his role as a "chance taker" has let him down and no longer leads to need satisfaction. His perception of this situation will lead him to the role consistent with his new perceptual field. He may develop a "drive with care" technique in place of the former "come close but not too close." This illustration assumes that only the required role is brought under doubt by our driver's accident. Of course, it will be recognized that if his concept of himself as a skillful driver is too greatly threatened, he may become not a safer driver, but a more dangerous one, to satisfy his need to defend his concept of self.

We have only begun to understand the importance of the phenomenal self in selecting and controlling human perceptions. In this chapter we have examined something of the role of the phenomenal self as a factor in perception. We have seen, too, that the phenomenal self is, itself, an organization of perceptions. In a later chapter we shall want to give much more attention to how the phenomenal self develops and its relationship to human feelings and emotion.

How the Self Concept Changes

As Raimy has pointed out, "the self concept not only influences behavior but is itself altered and restructured by behavior and unsatisfied needs." We have seen that the self concept is a stable organization. To say that it resists change, however, does not imply by any means that once it is established no further changes are possible. It is probable that throughout the lifetime of the individual change is constantly occurring in the self concept as he perceives the reactions of others to himself. In a sense, this is like learning about self through a mirror. He differentiates new aspects of self in terms of the reactions of those about him as they respond to his behavior.

The individual's own fundamental need requires change in his concepts of self. One cannot be truly adequate in a changing world without adapting to the changes going on about him. A static self concept existing in a moving world would soon be out of touch with the world about it. An adequate self must be stable but not rigid; it must be changing but not fluctuating.

THE NECESSITY FOR CHANGE

We have already suggested that the self is the product of the individual's experience. Each of us discovers who he is and what he is from events that have occurred in his lifetime, but most particularly from the ways he has been treated by those close to him in the course of his growing up. The process of self differentiation never ceases. We are continuously engaged in a process of self discovery, sometimes more rapid than others, but never completely absent from our experience.

The first step in the acquisition of new concepts must, of course, be some sort of experience inconsistent with existing self perceptions. The mere fact of living in a dynamic changing society imposes upon the individual a necessity for change. The varying roles the individual is called upon to play in the course of his interaction with his culture make it inevitable that sooner or later he will be subjected to experiences at odds with his existing self organization. This inconsistent experience may be perceived by the individual at any level of awareness. Thus, a person may be quite clearly aware that his new experience does not jibe with his existing phenomenal self. Perceptions inconsistent with existing concepts of self may also be experienced by the individual dimly and indistinctly as "doubt," as a vague feeling of tension, as a feeling that "something is wrong," "this is not me," or, more specifically, as a feeling of inadequacy or failure. This inconsistency may also be experienced in a positive sense as when one feels a sense of elation at a new skill mastered or new status achieved.

The ability to perceive difference between the self that the situation requires and the phenomenal self is dependent upon one's ability to see himself as others see him. As a member of a particular group or culture and responding to the world of things and events about him, the individual interprets these events in terms of his concept of the culture. Furthermore, he participates in this observation of himself, and he becomes more or less able to "see himself as others see him," or at least to see himself as he thinks others see him. When the author does not attend church on Sunday morning, he is aware of the fact that other people in his neighborhood look askance at such behavior. Similarly, the child as he grows older learns not only to behave in one way or another, but to evaluate his behavior in the terms of the culture in which he is reared. When he takes a piece of forbidden candy, he knows that his behavior is not acceptable. He not only behaves in a certain way but becomes able to interpret his behavior objectively, that is to say, in terms of the values of the culture in which he operates. This objective evaluation of his behavior in terms of the society in which he moves may or may not affect his concept of himself. For example, though he may evaluate his act of taking the candy as "stealing," he may continue to regard himself as a "good" boy. It is interesting that this is often exactly what seems to occur in many delinquents. Even though they may accept the label of "liar" or "thief" this acceptance is subject to the selective effect of the need for maintenance of the phenomenal self upon perception, which leads the child to defend himself by believing that his lying and stealing are "smart" or "good."

Unless awareness of discrepancy between the perceived self and cultural demand occurs, it is certain that the chances of change in the self are very slight. Almost anyone is familiar with examples of such lack of insight in everyday life. We see illustrations of this in such common expressions as, "Ye Gods! Can't he *see* what he's doing?"; "You'd think he'd know better"; and "Yeah! Just *try* and tell him." In such situations the individual's perceptions of self seem truly to have blinded him to the external evaluation of the facts.

Even the ability to see himself as others do is limited by the need for maintenance of the self concept. For example, in the illustration used above, the child who conceives of himself as good, but who has taken the forbidden candy, may deny in the most vociferous terms any suggestion that he is a "naughty" boy. Even though he "knows better" he must defend his concept of himself to protect his organization.

RESISTANCE TO CHANGE

The differentiation of new perceptions of self is comparatively easy when the economy of an individual does not already contain self perceptions in that area. Children who have not yet formed clear concepts of self in respect to a particular function are much more responsive to new experience than adults who have clearly differentiated phenomenal selves. When no preëxisting concepts of self interfere, the differentiation of new concepts is a simple concomitant of the kinds of experiences to which the individual may be subjected. Thus, repeated instances of success or failure in a particular area may quickly result in a self concept as adequate or inadequate with respect to that matter in a child who has no preëxisting concepts. The same experiences of success or failure experienced by a child who already has strong perceptions of self in this area may result in no appreciable change in the self concept whatever. Early experiences are likely to be highly important in determining the self concept because they limit the possibilities of later ones.

We have already seen in an earlier chapter that the fundamental need of each of us is to maintain and enhance the phenomenal self. The self concepts we seek to maintain, furthermore, are those currently in existence. The stability of the phenomenal self makes change difficult by causing us (1) to ignore aspects of our experience which are inconsistent with it or (2) to select perceptions in such a way as to confirm the concepts of self we already possess. As a result, changes produced by events inconsistent with well-differentiated self concepts are likely to be slow and laborious, if indeed they occur at all. What is more, the greater the importance of a particular concept of self in the economy of the individual, the more unlikely is any given experience to produce a major change.

A self concept resulting from many experiences over a long time may take an equally long time to change. The delinquent who has learned over a 14- or 15-year period that people cannot be trusted, or that he is unliked, unacceptable, an outcast, is not likely to respond at once to the first new or kindly experience the well-meaning teacher or social worker directs toward him. This is sometimes difficult for teachers and social workers to understand. A child with a long history of unhappy experiences develops a concept of self which is not easily open to change, and the harm that took so long to build up may take a long time to be reversed. A concept resulting from much experience requires a large amount of contrary experience to produce any basic change. Like a well to be filled up, even after a lot of dirt has been shoveled into the pit, the hole is still there and seems as deep as ever. One must shovel a long time before one begins to see any tangible results.

Persons who must work with deeply disturbed children often become discouraged and disillusioned because their well-meant acts of kindness or sympathy are rebuffed by the very children they seek to help. Their discouragement is the product of their own misunderstandings, however, and not a function of the perversity of those they seek to help. The child who has become a truly tough delinquent as a result of a lifetime of frustration, neglect, and failure develops a feeling about himself that he is unliked, unwanted, unacceptable, and unable. He has learned, too, that other people are not trustworthy. Expecting such a child to respond immediately to a single statement, "I like you, Jimmy," is like expecting to reverse Niagara Falls with a teaspoon! All his previous experience has taught him that he is unlikable and unacceptable and that people are untrustworthy—particularly when they say the very things he would like so desperately to believe but knows are not true. The worker who approaches such a child in this way had better be prepared to back up his spoken words by behavior, for he is certain to be tested if he is attended to at all.

Unfortunately, what often happens is something like this: The naïve or untrained worker approaches the child with a statement like that above, meaning in all sincerity what he says. The child finds such a statement completely inconsistent with his concepts of self and is impelled to reject the idea. At the same time, his experience has shown him that people are not to be trusted. As a consequence of these perceptions he rejects the proffered help or affection and may even attack or insult his benefactor. The astounded worker, in turn, seeing himself rebuffed so violently may conclude the child is incorrigible or hauls off and slaps him for his impertinence—thereby proving to the child what he has believed all along! Self concepts differentiated as the result of long and adverse experience do not change in a moment. Nor do they change as the result of words alone.

GRADUAL CHANGE IN THE PHENOMENAL SELF

While changes in peripheral aspects of the self concept may sometimes occur fairly quickly, changes in the important or fundamental concepts of self usually change only slowly and gradually. Such shifts may even occur so imperceptibly that the individual, himself, lacking the evidence of some striking event, may never be aware that any major change has occurred and assume that he always had the same attitudes he has now. Sometimes, too, the change in the way others treat the individual is so gradual that he is hardly aware of it and cannot put it into words. It is rare, for example, that the adolescent is suddenly conscious of being grown-up. In fact, it is more likely to be true that he still regards himself as a child far longer than is justified by his general development. This often results in behavior extremely annoying to adults who wonder why he doesn't grow up or "act his age." In time, with repeated evidence of his new status, however, most adolescents achieve a differentiation of the self more adequate to their new social status. It seems likely that gradual changes of this sort, as a result of repeated experiences, represent the most frequent type of change in the concept of self. Primitive societies, as a rule, handle this problem better by holding public ceremonies to dramatize the person's new adult status to the community and to himself.

Even changes in the self which at first glance seem to be quite rapid often turn out to be really very gradual. "Sudden" insights are more often than not likely to be based upon a whole series of prerequisite differentiations so prosaic as to be unnoticed but establishing the foundation which made the "insight" possible. A young woman who came for therapy with the author of this volume was the daughter of a minister. All her life she had led an exemplary life for the benefit of her family and the congregation. Going away to school and being forced at last to live her own life, she was deeply confused and upset. In the following series of statements from the eighth interview with this young woman, note how she struggles with her concept of herself and her relationship to the world about her as she attempts to differentiate just what she is.

Note, too, how a whole series of minor differentiations result finally in a "sudden insight" (shown in the last sentence in italics).

A couple of years ago I heard one of Dad's sermons in which he said, "A person has to like himself." From then on I took it for granted that I did. I decided I wouldn't change for anything—until this week, when I began wondering if I really did. I decided I liked myself but I also despised myself. Remember I told you I was afraid of failure because I had never really experienced it. Hooey! I've never really had anything but failure.

I've decided I'm a two-sided, two-faced person. I've always had to act one way although I felt another. I've always had to be something I'm not. I feel like a different person at home and away.

I'm not sure now what I'm like—I don't know what I am. I'm a man without a country. I don't think I ever knew really what I was. I give appearances, but down under I'm not that at all.

What is myself? It's funny how sure I was and now I'm not sure at all. I feel so miserable, afraid, and worried. I'm afraid of everything at the moment, but I can't find what I'm afraid of. I'm afraid to live like this for the rest of my life, but I'm even more scared as to what to do about it. I'm afraid even to think about it. The more I think, the more worried and scared I get—It gets worse and worse.

My problem is myself. Everything's wrong but I don't know what it is. What am I? I'm human, female, five feet seven, period. . . . I want to be sure but I'm not even sure of myself. . . . Maybe I know what I am but I'm afraid of it. I'm in a panic about myself.

I never felt I could be myself. I couldn't be because of my father's job. Now I know I must change myself, but what am I? I must know that.

This stared me in the face. I'm face to face with it, but I just can't do it. I keep getting this far and that's all. I'm stopped. One side of me says, "What can you do?" and the other side of me says, "You've got to, you've got to, you've got to." *It's a battle between what I think I am and what I really am.*

TRAUMATIC CHANGE

Changes in the self concept also may occur, but much more infrequently, with traumatic shocks in which the entire organization of the individual is threatened. This is well illustrated in the following case of a young woman from the files of a psychological clinic. As a child, she had been happy and carefree. She felt quite secure in her position and conceived of herself as a "good girl." One evening her parents had a rather wild party and she was put to bed with instructions that she was not to get out of it under any circumstances. Curiosity, however, was too much for her and she got up, lay on the floor and watched the evening's proceedings in the room below through a grating in the floor. Here she fell asleep and in the night was overcome by coal-gas fumes in the house. Later, she was discovered by her mother, who was furious at her misbehavior. The child hung between life and death for several days, during which time her mother did not let her forget that she would never have been in that condition had she been a "good girl" and done as she was told. This single incident was of such a traumatic nature that the child completely revised her self concept and accepted her mother's definition of herself. Even by the time she came to college, she was thoroughly convinced that she was indeed a very "bad" person. She had apparently developed a concept of herself as "guilty," and bowed to her mother's slightest whim because she felt she "owed" it to her. She gave up the career as a dancer she had wanted previous to her narrow escape, to enter religious education in the hope of someday "saving" herself. Thus, under the traumatic shock of possible complete destruction, a fairly violent change in the phenomenal self was brought about.

SOME CONDITIONS FOR CHANGE IN THE SELF

Whether or not a change is likely to occur in the perceived self seems to be dependent upon at least three factors. These are:

1. The place of the new concept in the individual's present self organization.
2. The relation of the new concept to the person's basic need.
3. The clarity of the experience of the new perception.

The relation of the new concept to the total economy. We have already seen in the preceding pages that not all concepts of self have equal value in the peculiar economy of a particular individual. Less important concepts of self (from the behaver's own view, of course) will be more easily changed by new experience than more central or personal concepts of self.

The relationship of the new concept to the subject's need. The phenomenal selves possessed by each of us are our nearest and dearest possessions. We have seen that the maintenance and enhancement of the phenomenal self is the fundamental need motivating our every behavior. It follows that new concepts of self which seem to the individual to satisfy this need are more likely to be accepted into his personality structure. Experiences which seem to the behaver to be threatening to his existing concepts of self (even if such experiences seem enhancing to the outsider) are likely to be rejected with great vigor. This means that other things being equal, change in the self is most likely to occur in situations which do not force the individual to self defense. Change can and sometimes does occur under threat, but generally speaking, the absence of threat increases the mobility of the self concept.

The clarity of the experience of the new perception. Change in the self concept can only occur as a consequence of some new experience of self. The more vivid such experience, the more likely is it to result in changes in self perception. In general, first-hand experiences are likely to be much more effective in producing self-concept change than are symbolic experiences. What happens to us directly is much more vivid and clear than the words that people speak to us. The experience of failing an examination, for example, is far more real than a parent's warning of the possibility of failure.

CHAPTER 9

The Availability of Perceptions in the Field

TO live effectively and efficiently in our modern society requires that we be able to cope successfully with the situations in which we find ourselves. It requires also that we be able to adapt and change our behavior to fit the varied requirements of the moment. In a world changing as rapidly as ours, anything less leaves us in danger of behaving inappropriately. The kind of adaptability and efficiency of behavior required for modern living can only occur if we have a field of perceptions maximally open to our use. Perceptions must be available to us when they are needed. Since behavior is a function of our perceptual fields, effective, efficient behavior can only occur from the widest possible field of perceptions. Whatever restricts and inhibits the perceptual field will have serious effects upon the individual's ability to deal with life.

Differentiation and Need Satisfaction

Whether or not satisfaction of need is possible for the individual will depend upon the differentiations he is able to make in his perceptual field. If it is necessary for me to be 20 miles from this spot in two hours, I shall certainly not be able to satisfy my need if the only means of travel I can differentiate is walking. Recently a new drinking fountain was installed in one of our college buildings. The need of the writer was momentarily frustrated until he had differentiated that *this* fountain worked by a foot pedal instead of the usual handle. How adequately we are able to satisfy our own and others' needs will depend upon the differentiations we can make in our perceptual fields. It is not enough, either, that perceptions should be *possible* in the field. They must also be available for use at the instant they are needed.

Whether or not it is possible for the individual to achieve need satisfaction will depend upon the level and character of the differentiations he is able to make at a particular instant. If these perceptions result in behavior adequate to meet life situations, need satisfaction is achieved and the individual feels happy, satisfied, and operates with a minimum of disturbance. If they are not adequate, he is likely to feel unhappy, frustrated, and ineffective and may even make his situation worse by the behavior to which such feelings lead him.

A great deal of the work of the clinical psychologist is directed at assisting clients to make more adequate differentiations than have previously been possible for them. The handling of parents who bring a bed-wetting child to the clinic is a case in point. If they have perceived his bed wetting as "Jimmy is just being nasty," their behavior toward him is bound to be a function of that differentiation. Seeing his behavior as "being nasty," differentiations involving punishment, restraint, shaming, or "teaching Jimmy to behave" are likely to follow. On the other hand, if the parents can be assisted to perceive Jimmy's behavior in other and more adequate terms, their behavior will be quite different. Even their future perceptions may be vitally affected. This is exactly what the clinician attempts to do. If the parents can be helped to regard Jimmy's behavior as that of a child who is "upset," for example, a whole new series of differentiations and, thus also, of behaviors becomes possible. Viewing his trouble as a result of being upset is likely to lead, for instance, to differentiations as to the nature of what is upsetting the child and may even lead to new perceptions by the parents of their own behavior toward Jimmy. Such changed perceptions make more adequate behavior possible.

The effectiveness of behavior is a direct outgrowth of the differentiations the behaver can make in his perceptual field at the moment he is called upon to act. People cannot behave in terms of perceptions they don't have. We have seen in previous chapters how the phenomenal field is affected by the individual's fundamental need as this need is expressed through the phenomenal self, goals, and values. In the remainder of this chapter we shall examine further some effects of need on the availability of perceptions in the field.

NEED ORDERS PERCEPTION

The phenomenal field is continuously ordered by need. Any event which seems to the individual to be related to the satisfaction of need will have a strong effect upon the rest of the perceptual field. This change in organization normally has the effect of increasing the availability of perceptions related to the need. What affects need satisfaction compels attention and cannot be overlooked. All of us have experienced the way in which our attention becomes narrowed to some pleasant event which we may be experiencing or, perhaps, only anticipating. It is well illustrated by the ordering of our perceptions when we are preoccupied. Under a very high degree of concentration the area of the phenomenal field open to differentiation may be quite narrow, and perceptions will be confined to this fairly limited area. A commonplace example may be seen in our failure to differentiate the clock's ticking in a quiet room. As attention wanders from the book we are reading we may suddenly become aware of the ticking, which has certainly been available for differentiation all the time. As we narrow our field again to resume reading, the perception of the clock's ticking is no longer a major part of our field. This narrowing of the field can often be observed in clinical work as well. Clients are often found to be so anxious to achieve a particular goal that they repeatedly rush blindly straight for it, being unable to perceive any more adequate manner of approach. They are like the chicken, so intent on reaching the food dish on the other side of the fence that it keeps sticking its head through the wire instead of going around the barrier. In the same way, people who strongly desire respect may brag too much and so lose the very acclaim they seek. Had such persons been under less pressure they might have been able to perceive more effective although perhaps less straightforward techniques to achieve their goal.

Tunnel Vision

This narrowing of the phenomenal field when need is strongly affected has been called "tunnel vision," because the effect upon perception is very much like looking at an event through a tunnel or tube. The events at the end of the tunnel are clearly seen while surrounding events are blocked out of the field of vision. Because of this effect some perceptions are very clearly experienced. Other perceptions one might make in the periphery of vision if attention were not so closely oriented, however, become unavailable. While it is often a desirable and necessary thing to be able to concentrate upon a particular perception or series of perceptions, the narrowing of the field can also make it more difficult to perceive events from a broader perspective. A good example of this is the famous story of Archimedes' discovery of the principle of specific gravity. According to the story, Archimedes was commissioned by his ruler to discover whether a crown was truly of pure gold as it had been represented by the goldsmith. Archimedes was furthermore instructed that he must not harm the crown in the process of his investigations. This was a difficult problem and Archimedes wrestled with it for days trying to discover a solution, but to no avail. Finally, after long efforts he gave up the search. Then, suddenly, while he was relaxing in his bath, the solution to the problem came to him—he could weigh the crown in water and measure the amount of water it displaced! Archimedes had discovered the principle of determining specific gravity. While working intently his attention had been so narrowed he could not perceive the solution to his problem. Relaxed in his bath, his perceptual field was more open and he was free to perceive a new relationship of matter not understood before his time.

When Archimedes discovered the solution to his problem, the story goes on to tell us, he was so excited he jumped from his bath and ran naked through the streets crying, "*Eureka*" (I have found it!). Apparently any situation in which we are deeply involved tends to cause a narrowing of the perceptual field.

This narrowing effect of perception when interest is high and widening of perceptions when we are relaxed is not restricted to scientists alone. Almost anyone has had similar experiences wherein during periods of much straining to find an answer, no answers would seem to come, only to find that they popped into figure in our perceptual fields at some later moment when, perhaps, we no longer had need of them. This often happens when one is trying desperately to think of a name. The harder one tries the more restricted become the possible names that come to mind. Later, when we are no longer trying, the name may come to us with no trouble whatever.

A fascinating example of the organizing effect of need on perception is to be seen in a study carried out at two of our universities. Following a particularly rough football game between Dartmouth and Princeton in which some spectators believed they saw a number of evidences of "dirty" play, Hastorf and Cantril carried on an investigation in each school as to the ways in which the game was perceived by the respective student bodies. On each campus editorials appeared in the student papers deploring the "dirty" play of the other school while praising the home team for its sportsmanship and restraint "in the face of great provocation." Movies of the game were shown in fraternities on each campus and the men attending were asked to record infractions of the rules made by each team. As with the editorials, each side saw what it was prepared to see! There are, of course, limits to the individual ability to distort any specific datum, but in such a case the organization of the perceptual field tends to be maintained by distortion elsewhere. Members of a Midwest alumni chapter, failing to find evidence of the atrocities they had expected to see, complained that they had been fobbed off with a censored film!

ENHANCEMENT VALUES OF RESTRICTION OF THE FIELD

It should not be supposed that the restricting effect of need on perception is all bad. On the contrary, the ordering of perception has an important value to the organism, making it possible for him to achieve need satisfaction. When a speeding car is bearing down upon us as we cross the street, it is no time for us to be musing about the beauties of spring. We need to be keenly aware of the threat to our existence and to deal with it precisely and quickly. Concentration on a limited part of the field under threat often helps us to cope more effectively with emergency situations. But the same effect can also be a severe handicap to adjustment in our society. Many of the adjustments we must make in our daily lives are not simple or direct problems of our physical relationship to things. Rather, they often involve highly subtle and complex relationships, frequently not clearly or directly discernible. Our forefathers could become angry at a stalled mule and might even get results by kicking him. The angry driver who kicks his stalled automobile, however, may gratify his feelings but is unlikely to improve his transportation.

If perceptions were not organized we would be at the mercy of every momentary shift of attention. Our fields would make no sense without organization. We would be so continuously distracted by the myriad changes in the external environment to which we are exposed at every moment of our waking lives as to make it almost impossible for us ever to accomplish anything. Restriction of the perceptual field *may* have adverse effects upon our capacities to behave effectively. More often than not, however, it facilitates our adjustment and assists us in coping with life by ordering and organizing our perceptual fields so that we are not will-o'-the-wisps at the mercy of every fleeting perception which comes to us. Ordering and restricting the field makes concentration possible and assists in the achievement of need satisfaction. Some degree of organization of the perceptual field is an essential to the development of an adequate self.

It is, of course, possible that the selecting effect of need upon perception *can* be inefficient and harmful. Many good things become harmful when taken in overdoses. There are people in our society who seek so strongly for money, prestige, or power over other people as to overlook more important and lasting values. Absent-minded professors may be concentrating so much on a paper they are writing as to overlook the importance of their students' problems. Some men may be so busy making a living for their families that they never have time to get acquainted with them. Others may be so intent upon achieving power and prestige among their fellows that they unthinkingly grind other people beneath their onrushing wheels.

Restriction of Perception and the Experience of Threat

Perhaps most destructive to human personality is the restrictive effect upon perception brought about by the individual's experience of threat. We have seen that whatever seems to the behaver inconsistent with his existing perceptions of self may be experienced by the individual as threat. Whatever seems threatening to an individual in turn, demands attention and produces a degree of tunnel vision in the perceptual field.

Everyone has experienced this narrowing effect on perception under threatening circumstances. It is commonplace to hear one's friends report: "For a minute, I couldn't think what to say to him!" "Honestly, that truck looked big as a house!" "I just kept doing the same thing over and over. I couldn't see anything else to do." "I kept looking and looking and couldn't find it and later on, when I found it, I saw it had been right under my nose all along!" The author recalls even at this date, years later, the threat he experienced one evening during his college days. I was driving back to town at the end of a delightful evening with my "date" and another couple when suddenly one of the tires blew out and the car began to careen wildly about the road. I can still recall, with much of the clarity it had when the accident happened, the picture that came to mind in those few moments fighting for control of the car. The perception I had most vividly in the moments following the blowout was a picture of myself standing before the father of the two girls, telling him his daughters were dead! The behavior of the car was far less threatening than facing the irate father! Fortunately, no smash-up occurred, but this was not due to the skillful handling of the car by the driver, for I made a number of serious mistakes. For example, though I "knew" better, in the stress of the moment I stepped hard on the brake, causing the car to swerve about the road. I had had blow-outs before, but with perceptions restricted to the relationship between myself and the father of my date, I was in no condition to behave in terms of more adequate understanding!

We do not need to rely upon testimonials concerning the effect of threat, however. The effect has been amply demonstrated in a large number of interesting psychological experiments. In a series of frustration experiments Hamilton found that both animal and human subjects under stress often were unable to perceive more than one line of behavior and this they used in rigid fashion despite the fact of its inappropriateness. Apparently, under great stress perceptions were so narrowed as to make it impossible to perceive better or more effective solutions. Other experiments have demonstrated that the experience of threat is accompanied by decreased efficiency and adaptability to a task, by adverse effects on learning and problem solving, and by perceptual inadequacy.

A vast majority of the threats we experience in modern life are not physical but social. We are less often threatened by things than by people. Such threats, furthermore, are seldom effectively dealt with by direct concentration on the threat itself. When one is threatened by his boss it seldom pays to tell him so. Direct attacks upon many of our modern threats often serve only to jam the machinery and increase the likelihood of our making further errors. In addition to increased errors and lowered efficiency, the experience of threat seems also to be accompanied by rigidity and intolerance of ambiguity. That is to say, under threat the ability of subjects to adapt readily when changed conditions are called for or to tolerate unsolved problems is seriously impaired. Paratroopers, for example, show impaired efficiency in perceiving before jumping, but after the jump has been successfully completed and anxiety is lowered, perceptual efficiency improves. Under threat, behavior becomes rigid and less fluid or adaptable to changing requirements. People under stress seem less able to cope with ambiguous or unsolved problems. They feel a need to have things definite and sure and in clear figure even though this may mean sacrificing accuracy.

Unfortunately, the restricting effect of threat in the phenomenal field simply complicates the resolution of problems. For adequate perception we need, not a narrow field of differentiation, but a broad one. Too narrow a field from which differentiations may occur results in repetitions of the same behavior time after time. This produces a characteristic behavior of threatened people often described as "compulsive" behavior.

Further Restrictions of Self Defense Upon Perception

In addition to the effect of "tunnel vision" upon the perceptual field, a second major factor restricting perception is brought about by the fundamental need to defend ourselves against attack. In the search for adequacy we have pointed out the need of each of us to maintain and enhance the phenomenal self. Under threat, then, we have no choice but to defend our self concepts when they seem to us to be severely threatened. Our phenomenal self after all is the only self we know. It is not just our dearest and most priceless possession. It is ourself. Without it we have no identity at all. Small wonder then that under threat we rush to its defense. We make excuses for our weaknesses, defend ourselves from criticism, and if pushed far enough, may strike out violently in retaliation against those who seem to be threatening us. One needs only to look about him to see numerous examples of self defense occurring in people everywhere. The child confronted with his misbehavior insists with vehemence upon his innocence, though we and he both know he did the act he is accused of. Husbands may defend with vigor threats to their concepts of self when wives cast aspersions about thinning hair or rounding figures. Wives are equally defensive of concepts of self as good shoppers, tasteful dressers, or fine cooks. Teachers are likely to be defensive when confronted with suggestions that they might be unfair or incompetent.

Attempts to defend the phenomenal self are not restricted to the individual's own self alone. People seek to maintain not only their immediate selves, but also those selves with whom they are identified. I defend not only me, but *my* child, *my* wife, *my* town, *my* country, *my* church, and those who are identified with these institutions or ideas. Indeed, these are all but extensions of myself, and in defending them I am but attempting to defend myself. In an interesting experiment on this question, Levanway asked subjects to rate themselves and others before and after a stressful situation. He found his subjects rated both themselves and their friends better under threat than when they were not under stress. Under threat we tend to "close ranks" and gather about us whatever strength we can.

This defense of the self concept provides a degree of stability to the self and makes the maintenance of identity possible. In this way self defense plays a vital and important role in need satisfaction. In the kind of world we live in, however, it can and often does have negative and destructive effects as well. The two factors, tunnel vision and the necessity for self defense under threat have far-reaching implications for human adjustment. Both factors contribute to making behavior static and unresponsive to the changing requirements of the world in which people live.

This nonadaptive, inflexible kind of behavior under stress has come to be known as "rigidity" and has captured the attention of many research psychologists in recent years. They have repeatedly demonstrated that rigidity is a concomitant of the individual's experience of threat and shows itself in decreased efficiency on intellectual tasks, an intolerance of ambiguous situations, and an inability to "shift gears" appropriately in moving from one situation to another. Some experimenters have even found rigidity to be closely associated with authoritarianism, dependency, and ethnocentrism. Apparently, threatened people have need to defend themselves by identification with strong institutions and figures, building up the prestige of their own groups and weakening that of others.

It must be apparent that this kind of rigid behavior produced by tunnel vision and the necessity for self defense is a far cry from the kind of behavior required for a great deal of modern living. Much of our adjustment to modern life requires not self defense, but self change. To live effectively in a technological, shifting, mobile society like ours requires of each of us the maximum of adaptability and resourcefulness to meet changing requirements. The achievement of a democratic way of life requires a free and open field of perceptions, untrammeled and unrestricted as can be. This will be true whether we are talking about an individual's adjustment to home, school, society, the world of work, or international relationships.

THE VICIOUS CIRCLE

The two effects of threat about which we have been speaking often lead to the permanence of behavior patterns in what has been called "The Vicious Circle." A phenomenal self which is incompatible with the demands of a social situation, for example, often leads to behavior not acceptable to the culture. People respond by rejecting or attacking the behaver, and this in turn forces the organism to greater defense of its position. The more violent the perceived attack the keener is the necessity for defense of the self. Furthermore, since it is often true that "the best defense is attack" the aggression of the society against the individual may result in aggression of the individual toward the society or its members, so that an unhappy state of attack and counterattack becomes established. This happens so frequently that in social psychology the principle that aggression results in return aggression has become almost a law of behavior.

One of the clearest examples of this vicious circle in operation may be observed in children who feel more or less rejected by parents. The child who has developed a concept of himself, whether justified or not, as unwanted, unloved, and unappreciated becomes aggressive toward his parents and seeks to regain his self esteem by punishing them or in some way demonstrating mastery over them. In this process he may utilize a very wide variety of techniques like temper tantrums, negativism, or any one of a thousand other fiendish devices. Parents, however, may be disgusted, shocked, or angry at such behavior and punish the child in an attempt to make him conform to the patterns of behavior they expect. From the child's point of view the threat inherent in his perception of his parent's behavior does not permit him to see the situation as they do. Their punishment is likely to appear only as further proof of what he already feels. This threat to self forces him to defend his position and his concept of himself is more firmly entrenched than ever. Thus he is driven to greater efforts in his attempts to gain a feeling of self esteem, which again may result in punishment, and so the cycle may be repeated over and over.

The resolution of this vicious-circle situation appears to lie either in some shift in the situation which reduces the threat to the phenomenal self or in aiding the individual to make some change in his self concept which will make him more adequate to deal with the present situation. Thus a delinquent may be treated by placing him in the more or less psychologically sheltered atmosphere of a foster home or by helping him to a new concept of himself capable of accepting his parent's behavior.

People under threat need the broadest possible field of perceptions from which to select appropriate behaviors. Yet the effect of threat is to make this kind of broad perceiving difficult, if not altogether impossible, so that the threatened personality may be reduced to repetitive unreasoning kinds of nonadaptive behavior under stress which, instead of relieving and solving the problem, may only serve to make it much worse. The delinquent, threatened and afraid of the police, is unable to communicate with the "cops" or to make an adequate adjustment to them when he confronts them. As a result he is quite likely to behave in ways that cannot fail to get him in trouble with the law. In the policeman's terms, "he seems to be asking for it."

Distortions upon perception may even have the effect of producing a feeling of threat where none exists. The child's feeling of guilt may cause him to behave in so guilty a fashion as to create suspicion in the minds of the adults who surround him. It is a commonplace observation that threatened personalities often behave in so exaggerated a manner as to call the attention of others to the very aspects they feel threatened by. This common behavior was illustrated by one of the writer's clients in psychotherapy, who said: "There are some things I sometimes don't want to tell you, so I try to hide them, but it's like trying to hide behind a tree. I sneak behind the tree so far I come right out into view on the other side!" "The wicked flee when no man pursueth." Threatened people with narrowed perceptions often bring upon themselves the very events they fear. They do, indeed, seem almost to be seeking their own destruction. In the complex society we live in a great many of the threats we encounter are not effectively met by direct, vigorous, or self-defensive action, and the utilization of such approaches may serve only to aggravate the problem.

The Intensity of the Experience of Threat

The important effects of the experience of threat upon the individual's perceptual field which we have been discussing occur not only when threats are perceived as violent or traumatic. Combs and Taylor, for example, have demonstrated that even with the mildest of threats to self, performance is measurably impaired. Any experience of threat, even of the mildest sort, seems to have its effects upon perception and produces an impairment of the efficiency of behavior. However, other things being equal, the more serious threats are likely to produce the more drastic and damaging effects. In general, the degree of threat experienced appears to be affected by at least the following four factors:

1. *Importance of the threatened concept of self.* You will recall

that the self concept is composed of many more or less discrete concepts of self. These concepts of self, moreover, vary widely in the degree of importance they hold in the particular economy of any individual. The degree of threat experienced by the person will be in part a function of the peculiar importance of the particular aspect of self under fire at any moment. The more important the aspect of self to the individual, the greater will be the experience of threat.

It is important to recall here that we are speaking of the danger to self *perceived by the behaver* and not that perceived by the outsider. From the point of view of the external observer an individual may appear to be under no threat whatever; yet from the behaver's own view he may be extremely threatened. A great many of our difficulties in human relations seem to stem from a failure to realize this important fact. The upper-middle-class female schoolteacher lives in a different world from her pre-teen-age boys. The values placed by upper-middle-class women on politeness, furthermore, are by no means shared by gang-age boys. Thus the teacher who calls a child before the class to learn to make introductions may, from her point of view, be "helping" George to get along in life. From George's view, however, this situation may appear as an excruciatingly painful threat to himself as a "regular guy," who is no "sissy"! The threats we feel are personal matters, the products of our own perceptions, and the degrees of threat we experience will be directly proportional to the importance of the peculiar aspects of self which seem to us to be threatened at any moment.

2. *Immediacy of threat.* A second factor affecting the degree of threat experienced will be the immediacy or closeness of the threatening event to self. Generally speaking, the closer, the more immediate the danger to the self perceived by the behaver, the greater will be the degree of threat he experiences. The examination coming next month seems much less threatening than the one tomorrow morning. The closer the event to self in time or space, the greater is the degree of threat which the individual is likely to experience.

The above statement seems a simple enough axiom, but it should be recognized that we are speaking here of psychological rather than objective immediacy. Objective evaluations of immediacy measured in terms of years, days, hours, minutes, or miles, yards, feet, or inches have little to do with psychological immediacy. Psychological immediacy does not refer to the external evaluation of distance or time, but to the individual's own experience of it. The cobra behind the glass in the snake house at the zoo is only a few inches from my nose, yet seems no great threat to myself. The same snake loose in a room with me, though 20 feet away, is a horrible and frightening threat to my being. Similarly, the man who is told today that he has only a few months to live may be more threatened by that fact at this moment than he will be two months from now on his deathbed. The immediacy of threat to self is a function of the individual's own unique perception of the situation, not the externally observable "facts." To understand the threat experienced by the individual it is necessary for us to perceive the world not through our eyes, but through his.

3. *Clarity of perception of danger: fear and anxiety.* Events perceived in clear figure are sharply experienced, while events differentiated only vaguely or as part of the ground of the perceptual field are less precisely experienced and result in vaguer, more diffuse kinds of behavior. Other things being equal, the experience of threat will be roughly proportional to the degree of clarity with which the disturbing event is perceived. Events only vaguely perceived as dangerous to self seem less threatening than those perceived precisely and sharply.

This relationship of the clarity of perception to the degree of threat experienced can perhaps best be illustrated in the distinction between fear and anxiety. Both of these words refer to the feelings we have when we are confronted with some sort of threat to our phenomenal self. People say they are "afraid" when the event which threatens is differentiated clearly and sharply in the perceptual field. Thus, we speak of being afraid of that car or that angry dog blocking our path, or of Joe Smith or Helen Jones. Fear is the word we use to describe those situations in which the object which threatens is clearly and sharply in figure. When the threatening perception cannot be so clearly differentiated, people speak of being anxious. Anxiety is thus a state of being threatened, but in which the object which threatens cannot, for one reason or another, be clearly and precisely differentiated. It is characteristic of people feeling anxious that they are unable to define precisely what it is that concerns and distresses them. They feel threatened, but they do not know by what.

This undifferentiated aspect of threat when people feel anxious is the very thing which makes it most difficult to deal with. Anxious people do not know what it is that threatens them and, as a result, cannot deal with the threats they feel with any degree of success. Helping people who feel anxiety clearly and sharply to see and understand the threats they feel is, in fact, a basic task of psychotherapy. One of the important things the psychotherapist does is to assist his client to explore his feelings and attitudes with great care until the client is able to pinpoint the cause of his distress, to bring the threat he feels into sufficiently clear perspective so that it can be dealt with. This is likely to be a painful process for the client, for the more clearly the individual perceives the danger to self, the greater is the degree of threat he is likely to experience. No wonder that therapy is often an extremely painful experience! Yet so long as the threats one feels remain undifferentiated and vague, they are difficult, if not impossible, to deal with effectively.

When the dangers to self are clearly and sharply in figure in the perceptual field, we say we are "afraid," and the threat we experience is likely to be similarly sharp and clear. When the dangers we perceive are only vaguely or diffusely differentiated in the perceptual field, we say we feel "anxious," and the threat we experience is similarly vague and diffuse. These two states represent the two ends of a continuum, but of course it will be recognized that there may be all stages of clarity of differentiation between these two positions, and the threat experienced by the individual will, other factors being equal, depend upon the degree of clarity with which he is able to differentiate the dangers to which his phenomenal self is exposed.

4. *Degree of threat as a function of personal adequacy: challenge and threat.* Finally, the degree of threat experienced by the individual will be a direct outgrowth of how strongly he sees himself as able to cope successfully with the emergency with which he is confronted. Other things being equal, people who see themselves as adequate are likely to experience threat less strongly than those who feel inadequate. Threat is the product of an inadequate definition of the self. When the phenomenal self seems adequate to deal with the situations with which it is confronted, there is no threat. Threat only exists when there is some feeling of inadequacy to cope. The degree of threat experienced will be an inverse function of the amount of adequacy felt by the behaver.

It is this degree of feeling of personal adequacy that distinguishes threat and challenge. When people feel completely adequate to deal with the problems that confront them, there is neither challenge nor threat. Behavior is likely to be quite perfunctory or carried out as routine. When the situations with which we are faced have not great possibilities for contributing meaningfully to our need for adequacy, they neither threaten nor challenge us. We do not ordinarily feel threatened or challenged by the breakfast set before us. We are not very hungry anyway, so there is little about it to enhance us. It is the same breakfast as yesterday and does not even have the interest of difference. There is no question of our adequacy to deal with the matter, and we behave toward it with little feeling of any kind.

We feel challenged when we are confronted by situations in which we feel fairly adequate, but in which we also see some opportunities for testing and enhancing our adequacy. There may even be some small degree of threat involved in the possibility that we might fail. This situation is exciting and challenging because the problem is perceived as one within our capacities and having inherent in it important opportunities for self enhancement. Let us take the example of a person asked to make a speech. When one is asked to make a speech and *feels fundamentally adequate* to the task, the request to make a speech may seem like an exciting and challenging opportunity to test one's adequacy, even as a means of building that adequacy further. There may also be a tinge of threat involved in the possibility that "it might not go over." Feeling fundamentally adequate to the task, however, the individual sees it as an opportunity for enhancement and further experience of adequacy. Hence he is challenged by the opportunity afforded him. Chances are, that feeling so, he will behave in a confident manner, will feel unthreatened by his appearance, and carry it off well.

People feel threatened when they are confronted with situations or ideas they feel fundamentally inadequate to cope with. The person who feels deeply inadequate when asked to make a speech perceives this request in a far different manner from the person we have just been describing. Feeling unequal to the task, the necessity to perform publicly holds nothing but threat for him. The more inadequate he feels, the stronger and more paralyzing is the threat he experiences. He tries to escape from the necessity of appearing through one excuse or another. If not successful in this, he approaches the speech with fear and horror. He may even be so frightened by the threat to which he has exposed himself as to be immobilized by his fear. We say, then, that he is a victim of stage fright. This failure may only serve to cause him to feel more inadequate than ever.

This same relationship seems to hold true not only for individuals, but for the societies they compose as well. Toynbee, the historian, points out that societies produce and progress when they are challenged, but make little progress when they are not confronted with problems or when the problems they confront are too overwhelming to be dealt with. Those societies, Toynbee points out, which are moved to action because they have problems to solve, yet which have sufficient adequacy to deal with the emergencies they confront, show the maximum progress. It would appear that societies, like individual people, respond to challenge but are paralyzed by threat.

What makes a matter challenging or threatening to a particular individual, it must be recalled, is a function of his own particular, unique ways of seeing himself and the situations in which he is involved. How it seems to some outside observer is irrelevant to the experience of threat. It is a failure to recognize this important fact that causes many of the breakdowns we encounter in dealing with other people. The teacher in the classroom, for example, may believe she is challenging a particular child to learn some aspect of a subject when in reality the child may be strongly threatened by the teacher's behavior. Or, the employer who gives his employees a "quota" of work to be completed in the belief that he is challenging them to greater efforts may be surprised to find that his workers do not see it that way at all. What seemed to the employer as a challenge to greater production and greater pay may seem to the workers only a threat to their dignity and integrity, a device to enslave them or make them produce beyond a reasonable level. Whether people feel challenged or threatened by a particular situation or event is a personal matter; a function not of the perceptions of an outsider, but rather of the behaver's own perceptions of adequacy or inadequacy.

The Sources of Threat

As we have said, people feel threatened when they perceive themselves as inadequate to deal with the situations in which they are involved. This feeling of inadequacy is a product of how the individual sees himself, the situations in which he is living and the interrelationships of these two. People may experience threat as a product of the inconsistency between self and the experience of the external world, or as a result of inconsistencies between two aspects of self.

THREATS ARISING FROM THE PERCEPTION OF THE SITUATION. A phenomenal self developed in a particular group situation, over a period of time, is an expression of the experiences of the individual in that group.

Threat to the individual may arise when, for one reason or another, the social group begins to treat him in ways incompatible with the ways in which he has grown to perceive himself. This failure of expectancy may occur slowly as in the case of the young man who conceives of himself as a "great man with the ladies," but who in reality is not. He may be led to act, because of such a self concept, in ways extremely obnoxious to the fairer sex. His tales of his conquests, his condescending air, and his "freshness" may even eventually turn the eligible women from him. After numerous attempts to get dates and a sufficient number of cool refusals coupled with a few occasions in which he is unable to find any companion for himself at all, our young man may begin to become quite conscious that something is wrong. He feels tension and threat. Almost everyone has had experience with this sort of slow change in perception of life situations. The adolescent's changing perception of the reaction of those about him toward himself is a type of experience through which all of us have lived more or less successfully.

People may also be threatened as a result of very rapid changes in the world about them. The loss of a marriage partner in an accident, for example, may suddenly confront the individual with perceptions extremely inacceptable and threatening. Threats may also occur when we change our jobs from one place to another. The present writer well remembers the shock of returning to graduate school as the lowliest of graduate students after a position of responsibility and authority in his home community. Such changes in the perception of life situations may suddenly present the person with concepts he cannot accept into his existing organization. We shall see later some of the ways in which the individual attempts to deal with such perceptions.

For the moment, however, it is important for us to recall that the production of new and inconsistent differentiations does not depend upon change in "real" situations alone. It is quite possible for such differentiations to arise although society continues to accept the individual on the same familiar basis. The pain experienced by many college students going home for the first time after a long period at college is a case in point. The treatment one gets from parents and friends is apparently no different than it has ever been, yet, since it is threatening to the student's new concept of self as an adult, the perception of this treatment may be radically changed and result in considerable anguish for the student. Similarly, the differentiation of a new idea may be extremely disturbing and even threatening to the individual. Many a student raised in a fundamentalist home has found the idea of evolution extremely disturbing because it is perceived by him to be inconsistent with previous ways of thinking about self and his relation to the universe. This is likely to be even more disturbing when others whom one considers to be important accept the idea without batting an eye.

Our culture values change much more than some others, and the attempts of our culture to "help" other less fortunate people have sometimes been more threatening than aiding. In parts of China, for example, where the population exists very largely on a rice and vegetable diet, it is customary for pregnant women to shift to a diet of fried chicken when they can get it. Small wonder then, that they rejected the public-health nurse who tried to persuade expectant mothers to eat vegetables. Vegetables indeed, when they had looked forward to special diets and special status for this mark of their maturity! Among people who feel it important that the body remain whole, surgery may seem worse than the disease it hopes to cure. Change can apparently be highly threatening, particularly when it runs counter to fundamental beliefs about self.

People may also feel inadequate because the circumstances they find themselves in suddenly seem overwhelming. Like the child lost in the city streets, people may sometimes feel threatened because the world they perceive is just too big and inexorable. This may be because the concepts they have of themselves are inadequate, or it may be that the situation to which they find themselves exposed will permit of no other interpretation. Like the psychiatrist in the *New Yorker* cartoon who diagnosed the young man, "As a result of my investigation, I can only conclude that you feel inferior because you are!" there are situations to which any of us may be exposed that permit of no other perception but that of our own inadequacy—at least at the moment we are called upon to respond. Without time for preparation most of us feel inadequate to deal with such cataclysmic events as hurricanes, earthquakes, epidemics, for example, or with such less wholesale dangers as speeding cars, falling objects, or others among the myriad emergencies of everyday life.

THREAT FROM THE UNKNOWN. People may also feel inadequate, not because things seem comprehensibly dangerous, but sometimes precisely because they are unable to comprehend whether they are dangerous or not. Some feelings of inadequacy occur because the individual is unable to determine the meaning of the situation in which he is involved. It is commonplace that what is unknown is often more frightening or threatening than that which is clearly perceived or understood, particularly when the individual is under the necessity of dealing with it. It is difficult or impossible to feel adequate when the expectancies of the situations in which we are involved are unclear to us.

To cope with life effectively, one needs to have a clear picture of the situation to which it is necessary to make an adjustment. The infant who is placed on the toilet and demanded to produce may be quite unable to comprehend the strange behavior of the adults who surround him or what it is that is expected of him. Putting pressure on him to respond only increases the feeling of inadequacy, and the whole process of toilet training may fail because the child is made to feel inadequate through inability to comprehend what is demanded of him. Adults, too, feel inadequate when they are unable to grasp the meaning of the situations in which they are involved. People in an office may feel threatened and inadequate when they do not know what is going on in the conference in the employer's office. Students feel threatened when they are unable to determine whether they have passed or failed the examination. It is a common experience to be "afraid of the dark," for it is difficult to deal with the unknown! It makes one feel inadequate. Throughout history, men have sometimes sought to escape this kind of threat by giving unknown events *some* kind of meaning, almost any kind of meaning, rather than be faced with the threat of the imponderable or incomprehensible. Thus lightning was attributed to the gods, and insanity to possession by the devil. Events without meaning or whose meaning is vague and unclear may cause feelings of inadequacy and threat in the perceiver.

Situations sometimes seem incomprehensible to the perceiver, not because meanings are unclear, but because meanings which do exist are too vacillating or rapidly shifting to make it possible to deal with them. The fulfillment of need requires an organized perceptual field. We feel more adequate when things stand still long enough for us to be able to comprehend them. The substitute teacher who must "fill in" for another in the middle of the semester often runs into this problem. The children, not comprehending the meaning of this new teacher, begin to try her out. They seek to discover the limits to which they can go. They try getting away with first one thing, then another. They keep on testing the limits until they have discovered where this teacher stands. When the substitute teacher helps the children to understand quickly and precisely what kind of person she is and how far they can go with her, she soon establishes an effective working relationship, the children feel secure, and the class gets under way again. If, however, she is vacillating and indecisive, if she permits things one day and "cracks down" on them the next, it becomes difficult for the children to discover the meaning of the situation and they feel inadequate to deal with it. Not knowing what to expect, they feel threatened and tense and so continue their explorations in an attempt to find out where the teacher is *now*. It has sometimes been said that people can adjust to almost anything so long as it stands still, and indeed there seems to be much truth in the statement. People feel inadequate and threatened when they are confronted with situations too vacillating or confusing to permit the discovery of meaning.

THREAT FROM INCONSISTENT PERCEPTIONS OF SELF. The effective satisfaction of need requires an organized self. The fact that the phenomenal self has many aspects, however, frequently makes the achievement of self consistency a difficult matter. Differentiations leading to enhancement of one aspect of the self may at the same time threaten other aspects. The individual may thus be placed in a position wherein his perceptions of what he has done as an expression of one aspect of self are seriously inconsistent and hence threatening to another concept of self. As a consequence he may show signs of tension arising from the threat he perceives. The more seriously the self is threatened by such differentiations, the greater will be the individual's feeling of threat and distress. As Murphy has observed, "the very activity which brings us one satisfaction reminds us constantly that it is depriving us of another—and this is especially true of ego values." Threat may arise from inconsistencies within the self even when two aspects of self are fundamentally enhancing.

THREAT FROM MULTIPLE ENHANCING PERCEPTIONS. A young minister we have known came to conceive of himself as a successful preacher and as a scholar. He made a very brilliant record in theological seminary, and indeed at the seminary he was both an excellent preacher and scholar. When he came to accept his first charge at a small community, however, he was almost a total loss to his congregation. His talents as a scholar were completely unappreciated. His most eloquent addresses went for nothing. In that community to be considered an excellent preacher required a homely, nonscholarly approach. When he was a successful preacher, he was most unscholarly; when he was most scholarly he was a total failure as a preacher. The poor man became more and more distraught at his lack of success and was at a loss as to how to deal with it. Unfortunately, his concept of himself as a scholar brought about a reaction to him in that community which belied and threatened his concept of himself as a speaker. Similarly, if he had been a good preacher in that community, his concept of himself as a scholar would have been threatened.

Threats arising from such inconsistencies are sometimes described as "conflict." It should be pointed out, however, that the term "conflict" is a term of external description. It is an outside observer's description of what he observes. The behaver himself does not experience conflict. He experiences threat to need satisfaction. He experiences threat to self maintenance from one or more differentiations of his self which he is unable to accept at that moment. This is Lecky's principle of Self Consistency. Such threatening differentiations may occur in rapid sequence and even be described by the individual as "conflict." In so doing, however, he is making an external observation of his behavior just as any outsider would. To state that the minister, in the example above, is in conflict with himself leads us to a ridiculous state of affairs. There is nothing conflicting about differentiating oneself as a good speaker and a scholar. Some of our most successful clergymen are both! Even in cases where two aspects of self appear to be in conflict, it will usually be discovered that one of these aspects is considered momentarily to be *not self* threatening self. Where inconsistent definitions of self exist in the same individual, it will usually be observed that one of these exists only at a low level of differentiation. Antagonistic concepts of self cannot exist at high levels of differentiation at the same time unless one is regarded as *not self*.

When two differentiations are perceived to be enhancing to the individual and can be achieved simultaneously, or in rapid order, little or no feeling of threat is likely to be experienced by the individual and he operates to realize the enhancement perceived. If, however, the realization of the two differentiations about self are not simultaneously or in quick order capable of realization, a very great degree of threat to need satisfaction may ensue. This is especially true where the realization of one may force the abandonment of another. The instant one is abandoned, it becomes threatening to need satisfaction and demands attention. The enhancing differentiation which is realized satisfies need, but the enhancing differentiation not realized threatens the self greatly. A good example of this is to be observed in the young woman in love with two men. Conceiving of herself as being loved by A and loved by B is enhancing to self. The decision to marry either A or B, however, immediately threatens self with a loss of the other. When adequacy can be achieved equally well through either of two goals, movement toward goal A means abandonment of goal B. The instant goal B is relinquished, however, the woman is threatened by its possible loss. Since she desires goal B, however, she moves to recapture it and now may find the same situation reversed. As a result, she may vacillate back and forth between her two suitors, unable to settle on either because of the threat of the loss of the other, until such time as either A or B is perceived as more enhancing than his rival.

MULTIPLE THREATENING PERCEPTIONS OF SELF

An even more threatening situation exists when the individual has two or more differentiations, all of which are highly threatening. For the sake of simplicity, let us suppose that only two such perceptions occur. In this situation the individual has no opportunity for self enhancement whatever. This is the state characteristic of many neurotics. An excellent example is to be observed on any college campus in what is sometimes called, "term-end-neurosis." The student who begins to feel failure bearing down on him is faced with two negative differentiations each of which is threatening. To stay at college and fail is unthinkable. It threatens his concept of himself. On the other hand, to withdraw from college and go home to face his parents and their expectations is also inacceptable. He is a failure if he remains; he is a failure if he leaves. Either situation is intolerable and threatening, but what is even worse, one or the other is inevitable. As the term progresses and the full realization of his jeopardy becomes greater, the necessity for defense of self becomes more pressing, and the student's activity becomes wilder and wilder. He engages in frantic behavior. Effective study becomes impossible. Finally, he may literally wear himself out and collapse before exams in "nervous exhaustion," and the school physicians send him home. This exhaustion is usually short-lived, because the moment the student arrives at home he is met with the sympathy of parents, the reassurance of relatives, and exclamations of "Poor boy, he worked too hard!" The threat and tension under which he has been operating disappears. He feels quite adequate once again and with a little rest he makes a quick recovery.

Another seriously threatening situation may arise when one aspect of self becomes differentiated and is recognized as inconsistent with another highly differentiated aspect. We have seen that inconsistent concepts of self may exist in the same phenomenal field so long as both are not simultaneously in clear figure. Antagonistic or derogatory perceptions of self produce feelings of threat and consequent defenses against such perceptions. Such inconsistent concepts of self may be kept from confronting each other in two ways. In the first place, the two concepts may be differentiated as applying to two different social situations. This is characteristic of the man who conceives of himself as a "good" and a "religious" man on Sundays, in deacons' meetings, and on religious holidays, but conceives of himself as a "good businessman" on weekdays. Sharp business practices, dishonesty, and even gambling may thus comfortably be engaged in on weekdays, while Sunday finds the same person sitting in a pew and piously following the dictates of his Sunday self concept. To conceive of himself in his Sunday self concept on Monday would prove extremely threatening to the weekday self concept and so must be strongly resisted. He may also be deeply disturbed if his minister calls on him at his place of business during the week, for this brings into figure concepts of self and of role out of touch with present experience.

THREAT FROM LOW-LEVEL DIFFERENTIATIONS OF SELF

A second way in which inconsistent self concepts may be prevented from confronting each other is through keeping one concept at a low level of differentiation so that it never appears in very clear figure. So long as one perception remains at a low level of differentiation, it may not greatly disturb another. We have seen that differentiations may be kept at a low level if they appear too threatening to the individual. This is true of perceptions regarding the self as well.

When one concept of self exists at a low level of differentiation and is antagonistic to another clear definition of self, the potentialities for threat are tremendous. If the individual behaves at some time in terms of his low-level differentiation, he may find that he has committed an act extremely threatening to a more clearly differentiated aspect of self. Such an act may bring an inconsistent concept of self into clear and inexorable figure, resulting in violent shock. The following case illustrates how this may occur. A young woman considered herself a "good Catholic" and conscientiously observed the rules of her religious faith. As she grew older, however, she desired more and more to marry but had very little opportunity to realize her goal. Finally, she met a man of her own religious faith who previously had been divorced. When he proposed she was delighted, and although she understood the ban of her church against marrying a divorced person, she was so intent upon her objective that this disturbing thought never appeared in very clear figure. For a while after marriage things went well, until one day a priest pointed out to her very clearly the position of the church. This brought the entire question into clear and inescapable figure in which both aspects of self were threatened by what she had done. To give up her husband was a threat to her concept of herself as a married woman, and to keep her husband was a threat to herself as a good and conscientious Catholic. For a time she vacillated desperately back and forth between these two concepts of herself. Finally, unable to find an acceptable solution, the poor woman collapsed and had to be hospitalized.

A self under threat has no choice but to defend itself. What is more, the very existence of threat makes the solution of problems more difficult. To resolve a threatening situation requires exactly the opposite of suppression and tunnel vision. It requires freedom to examine and to differentiate any and all aspects of the field in the search for a more adequate self.

Behavior Change Under Threat

While it is true that behavior under threat is likely to be rigid and narrow and defensive, this does not mean that under threat it is impossible to change another person's behavior. Far from it. Throughout history, man has discovered that threatening people is an effective tool for changing behavior. Since time immemorial many parents, teachers, priests, and political leaders, to say nothing of businessmen and military leaders, have used this method of dealing with people.

We have seen that threat leads to tunnel vision and the defense of the self. The effect of threat, then, is one of concentrating and restricting the area of the perceptual field to which an individual is responding at a particular moment. People under threat are likely to behave rigidly and unquestioningly and with a direct (perhaps even violent) response to the threats they perceive. This characteristic makes threat a most effective device for dictators. People under threat are likely to be so busy responding to obvious threats that they have little opportunity to explore those which are less obvious or which are purposely obscured by those in power. Every dictator has been keenly aware of the importance of giving people a clear-cut enemy.

People can and do learn under threat. People always learn when their need is seriously affected. Unfortunately, what people learn under threat is likely to be narrowly focused on the nature of the threat to which they see themselves exposed and may even lead to seeing threats where they do not really exist. The effect of threat is to concentrate attention on the threat perceived rather than upon the broader circumstances to which the threat is attached. A child we know was asked by her father what she "had learned in school today." "Oh, nothing," was the child's reply, "but was our teacher mad! Wow!" Clearly, this child *had* learned something. But also clearly, it was not at all what the teacher thought she was communicating! Under threat this child's attention was riveted upon the object which threatened her and she was in no condition to perceive from a wider frame of reference. What she learned was related to the nature of her angry teacher, a matter of concern to her at the moment of much greater importance than the structure of the United Nations, the physical geography of Wyoming, or how to do subtraction.

Threat lends itself well to dealing with people where it is desired to control and channel behavior. It may, for example, prove a useful device in teaching a child *not* to cross the street. It does not help much, however, in teaching him *why* he should behave so. Indeed, one of the important effects of threat is that it restricts "looking." It is the perfect device of the manipulator, for it provides a means by which human beings can be prevented from exploring widely while at the same time attention is held rigidly and unquestionably to those events the manipulator desires people to look at. It is the perfect tool for a regimented society.

A free society requires independent, thinking people of wisdom and perspective; it requires unthreatened citizens, people who are challenged but not threatened. A complex, interdependent society like ours requires people who are flexible, not rigid; who can perceive broadly rather than narrowly; who are not so bound to the necessity of self defense as to have little time or energy to devote to the problems of their fellow human beings. In our kind of society not all possibilities can be readily foreseen, and it is necessary for us to be able to rely not on the brains of a few, but on the interacting creative efforts of millions. Rigidity, narrowness and preoccupation with self defense are the very antithesis of what a fluid, open, dynamic modern society requires. Fear and threat have no place in such a society.

CHAPTER **10**

Learning, Forgetting, and Problem Solving

EFFECTIVE, efficient behavior requires that individuals be able to learn new things, to retain this learning over long periods of time and to solve new problems when confronted with them. Learning, remembering, and problem solving, however, are, like any other behaviors, the products of the individual's perceptual field. In particular, they are the direct outgrowth of the process of differentiation we have discussed in an earlier chapter.

Learning as Differentiation

When we speak of learning we mean the process by which an individual is able to change his behavior, usually in some more constructive fashion. Such changes are brought about by differentiation within the perceptual field. All learning of whatever variety has as its basic characteristic a progressive differentiation from a more general perceptual field. This is perhaps best illustrated by observing changes in the drawings of young children. Children draw what they know; that is to say, what they have learned. Observing their drawings, therefore, can provide us with interesting insights as to what is probably going on in the child's perceptual field. The differentiation characteristic of child learning is perhaps best illustrated in the child's drawings of a man. The earliest of such drawings are likely to be composed of little more than a head with appendages attached. Later, as the child grows and apparently differentiates more and more detail with respect to the adults who surround him, his drawings mirror this increased detail and we may find him adding fingers to arms, a trunk between legs and head, and the addition of feet, hair, and ears. Still later, when the child has differentiated still more details about adults, he may draw a man with a neck between head and trunk and various details of clothing. See Figs. 17, 18, and 19.

Fig. 17. Typical Early Drawings of Man. *Left:* Drawn by Alice K., age 5 years, 11 months, a shy retiring child who accepts adults only very cautiously and fearfully. *Right:* Drawn by Bill J., age 6 years, 5 months, born prematurely who shows lack of stable adult contacts and feels deeply rejected.

Fig. 18. More Mature Drawings of Man. *Left:* Drawn by Albert M., age 5 years, 10 months, a tense introverted child who accepts adults only very slowly and fearfully. *Right:* Drawn by George R., age 5 years, 10 months, a happy, active, relaxed child who shows little dependence on adults, and who had seldom held a pencil until this point.

Fig. 19. Drawings of Man Produced by Very Mature Children. *Left:* Drawn by David B., age 6 years, 0 months, well coördinated and almost too mature for his age, who prefers relationships with adults to peers. *Right:* Drawn by Helen S., age 5 years, 2 months, a very mature, adequate little girl who is a leader in her group.

The same development of differentiation and growth from a total field to a more and more precise kind of performance may be observed in handwriting, number concepts, reading, and vocabulary, to name but a few areas of a child's learning.

Learning at all levels at which psychologists have studied the problem is characterized by this process of increasing differentiation from a more general field. This is true whether we are speaking of the highly controlled laboratory experiments on "conditioning," "trial and error learning" on a less carefully controlled level, or "insight learning" of a problem-solving character where subjects are given a maximum of freedom. Pavlov noted in his famous experiment on the salivation of dogs that his subjects' first responses were highly irregular and vague, but as the experiment continued his dogs responded with ever-increasing regularity and precision as they were increasingly able to differentiate from the general field the most efficient response required. This differentiational character of learning in conditioning experiments has been illustrated repeatedly with many other animals, including man himself.

Experimental subjects who seem to learn by "trial and error" in running a maze or finding the proper means of escape from a puzzle box also show this differentiational characteristic of learning. Behavior which is quite general and vague at the beginning of the experiment becomes increasingly precise as the animal is able to perceive with greater and greater accuracy the "proper" solution to the problem. This will be true whether we are speaking of ants, rats, or men. The process can be clearly observed in examining the day-by-day productions of a child who is learning to write. Little by little over a period of time, as he is able to differentiate more clearly what is required and how to operate his muscular system to achieve those ends, his writing becomes increasingly precise. Most of us have forgotten how difficult a process this was. We have lived so long with an accepted ability to write that we have forgotten how slowly and painfully the process of achieving these new differentiations was at the time we originally learned them.

The reader can relive some of this early difficulty in learning to write and at the same time observe the differentiational characteristic of his own learning in action by learning a new skill such as mirror writing. This can be done by setting up a bridge of books, as in Fig. 20, in such a way as to make it impossible to see what one is writing unless he looks in the mirror. Now, if the reader will make four dots on a sheet of paper in the form of a diamond, he can place his paper in such a posi-

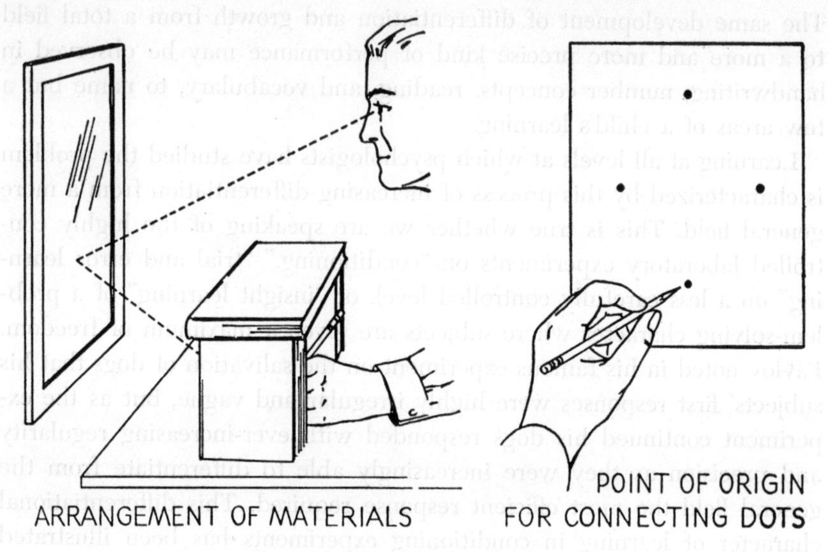

Fig. 20. Mirror-drawing Experiment.

tion that it can be seen only by looking in the mirror and can proceed to try to connect the dots he has made and so to complete the diamond. At once the experimenter will observe that he is behaving very much as the young child who is learning to write. He may, for example, find himself gripping his pencil for dear life, trying desperately to push it in directions it does not seem to want to go. He may even find himself chewing his tongue and making grimaces just as the young child does. His performance record, indicated by the pencil marks on the paper, can also be observed to be hesitating and tentative as he seeks to differentiate the proper solution to the problem (unless, of course, he goes through this process symbolically in his field without moving his pencil). With a little practice, however, the ability to carry out this task becomes rapidly more precisely differentiated and can shortly be done with a high degree of accuracy. This is a much quicker process than the way we originally learn to write, but then we are now adults with a great deal more experience to call upon than we had in those early days.

Some learning, at first glance, seems to occur "all at once" as a kind of sudden "insight." This seems to happen, for example, when we suddenly become aware of the solution to a problem with which we have been struggling for some time. On closer examination, however, it can be observed that this kind of learning, too, is a product of differentiation. What is happening here is the kind of differentiation producing synthesis and generalization, which we discussed earlier. A new principle or relationship is differentiated on an overall, generic level providing new meaning or relationship between two events not previously observed as related. The ape suddenly differentiates the box in his cage as something to stand upon to reach the banana hanging from the ceiling. The scientist differentiates a new relationship in the complex data with which he is dealing and experiences what the French have called an "ah-ha moment," in which previously differentiated perceptions are suddenly seen with a new meaning.

Actually, such sudden differentiations are the end product of long series of previous differentiations. This is perhaps best illustrated in the protocols of psychotherapy, in which it can be observed that the client's, apparently sudden, insight is really only a new differentiation of the interrelationship of two series of differentiations. A client may spend hours exploring his perceptions concerning his father and more hours exploring his perceptions concerning himself and his behavior, and then suddenly come to the "insight" that his own behavior has been caused by the kind of person his father was. Such an insight, however, although sudden and highly meaningful to the client, could only occur at the end of a long sequence of previous differentiations.

Learning as a Function of Need

Perhaps the most important contribution of the personalistic point of view to the psychology of learning is the recognition that learning, like all other experiencing and behaving, is an active process which results from the efforts of the individual to satisfy need. Whether we like it or not, people are always striving for the satisfaction of need; they are always learning. If they are to learn the attitudes, skills, and facts that are socially desirable, the situation must be arranged so that they can further their own ends by such learning. Mere presentation of material by repetition or drill is not sufficient. Habit and repetition are not, from the behaver's point of view, causes of behavior. As he sees it, he performs the act for the thousandth time for the same reason he performed it the second time, because it is the most effective way he knows of satisfying his immediate need. What any individual learns (differentiates) in a given situation is determined by the need of the moment. A child practicing the piano *may* be learning to play the piano better. He may also be learning how to give the appearance of practicing with the least possible effort. This relationship of learning to need raises difficult problems for educators. What teachers teach and children learn can often be maddeningly different because the immediate goals of teacher and child may be worlds apart. The best, most elaborate efforts to induce learning may thus come to be frustrated.

THE PROBABILITY OF LEARNING. We have already seen that the degree and direction of differentiation are always determined by the need of the behaver and the opportunities for differentiation that are available. Since the selections made by the individual in his perceptual field are always a function of his fundamental need, whether or not there is any learning at all will be dependent upon the operation of this need in the situations where learning is expected. Rats will not run mazes with any degree of precision without some need to do so. As a consequence, the experimenter usually makes certain that his rats are hungry and that their need is satisfied at the conclusion of the maze. In a similar fashion education has traditionally established a grading system by means of which students could be punished or rewarded for performance. Learning is always a function of need. But the need we are talking about is need from the behaver's point of view, not that of an outsider. Even hungry rats will not run mazes if their need to sleep is greater. Children with a desperate need to be accepted may find it more important to play with their neighbors than to pay attention to the teacher's lesson.

THE SPEED AND ACCURACY OF LEARNING. It is well known that the rate of learning may be accelerated by increasing the strength of the subject's need. It can also be accelerated by increasing the opportunities for the differentiation of essential cues and solutions. In general, the hungrier the rat, the more likely he is to learn the maze, providing the opportunities for making differentiations are not too limited. The effect of increased need upon learning has to do with increasing the intensity of effort and exploration. We can check this principle by observing our own behavior. When need is greater, we search harder and longer, and hence we are more likely to find solutions. Whether or not this exploratory activity pays off in increased learning, however, will of course be determined by whether or not the opportunities are such that the necessary differentiations can be made. No matter how hungry a rat may be, he will not learn the maze while sitting in his cage. Nor will a human being longing to sail a ship learn to do this effectively while plowing a field in Iowa.

Of course, there are limits to the degree to which the strength of need will affect the accuracy and speed of learning. If the individual's need is too great, his awareness of the need may become so acute and detailed that all other parts of the perceptual field fall into ground and further differentiation of those parts ceases. Under these circumstances the behavior loses its effectiveness or may even stop completely. Examples of this may be observed in people under panic when persons feel so threatened they become the victims of "tunnel vision." It is a common thing to find reports in our newspapers of persons being killed in panic because perceptions become too narrowed to make it possible for them to see the obvious solutions to their predicament. The drowning swimmer may be so intent upon keeping his head above water that he cannot permit himself to sink momentarily while he removes the heavy shoes which make swimming impossible. The frightened driver "freezes" to the wheel and cannot perceive what to do next. The person with clothing on fire seeks to run from the threatening flames and so fans the flames he seeks to escape.

THE LEVELS OF LEARNING. Aspects of the perceptual field may be differentiated in varying degree from ground to clear figure. As a consequence, learning may occur at any level of awareness, from a level so vague that the individual may not be able to report his experience to a level so clear and precise that the individual can report his learning with great keenness and certainty. Learning can occur at any level at which differentiation is possible. Many of the things we learn in life are never differentiated in sufficiently clear fashion that we could report them to other people. This can be demonstrated in such experiments, for example, as those on "unconscious learning," wherein it is possible to teach a subject to blink his eyes to the sound of a buzzer so faint that he is not able to report that he heard anything at all. The principle of learning at low levels of differentiation has been commercially exploited in the development of a record player with an under-pillow speaker which makes it possible for an individual to hear music, the lines of a play, or even factual information of various sorts while he sleeps. Later, when he seeks to learn these in a waking state, they seem easier to bring to clear figure apparently because they have already been perceived at a lower level of awareness.

THE PERTINENCE OF LEARNING. We have already seen in an earlier chapter that the degree to which any perception will affect behavior is a function of the relationship of that perception to the self. Events perceived as having little relationship to self have little effect upon behavior, while events perceived as being closely related to self affect behavior in marked degree. Even an event which is clearly and precisely perceived may have little effect upon the behavior of the individual if it is not also differentiated in some manner as having a meaning to the individual himself. The pertinence or applicability of learning will be a function of the perceived relationship to self.

There is a difference between knowing and behaving. It is familiar to any of us when we find ourselves saying, "Now I knew better than to do a thing like that!" A great deal of what people learn in school is of this character. Although concepts have been clearly perceived, the further differentiation of the relationship of these concepts to the individual's own need has not been perceived and as a consequence the individual does not behave in terms of what he "knows." Any student is aware that when he "needs to" he can learn a set of facts with sufficient clarity to be able to report them back to his professor on an examination, yet behave the following day as though he had never heard of the concept in his life. Learning proceeded as far as the student saw a need.

Differentiations may occur in any area of the perceptual field: in the self position, the not-self position, or at any point between. We can learn about events having little to do directly with self if we develop the desire to know about such matters. The objective observations and disciplined experimenting of the physical scientist are attempts of this sort to explore matters of interest with the least possible distortion from self reference. He "needs" to rule self out of the picture and so confines his differentiations to the not-self aspects of his field. In this fashion, the existing body of "fact" in a science may be built up. Such differentiations made in the not-self portion of the field, however, may never be perceived by the learner to apply to "real" problems of life. The author recalls some years ago congratulating a well-known child psychologist on the birth of his first child, then jokingly adding: "Now, John, you can talk like an expert." He was quite unprepared for his friend's reaction. John drew himself up and replied with icy coolness, "I don't think that will make any difference!" Apparently the learning of this eminent scholar was not perceived as having a practical bearing upon his own life and family. Differentiation is a function of need, and if the need is only *to know,* the effect of differentiation upon *behaving* may never progress beyond an esoteric level of abstraction.

Although differentiation can be made in the not-self portions of the field, it should not be supposed that learning can ever escape from the personality of the learner. Since the perceptual field is always organized with respect to self, differentiation and learning may occur with more or less reference to self; it can never occur unrelated to self. Even the disciplined scientist, making his observations with meticulous care to rule out self, is seeking by this very behavior to satisfy his very personal need for self adequacy as a scientist! Though it is helpful, even essential, for the solution of some of our problems that learning progress in these not-self areas, sooner or later they must be differentiated with relationship to self if they are ever to make a difference in the behavior of individual people.

The Economy of Learning

The major determinant of the kind and degree of differentiation which is immediately possible in any situation is, of course, the character of the existing perceptual field. A limiting factor, therefore, is always the degree of differentiation already attained. In our society, children differentiate the wheels from the rest of vehicles rather early and their drawings begin to show an awareness of how they are attached to vehicles at 5 or 6. An adult Australian aborigine from an island off the north coast where no wheeled vehicles existed, lumped all the vehicles he saw in Sydney as "houses that ran around." His reason for classifying them as houses was the fact that he saw people looking out of the windows. He showed no evidence that he had even seen the wheels, much less their mode of attachment. The same individual had very high skills as a hunter and tracker, which required a high degree of differentiation and observation of details.

The process of differentiation is quite regular and proceeds step by step, and it is futile to attempt to teach a pupil any detail for which he is not ready. An advanced 5-year-old who had noticed the wheel-and-axle relation was met by incomprehension and, finally, resistance when he attempted to get his kindergarten classmates to revise their less-differentiated pictures which showed the wagon box resting on the tops of the wheels. They were unable to see the difference between the two positions, and could not understand what he was excited about. It is quite probable that the lack of confidence in their drawings that appears in most children about the time they enter the third grade, is the result of misguided efforts by their teachers to get their drawings to conform to the phenomenal field of the teacher rather than that of the child. He learns that he is not making an accurate picture but is not able to see why it is not accurate. Schools where the teachers do not insist on their own personal adult "realism" do not produce this effect of discouragement and frustration.

The effective satisfaction of need is best achieved with the greatest possible accuracy of differentiation. Accordingly, learning proceeds to the point of ever more precise figure in the least amount of time. Need satisfaction does not stop here, however. Human need is insatiable and, once satisfied by events differentiated only a moment ago, continues the process of differentiation in ever new and more productive directions. Events learned to the point where they are differentiated in clear figure soon fade into the ground of the perceptual field, being replaced in figure by some new or more extensive differentiation. In Bryan and Harter's classic experiment on learning telegraphy a half century ago, beginning operators were found attempting to differentiate letters. As this was achieved, they began to "go after words." Following this, fair operators were able to differentiate phrases and even short sentences. The real expert, they found, finally reached a point where he had differentiated all of these aspects with such clarity that they became ground in his perceptual field, and he gave them practically no attention at all, which is to say, he did not find it necessary to call them into clear figure again. The expert operator even preferred to keep ten or twelve words behind his instrument, where he could perceive the larger, more meaningful pattern.

The economy of the organism requires that we be able to drop what has been differentiated in clear figure further and further into the ground of the field. If every event had to be new and clearly differentiated at every moment, need satisfaction, even the very existence of the organism, would be impossible. We are all familiar in our own experience with this movement of what has been learned from clear figure into the total field of our experience. In learning to drive a car, for example, starting, shifting, accelerating, and steering are each at first done painstakingly and with great concentration of effort. Later, as we learn to do these things effectively and smoothly, they become more and more a part of the total situation with which we are concerned. At first our need in driving the car was to differentiate how to turn it on. Having mastered this, the next problem became how to make it go. Later, when we had learned to drive very well, the whole business of driving became mere ground for the more important figures of where we want to go and how do we get there. What emerges into figure at one time may become ground for new figures the next.

DIFFERENTIATION AND HABIT

The apparently automatic behavior as a result of differentiations no longer in clear figure is called, in external approaches to psychology, "habit." Although such behaviors seem automatic, it should not be assumed that they ever occur without meaning or without some degree of awareness. Behavior is always a function of the total field and never exists without meaning. Habits in a perceptual sense are behaviors resulting from low-level perceptions in the phenomenal field. The assumption that habits are automatic and without meaning has probably come about because of the fact that the individual often does not seem to be keenly aware of his behavior at the moment it occurs. A confirmed smoker may suddenly find himself with a lit cigarette in his hand without having been consciously aware of, that is, able to report, the sequence of behaviors that have brought him to this condition. What has happened is that smoking, orginally a series of techniques for the satisfaction of need in clear figure, has now become part of the ground of his perceptual field as more immediate problems of need satisfaction arise into figure. The confirmed smoker's "habit" is a lower-level differentiation in the perceptual field. Its presence in the ground of the field, however, necessarily affects behavior even though it exists at a lower level of differentiation than the immediate events in figure for the individual at the moment.

The operation of this figure-ground relationship of habit is neatly illustrated in Dunlap's fascinating method of breaking a habit by practicing it. Dunlap observed that in typing he had developed a very bad habit of typing *hte* when he meant to type *the.* When he attempted to break this habit by practicing writing *t-h-e,* he found that his habit persisted. When, however, instead of practicing *t-h-e,* he practiced writing *h-t-e,* his unfortunate habit quickly disappeared. What apparently happened in this case was that Dunlap had developed perceptions which resulted in his writing *hte.* These perceptions at a low level of awareness in his field caused him to continue writing *hte* as he typed his manuscripts. The attempt to break his habit by practicing *the* did not help matters any, because it served to bring into figure the differentiation *t-h-e* instead of the differentiation *h-t-e* which was the real source of his difficulties. When, however, he practiced *h-t-e,* thus bringing this differentiation into clear figure, he was able to change it and the habit was broken. Behaviors operating from low-level perceptions often continue to persist until they are somehow brought into clear figure where they can be dealt with in a new fashion. Nail biting or thumb sucking are "habits" which may sometimes be dealt with effectively by practicing them directly and openly for a certain length of time each day. This brings the low-level differentiation into clearer figure where it can be dealt with. Events can be much more effectively dealt with in clear figure than when they remain as part of the ground. The same principle operates in psychotherapy when the counselor seeks to help his client to bring his anxieties into clear figure where they can be more effectively dealt with.

Remembering and Forgetting

Remembering and forgetting, like any other behavior, are functions of the differentiations the individual is able to make in his perceptual field. When a person is able to recall into figure differentiations he has made on a previous occasion, we say he "remembers." When he is unable to call again into figure differentiations he has previously made, we say he has "forgotten." Thus, we may define remembering and forgetting as functions of the ability of an individual to recall into figure events he has previously differentiated. As products of perception, remembering and forgetting will be affected, just as learning is, by those factors which control the processes of perceiving we have discussed in the previous chapters of this book.

Earlier in our examination of the nature of the perceptual field, we observed that differentiations once made are permanent. That is to say, perceptions once made have been made forever. Perception and differentiation are a one-way process and one cannot *un*differentiate or *un*perceive. A perception or differentiation has presumably been made forever. There seems ample evidence to demonstrate this permanent character of learning. Burtt found, for example, that Greek passages read to his infant son were "learned" more quickly at later periods in his son's life than similar passages which the young man had never heard before.

Other evidence for the permanence of learning may be found in the remarkable ability which many people show under hypnosis or under the influence of hypnotic drugs to remember with great detail events occurring at extremely early periods in their lives. Similarly, a large portion of the time of a client in psychotherapy is spent in recalling events he has long since thought he had forgotten. If what is once differentiated in the field is differentiated for all time, how then shall we explain the varying degrees with which we seem able to recall previous events?

Before looking at some of the factors which affect the degree of remembering and forgetting, it is necessary for us to recall that the perceptual field is differentiated in terms of the individual's unique and personal experience. The perceptual field is differentiated, not in terms of the experience of the outside observer, but as events are perceived by the behaver himself. Failure to understand this point may sometimes result in an assumption of a failure in memory which is really no more than a difference in perceiving as seen from the point of view of the behaver and the observer. Two people exposed to the same situation perceive this event in quite different fashion. On a later occasion person A may discover that person B reports quite a different picture of what happened. Since A assumes that his field is correct, he may then conclude that person B has "forgotten" what is quite obvious to A.

What can be remembered can only be that which was once perceived. To ask an individual to remember what he has not perceived is asking of him the impossible. Some of the frustrations adults suffer in attempting to deal with young children often arise from a failure to understand this fact. What adult has not experienced the frustration, for example, of asking a child "What happened?" and getting for an answer, "I don't know!" In the adult's world it seems inconceivable that anybody should have forgotten so soon what happened to him. We are likely to forget that the perceptions of children are far different from those of adults. A child confronted with a highly threatening situation, for example, may have differentiated little more than the overwhelming enormity of the threatening object and his own inadequacy to deal with it. Little wonder, then, that he finds himself confused still further by adult demands that he describe with accuracy and precision the what, why, how, who, and when of the situation in which he has been involved. What is going on here is not so much a failure of a child's memory as of an adult's understanding.

The perceptual field at any instant is, from the point of view of the behaver, his whole universe and consequently includes what he knows of the past at that moment and what he infers about the future at that moment. Like all other parts of the field, these memories of the past or expectations of the future will emerge into figure or lapse into ground in conformity with the needs of the individual and the activity he is pursuing. Like all parts of the field they are subject to distortion and modification by the major variables of perception we have discussed in Chapters 3 to 8 of this volume.

THE CLARITY OF AWARENESS

We have already observed that perceptions exist in the phenomenal field at all levels of awareness, from those so vague and indistinct as to be forever in ground to those, on the other hand, so sharp and precisely in figure that it becomes possible for us to express them even to other people through the symbolism of language. Other things being equal then, memory will be dependent upon the level of awareness of a given event in the individual's perceptual field. Generally speaking, we will be able to reproduce on demand most effectively and efficiently those events which have become, as a consequence of our experience, sharply in figure. Events in the ground are always more difficult to bring again into figure. This creates some serious problems for our courts and the legal profession. Two men standing on the street corner talking with each other, for example, may be aware of the traffic patterns surrounding them only as vague and indistinct movement. When suddenly two cars collide, their attention is immediately drawn to the collision and the events surrounding. Later, on the witness stand, they can give quite precise accounts of the position of the cars, their condition, and perhaps the behavior of the passengers immediately following the impact. Their perceptions of the events leading up to the accident, however, may be far less clear, even highly confusing, as this calls for differentiation of events never really clearly perceived. Unhappily, it is these very events leading up to the causes of the accident that are of most concern to the judge, jury, and attorneys involved in the case.

Several "laws of memory" have been developed as a result of extensive experimentation with problems of memory. Among these are the observations that memory is a function of frequency, intensity, and recency. That is to say that, other things being equal, what is likely to be remembered most easily will be that which the individual has experienced frequently, with greatest intensity, or most recently. These observations seem to hold true with respect to the differentiations an individual is able to make, providing we prefix each of them with the statement "other things being equal." Whether or not these principles apply in a given case will of course be dependent upon what has been previously differentiated in the field. Almost any of us have had experiences which illustrate that frequency of exposure to an event is by no means enough to guarantee adequate differentiation. For years we may walk the same street to work and never observe important details in the buildings along our way until we make a point of it. Similarly, it is possible in listening to a symphony orchestra almost to ignore the intense sound of the percussion instruments as we strain to hear the soft melody of the woodwinds.

THE EFFECT OF NEED ON MEMORY

What is remembered is always a function of the individual's basic need. As in all field change, the subject matter and degree of differentiation are determined by the need of the behaver and the opportunities for differentiation that are available. Like all items of awareness, memories are characteristically pertinent to the immediate problems of the individual and are not fortuitous or random. If we are distracted from our work by vagrant memories, it is because the work itself does not promise adequate satisfaction of our need. We are not always able to remember what we need but we do need what we remember.

The same characteristics of purpose and direction which select our memories also determine the relations within the remembered material. As in all cases of differentiation of the field, the sequence is from a relatively large and homogeneous figure, which usually cannot be verbalized, toward a more detailed but restricted figure, the process ceasing when the need is satisfied or the activity is abandoned. As a general thing, the first emergence in remembering is not of isolated objects or individuals but of generally meaningful events which are then differentiated into their necessary details. For instance, a freshman student remembers his fourth Christmas because he then got the sled which led to the accident he remembered.

Whether or not an individual can differentiate on a later occasion what has been previously differentiated will be affected by his need both at the time of the first experience and at the time that recall is demanded. We have already seen above that the individual's need at the time of the occurrence of an event will determine what is differentiated in clear figure at that time. In the case of the auto accident cited above, the need of the men on the street corner to talk with each other may have caused each to be in such clear figure to the other that neither participant could perceive with any degree of clarity what was going on about him. With a shift of interest to the actual collision, differentiations having to do with that event could occur with much greater clarity and precision.

The individual's personal need will also determine in large measure what is remembered on the occasion when it is later demanded. In general, we recall what we have a need to recall. When I need a drink, I recall where the drinking fountain is located. When I need a plumber, I recall the whereabouts of his shop. It should not be supposed, however, that simply because an individual verbalizes a need to remember that such a statement constitutes his real need. It may represent only that he needs to have us believe he is making an effort. We have already seen in our discussion of threat that events perceived as threatening to the individual may be refused admission into clear figure. Clients in psychotherapy, for example, may often be observed to be making what seems on the surface like a very intense and painful attempt to remember an earlier experience without success. They may even complain quite sincerely, "I need to talk about that. I wish I could tell you about it." The counselor, however, knows that what his client is expressing is not so much a need to remember as a need to be strong enough to deal with the event. What he is saying is "I wish I were adequate enough to permit myself to confront this question." The individual's statement of what he needs cannot always be relied upon as an accurate representation of the need he really feels.

Since only one event can appear in figure at a time in the perceptual field, the effect of need in focusing attention in one direction may make it impossible to perceive some other aspect of the field at that moment. This is what often happens in stage fright, when the individual's concern about himself and his performance become so clearly in figure that he cannot perceive his lines and later claims that he forgot them. If he has been well trained, this proves only a temporary lapse and he is soon able to turn his attention again to his speeches and get on with the play.

An intense need of any kind has this sort of ordering effect upon the perceptual field and may make it difficult for differentiations to occur. This happens not only with threat. It may also occur in periods of high anticipation. The joy of reunion with a loved one at the station may sometimes cause us "to forget" where we are and so behave in ways usually not appropriate for public display. Much forgetting and failure of memory is the product of this kind of focus of attention on aspects of the field determined by need at the moment.

OTHER FIELD EFFECTS UPON MEMORY AND FORGETTING

Since behavior is a function of the total perceptual field, what is remembered is always a product of the field state at the instant recall is demanded. We have already observed above how the level of differentiation in the field affects memory. Various factors having to do with other aspects of field organization will also determine what is remembered or forgotten.

What is remembered is always a product of the phenomenal field. As a result, a good deal of distortion may sometimes be imposed on memory either by the field existing at the time of the original event or, later, at the time it is to be recalled. Things are not always experienced in the same way by children and adults, for example, and thus the experience remembered may be quite different. The reader can test this for himself by discussing some of his childhood memories with the adults who were there. One can usually discover that some things he remembers never really happened at all. What is remembered can only be our experience of an event. This experience, moreover, is not equivalent to the physical occurrence but is perceived in terms of the individual's need and the state of his field at the time the event occurred. Unnecessary details are omitted and details necessary to the phenomenal event are added and "remembered" even if they were never seen or never existed.

Just as the existing field affects the perception of the event at the time of its original occurrence, so also does the need of the individual and his current field affect perception at the time of recall. It is a common experience to discover we have inaccurately remembered a name, a place, or idea on later occasions.

What the individual experiences when he is first exposed to an event is always a function of the total field at that instant. What he perceives is what best fits the existing field at that time. This is also true of what is remembered. The perceptual field is always meaningful and what is remembered is affected by the existing meanings in the field. It thus happens that a person reporting upon a previous experience may often be observed to distort his report in terms of what he now knows to be meaningful. This raises some additional problems and new causes of error for the psychology of testimony we mentioned earlier. Since the individual's field always has the feeling of reality, it is sometimes difficult to distinguish between an event that really happened and an event which now seems *reasonably to have happened.* Some things we remember not because they occurred but because it seems to us that they *must* have occurred.

This experience of the perceptual field in terms of what is meaningful is illustrated in the phenomenon of paramnesia or *déjà vu,* the feeling of having been in a place before although we know that fact is impossible. Almost everyone has experienced this feeling at some time or another. It may occur walking down the streets of a city in which we have never been before: we suddenly get the feeling of great familiarity with this street, even to the extent of being certain that we could describe what is around the next corner. Such feeling seems to come about in this way: traveling often over a particular street in our home town, we may differentiate, usually very vaguely, a pattern or series of houses or stores or whatever. Later, on a new street in a new city where we have never been before, if the pattern or series of stores or houses in this neighborhood has a degree of similarity to those in the old one, the total field response we may get includes the feeling of familiarity characteristic of the old setting. Ordinarily, an attempt to differentiate more precisely the cues to which we have been responding in the two situations will quickly make it apparent that they are not by any means alike.

The perceptual field is always meaningful and related to the satisfaction of need. Need, however, cannot be efficiently and effectively satisfied if it is only possible to deal with events that are in clear figure. As a consequence, much of our forgetting actually contributes to the efficiency of our behavior. For example, I need to know the names of the students in my classes and, if the class is not too large, within a few weeks I can manage to differentiate the names of most of the people in the group. When the semester is over, however, I have often been embarrassed by meeting a student whose name I could easily have called last week but now find myself quite unable to do so. The reason for this seems to be that with the end of the semester I no longer "need" to know the student's name. As a consequence these differentiations are difficult to make again when my perceptual field has become organized in a new direction. I have even been fascinated to discover that within a week or two after a class was completed I found great difficulty in calling the names of individual students whom I met about the halls of the university. At a reunion with the same class several years later, sitting about the table as we did on earlier occasions, however, I was delighted to find that I knew their names as I had during the days when the class was actively in session. Apparently the most important factor affecting memory is the need of the individual himself. Some politicians with very intense need to call people by name have been able to develop phenomenal abilities in this direction.

Reasoning and Problem Solving

Just as perception and learning differ only in the complexity of the differentiation required, so "problem solving" and "reasoning" also appear to be functions of differentiation. As an example of reasoning let us take the solution of the following problem. Dr. S. had rented a garage in front of which was an electric-light pole, about fifteen feet from the entrance. When he got into his car at 6:55 the next morning and began to back out to the street on his way to a seven-o'clock class he discovered the light pole by crumpling his right rear fender against it. The following morning he was very much aware of the pole and cut his car sharply to the left to avoid it, with the result that the right front fender scraped against the open garage door. Two major obstacles had now emerged from the ground, the pole and the door. A fence made it impossible to push the door farther out of the way and the pole could not be removed; so it was necessary for him to discover a path by which he could back his car from the garage to the street without striking either obstacle. It seemed quite likely that, by continuing to do the best he could to avoid these obstacles as he backed out, he would eventually learn (by differentiation of visual, temporal, and kinesthetic cues) to do so. However, such a course might require a considerable amount of time and cost more money than he could afford for repairs to the car. He was accordingly impelled to solve the problem more directly. Since he could drive into the garage without damage (because in driving ahead the field was more highly differentiated in terms of both visual and kinesthetic patterns), it was only necessary for him to discover some way of backing out along the same path. By noting (differentiating) two or three landmarks as he drove in at night it was only necessary for him to observe these points when he backed out the next morning. He had no more trouble during the rest of the summer, except for one morning when his alarm clock failed to ring. While he was backing out of the garage at 7:02 in a vain effort to reach a seven-o'clock class on time, the urgency of the situation became the figure in his field, the landmarks dropped into ground, and he backed into the light pole.

As in learning and perception, the first awareness was of the gross situation, and the essential cues and orientation points did not emerge into figure until the behaver became aware of his need for such details. The factors determining the degree and direction of differentiation were, again, the goal or need of the behaver and the opportunities for differentions that were available. Reasoning and problem solving, it would appear, are not something different. All behavior is in a sense problem solving. The important question is, what is the nature of a superior ability in this direction? How does one become more skillful or efficient?

Problem solving has to do with the individual's ability to perceive new, different, or more efficient aspects of a complex situation. Even the lowest animals are able to differentiate in this fashion in some degree. The ability to differentiate in this way on a symbolic level available to us as human beings, however, opens vast new horizons for effective and efficient differentiation, and hence need satisfaction. Operating on a symbolic level gives us a kind of shorthand in terms of which we have an immensely increased mobility of action.

As a consequence of the experience of past generations of thinkers, techniques of inductive and deductive reasoning have come to be formalized as particularly fruitful approaches to problem solving. The experience of more recent generations living in the midst of the marvelous accomplishments of the physical sciences have added the "experimental method" of hypothesis, experiment, and conclusion as the "right" approach to reasoning. Certainly these methods are useful devices by which it becomes possible to bring order and meaning out of large bodies of data. The attempt, however, to teach problem solving and reasoning by the use of such formal devices usually fails. What is logically reasonable is not always humanly practicable. The attempt to utilize some of these formal techniques of problem solving may even, sometimes, interfere with the process of reasoning by turning attention away from the aspects of the perceptual field in which the solution must be found. The field in which a problem must be solved is a field organized with respect to the problem. Preoccupation with a *method* of solving problems brings into figure aspects of the field having nothing to do with the actual solution of the problem. The solutions to problems after all can only be found in the field pertinent to those solutions. Two things cannot be in figure in the perceptual field at once, and when methods are in figure, concepts cannot be.

Improvement in reasoning and problem solving, it would appear, is not likely to be effectively brought about by formal methods. What improves capacity in problem solving are the same things which produce richness, variety, and availability of perceptions in the perceptual field. What improves reasoning and problem solving are the same factors which produce creativity, spontaneity, and the kind of free and open perceptual field which we have found is characteristic of the adequate personality. In later chapters on the problem of human capacities and the nature of the adequate personality we shall consider in much more detail the kind of perceptual field necessary for most effective reasoning and problem solving.

CHAPTER 11

The Nature of Capacities, Emotion, and Feeling

WE began this book with the premise that all behavior is a function of perception. To understand behavior, we said, it is necessary to understand how things seem to the person who is behaving. Accordingly, in the past eight chapters we have been systematically examining the factors which influence perception. In particular we have given a good deal of attention to seven variables having important effects upon perceiving:

1. The physical organism
2. Time
3. Opportunity
4. The effect of need
5. Goals and values
6. The phenomenal self
7. The restriction of the field

The first three are well known to us in our common experience and have also been extensively explored in the psychology of the last 50 years. These are factors affecting behavior that lie very largely outside the individual and are open to manipulation by those who surround the individual. Throughout man's history they have provided the primary bases through which people have sought to control or affect the behavior of their fellows. The latter four are factors inside the behaver and are open to external manipulation only indirectly and in limited degree. These four are functions of the phenomenal field and have only in recent years been greatly appreciated for the vital bearings they have upon behavior. All seven of these factors we know have important effects upon how people perceive. There may be others of which we are not now aware, for perceptual psychology is not very old, and it is only in fairly recent years that the problems of perception have been intensively or widely studied. It is conceivable that in the years to come we may discover still other important variables which will help us to push forward the frontiers of our understanding.

In the preceding chapters we have had to look at these variables of perception one by one; but, of course, behavior is never the product of any one of these variables operating alone. Behavior is always a function of the whole perceptual field at any moment, and the perceptions available to the behaver in his perceptual field will be the product of all of these factors.

All behavior, we have said, is determined by the perceptual field of the behaver at the moment of his behaving. How effectively a person is able to behave at any moment will depend upon the perceptions available to him at the instant he is called upon to act. Let us go back and look at that statement again. If the statement is true, it means that human capacities and abilities to behave are a function of the perceptual field, and the factors controlling human capacities will be the same factors as those which govern the process of perceiving! If behavior is a function of perception, then, the factors which govern perceptions will also determine the nature and degree of the abilities which any individual possesses.

Historically, we have been accustomed to think of human capacities and abilities as the direct products of heredity or of the strength, agility, or health of the physical organism. And, of course, when we are thinking of purely physical potentialities these observations hold true. One cannot jump, for example, without legs, and how far he can jump with legs will be dependent upon the strength and health of the organism which is doing the jumping. There must, of course, be a physical organism to operate, and the physical operation of that organism will be dependent upon the kind of structure it possesses.

We have already seen (Chapter 4), however, that human behavior cannot be understood solely in terms of physical structure. Our physical bodies provide the vehicles for perception and behavior and set important limits upon some types of behavior; they do not provide a sufficient cause for the understanding of *all* behavior. One must have the necessary structure of the throat in order to speak, but *what one says* is not to be understood in terms of the laws of heredity or the physiological make-up of the individual alone. Although the physical organism is essential for behavior, we must search elsewhere for a comprehensive understanding of the nature of behavior or of human capacities for behaving or misbehaving.

Previous generations of psychologists were deeply impressed by the successes of the physical sciences and often pined for the kind of precise measurements which those sciences found possible. It seemed only reasonable to them that human behavioral capacities must be limited in the same fashion as physical capacities, since both occurred in the same physical organism. To conceive of a limited organism capable of almost unlimited behavior seemed too mystical for scientific belief. Accordingly, the psychologists of 30 years ago were almost unanimous in describing human capacities as the direct product of the individual's heredity and physiological structure. It was thought then that children were born with certain specific potentialities of intelligence or aptitude. This potential, moreover, was conceived as fixed and immutable. A child could fail to achieve his inherited capacity, but he could certainly never exceed it. Many human abilities were conceived as inborn and, hence, as unchangeable.

In more recent years many psychologists have come to have grave doubts about this fatalistic conception of human abilities. Human abilities seem capable of far more change than had previously been thought. Numerous instances have now been reported which demonstrate that considerable changes in general level of achievement are possible. Programs enriching the environments of children deprived of affection and evidence of personal worth, for example, have shown measurable improvements in intelligence. Intelligence ratings have also been found to change positively following play therapy, and negatively with long periods in restricted environments. Human abilities no longer seem so exclusively the product of the behaver's genes as we once thought. It seems necessary now to consider a large number of psychological factors in addition to physiological ones.

This is not a denial of the importance of our physical beings in behavior, but a matter of seeing the contribution of our body structure in better perspective as one of a number of factors rather than the sole determinant of capacity. The contribution of physical factors to any behavior will vary widely from act to act, never reaching zero, but never serving as the full and sufficient explanation for behavior, either. We have attempted to diagram this in Fig. 21. The three bar graphs in that figure each represent a typical behavior. The shaded area of each graph represents the contribution of the physical organism to the behavior. Bar A might be such a behavior as climbing a rope, in which the physical strength and agility of the behaver will play a very large part. In this

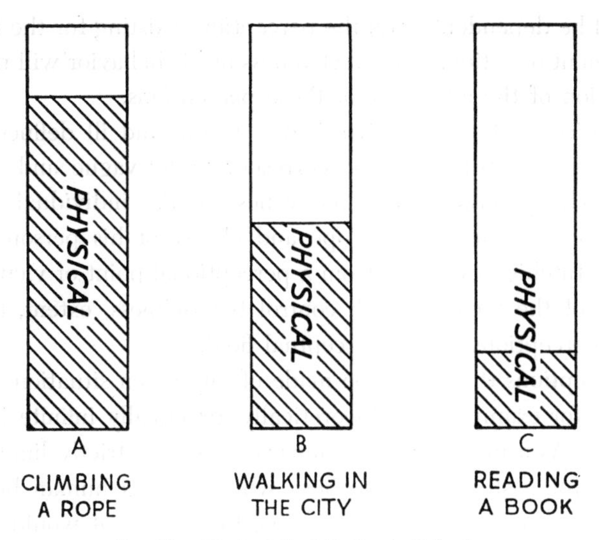

Fig. 21. Physical Contribution to Behavior.

instance, the physical condition of the subject determines in very large measure his capacity to behave effectively. Bar *B* represents a behavior in which the physical organism plays a lesser role as, for example, walking through a city. Here is a behavior which requires some degree of physical fitness, but not so much as climbing a rope. In Bar *C* we have represented a behavior like reading a book or making a speech, in which the physiological potentialities of the individual play a relatively minor role. By far the greatest portion of the things we do lie well within this latter sphere of operation, in which our physical bodies provide only the vehicle for behavior. How we behave, given the necessary vehicle, is a function of psychological or experiential factors like those we have been exploring in this book.

Intelligence as a Problem of Perception

By the term *intelligence* we ordinarily refer to the effectiveness of the individual's behavior. Intelligent behavior is behavior which effectively and efficiently satisfies the need of an individual and his society. Whether or not such behavior can occur, however, will depend upon the differentiations the individual is able to make in his perceptual field, which we have defined as "the universe of experience open to the individual at the moment of his behavior." In other words, the behavior of the individual will be dependent upon the perceptions existing for the individual at the moment of action. The effectiveness of his behavior will necessarily be a function of the adequacy of those perceptions.

If an entity in the perceptive field is vague and ill defined, the behavior of the individual will be correspondingly vague and lacking in precision. The precision and effectiveness of the individual's behavior will be dependent upon the scope and clarity of his personal field of awareness. Intelligence, then, from a perceptional point of view becomes a function of the factors which control the richness, extent, and availability of perceptions in the perceptual field.

The perceptions that could be made of any given situation, such as a stone wall, for example, are, theoretically, practically infinite in number and quality. As a matter of fact, however, we are strictly limited in our perceptions of a stone wall to those which we, as human beings, can make. We cannot, for instance, perceive the wall as it would appear to a man from Mars, or from the interior of an atom, or as it would appear to a centipede. What is more, we cannot even perceive it as it would appear to all people. Different people will perceive different aspects of the wall differently, even at the same instant. I can only perceive the wall, and hence behave toward it, in terms of the perceptions that I, as an individual, can make regarding it. I may, for instance, perceive it as a fine, sturdy fence enclosing my property, while a stonemason friend might perceive it as having been poorly designed or as having been built with too little cement in the mortar mixture. The perceptions open to my mason friend are the result of his unique experience. I, not having such experience, am incapable of those perceptions at this moment. Each of us is limited in perceiving by the richness, extent, and availability of perceptions in his unique perceptual field.

THE EXTENT OF PERCEPTIONS IN THE PHENOMENAL FIELD

At the instant of their behaving, people can only behave in terms of those perceptions which exist for them. In the example above, it might be possible for me to acquire the same kind of perceptions about stone walls as my mason friend. I could increase my own perceptions by a period of study or apprenticeship, for example. At the moment of behaving, *now,* however, I am limited by those perceptions which exist in my field. I cannot behave in terms of perceptions I do not have at that instant.

THE QUALITY OF PERCEPTIONS AS A LIMITING FACTOR

At any instant behavior will also be limited by the quality of the individual's perceptions. In the example above, the perceptions open to the writer and to the mason are by no means equal in quality. Even if these people had the same number of perceptions, the perceptions available to each would vary greatly in detail, richness, and meaning. The artist and the novice looking at the same picture might conceivably have the same number of perceptions, but the meaning or quality of these perceptions would be vastly different for the two observers.

THE AVAILABILITY OF PERCEPTIONS IN THE FIELD

Finally, the behavior of the individual at any instant will be determined by the availability of perceptions in his personal field at the moment of his behaving. The existence of perceptions in the phenomenal field is no guarantee that they will be available at a high enough level to affect behavior significantly at the instant they are required. Some perceptions may exist in the field only as *potential* perceptions. By this we mean those perceptions that exist in the individual's unique field of awareness and that, given the right circumstances at any particular moment, *could* rise into figure. The fact that a perception is potentially possible to any individual does not mean that it will occur at the moment of action. Even those perceptions that I can make potentially may not be active for me at any given moment. Potentially, I might be able, for instance, to perceive the wall in our example as a barrier to be gotten over, as an eyesore to be beautified, as composed of 687 bricks costing $80.27, or as providing pleasant shade on a hot day. These are all potential perceptions I am capable of making about the wall. They will affect my behavior, however, only when they are active or functioning in my field of perceptions. When I am beating a hasty retreat pursued by a neighbor's angry dog, perceptions about the shade, beauty, or cost of the wall, though potential, are not functional in affecting my behavior. I behave only in terms of my functioning perception of the wall as something to get over—and quickly.

The fact that particular perceptions may be potentially available in the field of an individual is by no means a guarantee that they will exist functionally at the moment of action. The capacity of the individual to behave at any moment will thus depend upon the extent and richness of his perceptions and the availability of those perceptions at the instant they are required. This extent, richness, and availability will in turn be dependent upon the seven variables of perception we have explored in earlier chapters (3-9). We have already observed how each of those factors controls the perceptual field.

The Maximal Limits of Behavior

What are the maximal limits of human capacity? At the lower level of these limits we know there are some unfortunates who have little more capacity for behaving than the bare minimum required to keep alive. Examples of this extreme degree of limitation would be the so-called "crib cases" to be found in many of our institutions for the mentally retarded. These are persons born with such drastic physical deficiencies as to be capable of little or no perception. They live out their lives in little more than a vegetative condition.

At the opposite extreme, what are the upper limits of human capacity? This is indeed a difficult question, for so far as we know no one has ever remotely approached the upper limits of perception. Indeed, the possibilities for human perception seem almost infinite. Given a healthy physical organism to provide the vehicle for perception, enough time, a stimulating environment, challenging and fruitful problems, and a non-restrictive self concept, there seems no end to the perceptions possible to the individual. Given eyes capable of seeing, who can say what are the limits of what may be perceived? Presumably one could perceive whatever one looked at, and there are no end of things to look at! Unlike the limits imposed on the physical organism by our physical structure, the limits of what *might* be perceived by a particular individual seem practically nonexistent. The potentialities of perception are infinite.

Apparently, people can go on differentiating new perceptions in their phenomenal fields from conception to death. Their perceptions during this period seem limited only by the seven variables of perception we have discussed earlier. One of these variables, of course, is the state of the physical organism, and with advancing age, failures of the physical organism may contribute to a reduced ability to perceive. Students of the aging process now believe, however, that the intellectual, behavioral capacity of the elderly need not deteriorate with age simply because the body is less capable of the kind of reactions it could deliver in its younger days. Indeed, they have collected many remarkable case histories of persons, like Oliver Wendell Holmes, who remained remarkably keen and productive to extremely advanced ages, sometimes even in spite of great physical deterioration. It would appear that some of the rigidities of aging are not so much questions of a slowing down of the physical organism as limitations on perception brought about by some of the variables of perception. Some elderly people seem limited by their perceptions of self. Seeing themselves as unable, unacceptable, or useless, they behave as though they were, though they may be enjoying perfectly good health. Some seem limited by their own feelings of threat at anything which resembles change in their accepted pattern of life, and they avoid exposing themselves to the necessity for change as much as feasible. Still others seem to have become the victims of their own goals and values, so that new events and new ideas have no place in their perceptual fields. Although deterioration of capacity may come with advancing age by reason of a failure of the physical organism, it now seems clear that this is not a necessary occurrence if other factors affecting perception can be kept operating in positive constructive ways rather than contributing to rigidity and narrowness of the perceptual field.

THE DEVELOPMENT OF SPECIAL CAPACITIES

In the course of differentiating perceptions throughout a lifetime each of us develops a unique field of perceptions richer or more extensive in some areas than the fields of our friends and neighbors and poorer and narrower in others. This unique pattern in the content of our field is brought about by the action of the variables of perception during the years of our growing up. The particular field we develop represents our own specialization, our own peculiar know-how, skill, or understanding. No one can respond to everything, and as a result our perceptions become more or less differentiated in these fields depending upon the kinds of experiences to which we have been exposed. Even the decisions we make from day to day have a directing and selecting effect upon the kinds of perceptions we can have and will have thereafter. If a young woman should decide to enter nurse's training, for example, it is unlikely that she will have many perceptions about calculus and topology during the next four years. Our perceptions become specialized by the very nature of the decisions we make.

For some people, this specialization of perception may proceed to extraordinary lengths so that they seem to have capacities far beyond that of ordinary mortals. A young man whom the writer tested at an induction center during the war illustrates the point very well. This young man was a newsboy on the streets of a West Virginia city. Although he had failed repeatedly in grammar school and was generally regarded as "not bright," he appeared on a national radio hookup as "The Human Adding Machine." He was a wizard at figures. He could multiply correctly such figures as 6235941 × 397 almost as fast as the problem could be written down. He astounded our induction center for half a day with his numerical feats. Yet on the Binet Test he achieved an IQ of less than 60!

People in his home town, who bought his papers, amused themselves by giving him problems to figure. When not so occupied, this young man entertained himself by adding up the license numbers of cars that passed his corner! He was a specialist in numbers. Apparently as a result of some early success in this field, he had been led to practice numbers constantly, eventually to the exclusion of all else. This was one area in which a poor colored boy could succeed and he made the most of it. His number perceptions were certainly rich and varied, but other things were not. Although he was capable of arithmetic feats not achieved by one in millions, he was classified on the intelligence test as dull. Such specialization or unusual richness of perception in a particular area of behavior is not magical. It is produced by the operation of the same factors governing perception as exist for the rest of us. In fact, most of us could probably duplicate the boy's feat if we were willing to give up most of our other goals as he did.

What Do Intelligence Tests Measure?

Intelligence tests are basically tests of achievement. No one has yet devised a means by which we can approach the measurement of capacity directly. Instead, we are forced to approach this problem indirectly by means of inferences from what we can observe. Intelligence tests are based upon the fundamental assumption that all people taking the test have had an equal opportunity to learn the things the test measures. Accordingly it is assumed that people who have learned more must have had more basic ability or capacity for learning. For example, if John and Mary, two children of equal age and the same general culture, are each given an intelligence test and John makes a better score than Mary, the test administrator would infer that John probably had somewhat more ability than Mary. How accurate the inferences made from such tests are is, of course, dependent upon the degree to which this fundamental assumption holds for the individuals being tested.

A great deal of research has gone into the development of adequate intelligence tests over the past 40 years, and test makers have sought continuously to refine their instruments, primarily through an attempt to find more valid items for these tests, items which could accurately be presumed to be part of the experience of all people taking the tests. This search for common items has been most successful for those age ranges during the school years. Earlier, during infancy, it is difficult to find common items of experience, but our public schools provide a considerable area of common experience (at least as it is seen by an outsider) for children. Consequently, during these years intelligence tests seem to have their greatest validity. After the school years when individuals are free to go their own ways as adults, this modicum of comparable experience rapidly disappears. As people grow up, marry, and embark in the infinitely diverse field of work, it is no longer easy to find common experience upon which intelligence tests may be constructed. The older one gets, the more unique he becomes. Intelligence tests, therefore, based largely upon materials drawn from the school years, sometimes show a leveling off or even a decrease in intelligence after age 16 to 18, the years when children characteristically quit school. Observing this drop, it was once assumed that intelligence ceased to develop after age 16, but we know better than to make such assumptions these days.

From a perceptual point of view, what intelligence tests measure is the phenomenal field. They do not measure this field directly, of course. Instead, they provide us with a sample of the individual's perceptions as these are expressed in the behavior of the individual taking the test. Since behavior is a function of the perceptual field, it becomes possible to infer the nature of the perceptions existing in a person's perceptual field from his behavior. This is exactly what intelligence tests do. From the behavior of the individual on the tests we infer the quality and extent of the perceptual field from which that behavior originated.

We have already defined intelligence in this frame of reference as a function of the quality, extent, and availability of perceptions in the perceptual field. Intelligence tests, then, sample these three aspects of the field. From the sample we may conclude what the whole field may be like. This sample, it should be recalled, is a sample of the state of things in the *current* perceptual field. It gives us an indication of the individual's present perceptions. Ability in this sense is a developmental characteristic, not an immutable or inherent or never-changing trait. In the degree to which the perceptual field is stable and unchanging, so our assessment of an individual's capacity will similarly be stable. We have already seen, however, that the perceptual field is characterized by some capacity for change, and in that degree intelligence or capacity will also be open to change.

In our culture many people have come to accept intelligence-test results almost as trustingly as a prescription from the family doctor. Important decisions are often made as a result of such tests. It is important, therefore, that we have a clear understanding of what tests measure and of the degree to which the results they provide us are accurate assessments of the capacities of people. We need, for example, to be very sure the sample of the perceptual field is indeed an adequate sample of what is there. It is conceivable, for example, that a test might sample so narrow a portion of the perceptual field as to cause completely erroneous conclusions about the individual's perceptions. Tests designed to sample a subject's perceptions about music or art, for example, might be totally inadequate as samples to determine the probable effectiveness of the individual in flying an airplane.

A second possible source of error in sampling has to do with the determination of what is worth sampling. Our own perceptions always seem the "right" ones to each of us. By whose standards, then, shall we take our sample—yours, mine, society's, the subject's own? For the most part our intelligence tests are based on the assumption that academic, upper-middle-class, intellectual perceptions are important. But are they? Can we assume that the expert machinist, who can perceive things "out of this world" for most of the rest of us about a piece of stock on his lathe, is less intelligent than a diplomat who perceives many things about foreign affairs? Can we be so sure of our values as to call one bright and the other dull? Can we blame the machinist for his lack of perception about foreign affairs without asking the diplomat to be equally skilled in the machinist's field of perceptions? In the past it has sometimes been assumed that primitive people are incapable of abstract kinds of perceptions. After studying the capacities of Tepehuan natives to deal with abstractions, McConnell comes to this conclusion; "It is far too easy to read simple mindedness into simple behavior. Merely because some primitive cultures may not demand complex abstract modes of behavior from their members does not necessarily mean that the primitive may not be able to function on a higher level whenever called upon to do so."

Intelligence, we have said, is the capacity for effective, efficient behavior. But who is to determine what is effective and efficient behaving? To a very large degree we adhere to an upper-middle-class definition of values in creating intelligence tests. Since middle-class professional people construct these tests, it is not surprising that the items they choose to test their subjects are derived from their own values. It is probably no accident that, almost without exception, psychologists make the highest scores of anybody on intelligence tests as compared with other professions. They should. They made the tests and included the items that are important to them.

IS THE CAPACITY FOR INTELLIGENT BEHAVIOR OPEN TO CHANGE?

It will be noted that all of the factors we have spoken about which affect perception are capable of some degree of change or manipulation. Even the effect of the physical organism upon perception is capable of variation within certain narrow limits, although, to be sure, it cannot be drastically shifted. The remainder of the factors in our list, however, seem open to fairly wide degrees of change. If this is so, it would appear to follow that the capacity for intelligent behavior can be created! This seems to be true within the limits to which the perceptual field itself is open to change.

Although it is well within the realm of possibility that the perceptual field and, hence, the capacity for more intelligent behavior, may be changed, it should not be assumed that this is either easy or quick. The field has a degree of fluidity and within the limits of that fluidity change is possible. We have already seen, however, that a major characteristic of the perceptual field is its stability, its resistance to change. The factors affecting perception vary in the degree to which they may be manipulated and controlled. There are ways, for example, in which we can provide people with different kinds of opportunities to perceive. There are things we can do to help people discover new and more adequate goals and values or concepts of themselves. It is even possible to deliver many people from the unhappy and restricting effects of threat. To make such changes, however, is neither simple nor easy.

Perceptions of long standing do not change rapidly. The child who has come to define himself as a person who cannot do mathematics as a result of ten years of failure does not change his ways of seeing himself in a moment. It took a lot of experience to build this self concept as a part of his perceptual field, and to organize the rest of the field to fit it; and it is quite likely to take a large amount of a different kind of experience to counteract it. The man who has believed for 40 years that his methods of farming or teaching are the "right" methods cannot be induced to change his goals and values in a moment. Perception is a function of experience. Long established and deeply meaningful experiences have a high degree of stability and resist change. As we have seen, the individual's need tends to produce behavior which corroborates his already existing concepts. Once perceptions have become firmly established in the field they tend to perpetuate themselves and this, of course, adds further to the difficulties of inducing change in the field.

The perceptual view of capacity we have been discussing in these pages is consistent with the position many psychologists have taken in recent years: that intelligence is open to a degree of change. They believe it is not so unchanging or limited by our physical heredity as we once thought. Several studies indicate that intelligence is capable of change, but that this change is not something which can be brought about quickly or easily or in unlimited degree. To produce such changes, however, requires major changes in the experience of the individual whose capacity is being studied. They have found, for example, increases in intelligence levels when children have been moved from the restricted environment of an "orphanage" or "children's home" to the richer experience of living with adopted parents. The reverse has also been found: that children committed to the restricted environments of some types of institutions show a gradual decrease in capacity. It has been found, too, that major changes are increasingly difficult as the person grows older. Intelligence levels then seem open to some degrees of change depending upon the experience of the individual. The point of view with respect to intelligence or capacity we have been discussing here is consistent with such observations and suggests, further, some possible reasons for the phenomena these psychologists have observed.

From a perceptual point of view, intelligence is not something static and unchangeable. But neither is it so fluid as to be open to rapid manipulation. Capacity, in this frame of reference, is a developmental characteristic affected and controlled by at least the seven factors of perception we have been exploring in this book. It is a function of the richness, extent, and availability of perceptions in the perceptual field and is open to change in the degree to which the phenomenal field itself can be changed. This view by no means offers hope that every child of low intelligence can be made normal. The perceptual field is not that fluid. On the other hand, we need to explore every possible avenue to the creation of intelligence and to push as far as we can go up every avenue that is open to us. The perceptual point of view may not be able to reverse the trends of a lifetime, but it can point the way to some challenging routes to explore.

SOME IMPLICATIONS OF THIS CONCEPTION OF INTELLIGENT BEHAVIOR

If the conception of intelligence we have been discussing is accurate, it raises serious questions about some of our common assumptions about intelligence and, at the same time, opens some exciting new possibilities for the treatment or education of persons we have often assumed to be beyond help. Perhaps we have been too impressed with the limitations upon growth and development which we observe in physical maturation.

We should explore to the very fullest the possibility that in those cases where we cannot demonstrate biologic impairment, the limitations upon intelligence may be psychological. If it turns out not to be true, we shall find out in time. We cannot afford to limit the places where we look by the preconceptions we have about the matter. Our responsibility here is too great. Education, to name but the most obvious of our social institutions, has in large measure predicated its goals and methods on a concept of humanity with certain static limitations on intelligence. If these limitations are not static, educators need to know that as soon as possible. The task of the scientist is to question, not to be content with answers. We cannot afford to accept an undemonstrated point of view that prevents us from asking questions.

Who can say, for example, what results we might be able to achieve by a systematic effort to remove or decrease the effectiveness of the limitations on perception discussed in this chapter? It is fascinating to speculate on the possibilities one might try in constructing a situation for a child, or adult, consciously designed to minimize the limitations imposed on perception by physical condition, environment, goals, the individual's self perceptions, and the effects of perceived personal threat.

If the position we have taken is accurate, it would suggest that there is much we can do (a) to free individuals from the restraints upon perception and (b) to provide the opportunities for perception to occur.

1. First and most obviously, we should be able to discover and make available to far more people the means to achieve better physical condi-

tion. We have already done a good deal in this area, but much needs yet to be done. Who can say, for instance, what completely adequate medical care for all our people or a more adequate diet for many might mean a generation hence?

2. If this discussion has merit, there lies the possibility of providing experiences for people that will make adequate perceptions possible. We have tried to do this in our schools, but have not always accomplished it. Can it be that the decreases in school success with advance through the school years is more a function of lack of meaning for students than lack of intelligence? Is it enough to assume that experience provided by us to the student is truly provided when he is free to experience it? Has the school child who is so worried about his relationship with his peers that he cannot perceive what his book is saying, truly been provided opportunity to perceive?

In our training of children of "low intelligence," we often provide situations wherein they are carefully taught to perform repeatedly a simple act. Is it possible that in so doing we may be further narrowing their fields of perception and building phenomenal selves that produce even narrower perceptive fields?

What kinds of environments could we construct that might more effectively result in increased perception? Such experiments as Lippitt and White have carried on with democratic and autocratic environments suggest some possibilities, but we need to know much more. Perhaps we could learn to build such environments from observing with greater care and understanding the methods of good teachers.

3. Who can say what possible effects might occur from a systematic release of the individual's perceptions by the satisfaction of his most pressing needs or goals? College professors insist they can produce more, which is another way of saying perceive more, when they have the leisure time to do so, when they are freed from the necessity of spending their time satisfying their needs for sheer existence. Can this be less true of others? It is possible that the child with strong desires for love, affection, status, prestige, or friendship might also be freed to perceive more widely and richly, if we could but find ways of helping him satisfy his need. Ordinarily we pay a good deal of attention to the physical needs of a child, understanding that with these needs unfulfilled he makes a poor student. Is there any good reason to suppose his psychological need is less pressing or less important in freeing him to perceive widely and accurately? We spend much time and energy trying to find ways of

"motivating" people or blaming them for not being motivated to do what we need them to do. We assume that if permitted to seek their own ends, people will not satisfy ours. Perhaps we should get further by helping them satisfy their need; they might then be free to satisfy ours.

4. Most of our educational methods are directed at the provision of perceptions for the student. He is lectured, required, shown, exhorted, and coerced to perceive what someone thinks he should. It seems possible that with equal energy devoted to the matter of creating new goals, and values in students, rich and varied perceptions might be more efficiently produced.

5. What effects might we be able to produce by providing experiences that build adequate concepts of self in children and adults? What differences in the richness and variety of perception might result from a generation of people with "I can" rather than "I can't" conceptions of themselves? What possibilities of increased perceptions and hence of increased intelligence might accrue to such a program? Clinical experience has demonstrated frequently how a changed perception of self as a more adequate personality can free children for improved school performance, for example.

What would happen if we were consciously and carefully to set about the task of providing experiences that would lead people to perceive themselves as adequate, worthy, self-respecting people? The child who perceives himself as unwanted, unacceptable, unable, or unliked perceives and behaves in rigid, defensive fashion. It should be possible to reverse this process and produce more adequate perceptions by systematic efforts at producing more adequate definitions of self. The possibilities seem tremendous, but we have scarcely scratched the surface of this problem.

Finally, if threat to the individual has as important effects as seem indicated in this discussion, helping persons to perceive themselves as adequate would seem a most important factor to consider in the release of the individual to perceive more adequately. The work of Rogers and his students in client-centered therapy has already illustrated to some degree what possibilities freeing the individual to perceive more adequately may accomplish through the provision of a permissive, nonthreatening relationship between counselor and client. We have already mentioned the effects Axline has reported following a permissive, nonthreatening form of play therapy.

The Phenomenal Self and Emotion

Psychologists have come to believe that there is some degree of emotion connected with every human behavior. Psychologists, however, did not always think this way. Experimental studies of the causes of emotional behavior have been made only in fairly recent times. For a long time fear and anger, as well as other emotions, were assumed to be innate responses to fairly definite situations. This assumption, which tended to discourage any efforts to modify emotional behavior by training, was first questioned by Watson. From that point on the psychologist's concept of emotion has undergone a rapid evolution. Today most psychologists approaching the problem from an external view have adopted a description of emotion as being nonspecific—a "disorganized response" on the part of the organism irrespective of the nature of the stimulus which sets it off. They point out that any person will become excited, afraid, or angry when he is in a situation which he is unable to control.

Most recently, a number of psychologists, perhaps best represented by Prescott and Leeper, have expressed disagreement with this view and have seen emotion, not as disorganized response alone, but as having an organizing and facilitating effect as well. These writers see all behavior as possessing more or less of the physiologic accompaniments of what is usually called emotion. They point out, for example, that even in slight emergencies there is some increase in all our bodily activities. Every human activity seems to be accompanied by some degree of emotional response.

It is probably the increased consciousness of personal power and effectiveness resulting from this heightened bodily activity that causes people to like excitement, adventure, and change, to ride on roller coasters, to travel for pleasure, and to go on blind dates. By placing ourselves in situations that automatically demand a moderate rise in body tonus, we secure a sense of well-being and physical power that is very satisfying to our fundamental need for enhancement.

In the presence of a problem of modest difficulty we raise our fuel consumption and output of energy above the "idling" rate which is sufficient for the maintenance of bodily temperature, and increase the activity of practically all parts of the body. With increasing demand for action on the part of the organism, the physiologic changes accompanying an emotional state are increased. This mobilization of the resources of the organism was described by Cannon as placing the organism "on a war footing." It results in making available the necessary energy resources required either for meeting or fleeing the threat confronting the individual.

It is interesting that the physiologic changes which occur under "emotion" are the same no matter how the individual may describe the emotion he is experiencing. A high degree of "emotion" is accompanied by a whole series of physiologic changes among which are the following: (1) sweating of the palms of the hands; (2) increased activity of certain glands, particularly the adrenals, which make it possible for the blood to coagulate more rapidly; (3) the release of blood sugar, which provides large stores of quick energy; and (4) the increase in heart rate and breathing, which makes great exertion possible should it be necessary. These changes occur, moreover, whether it is fear, anger, or the ecstasy of a first kiss that we are experiencing. Regardless of our description of the experience, our purely physiologic responses to "important" events is the same.

Our present view of emotion is thus to see it as a kind of acceleration of body processes, a mobilization of energy which makes it possible to meet the peculiar needs of the situations with which we are confronted. We might illustrate this by our behavior as we rise in the morning to go about our daily business. When we are asleep the energy output required of our bodies is very low. We need only to "keep our motors turning over," as it were. Now, when the alarm clock rings we are confronted with the necessity for more activity. We can no longer lie still. We have to move, and this movement requires more energy than we have been expending. Our body processes must be speeded up to take care of this new requirement. As we go through the accustomed activities of dressing, washing, shaving, eating breakfast, we need still more acceleration. Later on in the day, we may find ourselves confronted with exciting or threatening situations which call forth still higher degrees of acceleration of our bodily processes, as when we receive a letter from a sweetheart or narrowly escape being run down while crossing the street. At these times we may find our "heart pounding," our faces flushed, our breath coming faster. We "feel excited."

When our caveman ancestor walked down a forest trail and came face to face with a bear it was important to have available the necessary energy to deal with this sudden emergency. He needed accelerated body processes whether he fought with the bear or ran from him. Even in our modern life we have need for this kind of quick energy to make it possible for us to deal with emergencies like avoiding an oncoming car, getting out of the way of a falling tree, or running a race. Emotion in these situations has survival value. At other times, however, the effects of increased body tone may sometimes be more embarrassing than helpful. The student who is called "on the carpet" by the dean has little need for great acceleration of his body processes. Under the circumstances neither fighting nor running is appropriate. Similarly, in making a speech one needs some increase in bodily activity. Too much, however, can be downright embarrassing or may even be incapacitating, as sometimes happens in extreme fright. Release of large amounts of energy with no appropriate outlet can be a very exhausting experience. Accelerating an automobile motor on the open road gives a smooth, exhilarating ride. Speeding the motor with the brakes on shakes the car in unbearable fashion. Much the same sort of thing happens to human beings under the stress of great emotion.

It is even possible in a very high degree of acceleration that an individual may be immobilized completely. An observer may watch an approaching tornado with mild excitement. As the tornado comes closer, and it becomes clear that he is in its path, this interest may be heightened to even greater attention and activity as he seeks shelter. Finally, with the tornado upon him, it may even result in so great an emotion as to "paralyze him with fright."

EMOTION AND TENSION. In the past there has been a tendency to regard emotion as a cause of behavior. This appears to be a confusion of the symptom for the cause. Some writers have spoken of a child's aggressive behavior as being a *result* of its anger, or a mother's overprotection as a *result* of her love for her child, and it is extremely frequent to find references to behavior occurring "*because* the individual is afraid."

It is probably more accurate to say that emotion is a state of tension or readiness to act. This tension represents the reaction of the organism to the perception of the possibility of need satisfaction (self enhancement) or the perception of threat (maintenance of self.) Thus, emotion is a behavioral manifestation of the organism's attempt to satisfy need. As is true of any other behavior, tension, or emotion, may be regarded as an aspect of the activity of the organism in seeking adequacy.

What the individual describes as his emotion is actually his account of his personal relation to the situation. The greater the personal reference, the greater is the degree of emotional experience. It is well known, for example, that stage fright is a function of this personal reference. The greater the attention to self, the greater is the likelihood of crippling emotional reactions. If the speaker can use a common technique and "get his mind off himself" such emotional responses quickly disappear. Almost any school child is familiar with the stunt of getting another to blush by focusing the latter's attention on himself. The blusher may also be aware that he can quickly reduce his tension if he can turn his attention and that of others away from himself.

THE DEGREE OF TENSION EXPERIENCED. The person under tension is seeking satisfaction of need. The feeling of tension is the result of his awareness either of menace to his organization or to the possibility of self enhancement. The degree of tension experienced will vary widely dependent upon at least the following factors:

1. The perceived relationship of an event to the phenomenal self.
2. The psychological immediacy of the event.
3. The clarity of the perception.
4. The individual's feeling of adequacy to cope with the matter.

The first of these factors we have just been discussing. We might state it as follows: The degree of emotion or tension experienced by the individual will be roughly proportional to the perceived importance of the relationship of the event to the self.

PSYCHOLOGICAL IMMEDIACY AND EMOTION. The second factor affecting the degree of emotion or tension experienced will be the nearness in time and space of the threatening or enhancing object. Threats or enhancements occurring right now are perceived as much more menacing or flattering than those which are some time off. Atomic bombing ten years from now does not seem nearly as threatening as planes overhead today. The grade which comes at the end of the semester is not nearly so threatening in the first few weeks as it becomes during final exam week.

When we speak of the "nearness" of an event in time or space it should be clear that we are speaking of closeness as it appears from the point of view of the behaver, not an outside observer. This is a matter of "psychological" rather than physical immediacy. The tiger which I see through my binoculars a mile off will cause me much less concern than the one on the other side of that bush. In speaking of proximity in space it is necessary to think, not in terms of physical space, but in terms of psychological space. The tiger behind the bars at the zoo may be no further away than the one behind the bush, but in terms of my own perceptions he is, even so, at a very safe distance. This principle of the immediacy of threat is nicely illustrated in the neurotic whose anxiety increases markedly and whose attempts to escape become more frantic as he approaches in time and space the threat he perceives to himself. There are always more "nervous breakdowns" at a university just before final exams than at any other time.

All of the illustrations we have used here have been with respect to threat. The principle is just as true in terms of enhancement. When Christmas is six months away, the prospect of a picnic *today* is much more exciting to the child than the bicycle Santa Claus promises to bring next winter.

THE CLARITY OF PERCEPTION AND EMOTION. A third factor affecting the degree of emotion or tension will be the clarity with which the situation is differentiated by the individual as dangerous or enhancing to the phenomenal self. In newborn babies, for example, the awareness of environment is so vague that only extreme and sudden changes in it will arouse responses violent enough to seem emotional to others. As the child develops, differentiations become more precise, and sometime after he is six months old he may burst into tears at the approach of a stranger or when placed on the floor in a strange house. His parents may be quite at a loss to explain his behavior because he has never shown such reactions in similar situations before. The real reason for his behavior, however, is probably this: That he had not previously differentiated his environment with sufficient clarity to distinguish what was strange and different.

It is quite possible for an individual to be in the midst of a highly dangerous situation, yet feel no emotion or tension whatever. One can stand in the midst of a sunny field enjoying the country air without feeling in danger so long as one does not know that the field is impregnated with hydrogen-bomb "fall-out." An event unperceived is unexperienced and calls for no behavior in response. This is not just an all or none problem, however, for clarity of perception is a matter of degree and the emotion experienced is likely to be roughly equivalent to the clarity of perception, other factors being equal. Thus a vaguely perceived danger may produce a mild degree of tension. The clearer the perception of menace or enhancement, the greater is likely to be the accompanying experience of emotion.

THE FEELING OF ADEQUACY AND EMOTION. The degree of tension experienced appears to depend upon the individual's evaluation of the amount of enhancement or threat to himself he perceives in any situation. The novice at flying may be quite upset by the very thought of leaving the ground, while after such an experience he may even seek further opportunities to fly because he so enjoys the excitement. The pilot of his plane, on the other hand, may be quite bored with it all and find his job monotonous and dull. Since the threat or enhancement involved in any situation is for each of us a completely unique function, it is clear that the emotion we experience must also be different for each of us.

The amount of need satisfaction inherent in any situation will be dependent upon the relationship which the situation bears to the phenomenal self as observed by the individual. Obviously, the person who conceives of himself as a very effective and popular public speaker will have a very different approach to an invitation to speak before an audience from one who conceives of himself as inadequate or of queer appearance. For the accomplished speaker it can be truly said that the idea of anyone's laughing at him on the platform "never enters his head," while for the novice this thought may be very nearly paralyzing in the emotional response it calls forth.

The degree of emotion or tension experienced will be determined very largely by the individual's feeling of adequacy to deal with the event he perceives himself confronted with. The things we feel adequate to cope with do not have an emergency character in our perceptions. They seem far less frightening and distressing than those things which seem beyond our control or capacities. Individuals who feel generally adequate suffer much less the incapacitating effects of emotion than persons who feel generally inadequate. Persons with concepts of themselves as generally unliked, unwanted, unacceptable, unable, and unworthy often find the tension they experience so great that they may be unable to operate effectively and efficiently. Instead, they are in a continual state of emergency, and the emotions they experience are destructive rather than helpful in maintaining and enhancing themselves.

The Phenomenal Self and Feeling

Most of us in the course of our daily lives make no distinction between our "feelings" and our "emotions." In attempting to communicate with other people we talk about our feelings or emotions of hate, anger, love, fear, anxiety, appreciation, or grief without stopping to define more precisely what it is we mean. Other people in turn grasp pretty effectively what we are trying to say. Whether we talk about feelings or emotions is, in everyday life, a matter of no great moment. The important thing is that we be able to communicate effectively with other people so that they understand something of what it is we are experiencing. The psychologist, however, trying to understand the nature and dynamics of behavior, cannot be content with so free and easy a use of terms. To shed light on the problems psychology is attempting to deal with, it is necessary to distinguish more clearly and precisely the concepts we use. This does not mean that the layman is wrong and the psychologist right or vice versa. It means only that different degrees of exactness in description are required for different purposes. The layman uses terms in his way for his purposes, and the psychologist uses terms in other ways for other purposes.

From the psychologist's view, what are these things we call our "feelings"? When we speak of our feelings, we are seeking to convey the personal meaning of an event for us. When we say we are "so mad at Jim," we are trying to communicate to someone else the particular meaning our interaction with Jim has for us. This feeling, "so mad at Jim," is the best we can do to translate the full flavor of our perceptions about ourselves and our relationship to Jim at a particular instant. Similarly, when we say "I love you," "I was scared stiff!" or "I wanted to sink through the floor," we are attempting to communicate either to ourselves or to others the particular meaning of a particular situation as we experienced it. Feelings are a kind of shorthand description of our perceptual fields at a particular moment.

Feelings are our perceptions of ourselves, of the situations in which we are involved, and the interrelationship of these two. This is a great deal to attempt to express in a single word or two, and it is not surprising that most of us feel our spoken words never quite convey the full flavor of what it is we experience.

What we experience at any moment is, of course, our whole perceptual field. To convey this, however, is patently impossible. To manipulate our own perceptions or to communicate them to others we need a kind of symbol by means of which we can express our field state. To express these perceptions of ourselves and the state of our respective fields we have developed a large number of symbols to convey our meanings to others. We speak of feeling angry, tired, blue, gay, in love, anxious, afraid, grateful, and a thousand others. These represent our attempts to convey to others the personal meanings events have for us. They are our attempts to translate our own perceptual fields in a way that can be understood by others. The deeper, more pervasive the meaning for us, the less likely are we to be able to express it satisfactorily. Our perceptual fields are so complex and include such a myriad host of perceptions that it is a wonder we are able to convey as much as we do to an outsider who has not experienced it with us.

Since the individual's bodily self is always a part of his perceptual field, a very large part of what a person describes as his feeling is made up of his awareness of the bodily conditions he differentiates in the field at that moment. Our body states are always with us and always in some degree a part of the perceptual field. This includes, of course, awareness of our state of tension or acceleration, which we described as emotion in the previous section. Almost all of the feelings we express convey to our hearers some sense of our physical status. For example, when I say that "I feel fine," what I am describing is the nature of my field at that moment including the state of my body. This is my way of expressing to others the vague organization of physiologic conditions existing within me at the moment as well as perhaps my knowledge of having achieved something noteworthy. If I am pressed for further description I might say "I feel vigorous," "my body tone is up," or "I feel like I could lick my weight in wildcats." On the other hand, when I feel "blue," if pressed I would probably tell you that I feel "funny in the stomach," "feel tired," "heavy in the chest," etc. The more intense the feeling, the more of this awareness of body state is conveyed. The terms "rage," "hate," "fright," "love" all carry strong feelings of body state even to the listener. Some psychologists have rather plainly although inelegantly described these kinds of words as "gut words" because they seem to include so very large an experience of our visceral states.

What we attempt to communicate by our feelings, then, is the state of our perceptual fields including our state of tension or acceleration. Feelings differ from emotion, however, in that they symbolize *all* of the perceptual field. The degree of tension experienced would express very little to other people without some further description of what brought on this state. To say "I felt very tense" conveys very little until we add to this a description of the meaning of the tension for us. It makes a good deal of difference whether we are talking about a degree of tension brought on by another person as anger, fear, or love. Feelings always include the emotional condition as an important factor in the total perceptual state, but usually extend far beyond body status.

Since feelings always include emotion, we would expect that the intensity of feeling would vary in the same ways as emotion, and this is actually the case. Like emotion, the intensity of feeling is likely to be a function of: (1) the perceived relationship of an event to the phenomenal self, (2) the psychological immediacy of the event, (3) the clarity of the perception, and (4) the personal feeling of adequacy possessed by the subject.

Often feelings, which are really descriptions of perceptual field states, have been confused with causes of behavior. Actually they represent no more than the individual's differentiation of a part of his field in symbolic and often highly stereotyped terms. As descriptions it is clear they cannot be causes of behavior. When a person says "I did it because I felt like it," what he is describing in a vague way is his perceptual field at the moment of his act. When he says he "felt angry" and struck his assailant, or felt "afraid" and fled from the scene, his behavior was not motivated by the feeling but was a result of the perceptions existing in the perceptual field at the moment. In either case, his bodily state was probably identical, for we know that the physiologic aspects of any "emotion" are always the same in kind though they may differ in degree. As a matter of fact, if the threat to his organization was very great he probably was not even aware of his "feelings." It is a common experience that in moments of great stress we may act with extreme vigor and are often surprised to find we did not feel afraid till the moment of crisis had passed. This is probably due to the fact that we were not aware of our body state during the moment of crisis and only became so when sufficient leisure was reached for attention to be directed to body conditions. Being "afraid" is thus the individual's description of his state—his personal reference and has nothing to do with cause or effect of the behavior of the moment of action. The behavior is the result of the perceptual field, not the feeling which describes the field.

It should not be supposed, that the feelings *as reported by* an individual are necessarily the same as those he experiences. What an individual feels is an internal experience going on in his own private world. What he chooses to reveal of this sanctuary to an outsider may have a more or less accurate relationship to the feelings he really possesses. Even with the best of intentions, it is likely that he can never succeed in conveying the full flavor of his perceptual experience to another. It is even true that a large part of our time and effort is spent in preventing other people from knowing what it is we are feeling about particular matters. Most of us want to keep our private worlds intact, and even those whom we love and trust most can never be fully admitted to this inner sanctum. Feelings as experienced and feelings as reported to other people are by no means one and the same.

Some writers have made a distinction between "intellectual" behavior and "emotional" behavior. They point out that some things we do seem to be the result of our thinking about things, while other activities seem to be the outcome of how we feel about things. This is, of course, a false dichotomy. We cannot separate intellectual from feeling functions. All our behavior is always a function of the total perceptual field at the moment of behaving. Some events seem to us to be more closely related to ourselves and may be accompanied by more or less tension. In this sense, some events are more likely to be matters about which we have definite feelings than others, but no behavior can ever be purely intellectual or emotional. All behaviors are a product of our perceptions and all involve a greater or lesser degree of acceleration or tension.

In this discussion we have talked primarily of the individual's own feelings. We have said that the words he uses to describe his feelings are symbols by which he tries to convey something of the nature of his perceptual field to other people. Other people use similar words to describe the state of their perceptual fields in their turn. We thus become aware, not only of our own perceptual fields, but also to some degree of the fields of others through this kind of communication.

But language alone is by no means the only source of information about the fields of others. We are able to understand a great deal about how other people feel from the clues they give us through their behavior. Observing other people's behavior (including, of course, what they have to say, which is a kind of behavior too), we are able to infer something of what they are feeling and this makes it possible for us to understand something of the nature of the perceptual field which lies behind their actions. This ability to "feel like another" or to "place oneself in another's shoes" is called *empathy*. It is a talent possessed in some degree by all of us, although some of us have developed it far more than others. It is an important factor in communication and in effective human relations.

CHAPTER 12

The Adequate Personality

ADJUSTMENT AND MALADJUSTMENT

Our unceasing striving for feelings of worth and value places all of us under the necessity for adjusting to something at every moment of our lives. Some of us are more successful in achieving need satisfaction than others, but none of us is ever granted leave from the struggle for any length of time. In the course of this never-ending search we may behave in countless varieties of ways. Other people looking at our behavior may describe us as adjusted or maladjusted, depending upon the degree to which our behavior conforms to their peculiar values. From our own points of view, however, we do not describe ourselves as adjusted or maladjusted unless we are students of psychology or persons who are accustomed to trying to see themselves "objectively." Most of us describe ourselves in terms of our "feelings." We say we are happy or unhappy, satisfied or dissatisfied, angry or in love, depending upon the extent to which our need is being satisfied, and upon our progress toward the goals through which we are seeking to satisfy it.

The terms "adjustment" and "maladjustment" are terms from an external frame of reference. They are objective terms used to describe behavior as it appears to an outside observer. More often than not they are applied to evaluations of the extent to which an individual's behavior conforms to social expectancy. This approach to the nature of adjustment is a static one. It establishes a "norm" for behavior and thereafter judges individuals as "adjusted" or "maladjusted" depending upon their degree of conformity to such norms. Almost inevitably labels of "bad" and "good" also become attached to behavior of one variety or the other.

While the terms "adjusted" and "maladjusted" have a real usefulness in an external setting, they are likely to prove inadequate in helping us to understand the behavior of a unique human being. Many a "maladjusted" individual appears to be quite well satisfied with himself and many a seemingly "well-adjusted" person may actually be a desperately unhappy individual who conforms to others because he lacks confidence in himself. What brings the person to the psychological clinic is not the situation as it is seen by others, but the situation as he sees it himself. The case histories in any clinic reveal dozens of persons whom others would judge to be quite well adjusted, but who still feel so ineffective or unhappy that they seek the assistance of the psychologist. It even happens that persons tortured and driven by feelings of inadequacy have sometimes been pointed out with pride as examples of industry and perseverance for our children. On college campuses, homosexuals have been voted the "best-adjusted girl in our sorority." External observations are by no means adequate in understanding the particular human being.

Though the concepts of "adjustment" and "maladjustment" are useful in an external frame of reference for the classification of behavior, they have little value to the behaver himself. People behave according to their feelings or perceptions at any moment and it is seldom that "adjustment" per se is the goal toward which an individual strives. Who, after all, wishes to be average? Most of us may have to settle for such a state, but few of us are content to remain there if any other possibilities seem open to us. Adjustment in the normative sense is hardly desirable as a goal for society either. A society all of whose people were busily engaged in seeking to be average would soon find itself hopelessly outmoded and sitting still while the rest of the world passed by. We need a concept of adjustment which represents an achievement to strive for; a concept which defines the *best man can be* rather than the average of what he has been.

Actually, the best he can be is what each one of us is striving for in everything he does. The goal of all behavior, we have seen, is the achievement of personal adequacy. The search for the maintenance and enhancement of self is never ending. It is a dynamic, active search, a continuous striving to become the ultimate of which one is capable. Other authors have called this active "seeking to become" by such names as: "growth tendency," "self-consistency," "self-realization," "self-actualization," and "self-fulfillment."

Though each of us strives continuously to achieve an adequate personality, it should not be supposed that such an end is ever reached. On the contrary, this is a goal toward which all of us struggle but at which none of us ever arrives. Adequacy is a mark we can achieve only in degree; some of us more, some of us less, but none of us ever completely. Some unhappy people live out their lives with little or no feeling of adequacy, while other people achieve high degrees of satisfaction and pleasure from feelings of adequacy in very great measure. But not even the most adequate man who ever lived was able to achieve the fullest possible extent of adequacy. So long as life exists there is room and need for further effort.

What Is an Adequate Personality?

There are two ways in which we can attempt to examine the adequate personality. We can look at such a personality in terms of his observable behavior. We can ask, "How does such a person behave?" or "What are the particular behavioral traits that characterize an adequate person?" This is the approach taken by Maslow, who has attempted to study a number of self-actualizing persons with an eye to discovering the kinds of behaviors typical of such people. Since behavior is a function of perception, we can also approach the study of the adequate personality by an exploration of how such persons perceive themselves and the world in which they live. This latter approach is more consistent with the point of view of this book, so let us begin our exploration by examining how the adequate personality sees himself and the world. Having examined the ways in which adequate personalities perceive we may then take a look at the kinds of behaviors characteristic of such people.

The Perceptual View of Adequacy

Generally speaking, we could describe the adequate personality in perceptual terms as one who has achieved a high degree of need satisfaction. These are people who feel generally capable of coping with life, who have developed phenomenal selves so defined as to be highly successful in the achievement of effective maintenance and enhancement of self. They see themselves in essentially positive ways and as a consequence are free and open to their experience, able to accept both themselves and others and to identify strongly with their fellow men. Adequate people feel strong enough and safe enough to cope with life openly and directly with a minimum of threat and fear. They see themselves and the world in which they live more often than not as exciting and challenging. Life does not seem too much to such people. Events seem to them to lie well within their own capacities, and they feel capable of dealing with life effectively and efficiently. Indeed, they might almost equally well be called nonthreatened personalities.

Examining more closely the perceptual fields of adequate persons it seems possible to differentiate three major characteristics: (1) Adequate persons perceive themselves in generally positive ways. (2) Adequate persons are more capable of accepting and integrating their perceptions in the phenomenal field. (3) Adequate persons are capable of wide identification of self with others. It should not be supposed that these are discrete characteristics capable of operating by themselves. On the contrary, the perceptual field is a unitary organization, and the operation of these three factors is so mutually interdependent as to remind one of the old adage about "which came first, the chicken or the egg?"

POSITIVE SELF PERCEPTIONS

The self concept as we have described it is an organization of self meanings or ways of seeing self, varying in importance or centrality in a given individual. The basic need of each of us, moreover, is to maintain and enhance this self. Adequate personalities have achieved a considerable degree of such need satisfaction. They see themselves more frequently in enhancing than in destructive ways. In our society this usually means that adequate people see themselves, among other things, as liked, wanted, acceptable, able, and worthy. They perceive themselves as persons of dignity and integrity who belong and contribute to the world in which they operate. Their phenomenal selves are, for the most part, defined in positive ways as adequate to deal with those aspects of life important to the achievement of need satisfaction in their culture.

In another culture, to be sure, adequate people might perceive themselves differently. Most of us would feel woefully inadequate in a society which valued skill in the war dance, for example. Within the confines of the society important to him, however, the adequate personality perceives himself as capable and effective. The majority of the concepts of self which go to make up his peculiar phenomenal self are positive and appropriate to the culture in which he lives out his days.

This is not to say that adequate personalities are incapable of negative self perceptions. On the contrary, they may very well have negative concepts of self within the total organization of the phenomenal self. An adequate person might conceivably have within his self organization such concepts of self as: "I am not a very attractive person, I am thoroughly disliked by my father-in-law, I am a terrible golfer, joke teller, and typist." Negative concepts of self are not absent in the total organization of the adequate personality. They are present, but do not color and distort the entire organization. Such percepts maintain their proper perspective as parts of the self concept, but do not overbalance it. A very large part of the assistance rendered to people in psychotherapy consists primarily of helping them to gain a new perspective of self so that negative self perceptions do not exert an undue influence upon the organization of the phenomenal self. Adequate personalities have essentially although not exclusively positive concepts of self.

Concepts of self, we have seen, vary not only in number but also in centrality or importance to the individual. Adequacy is not simply a function of the *number* of positive perceptions; it is a function of the *importance* of the concepts of self possessed by a given personality. The important or central aspects of self have a greater effect on the total economy of a personality than do peripheral or marginal self percepts. It is being spurned by *the* girl which depresses the lover, although he may be attractive to dozens of others. A thousand good acts may be insufficient to counteract the feeling of guilt from a single act of years past. The child's perception of what his playmates say of him may be of far more importance than his teacher's good opinion. A plumber coming to fix the radiators in our play-therapy room was shocked to discover the freedom permitted our young clients. The idea of permitting a child to wet on the floor was completely repugnant to him, and he criticized our "damfool" notions in no uncertain terms. This attitude on the part of the plumber bothered us very little. Had the same ideas been expressed by an honored and respected colleague, our reaction would have been very different. We do not care much what a plumber thinks of our professional techniques; we care very much what some psychologists think.

A self concept organized of many positive self definitions provides the individual with a great resource for dealing with the vicissitudes of life. Many positive self perceptions give the individual a feeling of adequacy and confidence, so that he approaches the events of life with an essentially positive, assured bearing which, in itself, is an important head start. Research on leadership suggests that leaders generally possess more favorable attitudes toward self and others. The very presumption of success is likely to make success more likely. Moreover, positive self perceptions are conducive to still further perceptions of the same order.

This is a common observation which finds its place in our folk sayings: "Nothing succeeds like success," "Them as has, gets," "The rich get richer and the poor get poorer."

The positive self perceptions characteristic of the adequate personality act also as a reservoir against which negative, damaging experiences are perceived in a more accurate and realistic perspective. Because the self is overwhelmingly defined in positive terms, most negative self perceptions can be readily assimilated in such a reservoir with little or no disturbance to the whole structure. Negative events can be accepted and taken in stride. Feeling fundamentally self confident, the adequate person is less ruffled by unhappy events. He finds it possible to take criticism calmly and to evaluate it clearly. Instead of being disorganized by minor self-damaging experiences, negative percepts are evaluated against the larger mass of basically positive experience, in which perspective they seem far less important or overwhelming.

Since adequate personalities do not feel deprived, they have far less need to defend the self against external attack. Assaults upon self do not seem crucial or overwhelming. Rather, they seem well within the capacities of the self to cope with and even, if they are minor attacks, may be perceived by the adequate personality as exciting and challenging opportunities to test his mettle. For adequate persons, self testing can itself be an exhilarating experience to be met with interest and joy. For such people the trying is often more exciting and enhancing than the achieving. The possession of a large reservoir of positive experience of self provides the individual with a vast security to be used as a base for adventure and a firm foundation for meeting even the more difficult aspects of life with courage.

This fundamentally positive self organization seems characteristic of "well-adjusted" people seen from an external frame of reference as well. Numerous studies of "adjustment" have demonstrated that well-adjusted persons have essentially positive attitudes toward self and others, while the reverse is true of "poorly adjusted" people. Psychological health seems basically determined by the adequacy of the individual's self definitions. Effective living is closely allied to personal feelings of dignity and integrity, to feelings of worth and self actualization.

ACCEPTANCE AND ADEQUACY

A second major characteristic of the adequate personality is his ability to accept any and all perceptions into his awareness. As Rogers has pointed out, an individual confronted with a particular event may deal with it in any of three ways. The experience may be: (a) symbolized, perceived and organized into some relationship to the self; (b) ignored because there is no perceived relationship to the self structure; (c) denied symbolization or given a distorted symbolization because the experience is inconsistent with the structure of the self. The first of these methods of dealing with perceptions is what we mean by acceptance. An adequate personality is one capable of admitting any and all experiences and of integrating this experience into his existing self structure. Such a person can acknowledge his experience, allow it entrance to his consideration, and relate it in some fashion to the existing concepts he holds of himself and the world about him.

This characteristic is so important a factor in the perceptions of adequate personalities that in the earlier edition of this book the adequate personality was defined solely "as one capable of accepting into its organization any and all experience of reality." While acceptance is certainly an outstanding characteristic, it is hardly sufficient to define the adequate person in those terms alone. Acceptance is, itself, a function of the extent and nature of the already existing perceptions in the field. In the section just above we have seen that the adequate personality has a phenomenal field containing many positive self perceptions. The very existence of these perceptions makes acceptance more likely. Acceptance is thus a characteristic of adequate personalities derived from and largely made possible by the individual's positive experience of self. Because such persons have a reservoir of positive experience they are able to accept. Acceptance, in turn, makes possible even greater adequacy.

Adequate personalities do not feel a great need to defend themselves against their experience. They have an openness or readiness for new experience and are capable of reorganizing the phenomenal field to make most effective use of it. This willingness to confront experience has sometimes been confused with resignation. Adequate personalities, however, are by no means resigned. On the contrary, they are quite likely to be among our most important agents of social change. A readiness to admit the *existence* of an idea by no means implies its adoption. The acknowledgment of the presence of an event must be the first step to effective action. The readiness to receive and consider the facts about Communism, for example, does not mean a whole-hearted or even a faint-hearted conversion to such ideals. The acceptance of the facts may actually be the first step in a vigorous defense against such concepts. Acceptance refers to the admission of evidence, not a commitment to a line of action.

Clearly acceptance, in the sense we have used it here, is a *sine qua non* for effective, efficient, satisfying behavior. The individual able to accept is open to all experience. He has fewer limits imposed upon what he can explore and examine. He has less need to defend or distort his experiences and so is capable of examining even that which is too frightening or unpleasant for less adequate personalities to consider. This straightforward, uncomplicated kind of relationship to his experience gives the adequate personality a tremendous advantage in dealing with life, for behavior based upon more and better evidence will almost certainly be more effective, efficient, and satisfying in the long run.

This open, "all-the-cards-on-the-table" kind of relationship to events occurring about him is just as characteristic of the adequate personality's approach to perceptions about himself. Adequate personalities are just as capable of accepting their experience of self as of events in the not self. Maslow has expressed this relationship as follows:

> They can accept their own human nature with all its shortcomings, with all its discrepancies from the ideal image without feeling real concern. It would convey the wrong impression to say that they are self-satisfied. What we must say rather is that they can take the frailties and sins, weaknesses and evils of human nature in the same unquestioning spirit that one takes or accepts the characteristics of nature. One does not complain about water because it is wet, or about rocks because they are hard, or about trees because they are green. As the child looks out upon the world with wide, uncritical, innocent eyes, simply noting and observing what is the case, without either arguing the matter or demanding that it be otherwise, so does the self-actualizing person look upon human nature in himself and in others.

Taylor and Combs, for example, found this ability to accept self to be highly related to adjustment. They asked a group of fifth grade children to indicate on a list of 20 unflattering statements, probably true of all children, those which each child believed were true of himself. When these results were next compared to the same child's scores on a test of adjustment, highest scores were found among the best-adjusted children and vice versa. The better the child's adjustment, the more unflattering truths he was able to accept about himself! The admission of the existence of unflattering truth about self is often the first step toward more effective behavior. Indeed, many churches recognize this age-old principle, and utilize it in the confessional in the belief that confession (acceptance of the fact) of sin is the first step toward reformation.

Acceptance of self should not be confused with "liking." Some experimenters, for example, have attempted to measure self acceptance by asking subjects to indicate the degree to which they liked certain characteristics about themselves. But acceptance is no more related to liking than it is to resignation. Acceptance has to do with the admission of fact, the acknowledgment of existence, and has nothing to do with liking. The adequate personality may accept the fact, for example, that he is sometimes nasty to his children, but this hardly means that he likes himself so! Liking and disliking have to do with judgments about self, while acceptance is nonjudgmental. It has to do with the consideration of evidence, not its evaluation. The adequate personality neither overvalues nor undervalues self. He is maximally able to put his "self" on the block for examination and scrutiny like any other datum. Research on the outcomes of psychotherapy corroborates this characteristic of adequacy. The data show that as clients get better (and presumably more adequate) their capacity to accept both self and others increases markedly.

While acceptance is most notably characteristic of the perceptions of adequate persons, it is also characteristic in more or less degree by every human being. It is only through some degree of acceptance that any individual is able to profit from his experience. What distinguishes the adequate personality from his fellows is that he has achieved this ability in greater degree than the rest of us. The effect of a capacity for acceptance, furthermore, is cumulative. The wider, richer experience made possible by acceptance contributes to an ever more adequate phenomenal field and phenomenal self. In turn, the kind of self assurance possessed by the adequate person places him under less need to deny or distort his experience and thus leads to still further achievements of adequacy. A phenomenal self becomes adequate in part by acceptance; and the more adequate a person feels, the more acceptant he becomes.

THE ADEQUATE SELF AND IDENTIFICATION

We have constructed so far a definition of an adequate self from the individual's own frame of reference. But no individual in our society lives in isolation. Whether or not any person achieves need satisfaction does not depend upon himself alone but upon his interaction with his environment and the society he lives in. Presumably an individual could get along for a time on a desert island without other people, but few of us would choose such an existence. The concept is in large part a definition of the relationship between the self and society and must be in harmony with that portion of the culture important to the individual. We are so entirely dependent upon the good will and coöperation of others in our society that it would be impossible to achieve feelings of adequacy without some effective relationship with them. The adequate personality must be capable of living effectively and efficiently with his fellows.

The self, we have seen, is not a static and unchangeable organization. Rather, it is a more or less fluid organization capable of change and redefinition in the light of the individual's experience. The self may, for example, be so narrowly defined as to exclude some aspects of self which are apparent to others. It sometimes happens, for example, that handicapped persons may define themselves in such a way as to disown their handicaps. Similar physical manifestations of a restricted self definition can be found in hypnosis when a subject is told he cannot feel what is happening to him. With such a restricted self definition, he may not respond at all to a cigarette burn, for it does not seem to him to be happening to him. All of us are familiar with persons who have defined themselves in such a way as to deny some of their less pleasant characteristics.

Fortunately, the self may also be defined in ways that extend beyond the confines of self, so that one may, almost literally, rise above himself. We may extend the physical confines of ourselves when we point with a stick and we have a feeling of touch, not in our fingers but at the end of the stick. We may extend ourselves also by the use of a gun, a telephone, or a letter. Having written to another person, we say: "I told him . . . ," although it was the letter that did so. The business world is dependent upon the extension of self we achieve by signing our names to a contract. Most important of all, however, is the kind of self extension we achieve through identification with other people. In the course of growing up, each of us becomes more or less identified with large numbers of people and events, sometimes only remotely, but sometimes, too, so closely as to make it almost impossible to distinguish between "me and thee." People become identified with parents, husbands or wives, teachers, institutions, towns, races, nations, and a million other categories. These identifications become basic parts of self and we therefore speak of *my* daughter, *my* country, *my* fraternity, *my* race, *we* Southerners, or *us* Texans. Whatever the identification, it becomes part of an expanded self.

What is more, since the fundamental need of the individual is to maintain and enhance the phenomenal self, whatever the self is identified with must also be maintained and enhanced. Praise heaped upon those with whom we are identified is received as though it were personally earned. We rejoice at the winning of *our* team, the happiness of *our* wives or husbands, and we share the tragedies of *our* friends and neighbors. The individual behaves toward those things, people, or places with which he is identified as though they were, in truth, himself. The doctor cannot operate on his daughter any more than he can on himself. The psychologist can understand somebody else's children with greater objectivity than his own. The maintenance and enhancement of self becomes extended to those with whom we are identified, and the satisfaction of our own need becomes almost indistinguishable from the satisfaction of theirs, too.

To some people first exposed to the idea that each human being is insatiably seeking the maintenance and enhancement of self, it appears that people must indeed be extremely selfish beings intent only upon self gratification. This is only true, however, for the isolated personalities, the rejected hangers-on of our society. The stronger an individual's identification with others, the more certain it is that in seeking his own maintenance and enhancement he will be seeking that of others as well. He must, for they are one and the same. The need for adequacy in the individual extends to the people, things, places, events, and ideas with whom and with which he becomes identified. The more adequate the personality, the broader and deeper will be the relationships he has discovered between self and others. The more adequate the personality, the more likely he is to feel a sense of oneness with things and people about him. Adequate personalities behave in ways beneficial to all of us, not because it is a good thing to do, but because behaving so is a normal and natural expression of themselves. It is not the adequate people we need to fear in our society; they are likely to be so closely identified with us that they seek our needs along with their own. It is only the people that do not feel they belong who see no need to consider the good of others and to abide by the rules. It is the inadequate persons, the deprived, the rejected, the alone in our society who, seeing themselves apart from the rest of us, can behave in ways that are dangerous and destructive.

Psychology has long pointed out that the development of the child is from a state of egocentricity as an infant to altruism as an adult. That is, the very young child is primarily concerned with gratification of his own personal need. He wants what he wants when he wants it! Nothing is more tyrannical than a newborn baby. Even a child's parents are only objects to him at first, and it is only with time that he learns to identify himself with a particular person as *Mother* and a particular person as *Father*. Later he comes to identify himself with others of his family, then his neighborhood, his school, and after a time, with his town and country. The growth of an adult human being is a process of increasing identification with the world about him. Little by little over the years of his existence each human being discovers his unique relationship to people and events. Some people, like the saints, have developed this feeling of identification to a degree wherein they could feel at one with all mankind or even with all life. Some, like the criminals or the insane, live out their lives in isolation. Most of us lie somewhere between in our capacity for identification.

The more adequate we become, the greater the identification we achieve. Acceptance of self is closely related to acceptance of others. The modern closely interrelated society requires that effective citizens be deeply aware of their fellows and behave responsibly toward them. Adequacy requires both the discovery of self and the discovery of others.

The Trait Versus Perceptual Approach to Understanding Adequacy

It is the basic premise of this book that all behavior is a function of perception. It would follow, then, that the perceptual characteristics of adequate personalities should have their counterparts in behavior. And indeed this seems to be true. We have described adequate personalities as those who: (1) perceive themselves in essentially positive ways, (2) are capable of acceptance of self and others, and (3) perceive themselves as closely identified with others.

The more adequate the personality, the more these ways of perceiving self and the relationship to the world about him will be characteristic of the individual's phenomenal field. Such perceptions in turn will often cause such persons to behave repeatedly in certain ways. Behavior may even become so predictable and characteristic as to be described by the external observer as "personality traits." Similarly, because they perceive in more common ways, the behaviors of several different adequate persons are likely to be highly similar. Thus, certain kinds of behavior seem fairly generally characteristic of adequate persons. It should not be presumed, however, that these common kinds of behaviors are *always* present in every adequate personality. Nor can they be used as criteria to determine the degree of a given person's adequacy. Behavior is always a function of the individual's total field at the moment of action, and similar perceptions in the fields of different people will not necessarily result in identical behaviors. A way of behaving which deals satisfactorily with one problem may be totally inappropriate for another. Therefore we cannot judge adequacy solely on the basis of the presence or absence of particular traits. Truly adequate people are not rigid personalities. They have sufficient fluidity of perception and action as to be maximally effective in the situations to which they are exposed. This kind of effective interaction requires a high degree of sensitivity and openness to change when such change is necessary. As a consequence, the behavioral traits of such people cannot be employed as guides for the behavior of everyone else.

Those people in our society charged with the responsibility for helping others to grow and develop into effective, adequate citizens need to understand very clearly the difference between an external trait approach to the question of adequacy and a personal, perceptual approach. The achievement of adequacy is the fundamental need of both the individual and his society. Whatever we believe about the nature of the adequate personality, therefore, sets the goals for our personal growth as well as the goals toward which we strive in helping others to achieve adequacy in our homes, schools, or community life. An understanding of the nature of adequacy solely in terms of the ways adequate people frequently behave leads directly to attempts to catalogue "good" ways of behaving, and then to an attempt to teach these ways to others.

Such a trait approach to helping people often fails because it is exclusively concerned with *what people do.* What people do, however, is only a symptom or the expression of the dynamic factors within the individual that produce his unique ways of behaving. Assisting others to achieve adequacy, therefore, by means of telling, exhorting, or "teaching" people how they should behave ordinarily has little chance of success. What seems appropriate to do in a given circumstance is always dependent upon the individual's need and the state of his perceptual field at the moment. Few of us behave inadequately because we do not know better. Mere knowledge of how adequate people behave is of little value to other people because it seems to have little relevance to their own peculiar needs and problems. Much as we may admire what our heroes have done, such action may seem too difficult, impossible, or irrelevant and inappropriate to the situation *we* perceive ourselves to be confronted with.

It is the fundamental thesis of this volume that behavior is a direct function of the individual's perceptual field and change in behavior can only occur when some change has occurred in how people perceive. In the following pages we have tried to describe some of the characteristic behaviors which seem typical of many adequate personalities. These "traits of adequacy" are interesting observations about adequate personalities made from the point of view of the external observer, and they give us clues to how adequate persons are likely to behave in our society. Interesting as these traits may be, it should be kept in mind that they do not provide satisfactory or effective direction for helping others to achieve greater adequacy. They are products, not causes. The perceptual characteristic of adequate personalities we have outlined above will provide us with far more dynamic and applicable guides to effective action. When people can be helped to see differently, they will behave differently. If people can be helped to perceive themselves and the world they live in more adequately, they will behave more adequately as well. With this reservation in mind, let us now look at some of the characteristic ways in which many adequate people behave.

Some Behavioral Characteristics of Adequate Persons

MORE EFFICIENT BEHAVIOR

Adequate personalities behave more effectively and efficiently than their less adequate fellows. The great reservoir of positive perceptions and the capacity for acceptance of self and the world gives the adequate person a tremendous advantage in dealing with life. Being under no great necessity for self defense he has less need to distort his perceptions or to select them in terms or his peculiar unfulfilled goals or desires. He is able to behave more effectively and efficiently because he behaves in the light of more and better data. Being more open to experience, he has a wider phenomenal field on which to base his behavior. He is able to behave more often from choice than from necessity.

Maslow, in a study of self-actualizing persons, has described such people as follows:

> The first form in which this capacity was noticed was an unusual ability to detect the spurious, the fake and the dishonest in personality, and, in general, to judge people correctly and efficiently. In an informal check experiment with a group of college students, a clear tendency was discerned for the more secure (the more healthy) to judge their professors more accurately than did the less secure students.
>
> As the study progressed, it slowly became apparent that this efficiency extended to many other areas of life—indeed *all* areas that were tested. In art and music, in things of the intellect, in scientific matters, in politics and public affairs, they seemed as a group to be able to see concealed or confused realities more swiftly and more correctly than others. Thus, an informal experiment indicated that their predictions of the future from whatever facts were in hand at the time seemed to be more often correct, because less based upon wish, desire, anxiety, fear, or upon generalized, character-determined optimism or pessimism. . . . They are, therefore, far more apt to perceive what is "there" rather than their own wishes, hopes, fears, anxieties, their own theories and beliefs or those of their cultural group.

In the dynamic relationship of perception to behavior, more adequate perceptual fields must necessarily result in more adequate behavior. People who perceive more efficiently will behave more efficiently. The individual who is able to behave from a phenomenal field open to more data has a great advantage over the rest of us. He is able to play a better game because he holds more and better cards. With more data available, adequate personalities are able to penetrate more directly and sharply to the heart of problems. They often possess an uncanny ability to place their finger on the core of issues and are thus able to deal with matters more precisely and appropriately. Their perceptions are less complicated by extraneous events, personal goals and values, or the necessity for immediate self gratification.

Because adequate persons feel fundamentally secure they are able to evaluate themselves more accurately. Their levels of aspiration are far more likely to be realistic and attainable. They are able to deal with events, and with themselves, with greater objectivity and equanimity. Feeling secure within himself, the adequate person has less need to hide from the unpleasant and can feel more comfortable with himself even when under attack. This fundamental security makes it possible to deal with events with less "personal axes to grind." It even makes it possible for the adequate person to risk himself. He is capable of placing himself in a poor or unflattering light if necessary, and this makes possible the consideration of evidence not open to the individual who is fearful and defensive of self. Adequate people are able to be and to give of themselves with courage and conviction.

Adequate personalities do not *need* to have an immediate answer to problems. They are capable of what Frenkel-Brunswik has called "toleration of ambiguity." That is, they are able to live comfortably with an unsolved problem. They do not *need* to have an answer at once. Consequently, they are less likely to accept partial solutions to problems as sufficient or final. With a backlog of security in their own feelings of adequacy, they are not easily upset when confronted by events whose meanings are not immediately apparent. They do not ignore such events in the hope that "if I don't notice it, it will go away." They do not find it necessary to deny that an event has happened, nor do they find themselves compelled to "explain it away." Because they do not *have* to have an answer, they are able to consider wider samples of evidence and to deal with events with far more patience than the rest of us.

The individual who is capable of seeing in broader perspective and with less necessity for arriving at foregone conclusions obviously has a wider choice of action. He can deal with matters more objectively and leisurely because there seems to him less at stake. As a consequence, such people are likely to make fewer mistakes and run up fewer blind alleys. The value of this capacity for society can hardly be overestimated. We need such talents to prevent our becoming the victims of unfortunate concepts adopted because they are convenient or fit the existing patterns of thought.

SPONTANEITY AND CREATIVITY

Closely associated with the greater efficiency of behavior of the adequate personality, and growing out of the same basic characteristics of the phenomenal field, is the capacity for spontaneous creative behavior. The reservoir of positive perceptions and the ability to accept new experience provides a firm basis from which the adequate person can launch into new and different areas of experience. It is the secure people who can take chances. They do not have to maintain rigid, narrow lines of operation. A rich self can afford to be extravagant, a poor one must shelter and protect his investments with scrupulous care and conservatism. Adequate people have far less need to defend themselves and consequently are able to devote much greater time and attention to wider fields of experience. Feeling fundamentally secure, they are capable of experimenting, branching out, extending themselves to the limit. They are even capable, when necessary, of placing themselves in jeopardy for the sheer joy of testing their own limits. As a consequence such people are to be found among the most spontaneous and creative people of every generation.

It is, of course, possible for people to break with the conventional from motives of weakness or fear. It has happened that people have made important contributions to human advance out of motives that were purely hostile. A man may, for example, develop a new technique out of anger at a supervisor or a desire to embarrass his foreman. People may also be creative out of an attempt to rebel against the existing system or from a desire to break out of the sheer monotony of existing patterns. The creativity of the adequate personality, however, does not seem to stem from this kind of rebellion. Rather, the spontaneity of adequate persons seems an outgrowth of their basic security and courage to break with tradition and orthodoxy, not because they feel deprived or deficient, but out of an opposite feeling of inner strength and security which permits them to risk themselves in experimentation.

This originality of adequate persons is what one would logically expect as a consequence of the broader, richer phenomenal fields characteristic of such people. With wider fields available and less need for self defense, adequate people sometimes seem to fairly "pop with ideas." They are capable of seeing relationships not seen by others. Their more efficient perceptions make it possible for them to penetrate more effectively to premises while others are still muddling about with techniques. Persons dealing with the *essence* of ideas rather than their forms are far less likely to confuse means and ends. They can concern themselves with problems and issues and avoid being so bogged down in detail as to miss the major aspects. Because they operate from more inclusive frames of reference, they can often perceive more adequate, creative, and original solutions to life problems.

The kind of openness to experience we have been discussing has another effect upon the behavior of adequate people. It makes possible a capacity for wonder and a sensitivity to events that makes a thrilling experience of much that may appear humdrum and ordinary to others. Maslow speaks of this as a continued freshness of appreciation and describes it as follows:

Self-actualized people have the wonderful capacity to appreciate again and again, freshly and naively the basic goods of life with awe, pleasure, wonder, and even ecstasy, however stale these experiences may have become to others. Thus, for such people, every sunset is as beautiful as the first one, any flower may be of breath-taking loveliness even after he has seen a million flowers. The thousandth baby he sees is just as miraculous a product as the first one he saw. He remains as convinced of his luck in marriage thirty years after his marriage and is as surprised by his wife's beauty when she is sixty as he was forty years before. For such people, even the casual workaday, moment-to-moment business of living can be thrilling, exciting, and ecstatic.

It will be recognized that the freedom of the phenomenal field characteristic of adequate personalities, their clearer, more accurate perceptions of events, and their capacity for originality are synonymous with what we usually mean by intelligence. In Chapter 11, we define intelligence as a function of the richness, extent, and availability of perceptions in the phenomenal field. The acquisition of such a phenomenal field is enormously enhanced when people feel adequate.

THE AUTONOMY OF ADEQUATE PERSONALITIES

Adequate persons often seem characterized by a much higher degree of independence of the social and physical forces which bind many of the rest of us. They seem less in the grip of external events and respond more to inner wellsprings of understanding and motivation. They have a profound respect for the dignity and integrity of themselves as well as of others and so utilize themselves and their experience as the basic frame of reference for much of their behavior. As a result, they are able to break loose from many of the petty tyrannies of their surroundings to deal with events straightforwardly and uncomplicatedly. This autonomy seems a direct outgrowth of the individual's openness to experience and trust in self.

We have already observed that the characteristic openness to experience of adequate personalities provides such people with a much wider, less complicated, more precise and accurate perception of events. As a consequence the behavior of adequate people is likely to be more effective and efficient than that of his less gifted fellows. This greater accuracy of perception produces more effective behavior and need satisfaction and is likely to cause the individual, over a period of time, to have an increasing trust in himself and his own capacities and perceptions. Such a trust is likely to be fostered further by the appreciation and admiration of other people who perceive and react to his behavior. The adequate personality discovers in one fashion or another that his self is a highly trustworthy, effective instrument. As a result he comes increasingly to trust his perceptions of self and the world about him. He discovers that his feelings, attitudes, beliefs, and understandings are more often than not effective and efficient guides to behaving. He utilizes himself and his experience as the frame of reference from which to observe and judge other events. He learns to appreciate himself as an ongoing, sensitive, trustworthy process. Instead of defending himself against his experience or dealing with life at arm's length, he finds he can immerse himself in events, confident of his ability to assimilate and grow with interaction. This straightforward, uncomplicated relationship to life and to self makes possible a greater awareness, a quicker perception, and a more accurate judgment of all aspects of experience, including self.

It is this greater openness of experience and trust in self which seems to provide the adequate personality with a high degree of personal autonomy. He learns to use himself and his experience as his frame of reference for dealing with life and is far freer from the pressures and demands of his environment. Flowing smoothly with life, he finds it less necessary to utilize his energies in purely "coping" activities. Being closely in touch with events and able to trust his own experience, the adequate personality finds living far less complicated. He does not have to "deal with" life so often. Rather, he discovers that need satisfaction can be attained effectively and satisfyingly through simple expression of self in response to events, with little need for the complications of coping or manipulating.

Maslow has described this autonomy as a matter of "growth" rather than "deficiency" motivation:

> One characteristic of self-actualizing people which to a certain extent crosscuts much of what we have already described, is their relative independence of the physical and social environment. Since they are propelled by growth motivation rather than deficiency motivation, self-actualizing people are not dependent for their main satisfactions on the real world, or other people or culture or means-to-ends or, in general, on extrinsic satisfactions. Rather they are dependent for their own development and continued growth upon their own potentialities and latent resources. Just as the tree needs sunshine and water and food, so do most people need love, safety, and the other basic need gratifications which can come only from without. But once these external satisfiers are obtained, once these inner deficiencies are satiated by outside satisfiers,

the true problem of individual human development begins, i.e., self-actualization.

This independence of environment means a relative stability in the face of hard knocks, blows, deprivations, frustrations and the like. These people can maintain a relative serenity and happiness in the midst of circumstances that would drive other people to suicide They have also been described as "self-contained."

The feeling of adequacy to deal with external events makes such events less urgent. This in turn makes possible a high degree of concentration. Adequate personalities are, therefore, likely to be far less distractable. Their capacity for detachment from external demands makes it possible for them to devote their attention to problems with an intensity and devotion seldom achieved by less well-actualized persons. Indeed, so intense is this concentration that it sometimes seems to outsiders to indicate a lack of concern for human values. While adequate personalities do seem to have less "need" for other people on occasion, it would be a serious mistake to conclude that such people are disinterested in human affairs or human values. Quite the contrary is true.

THE COMPASSION OF ADEQUATE PEOPLE

The capacity for acceptance does not apply solely to impersonal events. Adequate persons are equally acceptant of people. Their perceptions of human beings are admitted to awareness with the same lack of defensiveness and distortion as any other perception. Having little need to be defensive, adequate persons find it possible to perceive and behave toward their fellows with a minimum of hostility. They accept people for what they are: human beings with interesting individual quirks and characteristics, to be comprehended without fear, hatred, or distortion.

When the factor of identification is added to the acceptance characteristic of adequate persons, another quality is produced. Identification, combined with a capacity for acceptance, gives adequate persons a deep and extensive feeling of being "one with" their fellow citizens. This feeling of oneness, or empathy, makes them capable of great understanding, for, in a sense, they share in the experience and feelings of others far more surely and intensively than less adequate persons. This ability to "place oneself in another person's shoes" makes it possible for adequate persons to understand their fellows and to communicate with depth and intensity of feeling. It also facilitates the achievement of a broad feeling of oneness with mankind in general. In a study of self acceptance, Berger found, for example, positive correlations between these feelings about self:

1. Relies on internalized values and standards.
2. Has faith in capacity to cope with life.
3. Assumes responsibility for and accepts causes of own behavior.
4. Accepts praise or criticism objectively.
5. Does not deny or distort feelings, motives, abilities in self.
6. Sees self as person of worth on equal plane with others.
7. Does not expect others to reject him.
8. Does not regard self as queer or abnormal.
9. Is not shy or self conscious.

And these feelings about others:

1. Does not hate, reject, or pass judgment on others when different from self.
2. Does not attempt to dominate.
3. Does not assume responsibility for others.
4. Does not deny worth or equality of others.
5. Shows desire to serve others.
6. Has active interest in others, desires to create mutually satisfactory relationships.
7. In advancing self is careful not to infringe rights of others.

The feeling of identification has a further effect. When one is strongly identified with others, what he does to actualize self is likely to contribute also to the actualization of those with whom he is identified. Adequate persons have much concern for other people, which shows itself in humanitarian interests and in close association with some of our great attempts at social welfare. Adequate persons are often motivated by love, understanding, and compassion for their fellow man. With less pressing need to demonstrate their adequacy or to strive desperately in areas in which they feel deprived, adequate persons are free to accept, appreciate, and love other people. They do not find it necessary to use others for solely personal gratification and, as a consequence, can devote themselves more fully to other people. They have the capacity to "give of themselves."

The capacity for compassion characteristic of adequate persons extends to themselves as well. Adequate persons have less feelings of guilt and failure, in part because they are more successful, effective people, but also because they are more realistic and accepting. They do not expect themselves or others to be what they are not. They accept their fundamental humanity and forgive themselves as well as others for the limitations of human frailty. Such compassion for self releases the individual and makes possible an open, accepting relationship with the world about him.

One outgrowth of the combination of acceptance and identification in adequate personalities is a greater responsibility and humility where others are concerned. With less pressing need for self aggrandizement they can be content with secondary roles. They are under less compulsion to prove themselves at the expense of others. On the contrary, with strong feelings of identification they behave with characteristic concern for their fellows. For these people the golden rule is not an ideal human relationship to be achieved, but a way of living that occurs as a normal outgrowth of the nature of such personalities. Compassion, understanding, responsibility, and humility are not blindly sought as desirable goals for behavior. Rather, such characteristics are a natural outgrowth of the capacities for acceptance and identification typical of their processes of perception and the fundamentally positive phenomenal selves they possess.

The Adequate Self and His Society

Since each of us lives inescapably embedded in one or more societies, it is necessary that people satisfy both their own and society's needs. The adequate self from *both* the individual's point of view and society's must necessarily be in touch with the expectancies of the members of the society in which he operates. These expectancies will vary considerably within a particular culture. What is expected of a child is considerably different from what is expected of an adult. Expectancies for men are different from those for women. What is expected of the banker is different from what is expected of the dog catcher. What is more, the amount of deviation permitted an individual before he is brought under social controls will vary widely within a particular culture. Women in our culture are permitted a good deal of experimentation and license in choosing clothing, but far less in choosing sex partners. The adequate differentiation and acceptance of such aspects of his world into the organization of the self is a necessity if the individual is not to find himself threatened by his environment and so made unhappy, uncomfortable, and ineffective in dealing with it.

Interestingly enough, an adequate self in the terms in which we have described it will produce an individual who not only satisfies his own need, but will operate to the ultimate satisfaction of his society as well. Every individual lives in and is dependent upon society. So long as his behavior is consistent with the expectancy of the members of society he operates smoothly and effectively and with a minimum of threat to himself from that society or to the society from himself. Adequate personalities, we have seen, are maximally open to experience. The individual with an adequate phenomenal self will react quickly and easily to his society. Since he is dependent upon his society in large part for his need satisfaction, he cannot operate in ways which would be destructive to it. When threats do occur from his society, he is capable of accepting them and modifying himself accordingly.

For every antisocial act there is a penalty imposed either by society or, worse still, by the individual himself. If he is free to make all differentiations, these penalties must necessarily be examined by him. Since need satisfaction requires the absence of threat, the likelihood of action being taken which results in greater threat is impossible. Note in the following transcript from counseling how in her attempts to find a solution to her problem a young woman examines and rejects behaviors inacceptable to herself and to society.

A college student who had not been doing as well as she expected had sought all sorts of answers in the course of her counseling. She consciously and clearly examined the possibilities of quitting school, of developing a "nervous breakdown," or of running away, and eventually rejected all. Finally she came to the counselor's office elated over a solution which went roughly as follows:

STUDENT: I'll drop some of the work I'm doing now. That will give me time to get good grades in the rest. Then, I'll come back this summer and make it up and be right up with my class in the fall.

(Examining the plan from every angle, she left, still elated. Six days later she was back.)

STUDENT: I felt so good about that plan and then I didn't want to do it at all after I saw you. So, I decided, I'm going to get my work done—all of it.

COUNSELOR: You discarded your plan?

STUDENT: I feel more confident now. I'm going to get it done. That other decision—I really had a guilty conscience after I left you. I thought, maybe I'm just making excuses. That decision was just a way out. Just making the decision helped me. It affected me just the opposite. I felt terribly guilty.

COUNSELOR: You felt you were not being honest with yourself.

STUDENT: It taught me I'm no different if I'm slow. It's better that I do what I can and take the consequences. I decided that the next day and I haven't had the jerks since. (Client had had a severe shoulder tic diagnosed by her physician as chorea.)
COUNSELOR: You feel you must accept yourself then.
STUDENT: I do. I'm slow and average. Now I'm utilizing time I never did before. I feel more confident. This is the most difficult adjustment I've ever had to cope with. That other decision was just making excuses. It's unfortunate I'm slow but I'll just have to work harder. Since I've gotten through this, I'm sure I can get through anything.

A similar excerpt involving possible suicide is presented on page 49. Note that differentiation and acceptance in both cases includes the social situation and that even the possibility of suicide, which removes the person from society, does not remove him from its controls. A social being must necessarily adjust to the demands of society or remove himself from it. If he identifies himself with society he cannot deny it, for to do that is to deny himself. Since he lives in and is dependent upon society for his welfare, his own maintenance and enhancement will lead to that of the members of society as well, providing he is free to make adequate differentiations and to accept these into his concept of self. Persons unable to differentiate freely or with an inadequate self concept are unsatisfactory to themselves and to society. The high degree of identification of adequate people with their fellows assures a relationship between self-actualizing people and their societies of mutual enhancement with a minimum of friction, hostility, or destructiveness.

ADEQUACY DOES NOT DEMAND CONFORMITY

It should not be supposed that because adequate persons have a close and sensitive relationship to their societies that they must necessarily be conformists. The adequate personality is so open to his experiences that his adjustment is often to a larger society rather than to a restricted subgroup. Thus, he might be out of harmony with a smaller group but in a closer relationship to broad human goals. The spontaneity and creativity of self-actualizing people would not permit complete conformity. Adequate persons are possessed of great dignity and integrity. Their characteristic goals have little or nothing to do with conformity or its lack. Conforming or rebellious behavior is for these people merely a by-product of their movement toward goals satisfying both to themselves and to their fellows in the long run. In the process of seeking such goals adequate persons may be conventional or unconventional as demanded by the situations they encounter in their search for mutual self enhancement. Conformity as an end in itself may never enter their phenomenal fields at all.

As we have said, society has little to fear from adequate personalities. It is not the people who feel liked, wanted, acceptable, and able who cause difficulties for the rest of us. The individuals in our culture who represent an ever-present danger are those unfortunates who see themselves as unliked, unwanted, unacceptable, and unable, who are incapable of acceptance and who have little or no feeling of identification with the rest of us. Adequate persons provide leadership and the dynamic force which makes possible both their own good as well as that of their fellows. They often become the focal points around which many of the rest of us can rally to combine our efforts toward the achievement of important social goals. In a very real sense such people provide the backbone of democracy. They are the kind of people a democracy seeks to produce and are at the same time the kind of people upon whom the success of a democracy depends.

How Adequate Selves Develop

In Chapter 7 we have seen something of how the self concept develops as a result of the perceptions of the individual while he is growing up and particularly of his perceptions of the people who surround him in his formative years. Adequate personalities develop their concepts of self in the same fashion as their less adequate fellows, from the experiences they have throughout their lives. Adequate people, like any others, learn who they are and what they are from the things that happen to them. What makes an adequate person seems to be the peculiar kinds of experiences he has had.

Important as the question is, we have little precise experimentation leading directly to answers to the problem of how to produce adequate personalities. However, much of the great body of research already accumulated in the field of human growth and development sheds light on this question. From that research we can discern certain guide lines which give us clues to the probable production of adequate personalities. These clues are closely related to the three characteristics of the perceptions of adequate people we have been discussing in this chapter.

THE POSITIVE EXPERIENCE OF SELF AND THE WORLD

Adequate personalities, we have seen, have generally positive perceptions of themselves and the world in which they live. They see themselves as people who are liked, wanted, acceptable, and able, living in a world with which they can cope. Such concepts of self do not arise in a vacuum. They are the product of the experiences of the individual in his development. Nor does one have to be an expert to design a kind of program which would be likely to lead to such a characteristic way of seeing self and the world. The kind of experience needed to produce this kind of self definition is apparent from the definition itself. One needs only to ask:

How shall a child feel liked unless somebody likes him?
How shall a child feel wanted unless somebody wants him?
How shall a child feel accepted unless somebody accepts him?
How shall a child feel able unless somewhere he has success?

In the answers to these questions lie clues to ways in which it may be possible to construct life situations more likely to lead to adequacy.

Positive self definitions can arise only from positive self experience. Similarly, a positive view of the world is likely to be found only in those who have found their own experiences with the world to be generally enhancing.

THE CAPACITY FOR ACCEPTANCE

The capacity for acceptance, we have seen, is in large part a function of the existence of a generally positive phenomenal self. Positive self concepts make possible greater acceptance. Acceptance seems to be a capacity one can "learn" given the right kinds of circumstances. We know, for example, that people can be more accepting of themselves and other people in the absence of threat. As a result, many teachers and counselors have learned to create warm, permissive, nonthreatening atmospheres for their students and clients, and this kind of atmosphere in turn makes possible a greater degree of acceptance by the subject. Whether or not acceptance is possible is very largely a question of the degree to which one feels safe and secure. The greater the degree of personal security felt, the greater the degree of acceptance.

There is research evidence which indicates that people can, indeed, learn to be more accepting as a result of being given the right kinds of opportunities. The experience of being accepted in therapy has been found to be followed by an increased ability of the client to be accepting in his turn. Similarly, teachers know that when they are successful in creating situations where children feel free to talk and to look at controversial matters without fear or censure, the children become better able to deal with people in a similar manner in other settings.

IDENTIFICATION CAN BE LEARNED

Finally, the identification characteristic of adequate personalities seems open to considerable modification. People can "learn" to identify with wider groups of people. Experiences can be provided for them which make a high degree of identification possible. Many a Southerner forced to work side by side with Negroes in the armed forces during the war came to appreciate his colored "buddy" in a way that would never have been possible had he spent those years in his home community. This is only one of many instances which could be cited of persons learning to identify with people of different races, creeds, and religions in all parts of the world. The literature of social psychology is particularly rich with examples of situations in which people learned to identify with one another.

Interesting techniques have been devised by some workers to provide people with experiences of identification and increased understanding of how things look to others. Rachel David Du Bois, for example, has developed a method of inducing people to share one another's fields through remembering a common experience they have had. People interested in group process have developed other methods like role playing and psychodrama. Psychotherapists have found ways of teaching themselves to empathize with their clients.

The Adequate Person in Crisis

Throughout this chapter we have seen that the adequate personality has more effective, efficient, and dependable relationships with the world about him. Nevertheless, there are those who loudly proclaim the virtues of failure, rejection, and humiliation as devices to be liberally used in the training of the young on the theory that the intense experience of failure and indignity "toughens" the individual and makes him strong in the face of later adversity. Nothing could be further from the truth. The idea seems to have arisen from the fact that successes, to be enhancing must be over great difficulties. The uncritical observer, seeing the difficulty as the common element in the development of great people, advocates difficulties without worrying about success. This is like the man who, having acquired hang-overs from Scotch and soda, bourbon and soda, rye and soda, and gin and soda, gave up soda. The best guarantee we can have that an individual will be able to deal effectively with crises lies in the degree of his personal adequacy. Even those who most staunchly defend the "school of hard knocks" mostly advocate it for other people's children.

Adequate personalities are the products of positive experience. What is destructive to human dignity and integrity, what indoctrinates people with false perceptions of themselves as people of little worth, respectability, or capacity represents a tragic waste of human potential. Worse still, it produces people who constitute an ever-present danger to the rest of us in the interdependent, coöperative environment of modern society. Adequate personalities are not a luxury in our society, but a continuously increasing necessity. Indeed, it can be argued that societies themselves are no more than means by which people may band together to achieve greater personal adequacy. As a consequence, it is necessary for us to search always for new and better ways of providing people with the kind of positive experiences and relationships which contribute to their adequacy. The best guarantee we have that people will operate effectively to fulfill their own and other people's needs is that their own need for feelings of worth and value has been adequately filled in the past. This principle has vast implications for every phase of human relationships, whether we speak of child-rearing practices, educational method, labor-management relations, or the relationships of nations with one another.

CHAPTER 13

The Inadequate Personality: The Dynamics of Failure

IT would be nice if we were able to construct in our time a society all of whose members were adequate personalities. Unfortunately, we have not yet progressed that far. There still exist in our culture inadequate personalities who eke out an existence with little or no satisfaction either to themselves or to anyone else. Some of these attract our attention by careers of violence and revolt. Others live out their lives in silence and despair. The most inadequate we call mentally retarded, criminal, or mentally ill; and these fill our institutions, our jails, and our mental hospitals to overflowing. Such unhappy people represent a drag upon the rest of us and a pitiful waste of human potentialities.

Inadequate personalities are those who regard themselves as unable to achieve need satisfaction. They are people who feel unable to cope with life in one or more important respects. Inadequate personalities develop in the same manner as adequate ones, as a result of the peculiar experiences they have had in the process of their growing up. Whereas adequate persons see themselves as capable of coping with life, inadequate people have grave doubts about their capacities to deal with events. Their experience has taught them that they are more often than not unliked, unwanted, unacceptable, or unworthy. Seeing themselves in these ways, inadequate personalities find living a difficult and hazardous process in which they must constantly be prepared for emergencies. They feel threatened so much of the time that we might well use the term "threatened people" as synonymous with inadequate personalities.

The problem of inadequacy, however, is not just a matter of the very inadequate, nor is it a matter involving only the other fellow. Most of us are more or less inadequate from time to time, just as most of us are more or less adequate. Adequacy is a continuum extending from very little to very much. (See Fig. 22.) Though all of us are continuously and insatiably striving for adequacy or self actualization, none of us

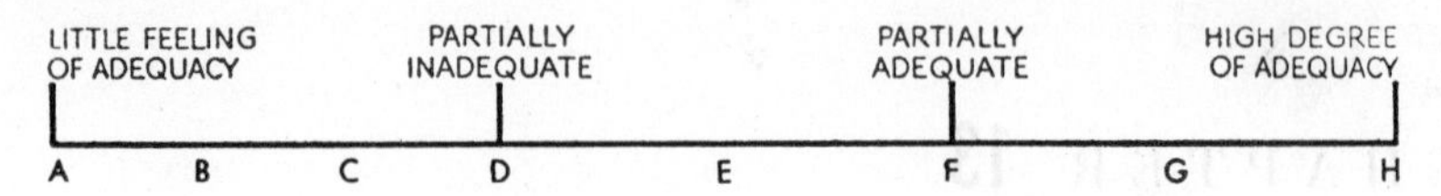

Fig. 22. The Adequacy-Inadequacy Continuum.

ever achieves this goal entirely. Most of us exist somewhere on the continuum schematically represented in Fig. 22 between *D* and *F*. A few people in our world, like the Lincolns, Gandhis, or Albert Schweitzers, achieve a high degree of self actualization and manage to reach such high plains of adequacy as indicated by the general area *G* to *H* on our continuum. At the opposite end of the scale are those people with little or no feelings of adequacy, the neurotic, the criminal, and the psychotic. The "neurotic" personality might be represented on our adequacy rule in the neighborhood *C* to *D*. Although they feel severely threatened, such people nevertheless feel a sufficient degree of adequacy to make it possible for them to go on struggling and fighting for better things. At the very lowest levels of adequacy in our society are the psychotic and the violently criminal personality, represented on our chart at points *C* to *A*. These are the people so severely threatened and inadequate as to be driven to extreme devices to achieve even the smallest measure of adequacy.

It should not be supposed that the above chart represents a discrete classification of adequacy and inadequacy. None of us ever achieves a full measure of adequacy, on the one hand, or escapes from some measure of inadequacy, on the other. In the previous chapter we described the adequate personality and some of his characteristics. In this chapter, we shall turn our attention to the other end of the continuum to examine the nature and characteristics of inadequacy.

Perceptual Characteristics of Inadequate Persons

We have seen that the perceptions of adequate people are characterized by: (1) an essentially positive phenomenal self, (2) a capacity for acceptance, and (3) a high degree of identification with others. We would expect to find that the perceptions of inadequate people were characterized by the reverse of these criteria, and this is exactly the case.

A FUNDAMENTALLY NEGATIVE PHENOMENAL SELF

Inadequate people see themselves in generally negative ways. As a result of their past experience they have come to define themselves. for example, as unworthy, unwanted, unacceptable, and unable. This is, of course, not true of all of the perceptions such people have of themselves. It is, however, likely to be true of those aspects of self which seem to the individual most important or central to his self structure.

A self defined in negative terms is a poor instrument for dealing with the vicissitudes of life. It leaves one helpless and fearful before the demands of living. It provides but a shaky and tenuous foundation for effective existence. The smaller and more insignificant the self, moreover, the larger, more overwhelming, and threatening are the problems with which such a person sees himself confronted. Life need not be threatening to the adequate individual with a strong and positive phenomenal self. The self concept made up of many negative self definitions, however, finds itself in constant danger from external events. Such a self lives in perpetual jeopardy.

The inadequate self may find it necessary to live a life of continuous, belligerent, aggressive seeking for self enhancement in a desperate effort to demonstrate to himself and all the world that what he feels to be true is not so. This is characteristic of many criminals and neurotics. Such people find no rest or contentment, for life is a continual contest in which they daily run the risk of destruction. If the self is defined in too negative a fashion, the individual may even give up in despair. He may accept himself as defeated and incapable of dealing with life, and content himself with a lackadaisical existence pushed about by whatever forces are exerted upon him. Many psychotics and mentally retarded people show this kind of reaction. This intimate relationship between the individual's feeling of adequacy and violence of behavior was demonstrated by Balester in a study of the self concepts of delinquents. He found adults had more positive self concepts than juvenile nondelinquents, nondelinquents perceived themselves more positively than first-offender delinquents, and these latter, in turn, possess more positive self concepts than "repeaters."

Human need for personal adequacy is insatiable, and threat to the self must be met with some kind of response. Much of what we describe as "maladjusted" behavior is the individual's "loud protests against the crushing of his psychological bones, of one's true inner nature." What is more, the greater the threat, the greater will be the response, so that threatened people almost always overreact and behave in exaggerated ways. They smile too broadly, try too hard, compliment too much, protest their innocence too forcefully, brag too blatantly, give too little or too much, because they are continually faced with the necessity for proving their adequacy.

We have seen in an earlier chapter that when individuals feel threatened their perceptions are affected by two phenomena: tunnel vision and the necessity for self defense. Unfortunately, each of these effects markedly reduces the individual's ability to perceive effectively and efficiently. Tunnel vision reduces the field from which behavior may be selected, while the necessity for self defense makes change difficult or impossible. Adequate behavior requires not a narrow, restricted phenomenal field, but an open, rich, and maximally free field of perceptions. The experience of inadequacy provides a poorer, more restricted field from which the individual must select his behaviors. It is not surprising, therefore, to find that inadequate personalities are often characterized by rigid, inflexible patterns of behavior or that they are quite likely to be inaccurate in their assessment of themselves and the world about them.

LACK OF ACCEPTANCE

The necessity for self defense imposed upon the phenomenal self by the experience of threat makes difficult or impossible acceptance of new or conflicting perceptions into the perceptual field. Most of us have experienced this phenomenon when, perhaps in the heat of an argument, we found it difficult to understand or even to hear what our antagonist was trying to express. The fundamental need to maintain and enhance the phenomenal self requires self defense. As a consequence, threatened people reject unflattering or self-damaging perceptions and seek those which assuage wounded self perceptions or help to bolster the self against the threat experienced. When this happens, many important differentiations may not be accepted into the phenomenal field or, if they already exist in the field, may not be accepted into clear figure.

This inability to accept important aspects of his experience has unhappy effects upon the individual's capacity for effective behavior. He is forced to behave on the basis of restricted or partial evidence. Behavior originating from only part of the data must necessarily be less precise and effective than that arising from a wider, more inclusive frame of reference. Like trying to build a house with but part of the necessary lumber, the product is unsatisfactory to everyone concerned. Inability to accept the data of their experience often produces a rigid, vicious-circle kind of behavior which seems only to prove to inadequate persons their own inadequacies. The pattern goes something like this:

1. A person behaves in terms of his phenomenal self.
2. This behavior is rejected by those with whom he comes in contact.
3. Rejection, in turn, may so threaten the individual that he is forced to defend himself with great vigor and is unable to accept the evidence of his rejection. As a consequence, he behaves even more strongly in terms of his existing phenomenal self.
4. Such behavior, of course, only intensifies the rejection of his fellows, bringing more threat to himself, an even greater need for self defense, and progressively less ability to accept the facts of his situation.

Just such patterns of perception and behavior cause many inadequate personalities to behave in ways that produce the very reactions in others which corroborate their own already existing beliefs. Thus the delinquent may attempt to force people to respect and notice him by an attitude of toughness or belligerence which only intensifies the wrath of society against him. Some psychologists have seen this, erroneously we believe, as a drive toward self destruction.

The inability of inadequate persons to accept threatening perceptions does not apply only to perceptions of the situations in which they find themselves. Lack of acceptance also distorts their perceptions of themselves. For effective behavior, people need to change their concepts of self on occasion as demanded by new experience, new times and places. Threatened personalities find this extremely difficult. The dire necessity for self defense may preclude the acceptance of new concepts inconsistent with existing self definitions. Common examples of this effect may be observed in the woman who cannot accept her fading youth, in the child unwilling to accept the responsibilities involved in growing up, in the worker unable to change with changing methods and techniques, or in the student so unable to accept the evidence of his inadequacy that he must maintain his failures are due to teachers who "had it in for him." This tends to keep the phenomenal self a static and rigid organization, a characteristic which only increases the likelihood of its being threatened by the changing world in which all of us live. A phenomenal self incapable of accepting change in itself is practically certain to become increasingly out of touch with the world and therefore increasingly inadequate and threatened.

INABILITY TO IDENTIFY BROADLY WITH OTHERS

Inadequate persons do not possess strong feelings of identification. Indeed, it has often been observed that severely threatened people, like criminals and the psychotic, are fundamentally lonely people. Often they do not have so much as a single person in their lives whom they feel really respects them. Mostly, they have been unsuccessful in their relationships with others. Extremely threatened people, like hardened criminals or certain kinds of psychotics, may even attempt to destroy any possibility of developing such identification. Other people are perceived only as dangerous and so to be avoided, or as victims to be manipulated and used.

Threatened people are likely to be selfish or egocentric. The experience of threat focuses attention upon the self and its maintenance and enhancement, so that there is little opportunity for broader, more outgoing kinds of perceptions like those required for identification. What is more, the poorer, more meager the phenomenal self, the greater will be the necessity for its defense and the less likely is there to be any extensive feeling of oneness with others.

Just as each individual grows up with a self concept which is in large part the product of how he has been treated by those important to him in his growing years, he also develops perceptions of what other people are like. Depending upon his experiences of them, he comes to feel that other people are essentially friendly or unfriendly, warm or cold, interesting or frightening, pleasant or unpleasant. It is characteristic of deeply inadequate persons that their early experiences with others have been unsuccessful. The same unhappy relationship with an adult from which a child learns that he is unacceptable or unable may teach him also that people are unfriendly, dangerous, or untrustworthy. Small wonder then that inadequate people have little feeling of identification with others. A low opinion of self is likely to be associated with a fear and distrust of others. To feel unacceptable is to perceive others as unaccepting, as unfriendly. The inability to accept self is therefore strongly correlated with inability to accept others. This relationship between self acceptance and ability to identify with others is also demonstrated in the progress of psychotherapy, where it is repeatedly found that as persons are aided to greater acceptance of self they show a concomitant increase in positive feelings toward other people.

People with little feeling of identification with their fellows are unlikely to be deeply concerned about them. This is perhaps observable in its most extreme form in the case-hardened criminal, who feels not the slightest compunction at harming another human being. He may even enjoy it. After all, when you don't belong to the club, you don't have to abide by the rules, pay your dues, or defend the membership! And when the club has blackballed you, you owe them no sympathy. Inadequate personalities do not develop in a vacuum. They are produced from interactions of the individual and the world in which he lives.

Techniques of Dealing with Threat

The experience of threat is an event which cannot be ignored. Threat to the self requires some sort of action, some technique for dealing with the experience. Many of these techniques are familiar to all of us and can be seen in daily behavior. They may be simple and transitory devices used only on rare occasions by mildly threatened individuals, or they may be fixed and permanent methods of dealing with life employed by the deeply disturbed personality. These techniques have often been described by psychologists as "defense mechanisms," a term which itself implies the attempt of the organism to deal with a threatening situation. Such techniques seem to fall in three general categories:

1. The phenomenal self may be reorganized to include the threatening perception.
2. Perceptions may be denied acceptance into the organization of the phenomenal field.
3. Perceptions may be so selected or modified as to be consistent with the existing organization.

REORGANIZATION OF THE PHENOMENAL SELF

We have seen that the adequate personality is characterized by an ability to accept any and all differentiations into the phenomenal field. When a threatening differentiation can be so accepted, threat no longer exists. It is only those perceptions refused acceptance which continue to appear threatening. The inclusion of a new differentiation into the field, however, will necessarily result in some degree of reorganization of the existing structure. Sometimes this will be very great, sometimes only slight. The individual confronted with a personal criticism by his employer, for example, may find himself faced with a disagreeable threat to self. The appropriate thing to do in these circumstances is to accept the perception, evaluate its accuracy, and modify one's behavior if necessary. This is what the essentially adequate personality does. Unfortunately, this kind of reorganization of the self is not so easy to accomplish if threat is very great or the personality fundamentally inadequate.

The acceptance of all pertinent evidence leaves the individual in a far stronger position to deal with life. It leaves him open to adjustment and the possibility of change to meet the shifting exigencies with which he is bound to be faced from time to time. Reorganization of the self permits the inclusion of new data and a relationship with the outside world characterized by a maximum degree of accuracy and realism. One is always able to deal more effectively with life when he is in possession of more evidence. The reorganization of self in the light of one's experience keeps the self in closer, more intimate contact with the world in which one lives and moves.

This method of dealing with threatening perceptions is likely in the long run to offer the greatest satisfaction to the individual. Unfortunately, it is not always possible, particularly for the threatened, inadequate personality. Acceptance of threat and reorganization of the self are the very events the threatened personality seeks to avoid. Inadequate personalities are characteristically incapable of acceptance. The more inadequate the individual feels, the less he is able to utilize this approach to dealing with his threatening perceptions and the more likely he is to be driven to the use of some less productive but, from his point of view, safer technique of dealing with threat.

DENIAL OF THE RELEVANCE OF THREATENING PERCEPTIONS

A second, but less happy means of dealing with threatening perceptions is simply to deny their relevance to self, thus escaping the necessity for dealing with them at all. This may be brought about in three general ways familiar to all of us in their milder forms. The threatened person may deny the relevance of a threatening perception by:

1. Denying its existence completely. "It isn't so!"
2. Accepting the possibility of its existence, but denying the relationship to self. "It doesn't refer to me!"
3. Postponing the matter in space or time. "I don't have to deal with it now."

DENIAL OF THE EXISTENCE OF THE EVENT. This method of dealing with threat is accomplished by insisting that the threatening perception simply does not exist. Galileo, for example, was persecuted for his insistence that the earth revolved around the sun. The scholars of his day found this idea so repugnant and so threatening to their way of life that they dealt with the matter by insisting that the event was not so. What was more, because Galileo threatened them so by insisting that it was true, they found it necessary to bring him to trial and to force him to recant his idea. Man's history has been replete with examples of this "ostrich-like" method of dealing with threatening events. People found great difficulty in accepting Darwin's ideas about evolution, and Einstein's concepts of relativity, time, and space were laughed at and ignored by many when they first appeared.

Such methods of dealing with threatening events are not limited to earth-shaking discoveries or to deeply threatened people. Almost any of us, even the most adequate, may utilize such a method of dealing with threat, at least momentarily, if the threat we experience is sufficiently great. Any of us might find ourselves on occasion refusing to admit the death of a loved one or the approach of our own demise. The technique is also common among children who may find it necessary to object violently to the idea that "there is no Santa Claus"! Matters which do not exist do not have to be dealt with, and an inadequate phenomenal self may find it necessary to ignore the existence of threatening events.

We may even anticipate the possibility of such events and avoid or resist entering the situation where they may occur. One of the most common examples of this method of dealing with threat may be observed in the mechanism psychologists call *negativism.* It is particularly common among children, but often exists in adults as well. Negativism can often be used as a positive device for controlling other people. Thus a threatened self may be able to forestall the necessity of experiencing a disturbing event and may even be able to restore the self to a feeling of personal worth through forcing others to give in. In this way, a feeling of mastery may be obtained from one element of the situation while at the same time avoiding the necessity for dealing with another. For example, before going to bed one evening a young boy complained that it was much too early to retire. This was threatening to his concept of self. He attempted to point out to his father that it was unfair to expect him to go to bed when it was still light, especially for such a big boy as he. When these arguments proved of no avail he rebelled and said "No!" to brushing his teeth, washing his face, taking off his clothes, and picking up his toys. He even went so far as to say "no" when asked if he wanted to be read to (a decision he quickly regretted and only saved face at the last moment by changing his "no" to refer to his father and not his mother). Having been threatened by his parents' failure to regard him as he regarded himself and being overpowered by the might of adults, he sought a means of restoring his feeling of self esteem by mastering his parents through negativism. Even as he said "no" while standing with his back to his father at the basin, his father could observe in the mirror the delight written all over the child's face. The enhancement of self achieved by such tactics is often far more pleasurable than the minor losses one may sustain by the negativism. This is true of adults as well. Strikers out for weeks for an extra cent per hour count nothing lost if in the end their tactics of refusing to coöperate achieve their goal, even though it may take years to recoup their losses on the new pay scale.

DENIAL OF THE RELATIONSHIP TO SELF. A variation of the denial of relevance may be found in the relegation of threatening perceptions to the not self. This is a common device seen in daily life in the bland assumption that new rules and regulations, "of course," do not apply to us. It may be observed, too, in the phenomenon pointed out by Freud, that we discover in others the characteristics we deplore in ourselves. We may also find it possible to deal with threats in this fashion by the common excuse that "it was not our fault."

Techniques of denial may often be extremely effective for a while. Sometimes, too, they are extremely useful devices which protect us against minor upsetting perceptions. When we "forget," for example, it may be that after a time the situation will change and it will no longer be necessary for us to remember anyhow. Or, when some unacceptable aspect of ourselves is relegated to someone else, we may discover at a later date that we have changed in the meantime and the threatening perception is no longer applicable. In either event, the situation has been met with a minimum of difficulty. The self has been successfully maintained intact. Though such methods of dealing with threat have momentary value to the individual, they may sometimes only make things more difficult to deal with on later occasions. When perceptions are very important they are likely, sooner or later, to be forced upon us in one form or another. Society will usually see to that.

Another method of dealing with threat by denying relationship to self is nicely illustrated in the technique of *projection*, in which the threatening experience is avoided by relegating it to someone else. Mr.

Allen may have extremely aggressive feelings toward his wife and children, which if brought into clear figure would shock and frighten Mr. Allen himself. One way of dealing with such feelings may be to dissociate himself from these ideas by attributing them to someone else. Indeed, if he can manage to attribute similar feelings toward him on the part of his family, he may even be able to justify his own ill will. Still another way of dissociating himself from his threatening feelings may be to express exaggerated concern for his family's safety and comfort. If we place Mr. Allen in a situation where he is under no threat from those around him or in which he may behave without restraint, however, it is likely that he will reveal much more of his real feelings to the eyes of a practiced observer. Thus he may be able to "let himself go" in a play, because a play is "only an act," or in telling of his childhood, for "you can't blame a man for what he did as a child," or in telling a story, for then "it is only a story." It is just this release from the restraints of objective reality that makes projective instruments so revealing of the fundamental motivations of the person's personality.

But projection occurs not only on projective tests. It is often utilized by the individual in daily life. Through identification with others (and thus protection to the self) it may be possible to find vicarious pleasure or self esteem in blaming others who do those things he would like to do himself. It has been reported, for example, that the founder of a famous society advocating kindness to animals used to walk the streets of New York with a horsewhip to use on drivers who beat their horses. The guilty are often the most avid reformers. Criticizing behavior of others, they absolve themselves from feelings of guilt and, as fighters against evil, justify their use of techniques differentiated as shameful or evil when used by others. Projection gives the individual self justification for operating free of normal social controls.

POSTPONEMENT OF THE THREATENING PERCEPTION. The relevance of threat to the self may also be reduced by postponing its effects in time, in space, or in clarity. We have seen in a previous chapter that the experienced magnitude of threat is a function of its psychological immediacy. Generally speaking, the more immediate the event to self, the greater is the experience of threat. One means, then, of reducing the experience of threat is to postpone it in one fashion or another. This postponement may be affected in time by putting off the critical event until some later occasion. The failing student may thus reduce the immediate distress of facing the dean by putting off seeking an appointment till "tomorrow" or "after the week end." Procrastination is a time-honored device by which the threats of decision making can be alleviated, and it has been used at one time or another by almost everyone.

One of the most interesting and important of these techniques in the psychology of human adjustment is suppression. This is a method of dealing with threatening perceptions by holding them at a lower order of differentiation. Perceptions which would require too great a change in the self cannot come into clear figure. The need of the organism for self maintenance will not permit this, and the perception may be held in the field at a low level of differentiation. This does not eliminate the threat, however, for a suppressed differentiation is still in the phenomenal field. Nor will the need of the organism permit a threat to exist without action on the part of the individual. As a result, the threat, although not clearly differentiated, keeps the organism continuously in a state of tension or distress. This produces the state we have previously described as "anxiety," in which the individual feels threatened but is unable to clearly discern the threatening object or event. This is particularly characteristic of the neurotic who complains of being afraid, anxious, and uneasy but is unable to tell us what he is afraid of.

The failure of threatening events to emerge into figure is not surprising, since if the threat is very great clear perceptions may be too frightening to accept. A good example of such failure of differentiation is to be seen in the young child's insistence on his parent's goodness and power, often, in spite of many obvious proofs to the contrary. To conceive of his parents, on whom he is dependent, as being confused and weak in a terrifying world may be just too much for the child to take. Accordingly he is forced to deny or protest suggestions which imply his parent's weakness.

Persons who feel threatened by poorly differentiated experience often seek one activity after another in a frantic effort to keep from giving attention to themselves and their problems. Such an approach may be observed when we attempt to "snow under" a threatening perception by a series of enhancing techniques that reinforce a damaged phenomenal self. This is the sort of thing that occurs when a man who has been insulted by his wife at breakfast, drives to work at breakneck speed, gets in an argument with his foreman, or "tells off" his best friend. He attempts to reëstablish his feeling of self esteem by wildly seeking momentary superiority over people or objects most available at the time.

It is comforting and reassuring—and sometimes necessary—to emphasize our strengths in moments of weakness or inadequacy. This seems to be an attempt to prevent low-level differentiations from becoming clearly (and so, more threateningly) defined. By maintaining a high degree of attention on other things, it is possible momentarily to avoid the threatening perception. When vigilance flags, however, the need of the individual to maintain and enhance himself tends to bring these differentiations into clearer figure. Persons caught in this merry-go-round remind one of the policemen at the parade, who keep pushing the spectators back only to have them press forward again sometimes one at a time and sometimes in whole batches at once.

The following case of Nancy summarized from the files of a mental-hygiene service illustrates this effect. As a girl, Nancy was very tall and not very attractive to boys. In addition, her family were well-known "intellectuals" who taught their children the importance of being *controlled.* As a result, Nancy grew up with the idea that she was something very special in womanhood, destined for great things and as a professional person several cuts above the ordinary female. This concept of herself was very reassuring and gave her a good deal of self esteem while she was growing up. Nancy married a man who was also an intellectual and who was very proud of her in her job. All went well with this sort of arrangement until Nancy discovered she was pregnant. This was a very threatening perception, and she refused to accept the idea because it did not fit her existing concept of self. Up to the day the baby was born, Nancy never mentioned her condition or made any attempt to prepare for the baby; she merely redoubled her efforts on her job. But babies have a way of arriving in time and she could not forever deny its existence. With the coming of the baby she was faced with an even worse threat to her concept of herself and to her hopes of enhancing it. She had to give up her job to care for the child. Who ever heard of intellectuals who washed dishes, or nursed babies, or made beds? Such ideas were completely foreign to the kind of person she thought herself to be. As a result, Nancy rejected her child and began a whirl of activity that kept her busy from morning till night. She could not stand being with other women who talked about their children. She no longer had her work to give her self esteem, and she could not achieve it at home. So Nancy neglected her housework, put her child in a nursery school, and became a well-known public speaker in her community. She became a veritable dynamo of energy, racing about from meeting to meeting until at last her physical resources gave out and she collapsed in "nervous exhaustion."

SELECTION OF PERCEPTIONS CONSISTENT WITH THE SELF

A third class of techniques for dealing with threatening perceptions is the selection of perceptions in such a way as to be consistent with the existing phenomenal self. Perceptions threatening to self may be so selected as to appear, not threatening, but even enhancing to the phenomenal self. This is the sort of thing that occurs when an insult is taken as a compliment. All of us use this technique day after day, so smoothly that we succeed in fooling ourselves. The reason a student leaves his work until the last minute is not that he doesn't want to study. Perish the thought! He leaves his work till the last minute because "there was just too much to get done," because "the fraternity had a house meeting," or because of any number of other more satisfying reasons. And this is true of professors as well. Students' papers may not get marked, not because the professor hates to grade papers, but because of the pressure of "important" work to be done, or the "need to take a day off now and then," or even because it doesn't really matter, "the students don't mind."

This distortion of perception to bring about greater consistency may (1) be applied to the threatening perception, so as to reduce the degree of threat it poses, or (2) the threatened person may select his perceptions of self in such a manner as to increase his feeling of adequacy and reduce the threat experienced in that way.

THE DISTORTION OF EVENTS. It has sometimes been said that there are two ways in which a person may react to a new idea: he may discount it by saying, "Why, there's nothing new about that. We've known that for twenty years!" or he may minimize it by saying, "It's just a silly new fad. It will soon pass away!" Either way it is no longer necessary to deal with the concept, and the threat has been dealt with, at least for the present. Distortion makes events seem less threatening by bringing them in line with existing concepts of self, and results in certain types of adjustive behavior which psychologists call the *sour-grapes reaction, rationalization,* or *compensation.*

The amount of distortion shown by an individual is proportional to the degree of adequacy he feels. The greater the feeling of inadequacy the greater the incidence of distortion. An interesting study by Friedenberg of student perceptions of self and the university demonstrates, for example, that successful and unsuccessful graduate students see themselves and the university quite differently. The successful students showed much self determination and acceptance of self and saw the university's purposes as consistent with their own. Unsuccessful students, on the other hand, had less self acceptance and less self determination, and saw themselves as cash customers of the university frustrated in the legitimate pursuit of their goals.

The sour grapes reaction is a technique of dealing with threat which gets its name from Aesop's famous fable of the fox and the grapes. Like the fox in the fable, persons may console themselves over prizes they cannot win by concluding they weren't worth having anyhow. People may thus assuage their disappointment by deciding that the more expensive house "would probably have cost more to heat," or that the missed play "was probably no good anyhow," or that the lost opportunity "would probably have turned out to be a dud." By belittling the importance of the goal, the failure to achieve it ceases to be a sign of failure and inadequacy.

A similar method of dealing with threat is that of *rationalization.* It represents a selection of perceptions in such a fashion as to be consistent with existing concepts of self. We are ordinarily aware of our rationalizations only after the need for them has passed. We may perceive a threatening concept as consistent with the self by selecting those aspects which are self enhancing and ignoring those which are not. The individual finds "good" reasons for the "real" reasons for his behavior. For instance, a woman goes shopping and finds two dresses in which she would be very attractive. She buys both dresses and thus achieves an enhancement of self. When friends remark, "Oh, you bought *two* dresses," this may represent a threat to her concept of herself as thrifty, and our shopper replies, "They were such a bargain, I couldn't resist them." Thus she achieves not only a dissolution of the threat but even an enhancement of self as a thrifty shopper who knows how to take advantage of a bargain!

Rationalization is so common that most of us are not aware of the existence of such distorted perceptions. Even when they are brought to our attention it may be very difficult for us to accept them as rationalizations, for to do so may threaten our existing organization. The man who buys a new car, for example, and gives as his reason for this behavior that the old one was beginning to use too much oil, will probably object to our pointing out that the expense of 20 quarts of 40-cent oil in a year's time hardly justifies an expenditure of several thousand dollars in turning the old car in. Such an admission is likely to be a threat to his concept of himself as a smart businessman and, furthermore, may force the admission that the real reason for getting the new car is because it increases his self esteem. To increase one's self esteem is not a socially acceptable reason for buying a car. Such selective effects of the phenomenal self upon perception may be seen in thousands of daily acts illustrated by the following statements:

"Let's go to the movies. A fellow gets stale when he studies all the time."
"Who wants to be a Phi Beta Kappa—a bunch of greasy grinds."
"A little nip now and then is a good thing for a man."
"Nobody really pays any attention to those silly speed limits."

In *compensation* the individual may make quite open and unrestrained attempts at mastery, often with the full support and encouragement of the culture. In fact, in America we take much pride in the great compensators. We point out to our children from the earliest days of schooling the examples of Steinmetz, the hunchback; Cunningham, of the burned legs; Edison, the deaf; Lincoln, the poor; Demosthenes, the stutterer; and Roosevelt, the cripple. These we delight in setting up for our children as guideposts to great achievement, and the implication is clear to "go thou and do likewise." We have succeeded so well in implanting this concept of compensation that it has even become a common notion that anyone who accomplishes something must certainly be a bit queer!

Compensation may appear in either of two common forms, known as direct and indirect compensation. In direct compensation the individual attempts to achieve self esteem or mastery by refusing to accept the threatening differentiation. He denies that any handicap exists, and acts accordingly. His phenomenal self is defined as though the handicap were not a part of himself. In so doing he must deny the proof to the contrary which appears in the reaction of others toward him. A young woman in a small Ohio town who severed the major nerves leading to her legs in an automobile accident the night before she was to have been married, refused to accept the idea that she could never walk again. The author vividly remembers this girl's pathetic efforts to force herself to walk in spite of her hopeless condition. She had a pair of parallel bars built on her porch and daily spent hours dragging her legs behind her as she went hand over hand along the bars. She refused to give up her fiancé because she could not accept the notion that she would never walk. Nor would she marry him, for that would not be fair to him until she was able to walk again. This state of affairs continued for several years until finally she released her fiancé from his promise, gave up her attempts to walk, and died a very short time after. Not all cases of direct compensation end so tragically. Many people, like Glenn Cunningham or Theodore Roosevelt, find it possible to make such improvement through the extreme efforts which such a technique can produce that eventually the threatening handicap is, in fact, overcome.

In indirect compensation a person possessing a handicap may be driven to seek self esteem in other areas entirely. Thus, a child who feels incapable of participation in the usual playground sports may find satisfaction in being the brightest child in class—or the worst. Oftentimes, such compensatory behavior may be far more potent than behavior not so driven, for much more is at stake. It is probable that the amount of energy expended in compensatory activity will depend upon the importance of the threatening self perception in the economy of the individual's particular organization. So long as the perception cannot be accepted into his organization it remains threatening and disturbing to him. He must defend himself at all costs against the threat which he perceives. Nor does it matter whether the handicap is real or imagined from an outsider's point of view. If the perception exists in the field, it is real to the behaver and that is the only point that matters to him. The more threatening the perception, the greater the amount of energy which will be expended in attempting to deal with the problem.

In indirect compensation the individual has given up attempting to deal with the self-threatening perception directly. He recognizes that he is helpless before it, yet cannot accept it as part of his organization. He attempts to rehabilitate his damaged concept of self by "snowing under" the threatening perception with a series of other enhancing perceptions. The girl who is homely may find solace and comfort in extraordinary achievements as a student, as an athlete, as a comic, or in any of a thousand other ways. Since the fundamental perception cannot be accepted, however, it remains in the field and continues to threaten, requiring ever new heights of accomplishment to give a feeling of adequacy. It is only with continued success that the threat can be prevented from arising into figure. It is interesting that society often profits greatly from the tremendous efforts put forth by such persons. Many compensators make great contributions in all walks of life. In spite of the external evidences of success, however, the compensating individual may feel extremely unhappy and inadequate in the very midst of his successes. It is only with the acceptance or elimination of the original negative self perception that real "peace of mind" can occur.

DISTORTION OF THE PERCEPTION OF SELF. Threatened personalities may sometimes be observed to deal with the threats they perceive by selecting perceptions of self which help them feel more adequate. This is, of course, characteristic of all people, but the greater the threat experienced, the greater the necessity for selection. In a previous chapter we have seen how this may be accomplished through the use of drugs or alcohol, which give a spurious, but satisfying, feeling of adequacy at least temporarily. Under these circumstances, the self may be perceived as stronger or more adequate, and the world seems therefore less frightening and more nearly within the capacities of the individual. One can also make himself feel more adequate to deal with certain kinds of threatening situations by arming himself with a knife, a gun, or a club. Another means of increasing one's feeling of adequacy is to identify oneself closely with some other stronger personality or group. In this way it is possible to add the adequacy of others to one's own perceptions of self. Exaggerated needs to conform, for example, have been shown to be closely related to feelings of inadequacy.

Simple regressive techniques are often used in much the same way to increase feelings of adequacy. When perceptions are threatening, many of us fall back upon concepts and techniques which have helped us to feel adequate in former situations. The housewife who formerly found her tears could change her mother's mind may utilize these again in moments of stress when her husband does not treat her in a manner to which she feels she is entitled. Such techniques are not labeled by the individual as regressive, however. That description would be much too threatening. They are labeled as "regressive" only by outside observers who realize that they are not appropriate in the new situation.

Children, faced with the necessity for growing up, sometimes find the business of maturing extremely threatening. This may be particularly true when the child is subjected to a great many demands which are difficult for him to meet. The resulting feelings of inadequacy are threatening, and the child appears to adopt a self definition at a younger age as a means of excusing his behavior to himself and achieving the self enhancement characteristic of former times. When one is younger he cannot be expected to do so much and the demands being imposed upon him appear less threatening. By defining oneself at a lower age, the threats perceived can be given up—they no longer apply. The child who finds going to school threatening may thus regress to an earlier age level where one is not expected to go to school. At such a level he can feel adequate again. The toilet-trained child may lose his newly mastered skills with the arrival of another child or when subjected to such an upheaval as moving from one home to another. It may often be seen that children subjected to a great many demands in the early school years may show such "regressive" behavior. They may want to be rocked or sung to as a means of gaining comfort and reassurance that had value in other days. When demands become too heavy there is much comfort and reassurance in such redefinitions and many threatening situations can be avoided.

Various forms of fantasy may give similar feelings of mastery and offer opportunity for the self concept to operate without the disillusioning impact of threatening differentiations. Daydreaming, moviegoing, some types of reading—all offer avenues for temporary enhancement which the actual situation does not appear to provide. Such flights of fantasy are common to all of us and appear to be motivated by our attempts to achieve some feelings of self esteem or self enhancement. In daydreams we may be anything. We are relatively free from the impact of immediate external events and are free to manipulate ourselves and the world pretty much as we please. This manipulative function also makes fantasy extremely useful to us. As we bring external reality more and more into the phenomenal field, fantasy shades almost indistinguishably into planning, so that the fantasies of yesterday become the actions of today and the achievements of tomorrow.

Children frequently employ fantasy as a means by which the environment can be manipulated and controlled, and it is helpful to many children in assisting them to find meaning in the world about them. In play therapy, for example, a child may be observed to spend hours manipulating various elements of his environment with which he may be having unusual difficulty. In the process he may discover new ways of dealing with his environment or new definitions of self more adequate to deal with the environment he faces.

While fantasy has value as a device for manipulation and for the achievement of self esteem, it may also represent a clinically undesirable type of activity, and it is necessary for the clinician to have some measure by which it is possible to determine when this "danger point" is reached. From a phenomenological point of view, that point is reached when the individual finds the world of fantasy more real than his experience in an external world. The critical point is thus a matter of the attitude taken by the individual toward his fantasies. In extreme cases the threat resulting from the individual's perceptions may sometimes be so great as to leave him no other recourse but to cut himself off from external reality entirely to seek a more friendly environment in a world of dreams. There, he may divorce himself from threat and create a world which is far more pleasant.

But not all daydreams are pleasant. Sometimes they are reported as fantasies in which self punishment is the major consideration. At first glance it would seem difficult to understand how such fantasies could contribute to the maintenance or enhancement of the phenomenal self. Yet this is exactly what seems to occur. In such apparently self-destructive fantasies we may often find the self concept defined in a way which might roughly be described as "I am guilty." With such a self concept it is not surprising that the individual may find real satisfaction in berating himself in fantasy. It is what he deserves in his eyes. By atonement he achieves enhancement of self! Furthermore, there are certain advantages in such self punishment in fantasy, for one can be punished to one's heart's content with a minimum of real danger to the self, whereas if one sought punishment in the world of reality it is quite likely he would find his experience too threatening and out of control. The recognition by the individual of guilt and shame are ways in which he rises above his self. By such recognition he is enabled to feel superior to what he once was or has been. He achieves enhancement of self by thus dissociating from guilt and, by punishing himself, becomes the punisher rather than the punished. Thus behaviors which appear to the external observer to be operating against the individual's own best interests may be, from the behaver's own point of view, enhancing to self.

The Frightened Ones—The Anatomy of Neurosis

To adjust successfully to the varying problems of life requires of the individual a phenomenal field maximally open to experience. Adequate people are able to differentiate themselves and the world about them with accuracy and efficiency. Unfortunately, when people are severely threatened this optimal relationship with experience is no longer feasible.

For the severely threatened, inadequate personality the processes of differentiation and acceptance break down. The ability to perceive and to reorganize the phenomenal field becomes seriously hampered. The more inadequate the personality, the less accurate are his perceptions of self and environment. This does not mean that threatened persons are unable to differentiate *all* events accurately. Actually, even the most seriously disturbed person is able to perceive many events about him with sufficient accuracy to make some degree of operation possible. Things in which he is not deeply involved, for example, may be perceived quite effectively. His difficulty arises primarily with respect to perceptions in which he feels his own adequacy is at stake.

The outstanding characteristic of the inadequate or severely threatened personality is the inability to accept perceptions. Neurotic patients, for example, are always the victims of a distorted perspective. The neurotic mother believes she is a "bad" mother because she has made some mistakes with her children. The neurotic typically overreacts to situations. He suffers great guilt over some act which would have bothered other people very little. He feels *totally* guilty although the rest of his life experience may be spotless. Almost without exception the neurotic clients of the psychotherapist turn out to be people who see themselves in exaggerated and distorted perspective. They feel that as they are, they are unacceptable, unworthy, or unable to an extent completely unjustified by an outside appraisal. Distorted perceptions, it is clear, are unlikely to prove effective in helping individuals to new and better adjustments. To deal effectively with life requires the clearest possible perceptions of oneself and his relationships to the external world. The failure of adequate perception is the most obvious of the characteristics of inadequate personalities, and at the same time, the most vital factor in serving to keep them inadequate.

Strong feelings of inadequacy are likely to be accompanied by more or less violent attempts by the individual to achieve a greater feeling of adequacy. So long as these struggles for adequacy operate within the individual or result in behavior within the limits of tolerance established by his society, the inadequate person is considered "neurotic" or "maladjusted." When, however, the individual's search for adequacy leads him to behavior threatening or destructive to persons or property, he may be considered delinquent or criminal and subject to the penalties of an outraged society. Both delinquent and neurotic, however, are motivated by the same basic feelings of inadequacy. Each seeks in the best ways he can to achieve a more adequate self. Though the behavior each manifests differs markedly, each suffers the same fundamental complaint, a frustrated, limited self. Where once the criminal and delinquent were regarded only as dangerous or bad and locked up to isolate them from society, modern approaches recognize such disorders as requiring treatment rather than punishment.

Neurosis, maladjustment, delinquency, and criminality are personality problems occurring in human beings unable to find more effective and satisfying means of achieving self actualization.

ANXIETY AND INADEQUACY

Whenever the self is perceived as endangered, the organism is placed on a "war footing," and this will be true whether the threat which the self perceives is clearly differentiated, as in the case of fear, or when only vaguely differentiated, as in the case of anxiety. Anxiety and its accompanying tensions are the inseparable partners of inadequacy feelings. Indeed, anxiety is so constant a characteristic of neurosis that it has sometimes been treated as though it were a cause of such behavior. Anxiety, as we have used the term, however, is not a dynamic, but a feeling which the individual experiences when confronted by a vaguely defined threat to his phenomenal self.

The anxiety feeling experienced by the individual may be more or less clearly attached to some perception or may be vague and unattached to any perception. The former is the kind of anxiety found in a phobia, in which it seems to accompany some specific object or event. When it is experienced without any apparent reference to a specific object or situation, it is sometimes called "free-floating" anxiety and is likely to be found in more generally threatened personalities. Let us examine the dynamics of a phobia as an example of how this kind of perceptual failure operates in producing threat and anxiety.

A young man had a very severe phobia for knives. The very sight of a knife in the hands of another person was enough to make him extremely uneasy, sometimes to the extent of begging others to put the knife away. This fear was extremely embarrassing to him and often made him the butt of unpleasant jokes among his friends. The young man himself recognized that his fear was quite unnecessary and even extremely silly, but at the same time he could not help feeling upset and frightened by the sight of a knife. He could not remember any good reason why he should be afraid of such things. This is a typical picture of a phobia.

Such fears are characterized by an unreasonable dread or anxiety attached to one or more fairly specific kinds of situations. Almost always, they are regarded as silly and unreasonable by the person who has the phobia, and it is characteristic that he is quite unable to recall the origins of his behavior.

In the case of this young man, the feared object has been strongly differentiated as an object to be avoided at all costs. The threatening aspects of the situation, however, are not so clearly differentiated. He feels anxious but cannot tell why. The reason for this failure of differentiation usually lies in either or both of two possibilities. First, the origin of the fear may have occurred so early in the life of the individual that he did not possess the necessary symbols which would make its differentiation possible. For example, a child who is frightened by some object might perceive it clearly but have no symbols with which to differentiate it from the guilt feelings which existed in the situation. The differentiation of "guilt" clearly requires an ability to deal with abstract symbols not possessed by young children till a later period. Later in life the individual may feel unreasonably fearful or anxious about the object long after familiarity with it should have taught him there is no need to fear it. The object can be clearly identified but the guilt feeling is still an aspect of the total situation.

A second possibility which may cause a threatening situation to fail of clear differentiation on a later occasion may be that the perception is too threatening. As we said in discussing "suppression," threatening perceptions may not be clearly differentiated because their acceptance into figure would require too great a reorganization of the self. As an example, a child whose parents have severely threatened him with loss of their love and affection may find this idea so painful and threatening to his organization that he resists any tendency for that aspect of the situation to rise into clear figure.

Let us see how these points apply to the case of the young man we mentioned above. In therapy the young man with the phobia for knives revealed this story of the origins of his strange behavior: As a young child he felt deeply rejected by his mother and felt a very great need for her love and affection. Unfortunately, this was not always easy to obtain, because his mother was extremely critical, unpredictable, and often very "nervous." He had been repeatedly warned by his mother that under no circumstances was he ever to touch a knife. One day, however, this youngster overheard his mother complain that she did not have a sharp knife in the house. Desperately seeking to please her, he took several of her kitchen knives to the curb in front of the house to sharpen them. He looked forward to the commendation he would receive for his act. In the process of sharpening the knives, one of them slipped and nearly severed the child's finger. Attracted by his cries, his mother rushed from the house in a panic, picked up the child and rushed him into the house, spanking him on the way and making it evident he was a *very bad boy.* She pointed out in no uncertain terms that this would never have happened had the child done as he was told. All this was terribly threatening. The child felt he had committed an unforgivable sin which caused his mother to reject him. From this incident, knives were differentiated strongly as objects to be avoided at all costs, but the concept of himself as guilty was by no means so clearly differentiated, probably because he had no symbols in which it could be brought to figure and (or) because bringing such feelings clearly into figure would have represented an intolerable threat to his phenomenal self. In later life it was often necessary to use knives for one purpose or another, and the young man was able to do this but never without a vague feeling of anxiety. Although he regarded his fear as silly in a grown man, he could not avoid his uneasiness and was often driven to certain impulsive behaviors which he was quite at a loss to explain. When, in the course of therapy, he was able to examine this early situation carefully and come to a clear differentiation of his feeling of guilt, he was able to reorganize his perceptions so that he no longer felt unworthy and unacceptable in the presence of a knife. As an adult he felt adequate to deal with the knife, and when he had clearly differentiated the threatening aspect he was able to accept this too into his organization. When this had occurred he lost his phobia completely.

NEUROSIS

The undifferentiated threat we have been discussing as characteristic of phobias is also the major characteristic of the neuroses. In fact, the primary difference between a neurosis and a phobia seems to lie in the fact that the threatening perception in a phobia appears primarly attached to one or more fairly specific objects or situations, while in neurosis the undifferentiated threat may be quite general and catastrophic. A very neurotic middle-aged schoolteacher came to a psychological clinic for assistance. She complained of constant tension, inability to sleep, and vague aches and pains for which her doctors could find no physiologic reason. She found it necessary to dose herself with all manner of medicines and complained of being in constant dread of something which she could not define. She was unable to concentrate on her work and found herself extremely overemotional, laughing or crying almost uncontrollably on the slightest pretext. Under therapy the following facts began to emerge.

She had always been a very popular and good-looking young woman, but was also under the domination of her mother to an extreme degree. As a result, although she had had numerous offers of marriage she was never able to bring herself to make the break from home. This state of affairs continued for some years until she began to be less attractive to men and her chances of marriage became fewer and fewer; finally she found herself 40 years old with no potential suitors left. About then, her mother began to show definite signs of age and it became apparent to the teacher that the time was not far off when she would be all alone in the world. She began to feel vague dreads of something she could not quite discern. Her behavior became compulsive and erratic and she felt constantly tense and uneasy. About this time her principal, a married man of her age, began to show her marked attention and finally asked for a date. The two became more and more intimate. Other people began to become suspicious and the threat of scandal and loss of position made matters even worse. The teacher became more and more frantic and more and more "neurotic" in her behavior.

In the course of counseling with this teacher it became clear that she reveled in the attentions she received from her principal although she knew full well the price she might have to pay for her clandestine affair. These aspects of her situation were clearly and sharply differentiated. Her feeling of guilt with respect to the possibility of breaking up her principal's family was similarly clearly perceived. In spite of this, she still felt that she could not give him up and continued to feel anxious and tense, although somewhat less than previously. She acted like a schoolgirl. She was radiantly happy in her intrigue and her mannerisms and affectations were those of a woman of 20 although she was twice that age. She was violently opposed to revealing her true age and went to football games and parties with teachers half her age, while at the same time speaking of people of 40 as "old-fashioned" and severely criticizing her contemporaries on the job. She acted 20 because she needed to regard herself as 20. She conceived of herself as still young, attractive, and desirable, and this led her to behave in ways often ludicrous to external observers. With such a concept of herself she could not give up her lover, for he probably represented her very last chance. To give him up would mean resigning herself to being an "old maid," would mean acceptance of herself as growing old. This was the vague dread that she could not face. With such a self concept she was beset on all sides with proof from the world about her that her concept of herself was just not so. She was kept so busy defending herself from the various onslaughts on her established position that change became impossible while threats became more and more pressing. The threat became larger and larger, becoming so much a part of her field that she acted fearfully in many situations, even those having no apparent connection with her dilemma.

To examine the dynamics involved, let us reduce this case to its basic elements. This woman conceived of herself as a teacher, which occupation was absolutely essential to her as a means of making a living. She regarded herself, also, as desirable, as young, as marriageable, and as essentially moral. She needed to maintain and enhance all these self definitions. But behavior which led to enhancement of one important aspect of self as young and desirable faced her at once with the terribly threatening perception of being immoral and unemployed. To give up her man was equally intolerable and threatening. At the same time external events were pressing for a showdown. She felt more and more threatened. What is more, the threat she felt made the broader examination of her field impossible, so that no solution was perceptible anywhere. She suffered from extreme anxiety. Since the perception of a solution was impossible, obviously, none could occur.

The major characteristics of this case are almost identical with the picture presented in the results from "experimental-neurosis" studies with animals. Shaffer, for instance, summarizes these results as follows: "First, the animal becomes unable to discriminate, losing even the older more habitual differentiations that have been formed previously. Second, he shows an irrational spread of response salivating for stimuli only incidentally connected with his training. Third, the animal gives evidence of tension and of emotional responses. . . . The same characteristics are seen in persons who are neurotic, unintegrated and predisposed to maladjustments." It is probably no accident that all of the work in "experimental neurosis," from Liddell's sheep and Pavlov's dogs to Krasnogorski's children, shows "neurosis" occurring when differentiation of adequate response is impossible.

DYNAMICS OF NEUROSIS

The dynamics of a typical neurosis seem to follow a pattern somewhat as follows:

1. One or more aspects of the phenomenal self become severely threatened either (a) by the perception of external events or (b) by the perception of the individual's own behavior motivated by another aspect of self.

2. These threatening perceptions cannot be accepted into figure and are maintained at a lower level of differentiation. This keeps them vague and diffuse. But they do exist in the field and so affect behavior.

3. Such "suppressed" differentiations continue to threaten the self although vaguely and unprecisely. The individual experiences anxiety.

4. The need of the organism to maintain its phenomenal self will not permit threatening perceptions to exist in the field without solution. Even low-level perceptions continue to motivate the individual, and if these cannot be fitted into the organization they keep him in a continual state of emergency so that he feels tense and emotional.

5. The individual's behavior proceeding from these vague and diffuse low-level perceptions will be similarly vague and lacking in precision. This inefficient behavior is unlikely to provide adequate solutions to his problems. Indeed, it is even likely to make things worse or more complicated than ever, bringing on a kind of vicious circle in which the experience of threat makes precise differentiation impossible, which in turn makes effective behavior unlikely, which does not resolve the threat and only increases the likelihood of ineffective perception. Such a circular pattern of perception and behavior may go for years without resolution. Large numbers of unhappy and maladjusted people in our society are caught in just such a cycle as we have been describing above. Having come to see themselves, for one reason or another, in inadequate ways, they become deeply threatened and frustrated, living large portions of their lives in grim attempts to achieve a measure of adequacy they do not feel. The pattern of a neurosis we have just been describing would serve equally well to describe the dynamics of delinquency. In the case of the teacher described above the same feelings of inadequacy that led to "neurotic" behavior produced a number of delinquent acts as well.

If neurosis and maladjustment, delinquency and criminality are, as we have suggested, the product of inadequate perceptions of self and the world people live in, it would seem to follow that the treatment of such disturbances must be based upon helping inadequate personalities to new and more satisfying perceptions of themselves and their relationships to the world. This is exactly what modern methods of psychotherapy seek to accomplish for all of these disturbances. Although there are a number of different schools of thought about how to treat extremely threatened personalities, all schools agree on the necessity for producing some kind of change in the ways in which the individual sees himself and his world. Psychotherapists help their clients to explore their perceptions of themselves and the worlds they live in to the end that they may discover new and more satisfying definitions. Since the experience of threat looms so large in the dynamics of inadequate personalities and serves to complicate the problem of adjustment, most psychotherapies also include one or more methods by which clients seeking treatment can be at least temporarily protected from threat.

The Desperate Ones—The Dynamics of Psychosis

The existence of threat in the individual's phenomenal field cannot be ignored. It must be dealt with. The greater the experience of threat, the greater must be the attempts of the organism to find resolution. Mild threats may require only mild kinds of behavior, but extreme degrees of threat are likely to call forth increasingly bizarre and violent behavior on the part of the individual attempting to seek adequacy in a too threatening world. Severely threatened persons like neurotics may act in ways that sometimes seem to us to be odd or unnecessarily intense. Such people are not the most inadequate persons in our society, however. Though they feel inadequate in ways important to them, they do not feel totally inadequate or defeated. Consequently the methods they use to achieve feelings of adequacy are likely to remain within the tolerance of people around them. Persons who feel more deeply inadequate and threatened are likely to use much more extreme ways to achieve a measure of adequacy. At times these methods may even become so upsetting or dangerous to themselves or to the rest of us that such people have to be isolated.

The most threatened, desperate individuals in our society are those we describe as psychotic, mentally ill, or the more violent and dangerous criminals. These are the desperate ones, the people unable to find more than a modicum of need satisfaction. They differ from the neurotic in the degree of inadequacy which they feel and the techniques they use to deal with the threats they experience. They feel so deeply inadequate for one reason or another that they live almost constantly (from their point of view) in the shadow of destruction. They feel desperately unable to cope with the threats they perceive and find little opportunity for successful or satisfying fulfillment of need. The extremity of the threats which they experience, moreover, calls for heroic measures in coping with life.

It is not our intention to enter upon an extended discussion of the psychology of psychosis here. The variety of techniques used by deeply inadequate personalities are almost limitless. In kind, they extend all the way from simple techniques of rationalization to some of the most bizarre and imaginative devices of which the human mind is capable. The particular symptoms of a particular individual may range from a single repeatedly used technique to a wide variety of techniques used in rapid succession. To deal with these extensively would be beyond the scope and purpose of this volume. Instead, we shall content ourselves with a few illustrations of how some common techniques of dealing with threat are utilized by extremely threatened, inadequate personalities.

The particular symptoms observed by outsiders examining the behavior of extremely inadequate personalities are the outward manifestations of the individual's attempts to deal with the threats he perceives. They are the techniques he uses as his peculiar means of achieving need satisfaction under great difficulties. He may use them in the same ways less threatened people do or he may use them in much more extreme degree or with variations undreamed of by more adequate persons. Desperate feelings, after all, require desperate measures, and what seems quite normal in a minor degree may become bizarre and outlandish when pushed to an extreme. Punishing others by failing to speak to them is usually permissible; punishing others by murder is seldom tolerated, at least in our society. The mildly threatened individual may find it assuages his wounded self to find a "good excuse" for failure. He explains that he "wasn't feeling well," "forgot," or "someone interfered" in his achieving his goals. The more threatened individual may do exactly the same thing in extreme form when he explains that "someone is controlling him against his will," he "was in Afghanistan on a secret mission for the President" at the moment he was called on to perform, or perhaps he may explain in great detail how "certain persons have cunningly arranged" just this sequence of events for his discomfiture.

In general the peculiar techniques of dealing with threat used by the psychotic may be classified in two of the categories we described earlier in this chapter, namely, (1) threatening perceptions may be denied relevance to the self in one form or another, or (2) perceptions of self or the world outside may be so distorted as to fit the existing organization of the phenomenal field. Let us examine some of the ways in which such techniques may be used in extremely inadequate personalities.

DENIAL OF THE RELEVANCE OF THREAT

The experience of threat may be dealt with by denying its relevance to the self. This may be accomplished, we have seen, either by relegating it to someone else or by denying its existence at all. This is typical of some forms of schizophrenia. Many such patients appear to feel so inadequate that any event, no matter how insignificant to the outside observer, is perceived by them as extraordinarily threatening. The slightest word or phrase, even the lift of an eyebrow in those important to them, may be interpreted as threat. The whole external world seems just too threatening to tolerate.

Some schizophrenics solve this problem by retiring within themselves and relegating more and more of experience to the not-self aspects of the field. Although Maslow has approached this problem from a different frame of reference, his description of the schizophrenic lies very close to our own conception of these states. He describes them in part as follows: "The evaluation of reality, as regards both social customs and perceptions, is disturbed partly because . . . the patient seems to follow a formula which implies: 'Reality does not matter; only what I desire matters.' This results in the absence of shame and the disregard of restriction common to normal human beings." From the patient's own point of view, of course, he is not denying reality. On the contrary, so far as he is concerned, he is living in the only reality: that of his phenomenal field.

In its milder forms this withdrawal from life may be observed in simple schizophrenia, in which the person adopts an attitude of "it doesn't concern me" and often becomes apathetic and dull. Many hobos present this picture. A young man known to one of the authors showed an interesting pattern of this type. All his life until he came to college he had been protected and petted by an oversolicitous mother. He became almost entirely dependent upon her, and in his college years he made a remarkable academic record. All his out-of-class time was spent at home with his devoted and adoring mother. In his last year of college she remarried, and the young man set out after graduation for his first teaching position. Within a few days he walked out of class and never returned. He was picked up wandering the streets of a town some distance away. In the hospital he was coöperative and pleasant and when attention was paid to him he would converse intelligently on a wide variety of topics, always on a high intellectual plane. The moment the topic of conversation was steered toward himself he would skillfully avoid the reference and skip off to another topic with less personal reference.

When put to work on the farm, this young man would go along willingly, would start hoeing at the beginning of a row, but when he reached the end would lie down. He was through for the day. No amount of urging could induce him to work any longer. When he was discharged from the hospital to a job in a gas station he worked three hours, then wandered off for several days. He was picked up some distance away. When returned to the hospital he sat by himself with a fixed smile for hours until someone stirred him enough to get him talking on some subject. He delighted in talking to groups of students touring the hospital and discoursed at length with them in their own campus language. Thus, when opportunities were presented to him for self enhancement without overt effort, he would rise to the occasion and was willing to remain in contact with external events. However, the moment that he was thrown in any degree upon his own resources, or when it became necessary to react more than passively to his environment, he retreated into his apathetic and disinterested pattern of behavior. When he felt adequate, he acted normally. When he felt inadequate, he retreated into his protective shell. It seems likely that the loss of his mother's protection and aid left this young man so poorly equipped that the necessities of assuming personal responsibility became a very real and violent threat to his existence.

Perhaps the most extreme example of this withdrawal of the individual and refusal to operate in external reality is to be observed in catatonic types of schizophrenia. In this state, denial of the relevance of threat may even involve separation of the self from the physical body. It becomes possible to stick the patient with pins, to mold him almost at will without his slightest response. He behaves as though he felt "it doesn't concern me in the least." He acts like an innocent bystander with respect to his own body conditions. The catatonic behaves as though his phenomenal self were completely apart from this world. He treats outside events as irrelevant and immaterial. He may sit quietly while his room burns. He sees the fire but, since it has no relation to him, it does not spur him to action. Occasionally, however, he may suddenly return to contact with objective reality with violent excitement and impulsive activity. Such returns appear to occur when the individual shifts his techniques from a withdrawal from threat to an attack upon it. Such sudden returns to contact seem to be associated with increased feelings of adequacy.

It will be recognized that the denial of the relevance of threat is a major characteristic of criminals as well. The assumption that the normal controls of society do not apply to him leaves the desperado free to behave as he desires. Or if he is really threatened and has little sense of identification, some threats may be eliminated by eliminating the persons who produce them. The methods he uses to deny the relevance of threat are often the very factors which cause some individuals to be considered criminal rather than psychotic.

DISTORTIONS OF PERCEPTION TO FIT EXISTING FIELD ORGANIZATIONS

Like all people, seriously inadequate personalities attempt to deal with threat by distorting their perceptions of themselves or the world they live in in such a manner as to be consistent with the existing field organization. Many psychotic states are characterized by such distortions. They exist as hallucinations, delusions, and obsessions of one variety or another. Though we describe such distortions as false or unreal, it should not be thought that they seem so to the persons who experience them. Quite the contrary, to the individual at the moment of having such perceptions, the experience is real and vital.

Perhaps the best illustration of the distortion of external events is to be observed in paranoia. This is a psychotic state characterized by great suspicion of others and often highly fanciful delusions of persecution. Here the threat to the individual's phenomenal self may become so great that it is involved in every slightest activity in which he is concerned. He perceives threat in everything; the letters he receives are summonses to court, his friends are out to "get him," all the world is lying in wait for him. His feeling of being threatened colors a very large share of his perceptions. It appears to him that he is threatened by even the smallest details of his surroundings. Alone in this threatening world, the paranoid patient often spends much time in scheming to get the better of the host of enemies by whom he feels he is surrounded. Everything must be given an explanation and even events having nothing to do with him are seen as oriented toward self. He suffers delusions and hallucinations and, to all intents and purposes, he is indeed alone against the world.

Unlike some of the other psychotics, the paranoid patient lives in the midst of his threats instead of withdrawing from them. He often remains more or less in touch with many aspects of external reality but builds a keen and often highly logical defense against those perceptions which appear to him most threatening. Some paranoid patients may be quite normal with respect to much of their daily living and feel threatened only when some event is perceived as relating to those areas in which they feel vulnerable. Paranoids frequently organize their field so completely that they are able to pluck enhancement out of the threat. Once they have explained their failures and feelings of inadequacy by believing that they are surrounded by enemies, it is almost necessary for them to ask themselves: "Why am I so important that so many people spend their lives conspiring against me?" It should not surprise anyone that many paranoids come to believe that they are God.

MULTIPLE PERSONALITIES

Distortions which maintain the organization of the phenomenal field may affect the individual's perceptions of self in other ways. Behavior resulting from one concept of self may be unacceptable and threatening to another aspect of self. Under these circumstances perceptions of self may be so distorted as to keep such diverse self perceptions from existing simultaneously. This appears to be illustrated in an extreme form in what are often described as *multiple personalities.* In a mild form this separation of self was illustrated in the case of Helen, a little girl known to the author. Helen had developed another personality, Marie. Helen was an extremely "good" child who always did as she was told. She was in every way a delight from an adult point of view. Marie, on the other hand, was a "naughty" girl who said "bad words," who sometimes wet her panties, who slapped her little brother, and who was generally responsible for most of the quarrels among the children of the neighborhood. This dual personality had been brought on by the birth of Helen's little brother and the child's consequent attempts to gain self esteem. Finding herself no longer the "apple of her parent's eye," she sought to achieve self esteem in new ways. These attempts were met by her shocked and horrified parents with many statements that she was a "bad" girl and were accompanied by moralistic reproof and severe punishment. Such proof of her immorality could not be accepted by Helen, who had always regarded herself previously as a "nice" girl. Yet the proofs could not be done away with. Her own parents in whom she trusted *insisted* that she was a bad girl! Her "naughty" behavior, moreover, was extremely satisfying and made it possible to regain a feeling of enhancement necessary to her. She could neither accept her behavior as bad nor go on believing herself good. A multiple personality solved the problem for Helen. Helen did not have to feel guilty at what Marie did, while Marie could do things that gave the child immediate satisfaction without threatening Helen. When the child's parents were helped to remove the threats and pressure from Helen, when they had accepted their little girl's behavior, and when they had provided new ways in which Helen could gain self esteem, Marie disappeared and has never been heard from since.

T. W. Mitchell and Gardner Murphy have made a distinction between two general types of multiple personalities. In Type I, the two or more personalities are widely separated, and the individual operating in either frame of reference has little or no apparent knowledge or memory of the activities of the other. This state of affairs appears to exist when both A aspect of self and B aspect of self are inadequate, that is, too threatened by the perception of their counterparts to be able to accept their perceptions into the organization. In this case, A will not even "know" what B has been up to. Nor will B have any apparent knowledge of A's activities. It should not be imagined, however, that this is a "real" difference in personalities, for under hypnosis or some other method by which the individual can be made to feel unthreatened, both personalities can be recalled and described by the individual.

In Type II, personality A is able to recall the activities of personality B, but B is apparently unaware of the activities of A. Murphy summarizes Morton Prince's "BCA" case as follows: "[BCA] after recovery wrote her autobiography as a double personality. . . . A was sober, serious, reserved, afraid of life, and of herself, 'full of metaphysical doubts and fears, full of scruples.' B was jolly and carefree, healthy and vigorous. When B suddenly disappeared, A was often shocked to find herself confronting a wineglass or a cigarette. B, however, knew all about A, pitying and despising her thoughts and attitudes, of which B always had complete and direct knowledge." We have here what Murphy has called a "restricted" and a "relaxed personality." In perceptual terms we would call them threatened and nonthreatened, respectively. The already threatened personality cannot tolerate new threatening perceptions, while the less threatened personality finds it possible at least to accept new threats into figure, even though they may be rejected and despised. Whereas in Type I we have been discussing two aspects of self each highly threatening to the other, in Type II we have a highly threatened self definition and a less threatened one.

This restricting effect of threat is nicely illustrated in W. F. Prince's classic case of Doris Fischer. Over a period of time Doris developed four fairly distinct personalities. The original Doris was a "good" girl who ordinarily did quietly what was demanded of her. She was a restricted, introverted personality deeply attached to her mother. The second of Doris' personalities appeared when she was about 3 years old, following a traumatic experience in which she was brutally thrown to the floor by her drunken father. Following this experience, Doris developed a second personality, Margaret. Margaret was quite a different person than Doris. She was active, carefree, mischievous, and constantly engaged in aggressive behavior of one sort or another. Margaret knew about Doris, disliked her intensely, and even punished Doris on occasion for playing with Margaret's possessions. Doris, however, apparently knew nothing of the existence of Margaret. The third personality came into being when Doris was sixteen. Doris' mother died then, quite suddenly. This was too much for the young girl. She was deeply shocked and distraught, and "Sick Doris" appeared on the scene. This new personality was an extremely threatened one, a highly restricted drudge who went about her tasks without imagination and little or no response. "Sick Doris" seemed to know nothing of her other selves.

At the time Prince worked with this patient then, she had three distinct personalities—Sick Doris, Doris, and Margaret—arranged in order of the increasing freedom of the personalities. It is interesting that the more threatened personalities "did not know" of the less threatened ones but the freer personalities were apparently aware of the more restricted ones. Finally, under hypnosis, a fourth personality made its appearance. This was "Sleeping Margaret." Sleeping Margaret was the most unrestricted and unthreatened of the four personalities. She knew all of the activities of her other selves and was able to converse at length, in detail, and with much objectivity about each of the other three. Thus the multiple personality seems to be an attempt to maintain the phenomenal self through acquiring another self, adequate and able to do what is impossible or inappropriate for the original. Extremely threatened personalities may find it possible to achieve a degree of adequacy by assuming a different identity.

Closely related to such distortion of self perception is the assumption of new, more adequate personalities unrelated to the original self. Many mental patients appear to find another solution to the problem of threat in various "delusions of grandeur." Feeling inadequate to deal with the world as themselves, it is sometimes possible for them to achieve a feeling of adequacy and even of invincibility by adopting a ready-made and proved self from history, religion, or mythology. Thus, if George Smith is not adequate to deal with life as Smith he may become George Washington instead. There is no doubt in either his mind or those about him of Washington's adequacy.

Perhaps the most extreme distortions of self perceptions are to be observed in some types of psychosis in which the organization of self seems shattered, or so wildly fluctuating as to leave the individual completely confused and with little or no frame of reference from which to operate. This kind of disorganization of self perception may be seen in some types of schizophrenia generally characterized by disorganization of thinking and often by rapidly shifting and changing behavior on the part of the patient. These patients seem characterized by self concepts which appear to have lost the stability characteristic of those of the normal individual. They appear to feel threatened in many aspects of self, so much so that they cannot accept any consistent evaluation of self. They appear to be confused as to who and what they are, and feel inadequate in many ways. The definition of the phenomenal self seems almost to be shifting and changing quite out of the patient's control, and his ideas and actions may shift rapidly from moment to moment. Often it is possible to observe in the so-called "word salads" of such patients a train of coherent thought which appears to rise to the surface and then disappear in a jumble of other ideas only to return again later in the passage. This sometimes appears as though the patient's field had a momentary organization which slipped away, and returned, and slipped away again, over and over.

CHANGING FEELINGS OF ADEQUACY

It is interesting to note how the techniques used by very inadequate personalities change with varying degrees of feelings of adequacy. With increased feelings of inadequacy, techniques become increasingly violent, bizarre, or withdrawn. As feelings of adequacy increase, techniques become more socially fitting, acceptable, and active. This is nicely illustrated in the following case known to the author. Bill Johnson was an extraordinarily successful businessman. He was known in his community as a veritable dynamo of energy. He was athletic, hearty, and a rather dominating sort of person. He seldom listened to other people but usually had good ideas of how things could be accomplished and the energy with which to follow them through. By virtue of his tremendous energy and frequent flashes of brilliance he rose rapidly in the X Corporation through a whirlwind development of the sales department. He finally became vice-president of the corporation. He was a promoter of no mean ability. His family was inclined to breathe a sigh of relief when he was away from home, for even in the family setting he continued his whirlwind methods of operation. He seldom slept more than four hours a night. He looked like a very promising young man until the president of his corporation began to feel threatened by the extraordinary rise of his junior officer. The corporation president began to block Bill Johnson's ambitious efforts at every hand. Bill became wilder and wilder in his efforts to achieve his ends and finally precipitated a showdown with the board of directors. He lost, was forced to resign his job, and retired to his home a very sick man. For many months he was in the depths of despair, feeling himself a complete failure. He felt inadequate to attempt the simplest thing and slept 12 or 13 hours a day.

A few months later he was offered an important position with a government agency in a distant part of the country. Almost overnight he was a different man. He packed up his family and was off to the new location. He had hardly arrived before the same cycle began all over again. Once more he was a dynamo of energy involved in all of the affairs of his community. Again he rose rapidly to a position of considerable responsibility in the new agency until he had reached the top. It was impossible to go further in this job, after three or four years, without participating in politics and being elected to the next highest office. Without batting an eye he became a politician overnight and ran for election. Unfortunately, he lost by but a few votes. Immediately after election he collapsed and was hospitalized for almost a year in a deeply depressed state.

The dynamics of Bill Johnson's case appear to be as follows: Bill Johnson is possessed of a concept of self as inadequate. This concept, however, is intolerable to him and he strives in countless ways to "snow under" such threatening perceptions by a ceaseless round of activity.

He attempts to prove to himself that he is better than he feels he is. Often he is successful at this sort of thing for long periods of time. So long as he remains physically healthy and has reserves of energy to call upon, he continues his wild course of behavior. He literally runs away from his problem by doing things, *anything*. When his physical resources collapse, however, he no longer feels adequate. He has not the energy with which to carry on his frantic behavior. He is forced to slow down in spite of himself and is, at once, faced with the very threatening perceptions he seeks to avoid. In a very real sense his immobility robs him of his best defensive technique. He feels depressed and woefully inadequate. Such depressions are often their own cure, however, for they prevent him from being active and over a period of time his physical resources may return. Now he can feel adequate again, and some little success sets him off on the business of convincing himself once more that what he believes to be true is "just not so." When Bill Johnson felt more adequate, he behaved more adequately. Unfortunately, even when he was operating in high gear, he still felt basically inadequate.

TREATMENT OF PSYCHOSIS

Even the most threatened, withdrawn psychotics can sometimes be induced to come out of their protective shells and return to fuller "contact" with the outside world when they can be helped to feel more adequate and secure. When such patients are treated in a warm, nonthreatening atmosphere for long enough periods, they can sometimes be induced to carry on conversations with others or to make halting attempts to renew relationships they have rejected for years. Many mental patients seem to get well when they are hospitalized, even though they have had no formal treatment whatever. Sometimes the very fact of hospitalization removes the patient from the threatening relationships of his daily life. In the sheltered atmosphere of the hospital he then is able to feel more adequate and, temporarily separated from his inadequacies, may find it possible to relax and differentiate new self definitions more satisfying than those he held before. Unhappily, this does not always occur. Frequently the patient improves in the sheltered atmosphere of the hospital only to suffer a relapse when he is plunged back into his normal setting and finds himself once more confronted with threats that seem just too much for him to bear.

Once it was customary to treat inadequate personalities as the psychotic or criminal by locking them up or subjecting them to various forms of punishment or horrible experiences of one sort or another in the hope of frightening them back to a semblance of normality. Occasionally these methods worked, but more often the patient became worse if he succeeded in surviving at all. This is what we would expect in the light of our current knowledge of the effects of threat. Modern treatment of seriously inadequate personalities is a far cry from the primitive techniques of a generation ago, and the past 20 years has seen great changes in the operation of our institutions for the criminal and the psychotic. New understandings of the psychology of these desperate ones has made it possible to devise new methods of treatment for severely inadequate persons with far greater chances of success than formerly. The most successful of these new methods assist the individual in one way or another to differentiate new and more adequate concepts of himself and the world in which he lives. This is, of course, neither simple nor easy. Rather it is often a long, painful, and difficult process of self redefinition requiring patience and skill on the part of the therapist and his coworkers as well as a high degree of courage and perseverance on the part of the patient. Given a chance, however, the individual's own need for adequacy will impel him toward better health if the ways seem open to him. In recent years we have found better and better ways to help such desperate persons to find greater adequacy and to achieve a larger measure of self actualization.

PART II

The Perceptual Approach Applied

So much of our lives is concerned with human relationships that any change in our beliefs about the nature of man and his behavior must, of necessity, have tremendous implications for all aspects of our social existence. This has always been true throughout man's history and is just as true today. Whatever we believe about people must inevitably affect the ways we behave toward them. In the previous chapters of this volume we have developed a frame of reference for the understanding of behavior. It is time now to look at some of the implications of these concepts for dealing with the great human problems of our generation. Practice provides the test of theory. Theory opens the doors to new possibilities in practice. No matter how consistent and plausible a theory may be, it is of no value if it does not contribute ultimately to the improvement of practice. If the point of view presented in the preceding chapters has any value, it should be manifest in a contribution to improved understanding and action.

What, we need to ask, has this view of behavior to offer for dealing with some of the practical problems of man's relationships with his fellows? In the pages to follow we shall attempt to answer this question by exploring the implications of a perceptual view of behavior as they apply to several important areas of human action.

CHAPTER 14

Some General Implications for Human Relations

The Facts of Human Relationships

The facts of human behavior, we have seen, are not the facts that exist for others but the facts that exist for the behaver. If it is true that people behave according to how things seem to them, then it is the things people believe which are the facts of human relationships. In this sense, seeing is not only believing; seeing is behaving! A fact is not what is; a fact is what one *believes!* The data with which we must deal in understanding and changing human relationships, then, are feelings, attitudes, beliefs, and values. The citizen who voted for the Democratic candidate did so in the belief that he was the better man. Millions of Republican voters disagreed. Each voter behaved in terms of what seemed to him to be so. Which voter was correct we shall never know, but each behaved as though his own *belief* were the fact of the matter.

Many Russians believe we are a nation of "capitalistic warmongers bent upon world domination." Many of us, on the other hand, believe the Russians to be "fanatics who will stop at nothing to achieve world domination." Each nation behaves as though its assessment of the other were an inescapable fact. We are shocked by Russian perceptions of us and deeply hurt that we are regarded with such suspicion. How people perceive, however, is not a matter to be ignored or to feel hurt about. Perceptions are not matters to deplore. If it is true, as we have postulated, that behavior is a product of perception, then they become the basic data of human relations and the facts with which we must learn to deal.

To regard the facts of human behavior in this way is likely to prove extremely distressing or difficult to some people. Though the idea that people behave according to how things seem to them is simplicity itself, there are strong factors both in ourselves and our society that make this quite difficult to accept. We have been so impressed, for example, with the magnificent achievements of the physical sciences in our society that many of us have come to regard the "objective" world of the physical sciences as equivalent to reality itself. This view of events has served our society so well in dealing with the problems for which it is appropriate, that many people have come to believe the objective approach is the only possible method of observation worthy of consideration.

It is a natural thing to attempt to apply the methods with which we have been successful in the past to problems we meet in the present. There is a glorious definiteness about dealing with "things." They stay where they are put and behave in comfortable, predictable ways, and we would like people to behave so too. Because of this former satisfying experience it is a temptation to extend the methods we have found so useful to the new area of our interest. We fail to understand that different problems require quite different approaches.

It is difficult for us to approach human relationships from a perceptual view, for another reason. Our own perceptions always have so strong a feeling of reality that it is easy to jump to the conclusion that they must be real to others as well. If others do not see as we do, we may even regard them as stupid, stubborn, or perverse. It is hard to set one's own experience aside, yet it is difficult to see how effective human relationships can be built without a clear recognition of the personal character of perceptions. The first step toward the solution of our human problems seems to require a willingness to grant that "How it seems to me may be different. I, too, could be wrong!" Humility, it would seem, is more than a nice idea. It is an essential to effective communication!

Still another factor makes the perceptual approach to human relationships difficult. That is, the widespread feeling in some quarters that the admission of human feelings, attitudes, and perceptions as behavioral data flirts with the mystical and runs the risk of being "unscientific." No real science, however, can afford to ignore data relevant to its purposes simply because they are difficult to measure or do not lend themselves to treatment by orthodox means. If behavior is a function of perception, then a science of human relationships must concern itself with the meaning of events for the behaver as well as for the observer. Human feelings, attitudes, fears, hopes, wants, likes, and aversions cannot be set aside while we deal with objective events. The subjective aspects of human experience cannot be suspended from operation. Perceptions are the very fabric of which human relationships are made. They are the crucial facts with which we must deal in attempting to solve our most pressing problems. If we do not currently possess the means of studying perceptions effectively, then we need to get about the business of finding out how without further delay. Time presses upon us.

Man as Responsible Agent

A second broad implication of the perceptual approach has to do with the way in which we regard man and his relationships to the world in which he lives. One of the earliest conceptions of the nature of human beings held that man was a completely independent and responsible agent. People in those times, looking at themselves and their fellows, observed that human beings made decisions. They concluded from these observations that man was, therefore, a creature entirely responsible for his behavior. Whatever he did arose entirely from within himself. If a man misbehaved, it was his fault that he did so. He was thoroughly and inescapably to blame for his acts.

With such a conception of what man was trying to do, it is not surprising that education in those days was a gloomy, coercive affair in which children were "taught," *made* to behave. And no wonder—salvation was at stake! Nor is it surprising that adults believed quite thoroughly that people deserved what happened to them. Since man was utterly responsible, punishments were harsh and severe. Little sympathy was wasted on the criminal, the sick, or the insane. Indeed, that such misfortunes befell a man only served to prove how bad he must have been! Parents were blamed for their failures to correct a child or to force obedience, not for their failures to provide a child with love and affection. When a child misbehaved it was because the child was bad and parents were sympathized with or pitied. If they were blamed at all, it was for failure to force obedience, teach manners, or "bend the twig properly." We still have in our society people who believe that criminals and even nations should be punished severely for their misbehavior.

Whereas the concept we have just been speaking about held that man was completely responsible for what happened to him, another concept commonly held even today sees man as the *victim* of his environment. He is what he is because of what has happened to him. Unfortunately, this point of view, while making possible great strides in some aspects of human living, has, at the same time, made it difficult for us to understand some of our most pressing problems. It has given rise to a mechanistic conception of human beings as physical objects whose behavior is the result of forces acting upon them. It has largely dehumanized psychology, making of human beings little more than objects to be manipulated at will. In this view human beings are often compared to steam engines, automobiles, or other pieces of machinery. Man is thought of as a passive automaton, buffeted about by the circumstances surrounding him.

Such a view of behavior places the responsibility quite outside the individual himself. The implications of this view are widespread throughout all phases of our society. Perhaps no group is more affected, however, than our defenseless, unorganized parents. As low man on the totem pole, the responsibility for all our social ills is laid squarely at their door. Whatever institution is criticized for its failures to deal with people effectively sooner or later ends by blaming the parent. The parents, having no one to whom to "pass the buck," are stuck with it! The best a poor parent can do is to blame it all on his spouse's side of the family. But if behavior is truly a function of environment only, then parents can no more be held responsible than other agencies in society and the people *really* responsible are our forefathers clear back to Adam or the first living organism!

The view of man's behavior we have adopted in this volume helps us to resolve this dilemma. We have seen in Chapter 3 that man is continuous with his environment, but we have also seen that he is never free from the dynamic, creative force of his fundamental need for adequacy. This gives us a view of man neither so completely responsible for his behavior as the first view we have cited above, nor on the other hand so willy-nilly at the mercy of his environment as the second would lead us to believe. He is part controlled by and in part controlling of his destiny. It provides us with an understanding of man deeply and intimately affected by his environment but capable also of molding and shaping his destiny in important ways. Such a view fits more closely our own experience and is an understanding broadly significant in helping us find solutions to some of our great social problems.

Two Approaches to Dealing with Human Problems

THE FENCING-IN APPROACH

The differences between the environmental and perceptual views of behavior are nowhere so clearly marked as in the kinds of methods they lead to in dealing with human relationships. The environmental approach to behavior has led us to believe that almost anything can be accomplished in dealing with people if we are sufficiently skillful in the manipulation of the proper forces at the proper times. Its adoption results in an approach to human problems based upon control of environment and has produced a way of dealing with people familiar to anyone who has ever visited a stockyard or driven the cows home from pasture. One goes down the lane from the barn and carefully closes all the gates where he does *not* want the cattle to go and opens the gates where he *does* want them to go. In the pasture the cattle are set in motion by creating an annoyance behind them, thus driving them forward up the path prepared for them.

While the fencing-in technique works fine with cattle and sheep, it often breaks down with human beings. People, being somewhat smarter than cows, have a disconcerting way of discovering that the "right" way often leads to places they would rather not go. They are just as likely as not to jump the fence, open gates that were overlooked, and generally behave in the most unpredictable and "uncoöperative" ways. In spite of its frequent failure, however, this fencing-in philosophy of human relationships is applied in dealing with people throughout our society: in advertising and selling, in labor-management discussions, in administration, in our legislatures, and even in our diplomacy of power politics, buffer states, and vetoes. It is common practice in our schools, our churches, and our homes. If we believe that human behavior is alone a function of the forces exerted upon people, a philosophy of force and coercion naturally follows as the appropriate means of dealing with our fellows. Such force may be expressed as naked power. It may also be clothed in a velvet glove as "friendly" advice, reward for "proper" behavior, or various more or less subtle forms of reward or punishment.

The fencing-in approach moreover, raises an additional serious problem, for it requires that someone must know what the "right" goal is in order effectively to manipulate the required forces. Someone must know where the people *should* go. This calls for a leader or great man, to chart the proper path for the common people. Such an approach sometimes works fairly well when the right answers are known and leaders are essentially benevolent. Unfortunately, right answers to human problems are remarkably elusive and great men are as often wrong as right. Despite the fact that this essentially manipulative method of dealing with people seems hardly compatible with our democratic ideals, it nevertheless may be found operating even in some of our most "democratic" institutions.

THE GROWTH APPROACH

If the view of human behavior we have been exploring in this book is accurate, it calls for a very different approach to human problems from the one above. How people perceive themselves and the world in which they live is an internal, personal matter. What people believe about themselves and their environment is not directly open to manipulation. A man's perceptions arise within himself. We cannot *make* people perceive. Effective, satisfying human relationships can only be developed through helping ourselves and others to perceive more freely and accurately. Man is not a puppet bandied about at the mercy of the forces exerted upon him. On the contrary, he is a creature of discretion who selects his perceptions from the world he lives in. He is not the victim of events but is capable of perceiving, interpreting, even creating events. Such a conception of human beings requires a very different approach to working with people than the "fencing-in" technique we have outlined above. It calls for the development of understanding rather than manipulation; for freeing communication, in place of coercion; for stimulating mutual exploration and discovery of goals and means, as opposed to servile dependence on an elite.

The perceptual view sees man as a growing, dynamic, creative being continuously in search of adequacy. Instead of an object at the mercy of environment, he is, himself, a purposive agent engaged in a never-ending business of becoming. People in this sense are processes rather than objects, growing rather than static, and call for the same kind of treatment we accord other growing things. To grow a good plant, for example, we acquire the best seed we can get, plant it in the best ground we can provide, surround it with the very best conditions for growth we can produce; then we get out of its way and let it grow! In a similar manner, the perceptual view leads to methods of dealing with people which recognize the internal character of perception and seek to affect behavior through processes of facilitation, helping, assisting, or aiding the normal growth strivings of the organism itself.

Since perception is an internal process not open to direct manipulation from without, change in behavior cannot be brought about directly but only through the kinds of experiences people are exposed to. From a perceptual frame of reference therefore, the emphasis in dealing with people is upon the creation of *kind of situations which facilitate or assist the process of perception change.* Good teachers know, for example, that children cannot be *made* to learn. Children, however, can and will learn when teachers are successful in creating experiences which encourage and assist the learner in his search for adequacy. Our frame of reference calls for an approach to human relationships which seeks change in behavior through change in perceiving rather than through a direct attack on behavior itself. It emphasizes in practice techniques of communication, persuasion, learning, and discovery rather than the employment of force, coercion, or various forms of manipulation.

Since perceptions are more directly causative of behavior than environmental manipulation, methods of dealing with people dependent upon changing perception rather than controlling and directing behavior are likely to be more permanent and trustworthy on later occasions when pressure and coercion are no longer present. Although it is of course possible to make people behave as desired by the application of sufficient force at the right time, such behavior cannot be counted upon to occur at times when the force is no longer applied. What people *believe* they carry about with them, but environments are external and therefore can be left behind.

The perceptual approach seems particularly effective when applied to problems of human relationships in group settings. Because it recognizes the unhappy effects of threat upon perceiving and seeks to challenge people without threatening them, conflict among the members of the group and with outsiders as well is likely to exist at a much lower level. Conflict is heightened when people feel frustrated, inadequate, or coerced into moving in directions they do not wish to go. As a consequence resistance is likely to be high and change occurs only slowly and painfully, if at all. A philosophy of group operation based upon helping, aiding, assisting, however, keeps frustration at a minimum so that conflict is not so likely to occur. Even when it does occur, the elimination of threat provides little to support it and it soon fails of its own weight.

Such approaches to human interrelationship, furthermore, actually create leadership in groups rather than being dependent upon leadership provided from without. Where human dignity and integrity is respected and valued, when people are treated as though they were able, given assistance and help in their search for adequacy, and confronted with challenging tasks, creativity and spontaneity result. It should not surprise us either that under such circumstances the solutions people find to problems are likely to be of superior quality. And why not? Groups operating on a growth philosophy are not restricted to the solutions which occur to a single leader; the groups themselves create leadership and release human potentialities. What is more, persons who have experienced these kinds of human relationships are far more likely to have faith and trust in their fellows and to be capable of identifying and empathizing with others.

To some this approach to dealing with human problems as a process of facilitation of perceptions seems highly disappointing and much too slow to be capable of solving important problems. A helping, assisting, freeing approach seems somehow to smack of anarchy and laissez faire. They have little assurance that people will arrive at the "right" answers to problems without someone to decide what these are and arrange matters in such a fashion as to make sure that everyone gets there. As a matter of fact, the emphasis upon processes and facilitation in the long run seems much more likely to supply us with better solutions, for it has the advantage of producing an open, rather than a closed, system of thought. Whenever we choose a particular set of goals or values for people and then set about deliberately to achieve these ends, we are operating in a closed system. Such systems seriously restrict the field from which we can make our selections. Rogers, in a discussion of this principle applied to the science of human relationship, has described closed systems as follows:

> . . . If we choose some particular goal or series of goals for human beings and then set out on a large scale to control human behavior to the end of achieving these goals, we are locked in the rigidity of our initial choice, because such a scientific endeavor can never transcend itself to select new goals. Only subjective human persons can do that. Thus, if we choose as our goal the state of happiness for human beings (a goal deservedly ridiculed by Aldous Huxley in *Brave New World*), and if we involved all of society in a successful scientific program by which people became happy, we would be locked in a colossal rigidity in which no one would be free to question this goal, because our scientific operations could not transcend themselves to question their guiding purposes. And without laboring this point, I would remark that colossal rigidity whether in dinosaur or dictatorships has a very poor record of evolutionary survival.

Implications of an Immediate View of Causation

The perceptual frame of reference provides an immediate rather than a historical understanding of the causation of behavior. It suggests that, since perceptions exist only in the present, it should be possible to deal effectively with behavior through an understanding of present perceptions even if we do not know anything about the individual's past! If true, this notion has vast implications for our methods of dealing with people everywhere in our society. On the surface this statement seems quite contrary to the widespread belief that any attempt to deal with a human being must be preceded by a detailed analysis of his previous history. Actually, both immediate and historical views are quite accurate descriptions of human behavior and not at all antagonistic. Although the perceptual view of behavior is concerned primarily with present perceptions, this is not to suggest that the past is unimportant. On the contrary, one of Freud's great contributions to our understanding of behavior was his observation that behavior is a product of past experience. The principle seems just as true today as it ever was. Behavior is *historically* a function of what has happened to us in the past but *immediately* a function of our present perceptions. A child brought up in a family where he was often rejected and treated as unimportant may grow to manhood with deep feelings of unworthiness or inferiority. These feelings (ways of seeing) may in turn motivate much of his present behavior. What has happened to him in the past has produced his present ways of perceiving. A knowledge of his past thus *explains* his present perceptions. It is possible for us, however, to interact effectively with him even if we have no knowledge of his past whatever, providing we understand how he is presently perceiving.

For several generations Freud's observation provided the principal direction for hundreds of experiments and investigations into the nature of behavior. As a result of these studies, we have acquired a vast store of information about the ways in which human beings grow and develop, become adjusted or maladjusted, effective or ineffective. Workers in the helping professions like social work, psychotherapy, education, and counseling were particularly affected by this observation and many came to feel that careful studies of the life span of their clients was an indispensable requirement for properly carrying on their functions. The case study, the anecdotal record, and free association became fundamental tools for carrying out their roles.

There can be little doubt of the essential accuracy of Freud's principle, but it has severe limits when applied to problems of treatment or learning. An understanding of how an individual got the way he is today is not always helpful in guiding us in the determination of where to go from here. Gordon Allport once suggested, "People are busy living their lives forward, while psychologists busily trace them backward!" The perceptual view makes it possible to break away from this unhappy preoccupation and opens vast new avenues for understanding and dealing with human interrelationships. It releases the applied worker from the necessity of accumulating quantities of information formerly thought essential. There is, after all, very little we can do about a person's past. There is a great deal we can do about people's present perceptions.

PERCEPTION AND ENVIRONMENTAL CHANGE

A second significant implication of the immediate view of causation is the freedom it gives us to deal with human problems without the necessity of environmental change. Environments are not always amenable to manipulation. There are serious limits to the degree to which they can be changed to suit the need of individuals. A way of dealing with human problems which is not dependent upon environmental change therefore opens vast new possibilities for solving some of our most knotty social problems. We are beginning to discover that when we find ways of helping people change the ways they see themselves and the world in which they live, it may not be necessary to change their environments. For instance, parents who see the need for better schools are more likely to get them through their own efforts. Children aided to see themselves more adequately can live effective lives even though outsiders may be unable to make basic changes in distressing family situations. Following play therapy, for example, in which children have been helped to perceive themselves and their parents more adequately it is not uncommon to find changes occurring in the child's family despite the fact his parents have not been involved in treatment themselves. Apparently, as the child feels better he behaves better and this in turn affects the feelings toward him of those who surround him.

This is not to suggest that improvements in housing, parent education, or the provision of food, shelter, and clothing for the needy are either unnecessary or undesirable. Such devices will always be important approaches to social problems. In fact, it frequently happens that changes in environment will be accompanied by important changes in perceiving. The understanding that people behave according to how things seem to them does not discard other approaches. It simply opens another avenue by which we may contribute to human happiness and development.

If behavior is a function of present perceptions, however, then there is something that can be done about *any* individual, even those from the worst backgrounds. It means that whatever we do in interaction with other people is *always* important. The behavior of people toward each other can be helpful or hindering, constructive or destructive in greater or lesser degree. We need not throw up our hands in despair over inability to change the past or control all aspects of present environment. The interactions of people need not be trivial and unimportant no matter what the previous experience of an individual may have been. Fritz Redl once commented in a speech that the distance between a naughty boy and a hardened delinquent was a very long way. Redl then went on to exclaim, "If we could just keep 'em naughty, what a wonderful thing we have done!" Although we may not always be able to produce deep and meaningful changes in those who surround us, whatever we do is worth doing, even though it may be sometimes too little or too late to make the kind of difference we should like.

THE IMMEDIACY PRINCIPLE IN PROFESSIONAL WORK

The importance of this principle is nowhere so appreciated as in the professional work of teachers, social workers, and psychotherapists. To many teachers, for example, this idea opens the doors to vast new possibilities for helping children with problems. It means no child is hopeless. There are things which can be done to help even the most unhappy and maladjusted child right in the classroom. To many discouraged teachers it brings new hope that their jobs are important, that they can be, and often are, effective in helping children grow. It means teachers can help children in school even though they have no control over the child's outside environment.

This is no small matter. Teachers for a generation have been made to feel they are powerless to help children who come to them too late or who are present victims of unfortunate home environments. The perceptual view of behavior emphasizes that present experience in the classroom can affect a child's perceptions in the same fashion as his experiences outside the schoolroom. The child who sees himself as unliked, unwanted, unaccepted, or unable can be helped by the teacher's own behavior toward him even though neither he nor his teacher may have any idea whatever of how he came to feel as he does. You do not have to be an expert to know what to do with a child who feels unliked, unaccepted, or unable!

The principle that behavior can be changed without full knowledge of the past seems equally promising for the field of social work. Much of the social worker's time and energy, to say nothing of shoe leather and carfare, has often been spent in the painstaking collection of mountains of data about the histories of clients. While much of this is necessary, much, too, is not. Such collection of data is often regarded by the social worker's clients as unwarranted and malicious snooping, and such attitudes immeasurably increase the difficulty of establishing a helping relationship. Seeing behavior as a function of present perceptions makes it possible for the modern social worker to dispense with much of this. As a result he appears in the eyes of his client far more understanding and sympathetic.

Like the teachers, social workers have often felt themselves powerless to help clients enmeshed in harmful environmental circumstances. Frequently they have become depressed and discouraged because so little could be accomplished in changing the conditions they observed. With this point of view, however, new possibilities are open to the social worker for helping clients to change their perceptions even though it may not be possible immediately to change their present conditions. Indeed, it often happens that when clients change their perceptions they find more ingenious and effective ways of helping themselves than any outsider could contribute.

The emphasis upon present perceptions rather than past experience has also produced changes in our approaches to counseling and psychotherapy. Once it was considered impossible to help a disturbed child without first producing fundamental changes in his parents. This is not always possible, however, and in the past such children often had to be charged off as bad risks. The perceptual point of view opens new possibilities. Psychotherapists are now finding it possible to help children to new adjustment and happier lives even when there is little opportunity to make fundamental changes in family structure. Methods of play therapy, for example, dependent solely on assisting children to explore present perceptions of themselves and the world they live in, have produced startling results in aiding disturbed youngsters.

The principle has proved equally effective in assisting adults with their problems. About 1942, Dr. Carl Rogers proposed a method of psychotherapy based on helping his clients explore their present ways of seeing themselves and the world in which they live. These methods have since been subjected to much research and have proved remarkably effective in a wide variety of cases. The method is based upon helping the client to explore his ways of seeing himself and his world in an atmosphere of warmth and understanding. The therapist avoids probing and exploring his client and instead assists his client to explore himself. The method is known as client-centered therapy because of this emphasis upon the client's rather than the therapist's understanding. Using such methods, it seems possible to help many clients without extensive delving into the past. To many, the idea of helping people to better adjustment without a thorough understanding of the client's past history seems highly unorthodox, even irresponsible. Viewed from our former ideas about the nature of human behavior, such objections appear sound. From the perceptual view of behavior, however, such methods make good sense.

Implications of the Need for Adequacy

In Chapter 3 we have described the basic human need as the search for adequacy. In later chapters we have examined in some detail how this need operates in the insatiable striving of the organism for maintenance and enhancement of the self. We have seen, too, how it may be fulfilled in the adequate personality or frustrated in the inadequate one. Such a view of human need has important implications for the ways in which we view our common human problems and the kinds of ways we choose for dealing with them. If it is true, for example, that all human beings are motivated in all times and places by a need to be adequate, then much of the blame we are accustomed to heap upon other people for the stupidity, perverseness, or viciousness of their motivations is completely futile. Who, after all, can blame a man for seeking to be adequate?

People are always motivated from their own points of view. What we mean when we complain of the goals sought by some of our fellows is really that they are not motivated to seek the goals we *happen to think are important.* Even the neurotic, the criminal, and the insane are seeking in their own desperate ways to achieve the greatest possible degree of adequacy that *seems open to them.* The murderer at the moment of his act perceives what he is doing as the very best thing he could do under the circumstances, perhaps, even, the *only* thing he could do. The problems of human relations, then, are not so much a question of motivation as a problem of helping people to perceive more clearly. When people are able to perceive more adequately they will behave more adequately, too.

The basic character of human need is essentially positive rather than negative. Given a decent break, the need of the individual will drive him toward essentially positive goals and values. We have already seen that the truly adequate personality cannot behave in ways that are destructive either to himself or to his society in the long run. So long as people live in society and are dependent upon other people, the search for adequacy must include the adequacy of others as well. Whether the behavior it produces is "good" for the individual and those about him will depend upon the ways in which he has learned to perceive himself and his fellows as a result of his past experience and the richness, scope, and availability of perceptions in his present phenomenal field. A positive view of human motivation leaves little room for wasting time on futile blame and castigation and turns attention to the importance of human compassion and understanding.

That the essential character of human motivation is positive by no means guarantees that it will only result in positive kinds of behavior. The ways a dope peddler uses to seek adequacy are certainly destructive. The problem is not with the nature of his need, but the means he has perceived to achieve it. Negative acts may of course be produced by inadequate ways of perceiving. The problem of human relations becomes one of freeing people to perceive themselves and the world they live in in more adequate terms.

MOTIVATION AND ETHICAL VALUES

This essentially positive view of motivation has another important implication for human relationships. It means the faith in our fellows demanded by our democratic society is not an idle dream but finds its justification in the nature of the organism itself. Faith in others is justified, even demanded, if the basic motivation of people is for adequacy. Our democratic credo holds that when men are free they can learn to rule themselves. We could not afford to grant men freedom in the kind of interdependent society we live in if the basic human need was not for adequacy. It is because men fundamentally seek adequacy that we can afford to trust them with freedom. When the credo fails, it is not because men's motivations are bad, but because we have not been successful in finding ways truly to set them free.

Like the concept of faith, other ethical values we are accustomed to think of as "good" arise out of man's need for adequacy operating in an intensely interdependent and coöperative society. Living alone on a desert island, an individual might seek adequacy with no concern for such human values as love, respect, or the dignity and integrity of others. Living in a modern interdependent culture like ours requires strong feelings of identification with others, for adequacy cannot be achieved alone. As a consequence man's experience has led him to exalt those values like brotherly love, respect for one another, charity, justice, and friendship which facilitate human interaction, while condemning those which debase individuals or impede the achievement of adequacy. Ethical values are no accident but the product of long and painful experience. Our world would be in chaos if ethical values were held in low esteem by any large number of persons. In the kind of world we live in and with men motivated toward the maintenance and enhancement of self, love, respect, and the dignity and integrity of man become more than fine ideals to be sought after; they become absolute essentials to the very existence of life.

The Attack-Appease Dichotomy

Finally, if the concepts of this point of view about people and their behavior have any validity, they give promise of helping us to perceive some reasonable alternative to the horrible choice of attack or appeasement we are usually offered as modes of dealing with human problems. Ever since Munich we have behaved as though there were only two possible ways of dealing with human problems—attack or appease. These are the choices that usually occur to us for dealing with the great issues of our day. Appeasement, however, has become a word of scorn, a new "cuss word" of our generation. We were all so badly burned by the Munich Conference and its disastrous consequences that we have firmly resolved never to be caught in that way again.

But much as we despise appeasement, we are equally repelled by its opposite. Though we are willing to defend ourselves with vigor and determination, attacking others without provocation is as repugnant to us in one direction as appeasement is in another. We are essentially a peace-loving people. Attack seems the method of the bully or the desperado and its use seems morally indefensible. In agreement with other nations, we have decided that attackers are aggressors and aggressors are outlaws.

If it is true, as many would have us believe, that we can only attack or appease, then indeed we are in a fearsome dilemma. Appease, and we lose all we stand for. Attack, and we become outlaws in the eyes of the world. Either way we lose. This is the Hobson's Choice we are offered for dealing with the great problems of our time. What is more, there are many who would have us believe there is no alternative. Any slightest gesture of good will toward nations or people with whom we disagree, or acceptance of a point at argument, runs the risk of being hysterically labeled appeasement. You either attack or appease, they tell us, and it soon becomes clear that there is no middle ground; appeasement is anything less than outright attack!

If attack and appeasement appear in our eyes as the only approaches available, we must perforce choose one of these as the appropriate method of coping with our problems. We can only behave, after all, in ways that occur to us. If there are other and better approaches to our problems, we need to be clearly and sharply aware of their existence lest we become the unwitting victims of our own misconceptions.

Is there an alternative to this fearsome dilemma? Out of the understandings we have been developing in this volume about human behavior, I believe there is. Essentially, it is an approach to human interaction which says in effect: "I am a person of dignity and integrity. I believe you are too. I have no need to attack you nor will I permit you to attack me." This is a position which is neither attack nor appeasement. It is not concerned with winning or losing. It is solely concerned with the maintenance of human dignity and the preservation of freedom for people to grow and develop to greater adequacy.

Appeasement interferes with the achievement of adequacy. It destroys the dignity of the appeaser. Attack violates the integrity of others and brings into being the negative effects of threat. The position we speak of maintains the dignity and integrity of the behaver without either violating the rights of others or relinquishing one's own in the process. It is a position of strength and security which stands *for* something as well as against something. This is a position consistent with man's fundamental need for adequacy. It is consistent too with what we know about threat and its resolution. It accepts the fact of differing human perceptions and seeks to avoid as much as possible the negative effects of threat on perceiving. It is a position equally applicable to relationships between individuals or nations.

It will be recognized at once that this position is by no means new.

It has been practiced by many throughout our history. It is the way of life advocated by the great religions. It is the method of Schweitzer and Gandhi and in lesser degree of all of us in our better moments. Each of us knows of people who behave this way. We even behave so ourselves sometimes, and now and then we rise to our full stature collectively and behave so as a nation as well.

Strangely enough, in spite of its simplicity and age this method of dealing with people is an approach without a name. We do not have an adequate word to describe it. This is a great tragedy, for it is difficult to deal effectively with matters without clear and precise terms by which we can refer to them. We can, after all, only deal with events in ways that occur to us, and ways that are clearly symbolized come much more readily into figure. *Attack* and *appease* are unequivocal and easily understood. As a result they come easily and quickly to mind when people are confronted with problems. We need an equally sharp and distinctive term for the kind of relationship we are speaking of here. Perhaps it is because we do not have a proper name for this approach that it seems so little understood and is so often overlooked as an alternative.

The alternative to the devil's dervish of attack-appease, we have suggested above, is a position which declares the dignity and worth of all people, including the self. It seeks the achievement of adequacy for all instead of the achievement of adequacy for some by the humiliation of others. It requires behaving in ways that are at the same time nonthreatening to others and expressive of the value of self. To be able to accept ourselves and other people in this way requires a high degree of personal security. It calls for a deep feeling of one's own worth and integrity. It requires of us both as individual people and as nations that we keep physically fit to resist aggression and to provide us with a healthy vehicle for our beliefs. Equally important, it demands a willingness to examine and reëxamine fundamental convictions and beliefs, making them ever clearer and more precise. To accomplish this we will need to appraise ourselves and our understandings with precision and courage. Doubt and vacillation will leave us wide open to threats from without. Firm beliefs and convictions, which is only another way of saying personal meanings or perceptions, are the best guarantee of consistent behavior toward other people as well as courage and determination in self. Persons with convictions and beliefs will not be easily panicked by show of force, nor will they be push-overs for false propaganda.

To behave in this way is not easy. It calls for a high degree of personal security, acceptance of self and of others, and a wide identification with other people, all characteristics of the adequate personality we discussed in an earlier chapter. The more adequate people we can produce, the more likely we are to find adequate solutions to our human problems. Attack and appeasement are methods of desperation and resignation, approaches to human problems of the threatened and the weak. To behave in the alternative fashion we have described above requires that we seek, on the one hand, the production of the largest number of adequate personalities possible in our generation and, on the other, that we be keenly and continuously aware of the existence of better methods of dealing with human problems than appeasement or attack.

CHAPTER 15

The Individual and His Society

THE ideas we hold about what people are like will have particularly far-reaching consequences in the ways we attempt to solve the great international and social problems of our generation. Theories of history or economics which are based upon inadequate principles of human motivation and behavior can have catastrophic results if they become part of national policy. An example is the theory of Aryan superiority, which not only helped plunge Germany and the greater part of the world directly into World War II, but was doubly disastrous to Germany by causing its leaders to underestimate Russia and conduct a war in such a way that they turned a potential victory into an overwhelming defeat. The ideas we hold about the nature of people inevitably affect our dealings with them. Even with the best of intentions inadequate concepts of what people are like can lead us to the adoption of techniques of dealing with them that may delay or defeat the very ends we hope to achieve. Well-meaning people have sometimes been led, for example, into action on matters of racial integration, labor-management disagreements, or community reform which, instead of moving matters forward, only served to inflame feelings and push people into defensive positions that slowed down the achievement of the very goals they sought.

Effective methods of dealing with human problems must be predicated upon accurate observations of what people are like and why they behave as they do. In this book we have set forth a way of looking at behavior. If this way of looking at human beings is accurate at all, it should have important implications for problems of human society and social action. Let us examine briefly the nature of some of those implications in this chapter.

The Personification Myth

It is a common practice among many people in our society to think of groups or other societies as if they could be understood as single persons. We think, for instance, of America, Britain, Russia, of labor, and capital, of the American Legion or the Knights of Columbus, the Catholics, the Baptists, etc. Each social unit then tends to be thought of as motivated by needs and motives for self preservation and aggrandizement which frequently have nothing to do with the needs and motives of its individual members. On the basis of the observer's bias and experience each group unit is endowed with a characteristic personality, and predictions of its future behavior are based upon this personality. Unfortunately, these group personalities are necessarily oversimplified. Any foreign statesman who predicts the behavior of the British government by thinking of the British empire as either "Honest John Bull" or "Perfidious Albion" is sure to make grave and serious errors. Neither the concept of America as the "unselfish good neighbor" nor as the "hypocritical Yankee imperialist" is adequate for predicting the behavior of the United States in world affairs.

On a consciously superficial level of speech such personification of groups is convenient and permissible, but if we are looking for a frame of reference which will allow us to predict changes in the way a group behaves, the device of group personification is a complete failure. When the entire group is treated as a unit the dynamics of action within the group are ignored and obscured, and, as a consequence, there are no means of studying or predicting the changes within the group which lead to changes in its behavior. In order to appreciate the disadvantages of thinking of "the Russians," "the English," or "the Arabs" as a monolithic unit, it is only necessary to think of the difficulties which are encountered by a foreigner who thinks of "Americans" as an undifferentiated group, all the members of which have the same characteristics and motives. Although societies are, of course, composed of persons with more or less common motives, the attempt to deal with groups as though they were single people is almost certain to lead to chaos.

Societies are formed as the products of human interaction in seeking need satisfaction. Recognizing this fundamental characteristic of societies, Adam Smith observed that men seemed to have deep needs for food, clothing, and shelter. Beginning with this assumption about human needs, he then proceeded to derive the basic principles of classical economics by deciding how such an hypothetical "economic man" would logically behave. In this way Smith was able to derive a system of causal principles which were to a considerable degree transferable from one situation to another. Unfortunately, his fiction that the only motives of behavior are economic does not correspond to the facts. As a consequence, the predictions of conventional economics are reliable only in those circumstances where people are seeking financial profit to the exclusion of all else. Note the frustration of conventional economists, for example, in dealing with labor-management problems when the real goals are mastery or power rather than food, shelter, or clothing. However, within the field to which he limited himself, the deductions Smith made in *The Wealth of Nations* constitute an internally consistent contribution which made it possible to predict, with fair accuracy, the behavior of people under certain restricted conditions.

In the nearly two centuries since Adam Smith published *The Wealth of Nations* a great deal of psychological research has taken place. If the picture of human motivation and behavior which we have presented in this volume is more accurate than that used by Adam Smith, it should be possible for social scientists to derive, by methods similar to those he used, causal principles of social behavior which will be more inclusive and more accurate.

Smith's approach to understanding his society by beginning with the fundamental needs of human beings seems like a fruitful and useful approach. The weakness of his approach lies not in his method of dealing with the problem but in the unfortunately narrow conception of human needs with which he began. What people need, we have seen, runs far beyond the material things of food, clothing, and shelter. What implications does a more inclusive conception of human motivation have for understanding human societies or the relation of the individual to the social group?

Principle I

Individuals tend to seek adequacy through identification with people seeking need satisfaction in ways similar to their own. It is this discovery, that by banding together with other people one's own need satisfaction can be more adequately attained, that is responsible for the formation of groups. The principle is true in all societies, but it is particularly active in highly coöperative, interdependent societies like our own. In our world it is practically impossible for individuals to achieve much in the way of need satisfaction except through the medium of some kind of group membership. The importance of people and of groups is one of the earliest concepts we teach our children.

The mere existence of common goals, however, is not a sufficient explanation for the formation and continuance of a group. Groups form and continue only so long as the association seems important to the individual in the satisfaction of his need. Millions of children, but almost no adults, have eaten spinach to be like Popeye. Popeye can be a hero to a child, but he is only an amusing character to most adults. People do not join *just any* group. They identify with those people and those groups which seem to them important and which most effectively contribute to the individual's own achievement of greater feelings of adequacy. The gang of the juvenile delinquent provides him with feelings of adequacy which he cannot achieve in other more established institutions of his society. As a consequence the delinquent associates himself with those people most likely to provide him with feelings of self enhancement and status, even though from some outsider's point of view such action may seem to be leading to an end directly the reverse. People come together in groups which provide them with increased opportunities for achieving adequacy.

Although persons band together for the more effective achievement of need satisfaction, and may even sacrifice some minor goals for the greater adequacy afforded by group membership, need satisfaction is always an individual matter. The individual search for need satisfaction is never totally surrendered to the group. Even when persons have become important members of a group, the need for personal adequacy may cause them to behave in highly individual fashion when it seems to them that adequacy is affected. This is particularly well illustrated in some of the reports about human behavior arising out of the experiences of World War II. Under the great stress of war, people may move in highly individual directions if this seems more likely to produce personal adequacy for them. Following the war, for example, thousands of young German women who had been raised in highly moral middle-class families turned to prostitution when this seemed the only method of escape from starvation. In the stress of prison conditions group structure and discipline often broke down as individuals desperately sought to remain alive even at the cost of rejecting lifelong ties with other people. Although need for adequacy may sometimes cause us to move in directions at odds with a group we belong to, most of us find our major sources of need satisfaction in some kind of group setting.

Principle II

Persons banded together in groups for the mutual satisfaction of need find their group purposes most effectively advanced by the development of group organization. Persons coming together for need satisfaction soon discover that their ends are best achieved through the development of some kind of organization and structure. At first this organization is vague and not highly crystallized. It may be no more than a highly informal kind of structure in which various roles and functions are simply understood by group members.

As time passes, different people within the group soon acquire roles and responsibilities as a result of the experience of group members with each other. Certain members characteristically behave in certain ways, and other members of the group observing this develop a kind of expectancy for such behavior. This expectancy in turn calls for certain kinds of behavior on the part of the individual. Eventually this kind of differentiation of the membership may develop into a much more complex kind of organization in which various kinds of status positions and group structures are spelled out in great detail.

As a result of the movement of individuals toward common goals and the group members' interaction with each other, groups also develop values and norms which become quite characteristic of the group. As group members seek for the satisfaction of need in the group and, particlarly, as they interact with each other, common values, goals, beliefs develop. At first, these may be quite informal "understandings." Gang members develop a common abhorrence of "squealing." Workers on a job may set quotas for production levels. After a while such common values and standards may even become crystallized into passwords, slogans, customs by which group members can be distinguished from those who are not members of the group. Eventually, common values within a group may be written down as laws, regulations, or rituals.

Principle III

People tend to withdraw from groups whose approval they are unable to win or which no longer satisfy need. So long as membership in a group continues to provide the individual with need satisfaction in important ways, people tend to remain members of groups. When, however, membership in a group no longer satisfies need or when membership in a group becomes frustrating to individual goal satisfaction, groups disintegrate or evolve into some other kind of group which more effectively satisfies need. Toynbee points out that new civilizations arise when the previous civilization is abandoned by its proletariat. The origin of Western civilization, for instance, came in the adoption of Christianity by the oppressed proletariat of the Roman world. This principle functions just as effectively on the levels of the family, the social club, or the casual conversational group. An example may be found in children who find themselves unable to live up to the expectancies of parents and so violently reject the goals of social groups their parents value. It may also be observed in the loss of interest in the sorority or fraternity characteristic of many college students upon graduation.

Mere membership in a group does not guarantee that an individual necessarily possesses a high degree of identification with that group. Experience following the Korean conflict seemed to show that many young men who succumbed to so-called "brain washing" were young men who had never had any real understanding of the nature of democracy or any high degree of identification with the principles and morality of a democratic system. By purposefully breaking down group organization and group loyalties in the prison camps and encouraging individual search for need satisfaction, American soldiers could be made easy prey of propaganda, particularly when presented by earnest, sincere teachers speaking from deep conviction. Stripped of group support and with few firm convictions of their own, many young men accepted the "good" explanations offered them because they had no better ones of their own. Having little identification with their home group to begin with, they were fair game for the adoption of ideas and values espoused by people of another group who believed what they were saying with sincerity and conviction.

People do not move in single groups. Each of us lives and operates in many groups, moving in and out of varying spheres of influence from one group to another throughout our daily lives. Thus we may have membership in a family, a neighborhood group, a church group, a play group, a political party, a club, fraternity, profession, nation, civilization, etc. In each of these groups, what is more, we are expected to espouse differing values, standards, traditions, customs, and the like. Each group will allow differing ranges of permissible deviation from the values they hold dear.

The group with which we play tennis may be quite uninterested in our religious beliefs and quite willing to permit us a great deal of latitude in questions of morality, providing only we do not cheat at keeping score. Our church group on the other hand may be little concerned with our sportsmanlike behavior but very much concerned with the problems of basic morality which we evidence.

The mere fact of existence in these multiple groups creates interesting problems for the individual, since one of the necessities for adequacy is a degree of consistency in our personal beliefs, attitudes, and convictions. Membership in a number of different groups makes it almost a certainty that sooner or later the individual will run into some kind of conflict among the beliefs and values of his various groups. Sometimes antagonistic group values can be held successfully apart by a kind of compartmentalization, as when our prejudices and our religious beliefs are held safely apart by avoiding the consideration of problems of prejudice when we are in church and failing to apply the teachings of a church in dealing with persons of other races or religions when we act in public.

Conflicting norms and beliefs, we have seen in an earlier chapter, are likely to prove highly threatening. When the standards and norms of the groups to which we belong are brought into serious conflict, therefore, the experience is likely to be painful. Under these circumstances the norms the individual adopts and the groups with which he remains will be those which satisfy his basic need most strongly. Confronted with conflicting values the individual is most likely to stick to those which seem to him to be most meaningful. More often than not these are also likely to be those he has held for the longest periods of time, other things being equal.

Principle IV

Identification of an individual with a group leads him to adopt and defend the standards and behavior of that group. To think well of himself it is necessary for a person to think well of his group. This introduces a measure of distortion to the individual's perceptual field and becomes an important factor in breakdowns of communication. An attack upon the group is an attack upon self, and the strength of reaction to the attack is a function of the degree of threat. Criticism of the group by a fellow member stirs much less violent response than attack of the same sort by an outsider, who is presumed to be hostile to the whole group. A teacher, for instance, who has himself criticized features of the educational system, may resent such criticism from outsiders because he feels he is part of the system. Criticism by foreigners is universally resented. Similarly, aggrandizement for the group is aggrandizement for self. *My* team's victory is mine too. The accomplishments, prestige, and glory of those with whom we are identified are fulfillment for us as well.

Since each individual accepts the reality of his own perceptual field, the customs and attitudes of his own group are judged as objectively superior and other people and other groups are judged by these standards. Each must think well of his group. Americans, for instance, commonly place a high value upon houses with modern plumbing. As a result, many American soldiers consider that the Germans are superior to the French, who are less able to afford such luxuries. The boy who has identified himself with the predelinquent gang has a different system of prestige values from the boy who has identified himself with the Boy Scouts or who thinks of himself as a responsible citizen. They admire not only different institutions but different individuals and types of success. As a consequence they are not responsive to the same social controls.

When an individual becomes identified with a group he tends to adopt the standards, customs, traditions, etc., of the group as the bases for his own judgments of events occurring thereafter. Existence in a particular group sets many expectations for the individual and in large measure determines his levels of aspiration. Such bases for judgment and evaluation adopted with membership in a particular group become the standards by which the individual judges persons outside. Members of a group accept and approve those individuals who seem to them to be important. That is, an individual who is able to behave in ways admired by members of the group will be sought as an associate, providing his acceptance will enhance the self concepts of the members. Individuals who behave in ways condemned by the group are avoided and rejected.

Other groups are likely to be judged good or bad depending upon the degree of likeness which those groups have to the values and standards of one's own group. This social distance is well illustrated in the class structure of many societies. Social classes are distinguished primarily by the behavior of their members. Individuals who are able to behave in conformity with the standards of the group are accepted, and individuals considered uncouth are rejected. Contrary to popular opinion, money does not automatically give advancement to a higher social class. It merely makes it possible with training to behave in ways that are admired by such a class. In Yankee City, for instance, the upper-uppers were almost exclusively members of families which had had two or three generations to perfect and master the class behavior. The wealthiest man in town was upper-middle class because he did not wish to change his behavior and insisted that his children conform to middle-class standards as well.

It is readily apparent that these principles confer a continuity, consistency, and conservatism upon the behavior of groups, which agree with empirical observations. This consistency is acquired, not from some mysterious quality of a group *per se*, but through the dynamics of the efforts of individual members to achieve adequacy. The effective factors in determining the individual's behavior toward society are, as for all behavior, his need, his perceptual field at the moment of action, and the potentialities for differentiation that exist in the field.

The Psychology of Culture Change

The same principles that govern the relation of the individual to the groups and institutions he encounters also govern the transfer and adoption of culture elements and techniques. Linton has pointed out that the factors most important in determining the introduction of cultural novelties are: (1) the prestige of the individual under whose auspices the novelty is introduced, (2) the prestige of the inventor or donor society, and (3) the effectiveness of the trait or techniques in the local environment. In other words, an individual in one culture adopts those aspects of another culture which make possible the enhancement of his phenomenal self. These are selected in terms of his existing field. Alcohol, for instance, was a boon from heaven in the eyes of the Plains Indians, who lived in a world where men became great and found power in dreams and delirium. The Hopi, on the other hand, living in a field of complete but fragile order and regularity, where a single mistake in the ritual dance might shatter the universe, saw alcohol as a tremendous menace and rejected it.

It is a well-established principle of anthropology that cultural elements which fit the pattern of the recipient culture are transmitted without obstacle, and that elements that do not fit the pattern are rejected or accepted only after modification and distortion. For instance, firearms are immediately transmitted to hunting societies which have a surplus for barter, printing presses are rejected, and alarm clocks are accepted only as ornaments. This is a normative application of the psychological principle we have cited earlier, that new entities or characters are selected in accordance with the individual's need and are modified or distorted by their relation to other parts of his field.

THE PSYCHOLOGY OF INTERGROUP RELATIONS

Since each individual customarily regards his own view of the world as true, just, and real, he is apt to regard the behavior of other people as more or less mistaken and in error. This is especially true if he is observing people of a markedly different culture, since by their failure to conform to his standards they inevitably stamp themselves as ignorant or evil or both. Contacts between different cultural groups are almost always uncomfortable because of the difficulties of communicating which tend to make individuals on both sides feel frustrated, inadequate, and often suspicious, unless one group is so clearly superior in power that the question of comparative force is not even considered. It can be taken as a basic principle that no minority group is the object of attack until it becomes large enough or powerful enough for the majority group to feel threatened.

Communities and schools which pride themselves on absence of intolerance and prejudice almost always prove to have only a few members of the minority group in residence. Under such circumstances the minority members may even have added prestige as exotic individuals. When minority groups become threatening to majority groups it is not of course necessary that the minority should be the actual source of the threat; but it is necessary that the minority group be large enough or powerful enough for the members of the majority to believe that it is a threat, so that it can become a reasonably convincing scapegoat. If the minority group is small, its members are more easily differentiated from one another and tend, therefore, to be treated as individuals rather than as group members.

Under threat the members of groups tend to respond by an accentuation and idealization of the group characteristics. It is only by placing emphasis on their differences from the other group that they can feel superior to it. See, for example, the great upsurge of Zionism after the horrors of Nazi atrocities and the glorification of color in the Negro press. Despite the insistence of social scientists on the fallacy of white supremacy, when racial tensions are aroused the old arguments of Negro inferiority are sometimes paraded anew in the public press.

The claim to be a master race is an effort to enhance the threatened phenomenal selves of group members. Propaganda stressing "encirclement" is a common technique of governments wishing to create a greater feeling of unity in their own group. Both Hitler and the Russian Communist leadership have used it with conspicuous success, and it is not unknown in America. It is most eagerly accepted by those members of the group who are most in need of self enhancement. As a general thing, group conflict is at its maximum between the lower levels of the conflicting groups, especially if these levels are the victims of aggression and domination within their own groups. In our own South, for example, the most violent reactions to the threat of school integration have occurred among the "poor whites," while middle- and upper-class whites with less need for self enhancement adopt a more moderate view.

The Resolution of Group Conflict

In thinking about problems of group conflict it is always a temptation to fall into the error of believing that the responsibility for such conflict is exclusively a responsibility of sick leadership. This is rarely ever the case, however. Individuals become leaders in groups because they seem to the members to be capable of leading the group to those goals which it holds dear. Leaders could seldom remain very long in positions of leadership if they did not represent the fundamental needs and desires of their group members. The abhorrence of dictatorship, characteristic of much of our thinking in this country, leads some people to the dangerous assumption that societies operating under a dictatorship are doing so totally without the support of the people in that society. Because we find this form of government unacceptable ourselves, it is easy to jump to the conclusion that persons living under dictatorships do not like them either. It is necessary for us to understand, however, that even a dictatorship exists because it supplies need satisfaction to its people. It is a temptation to believe that the Russians do not like their form of government and would not fight for it. To build a national defense on any such assumption, however, could conceivably prove to be disastrous. Although the Russian standard of living may be considerably below that of our own, it is probable that the average Russian today is better off than he has ever been in his previous history. From his point of view, his government is meeting his needs.

The goal of society is to meet the need of its members. Whether or not it is successfully meeting need, however, can only be judged by those persons having membership in the society. Even though a society may seem to some outside observers to be less adequate in providing need satisfaction for its members than some other society, this information is irrelevant and immaterial insofar as the members of a given group are concerned. People can, after all, only behave in terms of that which they know.

THE GOALS OF CONFLICT RESOLUTION

In earlier chapters of this book we have seen that when individuals are threatened, two negative effects upon perception ensue: (1) perceptions become narrowed to the object of threat, so that it is difficult for individuals to see broadly and clearly, and (2) individuals are forced into more and more rigid defenses of their existing perceptions. These unhappy effects of threat and counterthreat are bad enough applied to individuals in interaction. When these same effects occur to large numbers of people acting in groups, societies, or civilizations they carry implications of possible death and destruction too devastating to comprehend. Once war could be regarded as a kind of gentlemanly pastime in which comparatively small numbers of people were hurt. With the destructive power available to groups in our generation, however, the prevention of group conflict once it has occurred, or the resolution of such conflict, represents a major problem of our generation. In the light of the principles of behavior developed in this volume what can we say of the resolution of group conflict?

Once the threat-counterthreat spiral has gotten well under way the process is difficult to reverse. In the long run there seem to be only two alternatives to the resolution of such deep-seated conflict. One of these is the dissolution of conflict through assimilation or amalgamation of the conflicting groups. This may occur through the assimilation of one group by the other or through the development of a third group in which the conflicting groups can find similar goals and values. The United Nations represents this kind of a group. A number of examples of the assimilation of conflicting groups may be seen in our own history. At one time the Irish were regarded as uncouth and distinctly undesirable. On occasion these feelings even broke out in open violence. With the assimilation of the Irish culture into the American culture, however, St. Patrick's Day and the idealization of Ireland have become American traditions. As soon as the Irish were accorded a respected status, amalgamation could take place without loss of self esteem on either side. Such amalgamation of groups, it would seem, must be the eventual long-term outcome of the resolution of group conflict.

When groups amalgamate, the smaller group will ordinarily move farther and make more modifications of culture than the larger group. The comparative degree of shift may be roughly considered as inversely proportional to the population ratio of the two groups. If group A makes up one-fifth of the population and group B four-fifths, in a condition of nonselective movement and intercourse members of group A will have to adjust to members of group B four times as often as individual members of group B will meet and adjust to members of group A. If, as actually happens, the personal relations are selective, the process is slowed but the ultimate result is not affected unless contact between the groups is cut off altogether. This principle is only normative, like the others we are deriving in this chapter. What will actually happen always depends upon the phenomenal fields of the particular individuals involved. For instance, if the minority group has superior power and prestige in the eyes of a substantial number of the majority, the majority culture will shift farther because their members will move more than halfway in their contacts with minority members.

The second way in which group conflict can end is by reducing one group to impotence. This may be accomplished by destroying one group or by so reducing its size or importance that it no longer threatens. This is what wars have attempted since time immemorial. It is what Hitler attempted with the Jewish minorities. It is basic to the concept of "divide and conquer."

This is a hard alternative to contemplate, and it may appear to some that there might be an intermediate stage between the two long-time solutions to conflict, based on continued separation with avoidance of conflict through mutual respect and confidence. This is a desirable goal and one we should strive to achieve. Such a condition can be only temporary, however, since mutual respect encourages and makes possible the movement of individuals from one group to the other, and with such movement eventual assimilation of the two groups becomes inevitable.

MEANS OF REDUCING GROUP CONFLICT

Fortunately, while group conflict and suspicion are inevitable in some degree as long as groups exist, there do appear to be means by which the intensity of the conflict may be greatly reduced and eventual assimilation speeded. Conflict between groups is, in some degree, the result of aggressive and dominating behavior within one or both of the groups. Individuals who are unable to secure adequate satisfaction of need in their own society often seek such satisfaction by dominating and aggressive behavior against members of weaker groups. It is quite possible, therefore, that the most effective way of reducing group conflict would be the reduction of domination and aggression within the groups themselves. Individuals who achieve a satisfying degree of adequacy within their groups will find little need to dominate and harass other groups. Adequate people, as we have seen, are characterized by acceptance and identification, both antithetical with conflict. It would thus appear that an important means of eliminating conflict lies in helping groups to provide real opportunities for growth and need satisfaction for their own members.

Since conflict between groups is always carried on by individuals who think of themselves and their antagonists as group members rather than as individuals, group conflict can also be prevented by increasing the opportunities for the members of the two groups to differentiate one another as individuals. A major function of military training and indoctrination is to induce the individual to regard himself as a soldier rather than a civilian. Since a person's behavior is determined by his phenomenal field, it is impossible to get him to act as a soldier until he conceives of himself as one. Furthermore, if he thinks of himself as a soldier, acts which are taboo to him as an individual are not only permissible but, in many cases, mandatory. Europeans who have seen Americans only as soldiers may be expected to have a very erroneous picture of Americans, if by Americans we mean individual civilians. In the same way, a person who thinks of himself as a white in contact with a Negro will behave very differently than if he thinks of himself as John Smith in contact with Ed Jones.

The perception of other group members as individuals is increased when it is possible to encourage members of the minority to scatter themselves as widely as possible among the members of the majority. This is, of course, impractical where group feelings are already strong, since it is a step toward abandonment of the minority-group institutions and cannot, therefore, be taken under threat.

Another way of fostering the differentiation of members of the conflicting groups as individuals is by increasing the possibilities for communication between them. Communication, however, is possible only when there is an overlapping of cultural fields so that there is a common area of meanings. From this point of view the practice by which books and motion pictures about foreign countries emphasize the strange and exotic can be expected to achieve little or nothing toward promoting tolerance and good will. The "Man Bites Dog" concept of news is of little help in fostering this sort of understanding. The emphasis of news-gathering agencies upon the bizarre and the different may even contribute to the intensification of group conflict.

On the other hand, a motion picture or story which shows the people at their daily work and children at their games promotes fellow feeling, if the work and games are those familiar to the audience. An interesting and effective means of promoting fellow feeling among members of different groups is that used by Rachel Davis DuBois. Instead of talking about the problems on which they suspect differences, they are asked to talk about their childhood memories—"talk about bread, for example." As soon as members of both groups have told about common experiences in making, tasting, or smelling hot, crusty bread they feel as if they have spent their childhood together and are members of a common group. Common experiences make possible a common feeling, and citizens of the same state, who would not stop to speak if they met at home, have a feeling of close kinship when they meet in a foreign land. A common language is a great advantage, especially if it is spoken with a common accent.

Another way of reducing conflict between groups is to provide them with a common objective or enemy. The need for action in the common cause makes all individuals in the previously conflicting groups important to one another through identification with the common cause. This technique of providing a common enemy is, as we have said before, often used more or less consciously by political groups and nations as a means of reducing tensions in their own ranks. Threat prevents disintegration of the group relationship, since all threatened individuals seek shelter and support from one another.

A more productive method of reducing group conflict lies in the development within a society of individuals who feel adequate to deal with their perceptions. We are afraid of that which we do not feel capable of handling. What we feel adequate to deal with does not threaten us. Thus the society which can produce adequate phenomenal selves in its members can tolerate or accept difference in others, and group conflict will thereby be reduced or disappear. A society composed of nonthreatened, nonthreatening personalities will not be in conflict. Such a society need not depend exclusively on attack or appeasement as the only solution to problems.

PROBLEMS OF GROUP AND INDIVIDUAL ASSIMILATION

Groups do not associate with another group as groups. The process of assimilation of groups really consists of the assimilation of separate individuals. An individual seeks admission to a new group, as we have said, if he so respects and admires the members that he would secure self enhancement through identifying himself with them, or if membership in the group will otherwise aid him in the satisfaction of need. Compare the complete and rapid assimilation of German immigrants in the United States, where the standard of living is higher than in Germany, with the unassimilability of Germans, even after hundreds of years, in eastern Europe, where the standard of living of the local culture is lower than that of the German culture. What the individual thinks of himself is the important factor in determining his search for assimilation and membership. Any person will seek membership in the new group more actively if he feels that he is acceptable to the members; and he is more apt to withdraw from his original group if he is threatened or humiliated within that group.

In the same way, an individual seeking admission to a group is assessed and accepted or rejected, not by an impersonal group but by individual members, each of whom considers the candidate in the light of his own need. If the membership of the candidate in the group will enhance the phenomenal selves of the individuals, he will be accepted. As a general thing, anyone advancing from an "inferior" to a "superior" group is handicapped by his previous membership in the "inferior" group so that he must have unusual qualities and abilities to gain acceptance. If he shows obvious physical or behavioral characteristics of the "inferior" group, he must counterbalance them with tremendous prestige in the eyes of the new group. He will be aided further by a personality that does not actively dominate or threaten the self esteem of the members of the group he seeks to join. It will not be a handicap and may even be an advantage if he threatens outsiders, provided he does it in a socially acceptable way. Artists, writers, athletes, and members of the professions, if successful, have unusual opportunities for social mobility because they are admired by so many people. The American public schools and, in particular, the high school athletic teams, by providing able individuals with opportunities for winning prestige, are an important factor in social mobility and group assimilation. It goes without saying that any society must provide opportunities for mobility if the most able individuals are to reach the positions where they will be of most benefit.

What Is a Good Society?

LACK OF AGREEMENT IN DEFINITION

As we have said above, one of the principal barriers to international coöperation among peoples, all of whom sincerely desire a better world and a better society, is the lack of agreement among the various groups as to what constitutes a good society. The representatives of each culture, considering their own version of society as fundamentally right and true, believe that the better society can only arise from a further development and modification of their own. This is true whether they be Iranian or Hindu, Russian or American, Berber or Eskimo. To the true representative of each, any other society is manifestly inferior to his own.

The United Nations must continuously struggle with this problem as it tries to achieve harmony and coöperation among individuals or nations which have as diverse pictures of the better world as do the various cultural blocs and groups of which it is composed. Such a conflict of ideals and values is almost certain to result in political conflict in which each bloc is chiefly interested in defending the integrity of its own society against the social reforms of the other blocs. To make matters worse, even when delegates may personally achieve a degree of understanding of other views they may be unable to act upon their changed perceptions because they are instructed rather than free delegates. Under such circumstances international conferences are chiefly concerned with obstruction rather than coöperation and often end either without agreement or in a mutually distasteful acceptance of the status quo. It seems likely that in years to come we may discover that the most truly effective work of the United Nations is not produced by the Security Council or General Assembly but by those backstage agencies which operate with little fanfare to improve communication and raise standards of living and health.

Real coöperation for world betterment can arise only out of common goals. This is to say, there must be mutual agreement on the ends which are to be attained. All groups sincerely desire a better society. But there can be genuine coöperation only among individuals who are able to look beyond the particular devices and techniques used in their own societies and focus their attention on the ends themselves.

THE GOOD SOCIETY SATISFIES NEED

What are these ends? We have already given two answers. The purpose of society and of social institutions, we have said, is the satisfaction of human need. The basic human need is the preservation and enhancement of the phenomenal self. If these two assumptions are correct, we have here a culture-free criterion by which the comparative goodness of societies can be determined. A society is good to the degree that it enables its members and neighbors to live with health, security, self respect, and dignity. It is good in the degree to which it aids its members to the development of selves adequate to deal with the world that surrounds them. A society is bad to the extent that it fails to provide these things for its members or removes them from its neighbors. The inadequate self will feel threatened and will threaten others in turn.

The society must be judged primarily by the degree to which it satisfies the need of its least important members, since the nonsatisfied members of any society are, like cancer cells in the body, a source of danger to their fellow members and to the social organization itself. For this reason one criterion of a good society is the extent to which it makes less necessary the use of techniques for satisfying need like domination and aggression which give satisfaction to one member only by depriving others. These are techniques of the inadequate phenomenal self. Socially, such techniques may be thought of as attempts to lift the society by its bootstraps; as the aggressor enhances his phenomenal self and goes up, the victim goes down. When the domination is institutionalized on a grand scale with a noticeable ruling class and hierarchy of domination, the eventual result must be a revolt of the common man from within the group or aggression against persons outside the group. A society which fails to satisfy the needs of its members is therefore not only not good for them; it is also a source of danger to its neighbors. In a good society there can be no unimportant members. The criterion of a good society is the amount of self actualization it succeeds in fostering in its members.

The good society must be dynamic. It cannot be described in terms of its institutions. All planners of Utopia, except More himself, have made a fundamental mistake in conceiving of a society which reaches an ideal state and remains unchanged thereafter. No static, unchanging Utopia can be the psychologically satisfying "good" society which we are seeking. The culture of such a society must be dynamic and flexible rather than static, because the individual's need for the maintenance and enhancement of his phenomenal self can never be completely satisfied. No matter how successfully he solves his problems and builds up his feeling of strength and security, no successes and no recognition can be enough to give him the permanent feeling of adequacy and self assurance that he seeks. Further achievement and growth are always necessary. As a result no society which attempts to remain static can adequately satisfy the needs of its members.

Since it is the function of societies to assist their members to need satisfaction, there can, of course, be many "good societies," almost as many good societies as there are ways of achieving self maintenance and enhancement. Furthermore, since human need is insatiable, "good" societies must be continually changing. Each must find ever new, more effective and satisfying ways for helping its members to achieve self enhancement.

In the previous chapter, we have contrasted the closed and open systems of thought in dealing with human problems. It will be recalled that the closed system is dependent first upon the determination of some manifest objective and thereafter upon the control of events to achieve these preconceived ends. The open system, on the other hand, had as its goal the process of growth and discovery itself rather than some more specific manifest objective. Its techniques of operation, furthermore, were concerned less with the control of events and more with the facilitation of growth, exploration, and discovery. This open system of dealing with human problems seems highly consistent with the kind of good society we have been describing here. The goal of a dynamic society is to create the optimum conditions for individual growth and achievement of adequacy. Such a society would avoid the dangers of a planned society, which sooner or later must find its plan no longer adequate in a changing world. A dynamic society, concerned fundamentally with setting men free, seems far more likely to evolve and change with the march of human events.

Culture Change—A Problem of Changing Individuals

What can be done to make society better? First, it will be necessary to recognize that there can be more than one "good" society. Any society which satisfies the above criteria is a good society, and it would be impossible to say that any society now existing could not develop into a good society. Very definitely, attacks upon other societies can not make them into good societies. People are not free to change under threat, and a group under attack simply accentuates its destinctive characteristics. A good society can only grow where there is a minimum of conflict between societies, so that the people of each feel free to move and change.

There are three ways of changing a culture. One way is to abandon it en masse, to give it up. Since we have mastered no alternative culture, such a course would cause the death of most of the members of our society as its institutions for the production and distribution of goods cease to operate. Another way to change a society is by revolution. Since people have learned to manipulate only the culture in which they have been living, human revolution results in surprisingly small changes in the culture pattern itself, although it often results in a more efficient and intelligent government. A good example of this may be seen in the Russian Revolution. Following an international period of westernization and democracy, the USSR has tended more and more to revert to the governmental and productive systems of czarist Russia, substituting the G.P.U. for the Cheka, a dictator for the czar, and the collective for the landed estate. It was apparently impossible for the new rulers of Russia to make a fundamental change in the culture of Russia because it was the only culture that they and their people had learned. Though revolutions can often produce changes, they rarely seem worth the price, owing to the high death rate during the initial stages. At this time sweeping changes in the society are being attempted and a great deal of disturbance and dislocation results.

The only alternative seems to be a continuation of the slow process of change in the ways individual people perceive. Since societies are composed of people and people only change when perceptions change, it follows that to change a society we must find ways of helping individual people change the ways in which they perceive. Individuals are often likely to feel weak and puny before the staggering requirements for changing a culture by means of revolution. Even if the price of change by revolution were not so exorbitant, it would still be true that very few of us would ever give up the struggle entirely. If, however, the most fundamental and permanent changes in society occur through the slow processes of evolution and changes in individual people, then every individual, no matter how great or small, has important effects upon social change.

The Individual as an Instrument for Social Change

Societies are the product of human interaction and every human interacting is part and parcel of the product. How effective any individual can be, therefore, as an instrument for social change will depend upon what kind of a person he is and the degree to which he behaves so as to contribute to the achievement of adequacy in others as well as in himself. It is a little disconcerting to find that the most effective means most of us have to change our societies is to change ourselves. It is so much more comfortable to change the other guy. An adequate society can only exist if its members are adequate people. One of the ways, therefore, in which we can contribute to social change is through the achievement of an ever greater degree of personal adequacy. Only then, when we have achieved some degree of self respect, dignity, and integrity in ourselves, are we likely to perceive and respect it in others as well.

Since societies are made up of people in interaction, we can also affect our societies through the impact of our behavior on our fellow group members. When our behavior contributes to the adequacy of others, it contributes also to making the group successful. Whether we behave in positive or negative fashion as a group member, however, will be determined by the way our own behavior is perceived by our fellow members. The ways we behave in interacting with our fellow human beings have a vital bearing upon the kinds of perceptions which make up their perceptual field. Not all of our behavior will, of course, be of equal value in producing changes in the perceptions of other people, but neither is our behavior ever entirely unimportant. Someone once observed that the only immortality any of us can achieve is carved out through the impact of our behavior on other people. While we cannot be responsible for the behavior of people who are dependent upon us, we ourselves can behave in ways that are constructive, destructive, or of no account at all in their effect upon others. We have a degree of choice in how we behave toward others and can learn to use ourselves effectively or ineffectively as instruments of social change.

To produce an optimum degree of effect upon our society we need to learn to behave in ways that contribute maximally to human adequacy and minimally in the production of threat. This relationship of the individual to his group has been diagrammed in Fig. 23. In this figure the

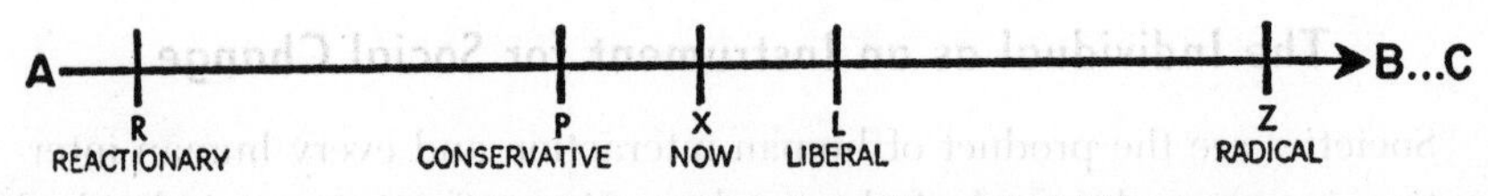

Fig. 23. The Individual and His Relationship to Social Movement.

movement of society is expressed by the line *AB;* with society moving from *A* to *B* in the direction of some ultimate *C*. The present position of society in this diagram is indicated by the line *X,* also marked "Now." What then is the effect which an individual's behavior may have on this movement at varying points? The person who operates at point *P* is only in small degree behind the movement of his society. This is the position of the conservative. Much further behind society's current position is the reactionary (point *R*), who may be so far out of touch with the existing situation as to act as a considerable drag upon the process of change. If such people represent too great a threat to the societies to which they belong, however, these societies find ways of ignoring them and in some manner reducing them to a position of impotence.

Persons at the opposite end of the scale, operating at point Z, may be so far out of touch with the expectancies of their society in the other direction that their behavior may constitute a serious threat to the membership. Under these circumstances the society seeks to protect itself from such threats by reducing these people to impotence in one form or another, by walling them off, by counteracting their effect, or by outright destruction if the threat is great enough. A few persons operating at extreme positions may become martyrs and so serve an important function in dramatizing a concept or idea, sometimes at the price of their own destruction. Even so, if their message is to be at all effective it must eventually be carried by others more closely in touch with the realities of the social scene. More often than not the radical has a negative effect on his social group. By threatening his society he forces it to defend its position or even to retreat from its forward progress. Individuals operating at point *L* (the liberal position on our scale), while somewhat in advance of the current position of society, are nevertheless also sufficiently in touch with it so that they do not appear to the society to be seriously threatening. It is probable that persons operating at this position produce the maximum degree of progress in a society.

It should be clear that we have been talking about the relationship of the individual's *behavior* to his society's position. This does not place limits on how people may *think* or *believe*. The individual's impact upon the phenomenal fields of other members of his society occurs through the medium of his behavior as it is observed by those he comes in contact with. Individuals in a free society may think or believe as they please and do not become threatening to their society until such times as their behavior warrants. Thus, on our diagram a person may think far out at point *B* if he wishes, so long as he does not threaten his society by his overt acts. This is the position adopted by many pro-integration Southerners living in deeply prejudiced anti-Negro communities. They recognize that to work effectively for the principles they believe in, they must govern their behavior in terms of the tolerance levels of their communities. To stand on a soapbox in the village square and preach their beliefs would so deeply threaten many of their neighbors as to bring upon themselves social controls which would make it impossible to exert any further influence whatever. Accordingly, they adjust their behavior to the realities of the situation, learn to exert an influence toward the goals they espouse in ways less likely to threaten the social groups they hope to move. In such fashion they maintain their own integrity while at the same time exerting a maximum influence for change.

It will of course be recognized that the conditions we have been speaking of are relationships of the individual to a particular group. The same concepts may appear quite differently to different groups and what seems radical to one group may appear downright conservative to another. In moving from group to group, therefore, the individual must adjust his behavior in dynamic adjustment to the tolerances and expectancies of the groups he is in. Though operational levels may change, the optimal relationship for effective action remains a position in touch with the realities of the group yet moving onward at a pace with a maximum of challenge and a minimum of threat.

The "good" society is one whose members contribute maximally to the adequacy of their fellows. This means that effective action of individuals must be that which contributes to ever greater adequacy of self and others. We have described adequacy in this book as a function of positive self reference, acceptance, and identification, and intelligent action as arising from a perceptual field rich, extensive, and available. A free people can only remain so as long as they are able to perceive freely and broadly. All the more reason why we need to protect our freedoms with eternal vigilance, lest we become the prisoners of our own misperceptions. While there is in our environment unobstructed opportunity to see and understand, and within ourselves no fear of looking, progress can always be assured. A people can be held in bondage only so long as their perceptions can be limited or controlled, a fact well understood by any dictator. How any person behaves in moving toward such goals is necessarily a purely individual matter. There are no "right" ways for all people. Rather each person must discover those *best ways for him.*

CHAPTER 16

How People Can Help Themselves

WHAT are the implications of a perceptual view of psychology for the individual's own efforts at need satisfaction? How much control can an individual exert over his own destiny? In this point of view we have postulated that all behavior is a function of the perceptual field. We have seen, too, that perceptions are selected by individuals in the light of their fundamental need for adequacy. The fact of this selectivity makes possible a measure of control by the self over its own destiny. But how much control?

THE FALLACY OF REVOLUTIONARY CHANGE

The individual's basic need for adequacy requires a stable perceptual field. A perceptual field constantly shifting and changing in its basic characteristics would make it impossible for the individual to achieve any need satisfaction whatever. The basic need of the organism for the maintenance of organization forces each of us to protect ourselves against sweeping changes in self. We cannot "lift ourselves by our bootstraps" overnight. Nevertheless, it is apparent that people do change and, looking back, we can perceive that we, too, have changed. Such changes, however, are seldom ever violent or all-inclusive. Rather, clinical experience would indicate that even when major changes *seem* to happen, this evaluation of things is probably an artifact of the point of observation. When sweeping changes appear to occur they are ordinarily only the dramatic last step in a long series of many small changes.

The stability of the perceptual field is an essential to the achievement of adequacy. Changes in the self come about only slowly and over a considerable period of time. This is not to say, however, that there is not room in the perceptual field for movement and change to occur. As a matter of fact, the self is in a constant process of change throughout its existence. There is always a degree of freedom in the selection of perceptions, a certain amount of "slack" within which choice may occur. It is even possible that if this "slack" is consistently taken up in the same direction over a period of time, a considerable degree of change in the self may be brought about. As C. W. Hunnicutt once put it, "Even in the worst situation, there is always room to wriggle. If you would like to find out how free you are, try wriggling!" Dr. Hunnicutt's advice seems to apply very well to the perceptual field and the possibilities of self change. So long as there is opportunity for selection, there is room for change. The problem of self improvement becomes a question of maintaining a maximally fluid field, on the one hand, and making full use of the "wriggling room" permitted by such a field, on the other.

The Cumulative Effect of Selection

The perceptual field is the product of all the selections within the field that have gone before. As we have seen in an earlier chapter, the selections an individual makes in the process of his growth and development both narrow and expand the possibilities of his future perceptions. The decision to live in the country rather than in the city automatically eliminates certain kinds of experience which can only be gained in the city. On the other hand, it makes possible having the kinds of experiences which cannot be gained in the city but only in the country. The phenomenal field existing at any particular time is a product of all its previous selections. Its current rigidity or fluidity will likewise be a product of the individual's previous selections. The selections made today will similarly affect the rigidity or fluidity of the phenomenal fields of the future.

Effective self help is seldom a question of *making* oneself behave. This is a manipulative approach and is seldom likely to be effective because it deals with perceptions unrelated to dynamic events. For example, I may promise myself "next time I meet Mr. X I will not fidget around in such an impolite manner. Instead I shall listen to him carefully, even if he is a terrible bore." Such an approach to self change is almost bound to fail because it does not deal with the perceptions producing my behavior. The perceptions immediately producing my behavior are my perceptions of Mr. X, of what he is saying, of the situation in which we are involved, and a thousand other events. Indeed, if I persist in trying to change my behavior by concentrating on me, next time I see Mr. X I shall almost certainly convey to him my lack of interest in what he is saying by being preoccupied with what I am doing. I cannot respond effectively to him while perceiving exclusively me! The direct attempt to change behavior is seldom likely to be very effective because it does not deal with causes. The causes of behavior, we have seen, lie in the perceptual field, and the way to change behavior, it follows, must be through changes in perception.

Many people seeking to produce changes in self quickly find themselves bogged down in a morass of self evaluation, self analysis, self criticism, and self judgment, which is seldom very helpful in producing change. It seems a logical thing to do to begin the business of personality reconstruction with a careful diagnosis of the present state of affairs. This is the objective, "scientific" way. It is the approach we are used to in dealing with problems of physical health. It is the method we try to apply to our jobs and to certain intellectual pursuits. Although diagnosis, evaluation, and analysis seem logical, however, they often turn out to be of far less assistance than we might have hoped. This kind of approach to self help turns attention on the self as an object, but whenever people behave, the self is not an object but a process.

The factors affecting behavior, we have seen, are not the objective facts but the perceptual facts. The more closely events are perceived to self, the less objective people are able to be. I can be objective about your wife or your problem but not mine. When we deal with self we must be concerned primarily with those perceptions we call feelings, beliefs, attitudes, values, and convictions. Few of us, after all, misbehave because we do not "know" better. Important changes in the self are seldom brought about by deep introspection or highly critical self analysis. Like learning to dance, so long as one watches his feet he falls all over himself. When he learns to listen to the music and respond to its rhythm he gets along far better. In a similar manner preoccupation with self is seldom helpful.

Contrary to what the layman often believes, modern psychotherapy tends to avoid self evaluation and is concerned instead with the exploration of the client's goals, purposes, and perceptions of the world in which he lives. Indeed, one of the signs of successful therapy is increased acceptance of self. A great deal of psychotherapy is concerned with assisting clients to better perceptions, to appreciate and value self. The place to begin self help, it appears, is not with an exploration of "goodness" or "badness" of self but with questions of purpose and values: "What do I think?" "What do I believe?" "What seems to me to be so?"

The Willingness to Look

Long ago Freud pointed out that we never do anything unless we would rather. To accomplish some change in self, then, it is necessary for the individual to feel it is important and desirable to do so. To produce a perceptual field open to change, the first step required of the individual will, of course, be a willingness to look. The individual who is unwilling to look will almost certainly be unable to see. The first step in achieving a field open to change is the feeling that it is an important, enhancing, and desirable goal to accomplish.

Such a decision to explore one's field may even be highly painful. The need of the individual is for adequacy, and the perceptual field he has at the moment is the most adequate he is able to contrive. The development of a richer, broader, more fluid field means seeking new experience and new perceptions, confronting belief with belief, even placing oneself in predicaments for the risky joy of finding one's way out. It calls for valuing present adequacy less and future adequacy more. Such a program is not easy, for it requires placing oneself in jeopardy. This kind of flirting with inadequacy requires courage and determination, even willingness to put oneself in the position of being hurt.

Effective self help is dependent upon finding ways of seeing differently, with the understanding that when we see differently we will behave differently. It requires subjecting ourselves to new experiences not only of an intellectual character but at a deeper level of feeling and meaning as well. It is not enough just to know that something is true. It is also necessary to discover the meaning of that fact for oneself, and this is an active process of trying and failing and trying again and succeeding. Exploration, whether of strange lands or one's own personality, can seldom be accomplished by insisting on the status quo.

The Adequate Self: Goal of Self Improvement

We have already seen that each of us is continuously seeking to be a more adequate personality. We have also examined in an earlier chapter the characteristics of an adequate personality. In that analysis we found that three kinds of perceptions were typical of the adequate personality: (1) an essentially positive regard for self, (2) the capacity for acceptance of self and of others, and (3) the ability to identify broadly with other people. While, of course, no one can hope to begin perceiving like this all at once, each of these ways of seeing can be approximated by any of us over a period of time.

Each of us has it within his capacities to seek the kinds of experiences which will open and enrich his perceptual field and keep it essentially fluid and free. Each of us, too, can learn to avoid the kinds of experiences and events which narrow, restrict, or make the perceptual field more rigid. It is possible to seek experiences which will help us to feel more positively about ourselves, to accept ourselves and others more fully and completely, and it is, of course, possible for us to identify more closely with larger groups of people if it seems important for us to do so. Maslow has pointed out in connection with his study of adequate personalities that such people seem to be characterized frequently by what he calls "peak" experiences. Peak experiences, for Maslow, are those in which people live life to the hilt, sometimes only momentarily, sometimes for much longer periods of time. They are experiences in which people feel intensely, see broadly, communicate deeply, or respond completely. Apparently, the more often people are able to have these kinds of experiences, the stronger, more adequate, more self realizing they become.

Even though it is not possible for all of us to experience such peak moments in life with great frequency, we can learn to value and cherish them when they occur. Indeed, the very fact of valuing them is likely to contribute to their greater frequency. In addition, there are other, less dramatic but equally important, ways in which we can contribute to making our perceptual fields rich, varied and available.

Earlier in this volume we described a number of factors affecting the perceptual field and hence individual behavior. These factors, we have seen, provide valuable keys to the problem of behavior change. They also provide us with important hints as to ways in which we can exert some control over our own achievement of adequacy.

MAINTAINING A HEALTHY ORGANISM. One of the most obvious ways in which we can contribute to our own adequacy is through care of our physical being. While it is possible for a broken-down or outmoded vehicle to get us to the places we would like to go, other things being equal, an efficient, active body is far more likely to provide a minimum of restriction and a maximum freedom of movement for participation in new experience. Most of us already know a good many things we could do to improve our physical conditions. We are aware of the importance of diet, frequent checkups, exercise, and the like. Indeed, we are so continuously bombarded with information about the maintenance of physical health that one would have to be a hermit to be unaware of many things he can do to improve his physical condition. The problem is not a lack of information but a matter of valuing health sufficiently to make it seem desirable and enhancing to apply what we know to our own situations.

TIME AND ADEQUACY. Changing perceptions and hence behavior takes time. This is particularly true of perceptions of long standing or those which are closely related to the self. The more important or central the perception in the field, the more time it is likely to take to make any significant changes in it. A great many attempts which people make at self improvement fail for lack of understanding of this important fact. A human being is a growing, dynamic organization, and growth is a notoriously time-consuming process. Just as the teacher must pace the demands she makes on children to their existing levels of capacity and readiness for change, so too, as individuals, it is necessary that we adjust the demands made upon self to that which can be properly tolerated and assimilated. The attempt to hurry growth beyond a reasonable degree of acceleration may only contribute to frustration and failure.

A good deal of human unhappiness and maladjustment seems due to the individual's inability to accept the fact that it takes time to "become." The young mother must be a good mother *today*. The adolescent discovering religion is overcome with remorse because he is not as "good" as he should be, instead of seeing his church's teachings as something to strive for. Much remorse and guilt are produced by the individual's inability to accept his mistakes. Often he demands of himself that he be today what he can only hope to become some day in the future. One of the essentials for effective self improvement seems to be a degree of compassion for oneself, willingness to permit one's self to "be" while he goes through the process of "becoming." Just as the psychotherapist learns to accept his client and to move at a speed his client can tolerate, so the individual seeking to help himself needs a degree of compassion and self acceptance which will make it possible for him to move with maximum freedom.

Generally speaking, self improvement proceeds more smoothly and effectively when we do not attempt to move at too fast a pace or too far at a time. Attempts to move too far too quickly oftentimes simply result in increased anxiety, which can sometimes be even more crippling than the particular facet of self which we seek to change. Self help is most likely to be effective when we try what we can do easily and naturally. Whatever we seek to do needs to be consistent with the kind of person we are. The author recalls his first teaching job when, fresh out of college, he took over a junior high school class in the middle of the semester. Much of his course work in the teacher-training institution had convinced him that a good teacher was a "pal" to his students. The ensuing chaos produced by his attempts to deal with his classes in a way they could not accept, and which was not consistent with his personality structure, was complete. Like thousands of beginning teachers before him, he was soon disillusioned and discouraged by the complete failure of his attempts at teaching. In time, however, he came to perceive that he could be effective only when he was doing what "fitted." The attempt to change oneself too violently, too quickly, or too greatly in too short a time is responsible for a great deal of the disillusionment and despair of many beginners in whatever profession. The methods people use must be consistent with the kinds of people they are.

CREATING OPPORTUNITIES FOR PERCEIVING. Since perceptions are the product of experience, there is no more fruitful way of affecting or changing perception than through the medium of some kind of new experience. It is rare that we are successful in changing perceptions either in ourselves or others simply by a process of telling. Perceptions do not change simply by "willing" unless this process is accompanied by some kind of experience as well. Although individuals can seldom change their perceptions directly, it is possible for us to make changes in the ways in which we perceive through the kinds of experiences we seek. This can be done in two ways. In the first place, it is possible for us to change perception by exploring our old experiences to discover new meanings from them. This often happens in some kinds of group discussion. Engaging in successful group experiences, the members may discover that their perceptions of things which have happened to them in the past have changed as a result of bringing them out in the open where they can be explored and subjected to the impact of other personalities and other ideas. Old meanings can also be explored in solitary fashion. Many a fine new perception has been differentiated while people were quietly "musing" or permitting their fantasies to run riot as one often does in daydreaming. This sort of exploration of one's field can also be done more purposefully, as when we set ourselves the task to "think through" an idea. Many creative activities like painting or music or writing may serve to provide us with important and fruitful opportunities for perceptual exploration on a symbolic level.

Secondly, perceptions can be changed as a consequence of seeking new kinds of experience which will produce new kinds of perceiving. Perhaps one of the most important ways in which individuals can assure new perceptions is through the deliberate breaking out from accustomed patterns. The experience of thousands of white children in our South going to school for the first time with Negroes must inevitably affect the beliefs, values, and goals developing in their perceptual fields. Many adequate personalities seem to be possessed of a kind of *joie de vivre* or an attitude of open enthusiasm for new experience, new ideas, new problems. Such people seem to enjoy getting into predicaments for the sheer thrill of getting out of them again. The very valuing of such experience is likely to contribute to greater adequacy. Within reasonable limits the experimental approach of trying something new and different from time to time is a fruitful way of breaking out of old ruts and exposing oneself to the necessity for perceiving things in new ways. Often those instances when we have dared to thrust ourselves into new experiences may lead us into high adventure that adds new sparkle and meaning to life. This calls for a kind of campaign against rigidity and ossification. One can tear up last year's plans and start all over, take that trip one was always going to take and never did, meet those persons we have often thought would be interesting.

There is of course a limit to the degree to which we can uproot ourselves and provide ourselves with new experience. If such an uprooting occurs too violently, instead of challenging ourselves we may find that we have only threatened ourselves. New experience for ourselves, like new experience for any other growing, learning thing, is only of value when it is provided at a rate at which it can be assimilated. We rarely make progress in human personality by revolution. On the other hand, there is unlikely to be change if we fear it so much that we must sit at home surrounded by ever higher, tighter walls of protection.

In order to be free to seek new experience it will be necessary to shake ourselves loose from the very common fear of making mistakes. Some of us have been taught quite thoroughly in the years of our growing up that mistakes are reprehensible, perhaps as a consequence of being raised in a school system that values only "right answers." For some, the fear of failing may be so great as to immobilize or prevent them from having important experiences because they *might* make an error. Such an attitude is not likely to be conducive to seeking new experience. The fear of making mistakes is far more likely to produce a high degree of rigidity and ultraconservatism. When people are not permitted to make mistakes they may also be robbed of the very activities which make possible the discovery of new and better perceptions. One can learn responsibility, for example, only by being given responsibility. The individual who is given no opportunities to try because he, or those who surround him, feel too apprehensive of failure, may be robbed of the very experience through which he could discover new and more satisfying relationships.

It even seems helpful on occasion to foster an attitude of *expecting* to make mistakes, for the freedom this gives the individual to break loose from established patterns and to experiment and try. "Cap" Tracy was a woman of tremendous energy and deeply loved by all of the people in the slum section of Cincinnati in which she served for years as school principal. "Cap" Tracy spent her life serving the community and its children, many of whom were brought up under the most appalling of conditions. Several years ago she stood talking with the author and a bright young teacher who was having her difficulties starting out in her profession. As the young woman bewailed the enormity of the problems with which she was confronted, the older woman quietly suggested several things she might try. Finally, in despair, the young teacher burst out, "Oh, but I couldn't try those things. I'd be so afraid of making mistakes!" At this "Cap" put her arm around the girl and said, "My dear, down in my neighborhood I've seen God make so many mistakes that I'm sure He'll allow you a few." Perhaps it is an attitude something like this which we need to foster for maximum perception change.

THE FULFILLMENT OF NEED AND ADEQUACY. A fourth clue to self help may be found in the effect of goals and values upon the perceptual field. Those differentiated by an individual in his search for adequacy have a profound effect upon his later perceptions and upon the effectiveness of his behavior. While it is true that the individual's goals and values always seem to him to lead to need satisfaction at the moment of his behavior, the ones he selects from his perceptual field are by no means equal in their power to assist him to a feeling of adequacy in a longer view of things. The young delinquent who has differentiated "getting the best of the cops" as a means of feeling more adequate may indeed achieve a momentary feeling of adequacy, but if such a goal persists it is almost certain to result in a destruction of adequacy in the long run. Although any goal or value may conceivably contribute to an individual's feeling of adequacy momentarily, not all have equal potential for the achievement of need satisfaction in a broader perspective.

The human being's need for adequacy is constant and insatiable but the goals, techniques, and values differentiated by individuals, through which the need for adequacy is achieved, are open to change and modification. Unfortunately the goals men differentiate to satisfy need are sometimes confused with need itself. One may hear it said, for example, that another person "needs" to get drunk, to drive too fast, to be sexually promiscuous, to be rich, powerful, or eat too much. While it is of course true that an individual may achieve a momentary feeling of adequacy through any of these goals, seeing them as "needs" invests them with a kind of monolithic immobility which almost precludes the possibility of any change. The goals and values men differentiate are by no means synonomous with need. They are expressions of need and hence are open to change.

The very perception of this distinction between need and goals provides the individual with a key to self help. The mere fact of perceiving "I do not *need* to do this" or "I need to be adequate but not necessarily in this way" in itself provides a freedom to explore new and more satisfying means of achieving need satisfaction. The very perception that "I do not *have* to be married, or a doctor, or richer than my neighbor" in order to achieve adequacy, opens the doors for the consideration of new possibilities and new directions. The problem of changing goals and values is not one of seeking their control. Rather, it is a problem of seeking experience which makes possible the selection of new perceptions or the modification and extension of old ones.

THE DEVELOPMENT OF POSITIVE GOALS AND VALUES. While the individual's goals and values are not open to violent or sweeping changes, like any other perceptions they are open to modification and change with different experience. Although this change is not great, there is always "room to wriggle." Certain kinds of values themselves seem to contribute to the achievement of greater adequacy, and new possibilities for self help seem open to us when such values become part of the individual's organization. Certain kinds of goals and values, when differentiated by an individual, have continuing effects upon the nature of his phenomenal field. The mere fact of valuing change more than the status quo in itself leaves an individual more open to the possibilities of changes in perception. There are a number of such positive values which have an effect upon the selection of perceptions in such a way as to be more likely to produce greater adequacy than others. Some of these seem to be as follows:

1. The individual who values the testing of his own perceptions is far more likely to achieve changes in his goals and values that will lead to greater adequacy than the individual who holds his perceptions as a sacrosanct preserve which must be kept intact at all costs. An attitude of "willingness to look" is, itself, a first important step in the achievement of better, more satisfying values. One is after all unlikely to learn to swim if he is unwilling to get his feet wet. Goals and values can often be effectively changed and modified by confronting one with another in a search for ever greater consistency. The adequate personality is characterized by internal consistency, and such consistency is in part achieved as a consequence of confrontation of values. Unfortunately the confrontation of value with value within a particular personality is not always easy to achieve and may even prove highly painful. Sometimes it is far more comfortable to keep values and goals neatly pigeonholed where they cannot be trotted out side by side and seen together. It seems clear that little change in perceiving is likely to occur in the absence of a "willingness to look." Placing a high value on "looking" seems a first essential to the achievement of greater adequacy.

2. The achievement of adequacy in a changing world requires a perceptual field open to change. Rigid, restricted phenomenal fields, we have seen, are associated with inadequacy while breadth and fluidity of field are characteristic of adequate personalities and provide the basis for intelligent behavior. People then who value a fluid, open field are far more likely to be able to respond effectively and efficiently to the shifting demands of a dynamic society. Even scientists may sometimes succumb to the temptation to rule out data which may be uncomfortable or upsetting. It is often easier to deny the existence of events than to make the adjustment to them. Thus the chemist or biologist who carefully considers the variables involved in his field of knowledge may continue to utilize outmoded and inefficient methods of teaching his subject, even scoffing at the findings of educators about the nature of the learning process, although such findings may be supported by mountains of data.

There are two ways of approaching new ideas that may often be observed in people about us. One is to say: "There is nothing new about that. We've known that for thirty years!" The other is: "It's only a fad. It will soon pass away!" Either of these approaches permits ignoring the data and going about one's business undisturbed. Such behavior may often contribute to momentary comfort, but whenever we ignore data we do so at our peril. An open, fluid perceptual field is an essential to the achievement of maximum adequacy, and the first essential in developing such a field, it appears, is the possession of an attitude that it is important to do so.

3. The characteristics of the adequate personality provide some further clues to the kinds of values which may be likely to produce greater adequacy in ourselves. The adequate personality is characterized by a positive view of self, by the capacity for acceptance, and by a high degree of identification with other people. If, then, we can adopt these characteristics as desirable goals, they provide us with selective criterion for further perceptions which we may be able to make. Individuals who value acceptance highly are far more likely to be open to their experience. Similarly, the individual who values identification with his fellow men is much more likely to achieve this than one who finds it necessary to cut himself off from his fellows.

4. Finally, the individual who has determined which of his values and goals are most important to him and which are of lesser value has taken an important step forward in the achievement of adequacy. The goals and values we hold vary greatly. Not all are of equal importance, and the individual who persists in trying to treat them as though they were soon finds himself hopelessly bogged down in confusion. If he has an unclear conception of his values he finds himself buffeted about like paper in the wind by all of the forces impinging upon him from every side. Under such circumstances people do not become what they can be: they become what they are made.

When perceptions are vague and unclear, behavior is also. When we do not know what is important, behavior must be as haphazard and inconsistent as our perceptions. The failure of administrators, teachers, politicians, clergymen, and parents can often be traced to faulty perceptions of what is important. Thus, in dealing with those they are responsible for, they behave ineffectively and futilely. When what we believe to be important is out of touch with the realities of the situations in which we are involved, we can only flounder about like a ship without a rudder. Not all things are equally worth while, and human efficiency and the achievement of self realization require clear concepts of what is important.

THE PRODUCTION OF CHANGE IN SELF. Since the self is a perceptual organization, it too is open to a degree of change like any other perceptions. The central, all-pervading character of the self in a human organization, however, does not permit the kind of wide variations in perceiving that may occur in not-self aspects of the field. It is always easier to change what one thinks of others than to change what one thinks of oneself. Despite this resistance to change in the self concept, however, there is always some room to maneuver. Through an individual's experiences it is possible to bring about changes in the self organization in the direction of new and more adequate personality structure. This, of course, is not possible directly, but since the self concept is a function of experience it is possible to make important changes in the self by the kinds of experiences an individual is provided or provides for himself.

There is a common assumption that change in the self is often brought about by seeking to achieve an ideal self. Actually, this seldom turns out to be the case. The self ideal is nearly always a kind of report of what we might like to be which we provide for the examination of persons who have asked us about the matter. It is rare, however, that the self ideal has any very great dynamic effect in motivating the behavior of individuals. It seems logically true that if you want to get somewhere, the thing to do is to set up some clear-cut, manifest objective and go to work to achieve it. Actually, many such ideals are likely to have little effect on the individual or his behavior. Perceptions and behavior, we have seen, are immediate, whereas the kinds of self ideals we are encouraged to adopt are probably far removed from our present state in both time and quality. There is certainly nothing wrong with having lofty and distant goals for oneself, but unless such distant ends can be converted into more immediate and achieveable goals they will have little or no effect upon the individual. They may even succeed only in discouraging him entirely.

Most effective change is brought about in the self concept by more realistic and immediate perceptions. Clinical experience in psychotherapy would seem to indicate that miximum change in self is brought about not by the rejection of self, nor by longing for that which is beyond achievement, but through acceptance of self *as one is.* After all, we can only make changes in self by beginning where we are. The acceptance of self provides the platform from which it is possible to go somewhere else. In very large measure the difficulty of the neurotic arises from the very fact that he is unable to accept himself as he is and thus has no firm basis from which to move or frame of reference in which to interpret new events and directions. The psychotherapist knows that it is only when such a personality is more able to accept himself as he is that new and tentative steps toward becoming something else are possible. While it is, of course, not possible for the individual to accept himself just by saying he will, such an acceptance is more likely to occur if it seems a desirable growth-producing goal. So long as acceptance is seen as threatening and humiliating it is almost certain to be rejected.

Beginning from whatever self acceptance the individual is able to muster, change in the self concept becomes possible through the kinds of experiences he thereafter selects. We have seen in an earlier chapter that the self concept is a product of experience. We have seen, too, that the kinds of experiences individuals have are open to a degree of choice. However, just as it is necessary to begin with the self we are, it is necessary to select the experiences we would have in the light of what fits the people we are and the capacities we have. To force ourselves into experiences in which we are bound to fail will do little to increase our feelings of adequacy. In seeking new experiences it is necessary to choose those in which we stand a reasonable chance of success.

Effective change in self is a process of becoming involved in experiences or predicaments and working one's way out of them again. To do this successfully, however, requires a real appreciation of the personality in operation. The things we try must fit the selves we are. One of the greatest sources of discouragement in self help is the attempt to try to be what one is not or to do something in the way another person does it. The experiences we seek need to be selected in terms of our own personalities. To force ourselves into experiences in which we must be what we are not for any length of time is almost certain to result in increased feelings of inadequacy. Most people do not look their best in other people's clothes and even the best of mimics never becomes the person he mimics. To be successful in dealing with new events and new experiences we should expect to tailor them and remake them in the ways that fit ourselves most effectively and comfortably.

DEALING EFFECTIVELY WITH THREAT. Finally, for effective self help it will be necessary for us to deal with the unhappy effects of threat on the perceptual field. We have seen in several places in this book how the experience of threat forces self defense and narrows perception. To achieve self improvement it will be necessary then for us to eliminate these negative elements as much as we possibly can. While, of course, none of us can ever free himself from all threat simply by willing it so, like all other perceptions the perception of threat is open to some degree of modification.

In a sense, self change requires a kind of flirting with inadequacy, a willingness to open self to a degree of pain in the present in the understanding that greater adequacy may be achieved in the long run. The achievement of adequacy requires a degree of courage that makes it possible for a person to drop his barriers and venture outside his castle walls. Something must be ventured if there is to be any gain. This is, of course, not easy, for the fundamental need of the individual is the maintenance of self. But it is not impossible either. When individuals can perceive the possibilities of greater adequacy, the subjection of self to some degree of pain is seldom much of a deterrent.

Effective change in self requires a willingness to put oneself in the way of being hurt. This kind of courage and deliberate courting of threat, however, can also go too far. Indeed, it can even result in self destruction. Not all threats are worth seeking nor are all threats by any means equal in the degree of adequacy which they can provide for a particular person. In Chapter 10 we made a distinction between challenge and threat. People feel threatened, it will be recalled, when confronted with situations they do not feel capable of dealing with. People feel challenged, on the other hand, when they are confronted with situations lying within their capacities. Challenge offers opportunities for the experience of adequacy. Threat rarely contributes to the maintenance and enhancement of self. Individuals who value and seek for challenge contribute to an ever growing personal adequacy. With increasing adequacy many of the threats they formerly felt may even be experienced as challenges to be met with joy and excitement rather than with fear and dread.

The achievement of adequacy provides one with such strength and sureness of self that things outside seem far less threatening. The kind of continual testing of self we have been advocating is a far cry from the search for security which some people would have us believe is the mark of adequacy. It demands, in fact, a willingness to give up security, even to place oneself in jeopardy, for the experience of achieving a more adequate self. Security of self is achieved by a willingness, when necessary, to renounce the support of the familiar. To cross the street one must leave the security of the sidewalk. To achieve the security in self necessary to cross streets without fear, one must be willing to renounce the comfort and safety of what is for the greater achievement of what may be.

CHAPTER 17

The Goals and Purposes of Education

IN the complex interdependent world we live in each of us is increasingly dependent upon the intelligence and good will of an ever larger number of our fellow men. It is not surprising, therefore, that as our society has grown more interrelated and coöperative, education has also grown by leaps and bounds. From an institution once designed for the enhancement of a few in the leisure class we now seek an education "for all." It is no longer conceived as a luxury but as a stark necessity on which the welfare of all of us depends in greater and greater measure. Modern society simply cannot exist without a continuously increasing supply of more and more adequate people. The goal of education from society's viewpoint, then, is the production of adequate personalities, people who can be counted upon to behave effectively and efficiently and to contribute freely to the welfare of all. This is simply another way of saying that the goal of education is intelligent behavior.

This is a definition of the purpose of education which could hold true in all societies, for all times, and for all people. It is quite true that this statement of the desired result of education is more general than those which are usually given; but a more definite and specific description of the kinds of behavior which should result from education can be dangerous. Conditions change and any society which sets out to concentrate on securing a specific type of behavior from its citizens runs the risk of getting it under conditions where it is valueless or even undesirable. Other nations besides the Spartans have had this happen to them. For the good of our society and its members it is better to wish for intelligent behavior than for good penmanship, or the ability to diagram a declarative sentence, or any of the other limited objectives which may or may not be a valuable means of need satisfaction in the future.

Since education is always concerned with training a younger generation to assume responsibilities in an era the precise character of which we cannot foresee, its goals must always appear in general terms. To decide today in too specific terms what children should be tomorrow may run the risk of preparing them for a world that does not exist. So it is that we must be content with a goal of education concerned with the *production of intelligent, adequate people,* in the belief that if we can be successful in this general aim, the specifics can be solved as we reach them.

Advocates of all systems and goals in education agree on one thing: that, to be effective, it must result in a change in the behavior of the person educated. If no change results, the attempts at education have been unsuccessful. It is the primary thesis of this book that behavior is completely determined by the perceptual field at the moment of action. From this point of view, then, the process of education is fundamentally a process of change in the field. Behavior is determined by the field, and the way to change behavior is to change perceptions.

We have stated that the goal of education is the production of adequate, intelligent people. Earlier in this book we have defined adequacy and intelligence in perceptual terms. Let us stop here for a moment to review those definitions, because they will help us to define more precisely the goals of education.

The adequate personality we defined as one who (1) perceives himself in essentially positive ways, (2) is open to his experience or capable of accepting self and others, and (3) is strongly and broadly identified with others.

Intelligent behavior, we indicated, was the product of perceptual fields (1) rich, (2) extensive, and (3) maximally available when needed. These perceptual characteristics of adequate persons and intelligent behavior define more specifically the goals of education. An adequate educational system which produces these kinds of perceptual fields in its students is successful. A system which fails to affect these important criteria has failed.

THE INDIVIDUAL'S GOALS ARE PERSONAL

Fortunately, the individual himself is also seeking an ever greater degree of personal adequacy. Indeed, as we have seen, this is the basic need of the organism, motivating its every act. The problem of education arises, however, in the fact that while the student's goals are immediate and personal, the goals of education are frequently cultural and remote. This difference in perception of what adequacy entails accounts for any of the difficulties we have in the education of the young. A 10-year-old boy from a lower socioeconomic class intent upon the immediate satisfaction of need and a 30-year-old, middle-class woman teacher intent upon preparing the child for the future, for instance, are living in quite different worlds. The behavior which is of value to the teacher in the pursuit of her goals would be a positive detriment to the boy in the pursuit of his. For the middle-class schoolteacher it may appear important to be polite. Being polite, however, when one's adequacy depends on status and prestige in his gang could, from the child's view, prove dangerous to life and limb!

To control or change the behavior of any individual, it is necessary to change his perceptual field. The student's differentiations in his perceptual field, however, are not only directed toward the satisfaction of his need for maintenance and enhancement; they are directed toward the *immediate* satisfaction of this need. In the exploration of his field the differentiations which seem likely to achieve this end are continued and perfected, and the perceptions which seem less promising are abandoned as soon as their uselessness is perceived. People do work toward long-range objectives, it is true, but only in the general sense that these long-range objectives have determined the selection of the more immediate goals which they are currently trying to reach.

A student seeking self enhancement, for instance, decides to become a teacher. So he registers in a teachers' college. To graduate he must secure a passing mark in his educational psychology course. He comes to class. But he cannot postpone his need for self enhancement until he becomes a teacher. He must seek it in the immediate situation in the classroom in which his long-range efforts toward self enhancement have trapped him. Only to the extent that the situation in that classroom gives him immediate satisfaction of need will he become or remain an active participant. Lecturers who believe that their students are hanging on every word forget their own woolgathering at some of the lectures they attend. Children are no less human. A request to think about a problem the individual does not yet have rarely leads to serious or earnest effort on the part of anyone, child or adult. Even if he knows that he may have to meet that problem in the future there is little likelihood of active effort. We are all too much in need of immediate reassurance and enhancement to spend much time solving problems we do not have and pursuing "goals" we do not desire. Time enough for that later. Right now, we have to do the things which are important *now.* As a result children who do not own houses remain quite uninterested in the paper-hanging problems in arithmetic, and students who have elected psychology as a means to more and better dates are usually bored by lectures on learning curves or chronaxie.

Any given individual will differentiate from the field only that which helps him toward the satisfaction of need at that moment. When the student's immediate goal is reached, his differentiations in that direction naturally cease. He learns no more about anything than he finds necessary. This "laziness" and "inattention" to the demands of the teacher and the school seems reprehensible to the teacher. It may even seem perverse and abnormal. But from the point of view of the individual it is simply efficiency. Failure to learn what the teacher wishes does not mean that he has ceased to learn. It only means that he has turned to more promising objectives and is searching his field for ways and means of reaching them. If the subject matter presented by the school promises to assist him in the immediate satisfaction of need and is within his ability to differentiate, he will learn it. If it does not assist him or (the same thing) is beyond his capacity, he will discover how to evade learning it. Essentially the control of learning is in the hands of the student, not in the hands of the teacher.

The insistence of the child on pursuing his own immediate ends sometimes arouses a great deal of indignation from his elders, who are apt to feel that the only way to behave is to conform to their plans and thus minister to their needs; but the point of view of the student is necessarily different. It is quite likely that much of the conflict between pupils and teachers which still occurs in schools is due to the fact that the schools are run by people who are chiefly concerned with preparing the student for his functions in adult life and are filled with students who want to satisfy their needs here and now. Each group is apt to find the other quite obtuse and unreasonable.

IMMEDIATE NEED VERSUS PREPARATION FOR LIFE

"Preparation for life" is good sense, as far as it goes. It is obvious that the way to have time enough tomorrow is to do part of the work today. Parents expect their children to do just that in school. But there is a catch. The catch is, as we have pointed out already, that people differentiate from the field only what is helpful to the attainment of their present goals. And school children have different goals from adults, partly because they are children and partly because they are in that special type of institution which we call a school. As a result they discover those techniques and make those differentiations which are most effective in securing their self enhancement *in the school situation* instead of discovering those techniques and making those differentiations which will be most effective in the adult situation for which they are "being prepared."

This is a problem peculiar to a culture in which childhood is put aside as a nonproductive period and in which children are not allowed to become productive members of society. In most primitive societies, where the economic and social contributions of children are needed and welcome, the problem does not exist. In such societies the work of adults and children is so much alike that the solution of childhood problems is often equivalent to the solution of adult problems. The child, in striving for satisfaction of his immediate need, is automatically "preparing for future life" as well.

In a complex and highly specialized society like our own we cannot go back to the educational practices of primitive times. To do so would bring our civilization to a speedy end. However, we would do well to bring our children into closer touch with adult society by giving them greater opportunities to become participating members. This cannot be achieved by make-believe activities such as Boys' States and Junior Governments, although they both, along with sociodrama techniques, are a long step in the right direction. Student governments, if they really govern, are of great value to the participants. As a step toward social membership, work-study plans have been very effective in many vocational schools; but for the purposes of general education a much wider program is needed. The best training in citizenship, for instance, is secured by children actively engaged in activities they have devised for the betterment of their community. The practices of some Southern schools whose students have contributed to their communities by reclaiming waste land, doing contour plowing, establishing canning centers, and finding new markets for community products are outstanding examples of effective education. The activities mentioned can be planned and carried out by young people in their teens; and in almost all communities even younger children can make real contributions to the public welfare. To the extent that they can gain recognition and acceptance for these activities they will inevitably develop concepts of themselves and their surroundings which will be very beneficial to them and to society in later life.

This does not mean that a school program is without value unless the child is making an immediate contribution to the community. Even when the school program is, from the point of view of adults, almost purely make-believe, it can be of great value in preparing the child for adult life if it allows and helps him to attack his own immediate problems, whatever they may be. A school program which emphasizes the value of the individual and helps him to make effective adjustments to other people is truly preparing children for the future. The school can best guarantee that a child will develop into a nonthreatened, nonthreatening, and socially effective person by providing him with success experiences and a nonthreatening, accepting atmosphere. Having self respect now will help him to develop a self which will be less threatened in the future and therefore more adequate in exploring his environment and dealing with other people.

As long as our schools persist in attempting to direct the child into activities which do not provide him with opportunities for immediate self enhancement, children will show great ingenuity in avoiding these activities. They must do so in order to concentrate on their immediate personal problems, which are the only things important to them. The traditional school has countered this refusal to deal with material which has no personal value by inventing the conventional system of marking and promotion. This gives the nonenhancing material an artificial self reference through requiring its mastery as a condition for avoiding censure or for securing a satisfactory mark. This makes the material a matter of concern to the pupils who have differentiated success in school as a means of self enhançement and it is, after a fashion, learned. However, the victim of this trickery does not allow himself to be put upon. He maintains his integrity by dropping the material from his field at the earliest possible moment, usually as soon as the mark has been assured. This state of affairs often results in the pupil's disregard of the subject matter entirely except as a vehicle for gaining approval or avoiding disapproval. And what he does or how he behaves toward it will depend on whose approval he is trying to gain.

What, then, is the solution to this impasse? Here is the student, on the one hand, intent upon the immediate satisfaction of his need and the school, and on the other, charged with the responsibility of assuring his adequacy in the future. Some teachers have attempted to resolve this impasse by designing educational practices entirely in terms of the immediate needs of the child. Other teachers have attempted to solve the problem by ignoring the needs of the child entirely and concentrating solely on "training the child for the future." The first of these approaches makes of the teacher a nonentity and ignores the goals of society. The second makes a nonentity of the child and glorifies the goals of society. Clearly, neither of these extremes is likely to result in an effective and efficient educational system. Effective education is not content with the fulfillment of immediate goals. It is concerned as well with the creation of goals. The truly great teacher does more than tell us what we want to know. He inspires us too to want to know what a moment before we had never dreamed of. To achieve such goals in modern education means that we must be deeply concerned with the meanings existing on the part of our students.

Education Must Deal with Personal Meaning

The important thing in the determination of behavior is not the objective description of objects and facts in the phenomenal field, but the meaning that those objects and facts have for the individual. This meaning is found in the relationship of the object to the phenomenal self, in the role which the object or fact is felt to have in the satisfaction of need. The work of Norman Maier indicates that objects differentiated from the field as a means to one goal may be correspondingly harder to experience with another meaning. In his experiments Maier's subjects were asked to solve a problem involving the principle of the pendulum and were given a piece of string and a pair of pliers. Many of his subjects were so used to pliers as pliers that it never occurred to them they could be used as pendulum weights. They were unable to see the new meaning pliers could have because they were so fixed on the old one. It is, therefore, very important that the fact or object emerge with a meaning which will make it most useful for the future satisfaction of need. If it is differentiated as something to be avoided, it becomes less available for future use. If it is differentiated with too narrow a meaning, it will also be less available.

Unfortunately, material forced upon students without consideration of their present need and immediate goals tends to acquire a meaning which makes it less useful in the satisfaction of need than if it had never been studied. Since it does not assist the satisfaction of need, its intrusion into the field simply creates additional difficulty for the student. The demand that he abandon his current problems and turn to the study of the required material is pretty sure to cause him to regard that material as an obstacle to self enhancement, as something to be avoided, a negative goal. If he remembers it at all after the examination is over he remembers it with this meaning and behaves toward it accordingly. If we wish a child to like a new food we give him the opportunity to eat it when he is hungry, when it will acquire the meaning we wish it to have. We do not, if we are wise, offer it to him when it will not satisfy his need; nor do we force it upon him under circumstances which humiliate or disgust him. Some parents, it is true, do make such mistakes, but teachers should be better trained.

MEANINGS CANNOT BE FULLY VERBALIZED

The meaning of any object or event is the relation which it has to the self of the perceiver. It is his perception of its effect upon himself and his efforts at self maintenance and self enhancement. As we have seen, however, not all meaning can be fully verbalized. Many meanings exist at such low levels of awareness as to be unreportable. It is quite likely that our inability to communicate and share meanings with more exactness is due to our inability to find verbal symbols for such low-level experiences. As long as they remain ground they are undifferentiated and therefore incommunicable. The result is that we rarely are able to communicate meanings fully and accurately. Students who are taught by verbal means alone are sure to behave as if most of the material they study is without relation to themselves, as indeed it is, until they actually experience the situations the books and teachers are talking about.

In general, the problem of communicating meanings is so difficult that it is often much more practical to help students discover the meaning of objects and events by actual experience than to try to convey them verbally. Furthermore, the meanings are bound to differ from one person to another because the object or event will play different roles in different fields. It will have different potentialities for different people.

MEANINGS DIFFER FROM INDIVIDUAL TO INDIVIDUAL

No two people ever share the same phenomenal field. In any objective situation and from each school subject the individual selects only those aspects which are pertinent to the achievement of his goals at that time. Because each fact and field of subject matter thus has very different meanings to different people, efforts to reform education by changes in the curriculum, although they may be helpful, are bound to fall short of expectations. We cannot reform education by this method alone, because the same curriculum means so many different things to different people. For example, the famous "hundred books" can be extraordinarily rich sources of growth and enlightenment to students who have identified themselves with their own society and are seeking to understand it and its problems. The same books, on the other hand, are mere compilations of irrelevant and boring opinion to people who read them "to learn what great men have thought," "to become cultured," or to acquire college credit. In the same way a student in a Latin class may learn a great deal about Roman politics, or about poetry, or about basic grammar. He may also learn how to cheat without being caught, how to avoid being called upon by the teacher, or how to wiggle his ears to entertain the people behind him.

THE FUNCTION OF SUBJECT MATTER

It seems obvious, therefore, that any system of education which concerns itself only with the formal presentation of standard subject matter without considering the individual student's point of view will affect different persons very differently. Subject matter and methods which have a desirable effect on the development and behavior of one student may have a very undesirable effect on the development and behavior of another. As a result any formalized system of education whether method-centered or subject matter–centered, is too unpredictable and erratic in outcome to be safely used by a highly integrated, democratic society. In such a society one ignorant, maladjusted, or disaffected individual may menace the life and happiness of people all over the world. No member is unimportant. As a voter, as a producer, as an inhabitant of the same world, the behavior of each citizen affects the lives of all. In such a society the education of no individual can safely be left to chance. To confine our educational effort to the production of change in the not-self part of the student's phenomenal field is to leave far too much to chance. The series of diagrams in Fig. 24 may illustrate the point. The top one schematically shows the entire phenomenal field of an individual. The middle shows the external part of the field only. This is the part accepted by traditional education as its entire field of action. The third shows the external field as it is divided among various fields of subject matter, each taught without reference to the phenomenal self and with many gaps and some overlapping. For several years educators have recognized the inadequacy of the bottom situation and have at-

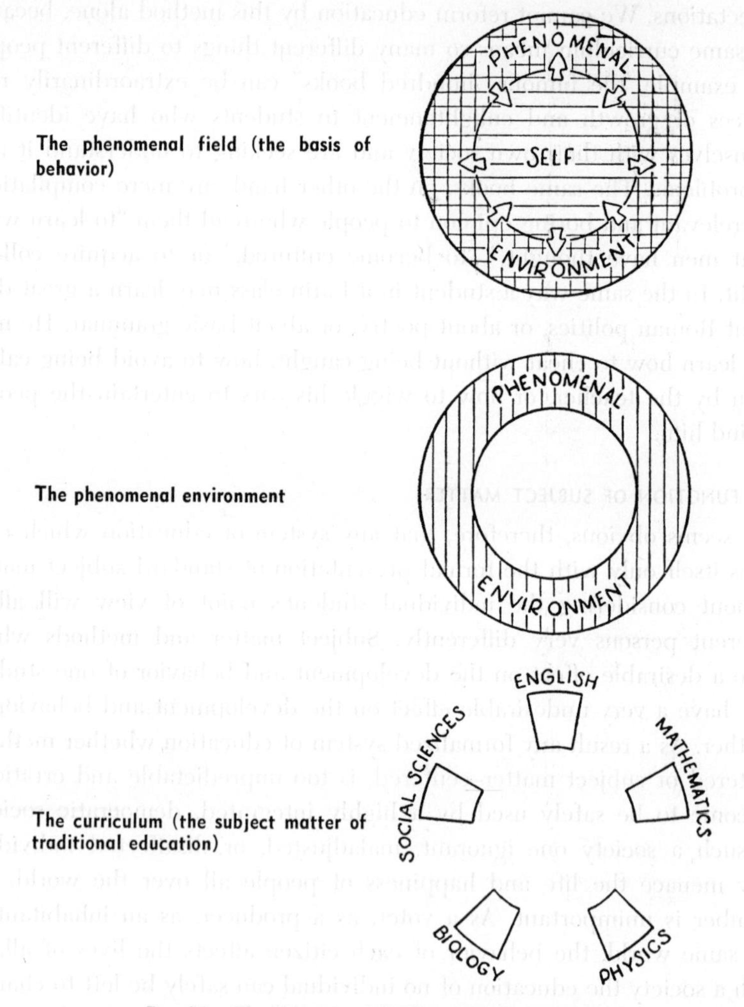

Fig. 24. The Phenomenal Field and the Curriculum.

tempted to remedy it by breaking down the subject matter boundaries and "correlating" the subjects to show the student their essential unity. If this could be done successfully, it would enlarge the field of education to the field shown in the middle diagram. But if our analysis of behavior is correct, even this would not help a great deal. To be really effective, education will have to accept the task of dealing with the whole phenomenal field of the individual, of producing changes in his perception of himself as well as in his perception of his environment.

This is necessary not only because of the dominant role which the phenomenal self plays in the determination of behavior but because of the organized and unified nature of the phenomenal field.

The Phenomenal Self

Since behavior must be appropriate to the phenomenal self, changes in the phenomenal self are invariably followed by changes in behavior. We have already cited instances of such changes in other chapters. Lecky has reported a number of cases of pupils who, after undergoing changes of the self concept, have made startling improvement in their level of achievement, often without tutoring: "A high school student who misspelled 55 words out of a hundred and who failed so many subjects that he lost credit for a full year, became one of the best spellers in the school during the next year, and made a general average of 91. . . . A girl who had failed four times in Latin, with marks between 20 and 50, after three talks with the school counselor made a mark of 92 in the next test and finished with a mark of 84. She is now taking advanced Latin with grades above 80."

The following case report, written by a teacher, further illustrates the important role played by the phenomenal self in behavior.

Roger is 12 years old, almost three years older than any other child in the class. He has failed three different terms in school and was passed into the sixth grade this year only because of his age. Achievement and other tests at the end of the year showed little improvement over what he accomplished on the tests given in September. He has had psychological tests three times: once when he was 7, again when he was 9, and once more this spring. Test results showed that he has normal intelligence and is abnormal in no way. He has never learned to read although there is no physical or mental obstruction to his ability to learn. He is far beyond the average child in his ability to converse and shows remarkable common sense and judgment for a child his age. He surpasses most of the class in reasoning out classroom problems not connected with schoolwork. He has a wonderful personality and is well liked by all the other children although the boys call him a sissy. Roger firmly believes that he was born without a brain and that it is impossible for him to learn. He will not attempt to do any kind of schoolwork which involves independent thinking and constantly attempts to foresee any challenge which might confront him before the school day even begins. Upon arriving at school he might say "If we do examples at the board today I'm not going up. I'll sit in my seat because I can't do them and only take up space at the board."

When Roger started to read in the first grade, the children laughed when he made a mistake and continued to laugh at his mistakes when none of his teachers corrected the other children. This occurred in more than the first grade. Roger at first laughed with them until he suddenly refused to read aloud any more. Since then he cannot even read silently. He dislikes school and has to be practically forced to school every day. His belief that he was "born without a brain" (and he sincerely believes this) excuses him from any thinking processes and so protects him from humiliation. He is no behavior problem as far as obeying rules, etc., and he is a very cheerful boy for, naturally, having no brain excuses one from the difficult things.

Roger was an only child until he was 7 and his mother did all the difficult things for him. When his brother was born, Roger demanded even more attention from his parents and, fearing he was jealous of the baby, the parents overworked themselves in showing their devotion. His mother tied his shoes until he was ten. I believe this dependence on someone to do all the hard things is one of Roger's problems now. Everything was made easy for him and all the difficult tasks taken over by his mother or father and now he is unable to do for himself.

He does not play with boys but prefers to play with girls. . . . The fear of failure in the boys' games undoubtedly keeps him from entering the sports. He can run faster than the girls and beats them at their games and to him this is better than being beaten by the boys. . . . Recently his mother called me to say that though he is signed up for two weeks at Boy Scout camp, he gets almost hysterical when it is mentioned and is begging to stay home. . . .

He is at the reading clinic on the Hill this year and there has been a decided improvement in his reading accomplishment. . . . The psychological tests have been bad for Roger, I think. These have naturally given him the idea he is different and that there must be something wrong with him, especially since he has had three. After his tests this spring (which his parents insisted upon) he came to school and said "Well, they gave me some more tests to see how dumb I was." His parents have never told him the results of the tests. . . .

We tried in school to help him gain more self-confidence but when his parents refused to let him take the bus to the city alone, would not allow him to go to the movies with a group of boys and girls on Saturday afternoon unless a parent was along, our work did little good.

The case of Roger illustrates quite well how the phenomenal self develops and how it affects behavior. This boy was treated as an incompetent by his parents, his classmates, and his teachers. He was placed in a situation where it was easier to accept this concept of himself than to reject it. As an incompetent at home he was waited on and protected. In school he found that the concept of himself as an incompetent was one which he could maintain because it was consistent with the way he was treated. His early efforts to behave as if he were competent were greeted with ridicule, so he fell back to a position he could maintain and became a boy "born without a brain," free from the responsibility of performing the tasks which led to humiliation. This self concept of incompetence as a student and as a boy not only caused his withdrawal from classroom activities and from competition with boys, it also became a determining factor in the further differentiation of his phenomenal field. Facts and experiences which threatened this self were rejected or were selected in conformity with it. His experiences at the psychological clinic, for instance, might have been a source of reassurance to another child. To Roger, however, they were supporting evidence which helped to maintain his phenomenal self and the stability of his field. This boy felt that to be able, to be normal, or to be masculine would be to be a failure because it would confront him with problems and responsibilities with which he felt unable to cope. It is no wonder that his teacher was unable to reassure him.

The case of Roger is unusual only in the clear-cut visibility of the mechanisms involved. It is easy to see in his case that the determining force which gave the individual character and direction to his behavior was the phenomenal self. Roger with a different perception of himself would have behaved very differently. So would any person.

This presents all schools and all teachers with a new responsibility. If we are to deal effectively with behavior we must consider what our students think of themselves. Indeed we must, if our assumptions are correct, frankly assume the responsibility for helping our students to perceive themselves in ways that will be more satisfactory to them and, through the resulting behavior, to others. The development of an adequate self by each student would seem to be a primary responsibility for us all.

THE ADEQUATE SELF AS A GOAL OF EDUCATION

In an earlier chapter we have seen that an adequate personality is characterized by three factors: (1) an essentially positive view of self, (2) the capacity for acceptance of self and of others, and (3) the ability to identify broadly with his fellow man. Since the self concept is a function of experience, what happens to students during their time spent in the educational system must be of vital importance in the development of the phenomenal self. Probably no other agency in our society outside the family has a more profound effect on the development of the individual's concepts of self. What happens to an individual in school is important to the production of an adequate personality. These learnings, furthermore, occur whether teachers plan for their occurrence or not. A teacher may ignore the effects of his behavior on a child's developing concepts of self, but the fact of his ignoring them does not eliminate the effect. An effective educational system can no more ignore the variables of behavior than the chemist can omit essential ingredients of his compound and expect to come out with the hoped-for product.

The ways in which the schools can assist their students in the development of satisfactory and desirable self concepts cannot be planned as a rigid syllabus of experiences or activities because the experiences and achievements which give self enhancement and confidence to a person at one stage of his life may be profoundly unsatisfactory to another person or to the same person at another time. Praise from the teacher, for instance, can represent either self enhancement or humiliation to different children or in different circumstances. It is possible, however, to make some assumptions about the general techniques that would be used by schools which deliberately set out to develop adequate self concepts in their pupils.

1. Such schools would provide each pupil with every possible opportunity to think of himself as a responsible citizen and a contributing member of society. They would see that he has the widest possible chance to identify with and be accepted by the socially desirable individuals and groups which he admires, so that he will feel accepted by and acceptable to society.

This seems to imply a need for democratic classrooms, where there is respect for the need, integrity, and potentialities of all members of the group and where all members feel free to express their opinions frankly and openly. It also implies an emphasis on coöperative activities which call for a wide variety of skills so that each student will have opportunities to gain a sense of self enhancement and personal worth from his contribution to the group. It implies a more appreciative attitude by adults, especially teachers, toward children's ambitions and achievements.

2. Such a school would provide its pupils with a wide variety of opportunities for success and appreciation through productive achievement. Under these conditions children would not only be able to gain self enhancement through the discovery of their talents and areas of strength, but would also be encouraged to discover their weaknesses and inadequacies under conditions in which they would feel adequate enough to acknowledge and deal with them.

3. It would provide its pupils with a maximum of challenge and a minimum of threat. It would stimulate and encourage the exploration of ever new fields of human thought, for nothing is quite as satisfying a contribution to personal feelings of adequacy than challenge successfully met and conquered. It need not be feared that children, in a situation where they are able to move freely toward self enhancement, will select activities which are "too easy" for them. Such activities do not lead to self enhancement and are chosen only when the individual is under threat. Under threat he attempts to protect himself from failure by reverting to an activity he has already mastered.

Other things being equal, more pupils will have opportunities for success and self enhancement if: (1) The achievements are evaluated by standards appropriate to the age and experience of the pupil. (2) The activity is chosen and planned by the pupils themselves. (3) The contributions of different members of the same class are so different in type that no comparisons are possible. (4) The activity is appropriate to the abilities, maturation level, and goals of the student.

The program of diversification of activities should not be prevented by the plea that the present subjects of instruction are of such unique importance that all must become proficient in all of them. Our society is one of coöperation among specialists. The United States census lists more than 35,000 occupations, each of which presumably calls for its own pattern of skills and abilities. It is to the advantage of our society that all of its members should think of themselves as responsible citizens and contributing members. It is not to the advantage of society that all have the same skills and items of information. Indeed, it is preferable that they do not.

The essential point is that the student, to acquire a satisfactory feeling of competence and acceptability, must grow up having success experiences and being accepted. Many students, it is true, do not win these experiences. But when we recognize that *every* student must have such experiences in order to become a happy and productive member of society, the defects of all but a few of our schools are at once apparent.

If it is important that students learn to perceive themselves as liked, wanted, acceptable, able, and responsible, then it follows that education must provide them with the kinds of experiences which help them see themselves so and avoid treating them in ways that destroy positive self feeling. If it is important that citizens grow up accepting themselves and others, then it is important that schools provide experiences of acceptance. It will be necessary to recognize that there are rejected children in schools as well as in homes. Finally, to achieve fully adequate people, education will have to aid young people in achieving the widest possible identification with their fellow men. This will require experience with others and interaction among peoples of a wide variety of race, color, and creed.

THE CREATION OF INTELLIGENCE AS A GOAL OF EDUCATION

The purpose of education, we have said, is the promotion of intelligent behavior. And in Chapter 11 we defined intelligence as a function of perception, the product of a phenomenal field rich, extensive, and maximally available. It follows that to produce an intelligent citizenry education must find ways of providing students with opportunities to become richly informed and fully free to utilize their perceptions to maximum advantage.

Human perceptions are the raw material with which education must work. How successful education is in accomplishing its goals will depend upon how effectively it deals with the problems of perception. The basic variables of perception which we have been discussing throughout this book thus become the raw materials with which the process of education must work. These variables, it will be recalled, are as follows: (1) the physical organism, (2) the effect of time, (3) opportunities for perception, (4) the effect of need, (5) the phenomenal self, (6) the effects of goals and values, and (7) the effect of restrictions on the phenomenal field. In the earlier parts of this chapter we have devoted a good deal of attention to discussing the effect of two of these variables upon the process of education, namely the effect of need and the phenomenal self. This is not to suggest that the remaining variables are less important. Rather, we have devoted so much space to them only because they are frequently overlooked and because they represent particular contributions of this frame of reference about behavior.

We do not have space here to examine in detail how each of the remaining variables is related to the problem of education. We have already discussed the operation of these variables at length in the early chapters of this book. In Chapter 11, we have raised a series of questions about ways in which our understanding of these variables might be related to the problem of creating intelligence. These questions are equally applicable to the problems of education in the creation of an informed citizenry. Educators and teachers in training may find it stimulating and exciting to attempt the application of these principles concerning perception to almost any aspect of education they choose. For the educator interested in experimentation with the teaching process, a perceptual understanding of these variables provides a veritable gold mine of hypotheses worthy of experimentation. Over the last ten years, for example, Combs has attempted systematically to apply some of these basic principles to understanding and practice in such areas as the construction of lectures, the training of counselors and guidance personnel, the development of group-discussion techniques, the solution of intergroup tensions, even, for a period, the task of a lobbyist in one of our state legislatures. Some of the thinking in the chapter to follow about the teacher and his relationships has grown out of this kind of attempt to apply what we now know of the basic variables of perception.

Similar experimentation on the part of Snygg has led to the following partial list of principles concerning the learning process:

1. In most schoolroom situations the chief motive of the children's behavior and learning is their need for self-esteem and a feeling of personal adequacy.
2. Activities and techniques which result in success and an increased feeling of self-esteem will be repeated; activities which result in failure or humiliation are avoided.
3. When children are confronted with a situation where the old techniques for satisfying their need for self-respect or security are not appropriate they will, if ready, learn new techniques for mastering the situation or, if unready, will use or discover methods for escaping from it.
4. Any child is ready to learn new techniques in situations which are not markedly different from situations he has already mastered. Any child is unready for situations which call for solutions quite unlike those he has already used and understood.
5. Attempts to teach children before they are ready are not only a waste of time but, by building up attitudes of avoidance, interfere with later learning.
6. Habit is not a cause of behavior. Acts and techniques are repeated only if they satisfy need. Habit is not the result of repetition but the result of success.
7. Repetition is not a cause of learning. It is true that some situations, such as those calling for the development of a new motor skill or a technique of solution completely new to the child, are ordinarily not solved at the first trial. In such circumstances most children must find themselves in the problem situation many times before they can find an adequate method of dealing with it. However, repetition sought by the child because he wishes to solve the problem has a very different effect from repetition forced upon him by the teacher. If repetition is imposed by the teacher in such a manner that the child is unable to notice progress or feels that he is failing, the result is invariably the discovery of a technique of avoidance.

8. Since the purpose of the schools is to develop each child to maximum capacity as a productive and happy member of society the real test of their success is not the degree to which the pupils can talk about desirable techniques or even the degree to which they are able to use them in school at the command of the teacher but the degree to which they voluntarily use them in their daily life outside of school. In other words, the attitudes which are acquired along with subject matter may be even more important than the subject matter itself.

9. The learning of any skill or item of subject matter is accompanied by the formation of attitudes by the pupil toward the subject, toward school, toward his teacher, toward teachers in general, toward adults, toward society, and toward himself which may be desirable or undesirable. As a result, how subject matter is taught may be even more important than what is taught.

10. Skills are better retained and more often used if they are learned under conditions similar to those in which they will be used.

11. Subject matter must be presented in such a way that each child shall secure a feeling of pride and satisfaction through its mastery. This involves an awareness of individual differences among children, not only in ability but in past experiences and present personality. It involves pacing the work for the individual child and it involves a wide and varied program of experiences in school so that each child will have an opportunity to feel successful in his work.

12. Since coöperation with others is a necessary feature of the work of all members of our society it seems desirable to provide many experiences where success can be obtained only as the result of the joint efforts of a group of specialized individuals.

13. The ideal program would be one in which the pacing of experiences is so appropriate that no experience ever needs to be repeated. It is not likely that this ideal will ever be attained but it is fair to assume that a program which requires large amounts of repetitive work is out of step with the normal development of the children and will result in techniques of avoidance rather than mastery. If a child fails to develop the desired attitude or skill as a result of an experience it should be assumed that what is required is a different experience.

The above statement of learning principles falls far short of completeness, since it only hints at the immense drive of the individual for self enhancement and self realization which makes him so unresponsive to the conventional methods and techniques of teaching. But it is not inaccurate as far as it goes. It can help us to decide what teachers can actually do to assist the education of their pupils. Such principles are only suggestive, and the interested reader may discover many more of particular interest and meaning for his own purposes and practices.

CHAPTER 18

The Teaching Relationship

IN former times teaching was conceived primarily as a business of gathering information and of imparting this information to students. The gathering process was accomplished through the collection of information in libraries, in museums, in research, and through bringing together in schools and colleges faculties of learned teachers. Education sought to impart information to students through such devices as books, lectures, demonstrations, art, and in more recent years, the vast field of audio-visual aids like film strips, movies, and television. Education has done very well in these gathering and imparting functions. It has done far less well in helping its students to discover the personal meaning of such information for their own lives and behavior.

This latter problem for education is comparatively recent. In a time when people were interested in educating only an elite, it was not necessary to worry about those people who came to the teacher wanting to know about things beyond what the teacher was prepared to teach them. It was enough to present students with information about the comparatively few subjects which then passed as marks of the educated man. The student's own desire to join the exclusive club of scholarship could be counted upon to produce the kind of active participation that would make learning effective. At about the beginning of the century, however, we decided to try something that had never been attempted before; we determined to educate everybody. Ever since we made that decision we have been faced with a very different problem, for the things *all* the people need to know about are so diverse that we can no longer restrict education to a few subjects satisfying to an elite. Nor can we be satisfied simply to gather information and make it available. Instead, we must now face the problem of how to help vast numbers of people translate a great variety of information into effective behaving. We must find better ways of helping people to *behave* better as well as to *know* better.

We are like the farmer who, when he was asked by the county agent why he did not attend local classes for the improvement of farming methods, replied, "Why man! I ain't farmin' now half as well as I know how!" Most of us know much better than we behave! We rarely misbehave because we do not "know" better. The translation of knowing into behaving is the most difficult and pressing task of education. Gathering and imparting of information can often be accomplished mechanically, but the business of helping people discover the personal meaning of information for them still requires a human interrelationship. This is the very heart of teaching, its reason for being.

Teaching: The Facilitation of Meaning Change

When modern education is criticized by the general public, it is most often for failures to present information. The presentation of subject matter, however, is so simple a problem that it offers comparatively little difficulty for most educators. Actually, both teachers and the public are concerned about the same thing; helping children to know and to behave differently as a result of their knowing. When young people do not behave in ways adults desire, the public often assumes it is because the proper subject matter was not taught. For the teacher, however, the problem is not one of presenting subject matter but of helping students discover and understand the *meaning* of subject matter so that it affects behavior. Teachers rarely fail for lack of knowledge of their subject. What most teachers feel a pressing need for is more effective ways of producing behavior change. "How," they ask, "can I do a better job of affecting the *meanings* of my students?"

Modern education is probably doing a better job with these matters than it has ever done before, but the demands made by the public upon our schools have increased at an even greater rate. Modern society requires much more intelligent citizens than formerly. We need vast numbers of informed and dependable people, and modern education has been given the task of providing broader, deeper, and richer education to veritable tidal waves of students. The demands of society upon its teachers have temporarily outrun the supply of people able to fill the immense new demands of our age, but the job remains the same—helping people to discover the personal meaning of events for them.

In Chapter 8 we observed that information affects behavior in the degree to which the individual discovers the personal meaning of such information for him. We have seen how the same bit of information may have widely differing effects upon the behavior of an individual, depending upon the degree to which that information is seen by him as bearing a relationship to his self. The more intimately one perceives the relationship of concepts to self, the more certain, the more profoundly does information affect behaving. This discovery of the personal meaning of ideas, values, experiences, or the accumulated culture of the race is the very essence of learning and the art of teaching is in helping people to make this discovery.

OBSTACLES TO THE EXPLORATION OF MEANING

Though the exploration of meaning is the goal of teaching, it should not be thought that this process is either easy or quick. Many students have even been thoroughly taught to *avoid* the exploration of personal meaning. Past experience has led them to protect themselves against the revelation of personal meanings. Most of us, for example, have been hurt at times in the past when we have exposed our feelings, attitudes, beliefs, or convictions to other people, and many of us have learned as a consequence to surround ourselves with a kind of protective shell from behind which we can deal with life at arm's length. This can happen even in institutions presumably designed to "help" people. The development of this kind of protective shell was nicely but unhappily illustrated in the case of a sorority group with whom the author worked some years ago.

A group of sorority women found themselves about ready to graduate yet extremely unhappy because, as they put it, at the end of their college careers they "knew many people, but had very few friends." As this group of girls explored the whys and wherefores of this sad state of affairs with the author, it became clear little by little how the situation had come about. The sorority to which they belonged has as its ostensible purpose "helping" the sisters to become the best possible kinds of people. Unfortunately, this "helping" often had quite an opposite result. For example, the sorority sisters would sometimes attempt to "help" one of their members by pointing out to her that the clothes she was wearing were not quite appropriate, or that she really ought to do something about the kind of voice she had, or the way she laughed, etc. This mistaken notion of how to be helpful was a standard procedure in the sorority. It did not take more than a couple of experiences in which a girl was treated in this way before she learned to protect herself from her too helpful sisters. As a result, conversation in the house was primarily concerned with "safe" subjects and the girls became masters at the *forms* of "gracious living." Girls learned to talk about things at a comfortable distance from self. They talked about what had happened to them, but not about the things they felt, believed, or wondered about. This kind of experience is common to many of us and has often caused us to surround ourselves with a shell of protection which makes it extremely difficult to examine our personal experiences or feelings except under very special and protected kinds of situations. It occurs in the classroom too. Good teaching must find ways of overcoming this kind of resistance to the exploration of personal meaning.

A second obstacle to the exploration of meaning, strangely enough, is a product of previous teaching. Some teaching seems almost expressly designed to ignore or discourage the exploration of personal meaning. Our generation has been deeply impressed with the necessity for being scientific, which, in the minds of many, is synonymous with "impersonal" or "objective." Indeed, we have been so impressed with the importance of objectivity that we run real danger of "throwing out the baby with the bath water." Science is sometimes treated as a modern sort of witchcraft. Objectivity, in the minds of some people, requires a dispassionate, selfless consideration of events directly contrary to what is required for the personal exploration of meaning. It is not uncommon to hear teachers say "What are the facts? I am not interested, Helen, in what you think about this matter. Just tell us what he said!" This overemphasis upon the "facts" and the accompanying discouragement of the individual's own conceptions may even be one of the most important reasons for some of education's most glaring failures. An educational system which rules out personal meaning runs a grave risk of becoming a meaningless ornament to life rather than an effective and satisfying way of changing and improving it.

Getting an education is an important American goal, and most students assume that their teachers know what they are doing. Teaching, therefore, which glorifies objectivity and the separation of self from learning is likely to be accepted by students as the "right" way. They fall into the system and learn "objectively," as their teachers desire, but maintain a wide gulf between their "education" and living. If they discover or even explore the personal meaning of ideas for themselves it is often in spite of, rather than because of, their educational experience. The methods teachers use may actually make learning more difficult.

Some years ago the author had a vivid experience of this principle in operation. On the first day of a new semester he explained that the class would operate as a seminar with major emphasis upon class discussion and exploration of ideas. About three-fourths of the class quickly informed him they knew all about that kind of class because they had had a course just like it the previous semester with another professor. The instructor was happy to hear this, thinking he would have to spend little time teaching the group the techniques of group discussion. Actually, the class was one of the most frustrating he had ever experienced. Each class would start off as though at the crack of a gun with everyone wildly waving his hand and wanting to speak. Everyone acted as though it were a matter of life and death that he should be sure to speak at each session. When students did get the floor, their talk was almost entirely descriptive. They spoke of what they had read, what they had seen in the papers, what had happened to them, ad infinitum. Almost never did anyone speak about what he thought, believed, felt, worried about, wondered, or was puzzled about. The discussion never was able to get off a purely descriptive, intellectual level. Students spoke always of things outside themselves, but never of things having any relation to self.

After several frustrating weeks, the instructor began little by little to piece together the reasons for this behavior. These students had learned to behave in this fashion because of the kind of experience they had had the previous semester. In another class the professor had told them it did not matter whether they participated in class discussions or not. But at the end of the semester when students came in to discuss their grades he would say, "Yes I see, Miss Brown, you believe you should have a B but, you know, you really did not participate very much this semester and I am afraid a C is all I can give you!" Following this kind of treatment, students came to their new class determined to participate if it killed them! The same professor had another interesting technique for handling a discussion. When one of the members of his class expressed an opinion he would turn gravely to the rest of the group and say, "Now class, why do you suppose Mr. Adams feels this way about this question?" and for the next half hour the class would take Mr. Adams apart piece by piece! Under this kind of treatment it did not take students long to discover that it was a very dangerous thing to talk about anything in class that revealed a personal feeling. In their new class, therefore, they each had resolved, as one student phrased it, "to participate like crazy but not about anything important!"

Effective teaching must find ways of helping students escape from the unhappy effects of past experience in the exploration of meaning. The walls people build to shut other people out unfortunately shut the builder in. Exploring meaning requires freedom to move, and effective teaching must find ways of helping students break down their defenses and open themselves to new experience. We have seen that intelligence is a function of a free and open phenomenal field. It is increased by freedom to perceive and diminished by that which inhibits and narrows experience. Good teaching must begin with the creation of an atmosphere that makes exploration possible.

The Atmosphere for Learning

To aid students in breaking down their barriers, on the one hand, and actively to engage in the exploration of meaning, on the other, requires an atmosphere conducive to such ends. Atmospheres, however, are not accidental, nor are they matters of physical environment alone. Atmospheres are created out of the interaction of people with one another. The climate for learning is the product of the kinds of interactions students have with teachers. The fact that a teacher is unaware of or doesn't care about the atmosphere he creates with his students does not change the fact. Atmospheres provide the stage upon which learning occurs and arise out of the interaction of teacher and student. They can be ignored only at the risk of making the process of learning haphazard and inefficient.

Even eminent scientists may sometimes be found expressing impatience with the idea of being concerned with what seem like extraneous issues in the learning process. The idea of taking student needs or classroom atmospheres into consideration in teaching strikes them as unimportant. This is like recognizing that an automobile needs a carburetor in its motor and air in its tires but insisting on starting on a trip without these no matter what! A scientist cannot ignore the variables that affect his processes. He can only learn to control them effectively. This is true of learning processes as well. The factors controlling learning still operate whether we take cognizance of them or not. Modern psychology has supplied us with some cues to what the atmosphere for effective learning should be. The following are some of these cues.

FREEDOM FROM THREAT

People can learn under threat, but we have seen that the effect of threat is to narrow perception to that which threatens and to force the defense of self. For most learning situations these two effects of threat are directly contrary to what we desire in an educational experience. We do not seek to narrow perception; education hopes to broaden and open perception. We do not want to encourage self defense; we want to facilitate change of self. The effects of threat seem directly the antithesis of the goals of teaching. Modern research seems to indicate that the effect of threat is to produce autocracy, rigidity, and intolerance, all destructive to the development of free and independent personalities.

It seems clear that an atmosphere conducive to effective learning must be one as free from threat as can be. This requires of the teacher a sensitivity to his own relationships with students and of his students with each other, for threat is a personal experience and can only be understood through the perceptions of the people who feel it. Great teachers have the capacity for creating situations in which threats remain at a minimum and students are encouraged to drop their defenses and engage in the exciting business of growth and change. Because threat is eliminated from the atmosphere of learning does not mean, however, that the situation is also without challenge. It will be recalled that in an earlier chapter we made a distinction between threat and challenge. At that time we pointed out that people felt threatened when they felt inadequate to deal with the events confronting them and challenged when they felt the situations they were involved in were within their capacities. The elimination of threat from the learning situation does not mean that teachers must coddle or shield their students. Quite the contrary, the task of teaching is to continually encourage and challenge students, to help students stretch themselves to their utmost. Students who are truly challenged do not need to be coddled or babied. As a matter of fact they are likely to surprise us by the capacity they have to place themselves in jeopardy for the sheer joy of self exploration and the achievement of greater adequacy.

The genius of good teaching lies in the ability to challenge students without threatening them. To do this effectively means that teachers must be sensitive to the impact upon their charges of what they do and say, for the distinction between threat and challenge lies not in what the teacher *thinks* he is doing, but in what the students *perceive* him to be doing.

AN ATMOSPHERE OF ACCEPTANCE

Generally, the absence of threat we have been speaking about is best achieved in situations which treat each person as an individual of dignity and integrity; situations characterized by warmth, friendliness, and acceptance of the student as he is. In this kind of atmosphere students can and will explore their personal meanings more effectively. Such an atmosphere is not created haphazardly, however, nor can it be expected to occur when the leader of the group is not sensitive to the meanings of his own behavior and personality as these affect the people he must work with. It requires a kind of self discipline, understanding, and sensitivity to other people far beyond that required in some other professions.

Modern research seems to indicate that acceptance of others is a function first of acceptance of self. People who cannot accept themselves are unable to accept other people. In order for a teacher to create an accepting atmosphere for students, then, it would appear he must first accept himself. While it is possible for a short time to create an atmosphere strikingly different from the personalities we possess, this is a most difficult deception to maintain for any length of time. To create a situation that is truly warm, understanding, and accepting, we are beginning to understand, requires a certain kind of person; not just someone who *knows* he should be these things. Good teaching requires that the teacher himself has discovered who he is and what he is and what he is trying to do, just as he is attempting to assist his students in discovering these things for themselves. It is only when people are able to accept themselves that they are able to engage with any great degree of freedom in exploring themselves. To make this possible, those who teach the student must themselves be capable of acceptance.

The good teaching atmosphere should be accepting, but some people have confused this word with resignation and have assumed that an accepting situation is one in which students are allowed to follow whatever whims meet their fancy. Some teachers have practically abrogated their responsibilities in an attempt to please their students. This is not the sense in which we use this word at all. Acceptance, as we have used it, is a dynamic word to describe an attitude of willingness to look at and consider the facts. It has to do with admission of data to consideration. A willingness to examine facts does not imply weakness and passivity. Resignation is an attitude of defeat. Acceptance is understanding without judging. It requires an openness to experience which provides the only sound basis upon which to progress. It is an attitude of taking people as they are and moving forward from this point. It accepts students where they are and serves as a starting point for learning. Acceptance of where a person is does not mean we must be resigned to leaving him there. The task of teaching is to help people move, change, and grow, and this is an active process encouraged by the kind of accepting atmosphere we have been talking about. Acceptance is conducive to the exploration of personal meaning. It is not a substitute for it.

THE IMPORTANCE OF LIMITS

All life situations have limits and the teaching relationship is no exception. In fact, the very existence of limits provides the structure for the teaching relationship and makes the exploration of meaning possible. Limits make possible the definition of relationships and the development of stable frames of reference. Without them we become lost and uncomfortable and learning is seriously disorganized. Anyone who has ever acted as a substitute teacher is keenly aware of the manner in which children explore the limits of a new teacher in an attempt to discover where *this* teacher stands. Those who have not experienced this as teachers may remember how they tried out the substitutes assigned to them. The attempt to discover the limits of new situations is characteristic of everyone placed in an unfamiliar setting. Experienced teachers know that when people are made quickly and surely aware of limits, everyone is happier and the attention of the class quickly reverts to the daily tasks. When limits are not made clear, or when limits vacillate, students are likely to continue the exploration of limits to find out *where teacher stands now.*

Limits have important growth-inducing values for people, and the lack of limits makes adjustment to new situations more difficult. A stable structure has important positive values in providing expectancies against which to judge one's behavior. Clear and reasonable limits provide important security values. In recent years some educators have been so impressed with the unhappy effects of threat and coercion upon the learning process that they have sought to decrease threat through making classrooms more permissive. In the attempt to be "permissive," some teachers, unhappily, have gone so far as to behave as though *any* establishment of limits were coercive. Of course, limits *can* be coercive, but they can also provide important structure and security, facilitating learning. The problem is not one of eliminating limits but of establishing limits which are clear, reasonable, and related to the exploration and discovery of meaning.

Teaching is a relationship, but there can be no relationship with a nonentity. The good teacher is not a shadow but an important and vital part of the learning situation. His personality, as it is experienced by his students, creates the atmosphere for learning. Teachers cannot abrogate their responsibilities by withdrawal and self effacement. Neither can they create an atmosphere conducive to learning by threat and coercion. The effective teacher is one who has learned how to use his own personality in establishing limits for learning that will be clear, reasonable, and maximally helpful in the encouragement of exploration and discovery of personal meaning.

The Provision of Information

The traditional task of education since time immemorial has been to induct young people into the accumulated culture of their age. To live successfully requires information, and the provision of information is a basic task of the educational process. An informed people is particularly necessary in a free society which permits its citizens to make decisions, for good decisions can only be made in the light of the pertinent information. But information is not only important for societal and governmental reasons; people need information about all kinds of things in order to make personal decisions and personal adjustments for effective living as individuals. Information is necessary for the satisfaction of need.

The search for adequacy, we have seen, is insatiable, and the information people require for the achievement of adequacy seems equally infinite. What is more, each of us is so unique and individual that the information we require to work out our destinies is a highly individual matter. Even in those instances where we have common requirements for information, we are likely to need it at quite different times. The teacher is thus confronted with the problem of how to supply a vast amount of information to people with widely differing needs at the same time.

The matter is further complicated by the interests of the teacher in his subject. He "knows" there is beautiful order in his discipline because he has discovered its logic and organization as a result of his own experience. He would therefore like to present this material in the neat orderly way it has come to have meaning for him. He is quite likely to be frustrated in this attempt, however, by the maddeningly haphazard way in which students want to know about things. They are just as likely as not to want information at the beginning that "should" come at the end of a long road of learning. Teachers often forget that the systematic understanding they have achieved followed a similar highly personal search for understanding. As a consequence, teachers and students sometimes pass like ships in the night, one sailing a course for system, the other charting his course by personal need. Sometimes both ships may arrive safe in the same harbor, but this is risky navigation at best.

Before information can have an effect upon behavior, the individual must perceive its relationship to self. He must discover its peculiar personal meaning. This means that efficient and effective teaching must relate information to the need of the learner. It is a comparatively easy matter simply to provide data. It takes real skill, however, to provide information in such a manner as to assist students in discovering its meaning for them.

The discovery of personal meaning requires some sort of activity on the part of the learner. People will learn what they "need" to know. Some teachers achieve this "need to know" through the use of artificial motives like grades or other varieties of reward and punishment. Artificial motives are rarely as effective as those arising from the student's own interaction with his teachers, fellow students, and the subject matter itself. The exploration and discovery of personal meaning is more effectively achieved through the kinds of atmospheres teachers create through their personal relationships with students. Good teachers are able to *create* desires to know. They have the capacity to relate information meaningfully to the perceptions of their students. By their own enthusiasm, interest, and understanding of both their subject and their pupils they excite similar interest in students. Good teachers do not deplore the disinterest of their pupils; they have the power to create interest.

The Reorganization of Meaning

The provision of information in an atmosphere conducive to exploration is not enough to insure that effective exploration of meaning will occur. It is the task of the teacher to insure that this process of exploration occurs. He must point the way to the importance of personal meaning change, must set an example of how to explore meaning, and must actively assist his students to make such exploration. We do not have space here to discuss all of the thousands of ways master teachers have worked out to accomplish these ends, but we can look briefly at several of the principles involved in these processes.

The techniques developed by good teachers down through the ages to assist and encourage students in the exploration of meaning are almost limitless. The particular techniques found useful by teachers are a highly individual matter. Each teacher finds his own best ways of operating as an expression of his own personality, goals, values, experience, and perceptions of the situations in which he is operating. Despite this highly individual character of the teacher's techniques there are several important general principles that seem common to the process of encouraging and assisting the exploration of meaning.

EXPLORATION TAKES TIME

The discovery of personal meaning is a process which seems to proceed best in an unhurried, unharried atmosphere. We have seen in an earlier chapter that perceiving takes time and good teachers are keenly aware of this fact. They know it is possible that the pressure of speed may destroy the process of exploration entirely. The organization and reorganization of perceptions in the phenomenal field is an active process best accomplished through some form of interaction of individuals with problems. The value of a learning situation can be completely lost by such an emphasis upon speed that the learner is reduced to passivity while subject matter is poured forth at a rate he is unable to comprehend. Almost any student has at one time or another been exposed to the teacher in such desperate haste to "cover the subject" that he succeeded in burying it forever.

GUIDING EXPLORATION

Teachers can point the way to exploration of meaning by actively helping students to explore the crucial aspects of learning—the personal meaning of events for the student. They may do this in two ways: (a) by learning to listen intently to what students are expressing; and (b) by holding up for the students' examination the crucial aspects of the events he is exploring, namely their peculiar meaning for the student.

Intent listening is something that many people have never learned to do. For many of us, listening is no more than waiting till the other fellow gets through so we can get a chance to speak again. Intent listening is quite different. It is an active process, not passive waiting. It is a matter of striving to comprehend the meaning of what another individual is attempting to express. To get an idea of how difficult this is, the reader may like to try a procedure devised by a group of graduate students in training as counselors. To teach themselves to listen carefully they required that no member of the group could express his own point of view until he had first stated the gist of the previous speaker's ideas *in a way acceptable to the previous speaker!* In this way they sought to discipline themselves in the art of listening. Good teaching requires a sensitivity to what students are expressing and this requires accurate hearing of what others are trying to convey.

Understanding what a student is seeking to express is not enough, however. Students need help in exploring their perceptions as well. Students will do this quite naturally when the atmosphere permits and when teachers demonstrate their willingness to explore their own perceptions. In recent years educators have been experimenting with a number of promising new techniques for helping this process along. Some of these, like techniques of role playing and psychodrama, have been borrowed from the experience of psychotherapists. Others have been derived from the work of psychologists and educators interested in group process and the techniques of group discussion. Still others have been devised by teachers experimenting with a wide variety of methods for helping students bring into the open and explore their own feelings, attitudes, beliefs, and convictions about themselves and the world about them. All of these techniques are dependent upon active exploration of personal meaning, not only of cold objective fact but also of feelings, attitudes, beliefs, convictions, doubts, questions, and concerns. When people feel *very* safe they may even explore their loves, hates, and fears. By holding up for examination the individual's personal perceptions of events, in an atmosphere which makes this possible, the student is helped to examine his perceptions and to organize and reorganize his phenomenal field.

ACCEPTANCE OF MISTAKES

Since exploration necessarily involves trial, practice, seeking, striving, and pushing into the new and unknown, it is bound to result in frequent error. Therefore, a learning situation which regards mistakes as affronts against God and man is hardly likely to encourage the exploration of meaning. Personal meaning can only be discovered in settings wherein one has the opportunity, indeed even the right, to make mistakes. An educational setting which cannot tolerate or permit mistakes imposes severe limits upon the freedom with which students can explore their own perceptions.

When students are not permitted the luxury of making mistakes, they may by the same action be prevented from learning the very things their teachers hope to achieve. A teacher the author once knew had to leave her classroom one day to visit the administrative offices. On leaving her class she told her students: "Children, I must go down to the office for a little while. I want you to be very quiet and go on with your work while I am gone." When she returned to the room a short time later, she found the place a bedlam. Sailing into the middle of the group, she expressed her displeasure in no uncertain terms, ending her tirade by saying, "I will never leave you alone again!" By this last act, she robbed these children of their only opportunity to learn how to behave when the teacher is not there! How indeed can one explore the meaning of responsibility and learn to be responsible without the opportunity to try? Making mistakes is an essential part of learning and where errors are not permitted there is likely to be little learning either. Most effective exploration of meaning is likely to occur where mistakes are expected and accepted as a normal, necessary part of the process.

APPRECIATION OF THE NEW AND DIFFERENT

The discovery of personal meaning is vastly encouraged in an atmosphere which assists people to look at the new and the different. This is not always easy, for this can be frightening and threatening. This is all the more true when new events and ideas are closely related to self. Any psychotherapist knows of the tremendous threat involved, for example, when an individual is confronted with unacceptable perceptions of self. Such threats are destructive to the process of meaning exploration. Good learning situations must find ways of eliminating threat on the one hand and of encouraging the exploration of the new and different on the other.

This kind of situation is created, in part, by the elimination of threat and the creation of an atmosphere of warmth and friendliness. It is created also by the teacher's own demonstration that he is willing, able, and unafraid to explore his own personal meanings. It is also fostered by an attitude which approaches the whole process of learning as an exciting, challenging, enhancing activity well worth whatever effort is expended. To create this latter attitude the teacher must be skillful in interpreting his subject in a fashion that makes it seem valuable and worth while to his students. He must be skilled in transmitting to them a freshness of appreciation, an enthusiasm for the new and the different, and a wonder and delight in their exploration. To do this well, however, is not easy unless it is a vital aspect of the personal meanings of the teacher himself. It cannot be put on like a cloak, for this fools no one. The teacher who does not himself have a wonder and appreciation for the new and the different is unlikely to produce such attitudes in his students, who might well say, like the Indian, "What you do speaks so loudly I cannot hear what you say."

As we have already seen, our educational system has often emphasized goals which do not encourage the exploration of meaning. It has even operated sometimes to discourage and prevent such exploration. Intellectual, disinterested examination has often been glorified as the "scientific" and therefore desirable way of dealing with events in spite of the fact that even the scientist only behaves so in his professional life, never in his private affairs. It is the personal meaning of things which matter to people, and schools which do not value personal meanings run a grave risk of dealing only with unimportant things. Large numbers of children in our society have learned to make sharp distinctions between ways to behave and things to be concerned about in school and out. They have learned too often that "what you learn in school has nothing to do with life." Small wonder, then, if school learning has little effect on performance.

Educators have long been disturbed by the problem of "transfer of training," which is another way of asking: "How do you get subject matter to make a difference?" The answer, as we have suggested in this volume, lies in helping students discover the personal meaning of matters for them. An educational system which seeks to produce change in behavior must value the importance of meanings, and its teachers must be skilled in helping students to explore and discover them.

The Teacher as Instrument for Behavior Change

The kinds of learning situations we have been speaking about in this chapter cannot be produced by force and coercion. Teachers cannot make changes in behavior directly. They can only serve as agents or catalysts in the process of change. This does not mean that teachers are any less important to learning. The task of teaching is the creation of situations conducive to the effective exploration and discovery of personal meaning. In the carrying out of this task the teacher may call upon a vast number of teaching aids, but in the final analysis there is no substitute for his own personality, which serves as the medium through which all he does is expressed. The efficient production of learning experiences for others depends upon the skill of the teacher in using his personality as an instrument for helping others learn.

There is no *one way* of creating relationships with students. As a matter of fact, the kinds of relationships teachers have with students are as diverse as human personality itself. One needs but to think of his own school experience and recall how differently his teachers behaved in accomplishing their results. Good teaching can occur though teachers be sweet or tough, lenient or strict, reserved or out going. What makes an effective teacher, it seems clear, is not the possession of some particular list of traits. It is not a kind of garment which can be put on or off as the season requires, nor is it a bag of tricks to be performed from time to time. People seem able to learn from a variety of teachers and methods. This was illustrated for the author in the conversation of three little boys he overheard at the end of the school year discussing their next year's teacher.

FIRST BOY: Hey, who ya got next year?
SECOND BOY: I got Miss Baxter.
FIRST BOY: Wow! I feel sorry for you!

And he launched into a long tale of how "awful" Miss Baxter was. Finally, as he wound up his tale of horror, the third little boy spoke up.

THIRD BOY: Oh, that's all right, Jimmy. You'll get used to her!

And indeed, this seems to be true. Children seem able to adjust to almost anything if it stands still! There is no kind of personality that all teachers should have. Good teaching seems, rather, to be a matter of effective use of the teacher's unique personality. There will be as many methods of teaching as there are kinds of teachers.

People are used to believing that teachers know how to teach. They are inclined to follow the lead of the teacher in the process of learning. As a result, the way in which the teacher behaves and the things he believes important are quite likely to be regarded by his students as signposts pointing the way to those things which should be important to students as well. One has only to observe the ways in which students seek to outguess the teacher on the final exam. They try in every way possible to discover what he wants, then try their best to give it to him. What the teacher believes to be important has an inevitable effect upon his own behavior and hence upon the behavior of students. Teachers reveal what they believe is important in spite of themselves. The teacher who does not feel the importance of helping students explore personal meaning will almost certainly not encourage his students to do so.

Whether teachers are aware of it or not, their behavior and their effectiveness as teachers depend upon their perceptions about themselves and the situations within which they are involved; particularly upon their beliefs, values, and convictions. Some years ago one of the authors was taken on a tour of a new school building by its proud principal. He was taken to see the shops, the bus-loading docks, the three gymnasiums, the cafeteria, the swimming pool, the public-address system; even the school's own barbershop for rural children. Finally, he was brought back to the principal's office without ever having been shown a classroom. When he pointed this out, the principal apologized for his oversight and called his secretary to lead the author to a classroom in operation. It was clear from his behavior what aspect of his job seemed most important to him! This was further illustrated a short time later when a little boy was brought to the office by a bus driver, who entered with the boy in one hand and the broken arm from one of the bus seats in the other. On the way to school the youngsters on the bus had begun pushing each other. This child had been pushed against a seat arm and had broken it. Now, knowing what we do about this principal's values, it does not take a psychologist to predict how he would behave toward this child! It is a foregone conclusion that he would be very angry—and that is exactly what happened. The principal behaved as though the boy had broken the principal's arm, and in a sense, the child had!

Effective teaching depends upon teacher perceptions. In particular, it depends upon the kinds of perceptions they possess about these things:

1. What people are like
2. The goals and purposes of education in our society
3. The adequacy of the teacher's own personality
4. Effective methods of encouraging learning.

WHAT PEOPLE ARE LIKE

When doctors believed that illness was the result of bad blood, many a defenseless invalid was bled to death. Teachers, too, can make less serious but no less certain mistakes in dealing with people, when the ideas they hold about their charges are false or inaccurate. Effective behavior can only be predicated upon accurate beliefs about the nature of human behavior. The beliefs teachers hold about what their students are like and why they behave as they do define the teachers' own relationships to them. It has been the purpose of this book to set forth one approach to understanding the nature of human behavior. Since education is, in a very real sense, applied psychology, it is our belief that every principle about people and their behavior we have stated in this volume has important meanings for educational practice. We obviously cannot explore all of these here. Let us, however, examine just two of the more obvious implications for teacher behavior growing out of the basic concept that behavior is a function of perception.

Teachers who understand that behavior is caused by present perceptions behave quite differently from those who believe that the causes of behavior lie primarily in the student's past. Teachers who see people's behavior as solely the product of history, for example, will need to acquire vast quantities of information and records about their student's lives. They are likely to judge pupils' capacities on the basis of previous performance and establish expectancies for them at similar levels. The students they face may be seen as already immutably fixed in capacity and the teacher's own contribution as comparatively minor and trivial. Seeing behavior as primarily produced by the influence of others, they are quite likely to demand coöperation of parents and to complain bitterly about parents who do not or cannot respond "properly." Too strong a belief in such a concept of causation may even result in disillusion and discouragement, for if the causes of behavior all lie in the past, the teacher's present role becomes unimportant and of little consequence. One advantage of such a belief, however, is that it provides fine excuses for teacher failure. After all, if behavior is caused by past history, a student's failures are the result of what other people have done before the present teacher got him and teachers can bury their failures by explaining, "What can you do with a child from a home like that?"

On the other hand, teachers who see behavior as the product of present perceptions will behave quite differently. They will need less detailed and extensive information about their students' pasts and will be much more concerned with understanding their students as they are For many teachers it will come as a great relief that they do not *have* to be amateur psychiatrists to carry on their jobs successfully. Seeing behavior as a function of perception makes human capacities much more amenable to change or modification, and the possibilities for education become immensely greater. Since perceptions are open to modification, there is hope for change and wider horizons for personal growth. Teachers are far less limited in what they can hope to accomplish with a particular student, and the role of the teacher is seen as a much more important one in human affairs. Seeing behavior this way, there is less need to feel discouraged or disillusioned and the possibilities for affecting human growth and development become far more exciting and challenging.

Teachers who see behavior as a function of the forces exerted on students will be led to seek ways of forcing and coercing their charges toward desirable goals. They will value "fencing-in" methods of guiding learning and techniques of reward and punishment. Argument and the weight of evidence will play a large part in their approaches to learning while emotion and feeling will probably be seen as disrupting and extraneous aspects of behavior having little to do with learning. Believing that people respond on the basis of the stimuli to which they are exposed, they must put much emphasis upon authority in their teaching, for someone will have to know where the students *should* go. Teachers who believe this way about human behavior will be heard making such statements as: "I told them . . . ," "I've got to get them to . . . ," or "You must make them see. . . ." Their concepts of "leadership" and "guidance" will often turn out on closer examination to be subtle techniques of coercion aimed at getting people to do what someone has already decided in advance "should" be done. Carried to an extreme, such a way of seeing behavior may even result in seeing students as things to be molded in some preconceived image rather than as independent people.

In contrast, teachers who see behavior as a function of perception are more likely to see themselves as "helpers" than "makers," and their students as dynamic and growing rather than objects to be manipulated. They are likely to value the process of learning as well as the product and to see themselves as assisters and facilitators in a normal stream of development. Students will be seen not as objects to do things to, but as people to interact with. Recognizing "feeling" as a kind of perception, attitudes and emotions, beliefs and conviction will play a much larger part in the business of teaching. The perceptual view leads teachers to be less concerned with reward and punishment and much more concerned with the motivational values of interest, challenge, and the creation of "new needs to know." Their speech will include much less of "I" and "you" and much more of "we" and "us." They will be more concerned with experience and less with telling, with questions and problems rather than answers and dicta. They will see their own roles as freeing and stimulating rather than directing and coercing. They will value more highly discussion, doubt, and uncertainty. Teachers who understand behavior as a product of perception will seek to understand their students as well as the subject, and the probability is that when they see their students as people, their students will return the compliment.

Whatever we believe is so has its inevitable consequences upon behavior. What teachers believe about people and their behavior must of necessity affect the ways in which they behave as educators. Effective teaching requires an accurate and realistic concept of the nature of human beings and the ways in which they grow and develop. The more accurate and useful the teacher's understandings, the more likely he is to behave effectively and efficiently. Some teachers develop such understandings as a result of experience and observation; others acquire their understandings from more formal educational experiences; but wherever they acquire them, no teacher is without them. Whether he is aware of the fact or not, every teacher's behavior is a direct outgrowth of his beliefs about what people are like. Accurate beliefs make possible effective teaching and satisfying experiences with education. Poor teachers unhappily remain the victims of their false perceptions.

THE CLARITY OF TEACHER GOALS AND PURPOSES

Behavior, we have seen, is never without purpose. The goals and values people hold have inevitable effects upon the ways in which they behave. How teachers teach is likewise affected by the particular values they espouse. Teachers who feel it is important to have a noiseless classroom will behave quite differently from teachers who believe it important that children be active. A belief that democracy requires every decision be made by the entire group will cause teachers who feel "democratic" teaching is important to emphasize group decisions. On the other hand, teachers who believe democracy is "treating everyone alike" may decry group decisions and establish common standards for everyone. No one can escape the consequences of his own beliefs, and teachers are no exception. The effectiveness of teaching then will be dependent in part upon the kinds of goals and purposes the teacher has differentiated in his phenomenal field and which thereafter serve as the producers of his behavior. To complicate matters further, society expects teachers to have adopted and to be motivated by many of society's values as well. This is fine so long as the teacher's values and those of society are similar. When society's values are different from those of the teacher or when society's values are unclear, teachers have a difficult task to find effective anchors for their own behavior in the classroom.

When teacher values are clear, teacher behavior is similarly clear and direct. When teacher purposes are fuzzy, confused, or vague the teacher's behavior is likewise confused and inexact. When teachers are frustrated and tense, it is almost never because they do not have a grasp of their subject matter. When teachers fail it is far more likely to be the result of a lack of clarity in their own perceptions about what is important. When people are vague about what is important, behavior lacks direction and purpose. If such vagueness is long continued, a vicious circle of frustration and tension may be set up somewhat like this: the teacher is unclear about what is important, so everything that happens in his classroom must be seen as important! Important things cannot be ignored or overlooked; they must be dealt with. So the teacher deals with everything. Other people seeing him deal with everything are likely to assume that is how it should be, or how he wants it, and therefore expect him to deal with everything. This expectancy only adds to the teacher's pressures, and he may soon find himself so busy he has *no time to think about what is important!* So it is that the teacher who has not clarified his beliefs may become the victim of his own indecision and kept so busy dealing with crises that he has not time to discover what is really important.

The teacher without clear values is in the same position as a friend of ours who operated a small machine shop. His company was repeatedly approached by large manufacturers to make small items they needed for their assembly lines. Many of these contracts were so "juicy" that our friend accepted them even though the plant did not have the necessary machines to make the items. Having accepted the contracts, he then rushed out to acquire the tools to make them. After this had happened a few times and the contracted items had been delivered, his company found itself with large, expensive machine tools that had to be kept running. To keep these machines running the manager had to rustle up new contracts and soon found himself constantly on the road desperately scouting the country for new contracts to keep his machines operating. The contracts that had seemed so promising produced a Frankenstein. The shop had been "tooled up" with so little direction and purpose that management was kept frantically racing about trying to keep a wide variety of unrelated operations going. It was not until the owner collapsed in exhaustion and spent months in the hospital that he had time to think about his plant's directions and purposes and develop some guides to when to say "yes" and when to say "no." In a similar fashion teachers without clear purposes may find themselves "tooled up" for such conflicting ends and values as to defeat their own purposes.

Teaching, as we have said, is a relationship, but there can be no relationship with a nonentity. Teachers must stand for something. Confused purposes lead the teacher to such inconsistent behavior that students are unable to discover where he stands, what he believes, or even what it is he wants of them. Under such treatment students can find no clear guides for their own behavior. If such confusion is long continued students may come to feel frightened and anxious and will then seek to avoid or defend themselves against the teaching relationship in whatever ways seem possible. Thus the teacher's own confusions are conveyed to his students. Without clear purposes the teacher may destroy the very relationship essential to effective teaching.

The discovery of clear values and purposes is not always easy. Some teachers do not even make the effort, but nobody behaves without them. Having adopted, either knowingly or unknowingly, a set of values and purposes usually acquired from their own experience as students, some teachers proceed forever after to behave unswervingly in terms of those purposes even when they may be grossly inefficient. This is what often happens with the college teacher who acquires his Ph.D. in the study of a particular subject and assumes that "anyone can teach" and the sole purpose of teaching is "to get his subject across." His narrow view of purpose makes him dull and uninspired and may defeat the very goals of education. At the opposite extreme are those teachers whose search for goals and purposes is so confused and vacillating that they are like will-o'-the-wisps blown helter-skelter from fad to fad. They never light long enough in one spot to permit the development of any sort of comfortable relationship with students.

The discovery of stable values and purposes is further confused by the fact that the society which the teacher represents is itself sometimes confused. Societies, like everything else we know, are subject to change, and this change is reflected in the institutions designed to serve social goals. During the time such changes are coming about there is likely to be a period in which values and purposes become confused as varying segments of the population pull and haul in one direction or another. Sometimes this is the result of old purposes being called into question and new ones set in their place, as when several generations ago we decided to educate not just an elite, but everyone. Such a profound shift in purpose is necessarily attended by a good deal of confusion as more and more people come to appreciate the full significance of the idea and readjust other values and purposes to conform to this decision. Sometimes, too, the shift in social purpose may be the product of new needs arising out of new problems for society, as illustrated in our current need for ever greater numbers of highly skilled scientists and engineers, a need which has placed new demands upon our schools and necessitated new thinking about purposes and values.

Other shifts and changes of purpose are going on in our society with respect to such questions as: How much of an individual's development shall education be charged with? What is the responsibility of home and school? Of church and school? Shall schools seek to indoctrinate a given way of life or promote the seeking for better ways? Shall schooling be general, cultural, specific, or practical? In addition, there are the vast questions posed by the nature of our ideals themselves and the changes in our thinking with respect to them as we slowly learn to translate the essence of the democratic ideal into practice. These are but a few of the questions about purposes teachers must settle each for himself.

The goals and purposes of the teacher will be translated into behavior in dealing with students. When these goals are consistent with the nature of human beings and with the purposes of our society, teaching is likely to be effective and efficient. This will be true whether teachers are able to state their purposes clearly and precisely to others or not. Beliefs continue to affect our behavior even though we may be unwilling or unable to state them clearly to other people. Some teachers discover their goals and values by a kind of psychological osmosis as a product of their own experience and never clearly brought into figure or symbolized in words. Others have arrived at their beliefs as the product of study and discussion on a more precise and "formal" level of operation. Whether teacher purposes are clear or vague, implicit or explicit, however, they inescapably affect the ways in which teachers behave and determine in large measure the success or failure of the teacher's efforts.

THE TEACHER'S PERCEPTIONS OF SELF AND ROLE

A third factor governing the success of the teacher has to do with the teacher's own concept of himself and of his role as a teacher. How a teacher behaves in the classroom depends not only on how he sees his students and the situation in which he is involved, but also, upon how the teacher sees himself. Like everyone else, teachers are seeking personal adequacy and their behavior will be deeply affected by the degree of adequacy they have achieved. Students are responsive to teachers' personalities and there is much evidence to show that well-adjusted teachers produce better-adjusted students while poorly adjusted teachers have negative effects upon those they teach.

We have already discussed the adequate personality in another chapter. Generally speaking, the characteristics of the adequate personality are also the characteristics likely to produce a mature, effective teacher. Such characteristics as seeing oneself positively, the capacity for acceptance of self and others, and a high degree of identification with others are just as much desirable qualities of effective teachers as they are of effective personalities. In very large measure, effective teaching is a process of sharing self with others. Inadequate personalities find this very difficult to do. The ability to involve and to share self with others is highly dependent upon the individual's own feelings of his personal adequacy.

Setting the stage for the effective exploration of meaning requires that teachers demonstrate by their own behavior that this is the road to learning. To set such an example requires that the teacher himself be unafraid to make such explorations. He must show that he has the courage to look at himself and his beliefs without being defensive. He must be willing to explore his own perceptions just as he seeks to have his students explore theirs without fear, hesitation, or embarrassment.

He must show by his own behavior that he believes the search for meaning is profitable, exciting, and worth the effort. He cannot do this solely by exploring his students; he must permit his students to explore themselves and the teacher as well.

In addition to the general feeling of adequacy a teacher has about himself as a person, his behavior will be a function of much more specific concepts he may hold about himself as a teacher. Teachers who see their fundamental role as one of judging or evaluating students will behave quite differently from teachers who see themselves as friendly representatives of society. Similarly, the behavior of teachers will vary widely depending upon whether they see their role as one of telling or of helping to explore, as requiring control or effecting release. Some teachers see their task broadly as having responsibilities in all aspects of a child's life while others see their functions as related only to the imparting of a particular group of ideas or concepts. Whatever the role perceived by the teacher, it plays its part in producing the teacher's behavior and determines in large measure the kinds of results he gets.

Modern teacher-training institutions have recognized this close relationship between what the teacher thinks and believes and his behavior in the classroom. As a result many training programs now emphasize techniques of group discussion and individual participation in an attempt to help student teachers explore and discover themselves and their roles in the teaching process. They have recognized that the adequate teacher is more than a technician; he is a kind of personality. The teaching of subject matter, they have found, is comparatively simple. Helping student teachers discover themselves as people and as educators is a much more difficult task, involving the student's own exploration of himself as an instrument for helping people to learn.

THE PERSONAL DISCOVERY OF ADEQUATE METHODS

The achievement of understanding of the nature of people and of the goals and purposes of education, and the development of personal adequacy are all essential to effective teaching but not enough. Good teaching is also a professional matter involving the ability to utilize effective methods of teaching. Many of these methods may be no more than good human relationships that are the common property of anyone, and to the extent that good teaching involves no more than these, it is indeed true that "anybody can teach." Other techniques of teaching call for specialized kinds of experience less likely to be found in everyday life.

Some people learn these as a result of their own experience, some from special training. Some never learn at all. Regardless of where and how it is learned, however, effective teaching is dependent upon the teacher's skill in the use of effective methods.

Psychologists and educators often argue loud and long over "good" methods and "bad" methods of dealing with people, as though the methods we use to deal with people could be judged separate and apart from the people who used them. This emphasis upon "methods" as goals of behavior has sometimes led to unfortunate results. A generation ago, for example, many child psychologists deplored the spanking of children as evil and destructive. As a consequence many parents, who knew no other means of helping a child to learn, felt frustrated and helpless in the face of their child's misbehavior. If they spanked the child in spite of such teaching, they were no better off, for then they were saddled with the guilt of being "bad" parents. Similarly, there is a good deal of discussion in educational circles these days over the question of "homogeneous or heterogeneous grouping," by which is meant whether children of similiar characteristics should be grouped together or whether classes should include children of widely differing abilities. Advocates of one or the other of these methods have sometimes behaved as though the methods themselves were "good" or "bad." No method, however, is one or the other except in relationship to the three factors we have been discussing above, namely, the nature of the student, the purposes of the teacher and schools, and the personality of the teacher himself. A "good" method employed by a teacher who is unable to use it effectively may be a very "bad" method for student and teacher alike. If a teacher cannot deal effectively with wide differences in his classroom, it is probably better that he be given a homogeneous group of students with less variability than that he be left floundering with a heterogeneous group he cannot cope with. Even a good method is only good if people can use it effectively. Insistence upon a "good" method for people who do not understand it or cannot use it may even have a negative effect by undermining the teacher's self respect and confidence to operate as a teacher at all!

Methods of teaching are individual matters closely related to the personality of the teacher who uses them. What works for one teacher may not work at all for another. The kind of clothes we wear seem to us to fit our particular selves. We feel awkward and uneasy in someone else's clothes and the probability is that we do not look well either. In the same way, the methods some teachers use successfully fail miserably for others. A stimulating and inspiring lecturer whom we know is a complete dud in trying to operate a discussion group, while another friend of ours is exactly the reverse. Some teachers can joke and play with their students and do so naturally and effectively. Other teachers are more serious and remote from students and they too get excellent results. It is apparent that teachers need methods; it is also apparent that there can be no such thing as *the method* of teaching. Effective teaching requires the sensitive use of a human personality as an instrument for assisting other people to new experience and new discovery. It must always be a highly unique and individual matter.

CHAPTER 19

The Personal Approach to Treatment

THERE was a time when society could afford to ignore its inadequate personalities. They could be written off the books with hardly a second thought. But no more! The kind of interdependent society we live in cannot afford maladjusted, unhappy people. The very existence of desperate, inadequate, defeated people in today's world is a drag and a burden on the rest of us. Their presence in large numbers may even prove to be destructive of the institutions and values we hold most dear. These are practical reasons for concern about inadequate, unhappy personalities. But even if these practical considerations did not exist it would still be important to provide help for them on purely humanitarian grounds.

WHO NEEDS HELP?

The world we have created is often bewildering and complex. Few of us are so completely secure as to be immune from the possibility of suffering a more or less severe period of inadequacy at some time in our lives. No one is so strong as to be completely above such eventualities. Subjected to the proper combination of unhappy circumstances there is almost nothing which we might not do. Any one of us, on occasion, may find that our concepts of ourselves, for one reason or another, are no longer adequate to assist us in achieving optimal need satisfaction. In any of the ways we have discussed in Chapter 9, we may become threatened or inadequate personalities. Given time, most of us are able to achieve a reorganization of self and so return to greater harmony with the world we live in. Fortunately, most of our difficulties are minor or temporary and we shortly regain our equilibrium.

Some people, however, may be unable to arrive at new definitions of self so readily and may continue for long periods to be threatened, ineffective, and unhappy. We might take the position that society has often taken with these people in past generations and ignore them, quarantine them, or kill them off. But to do so is to lose their potential value for society and requires great waste of time, energy, and expense, while still more persons are removed from productivity to take care of those who are deeply inadequate. A much better and certainly more humane approach is to help threatened people to new and more adequate definitions of themselves which will make it possible for them to live effectively and productively in the social system. To provide such help we need persons with deep understanding of human behavior, who are trained in methods of assisting inadequate persons to a better life. People have been helping each other in one form or another ever since the dawn of man. In this sense psychological treatment has been carried on more or less effectively as a part of the functions of teachers, parents, and the clergy for hundreds of years. More recently, we have seen the development of a number of helping professions which employ professional counselors and therapists under such varied names as: counselor, guidance worker, psychiatrist, social worker, school psychologist, visiting teacher, play therapist, and family consultant, to name but a few.

In practice, counselors, psychotherapists, teachers, social workers, and others engaged in the "helping" professions are called upon to assist several types of threatened personalities. Sometimes threatened persons themselves will ask for aid. They may be so inadequate that they are perceived by outsiders as needing treatment or they may be unhappy and ineffective personalities whom society does not recognize as problems at all. Sometimes the therapist may need to deal with persons about whom society is concerned, but who themselves may not feel the need for assistance. This latter class will include a great many children who are unaware of the possibilities of any other life than that which they are leading. It will include, as well, those persons so limited in the development of an adequate self as to be unable to seek therapeutic assistance on their own initiative. Treatment methods must be capable of assisting each of these groups of threatened personalities as effectively and as economically as possible.

What Is Psychotherapy?

THERAPY DEFINED

We have seen that human beings are constantly, insatiably striving for ever greater adequacy. Sometimes, however, the organism is blocked in its striving by internal or external factors which prevent maximum achievement of this end. Such blocking may occur either in physiological or psychological terms. For example, the organism's need to maintain organization may be blocked physiologically by a germ, an injury, or impairment of its function due to aging, malnutrition, or the like. Psychologically, such blocks appear to be due to failures of differentiation, particularly those involving the self. The new field of psychosomatics is demonstrating that there are even physical effects of psychologic blocking, and vice versa. Since the need to maintain organization is all-pervading, the organism not only can but must move toward health if it is free to do so. It is this freeing of the organism to move toward health with which therapy of any sort is concerned. We might define therapy as follows: *Therapy is the provision of a facilitating situation wherein the normal drive of the organism for adequacy is freed to operate.* In medical therapy the physician or surgeon provides this "therapeutic situation" by eliminating or inhibiting the blocking factor, or by building up the organism itself so that it may operate as efficiently as possible. We shall find this definition describes the process in psychotherapy as well.

PSYCHOTHERAPY DEFINED

Psychotherapy is that branch of behavioral science concerned primarily with behavioral adjustment. Like all other therapies, it too is directed toward freeing the individual to operate effectively. Psychologically, the threatened person's need is impeded, not by physical obstacles but by inadequate differentiations of people, events, ideas, and concepts. The individual's satisfaction of need is blocked when for one reason or another his concepts of himself and his perceptions of the world about him are inadequate to make effective need satisfaction possible. We might define psychotherapy therefore, as follows: *Psychotherapy is a relationship consciously and carefully designed to assist persons to an exploration of themselves and the world in which they live so that they may arrive at new and more adequate relationships between themselves and the world in which they operate.*

The goal of treatment is the development of more adequate personalities, of individuals having personal worth and value. This goal of treatment is also the basic need of the individual. This makes treatment a coöperative project in which a client seeks for greater adequacy and personal worth and his therapist helps him to achieve it. Adequacy and personal worth are not things that can be *given* to people, they can only be achieved. Consequently, modern psychotherapy is not a battle between an all-knowing therapist and a perverse, unwilling client; it is a process of assisting, helping, or facilitating the normal capacities of the individual for perceiving and differentiating. Although the goals of client and therapist are alike, it should not be supposed that psychotherapy is easy or entirely pleasant. It may be the most difficult and painful experience of one's life. I have often felt that my clients in counseling are among the bravest people I have known. It is not easy to reorganize self, but the dividends may be very great.

How Psychotherapy Differs from Other Helping Relationships

The problems of human beings are the just concern of so many groups and agencies that it seems unlikely that psychological treatment can ever be made the exclusive perogative of any one. Psychotherapy is a human relationship, and human relations are engaged in by everyone. Aiding people to change perceptions is everybody's business in a sense, and the only excuse for a professional therapist is the presumption that because of special training, understanding, or skill he can help more effectively than most. Professional treatment differs from other helping relationships in three respects: (1) The ordered purposeful character of the therapeutic situation, (2) the intensity of the relationship, and (3) the data with which it is concerned.

THE DISCIPLINED CHARACTER OF THERAPY

Many human relationships we experience in our daily lives help us to explore and discover new meanings about ourselves and the world we live in. Even the most casual kinds of human contacts may serve to effect important changes in our ways of perceiving. Most of these ordinary interactions involve two or more people, each seeking to satisfy his own need. This is what happens at a tea, where each person stands about enhancing himself in a polite sort of way, chatting about one thing or another, seeking to capture the interest of other people, then waiting more or less patiently while someone else seeks enhancement so he can get back in the game again. Similar interactions occur over the card table or the back fence, in "bull sessions" or casual conversations among friends in a thousand different settings. Each of these relationships provides the participants with important means of achieving enhancement of self.

The methods used by psychotherapists to aid their clients cover a vast range. Indeed, we know that almost *any* method will *sometimes* work with *some* people. Every now and then some new method of treatment bursts upon the public scene, attracting much attention and often heralded as the new panacea for all man's ills. These usually begin from some accidental discovery that a particular method worked effectively with several people, and thereafter the method is avidly tried by many others. Most of these unhappy persons are destined to be disappointed, but a few find the methods successful and their testimonials add to the prestige of the new approach. Success of the method may sometimes be quite phenomenal if enough people *begin to believe they will be helped.* Physicians are well aware that even some "physical" ills disappear when the patient believes strongly enough in the efficacy of the aspirin tablet his doctor prescribes for him.

It is not enough for the counselor to possess an armamentarium of methods that have worked in the past. Psychotherapy must be a precise, predictable process if human beings are to be helped in more than hit-or-miss fashion. Effective therapy must be predicated upon some underlying conception of the nature of human behavior, and its methods must be intimately related to those understandings. Modern psychotherapy is based upon the best understandings we are able to arrive at with respect to: (a) the nature of human beings and their behavior, (b) the nature and goals of the helping process, (c) tested methods of treatment, and (d) the nature and personality of the therapist himself. Each of these four variables of the therapeutic process has been given much study in recent years, and as we are able to find clearer and clearer understandings of each of these factors, modern psychotherapy has become a more and more precise and predictable process. Not all behavioral scientists see human behavior in exactly the same way. As a consequence a number of different "schools" of psychotherapy have grown up in recent years, each dependent upon its own interpretation of the four factors we have indicated above. Some of these have remained for long periods. Others have developed quickly and almost as quickly disappeared from the scene as they turned out to be based on fortuitous rather than predictable processes. Although the science of psychotherapy is new, we are nevertheless finding more and more effective ways of creating predictable and efficient helping relationships.

THE INTENSITY OF THE THERAPEUTIC RELATIONSHIP

Therapy differs from more casual relationships in concentrating upon only one of the members involved. The purpose of treatment is to help the client, and this requires that the counselor, teacher, or therapist subjugate his own immediate goals in the interest of his client, student, or counselee. This is not to say that the process provides no enhancement for the therapist. On the contrary, therapy has sometimes been facetiously defined as a situation in which "two people help each other." Therapists, of course, cannot suspend the universal action of the basic need to achieve maintenance and enhancement. Successful counseling is, itself, an enhancing experience for the counselor.

Fundamentally, psychological treatment consists in the provision of a good, helping, human relationship specially designed and concentrated for the peculiar requirements of a particular human being. Although there exist numerous schools of thought about how treatment ought to be done, and although each philosophy has developed its own concepts of what are appropriate and inappropriate methods of working with clients, all approaches seek to provide a good human relationship in one form or another. An interesting study by Fiedler found that experienced psychotherapists from different schools were more often in agreement about what constituted a "good" counseling relationship than were beginning-therapy students and experts from the same school of thought. This finding would seem to suggest that there is a "good" therapeutic relationship and that this relationship is arrived at by many therapists as a matter of experience irrespective of what school of thought they were trained in. Furthermore, in the same experiment, Fiedler found that "the man in the street," when asked to tell what he thought would be an ideal therapeutic relationship, described it in about the same terms as the "experts"! This would seem to imply that a good therapeutic relationship is not a magic quality, the exclusive prerogative of a specially trained few, but the crystallized, concentrated application of the best we know about a helping relationship for the assistance of a particular person in difficulty. This is usually not very different from what is good for any other individual but is provided for the patient with greater intensity and with particular reference to his peculiar need. It is not that people in psychological distress need a *different* kind of relationship, but rather that they need *more* of a *good* relationship than those who have less need for help.

THE DEPTH OF TREATMENT

Psychotherapy also differs from ordinary human relationships in the depth with which it is concerned. Earlier in this book we have seen that behavior is affected in the degree to which an individual discovers the personal meaning for him of any information, idea, concept, or experience. We have seen that the closer an event is perceived to the self, the more intense will be the individual's experience. The effective achievement of adequacy may require of the individual new perceptions at any point on this relationship scale. What is meant by "depth" in psychotherapy is simply the point on this continuum at which treatment is operating. The closer the exploration of the perceptual field to the self, the "deeper" the therapy. Depth of therapy is synonymous with personal reference or personal meaning.

We might think of all the data which a person needs in order to make an adjustment as lying upon a continuum stretching from information having a great deal of relationship to self at the center of the perceptual field, to information having little or no relationship to self at the outer edge (X to Y, Fig. 25). In order to live effectively in our society an individual will need to have information or data existing at all points along the continuum. Information at the extreme not-self end of the continuum has little or no effect upon behavior. This is the kind of information which bombards us every day and which passes in one ear and out the other.

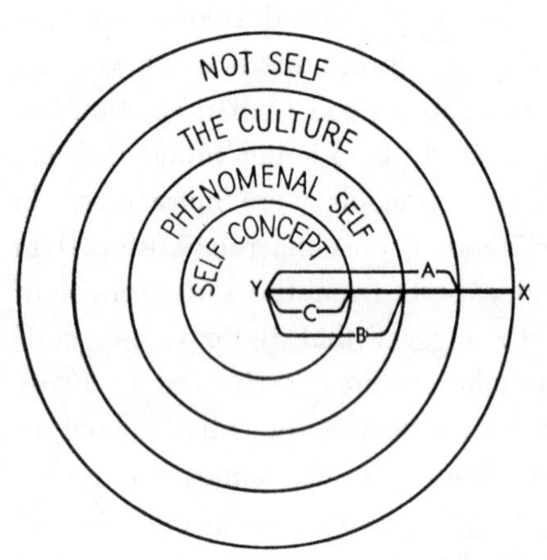

Fig. 25.

Data from the outside world and from the accumulated culture of our society, however, have a more important relationship to self. Here we need to discover the relationship to ourselves of the concepts and values accumulated by mankind in the course of his history. This traditionally is the primary task of education (section *A*, Fig. 25). It has the broad responsibility for helping the individual to develop an effective and satisfying relationship with the world around him.

Closer to the center of the perceptual field, people need to develop effective relationships with other people. These relationships are much closer to the core of self (section *B*, Fig. 25). Perceptions in this area have to do with the phenomenal self and the relationship of the individual to those people important to him. This is the area of the perceptual field of particular concern to group therapy.

Finally, at the very center of the perceptual field is the area of individual therapy (section *C*, Fig. 25). In this area the client is primarily concerned with discovering himself. The function of individual therapy is to assist the client to explore those very personal aspects of self involved in his self concept, values, ideals, etc.

Seen in this light, depth of therapy is a function of the personal character of the data under consideration. Education, group therapy, and individual therapy all deal with the perceptual field. Each attempts to aid the individual to explore the self and his relationships and varies from the others only in the area of its major concern. This is perhaps the most important distinction between psychotherapy and the functions of other agencies in assisting people to better adjustment. Therapy is only a more personal kind of exploration of the relationship of self to the external world. There are no clear-cut distinctions between individual therapy, group therapy, and education. These three kinds of adjustive experiences blend almost indistinguishably from one to another, differing only in emphasis. It must be clear from this analysis that therapy can never become the exclusive property of any profession. There can be no such thing as *the* psychotherapy. Psychotherapy is a "more or less" rather than an "all or none" activity in which many people in many professions engage in greater or lesser degree.

All therapies of whatever sort must affect human perceptions if they are to produce changes in behavior. The principles of perceptual psychology we have been exploring in this book will be found operating in whatever kind of psychotherapy we wish to examine. All methods of treatment will have a greater or lesser degree of consistency with our perceptual frame of reference. This will be true of much of psychoanalysis. It will be true also of the kinds of therapy advocated by such writers as Horney, Sullivan, Allen, May, Fromm, and many others. Perhaps most directly related to the views we have explored in this book, however, is the client-centered approach to treatment developed by Carl Rogers and his students. Indeed, so consistent is this view of therapy with the principles of perceptual psychology that, had it not developed prior to this frame of reference, it would certainly have had to be invented as an application of a perceptual view. The interested reader will find himself quickly at home in this field and a more detailed consideration of perceptual therapy can be found in many of the publications of client-centered counselors listed in the bibliography. In the remainder of this chapter we will confine ourselves to a few broad principles affecting the philosophy and practices of treatment growing out of a perceptual approach to behavior.

The Place of "Knowledge" in Treatment

We have seen in our discussion of the educational implications of a perceptual frame of reference that there may be a considerable disparity between what a person knows and what he does. Most so-called "maladjusted" behavior is not due to the fact that we do not know any better but that at the moment of action we *needed* to behave as we did. Not long ago I drove my car through a red light. Now, I am well aware that I should not go through red lights, but I did. Why did I? Because I was in a hurry to keep an appointment—I *needed* to behave as I did. Indeed, it wasn't until I had gone three blocks past the light that I was even aware of what I had done. My behavior was not a matter of not knowing, but of being unable to accept the perception at the moment of my action. The red light was perceived in the not-self portion of the phenomenal field because, had it been perceived as related to self, it would have been threatening to my satisfaction of need. Had I been able to perceive the red light as contributing to my need satisfaction, I would have stopped.

Knowledge is useful only if it is perceived as contributing to need satisfaction. It is even possible that some knowledge may place the threatened individual under greater threat than ever. Consequently, he will be driven to protect his existing organization and may, in the final analysis, be worse off than before. This serves to explain in some measure why it is that "telling people" is often violently resisted and may even result in increasing distress. Note how a client herself expresses this increased confusion from "telling" in the following excerpt:

CLIENT: You can think and think so long and you can try to talk yourself into things—you can tell yourself you are just timid, I talk myself out of it and philosophize and all that. I can forget for a while—for the time being—and then it comes back. Sometimes I feel so melancholy and then I tell myself I am just being self-centered, that there are many people worse off than I am. I might be blind for instance. I know it's silly to feel so badly about ordinary everyday things. It seems as though I should have control and not let things affect me so much. Maybe I'm not put together right—but I just can't. They told me I wasn't sociable enough with girls and ought to mingle with them more. And I try telling myself that is what I ought to do. But I can't seem to change myself that way—just by saying it to myself. It just makes more conflict inside and I don't have any satisfaction at all. (Pause) If by nature you're shy and retiring, you can work real hard and talk yourself into things sometimes and it may show on the outside but not on the inside. Then it hurts more than anything. Oh, I know psychology doesn't agree. It tells you a lot of things—they seem to think an individual can change and do anything he wants. I can't.

Somewhat later in counseling this client says:

CLIENT: They say when you know your faults and attack them—why you soon get over them. I've tried that for years but it's no good.
COUNSELOR: Mm hm.
CLIENT: It all sounds good in the books you read and the lectures you hear—but it doesn't work when you try to put it in practice. You just can't change a person to being boisterous and noisy when they are fundamentally shy. It can only be done on the outside. You can't force it on them, and I don't think you should. *It just makes a worse conflict than ever and that's all that remains—just the conflict.*

The meanings existing for the client must always be the major elements of concern in therapy, since it is change in these meanings that therapy is designed to foster. On the surface this seems like a very minor point, but it is amazing how often it has been overlooked in psychological and sociological treatment. It must always be recalled that client and therapist are operating in different frames of reference and what appears "good" to one may appear as exactly the opposite to the other. For example's sake, let us permit our imaginations to run freely for a moment and compare some common treatment techniques with what they *might* mean to the client:

TREATMENT TECHNIQUES	CLIENT MEANINGS
Telling a child to be good.	He thinks I'm bad!
Giving a needy client coal.	I can't support my family!
Warning a client to avoid daydreaming.	Good Lord! I'm going crazy!
Reassuring that "this is going to be all right."	He's afraid it isn't going to be all right.
Giving advice.	I can do that now—it's his responsibility—he told me to go ahead.
Foster-home placement.	They think my family is no good. Well, I'll show them guys!
Institutional placement.	I'm a real tough guy, I am. They gotta lock me up.

These seem like extreme examples, but unfortunately they often are not. The goal of therapy is to produce change in the client's meanings. Since behavior is a function of these meanings, therapy can only be successful if it produces a permanent change in meanings which will insure a consequent change in behavior.

To say that an individual in a severe psychological problem maintains his "maladjustment" because it gives him satisfaction is only partly true. It is not likely that he would enjoy and attempt to perpetuate this painful condition if he could perceive any better alternative. Rather, if he maintains his "maladjustment" it seems more likely that he does so because he *must* do so to maintain or enhance his phenomenal self in the situation as he sees it. Thus the client who says, "I know what I ought to do but I can't do it" is saying, in effect, that from a purely external or objective point of view, what he should do is clear, but from his own personal point of view his behavior is necessary to protect his organization. Knowledge can only contribute to need satisfaction if it is accepted into the individual's personal frame of reference. Therapy, to be successful, must produce some change in how people perceive. This is why treatment deals primarily with feelings, attitudes, convictions, and beliefs; what we sometimes call the "emotional" aspects of life. This is simply another way of saying that therapy is mainly concerned with those perceptions having a close and meaningful relationship to self. Successful therapy is rarely only a matter of helping people "know" better. Few of us misbehave because we do not know better. Like the farmer who told the county agent, "I ain't farmin' now half as well as I know how!" most of us already know far better than we behave. The problem of therapy is helping people explore their perceptions in such a way as to translate knowing into behaving. But how may this be done?

Two Kinds of Treatment

If the perceptual description of behavior we have outlined in this volume is accurate, it follows that all psychotherapy of whatever type must produce change in the client's perceptual field. Since change occurs through differentiation, to change behavior it will be necessary to bring about new differentiations either in the organization of the self concept or in the client's perception of the external world or both. This will be true whether we attempt (1) to assist a particular client to change his personal meanings by working with the client alone or (2) to induce a change in his field by changing his environment. Whether we work with the environment surrounding a client or with the client himself in a face-to-face situation our goal is the same. We hope to make possible new meanings in his perceptual field.

ENVIRONMENTAL TREATMENT

In Chapter 12 we described personal adequacy as a function of three things: (1) An essentially positive self concept, (2) a capacity for acceptance, and (3) a high degree of identification with others. Since therapy seeks to produce more adequate personalities, it follows that successful therapy must assist its clients to achieve a higher degree of these three characteristics than has been possible for them before. One of the ways in which this can be accomplished is by manipulating the environment in such a way that the individual is exposed to experiences from which he can learn to perceive himself in more positive ways, to be more accepting, or to identify more broadly with those about him.

Environmental therapy with children, for instance, often utilizes curriculum adjustment to make it possible for the child with feelings of failure and defeat to find success experiences. This gives him a new lease on his academic life, and he can then define himself and his abilities in more adequate terms. The same thing may be accomplished in foster-home placement. A child is removed from a home situation creating undesirable and harmful meanings to a foster home designed to produce different and more socially acceptable meanings in the youngster's perceptual field. Such methods are not confined to therapy. Families have been using environmental methods of dealing with children for ages. For instance, a certain family had tried for two years to get their 5-year-old to stop his persistent bed wetting but all to no avail. One evening while tucking in her son, the mother said "Son, when are you going to stop wetting the bed?"

The boy replied, "But Mom, I don't have to. I have a rubber sheet!" Once this meaning of the rubber sheet had been discovered, therapy was simple. Next day mother and son coöperated in making the bed and pointedly left off the sheet. And the child hasn't wet the bed since!

In environmental therapy the meaning changes we seek to bring about may be in the client's goals, his techniques, his self concept, his perceptions of others, or in all of these. In fact, it is probable that no change occurs in any one without some change in the others as well. Therapy on a goals-and-techniques level will often be all that is required to aid the threatened individual to more adequate behavior. Frequently it will be possible to assist the client to the differentiation of new goals and techniques which help him regain a feeling of adequacy and need satisfaction. So simple a measure as aiding an adolescent girl to discover more attractive methods of hair styling or helping an adolescent boy to a better understanding of the rudiments of etiquette in boy-girl relationships may go a long way toward helping them achieve greater feelings of adequacy and more effective behavior.

While many personality adjustments can be affected through change in the individual's goals and techniques, there is also danger that such a level of operation may be utilized when a more fundamental change is called for. Goals-and-techniques therapy is often palliative and, with the very threatened client, does not reduce the threat more than momentarily. With the self under threat in important ways, helping the individual only to the extent of discovering new goals and techniques may only result in making him dependent upon the therapist or, worse yet, cause him to feel he has not been helped at all. To help the man just out of prison to find a job may be only the beginning of therapy, yet, too often, it is as far as it ever gets. For deeply threatened personalities it is necessary that therapy aid clients to make fundamental changes in self organization. Sometimes this can be affected by environmental therapy, but unfortunately there are serious limits to this form of treatment.

LIMITATIONS OF ENVIRONMENTAL THERAPY

One of the most important of these limitations has to do with the varying worlds within which an individual moves. A growing child, for example, may be living in a number of cultural groups at once or in rapid succession, as illustrated in Fig. 26. His concept of himself, also, may have varying definitions with respect to each of the groups with which he comes in contact. In his earliest years, the child's self concept may be the result of his home experiences. The older he gets, however, the wider become the outside factors within which he moves as he passes from one cultural group to another. His self concept becomes defined with respect to his experience in these wider groups. At the same

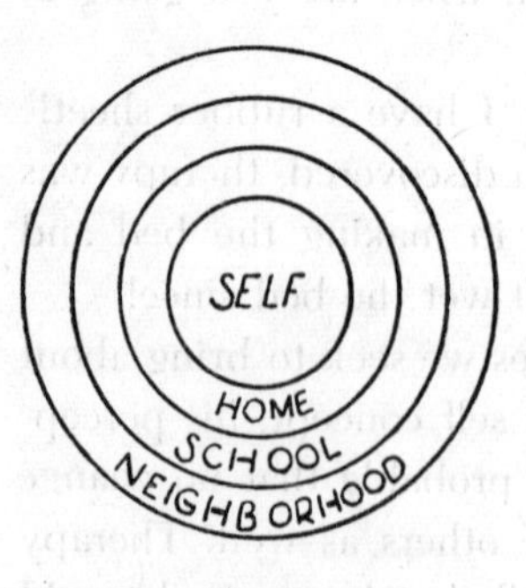

Fig. 26.

time, the possibility of producing changes in the external world to which he is responding becomes increasingly more difficult. While it may be possible for us to make some changes in small cultural groups, the amount of change we can produce in larger ones becomes progressively less as the size of the group increases. By the time an individual has reached late adolescence, change in his external reality has become very nearly impossible.

This principle is well illustrated in studies of foster-home placement. Studies of this type of treatment are unanimous in their findings that the earlier the child is placed, the more likely it is to be successful. Beyond the age of 9 or 10 such methods rapidly decrease in effectiveness. Change in environment offers possibilities for helping children but seems a distinctly limited and temporary measure for adolescents and adults. It is a simple matter to remove candy from the neighborhood of a sick child. The problems posed in removing alcohol from the environment of an adult alcoholic, however, is a quite different matter!

Environmental therapy can operate effectively only when a subculture to which the individual is responding is out of touch with a larger culture within which the individual is also behaving. For instance, it may be useful and effective to remove a child from a family situation which is in conflict with the demands of a larger social group. In this way the child might be placed, let us say, in a foster home which was consistent with the demands of the larger cultural group. But what about the situation wherein the child has a self concept considerably apart from both larger and smaller groups in which he moves? This problem often arises when delinquency of a child occurs in a middle-class family that is not only well accepted in the community but intelligent and well meaning in its attempts to do the right thing according to accepted standards. In such a case the family is already consistent with the larger cultural group definitions and the possibilities of environmental therapy are extremely limited. The same situation often exists in the case of a child with extremely severe feelings of jealousy and rejection, in a family situation where every effort is made to help him feel wanted in the family circle. Children often develop such feelings upon the arrival of a baby brother or sister in the family group. The child is not rejected but *he* thinks he is. Environmental treatment in a case of this kind is bound to be extremely limited. It cannot remove the sibling, and to remove the child from the home would only make matters worse. To send him off to school or to camp, for instance, may appear to him as absolute proof of what he already believes!

The aim of all therapy of whatever type must be to aid the individual to a self concept adequate to deal with wider culture patterns in which he will move as an adult. What is more, the eventual goal of therapy must be to free the individual to operate on his own without the necessity for continuing manipulations of the world about him. A mature society cannot reorganize itself for each individual within its framework. Treatment must, in the long run, develop in the individual the ability to adjust to whatever happens; not protect him from the world in which he lives. Successful environmental treatment must contribute to a more positive view of self, to self acceptance and increased capacity for identification. Treatment which results in a degraded self, in failure of acceptance, or in feelings of rejection and isolation may temporarily solve some social problems but at a price, in the destruction of human potentialities, too great to afford. Much environmental treatment is little more than palliative, resulting in the temporary control of behavior so that it remains within socially tolerable limits, but may be accompanied by personal feelings of dependence and inadequacy that create still greater problems in the long run. Planning for environmental therapy must be done with a clear vision of the *meaning* of treatment measures in the perceptions of those they are applied to.

Individual Treatment Through Perception Change

As we have seen above, there are serious limitations upon the degree to which treatment can be accomplished by manipulation of the environment. Fortunately, we do not have to rely on this alone.. Perceptions can be affected and modified by change in environment. They can also be changed without reference to the environment at all. A great deal of the unhappiness and inadequacy suffered by people who seek treatment is the product of unfortunate perceptions of self and the world in which they live, and there is little or nothing to be contributed to the solution of their problems by environmental means. With a change in perceiving, however, they may be helped to achieve greater adequacy. They may even change their environments themselves!

It sometimes happens that people may be unwilling for one reason or another to change their environments. We are all familiar with the ostensibly simple solution "Well, if you don't like your job—quit!" But we are also aware that changing the situation is not so easy. It may even produce more problems than it settles. Many of our adjustments have to be made within ourselves in the perceptions we have of ourselves and the world we live in. This is well illustrated in the case of a woman the author once worked with. Mrs. Mabel Sargent was 38 years old and had been married about a year. For many years before her marriage she had nearly given up hope that she would ever find a suitable mate. Then Mr. Sargent appeared on the scene! He was handsome, a bachelor, only five years older than she and well able to support a wife. Best of all he fell deeply in love with Mabel, and they were married after a year's engagement. The only drawback to this picture was Mr. Sargent's 73-year-old mother. Mr. Sargent had lived with his mother all his life in the family homestead, and when the couple were married they moved in there. The elderly Mrs. Sargent resented her new daughter-in-law with a vicious and bitter fury that appeared when the two women were alone in the house. In the presence of others, it was expressed in subtle innuendo and cutting remarks having a quite different meaning for the uninformed hearer than for the wife at whom they were directed. The elder Mrs. Sargent seemed to all public eyes, and to her son as well, a paragon of grace and virtue, deeply fond of her new daughter-in-law. Poor Mabel, caught in this fix, could find no way out. She could not give up the man she had pined for so long, nor could she dispose of the old lady, although she carefully considered this alternative in the course of treatment! She could not even talk about her problem with her husband or friends, who thoroughly believed old Mrs. Sargent to be a gracious and kindly person. For a year Mabel sought vainly for a solution, becoming more and more distraught and physically ill over her insolvable dilemma. Finally, in therapy, she was helped to adjust to her problem by changing her perceptions of herself and the mother.

She came to see herself as a stronger, more adequate person than she had ever imagined and her mother-in-law as the pathetic, beaten, self-pitying old woman she truly was. With such changed perceptions she no longer felt so threatened and could even, on occasion, feel sorry for the elder Mrs. Sargent. Insteady of fighting her situation she learned to accept it, even though it was sometimes unpleasant. Instead of permitting her mother-in-law to drive her away, Mrs. Sargent decided she was a lot younger and would "just wait the old girl out!" These changes in perception made it possible to tolerate an admittedly bad situation so that despite the impossibility of changing the external scene, it was possible to live an effective and satisfying life.

Perceptions—The Data of Therapy

The emphasis of perceptual psychology upon an immediate rather than a historical understanding of the causation of behavior has important implications for treatment. When we believed behavior was exclusively a function of the forces exerted upon the individual, helping people through psychological treatment required that the therapist discover the nature of the forces which had produced his client's behavior. This often made it necessary for counselor and client to spend long hours probing into the client's past, "reliving" the experiences that had molded him in his present form. If it is true, however, that behavior is a function of perception, then it should be possible to assist people to better adjustment by helping them change their perceptions even if the counselor has no knowledge of the past. If perceptions can be changed, behavior must also change.

Once it was considered impossible to help a disturbed child without first producing changes in a child's parents. Psychotherapists, however, are now finding it possible to help children to new adjustment and happier lives even when there is little opportunity to make fundamental changes in family structure. Methods of play therapy, for example, dependent solely on assisting children to explore present perceptions of themselves and the world they live in, have produced startling results in helping disturbed youngsters.

The principle seems just as effective in therapy with adults. If people can be helped to change present perceptions it is often unnecessary to explore past experience. In my experience as a counselor over the past 20 years, I have often observed that the clients who spend most time exploring the past are almost exclusively from the upper-middle class. They have grown up in a generation deeply imbued with Freud's concept that behavior is the product of the things that have happened to us in the years of our growing up. As a consequence, they explore what they believe to be the causes of their behavior. Clients from lower socioeconomic groups who have had little opportunity to learn this theory of causation, talk very little about their pasts. Instead, they start right off to talk about their current perceptions expressed as feelings, attitudes, likes, and aversions. In the process of such exploration they often discover new ways of feeling or perceiving and their behavior changes accordingly, even though I often do not know the details of how they got into their current difficulty. People who spend most time exploring the past in counseling sooner or later come to a point where they say, "Well, this explains but it doesn't change," or "Now I know why I feel like I do but I still feel so!" If it is true that people behave according to present ways of seeing, then it follows that it should be possible to help them to better adjustment by changing present perceptions. Knowledge of the individual's past may be helpful in this. It is not always an essential. For many educators, psychologists, social workers, and psychiatrists this idea opens whole new avenues of approach to the problems of mental health.

PSYCHOLOGICAL TREATMENT AS PERCEPTION CHANGE

The man in the street sometimes sees psychotherapy as a terrifying relationship in which a client surrenders most of his dignity, and certainly all of his privacy, to an imposing Svengali who somehow rebuilds personality by trickery and guile. Even those less influenced by movie versions of therapy often think of it as a relationship in which an all-wise counselor advises or directs a client in trouble. This latter is the kind of relationship most of us have experienced in our visits to the physician. We are accustomed to taking our physical problems to the doctor, acquiescing more or less willingly in whatever diagnostic procedure he feels is necessary and attempting to carry out whatever treatment plan he devises for us. Physical conditions can often be observed by outsiders, but human perceptions are another matter. People's feelings, attitudes, and personal meanings lie inside the personality and are not open to direct observation. As a result the counselor-client relationship is quite different from that of doctor-patient. In the doctor-patient relationship it is the doctor who knows and the patient who does not, but in psychotherapy it is the client who perceives and the counselor who does not! The important data for psychological treatment are the perceptions of the client. To be successful, psychological treatment must produce some change in the client's perceptions of himself and the world in which he operates.

Whatever the frame of reference of the therapist, the production of change in behavior requires that therapy assist the client to make changes in his personal meanings. To do this effectively treatment methods must deal in one fashion or another with two basic problems:

(1) It must provide a situation which makes it possible for the client to explore his perceptions, and (2) it must assist the client in this process to the end that he may achieve a more adequate self organization as quickly and surely as possible.

THREAT COMPLICATES THERAPY

Persons seeking therapy are persons under threat. This feeling of threat is of extreme importance to the eventual adjustment of the individual and to therapy. The very existence of threat may prevent the maladjusted person from improving his position. For example, the housewife who cannot accept her roles as housekeeper, cook, nursemaid, laundress, and a hundred others, but conceives of herself as something quite different, finds herself constantly confronted by the hard realities of daily life. These are likely to appear to her expressly designed to frustrate and to force upon her the very facts from which she would prefer to escape. The pile of laundry reminds her that she is the laundress, mealtimes demand that she be cook, and baby's insistent wail may threaten her concept of herself to the point where any aspect of her daily life appears threatening and coercing beyond endurance.

Under threat and the necessity for self defense, the individual fails to differentiate clearly and accurately. His differentiations are likely to be false and misleading and provide no adequate basis for change. The maladjusted housewife we have mentioned above cannot see her tasks clearly. The woman next door who sells face powder at the local department store may appear to have a much better, more meaningful, and important task than her own. Feeling threatened by her daily tasks, it is difficult for her to accept them. Perceptions become distorted and differentiations become misleading or result in false conclusions. It becomes difficult or impossible to convince her that her job is important, meaningful, and dignified. The more threatened she feels, the more unlikely adequate differentiation becomes.

To be effective, therapy must aid its clients to deal with such threats. Many treatment failures are a direct outgrowth of the counselor's ineptitude in understanding and adjusting his behavior to his client's perceptions. It is common knowledge, for example, that "welfare cases" are often extremely unsympathetic and "downright ungrateful" to the social worker seeking to help them. With the best of intentions, the worker inquires into the home life of his client, discovers he needs coal, food, or assistance in finding a job. These "needs" he then seeks to satisfy often with no realization that this treatment may appear extremely threatening. For to the client they may appear only as invasions of his privacy, proof of his ineptitude in caring for his family, or a slur upon his manhood.

When ideas presented by the counselor are not consistent with the client's fundamental personality organization, they represent a threat and he can do nothing else but resist them. Mittelmann and Wolff have checked this experimentally. By measuring skin temperature of the client during psychoanalysis it could be observed that he showed no fear reactions until questions were posed which placed him in a threatened position. The same principle is put to work in the techniques of "lie detection." The stronger, more convincingly, threatening concepts are forced upon the client, the greater is the necessity for his resistance. Thus advice, persuasion, personal influence, suggestion, and other such counseling techniques may be readily effective when the advice or information given is consistent with the client's already existing phenomenal self. When they are not consistent, they are likely to be disturbing and may actually impede his progress by producing greater confusion or, worse still, force him into an even greater defense of his position.

It must be remembered that the organization which the client is attempting to maintain is a unique and *personal* organization which the counselor can probably never hope to know in its entirety. Even information which appears to the counselor to be complimentary to his client may actually be disturbing to his organization and resisted by him. To attack the client's organization in counseling is an extremely easy thing to do. Almost anyone is familiar in his own experience with counselor attacks expressed in such familiar phrases as:

"Now just a minute, young man . . ."
"Really, now, it's not as bad as all that."
"Look how many are worse off than you are."
"I've had more experience than you, son. Now take my advice."

or even:

"You're not so bad off—let me tell you about my experience!"

When people are threatened it is not always readily apparent to an outside observer. Many persons have learned through long experience to hide their feelings from others. Since early childhood most persons have been taught to be "gentlemen and ladies" and the threats they feel are not likely to be apparent upon casual observation. When threatened by a counselor, therefore, they are likely smilingly to agree with him and beat a hasty retreat, reserving their opinion of him and his methods for their friends and acquaintances. Or when threatened the client may find security in complete dependence on the counselor and take no responsibility himself.

To avoid attacking his client, the counselor must be possessed of a high degree of sensitivity to how things seem from his client's point of view. He must be able to perceive and forecast the effect of any action he takes from his client's point of view. This is not a task for an amateur. Even with long experience and great sensitivity on the part of the counselor, the best of therapists cannot always avoid such threats.

While it is of course possible to bring about changes in people's perceptions through force and coercion, we have seen in Chapter 9 that this is often an extremely hazardous and unpredictable approach. Most modern therapies attempt instead to create a situation which facilitates change in perception by removing the client from threat as much as practicable. This may be done in environmental therapy, for example, when a threatened child is placed in a secure foster home or when a mental patient is removed from the pressures which overwhelm him in daily life to the protection of a mental hospital. In individual treatment it may be accomplished by the relationship developed between client and counselor.

THE COUNSELING RELATIONSHIP

This relationship is not a trick but a human interaction between counselor and client which makes possible the exploration of the client's perceptions and the discovery of new and more satisfying meanings of the self and the world. By this relationship the counselor creates a situation in which his client can be temporarily freed from the hindering and restricting effect of threat. He attempts to provide his client with a kind of sheltered atmosphere in which he can be free to explore and examine even his most fearful and distressing perceptions without fear of censure or blame. This is a "special" kind of relationship designed to remove the client from the threats and frustrations of daily life. Here is how a young woman deeply fearful of men described her feeling to her counselor: "In here I can talk to you. But if I were to meet you in the hall, you would be just another man and I couldn't talk to you at all." And another client describes it so: "Well, I don't know what it is when I am in here, but here I feel that I can be perfectly honest with myself.

I don't have to put on an act." By making the relationship as non-threatening to his client as possible, the counselor thus makes it possible for the troubled client to drop his defenses and to explore his perceptions of self and the world with less necessity for avoidance, distortion, or self protection. By freeing the individual from threat, movement is made possible.

The relationship of therapy is created by much more than an absence of threat, however. It involves a very positive, active expression by the counselor of his own concern, understanding, and compassion which does more than free his client from threat. It actively supports and encourages him in the exploration of himself and his world. If treatment is very deep or intensive this relationship becomes a strong and personally meaningful experience for both counselor and client. To explore one's deepest, most personal self cannot be done on a superficial level or at arms' length. It requires that communication occur at the most fundamental and personal levels of "heart to heart" understanding. Depth psychotherapy is an intense, emotional, that is to say personally meaningful, experience. It is this "emotional" experience that makes possible the individual's exploration of his unique and private self.

How this therapeutic relationship is created between a counselor and his client will vary greatly depending upon the nature of the client and his problems and the understanding, skill, and personality of the therapist. Most therapists do not learn to create such atmospheres easily or quickly. Effective counseling relationships are learned for most people only through intense study and arduous self discipline.

The Exploration of Meaning

Having created a situation which permits the client to explore his perceptions freely, therapy must next assist the client to make this exploration and to arrive at new and more satisfying self definitions. Warm, permissive situations and secure relationships with a counselor make it possible to talk about one's deeper feelings but do not guarantee that such talk will occur. Having established a relationship which makes change possible, successful therapy still requires that some change take place in the individual's perceptions of himself and his world. This may be brought about by environmental methods in which the therapist attempts to expose his client to new experiences designed to give him new perceptions of himself and the world he lives in. The school psychologist, for example, does this when he places a child having difficulty with a particular teacher in another classroom where he will have an opportunity to work out a more satisfying relationship. Similar principles underlie the technique of foster-home placement, wherein a child is placed in a setting likely to produce more positive concepts of self.

In the face-to-face relationship of counseling, the therapist may attempt to help his client redefine self through the medium of language. To assure maximum help from the counseling period, it is necessary for the therapist to assist his client to explore those aspects of the phenomenal field most likely to be of assistance in helping him to reorganize his self concept. The counselor must aid his client to explore the crucial aspects of the field, namely the particular relationships of the client's experience to the self.

The talk which goes on in the counseling hour is not aimless talk. It is talk about the self and its relationships to the outside world which the counselor encourages in one fashion or another. He does this by discouraging talk in some directions and encouraging that which explores the self: its feelings, attitudes, beliefs, and convictions, the personal meanings existing for the client. In effect, he says by his behavior: "Here is the place to look." All counselors do this in one form or another and every method of counseling has devised its peculiar techniques for bringing about this personal exploration of meaning. In client-centered therapy, for example, it is accomplished in part by the counselor's sincere and consistent sympathetic understanding and in part by his basic technique called "recognition and acceptance of feeling." By this is meant that the counselor responds to his client by recognizing and accepting how he *feels* about the events he is describing. This is sometimes described as "mirroring" the client's feelings and, in a sense, that is what the therapist does. He attempts to reflect the essential feeling expressed by the client in clear and understandable terms. Sometimes he will recognize and accept the client's feelings by practically restating what he has said. For example:

CLIENT: I get so mad at her sometimes. She does things like that all the time.
COUNSELOR: Sometimes you feel very angry at her. I can see how you might feel that way.

Sometimes, too, the counselor may respond to the feeling in terms quite different from those used by the client, as in the following:

CLIENT: Yes, it is not at all clear to me. Should I keep it out of sight or keep it out in the open? I still don't know.
COUNSELOR: There are advantages in either direction.

In either event, however, the counselor attempts always to recognize and accept the feeling being expressed by his client. But why should he respond to his client's *feeling?* Why not to any other aspect of his client's statement?

In Chapter 11 we pointed out that what the individual is describing when he speaks of his emotions or feelings is, in reality, his personal reference. For instance, when I describe myself as "tired," I am describing my phenomenal field at this instant. In large part, this is a description of my awareness of my body state but includes, as well, all other aspects of my field at this moment, including the fact that I have just looked at the clock and discovered how very late it has become. My "feeling" is the meaning of events to me at this time. When the counselor concentrates attention on the "feelings" of his client, he is helping him to explore and differentiate out of thc field the personal reference of events. This is why the therapeutic experience is likely to be a very emotional one. The more personal the exploration, the more emotional the experience will seem to be.

Many people in our society have been deeply hurt in the process of growing up, or have simply never learned to communicate with others on more than a fairly superficial level of meaning. They, almost literally, do not know how to look at themselves. In counseling, therefore, the therapist may have to "teach" his client where to look for the solution of his problems. He does this by the relationship he creates and the techniques he uses to direct the client's attention to the data of adjustment, that is, the individual's own ways of perceiving himself and the world about him. In emphasizing the client's feelings the counselor assists the client to an exploration of his field through an examination of the "meanings of events" for him. By recognizing and stating these meanings, clearly and sharply, he assists his client to further differentiations until, eventually, this process may arrive at those differentiations most troublesome or fear-producing for the client. Once that point has been reached new adjustments become possible.

This process of exploring meaning, which the adult carries on through the medium of language, is not available for children with vocabularies too limited to express their perceptions. Children can be helped, however, by therapy carried on in the language of play. Though children lack the vocabulary in terms of which to explore their perceptual field, they can achieve the same end through the manipulation of toys, paints, or the thousand and one materials at hand in a well-equipped play room. The play therapist provides the same facilitating atmosphere and assists the process of exploration of the child's own meanings expressed in his play activities. Thus, he might respond to the child sucking on a baby bottle: "Sometime, it is nice to be a baby. I know how you feel"; or to the child who has flushed the father doll down the toilet, "Sometimes you are very angry at the father doll." In this fashion he helps his young client explore his unique relationship to his world and in the process to arrive at more adequate ways of viewing himself and that world.

There is another way in which the relationship of psychotherapy helps the client to new and more adequate concepts of self. We have seen earlier that the adequate personality is characterized by three factors: a positive self, acceptance, and strong feelings of identification. By his behavior the therapist may be able to provide experiences for his client which help him begin to perceive himself as a more adequate person. The therapist treats his client *as though he were* lovable, likable, acceptable, and able. He accepts his client even when his client is unable to accept himself. This is an important experience for the inadequate personality. Self concepts are the products of our experience with the important people of our lives. Because his counselor treats him as though he were these positive things, little by little the client may come to believe in himself in these ways too. This does not, of course, happen quickly, for self concepts do not change so easily. Over a period of time, however, as he finds his counselor behaving consistently in these ways the client may begin to perceive himself in this light as well.

The warm, understanding relationship of the counseling experience and the deeply meaningful communication made possible by the personal character of the therapeutic relationship also provide the client with a strong feeling of identification. Perhaps for the first time in his life he finds it possible to identify successfully and meaningfully with another person, and this experience with the therapist increases the possibility of creating such relationships with other people as well. By his very behavior toward his client, the counselor is providing an important learning experience. In a very real sense he is teaching him to be adequate by treating him as though he were. For many threatened and inadequate personalities this is a new and wondrous experience. For deeply deprived personalities it may even prove extremely frightening as they feel desperately inadequate to deal with such strange and, in their experience, unusual behavior. Often they may be driven to test the genuineness of this relationship in ingenious and devious ways. To withstand this period of testing, the counselor must himself be capable of an extraordinary degree of patience, compassion, and firmness of position. This kind of experience in successful identification with the therapist can have tremendous value for the threatened and unhappy client. Through it he may be helped to identify more effectively with other people in his world.

With a clear differentiation of the relationship between self and the external world, facilitated by the creation of a situation that makes change possible and helped along by the therapist's assistance in the process of exploration of the field, the stage is set for a shift in the self concept. Under these circumstances such a redefinition of the phenomenal self and its relationship to external reality becomes not only possible but almost inevitable. But why should this be true?

The Outcome of Treatment—Self Reorganization

As we have seen, the threatened individual has a self concept inadequate to accept his perceptions of external events. Since his need is to maintain or enhance the organization of the phenomenal self, and since his perceptions of external affairs endanger that organization, he is driven to defend himself and is incapable of making any great change in the self concept. What is more, the selective effects of the self concept on perception makes the likelihood of any change in the self concept even more remote, for the client may not even be able to perceive the source of the threat to which he is exposed. Eventually, under these circumstances, the threat to the client's organization may become so great as to be almost intolerable yet he is unable to differentiate the nature of the terror to which he is exposed or what solutions are possible to him. The individual finds himself in a position where he cannot bear to remain as he is, yet cannot perceive any more adequate ways of behaving.

At this point in therapy we come to what appears at first glance a paradox—namely, that the same need to maintain and enhance the phenomenal self which brought the individual under threat in the first place operates to assist the client to a readjustment of his self concept and actually results in its change. Let us take an example to see how this comes about. Mr. Jones feels deeply threatened but cannot explain the source of his dread. So far as he is concerned he is just afraid of "something" but does not know what. Under these circumstances his need to maintain and enhance his organization causes him to defend his self concept, and he may be unable to perceive either the nature of the threat or the necessity for a reevaluation of his self concept in more adequate terms. In therapy he tells us of this threat which he feels but cannot "put his finger on." He describes it as vague and diffuse, and he is anxious and worried although he has nothing to worry about so far as he can see. As therapy progresses, he continues his exploration of his field and finally comes to differentiate clearly his own evaluation of himself and that of the events surrounding him. He tells us finally that he dislikes himself intensely. He feels he is a very unworthy person. What he is really afraid of is "What people will think of me?" Now with the situation clearly perceived, his need to maintain or enhance the phenomenal self brings him to a reorganization of his self concept in closer alignment with external reality. Anything else is impossible, for to remain as he is, is intolerable and keeps him under threat. The only thing which will remove the threat is to take the direction now clear to him as a result of his sharper differentiation of the situation. Before counseling, his need forced him to maintain his position because it was impossible for him to perceive that any other possibility existed. After he has achieved a clear differentiation of the situation in counseling it becomes intolerable to maintain his present self concept, and the maintenance and enhancement of the phenomenal self lies in making some change in its organization. Thus he may redefine himself as no better or worse than other men and really not such a bad person after all. With such a reorganization of self he may be able to like himself better and perceptions of external events will appear less threatening. In other words, if it becomes clear that enhancement of the phenomenal self is to be achieved by reorganization, the organism will move in that direction, providing the threat to his present position is dissipated.

It is just this sort of shift in the organization of the self concept which is characteristic of all successful therapies. While therapy is a device by which such changes are facilitated, the same types of changes are made repeatedly in the life of the average person. The very act of growing up involves a continuous process of reorganization or modification of the self concept as one moves from childhood, to youth, to manhood, to marriage, to middle age, and finally to old age. So long as the threat to the existing phenomenal self is not too great, reorganization continues smoothly as the person perceives the changes occurring in himself and his surroundings. Under extreme threat, however, the individual's self concept may become encysted. This often happens in children who feel threatened when parents push too hard for grown-up skills. When pressures become too great, individuals may feel so threatened and inadequate that they are forced to defend the existing self and so become incapable of change. The failing student in school may find the work demanded of him so overwhelming that he seeks to avoid it entirely, thus avoiding the very efforts that might solve his problem. Counseling is a method of breaking such a log jam and getting things moving again by making change in self definition possible once more. Psychological growth is a process of change in self definitions, and it is this kind of growth that treatment encourages and facilitates.

The Permanence of Change

Changes brought about in therapy may often be remarkably permanent. There is good reason why this should be true. Perhaps the greatest number of cases in which the self has become seriously threatened are due to the movement of the individual from one cultural group to another. This includes, of course, those many situations in which adult maladjustments are hang-overs from childhood self definitions. A great many of our maladjustments seem to arise from this early period of life when differentiations are far less clear than is true in adulthood, and when the child may even lack the necessary symbols in terms of which more adequate differentiations can be made.

A fundamental reorganization of self made as an adolescent or as an adult may, therefore, have a highly permanent effect for two reasons: (1) The individual has shucked off the inadequate self definitions imposed upon him as a child and is now better able to make clearer and more adequate ones than was possible to him in earlier days. (2) As a growing child, the individual moved into wider and wider cultural groups: from family to neighborhood group, to school, to gang, to social groups, etc. We have seen that this movement from one subculture to another is often the source of threatening perceptions, as the self concept formed in one group becomes inadequate to deal with the new group. When, however, the individual has reached adult status, he is no longer moving into such drastically different subcultures. His horizons have expanded and now include most of those groups in which he will move as an adult. Because he is no longer so likely to be moving from subculture to wider culture and because he has a greater differentiating ability, he is less exposed to new and upsetting relationships of self to the world about him. An adequate self definition effectively operating with people and events is less likely to be upset by ordinary exigencies of life. In fact, if emerging events are not too overwhelming, the experience of dealing successfully with them may be the very means by which even greater adequacy is achieved.

CHAPTER 20

The Exploration of Meaning

HOW effectively we are able to operate with other people and how adequately we are able to contribute our full share to the society in which we live will depend in large part upon the understandings we have about the behavior of others. The more understanding we have, the more efficiently we can govern our own behavior in living and working with them. Whether we are aware of it or not, we all have perceptions about other people. Such understandings may exist all the way from some vague feeling like "people are generally nice," or "most people can't be trusted," to the highly differentiated and precise descriptions of the research psychologist. Whether vague or exact, however, all of us behave in terms of what we have come to believe is "so" about other people and their motivations.

To understand the behavior of another person it is necessary to understand how things seem to him, to have some grasp of the nature of his phenomenal field. In particular, we need to know how he perceives himself and the world in which he operates. Perceptions, however, are an internal matter not open to direct observation by an outsider, and this, at first glance, might seem to confront us with an impossible task.

THE INADEQUACY OF INTROSPECTION

Logically, it would seem that if we would like to know how a person sees himself or the world about him, the thing to do would be to ask him. This is the technique, widely used in the psychology of 40 to 50 years ago, known as "introspection." Psychologists of those days, however, were forced to give up this method of approach to human meaning as too inaccurate and unreliable, and it seems no more useful for our purposes today than it did then. This is perhaps best illustrated by the difficulties we incur when we try to understand the phenomenal self of another by asking him how he sees himself. His reply is not a description of his phenomenal self, but rather his "self report."

The self report is the individual's self description as he reports it to an outside observer. It represents what the individual *says* he is. Like any other act, the self report is a behavior revealing in more or less degree what is going on within the organism. It is an expressive behavior produced by the perceptual field including the phenomenal self. The self report and the self concept, however, are by no means synonymous. One is a behavior, the other a perceptual organization which can be more or less closely approximated by inference from behavior. Confusion of these two concepts can lead to similar confusion in our thinking. There are even a number of experiments in the psychological literature designed to study the self concept but which, in fact, are studies of the self report.

The self report, like any other behavior, is a product of the individual's *total* phenomenal field. This perceptual field, it is true, contains all other perceptions of which he is capable as well. Any behavior is always the product of the individual's perceptions of himself *and his perceptions of the situation in which he is involved.* The self report, like any other behavior, is thus a product of *both* the subject's perceptions of self and of not self. How accurate a description of the phenomenal self the self report is likely to be is dependent at least upon the following factors:

1. *The clarity of the subject's awareness.* We have already seen that the phenomenal self varies in degrees of clarity. Some concepts of self at any moment are in clear figure while others may be immersed in ground. Thus the businessman whose concept of himself as a father is largely in eclipse during the hours he spends in his office may become keenly aware of himself in this role as he enters the door of his home. The concepts of self held by an individual vary widely with respect to their clarity at any moment, and whether or not they may be reported to others will depend in part upon whether they can be called into clear figure at the moment they are asked for. There may also be wide variations in the clarity of self perceptions of a more permanent character. Some concepts of self, for example, may exist only at very low levels of awareness for most of our lives. Still others, like the adolescent's slowly emerging concept of himself as an adult, may be quite unclear for very long periods of time. Attempts to report such undifferentiated perceptions to others may well prove impossible.

2. *The lack of adequate symbols for expression.* The perceived self

may also be unreportable because the individual does not possess the necessary symbols in which self perceptions may be adequately expressed. Despite the extent of our language there are times when it is impossible for us truly to express the richness of our experience in the limited vocabularies we possess. Words are notoriously inadequate to convey our full meanings. Even when we are able to express ourselves with some degree of accuracy we always run the risk that the words we use may not mean the same things to others as they mean to us. The degree to which the self report approaches the phenomenal self is thus open to all the errors involved in any other human communication and cannot be accepted as a one-to-one relationship without control of these variables.

3. *The social expectancy.* In our society it is customary, indeed, practically necessary, for the individual to hide his true concepts of himself even if he is able to report them accurately. Though a given person may think of himself as "very charming" or as "very stupid," he certainly would be most unlikely to express such feelings even under the most unusual circumstances. Each of us is always surrounded by the society in which he lives. We can never quite escape the effects of this society no matter how hard we may try. We are always aware of the approval and disapproval of others and the things we say about ourselves must always be more or less affected by these perceptions. Our perceptual fields are seldom free from such societal expectancies.

4. *Coöperation of the subject.* Subjects who are asked to coöperate in an exploration of their perceived selves have complete control over any attempt to approach the problem by way of self reports. If they do not wish to reveal an aspect of self, they can dissemble as they please or refuse to coöperate at all. They do not even have to reveal the fact of their lack of coöperation, if indeed they are aware of such a decision at all. A subject may agree to coöperate in an exploration of his self concept with the best of intentions, but be quite unable to give the desired information accurately for reasons of which he, himself, may not be clearly aware.

5. *Freedom from threat and the degree of personal adequacy.* Still another factor affecting the credibility of the self report will be the degree of personal adequacy felt by the subject. In general, the more adequate the individual feels, the more likely his self report will approach an accurate description of the phenomenal self, other factors being equal. The more threatened and inadequate the personality, the less is the

likelihood that he will be able to give an accurate report of his concepts of self. The more threatened, inadequate, or maladjusted the individual, the more vulnerable his concepts of self and the greater will be the necessity for him to defend the self. Poor as they may be, the concepts we have of ourselves are all we possess and the smaller, more insignificant our precious horde, the more vigorously it must be defended.

6. *Change in field organization.* Most important of all as a factor contributing to error in the use of the self report is the change in field organization brought about by the request for such a report. The organization of the phenomenal field when the individual is behaving with self only partly in figure is not the same as that when the self is clearly and sharply in focus. The reader can test this for himself. Until this moment he may have been intent on capturing the meaning of these paragraphs, but if we now ask him to tell us "how" he is reading, at once his field changes. A field organized with respect to the attainment of some goal outside the self is not the same as a field organized with the self in sharp figure. The very act of turning attention to self requires a reorganization of the field and this, of course, changes the character of what can be reported.

The Place of Inference in Perception Study

Understanding other people's perceptions is not new to us. Everyone has been doing this more or less successfully since childhood. Whenever we have to deal with other people, but particularly when we are trying to communicate with them in one way or another, we are sensitive to how they may be perceiving what we are saying or doing and we adjust our own behavior accordingly. In explaining an idea to a friend, we observe his reactions as we speak and adjust our explanation in terms of the inferences we make about how it is seeming to him. In a similar fashion, the teacher observes the child's reactions to the lesson and shifts and changes his own behavior accordingly to assure understanding of the point he seeks to convey. All of us develop this kind of informal sensitivity to the perceptions of others. Indeed, without it we could hardly continue to live in our complex, coöperative society. We make such inferences so automatically that we are seldom keenly aware of how we are doing it.

Children make such inferences when they deduce from the behavior of the adult that "Mother is angry!" or "Aunt Sue wants to kiss me." It is also what the grownup does when he infers that "John is not happy with Alice" or "the boss feels sore about something this morning." In a sense, people are always telling us about their perceptions by the ways in which they behave. Our problem is one of developing sensitivity to others and skill in making inferences from the behavior we are able to observe. These inferences provide the basis, the frame of reference, on which our own behavior can be founded when it is necessary for us to deal with other people. They provide the raw data for effective human relationships.

As a point of departure for estimating the potential effectiveness of such an approach in the prediction of human behavior we may take the findings of Sorokin and Berger, that individuals can predict accurately about 80 percent of their activities for the next 24 hours. These predictions were naturally made by the individual on the basis of his own perceptual field, and it might be a natural assumption that an outside observer, basing his view of the field on inference, would not do as well. As a matter of fact, the observer using the perceptual approach can often do much better than the subject himself.

The observer cannot, of course, reconstruct the subject's present field with the richness, warmth, and detail that it actually has. His most precise approximation of that field is only a plan or schema of its general characteristics. But in drawing inferences about the future field and the future behavior of the subject, he has two advantages that the subject does not have. For one thing, the observer's field includes not only his approximation of the subject's field but a great deal of other knowledge as well. The subject's predictions of his future behavior are based upon his present field exclusively, but the observer, with a broader field, can predict, as the subject cannot, impingements of new experience and their effect upon the field. Johnson, secretly planning to punch Smith in the nose, has knowledge of Smith's future field and behavior which is not, at the moment, accessible to Smith. So does Jones, who has just written Smith a letter asking for money, and Miss Anderson, who has just put an *F* on young Smith's report card. Of course, none of these people can accurately predict Smith's response to their advances from this knowledge alone. But they do have information pertinent to his future field which is denied him and, if they know him well, they can predict what he will do when the predicted events occur.

The observer has one other advantage over the subject. The subject is a prisoner within his own present field and is sharply aware only of the present figure. Material in the ground is at such a low level of awareness that it is available only in the form of vague feelings and "hunches," if at all. Even if the ground material has been in sharp figure in the past it has very little influence at the moment. On the other hand the observer, if he has had an opportunity to study the individual's phenomenal field in the past, is aware of a great deal of this material, once figure and now ground, which is out of the subject's reach at the moment, but which under predictable conditions, under the stress of another situation, will emerge into figure again. In other words the behaver himself can be aware only of his present field; the observer, who has his own field, can be aware of much of the subject's ground material which provides most of the raw material for the future field. Furthermore, since the observer can view the subject's field unemotionally, without personal involvement, he can be aware of the subject's characteristic distortions and use this knowledge in predicting the kind and degree of distortion of new material. The subject, again, cannot do this for himself because to him the distorted field is reality. In a situation where the subject is well known to the observer, and his field has been thoroughly explored by acceptable methods, and where the latter is also well acquainted with the situation in which the subject is to find himself, the prediction should fall little below complete accuracy.

Although most people develop enough sensitivity about the perceptions of others to make it possible for them to live fairly successfully, such undisciplined kinds of observation hardly suffice for professional workers. Teachers, social workers, psychologists, physicians, and others who have social responsibilities for dealing with human problems, need much more precise understandings of the perceptions of their students, clients, and patients than is required for the more casual relationships satisfactory for the purposes of the ordinary citizen. The inferences applied workers make about the perceptual fields of people call for much more disciplined and controlled observations. The research worker will need even more precise and accurate understandings than the applied worker for his highly specialized and exacting purposes.

What distinguishes the research worker from the applied worker or ordinary citizen is not that he seeks for something different in understanding, but only that he brings to the task a higher degree of care and precision. The researcher, the teacher, and the man-in-the-street all need to understand the perceptions of others. Most of us make inferences about others' perceptions in the vague and undisciplined ways we have learned in the process of our growing up, and this is ordinarily quite satisfactory for our daily purposes. The teacher, however, needs more precise understandings for his purposes and so must exert greater discipline and care in his observations. Such observations in turn will probably not be sufficiently precise for the research worker.

It should not be supposed that because each of these three approaches the problem of understanding perception with differing degrees of order and precision that one is "better" than another. On the contrary, each approach is useful and efficient for its own purposes. The methods appropriate to each of these levels is hardly suitable for the others. Thus the researcher finds the layman's ways too uncontrolled for research demands, while the layman finds the researcher's methods too detailed and cumbersome for the immediate action required in day-to-day and moment-to-moment living. The professional worker, on the other hand, uses methods lying somewhere between these extremes. His methods are at once more precise than the layman's and broader in scope than the researcher's.

In general, understanding the meanings of other people is accomplished by a process of observation, inference making, and testing of inferences. This is what the teacher does as he attempts to deal with the problem of Jimmy's difficulties in reading. He observes Jimmy read and infers, "It may be the child does not see well." Having made this observation, he checks his inference by having the child's eyes examined. If this proves inaccurate, he observes some more and makes other inferences. Perhaps Jimmy is not seeing the differences between *l* and *t*, or *n* and *m*. Or maybe the child sees the whole process of reading as a threatening failure experience. Through this kind of process of inferring and checking, the teacher is able to arrive at a workable understanding of how reading seems to Jimmy. This is the same kind of procedure used by mothers inferring why the baby is crying, or by psychologists attempting to diagnose the difficulties of a client. Through a continuous process of observing, inferring, testing, observing, inferring, testing, we may, over a period of time, come closer and closer to an accurate appraisal of the meanings existing for other people. Furthermore, we may do this informally, as we do in daily life, or we may carry on the process more exactly, exerting careful control and using highly refined techniques of observation and testing as the research scientist does in carrying out an experiment. At first glance this approach to the study of meaning may seem to some to be mystical and "unscientific." There is a widespread illusion that things can only be "true" or scientific if they can be physically measured. Actually, it is only when science is able to make inferences about things that it is able to progress beyond the immediate and the palpable to deal with the abstract and remote. A science limited only to that which is directly observable would never be able to deal with such matters as electricity, atomic physics, or the mysteries of human disease.

The making of inferences in itself is neither scientific nor unscientific. It is a technique of exploration. What makes a science is the care and discipline with which the data, whatever they may be, are collected, checked, and reported. The data used by the behavioral scientist studying the phenomenal self are exactly the same as those used by psychologists studying any other human characteristic, namely the observed behavior of the subject. For some purposes it is enough to deal only with behavior on this level as, for example, when we are trying to determine how many people taking the college entrance examination will probably graduate. When, however, we seek to predict what a *particular* individual will do, it is necessary for us to understand his motivations, desires, wants, goals, and perceptions of self and the world about him. The perceptual psychologist, interested in the study of meaning, accomplishes this by making inferences from the behavior he observes. Because he has different goals in view, he utilizes different methods of approach to his problem which make it possible to explore questions unapproachable in other frames of reference.

THE OBSERVER AS AN INSTRUMENT FOR RESEARCH

Human beings seem so much more variable than machines that a science which utilizes inferences for its data may at first glance appear hopelessly open to error. Indeed, it is true that the exploration of people's perceptions through a process of inference places a great deal more responsibility upon the observer than is true in the physical sciences. The making of inferences requires of the investigator that he be much more than a mechanist, concerned with the manipulation of external or physical factors alone. He must be able to see the world as others see it and be able to put himself in his client's place. This requires that he utilize his imagination and creative abilities to the utmost of his capacities while at the same time practicing upon himself the most rigid personal discipline with respect to his own prejudices and meanings. When inferences are made, the observer himself is acting as an instrument of research.

The direct observation of data, by itself, provides little help in the solution of problems in any science. There are, for example, no situations in which a single isolated datum is important. Nor do such data become much more useful simply by adding one to another. Data only become truly significant when subjected to the mediation or interpretation of human meaning. Creating a dynamic process from meaningless data is the indispensable function of the observer. Making inferences introduces a further variable to the process of observation, it is true. However, the use of human creativity in science does not produce an invalidation; only a further variable to be recognized and controlled. Properly used with full realization of its assets and liabilities, the human instrument deserves to be treated like any other fine instrument, with care and respect.

Exploring the Perceptual Field

How is it possible to explore so complex, unique, and apparently impregnable an organization as the perceptual field? Since the total field is made up of the individual's meanings of events past, present, and future, it may appear that the problem of understanding another's field is a completely hopeless task. Indeed it would be, if it were necessary for us to know and understand all the meanings of events for the individual in the course of his entire life history. Actually, the picture is by no means so bleak, for even without understanding the entire life history of an individual, many professional workers are making highly accurate predictions in their daily work.

While the exploration of the individual's total field in detail is almost impossible, the differentiations of certain aspects of the field are distinctly within the range of investigation. It will be recalled from our previous discussion that, while the behavior of the individual is always a result of the total organization of the perceptual field, certain differentiations become so important in the production of behavior as to serve as effective guides to what the individual will or will not do in any circumstance. These differentiations are the phenomenal self, the individual's perceptions of the world about him, and the goals, values, and techniques he has differentiated in the course of his experiences. These loom so large in the production of behavior that it is possible to understand how people behave with great accuracy once an understanding has been achieved of their character and operation in the individual's total field of meaning. It is these four major types of differentiation within the field with which perceptual diagnosis and research must be concerned: (1) the individual's self concept, (2) the meanings of certain external events for him, (3) the goals and values which he has differentiated to satisfy need, and (4) the characteristic techniques by which he attempts to reach his goals.

THE EXPLORATION OF THE SELF

Since the phenomenal self provides the very core of the individual's perceptual field, any understanding of the nature of the individual's field must, of necessity, be concerned with the peculiar organization of concepts which go to make up his self concept. We have seen that the self concept is composed of many definitions of self and that these definitions vary in at least two respects: (a) the degree of importance or centrality of the concept—that is, aspects of self will vary in the degree to which they seem to their possessor to be true, important, or basic aspects of his own personality, and (b) the specificity or generality of concepts—that is, one may wish to explore some broad sweeping aspect of self like a feeling of adequacy, or a more specific concept of self like the kind of driver he conceives of himself as being. The aspects of self we seek to explore will vary in terms of these factors. What is more, the techniques we use to explore these aspects will have to be chosen in the light of these considerations. Methods which help us understand the central or general aspects of the self may prove inadequate to aid us in understanding concepts of the self which are specific to particular situations.

What aspects of self are explored, of course, will be determined by the purposes of the observer. Different people will be interested in quite different portions of the same person's self structure. The teacher, for example, may be interested in the student's concept of self as able or unable to do mathematics. The parent, on the other hand, may be more concerned about a child's concepts of self as loved or accepted. The foreman in the plant may be quite unconcerned about such matters but be deeply interested in his employee's self concepts as a member of the production team or as a member of the union. The clinical psychologist, looking at the same person, may be particularly interested in those aspects of the self in which the individual seems to feel most inadequate or deficient.

Since behavior is always a function of the total phenomenal field, the same behavior can even be utilized by different observers working from quite different frames of reference to infer different aspects of self. Thus it is possible that the teacher, psychologist, parent, foreman, or casual acquaintance might each observe the very same behavior and infer from it quite different concepts of self. Nor would one of these inferences necessarily be more "right" than another. They might all be quite accurate although each represents only a limited aspect of self.

EXPLORING THE INDIVIDUAL'S PRIVATE WORLD

Since the individual's behavior is always a function of how he sees himself and how he sees the situation in which he is involved, a real understanding of the perceptual field of another will require that we know, in addition to his phenomenal self, something of this situation. We will need to explore the private world of the subject. Through the same process of inference, prediction, and testing used to determine the phenomenal self and its various aspects, we may discover the meaning of his world for a particular subject. Such inferences can be made with respect to some particular portion: how he perceives, for instance, a political candidate, a motion-picture star, a particular brand of laundry detergent, or his fourth grade teacher. Or we may be interested in a much broader sample of the phenomenal field, as, for example, when we seek to assess a person's intelligence.

THE EXPLORATION OF GOALS AND VALUES

In a previous chapter we have seen that the goals and values differentiated in the phenomenal field have an ordering and selecting effect upon perception. Goals and values, then, are important factors to be explored in assessing people's meanings. With a knowledge of the goals and values important to a subject we are in a position to make much more accurate inferences regarding the ways in which he is likely to perceive a given event. People who value Communism do not see the same events as they are seen by those who value Capitalism. Knowing the existence of such goals and values in a personality helps us to make far more accurate inferences as to the meanings governing his behavior and consequently to predict what he will do in many situations.

Traditional tests of attitudes, personality, interests, likes, and preferences provide interesting clues to the goals and values existing in a particular person's phenomenal field. Public-opinion polls, interviews, and questionnaires of a less formal character have also been used to assess perceptions. Understanding of an individual's goals and values may be informal as we make such observations in our daily contacts or may be carefully measured as the research psychologist examines them. In either case, our awareness provides us with important clues to his perceptual field, which in turn will make it possible for us to predict what he will perceive and how he will behave in other situations.

THE EXPLORATION OF TECHNIQUES

Other important meanings in the perceptual field are the techniques which the individual has differentiated as means of satisfying his need. Many of these become highly characteristic of people and an understanding of them makes possible a high degree of accuracy in the prediction of behavior. Floyd Allport and his students, for example, have carried on fruitful researches in the prediction of behavior from inferences made about "what the individual is characteristically trying to do." Using such inferences, or "teleonomic trends," as Allport calls them, experimenters have been able to forecast with amazing accuracy the behavior of their subjects. The techniques people differentiate as appropriate to satisfy their needs can provide important clues to the nature of personality if we can find ways of discovering what they are.

Ways of Exploring the Perceptual Field

A vast number of materials are now available to the student hoping to explore the phenomenal field. These range from devices like the Rorschach Ink Blots, which have a very simple structure, to tests like the Minnesota Multiphasic Inventory, an extensive and complex battery of statements about self. They range, too, from casual observations to highly organized and directed observations utilized by researchers in the psychological laboratory. Indeed, the development of new techniques for exploring perception is one of the most active areas of psychological research, and new instruments are developed almost daily. Many older techniques of exploration designed by social scientists in years past for quite other purposes may also lend themselves to the needs of the worker desiring to explore human perception. Even children's games and the methods of salesmen and interviewers, on occasion, have contributed to our insights. The number of these methods is so vast and sometimes so technical as to be impossible of inclusion in this book. We shall therefore attempt to do no more than suggest some of these devices and the ways in which they may be used for exploring perception.

OBJECTIVE DATA IN PERCEPTUAL EXPLORATION

The exploration of meaning must begin at the same point as all other exploration of behavior, with some kind of external observation. Though we are concerned with the individual's meanings, these are always meanings of something. It will be necessary, therefore, to begin our exploration with external observations from which it will be possible for us to make inferences as to the nature of the individual's perceptual field. For the most part these inferences will be of the character, "Now why did he do that?" "Under what circumstances would a person have done that?" or "What meaning would one have to have about this or that event to make one act like that?" Such inferences cannot be made in a vacuum. It will be necessary to use objective, external observations of behavior as the basis for interpretations.

Since the collection of objective facts has for so long been conceived as the primary task of psychology, the techniques for obtaining them are extremely numerous and, for the most part, so well known that we shall not pause at this point to do more than attempt to classify them. In general, they fall into three broad types: the observer's observations, the observations of others, and various forms of controlled observations.

In the first of these classes, the psychologist makes direct observations of the individual and his environment. He attempts to describe these in as nearly exact terms as possible. For example, the clinician working with a particular child may visit the child's schoolroom to observe his behavior in that setting, or he may visit the child's home with an eye to observing the home conditions which surround him, or he may make more or less informal observations in his own office, clinic, or laboratory. In any event, he is seeking to establish the nature of the objective facts by means of his own personal observations.

In the case of observations made by others, the psychologist accepts the report of other witnesses whom he regards as reliable. Thus, he may ask for reports from teachers, employers, friends, and acquaintances of his subject. Frequently these reports may also be obtained from court records, school reports, and various forms of documentary material. To assure a measure of greater accuracy these may, furthermore, be subjected to certain tests of reliability and validity.

The third group includes a tremendous number of special devices constructed for the purpose of making controlled observations. These constitute the traditional and most acceptable observations in the external frame of reference. The techniques used vary widely from attempts to control observations in life situations by such means as taking time samples, successive observations, and the use of laboratory experimentation, to various forms of traditional psychological tests. All are based on the same principle of attempting to obtain accuracy and regularity through the restriction and control of observation to the point where agreement in observation (reliability) is possible. Many of these are oriented toward establishing the relationship of the individual to the "normal" group. The number of these instruments now in use is so large that it would be impossible for us to do justice to them here. Instead of attempting such a discussion we shall push on to examine the nature of more strictly perceptual data.

Exploring the Individual's Personal Field

At least four techniques of investigation into the individual's personal meanings are already in more or less widely accepted use or show promise of possible development for that purpose. These are: (1) information obtained from the individual himself, (2) inferences from observed behavior, (3) the use of projective techniques, and (4) the protocols of therapy.

INFORMATION FROM THE INDIVIDUAL HIMSELF

People are always telling us about themselves, their feelings, attitudes, and ways of seeing. All kinds of expressive behavior may give important clues to the nature of the perceptual field, providing we can learn to look and to hear. What people have to say about themselves, their feelings, beliefs, attitudes, problems, worries, concerns, or even simple descriptions of events going on about them are all behaviors derived from the perceptual field. Reading such behavior backward, then, should give us important insights into the field states which produced them. Some of the kinds of data we can use for this purpose are the things people say about themselves and others in conversation, in letters and various forms of personal documents like diaries, journals, or autobiographies.

We have already seen in our discussion of the self report some of the pitfalls involved in accepting statements about self at face value or as having a one-to-one relationship to the phenomenal field. In spite of these difficulties, however, it is possible to use the subject's own descriptions of events, providing we remain keenly aware of the possibilities of error and make appropriate corrections. We can do this by concerning ourselves less with what is said and more with the probable meaning of such statements to the behaver. These meanings, for the most part, will be expressed in what the layman calls "feelings." It will be recalled from our previous discussion that feelings are the individual's attempts to describe his field state at any moment. Thus, by attending to the feelings which the individual is expressing, we may arrive at a more or less accurate description of the meanings which exist for him. This will be possible even when the words he uses describing himself or the events around him are intentionally distorted to give another impression. For instance, when a mother brings her 7-year-old son to the psychological clinic with the statement "My son is failing first grade. How can I ever face my friends?" it is not difficult to infer the meanings that exist in the mother's field or to decide whose self esteem is wounded by the child's failure. Frequently, such simple expressions may be more revealing of personal meanings than any number of more exact techniques of observation.

WAYS OF OBTAINING THE SUBJECT'S OWN REPORT. Techniques of obtaining the subject's own report vary greatly both in degree of structure and the degree to which they are revealing of the client's personal meanings. They vary in structure from unrestricted, casual conversations to highly restricted and exact responses like those on many tests or questionnaires. They will vary also in the degree to which they will provide data about personal meaning, depending upon the individual's need to protect himself.

INFORMAL CONVERSATION ABOUT SELF. Conversations may often be highly revealing of the person's meanings, particularly if he does not feel threatened by the circumstances in which he finds himself, or if he becomes so involved in a conversation that he loses sight of the potential threats which exist. It is a common observation that "bull sessions" and conversations with fellow passengers on trains and buses may often give the individual a sufficient feeling of temporary protection from threat that he is able to speak quite openly of even his deepest feelings. Sometimes, too, this occurs when a subject is extremely upset or angry, and when his field has become sufficiently narrowed so that he does not perceive the threat which exists in the larger field. Under the effects of alcohol a similar tendency may be noted. In this case, the absence of threat appears to be due to the blurring of the field rather than to an extreme narrowing, but results in the same failure to perceive threat. Certain drugs like sodium pentathol and sodium amytal also appear to depend for their effectiveness on this principle.

The practiced clinician soon learns to be on the alert for such expressions of meaning as they reveal themselves in the course of conversation. He learns to be particularly alert to such aspects of the person's behavior as varying tones and inflections of speaking, unusual modes of expression, and the degree of certainty or conviction with which the individual makes his statements. With experience, he learns that most people do not seriously call themselves "the black sheep of my family," for example, or express themselves vehemently about other people unless these things have important and often highly revealing meanings for them.

DIARIES AND LETTERS. These forms of personal documents have often been used in literature and in sociology but have only recently been of much concern to psychologists in the study of personality. Nevertheless, such materials in which the individual "talks to himself" are often extremely useful for purposes of getting at the meanings which motivate behavior. They may be much more expressive than what the client says in conversation, if in his letters, for instance, he is writing to others whom he feels he can trust.

In the following excerpts from an adolescent's diary note how meanings are expressed which would be most difficult to approach in a face-to-face conversation.

After six weeks of daily entries each saying "No job yet," "Still no job!" and the like, is the revealing entry:

I wish I could get a job!! What must Dad and Mother think? Here Sis has a job and I haven't!!

I felt disgusted with the whole world today.

The sooner I get out of this town the better I'll like it. It was all right for a while—but now! Gosh! It'll be great when I get to college and on my own hook.

Took Sally home from the library. She's not mad at me!! Gosh, it's great to love a girl like her!!

The three of us were not going to speak to any girls today! We all failed!

Joe got kicked out of the basketball game so I went with him. We resolved to always stick together.

THE USE OF AUTOBIOGRAPHY. Like diaries and letters, autobiography has not been extensively used in psychological research because of the common objections to the introspective method. Perceptual psychology, too, must reject the introspective method. The use of inference, however, makes possible the effective employment of a number of sources of data about behavior not available to more traditional approaches. Since perceptual research is not primarily concerned with the accuracy or inaccuracy of external evaluation but in the meanings of events to the individual, the very inaccuracies of autobiography may often become important facts for understanding the individual. This is particularly true in clinical psychology where the concern is with the individual's differentiations of the phenomenal self and its relationship to objective events. The clinician does not say, "This is not true in terms of the objective facts but is the way my client sees them and *that is important.*" *It is even possible that it may be the very inaccuracy of report that gives the clinician his important clues to personality.*

The use of autobiography in psychologiacl research may vary widely from highly uncontrolled materials on the one hand to such highly controlled assignments on the other as to resemble a questionnaire. Whatever their nature, autobiographies may provide us most important clues into the fundamental meanings which make up the individual's phenomenal field. Such insights into personal meanings as are revealed in the following small excerpt from an autobiography are a valuable source of information and ought not to be overlooked as valuable devices for exploring meaning:

When I was ten years old my father died very suddenly. As far as we knew he was all right, till one night he had indigestion, went to the kitchen for some soda, and fell over. He lived for about twelve more hours under an oxygen tent, and then died. It was a heart attack. So one minute I had a father and next thing I didn't have one. It was so sudden and unexpected that I couldn't believe it. It left me with a very insecure feeling, as though there wasn't anything stable that I could depend on. Things just happened after that. Then my mother's attitude and being away all day running my father's store after he died emphasized this feeling even more. My mother was adjusting to the shock by constant activity. So my mother's constant running around and doing things gave me still less to hold on to.

THE USE OF TESTS AND QUESTIONNAIRES. A great many tests in current use have important values for perceptual research. This is particularly true of some of the better personality inventories, which may often be highly revealing of individual meanings. For purposes of exploring the phenomenal field, however, the normative scores obtained from these tests will tell us little about the personal meanings of events for the client. Most test scores are external descriptions or summary statements of the subject's behavior traits. For the most part, the individual items of the inventory are likely to prove of greater value as sources of data about people's meanings. Most of our intelligence tests, for example, are in reality no more than tests of the differentiations characteristic of the subject. The trend in modern clinical use of such standard intelligence tests as the Stanford-Binet is to emphasize the study of test items while laying less and less emphasis upon total scores. In fact, the real measure of a good psychometrician lies in the degree to which the worker can make interpretations from the differentiations he observes in the item analysis of the test.

Standardized tests provide us with important means of making observations about people in a common setting and comparing these with the performance of others. For purposes of perceptual research and diagnosis, however, we may be less interested in the subject's status with respect to others who have taken the test than we are in what his peculiar and individual responses to the test items tell us about the meaning existing in his perceptual organization. In exploring personal meaning, therefore, we can also use a large number of unstandardized tests or even special tests devised for a particular problem or a particular person. The test is used as a vehicle for observing uniqueness rather than likeness or difference.

Many commonly used questionnaires and interest inventories may also prove useful in exploring the individual's perceptual field. As in other tests, the individual items of the inventories will usually be found to be more useful for exploring meaning than the normative scores they produce. Statements by the subject that he would rather be a plumber than an actor, or a pharmacist than a teacher, may render us much more important insights than a percentile score indicating a "tendency toward" some large field of work.

Even closer to the needs of perceptual research are such tests as the

Mooney Problems Check List and others of its type. Such tests ask the subject to indicate in a large number of problems, attitudes, ideas, or the like, those which he feels are of greatest concern to him. In this way a fairly direct approach is made to exploring the personal meanings that exist for the individual. Many of our modern attitude tests have similar important cues to offer for the exploration of meanings.

INFERENCES FROM OBSERVED BEHAVIOR

A second important source of perceptual data lies in the inferences it may be possible for us to make from the behavior we observe. This is a technique all of us use in daily life. When our hostess begins to be uneasy and finds it difficult to stifle a yawn, we must know that it is time to go home. In the same way, we are constantly modifying our behavior as we make judgments of what others like or dislike, as we infer what the car driver is going to do when we cross the street, and as we build our sales appeal on what we think our customers want.

UNCONTROLLED BEHAVIOR SITUATIONS. Observations may be made of people behaving in various kinds of uncontrolled situations. With children, for example, we can observe behavior in nursery school, in free play on the playground, or in any number of free and relaxed settings. With adults observations can occur at dinner, on the streetcar, or in any of a thousand other activities not under direct control of the observer. From such observations, if we are alive to the meanings which produce behavior, a great deal of insight may be gained into the nature of the individual's field.

THE USE OF CONTROLLED OBSERVATIONS. For the experimental psychologist who is testing a theory much more controlled observations must be necessary. Psychologists have been making controlled observations of subjects in a great variety of situations for many years. A great deal of this already published research may be found to be highly profitable when observed from a perceptual viewpoint. For example, a great many of the experiments conducted on the level of aspiration are distinctly pertinent to the problems of perception. The same is true of the interesting experiments in child behavior carried on by Lewin and his students. Observations of children made under such controlled conditions are often revealing of important dynamic aspects of behavior. For instance, the work of Barker, Dembo, and Lewin, who experimented with children's reactions to the interposition of a barrier between the child and an assortment of beautiful playthings, was designed to observe the behavior of children when confronted with frustration. These same experiments provide interesting data from which it is possible to infer a good deal about the personal meanings existing for these children, although such inferences were not the primary purpose of the experiment when it was designed.

EXPRESSIVE MOVEMENT AND CONVERSATION. If our fundamental hypothesis that all behavior is a function of the perceptual field is correct, then all activities of the individual should be revealing of meaning if we could but discover the means of interpreting them. This includes such expressive movements as writing, characteristic body gestures, or any other activity engaged in by the individual in the course of his daily life.

Even the subject's conversation about other people has vast possibilities for use as a device to approach the meanings of events for the individual. It is common observation that we respond to the behavior of others in terms of our own needs and meanings. Thus, even the most impartial Republican or Democratic newspaper cannot avoid a bias in its reporting. In the same way individuals are unlikely to be deeply concerned about behavior of others unless that concern is in some fashion meaningful to themselves. Actually, a person's conversation about other people is likely to be a very potent projection of his own attitudes and feelings if the observer is sufficiently keen to be aware of such meanings.

INTERPRETATIONS FROM PROJECTIVE DEVICES

To this point we have spoken of methods of exploring personal meaning in use from time immemorial. In more recent years, however, psychologists have opened a whole new means of approach to the exploration of the perceptual field. These are the projective devices. Since the individual's behavior is a function of his perceptual field, his behavior must be the result of the meanings which make up his field. If we supply a person, then, with a situation in which he is free to respond as he pleases, presumably he will invest the situation we provide with his own personal meanings. The stronger his need, the stronger should these meanings be expressed. This is the fundamental principle of projection and is the basic idea upon which a large number of modern methods for the exploration of personality have been constructed. Projective instruments are designed to confront the subject with some sort of ambiguous situation as an ink blot, a vague picture, an incomplete sentence, or an unfinished plot. In responding to such ambiguity the individual is necessarily thrown upon his own resources to interpret them, and the perceptions he reports in his responses give interesting clues to the nature of the perceptions making up his unique perceptual field.

Projective techniques have another aspect which further increases the likelihood that they will reveal the individual's meanings. This is the fact that most projective devices are designed to give the individual a feeling of protection which removes him from the threat involved in revealing meanings in ordinary life situations. By making the projective instrument a story, a play, or something of the kind, the subject is given a feeling of protection in that he can always pass off his responses as being "just a story" or a fantasy which "no one could possibly imagine had anything to do with himself." As a consequence, under this kind of protection persons responding to projective instruments often reveal to the skilled interpreter some of their most basic and personal meanings.

A vast literature has accumulated on the production, interpretation, and use of such instruments. Several hundred may be found in current use. Most of these are alike in providing some kind of standard setting to which subjects are asked to respond, but the designers of projective instruments have shown a high degree of ingenuity in the kinds of situations their subjects are asked to respond to. These range from the almost completely unstructured Stern "Cloud Pictures" to the highly structured and precisely controlled projections of some sentence-completion tests.

THE RORSCHACH INK BLOTS. Undoubtedly the best known and most widely used of the projective instruments is the Rorschach Ink Blots. This device consists of a series of ink blots to which the individual is asked to respond by telling the examiner what he "sees" in the blots. Whatever he says he "sees," of course, can only be the product of his own experience, and the meanings with which he invests the blots provide a revealing sample of the nature of his perceptual field. The typical Rorschach interview often provides a fascinating and helpful source of data from which it is possible to make important inferences about the perceptions of individuals. The Rorschach Ink Blots have been subjected to more study and research than any other projective instrument and over the years a number of systems have been devised for interpreting the responses of the subject to the blots.

PICTURE STORY TESTS. A more structured type of projective instrument is the Picture Story Test, of which the Thematic Apperception Test is perhaps one of the best known. These tests provide the subject with a series of pictures which are vague representations of social situations. Some, like the Thematic Apperception Test, are quite general in the kinds of meanings they seek to explore, while others are designed for use with particular groups of people or in certain limited kinds of situations. Symonds, for example, has produced a test for use with adolescents. Other tests have been constructed with pictures of Negroes to explore the dynamics of prejudice, or with pictures of children in school to examine the perceptions of children about school and teachers. Since all of us live in a society, and since our adjustment or lack of it is to the social situations in which we operate, the particular meanings social situations have for us constitute a major source of our problems. It is these kinds of meanings the picture story tests seek to explore.

COMPLETION TESTS. Another type of projective instrument in wide use is the Completion Tests. Instead of a pictorial representation these devices provide some kind of written statement purposely left incomplete, which the subject is then asked to finish. Sometimes these may be in the form of sentences like: "I used to think——" or "People often seem to me——" or "Teachers nearly always——." Sometimes the material presented to the subject may be a more lengthy description of a situation or predicament which the individual is then asked to resolve by writing out "what he would do."

An example of this type of instrument is the Situations Test designed to explore the perceptions of school administrators. The test consists of a short description of an interchange between an administrator and one of his teachers up to the point where some decision and action are called for. At this point the story ends and the administrator is asked to tell how he would have handled the problem. From this data it is possible to gain considerable understanding of how the administrator sees himself, his job, his school, his teachers, the children, and the curriculum.

ACTION TECHNIQUES. Still another kind of projective technique has the subject act out his perceptions in free play or in some more structured form of role playing or dramatic presentation. Psychodrama, for example, asks the subject to act some part either from his own or another person's life. The situations and roles he is asked to play may be quite freely chosen or they may be specifically designed by the examiner to explore some particular aspect of the individual's perceptual field. As a subject acts a role he automatically invests it with his own meanings and feelings and these provide important clues to his personal frame of reference.

PLAY DIAGNOSIS. With children, play provides an approach not possible by other means, since young subjects usually do not possess the necessary concepts to express problems verbally, even if they felt free to do so. Through play, the language of childhood, the child is capable of manipulating his environment and making differentiations not otherwise possible to one with so limited a vocabulary. For example, while it may be very difficult, if not impossible, for the child to define his own position with respect to his parents and the world about him in terms of language, in play he can manipulate both the dolls that represent his parents and the rest of the world to his heart's content and may be able to arrive at new perceptions and relationships in the course of such manipulations. The skilled observer can infer meanings which the child himself is unable to put in words.

The operation of the individual's need in restricting the perceptual field may often be most clearly observed in child play. Play is not mere manipulation but appears to be strongly driven in specific directions closely allied with the individual's own problems. For example, when the mother of one little girl went to a mental hospital and was confined for months, the child was not told where her mother had gone or why. In fact, the entire matter became a subject about which no one would speak. The little girl became more and more anxious about the matter and with the passage of time and no word from her mother, more and more of her play time was spent in playing "hospital." She developed a veritable passion for this type of play and induced other children in the neighborhood to participate with her as well. With the return of her mother to the family circle this play was dropped at once. The stronger the need, the more the behavior will be directed toward the satisfaction of need, whether it be in play or in any other behavior. The operation of this principle makes play diagnosis and all other free projective techniques remarkably sensitive for the investigation of adjustment.

That perceptions revealed in projective instruments are a function of the individual's need seems true but it should not be supposed that the perceptions revealed by the subject and those which activate his behavior in other circumstances are one and the same. It must be recalled that projective devices are specially designed to remove the ordinary barriers to the subject's expression and behavior. The Thematic Apperception Test, for example, asks its subject for "as dramatic a story" as he can produce. Since it is often presented as a test of imagination, the client is likely to take the examiner at his word and let his fancy roam freely and exaggeratedly in his story plots. As a result, the stories he tells are often unrestrained, bizarre, and even violent in the feelings represented. Since the client is protected by the very projection the test attempts to elicit and is encouraged in his fantasies, this is a perfectly natural consequence and requires that the interpreter be extremely wary of equating the strength of the feelings expressed in the projective instrument with the strength of the need existing in the client's perceptual field. Our behavior in daily life is a function of the *total* perceptual field, including our awareness of the normal controls of our society. Projective instruments *sample* the perceptual field under special circumstances with normal controls removed. They do not describe it fully.

Despite the difficulties posed by the use of projective instruments, they are the most exciting and productive means of exploring the perceptual field open to us. We have only briefly touched upon this fascinating field here. That is all we can do in this volume. The reader may wish to explore this matter much further through reference to some of the standard texts on projective instruments.

PROTOCOLS OF THERAPY

With the development of increasingly refined techniques of psychotherapy and particularly with the development of techniques of recording therapeutic sessions, a whole new field of approach to perception has been laid open. In the protocols of therapy we are given an opportunity to observe not only the state of affairs in the individual's organization at any one time, but also the nature and direction of change which occurs in that organization. Like the physician's use of radioactive particles in the blood stream or the use of the fluoroscope, the protocols of therapy give us a priceless opportunity to observe the innermost recesses of personality. As Rogers has pointed out: "The fact that these verbal expressions of inner dynamics are preserved by electrical recording makes possible a detailed analysis of a sort not heretofore possible. Recording has given us a microscope by which we may examine at leisure, and in minute detail, almost every aspect of what was, in its occurrence, a fleeting moment impossible of accurate observation."

In the course of therapy the client reveals a great deal of information relative to his characteristic organization. He talks of himself, of his ways of seeing things, of the meanings of events for him and in so doing reveals to the observer many aspects of the perceptual field. What is more, he does this often with great freedom and clarity. As was true of the projective devices, he feels protected by the counseling atmosphere and under the cloak of this protection can feel free to express his thoughts, desires, dreams, hopes, and plans.

In therapy the client is often free to explore the meanings of events in his personal organization with a minimum of distortion. As a result, what the client has to express will often represent an effective picture of his field from moment to moment. The following statements from the Case of Edith Moore show the meaning of events for the client at any moment, and make possible the observation of change (differentiation) in these meanings as the interview proceeds.

> I want to do this. I don't know why I can't get started.
> I don't know what stops me. There must be a reason.
> If I could find the reason, maybe I could accomplish something.
> I am afraid that people will say something that will hurt me.
> It is hard to put myself in a position where I know I will be hurt.
> And again I might not be hurt and then I would get over the fear.
> I want to avoid people's remarks. I ought to do it anyway then maybe it wouldn't be so bad the next time.

The possibilities inherent in this technique have only begun to be explored. It seems likely that the use of recordings for the investigation of the dynamics of group discussion might similarly lead to important insights into the perception of persons in a wide variety of social settings.

The exploration of human meaning, we have seen, is fundamentally a problem of learning to read behavior backward. It is possible to discover the meanings existing for people through a process of inference from the behaviors we see them engaging in. Some of the methods of doing this have long been a part of the "common sense" of the "average man" and with care and discipline can still provide us with means for understanding. Others are comparatively new inventions of the psychologist and psychotherapist requiring much more know-how and sophistication. For the man in the street, for the practical worker in human relations, or for the scientist in the laboratory, however, the fundamental problem is the same. The key to understanding behavior, whether it be our own or other people's, lies in large measure in the skill we develop in the exploration and understanding of the nature of people's perceptions.

References

The number of authors whose work has important bearings upon the point of view represented by this volume is so large that, to avoid extensive footnoting and protect readibility, it has seemed wise to handle the documentation of this text by means of this list of references. When the contribution of a particular author has been specifically mentioned by name, the reader may find the appropriate reference to his work by turning directly to the Bibliography. For the most part, the names of authors and detailed descriptions of research do not appear in the text itself. However, by the use of this list of references the reader may be guided to the appropriate bibliographical item pertinent to the discussion throughout these pages.

This book is printed with 39 lines to the page. The work of each author listed in the bibliography is indexed at the point in the text to which his work seems most relevant. Numbers preceding the name of the author refer to page and line of this volume. The number following the author's name indicates the item in the bibliography particularly referred to. Items listed immediately under chapter headings and without page and line numbers are general references of interest throughout an entire chapter.

To locate the points in the volume where the work of a particular author has seemed most pertinent, refer to the Index.

CHAPTER 1. The Challenge to Psychology

Page	*Line*	
		Allport, 19; Angyal, 31; Lewin, 361
3	18	Burkholder, 114
3	26	Combs, 148
4	37	Gerard, 252
4	39	Combs, 148
5	6	Mayo, 393
5	26	Allport, 19
5	37	Krech, 339
6	14	Angyal, 31; Halpin, 274
6	29	Dockeray, 192; Pratt, 457
6	31	Bettelheim, 69; Haller, 271
6	38	Allport, 20
7	22	Allport, 17; Cantril, 120; Lecky, 350
7	27	Allport, 19; Lewin, 363
8	4	Snygg, 544
8	12	Diehl, 189
8	19	Smith, 535
8	21	Worchel, 611
8	35	Angyal, 31
8	37	Cantril, 120
9	3	Lewin, 363
9	38	Schrodinger, 506
10	11	Murphy, 419
10	16	Hilgard, 288; Osgood, 433
11	13	Maslow, 387, 388
11	16	Allport, 15, 17; Lewin, 364
11	21	Allport, 16
11	36	Cantril, 120; Mowrer, 418
12	3	Sarbin, 500; Snygg, 544
12	35	Combs, 145
13	18	Combs, 145
14	6	Pavlov, 434
14	13	Combs, 145
14	28	Allport, 16; Cantril, 120; Schneirla, 506
14	36	Krech, 339

CHAPTER 2. The Perceptual View of Behavior

Page	*Line*	
		Bartley, 54; Blake, 37; Snygg, 544
16	8	Rogers, 490
16	11	Lewin, 361
17	6	Bernhardt, 67; Schneirla, 505, 504; Snygg, 543, 542, 547
17	11	Freeman, 234
18	11	Koffka, 332
18	31	Angyal, 31; Mowrer, 418
18	35	Allport, 19; Kelley, 325
18	38	Ansbacher, 32; Cantril, 121
19	10	Mowrer, 418
19	12	Cantril, 120; Halpin, 274
19	15	Schrodinger, 506
19	28	Koffka, 333
20	2	Lewin, 364
20	12	Koffka, 332; Lewin, 362, 366; Snygg, 541, 546
21	1	Ansbacher, 32; Frank, 230; Koffka, 333; Lewin, 362, 363; MacLeod, 379
21	4	Husserl, 302, 303; Landsman, 341
21	18	Bevan, 70
21	27	Allport, 17; Combs, 160
22	13	Mowrer, 418
24	7	Koffka, 332, 333, 334; Lewin, 362, 364, 366
24	15	Wertheimer, 599
25	17	Wertheimer, 599
25	19	Koffka, 332, 333
25	23	Schafer, 501
27	3	Angyal, 31; Koffka, 332, 333
27	6	Bartlett, 53; Wees, 593
27	8	Postman, 451; Syngg, 541
27	10	Snygg, 548
27	32	Smith, 535
28	4	Snygg, 548
28	11	Miller, 410
28	18	Freud, 239, 240; Levy, 360
29	6	Brigden, 101
29	23	Bruner, 106; Frenkel-Brunswik, 236; Lecky, 350; Levine, 357; Proshansky, 464
30	12	Bartley, 54; Bevan, 70; Blake, 87; Cantril, 121; Koffka, 332; Snygg, 542
33	6	Angyal, 31; Koffka, 332; Köhler, 334, 335
33	11	Dashiell, 177
33	36	Dashiell, 177
35	11	Gibson, 255
35	15	Halpern, 273
35	20	Chein, 131; Sarbin, 500
36	1	Elkin, 205; Rogers, 489; Sorokin, 552
36	4	Allport, 14; Perrin, 436

Chapter 3. What Do People Need?

Page	Line	
38	20	Gerard, 252
39	4	Fromm, 245
41	8	Schrodinger, 506; Gerard, 252; Goldstein, 257
41	19	Dashiell, 177
41	22	Cannon, 119; Dempsey, 186
41	38	Richter, 474
42	6	Goldstein, 257
42	10	Lecky, 350
42	19	Cannon, 119
42	33	Fletcher, 227; McKellar, 403
42	37	Freeman, 234
43	24	Combs, 160
44	33	Bertocci, 68; Lecky, 350; Raimy, 468
45	9	Anderson, 28
45	14	Frank, 229
45	22	Murphy, 419
45	30	Axline, 41; Child, 133; Eriksen, 212; Fitts, 224; Maslow, 380
46	16	Cantril, 120
46	28	Snygg, 545
49	30	Murray, 422
49	32	Combs, 147; Freud, 239, 241
50	3	Carter, 127; Frank, 229
50	7	Benjamins, 64
50	36	Smith, 534
51	10	U.S. Federal Security Agency, 584
51	15	Wolfenstine, 609
51	31	U.S. Federal Security Agency, 584
51	36	U.S. Federal Security Agency, 584
52	18	Roethlisberger, 477, 478, 479
53	2	Roethlisberger, 477 (p. 86)
53	16	Roethlisberger, 477 (p. 185)
54	29	Levine, 357; Adler, 5
54	32	Carter, 127
55	2	Eriksen, 213
55	6	Evvard, 215; Hastorf, 281; Kutner, 340; Young, 613, 614, 615
55	7	Davis, 183
55	15	Franklin, 232; McClelland, 395; Sanford, 498, 499; Seymour, 514
55	21	Osgood, 433
55	24	Frenkel-Brunswik, 236; Eriksen, 211
55	28	McGinnies, 398; Postman, 452, 453
55	33	Levine, 356
55	37	Jahoda, 307
56	15	Weingarten, 594
56	36	Snygg, 545
58	4	Axline, 40

Chapter 4. The Physical Organism: Vehicle of Perception

Page	Line	
		Bartley, 54
61	4	Burkholder, 114; Gerard, 252
61	22	Cannon, 118
63	11	Bartley, 54
65	7	Dockeray, 192; Pratt, 457
65	24	Bartley, 54
65	28	Werner, 599
65	39	Bartley, 54
68	7	Bice, 72
68	22	Bexton, 71; Twersky, 583; Worchel, 611
68	39	Wapner, 587
69	36	Hebb, 283; Lashley, 346
70	31	Allison, 13
70	38	Goldstein, 257; Hebb, 283
71	4	Jensen, 312
72	24	Boas, 90
72	27	Terman, 567
72	30	Poull, 456
72	33	Davis, 183
73	24	Davis, 183
73	34	Levine, 357
74	10	McClelland, 395; Sanford, 498, 499; Seymour, 514; Young, 613, 614, 615
74	16	Franklin, 232
74	22	Mercer, 408
76	39	Geig, 251
77	14	Mussen, 425
77	16	Boas, 90
77	36	Mittelmann, 411
78	5	Alexander, 9; Selye, 511, 512, 513

CHAPTER 5. Time and Opportunity Affect Perception

Page	Line	
		Ames, 24; Bartley, 54; Blake, 87; Ittelson, 305
81	38	Pottle, 455
82	9	Combs, 146; Goodenough, 258
83	11	Husserl, 302, 303
83	36	Ames, 24
84	2	Brown, 104; Carmichael, 126
84	16	Ames, 24
84	20	Ittelson, 305
84	23	Kelley, 325
85	2	Ames, 24
85	5	Cantril, 123; Freeman, 234; Leeper, 352
85	37	Ittelson, 305; Kelley, 325
88	20	Banham, 48; Smith, 537
88	24	Riesen, 475
88	32	Davis, 185
88	37	Anderson, 29; Bruner, 104; Frank, 231; Leuba, 354; Schafer, 501
89	9	McGinnies, 398; Peterson, 437; Rorshach, 493
89	28	Cantril, 121; Ittelson, 306
89	32	Wapner, 587; Werner, 598
89	35	Murphy, 419
90	2	Tresselt, 581; Wever, 600
90	15	Cantril, 122
90	21	Sherif, 520
90	26	Bexton, 71; Wapner, 587
91	7	Johnson, 316
91	12	Cantril, 123; Carmichael, 126
91	14	Krasnogorski, 338; Maier, 384
91	30	Stagner, 555
91	34	Asch, 35; Mayo, 393
92	2	Lewin, 365; Sherif, 523
92	12	Davis, 179, 181
92	18	Davis, 185; Feingold, 218; Freeman, 233; Frymeier, 246; Goodenough, 259; Thompson, 273; Linton, 275
92	29	Bovard, 98; Kilpatrick, 326
92	31	Köhler, 335
92	39	Hallowell, 272; Marks, 385
93	5	Plant, 443
93	8	Benedict, 63; Bossard, 94; Mead, 406, 407; Plant, 444
93	15	Linton, 374, 376
93	18	Kardiner, 318; Slotkin, 532
93	21	Cowen, 165, 167; Henry, 284; McGinnies, 397, 399; Taylor, 565; Young, 612
93	25	Piaget, 441; Proshansky, 464; Shaffer, 515
93	32	Frymeier, 246
93	36	Kanner, 317
93	39	Bruner, 110
94	4	Cantril, 121
94	20	Wittreich, 608
94	35	McConnell, 396; Mussen, 423; O'Connor, 428
95	8	Lee, 351
95	11	Whorf, 602
95	16	Merker, 409
95	27	Sherman, 528
95	30	Asher, 37; Combs, 146; Frymeier, 246
96	12	Ambriere, 23; Gould, 264; Postman, 453
96	20	Murphy, 420
96	25	Bogardus, 91; Schein, 502; Sherif, 523
96	34	Clark, 138; Goodman, 261; Marks, 385
97	3	Kluckhohn, 331
97	33	Linton, 374
98	1	Mead, 406
98	35	Burtt, 115
99	34	Snygg, 541
99	39	Bartlett, 53; Smith, 537
100	5	Ames, 24; Ittelson, 305
100	31	Engel, 207; Immergluck, 304; Leuba, 354; Siipola, 530
100	39	Bagby, 44
101	2	Koffka, 332, 333; Leeper, 352

CHAPTER 6. Goals, Values, and Techniques

Page	Line	
102	14	Fischer, 223
102	20	Gould, 264
104	2	Hallowell, 272; Hartley, 277; Thompson, 573
104	21	Allport, 14
105	21	Diller, 191; Morse, 415; Murphy, 419
105	28	Allport, 14

Page	Line	
106	39	Snygg, 545
108	4	Bakay, 46; Carter, 127; Klein, 330; Morse, 415
108	11	Bartlett, 53; Bruner, 106; Carmichael, 126; Hastorf, 281; Mausner, 392
108	16	Kinsey, 328
108	30	Farberow, 216
108	35	Hull, 300; Leuba, 354
108	37	McClelland, 395; Sanford, 498, 499
109	2	Anderson, 29; Combs, 144
109	19	Siipola, 530
109	23	Bruner, 110; Combs, 151; Gilchrist, 256; Haigh, 269; McGinnies, 397, 398, 400; Postman, 452, 453
109	30	Beier, 58, 59; Bruner, 107, 108; Clark, 138; Cowen, 165, 168, 169; Levanway, 355; Marks, 385
109	34	Cantril, 121; Lazarsfeld, 349; Levine, 356; Morse, 415
109	37	Proshansky, 463
109	39	Bird, 84; Brown, 104; Evans, 214; Lindzey, 373; Slotkin, 532; Taylor, 564; Ugurel-Semin, 583
110	2	Hovland, 298
110	10	Allport, 21; Clark, 137; Frenkel-Brunswik, 235; Goodman, 261; Katz, 320; Kutner, 340; Murray, 421; Mussen, 424; Rokeach, 491; Sherman, 528
110	30	Maier, 380, 381, 382, 383
110	38	Allport, 21; Bills, 81; Frenkel-Brunswik, 237; Thistlethwaite, 571
111	4	Bills, 76
111	11	Barker, 49; Bills, 75; Cantril, 123; Child, 133; Cohen, 142; Gould, 264; Lewin, 367; Solomon, 550
111	24	Brown, 104; Chapman, 130; Child, 132
111	28	Jersild, 314
113	8	Diller, 191
113	19	Shaw, 516, 517
113	25	Allport, 14; Combs, 158; Sherif, 523, 524
115	11	Frenkel-Brunswik, 237
115	37	Rosenzweig, 496
117	30	Chowdhry, 136; Martin, 386; Sherif, 526
119	6	Crutchfield, 175
119	15	Coffin, 141
119	18	Jahoda, 307
119	34	Asch, 36; Bovard, 96; Cantril, 123; Centers, 128, 129; Thrasher, 574; Whyte, 603; Zorbaugh, 619
120	22	Ort, 432
121	11	Hartshorne, 279; Roethlisberger, 479; Sears, 509
121	23	Martin, 386

CHAPTER 7. The Development of the Phenomenal Self

Page	Line	
		Combs, 160; Frank, 229; Lecky, 350; Murphy, 419
122	21	Sullivan, 561
122	24	James, 308
123	4	Allport, 18; Ansbacher, 32; Freud, 238, 239, 240
123	16	Bertocci, 68; Combs, 160; Mead, 405; Norman, 427
123	31	Lecky, 350
124	30	Adler, 4; Balester, 47; Bertocci, 68; McQuitty, 404
125	22	Combs, 160
126	3	Blos, 89; Sullivan, 561
126	14	Friedman, 243; Hilgard, 287; Lecky, 350
126	16	Combs, 149; Mead, 405
127	20	Raimy, 467, 468
128	4	Ansbacher, 32; Combs, 149, 160
128	25	Sullivan, 561
129	23	Balester, 47; Hilgard, 287; McQuitty, 404; Raimy, 467; Taylor, 566
129	25	Lecky, 350
130	37	Anderson, 28; Balester, 47; Engel, 208; Farberow, 216; Neilon, 426; Raimy, 467
131	1	Lecky, 350
131	7	Blos, 89; Freeman, 233
131	16	Cowen, 166; Cruickshank, 174; Taylor, 565
131	26	Aidman, 7; Frenkel-Brunswik, 236

Page	Line	
131	38	Brownfain, 105
132	18	Davis, 182; Gerard, 252
132	22	James, 308
132	34	Carmichael, 125; Dewey, 188; Dockeray, 192; Haller, 271; Pratt, 457; Riesen, 475
133	10	Bruner, 100; Gesell, 254; Jersild, 313; Piaget, 440, 441
133	12	Ames, 26; Clark, 139; Gesell, 253; Shirley, 529
133	33	Aldrich, 8; Dewey, 188; Frank, 229; Hildreth, 285; Olson, 429
133	37	McGranahan, 401
134	12	Mussen, 425
134	22	Bice, 72; Diller, 191; Plant, 443
134	25	Kanner, 317
134	28	Sullivan, 561
134	34	Abernethy, 2; Havighurst, 282; Mead, 405
135	1	Aldrich, 8; Davis, 182; Jenkins, 311; Spock, 554
135	12	Baruch, 56; Driscoll, 196
136	23	Barker, 50; Kimball, 327; Piaget, 439, 440, 441; Ribble, 472, 473; Spitz, 553
136	27	Allport, 18; Bishop, 85; Bowlby, 99; Breckenridge, 100
136	33	Diller, 191; Skeels, 531
137	9	Dollard, 194; Keister, 324; Levy, 358, 359
137	34	Taylor, 564
138	5	Bice, 72
138	6	Snyder, 540
140	5	Kardiner, 318
140	24	Cantril, 122
140	34	Child, 132, 133
141	5	Davis, 180; Gould, 264; Horowitz, 295; Kardiner, 318; Kluckholn, 331; Lewis, 369; Linton, 376; Mead, 407; Murphy, 419; Sherif, 524; Warner, 588; Young, 612
141	23	Benedict, 63; Gordon, 262; Sherman, 528
141	35	Abernethy, 2; Butler, 116; Hollingshead, 293; Horowitz, 296; Lee, 351; Plant, 444
143	10	Axline, 42

CHAPTER 8. The Effect of Self on Perceiving

Page	Line	
		Combs, 150; Lecky, 350; Sullivan, 561
145	18	Murphy, 419 (p. 499)
145	37	Marks, 385
146	2	Bierl, 73
146	4	Huntley, 301
146	9	Werner, 598
146	39	Allport, 18; Bogardus, 91; Combs, 160; Cowen, 166; Mussen, 423, 424; Tagiuri, 563; Tolor, 575; Wispe, 607
147	4	Abernethy, 2; Adler, 5; Allport, 18; Combs, 150; Johnson, 316
150	8	Mussen, 425; Rosenstock, 495; Wispe, 607
150	21	Bertocci, 68; Bierl, 73; Bills, 75; Cowen, 167, 168; Postman, 448
150	27	Eriksen, 210, 212; Pearl, 435
150	36	Ames, 26; Anderson, 28; Bossard, 94
151	11	Sullivan, 56
151	18	Alexander, 11; Berger, 65; Chapman, 130; Cohen, 142; Dymond, 201; Fitts, 224; Sheever, 518; Stock, 560; Wieder, 604
151	25	Cruickshank, 174; Walsh, 586
151	27	Lecky, 350
152	2	Lecky, 350
152	25	Ames, 26; Axline, 40; Bixler, 86; Monroe, 412
153	20	Combs, 150; Epstein, 209; Schmidt, 503
153	22	Lecky, 350
153	27	Brownfain, 105; Butler, 116; Cantril, 122
153	36	Berger, 65; Combs, 154; Cruickshank, 174; Fitts, 224; Hinckley, 289; Hovland, 298
154	8	Barry, 52; Calvin, 117, Diller, 191
154	15	Balester, 47; Fitts, 224
154	35	Dymond, 201; Epstein, 209;

Page	Line	
		Goodman, 260; Torrance, 579
155	1	Cantril, 122; Centers, 129; Stagner, 555
155	11	Cohen, 142; Frenkel-Brunswik, 237; Friedenberg, 242
155	26	Adler, 5; Farberow, 216
157	11	Raimy, 467, 468
157	24	Hartley, 278
158	13	Friedenberg, 242; Rogers, 482
158	22	Aidman, 7
158	36	Chapman, 130
159	39	Hartley, 278; Hastings, 280

CHAPTER 9. The Availability of Perception in the Field

Page	Line	
166	10	Hogan, 291
166	39	Masserman, 391
168	35	Hastorf, 281
170	23	Bowlby, 99; Hogan, 291; Janis, 309; Walsh, 586
171	12	Hamilton, 275
171	14	Bettelheim, 69
171	20	Ausubel, 38; Beier, 58; Bruner, 108; Davis, 184; Diethelm, 190; Eichler, 204; Gaier, 250; Hastings, 280; Korchin, 336; Laffal, 342; Lantz, 344; Lanzetta, 345; Postman, 450, 451
171	38	Allport, 21; Barker, 49; Brown, 103; Cowen, 165, 167, 168, 169; Frenkel-Brunswik, 237; Janis, 309; Korchin, 336; McGinnies, 397; Roethlisberger, 478; Rokeach, 492; Smock, 538
172	14	Katz, 322; McKellar, 403; Postman, 448
172	32	Alexander, 11
172	37	Levanway, 355
173	2	Keister, 323
173	14	Cowen, 168, 169; Frenkel-Brunswik, 327; Keister, 323; Lazarus, 347; Rokeach, 492; Smock, 538
173	20	Adorno, 6; Brown, 103; Dorris, 195; Frenkel-Brunswik, 237
173	23	Bettelheim, 69; Buchenholtz, 112; Eriksen, 210; Murray, 421
174	17	Bowlby, 99; Krall, 337; McCarthy, 394
174	36	Rogers, 483
175	4	Crandall, 171; Keister, 323, 324
175	33	Combs, 161
175	37	Bettelheim, 69
177	18	Beier, 58; Freud, 241; Liddell, 370; Zander, 616
177	21	Tomkins, 576
177	34	Ausubel, 38; Lantz, 344
177	38	Beier, 59; Freud, 239; Gaier, 250
178	1	Pomeroy, 445
178	8	Rogers, 482; Thetford, 568
178	21	Diethelm, 190
178	33	Bruner, 109; Friedenberg, 242
178	35	Chodorkoff, 135
180	2	Toynbee, 580
180	16	Flanders, 225
180	19	Coch, 140
180	39	Lanzetta, 345
182	16	Mead, 406
183	29	Ausubel, 38
184	15	Bergman, 66
184	25	Murphy, 419
185	14	Lecky, 350
187	6	Eriksen, 210, 211; Tagiuri, 563
187	29	Belmont, 61
188	36	Adorno, 6

CHAPTER 10. Learning, Forgetting, and Problem Solving

Page	Line	
		Hilgard, 288; Snygg, 544
190	20	Adams, 3; Barnhart, 51; Brigden, 101; Snygg, 544
191	10	Adams, 3; Lashley, 346; Pavlov, 434

Page	Line	
191	24	Crafts, 170; Perrin, 436; Schneirla, 504, 505; Snygg, 542, 546, 547
193	3	Adams, 3
193	15	Snygg, 539
193	30	Snygg, 544
193	39	Torrance, 578
194	24	Bernhardt, 67; Geig, 251; Hilgard, 288; Levine, 356; Pavlov, 434; Snygg, 542
194	28	Brigden, 101; Hilgard, 288
195	4	Zander, 616
195	11	Ausubel, 38
195	21	Miller, 410
196	10	Hartshorne, 279; Jersild, 314; Levine, 356
196	14	Horrocks, 297; Lewin, 365; Peterson, 437
197	20	Gibson, 255; Koffka, 332, 333; Köhler, 334; Postman, 451; Snygg, 541
198	12	Bernhardt, 67; Brigden, 101
198	17	Bryan, 111
199	1	Gibson, 255
199	32	Dunlap, 198
200	30	Bartlett, 53
200	36	Burtt, 115
202	3	Snygg, 544
203	17	Levine, 356; Lewin, 365
203	38	Peterson, 437
204	10	Bartlett, 53; Cantril, 123
205	20	Burtt, 115; Davis, 179
205	30	Smith, 537
206	6	Bartlett, 53; Thistlethwaite, 571
207	14	Maier, 380, 381, 382
208	6	Brigden, 101
208	17	Pottle, 455
209	10	Sheldon, 519

CHAPTER 11. The Nature of Capacities, Emotion, and Feeling

Page	Line	
		Combs, 146
211	19	Jensen, 321; Poull, 456
212	16	Jastak, 310
212	22	Freeman, 233; Ribble, 473; Schmidt, 503
212	28	Axline, 39; Boas, 90; Diehl, 189; Dorris, 195; Geig, 251; Goldstein, 257; Goodenough, 259; Gould, 264; Smith, 536; Stevenson, 558; Wellman, 595, 596
214	3	Bexton, 71
214	11	Clark, 139; Sherman, 528
216	35	Banhan, 48; Boas, 90; Carlson, 124; Terman, 567
217	13	Child, 132
218	30	Jastak, 310
219	2	Asher, 37; Wechsler, 591
219	38	Goodenough, 258
220	24	Asher, 37; Sherman, 528; Wheeler, 601
220	36	McConnell, 396
221	11	Stewart, 559
221	23	Axline, 39; Boger, 92; Feingold, 218
222	3	Cruickshank, 174; Davis, 185
222	17	Axline, 39; Skeels, 531; Wellman, 596, 597
222	19	Freeman, 233
222	24	Gordon, 262; Skeels, 531
222	29	Keister, 323
223	37	Davis, 185
224	4	Franklin, 232; Poull, 456
224	18	Boger, 92; Davis, 180
224	19	Bexton, 71; Freeman, 233; Keister, 323; Schmidt, 503
224	25	Gould, 264; Lewin, 368; Wieder, 604; Williams, 605
224	28	Bowlby, 99; Child, 132
225	33	Axline, 39; Rogers, 488
226	4	Lange, 343; James, 308
226	10	Watson, 589, 590
226	19	Leeper, 352; Prescott, 459
227	1	Cannon, 119
227	7	Funkenstein, 247; Mittelman, 411; Selye, 512
227	20	Selye, 511, 513
227	39	Cannon, 119
228	4	Carlson, 124; Funkenstein, 247; Gaier, 250
228	32	Mittelman, 411
230	20	Banham, 48
234	15	Aidman, 7

CHAPTER 12. The Adequate Personality

Page	Line	
		Allport, 16; Combs, 150; Maslow, 388, 389; Rogers, 481, 484
237	28	Combs, 150
238	10	Adorno, 6
238	22	Allport, 16
238	35	Axline, 41; Combs, 150; Goldstein, 257; Lecky, 350; Maslow, 389; Murphy, 419; Rogers, 481, 487; Sullivan, 561
239	7	Allport, 16
239	15	Maslow, 388, 389
239	37	Combs, 150; Rogers, 487
240	9	Balester, 47
240	23	Brownfain, 105
241	10	Rogers, 482, 488; Sheerer, 518; Sullivan, 561; Vargas, 585
241	37	Barry, 52; Bass, 57; Bell, 60; Bills, 74; Eriksen, 212; McQuitty, 404; Phillips, 438
242	12	Bills, 75; Hastings, 280; Mussen, 424
242	27	Benjamins, 64; Cohen, 142; Friedenberg, 242
242	32	Balester, 47; Combs, 150; Hanlon, 276; Kates, 319; Taylor, 564
243	2	Rogers, 482
243	27	Kates, 319
243	29	Friedenberg, 242; Goodman, 260
244	3	Chodorkoff, 136; Gage, 248
244	13	Berger, 65; Haigh, 268
244	15	Eriksen, 212
244	18	Maslow, 388, 389
244	30	Taylor, 564
245	18	Berger, 65; Haigh, 268; Hartley, 278; McIntyre, 402; Omwake, 431; Rogers, 481, 488; Sheerer, 518; Tagiuri, 563
245	27	Fey, 220
245	31	Barry, 52
246	11	Allport, 16
247	16	Bell, 60
247	30	Alexander, 11; Fromm, 244; Goodman, 260
248	20	McIntyre, 402; Phillips, 438
249	4	Bird, 83
249	30	Conrad, 162
249	32	Elkin, 205
250	39	Benjamins, 64; Eriksen, 212; Greer, 265; Hastings, 220; Kates, 319; Scodel, 508
251	2	Maslow, 388, 389
251	18	Friedenberg, 242; Norman, 427
251	32	Bills, 75; Brownfain, 105; Child, 132; Chodorkoff, 134, 135; Cohen, 142; Small, 534
252	6	Frenkel-Brunswik, 235; O'Connor, 428; Pearl, 435; Smock, 538
252	20	Kates, 319
252	31	Allport, 16; Rogers, 484
252	35	Gage, 248
253	6	Bass, 57
253	38	Maslow, 388, 389
254	29	Bass, 57; Rogers, 481
254	37	Cohen, 142
255	20	Maslow, 389
255	28	Maslow, 388, 389
256	28	O'Connor, 428; Stock, 560
256	36	Bell, 60; Bills, 74; Dymond, 202; Fromm, 244; Lindgren, 372
256	37	Norman, 427
257	2	Berger, 65
257	29	Bills, 74
257	36	Alexander, 11; Brownfain, 105
258	14	McIntyre, 402
259	3	Bills, 74; Stock, 560
259	13	Combs, 150; Greer, 265
260	24	Davidoff, 178; Sheerer, 518
261	19	Fey, 220; Fromm, 245; Kates, 319
262	10	Child, 132, 133
263	22	Dubois, 197
263	27	Axline, 41; Dymond, 199

CHAPTER 13. The Inadequate Personality: The Dynamics of Failure

Page	Line	
		Adorno, 6; Combs, 150; Sullivan, 561
267	4	Bowlby, 99; Calvin, 117; Combs, 150; Conrad, 162; Cowen, 166; Raymaker, 470
267	10	Barry, 52; Keister, 324; Walsh, 586
267	18	Dorris, 195; Friedenberg, 242; Friedman, 243; Kimball, 327; McGinnies, 399
267	24	Cruickshank, 174
267	27	Balester, 47
267	35	Maslow, 390
268	2	Bowlby, 99; Katz, 322
268	6	Chodorkoff, 135; Cowen, 168
268	16	Bills, 75; Child, 132; Hastings, 280; Hoffman, 290; Pullen, 466; Reeves, 471
268	28	Adorno, 6; Brown, 103; Cowen, 167, 168; Frenkel-Brunswik, 237
268	29	Taylor, 564
268	31	Benjamins, 64; Lazarus, 347
268	34	Bills, 80; Bixler, 86; Cohen, 142; Smock, 538
269	2	Bowlby, 99; Buchenholtz, 112; Crandall, 171
269	33	Calvin, 117
269	36	Adorno, 6; Cowen, 165, 167
269	39	Alexander, 11; Morse, 415; Warner, 588
269	27	Crandall, 171; Dymond, 199; Sullivan, 561
270	34	Calvin, 117; Rogers, 487
270	38	Fey, 220; Haigh, 268; Rogers, 488; Sheerer, 518
271	14	Hogan, 291
272	6	Berger, 65
272	30	Combs, 161; Dorris, 195
273	1	Adorno, 6; Bettelheim, 69
273	21	Eriksen, 210; Keister, 323
274	17	Combs, 161; Epstein, 209; Eriksen, 211; Keister, 324
274	22	Katz, 322
274	38	Crandall, 171
275	15	Murray, 422
276	6	Rosenstock, 495
276	11	Belmont, 61
276	18	Wechsler, 592
277	2	Cohen, 142
278	6	Banham, 48; Chodorkoff, 135
278	25	Child, 132; Murray, 421
278	28	Combs, 161
278	36	Adorno, 6
278	39	Frenkel-Brunswik, 236; Goodman, 260
279	1	Friedenberg, 242
279	19	Banham, 48
282	7	Buchenholtz, 112; Chodorkoff, 135; Epstein, 209; Lazarus, 347
282	20	Cowen, 169; Frenkel-Brunswik, 237
282	21	Hoffman, 290
282	23	Barker, 49
284	39	Buchenholtz, 112
285	5	Beier, 58; Bettelheim, 69; Chodorkoff, 123; Friedman, 243
285	31	Dollard, 194
286	18	Alexander, 9; Ausubel, 38
288	32	Freud, 239, 241; Horney, 294
288	34	Maslow, 390
290	29	Shaffer, 515
290	39	Krasnogorski, 338; Liddell, 370; Maier, 384; Pavlov, 434
291	33	Horney, 294
292	3	Pomeroy, 445
292	14	Freud, 239
292	22	Bettelheim, 69
293	7	Maslow, 390; McGinnies, 399
294	13	McGinnies, 399; Plant, 444
294	23	Epstein, 209; Maslow, 390
296	28	Friedman, 243
297	26	Thigpen, 570
298	15	Murphy, 419
298	29	Murphy, 419; Prince, 461
299	8	Prince, 462

CHAPTER 14. Some General Implications for Human Relations

Page	Line	
307	34	Gibson, 255
312	2	Adorno, 6
312	24	Allport, 16; Hoffman, 290
312	35	Asch, 34; Coch, 140; Gordon, 263; Johnson, 315
313	2	Bills, 78; Corey, 163; Katz, 321; Lewin, 365
313	33	Anderson, 30; Bell, 60; Chowdhry, 136; Coch, 140; Hollander, 292; Maas, 378
314	7	Allport, 16; Combs, 157; Corey, 163; Lippitt, 377
314	18	Lewin, 368
314	34	Rogers, 489
316	1	Allport, 16
317	19	Johnson, 315
318	24	Fiedler, 221, 222
318	37	Rogers, 485
320	2	Roethlisberger, 479
321	2	Fromm, 245

CHAPTER 15. The Individual and His Society

Page	Line	
		Sherif, 526; Snygg, 545
325	17	Burkholder, 114
326	35	Combs, 152
327	20	Smith, 534
327	26	Edwards, 203
327	34	Bovard, 97, 98; Centers, 128; Grossack, 266; Horowitz, 295; Precker, 458; Sherif, 523
328	4	Sherif, 525, 526
328	8	Centers, 129; Sherif, 521
328	21	Shaw, 516; Trasher, 574; Zorbaugh, 620
328	38	Bettelheim, 69
329	6	Centers, 129; Shaw, 518; Sherif, 522, 528
329	30	Ambriere, 23
329	38	Centers, 129; Goodman, 261; Hartley, 277
330	6	Toynbee, 581
330	16	Festinger, 219
330	28	Buchenholtz, 112
330	36	Combs, 152
331	12	Centers, 128
331	33	Allport, 21; Bierl, 73; Bogardus, 91; Centers, 128; Crutchfield, 175; Davis, 179; Flowerman, 228; Hovland, 298; Jahoda, 307; Precker, 458; Sherif, 522, 523
332	8	Bovard, 96, 98; Hartley, 277
332	12	Chapman, 130; Hallowell, 272
332	24	Asch, 35, 36; Bettelheim, 69; Centers, 128; Lazarsfeld, 349
332	33	Allport, 21; Marks, 385
333	4	Bogardus, 91; Davis, 181; Warner, 588
333	23	Linton, 374, 375, 376
333	38	Linton, 374
334	12	Coch, 140; Marks, 385
334	31	Davis, 181; Horowitz, 296
334	37	Adorno, 6; Hartley, 277; Lazarsfeld, 349
335	13	Snygg, 546
335	22	Bovard, 97; Chowdhry, 136
336	31	Sherif, 525
337	31	Snygg, 545
338	24	Kutner, 340; Mussen, 424
338	35	Davidoff, 178; Davis, 181
338	38	Sherif, 525
339	2	Bovard, 97; Coch, 140; Davis, 179; Snygg, 545; Thibaut, 569; Whyte, 603
339	18	Dashiell, 177
339	24	Kutner, 340
340	11	Lewin, 367
340	30	Linton, 376
342	8	Combs, 148

CHAPTER 16. How People Can Help Themselves

Page	Line	
349	11	Allport, 16; Rogers, 481
353	3	Diller, 191
353	11	Maslow, 388, 389
359	25	Allport, 16
361	18	Combs, 160

Chapter 17. The Goals and Purposes of Education

Page	Line	
		Kelley, 325
368	5	Bills, 81
369	11	Rivers, 476
369	20	Kelley, 325
369	36	Williams, 605
370	1	Olson, 430
370	6	Lifton, 371
370	26	Torrance, 578
372	9	Katz, 321
372	26	Asch, 34
372	37	Jersild, 314
373	22	Hildreth, 286
375	10	Lecky, 350
377	25	Benjamins, 64
377	33	Bovard, 95
378	18	Anderson, 30
378	24	Bills, 76
378	27	Bovard, 98; Coch, 140
378	33	Keister, 323
379	1	McCarthy, 394
379	30	Amatora, 22; Corey, 163
379	34	Howard, 299
380	12	Boger, 92
380	25	Bills, 76
381	10	Combs, 157
381	15	Tentative Social Studies Program, 566

Chapter 18. The Teaching Relationship

Page	Line	
383	11	Combs, 152; Kelley, 325; Moustakas, 417
385	15	Combs, 153; Gaier, 250; Torrance, 578
386	13	Janis, 309
388	12	Asch, 34; Bills, 77; Fiedler, 221; Gordon, 263; Schwebel, 507
388	19	Bills, 81; Bovard, 97; Thompson, 572
389	6	McCarthy, 394
389	14	Bills, 77; Combs, 158; Johnson, 315
390	2	Diller, 191
390	8	Faw, 217; Fiedler, 221; Johnson, 315
390	15	Asch, 34; Gordon, 263; Lippitt, 377
390	28	Alexander, 11; Amatora, 22; Anderson, 30; Bixler, 86
390	32	McCarthy, 394
391	12	Walsh, 586
391	18	Potter, 454
392	7	Lippitt, 377
393	30	Bovard, 95
395	25	Asch, 34; Axline, 40; Bills, 77, 78; Bixler, 86; Faw, 217; Fiedler, 221, 222; Monroe, 412; Roseborough, 494; Sheldon, 519
396	31	Coch, 140
397	39	Zimet, 617
398	10	Gordon, 263; Johnson, 315
398	15	Blocksma, 88
399	19	Anderson, 30; Blocksma, 88; Gage, 249; Preston, 460
402	19	Lepage, 353
402	39	Preston, 460
403	18	Corey, 163; Gage, 249
403	24	Combs, 158
406	21	Alexander, 11; Amatora, 22; Flanders, 225
406	35	Corey, 163
407	38	Wispe, 606, 607

Chapter 19. The Personal Approach to Treatment

Page	Line	
		Combs, 145, 151; Rogers, 482
414	5	Pugh, 465
414	34	Rotter, 497
415	19	Fiedler, 221, 222
417	34	Alexander, 10; Allen, 12; Freud, 238, 239, 240; Horney, 294; Rogers, 482, 485; Sullivan, 561
418	4	Brown, 102; Butler, 116; Combs, 143, 153; Haigh, 268; Porter, 447; Seeman, 510; Sheerer, 518; Snyder, 539, 540; Stock, 560
418	27	Horrocks, 297

Page	Line	
421	19	Rogers, 487
423	17	Rogers, 487
424	35	Combs, 150
426	8	Aidman, 7; Combs, 143, 151, 153; Howard, 299
426	26	Allen, 12; Amster, 27; Axline, 40, 41; Bills, 79; Moustakas, 416, 417
427	38	Snyder, 540
428	6	Pullen, 466; Rogers, 485
428	21	Pomeroy, 445
428	32	Haigh, 268
429	7	Mittelmann, 411
430	34	Butler, 116; Combs, 153; Rogers, 480, 486; Sheerer, 518
432	25	Bergman, 66
435	26	Hartley, 278; Pearl, 435; Rogers, 488; Stock, 560; Vargas, 585
437	11	Sheldon, 519
437	23	Combs, 156; Combs, 159; Conrad, 162; Fleming, 226; Hainowitz, 270; Hartley, 278; Pearl, 435; Thetford, 568

CHAPTER 20. The Exploration of Meaning

Page	Line	
		Allport, 20; Combs, 160
439	37	Bakan, 45
440	2	Bakan, 45; Boring, 93
440	14	Bills, 80, 82; Brownfain, 105; Calvin, 117; Creelman, 172; Taylor, 565
441	23	Abernethy, 2
442	22	Chodorkoff, 135
443	12	Sorokin, 552
445	20	Combs, 149
445	38	Allport, 20
448	29	Friedman, 243
450	21	Allport, 14, 15
450	33	Soper, 551
451	26	Cunningham, 176; Elkin, 205
453	33	Stephenson, 557
453	38	Allport, 20
454	24	Allport, 20; Grover, 267
455	9	Combs, 155
455	24	Allport, 20
456	28	Tolor, 575; Wells, 597
457	1	Arnold, 33
457	10	Dollard, 193
457	36	Lewin, 368
458	2	Barker, 49
458	12	Allport, 20; Barnhart, 51
458	23	Dymond, 200
458	38	Anderson, 29; Frank, 231
459	5	Bugental, 113; Elkin, 205
459	10	Combs, 147, 154, 155; Elkisch, 206; Masserman, 391
459	23	Stern, 556
459	25	Monroe, 412; Morgan, 414; Murray, 422; Symonds, 562
459	39	Rorschach, 493
460	3	Combs, 147, 154; Murray, 422; Symonds, 562
460	15	Zimet, 617, 618
460	17	Rohde, 490
460	26	Combs, 157; Zimet, 617
460	36	Moreno, 413
461	8	Axline, 41, 42; Despert, 187; Moustakas, 416; Pintler, 442
461	17	Amster, 27; Bach, 43; Bakay, 46; Baruch, 55; Bender, 62
462	22	Cronbach, 173; Rapaport, 469; Tomkins, 577
462	28	Combs, 159; Porter, 446, 447
463	2	Rogers, 487
463	10	Axline, 41; Baruch, 55; Frank, 231; Gaier, 250
463	29	Covner, 164; Rogers, 488

Bibliography

1. Abel, T. M. Free design of limited scope as a personality index. *Charact. & Pers.*, 1938, *7:* 50-62.
2. Abernethy, Ethel. The effect of sorority pressures on the results of a self-inventory. *J. Soc. Psychol.*, 1954, *40:* 177-183.
3. Adams, D. K. A restatement of the problem of learning. *Brit J. Psychol.*, 1931, *22:* 150-178.
4. Adler, A. Notes regarding the dynamics of the self. *Brit. J. Med. Psychol.*, 1951, *24:* 97-106.
5. Adler, A. *Understanding human nature.* New York: Greenberg, 1927.
6. Adorno, W. *The authoritarian personality.* New York: Harper, 1950.
7. Aidman, T. Changes in self perception as related to changes in perception of one's environment. *Amer. Psychologist,* 1948, *3:* 286.
8. Aldrich, C. A., and Aldrich, Mary M. *Babies are human beings.* New York: Macmillan, 1938.
9. Alexander, F. *Psychosomatic medicine.* New York: Norton, 1950.
10. Alexander, F., French, T. M., and others. *Psychoanalytic therapy: Principles and application.* New York: Ronald Press, 1946.
11. Alexander, T. Certain characteristics of the self as related to affection. *Child Develop.*, 1951, *22:* 285-290.
12. Allen, F. *Psychotherapy with children.* New York: Norton, 1942.
13. Allison, H. W., and Allison, Sarah G. Personality changes following transorbital lobotomy. *J. Abnorm. Soc. Psychol.*, 1954, *49:* 219-223.
14. Allport, F. H. Teleonomic description in the study of personality. *Charact. & Pers.*, 1937, *5:* 202-214.
15. Allport, F. *Theories of perception and the concept of structure.* New York: Wiley, 1955.
16. Allport, G. W. *Becoming.* New Haven: Yale Univ. Press, 1955.
17. Allport, G. W. *Personality.* New York: Holt, 1937.
18. Allport, G. W. The ego in contemporary psychology. *Psychol. Rev.*, 1943, *50:* 451-478.
19. Allport, G. W. The psychologist's frame of reference. *Psychol. Bull.*, 1940, *37:* 1-28.
20. Allport, G. W. The use of personal documents in psychological science. *Soc. Sci. Res. Coun. Bull.*, 1942.
21. Allport, G. W., and Postman, L. *The psychology of rumor.* New York: Henry Holt, 1947.
22. Amatora, S. A. Similarity in teacher and pupil personality. *J. Psychol.*, 1954, *37:* 45-51.
23. Ambriere, Francis. *The long holiday.* Chicago: Ziff-Davis, 1948.
24. Ames, A. *An interpretative manual: The nature of our perceptions, prehensions and behavior.* Princeton: Princeton Univ. Press, 1955.
25. Ames, A. Visual Perception and the rotating trapezoidal window. *Psychol. Monogr.*, 1951, 65-67.

26. Ames, Louise B. The sense of self of nursery school children as manifested by their verbal behavior. *J. Genet. Psychol.*, 1952, *81:* 193-232.
27. Amster, F. Differential use of play in treatment of young children. *Amer. J. Orthopsychiat.*, 1943, *13:* 62-69.
28. Anderson, Camilla M. The self-image: A theory of dynamics of behavior. *Ment. Hyg.*, 1952, *36:* 227-244.
29. Anderson, H. H., and Anderson, Gladys L. *An introduction to projective techniques.* New York: Prentice-Hall, 1951.
30. Anderson, H. H., and Brewer, J. Studies of teachers' classroom personalities, I. Dominative and socially integrative behavior of kindergarten teachers. *Appl. Psychol. Monogr.*, 1945, No. 6, 157.
31. Angyal, A. *Foundations for a science of personality.* New York: Commonwealth Fund, 1941.
32. Ansbacher, H. L., and Ansbacher, Rowena (eds.). *The individual psychology of Alfred Adler.* New York: Basic Books, 1956.
33. Arnold, D. L., and Mooney, R. L. A student's problem check list for junior high school. *Educ. Res. Bull.*, 1943, *22:* 42-48.
34. Asch, M. J. Nondirective teaching in psychology: An experimental study. *Psychol. Monogr.*, 1951, *65* (4).
35. Asch, S. E. Effects of group pressure upon the modification and distortion of judgments. In G. E. Swanson, T. M. Newcomb, and E. L. Hartley (eds.), *Readings in social psychology.* (2nd ed.) New York: Holt, 1952.
36. Asch, S. E. *Social psychology.* New York: Prentice-Hall, 1952.
37. Asher, E. J. The inadequacy of current intelligence tests for testing Kentucky mountain children. *J. Genet. Psychol.*, 1935, *46:* 480-486.
38. Ausubel, D. P., Schiff, H. M., and Goldman, M. Qualitative characteristics in the learning process associated with anxiety. *J. Abnorm. Soc. Psychol.*, 1953, *48:* 537-547.
39. Axline, Virginia M. Mental deficiency–Symptom or disease? *J. Consult. Psychol.*, 1949, *13:* 313-327.
40. Axline, Virginia M. Nondirective therapy for poor readers. *J. Consult. Psychol.*, 1947, *11:* 61-69.
41. Axline, Virginia M. *Play therapy.* Boston: Houghton Mifflin, 1947.
42. Axline, Virginia M. Play therapy experiences as described by child participants. *J. Consult. Psychol.*, 1950, *14:* 53-63.
43. Bach, G. R. Young children's play fantasies. *Psychol. Monogr.*, 1945, 59, No. 2.
44. Bagby, J. A cross cultural study of perceptual predominance in binocular rivalry. 1956 (to be published).
45. Bakan, D. A reconsideration of the problem of introspection. *Psychol. Bull.*, 1954, *51:* 105-118.
46. Bakay, Eva., and Shiller, P. H. Manipulative correction of visually presented figures. *Amer. J. sychol.*, 1948, *61:* 487-501.
47. Balester, R. J. The self concept and juvenile delinquency. Unpublished doctor's dissertation, Vanderbilt Univ., 1956.

48. Banham, Katharine M. Senescence and the emotions: A genetic study. *J. Genet. Psychol.*, 1951, *78:* 175-183.
49. Barker, R., Dembo, T., and Lewin, K. (Studies in topological and vector psychology: II.) Frustration and regression: An experiment with young children. *Univ. Iowa Stud. Child Welf.*, 1941, *18,* No. 1.
50. Barker, R. G., Kounin, J. S., and Wright, H. F. (eds.). *Child behavior and development; a course of representative studies.* New York: McGraw-Hill, 1943.
51. Barnhart, E. N. Stages in the construction of children's drawings as revealed through a recording device. *Psychol. Bull.*, 1940, *37:* 581.
52. Barry, J. R. The relation of verbal reactions to adjustment level. *J. Abnorm. Soc. Psychol.*, 1950, *45:* 647-658.
53. Bartlett, F. C. *Remembering: a study in experimental and social psychology.* Cambridge, Mass.: University Press, 1932.
54. Bartley, S. H. *Principles of perception.* New York: Harpers, 1958.
55. Baruch, Dorothy W. Aggression during doll play in a preschool. *Amer. J. Orthopsychiat.*, 1941, *11:* 252-260.
56. Baruch, Dorothy W. *New ways in discipline: You and your child today.* New York: Whittlesey House, 1949.
57. Bass, B. M., McGehee, C. R., Hawkins, W. C., Young, P. C., and Gebel, A. S. Personality variables related to leaderless group discussion behavior. *J. Abnorm. Soc. Psychol.*, 1953, *48:* 120-128.
58. Beier, E. G. The effect of induced anxiety on the flexibility of intellectual functioning. *Psychol. Monogr.*, 1951, *65,* No. 9.
59. Beier, E. G. The effects of Rohrschach interpretation on intellectual functioning of adjusted, questionably adjusted and maladjusted subjects. *J. Proj. Tech.*, 1953, *17:* 66-69.
60. Bell, G. B., and Hall, H. E., Jr. The relationship between leadership and empathy. *J. Abnorm. Soc. Psychol.*, 1954, *49:* 156-157.
61. Belmont, Lillian, and Birch, H. G. Re-individualizing the repression hypothesis. *J. Abnorm. Soc. Psychol.*, 1951, *46:* 226-235.
62. Bender, L. Art and therapy in the mental disturbances of children. *J. Nerv. Ment. Dis.*, 1937, *86:* 249-263.
63. Benedict, Ruth. *Patterns of culture.* New York: Houghton Mifflin, 1934.
64. Benjamins, J. Changes in performance in relation to influences upon self-conceptualization. *J. Abnorm. Soc. Psychol.*, 1950, *45:* 473-480.
65. Berger, E. M. The relation between expressed acceptance of self and expressed acceptance of others. *J. Abnorm. Soc. Psychol.*, 1952, *47:* 778-782.
66. Bergman, D. V. Counseling method and client responses. *J. Consult. Psychol.*, 1951, *15:* 216-224.
67. Bernhardt, K., and Snygg, D. The effect of cues upon the choice of the shorter path. *J. Comp. Psychol.*, 1937, *24:* 269-276.
68. Bertocci, P. A. The psychological self, the ego, and personality. *Psychol. Rev.*, 1945, *52:* 91-99.

69. Bettelheim, B. Individual and mass behavior in extreme situations. *J. Abnorm. Soc. Psychol.*, 1943, *38:* 417-452.
70. Bevan, W. Perception: Evaluation of a concept. *Psychol. Rev.*, 1958, *55:* 34-55.
71. Bexton, W. H., Heron, W., and Scott, T. H. Effects of decreased variation in the sensory environment. *Canad. J. Psychol.*, 1954, *8:* 70-76.
72. Bice, H. Factors in self concept of child with cerebral palsy. *Ment. Hyg., N. Y.*, 1954, *38:* 120-131.
73. Bierl, J. Changes in interpersonal perceptions following social interaction. *J. Abnorm. Soc. Psychol.*, 1953, *48:* 61-66.
74. Bills, R. E. Attributes of successful educational leaders. In R. L. Hopper (ed.), Interdisciplinary research in educational administration. *Bull. Bureau Sch. Serv.* Lexington, Kentucky: Coll. Educ., Univ. Kentucky, 1953, 16-38.
75. Bills, R. E. A comparison of scores on the index of adjustment and values with behavior in level-of-aspiration tasks. *J. Consult. Psychol.*, 1953, *17:* 206-212.
76. Bills, R. E. The effect of a value on learning. *J. Pers.*, 1952, *21:* 217-222.
77. Bills, R. E. An investigation of student centered teaching. *J. Educ. Res.*, 1952, *46:* 313-319.
78. Bills, R. E. Personality changes during student centered teaching. *J. Educ. Res.*, 1956, *50:* 121-126.
79. Bills, R. E. Play therapy with well adjusted retarded readers. *J. Consult. Psychol.*, 1950, *14:* 246-249.
80. Bills, R. E. Self concepts and Rorschach signs of depression. *J. Consult. Psychol.*, 1954, *18:* 135-137.
81. Bills, R. E., and McGehee, C. R. The effect of attitude toward psychology in a learning experiment. *J. Pers.*, 1955, *23:* 499-500.
82. Bills, R. E., Vance, E. L., and McLean, O. S. An index of adjustment and values. *J. Consult. Psychol.*, 1951, *15:* 257-261.
83. Bird, C. *Social psychology.* New York: Appleton-Century, 1940.
84. Bird, C., and Monachesi, E. D. Prejudice and discontent. *J. Abnorm. Soc. Psychol.*, 1954, *49:* 29-35.
85. Bishop, Barbara M. Mother-child interaction and the social behavior of children. *Psychol. Monogr.*, 1951, *65,* No. 11 (Whole No. 328).
86. Bixler, R. H. Treatment of a reading problem through nondirective play therapy. *J. Consult. Psychol.*, 1945, *9:* 105-118.
87. Blake, R. R., and Ramsey, G. V. *Perception: An approach to personality.* New York: Ronald Press, 1951.
88. Blocksma, D. D. Leader flexibility in group guidance situations. *Educ. Psychol. Measmt.*, 1949, *9:* 531-535.
89. Blos, P. The adolescent personality. New York: Appleton-Century, 1941.
90. Boas, F. The relation between physical and mental development. *Science*, 1941, *93:* 339-342.
91. Bogardus, E. S. Changes in racial distances. *Int. J. Opin. Attitude Res.*, 1947, *1* (4): 55-62.

92. Boger, J. H. An experimental study of the effects of perceptual training on group I. Q. test scores of elementary pupils in rural ungraded schools. *J. Educ. Res.*, 1952, *46:* 43-52.
93. Boring, E. G. A history of introspection. *Psychol. Bull.*, 1953, *50:* 169-189.
94. Bossard, J. H. S. *The sociology of child development.* New York: Harper, 1948.
95. Bovard, E. W., Jr. Clinical insight as a function of group process. *J. Abnorm. Soc. Psychol.*, 1952, *47:* 534-539.
96. Bovard, E. W., Jr. Conformity to social norms in stable and temporary groups. *Science*, 1953, *117:* 361-363.
97. Bovard, E. W., Jr. The experimental production of interpersonal affect. *J. Abnorm. Soc. Psychol.*, 1951, *46:* 521-528.
98. Bovard, E. W., Jr. Group structure and perception. *J. Abnorm. Soc. Psychol.*, 1951, *46:* 398-405.
99. Bowlby, J. *Child care and the growth of love.* London: Penguin Books, 1953.
100. Breckenridge, Marian E., and Vincent, E. L. *Child development: Physical and psychological growth through the school years.* Philadelphia: Saunders, 1943.
101. Brigden, R. L. Tachistoscopic study of the differentiation of perception. *Psychol. Monogr.*, 1933, *44:* 163-166.
102. Bown, O. An investigation of the therapeutic relationship in client-centered psychotherapy. Unpublished doctoral dissertation, Univ. of Chicago, 1954.
103. Brown, R. W. A determinant of the relationship between rigidity and authoritarianism. *J. Abnorm. Soc. Psychol.*, 1953, *48:* 469-476.
104. Brown, R. W., and Lenneberg, E. H. A study in language and cognition. *J. Abnorm. Soc. Psychol.*, 1954, *49:* 454-462.
105. Brownfain, J. J. Stability of the self-concept as a dimension of personality. *J. Abnorm. Soc. Psychol.*, 1952, *47:* 597-606.
106. Bruner, J. S., and Goodman, C. C. Value and need as organizing factors in perception. *J. Abnorm. Soc. Psychol.*, 1947, *42:* 33-44.
107. Bruner, J. S., and Krech, D. *Personal and social factors in perception.* Durham, N. C.: Duke Univ. Press, 1950.
108. Bruner, J. S., and Postman, L. Emotional selectivity in perception and reaction. *J. Pers.*, 1947, *16:* 69-77.
109. Bruner, J. S., and Postman, L. On the perception of incongruity: A paradigm. *J. Pers.*, 1949, *18:* 206-223.
110. Bruner, J. S., and Postman, L. The symbolic value as an organizing factor in perception. *J. Soc. Psychol.*, 1948, *27:* 203-208.
111. Bryan, W. L., and Harter, N. Studies on the telegraphic language. *Psychol. Rev.*, 1899, *6:* 346-375.
112. Buchenholtz, B., and Frank, R. J. The concepts of the self in acute traumatic neurosis of war. *J. Nerv. Ment. Dis.*, 1948, *107:* 55-61.
113. Bugental, J. F. T., and Zelen, S. L. Investigations into the 'self-concept.' I. The W-A-Y technique. *J. Pers.*, 1950, *18:* 483-498.

114. Burkholder, P. R. Cooperation and conflict among primitive organisms. *Amer. Scientist*, 1952, *10:* 601-631.
115. Burtt, H. E. An experimental study of early childhood memory: Final report. *J. Genet. Psychol.*, 1941, *58:* 435-439.
116. Butler, J. M. The interaction of client and therapist. *J. Abnorm. Psychol.*, 1952, *47:* 366-378.
117. Calvin, A. D., and Holtzman, W. H. Adjustment and the discrepancy between self concept and inferred self. *J. Consult. Psychol.*, 1953, *17:* 39-44.
118. Cannon, W. B. *The way of an investigator: A scientist's experiences in medical research.* New York: Norton, 1945.
119. Cannon, W. B. *The wisdom of the body.* New York: Norton, 1932.
120. Cantril, H. An inquiry concerning the characteristics of man. *J. Abnorm. Soc. Psychol.*, 1950, *45:* 490-503.
121. Cantril, H. The nature of social perception. *Trans. N. Y. Acad. Sci.*, 1948, *10:* 143-153.
122. Cantril, H. Perception and interpersonal relations. *Amer. J. Psychiat.*, 1957, *114:* 119-126.
123. Cantril, H. The prediction of social events. *J. Abnorm. Soc. Psychol.*, 1938, *33:* 364-389.
124. Carlson, A. J., and Johnson, V. *The machinery of the body.* (4th ed.) Chicago: Univ. of Chicago Press, 1953.
125. Carmichael, L. (ed.) *Manual of child psychology.* New York: Wiley, 1946.
126. Carmichael, L., Hogen, H. P., and Walter, A. A. An experimental study of the effect of language on the reproduction of visually perceived form. *J. Exper. Psychol.*, 1932, *15:* 73-86.
127. Carter, L. F., and Schooler, K. Value, need, and other factors in perception. *Psychol. Rev.*, 1949, *56:* 200-207.
128. Centers, R. The American class structure: A psychological analysis. In G. E. Swanson, T. M. Newcomb, and E. L. Hartley (eds.), *Readings in social psychology.* (Rev. ed.) New York: Holt, 1952.
129. Centers, R. Nominal variation and class identification: The working and laboring classes. *J. Abnorm. Soc. Psychol.*, 1950, *45:* 195-215.
130. Chapman, D. W., and Volkmann, J. A social determinant of the level of aspiration. *J. Abnorm. Soc. Psychol.*, 1939, *34:* 225-238.
131. Chein, I. The logic of prediction: Some observations on Dr. Sarbin's exposition. *Psychol. Rev.*, 1945, *52:* 175-179.
132. Child, I. L., and Whiting, J. W. M. Determinants of level of aspiration: Evidence from everyday life. *J. Abnorm. Soc. Psychol.*, 1949, *44:* 303-314.
133. Child, I. L., and Whiting, J. W. M. Effects of goal attainment: Relaxation versus renewed striving. *J. Abnorm. Soc. Psychol.*, 1950, *45:* 667-681.
134. Chodorkoff, B. Adjustment and the discrepancy between the perceived and the ideal self. *J. Clin. Psychol.*, 1954, *10:* 266-268.
135. Chodorkoff, B. Self-perception, perceptual defense, and adjustment. *J. Abnorm. Soc. Psychol.*, 1954, *49:* 508-512.
136. Chowdhry, Kamla, and Newcomb, T. M. The relative abilities of leaders

and non-leaders to estimate opinions of their own groups. *J. Abnorm. Soc. Psychol.*, 1952, *47:* 51-57.

137. Clark, K. B., and Clark, Mamie P. Racial identification and preference in Negro children. In G. E. Swanson, T. M. Newcomb, and E. L. Hartley (eds.), *Readings in social psychology.* (Rev. ed.) New York: Henry Holt, 1952, 551-560.
138. Clark, K. B., and Clark, M. P. Skin color as a factor in racial identification of Negro preschool children, *J. Soc. Psychol.* 1940, *11:* 159-169.
139. Clark, R. S., Heron, W., Fetherstonhaugh, M. L., Forgays, D. G., and Hebb, D. O. Individual differences in dogs: Preliminary report on the effects of early experience. *Canad. J. Psychol.*, 1951, *5:* 150-156.
140. Coch, L., and French, J. R. P., Jr. Overcoming resistance to change. *Hum. Relat.*, 1948, *1:* 512-532.
141. Coffin, T. E. Some conditions of suggestion and suggestibility: A study of some attitudinal and situational factors influencing the process of suggestion. *Psychol. Monogr.*, 1941, 53, No. 4.
142. Cohen, L. D. Level-of-aspiration behavior and feelings of adequacy and self-acceptance. *J. Abnorm. Soc. Psychol.*, 1954, *49:* 84-86.
143. Combs, A. W. Basic aspects of non-directive therapy. *Amer. J. Orthopsychiat.*, 1946, *16:* 589-607.
144. Combs, A. W. A comparative study of motivations as revealed in thematic apperception stories and autobiography. *J. Clin. Psychol.*, 1947, *3:* 65-75.
145. Combs, A. W. Counseling as a learning process. *J. of Counsel. Psychol.*, 1954, *1:* 31-36.
146. Combs, A. W. Intelligence from a perceptual point of view. *J. Abnorm. Soc. Psychol.*, 1952, *47:* 662-673.
147. Combs, A. W. A method of analysis for the Thematic Apperception Test and Autobiography. *J. Clin. Psychol.*, 1945, *2:* 167-174.
148. Combs, A. W. The myth of competition. *Childh. Educ.*, 1957, *33:* 264-269.
149. Combs, A. W. New horizons in field research: The self concept. *Ed. Leadership.*, 1958, *15:* 315-319.
150. Combs, A. W. A phenomenological approach to adjustment theory. *J. Abnorm. Soc. Psychol.*, 1949, *44:* 29-35.
151. Combs, A. W. Phenomenological concepts in non-directive therapy. *J. Consult. Psychol.*, 1948, *12:* 197-208.
152. Combs, A. W. The psychology of the college student. *In What Should Higher Education Be Doing in 1954?* Hempstead, N. Y.: Hofstra College, 1954, 31-35.
153. Combs, A. W. Some dynamic aspects of non-directive therapy. *Ann. N. Y. Acad. Sci.*, 1948, *49:* 878-888.
154. Combs, A. W. The use of personal experience in Thematic Apperception Test story plots. *J. Clin. Psychol.*, 1946, *2:* 357-363.
155. Combs, A. W. The validity and reliability of interpretation from autobiography and Thematic Apperception Test. *J. Clin. Psychol.*, 1946, *2:* 240-247.
156. Combs, A. W., and Cowen, W. L. Follow-up study of 32 cases treated

by nondirective psychotherapy. *J. Abnorm. Soc. Psychol.,* 1950, *45:* 232-258.

157. Combs, A. W., and Fisk, R. S. Problems and research needs in administration. *J. Soc. Issues,* 1954, *10:* 49-58.
158. Combs, A. W., Fisk, R. S., Fine, H. F., Zimet, C. N., Wiberley, J. A., and Nesbitt, D. A. The Syracuse studies. *J. Soc. Issues,* 1954, *10:* 5-24.
159. Combs, A. W., and Snygg, D. Implications of the phenomenological approach for the evaluation of psychotherapy. *Psych. Serv. Center J.,* 1950, *2:* 96-103.
160. Combs, A. W., and Soper, D. W. The self, its derivate terms and research. *J. Indiv. Psychol.,* 1957, *13:* 134-145.
161. Combs, A. W., and Taylor, C. The effect of perception of mild degrees of threat on performance. *J. Abnorm. Soc. Psychol.,* 1952, *47:* 420-424.
162. Conrad, Dorothy. An empirical study of the concept of psychotherapeutic success. *J. Consult. Psychol.,* 1952, *16:* 92-97.
163. Corey, S. M. *Action research to improve school practices.* New York: Bureau of Publications, Teachers College, Columbia Univ., 1953, 47-61.
164. Covner, B. J. Studies in phonographic recordings of verbal material: I. The use of phonographic recordings in counseling practice and research. *J. Consult. Psychol.,* 1942, *6:* 105-113.
165. Cowen, E. L. The influence of varying degrees of psychological stress on problem-solving rigidity. *J. Abnorm. Soc. Psychol.,* 1952, *47:* 512-519.
166. Cowen, E. L. The negative self concept as a personality measure. *J. Consult. Psychol.,* 1954, *18:* 138-142.
167. Cowen, E. L. Stress reduction and problem-solving rigidity. *J. Consult. Psychol.,* 1952, *16:* 425-428.
168. Cowen, E., and Beier, E. The influence of "threat expectancy" on perception. *J. Pers.,* 1950, *19:* 85-94.
169. Cowen, E. L., and Thompson, G. G. Problem solving rigidity and personality structure. *J. Abnorm. Soc. Psychol.,* 1951, *46:* 165-176.
170. Crafts, L. W., Schneirla, T. C., Robinson, E. E., and Gilbert, R. W. *Recent experiments in psychology.* New York: McGraw-Hill, 1938.
171. Crandall, V. J. Induced frustration and punishment-reward expectancy in thematic apperception stories. *J. Consult. Psychol.,* 1951, *15:* 400-404.
172. Creelman, Marjorie. Accuracy of the concept of self as a criterion in differential diagnosis. *Persona.,* 1949, *1* (2): 21-25.
173. Cronbach, L. J. *Essentials of psychological testing.* New York: Harper, 1949.
174. Cruickshank, W. M. Qualitative analysis of intelligence test responses. *J. Clin. Psychol.,* 1947, *3:* 381-386.
175. Crutchfield, R. S. Conformity and character. *Amer. Psychologist,* 1955, *10:* 191-198.
176. Cunningham, Ruth, and others. *Group behavior of boys and girls.* New York: Bureau of Publications, Teachers College, Columbia Univ., 1951.
177. Dashiell, J. *Fundamentals of general psychology.* Boston: Houghton Mifflin, 1937.

178. Davidoff, M. A study of empathy and correlations of prejudice toward a minority group. *Purdue Univ. Stud. Higher Educ.*, 1949, No. 67.
179. Davis, A. *Social class influences upon learning*. Cambridge, Mass.: Harvard Univ. Press, 1948.
180. Davis, A., and Dollard, J. *Children of bondage: The personality development of Negro youth in the urban South.* Washington, D. C.: American Council on Education, 1940.
181. Davis, A., Gardner, B. B., and Gardner, Mary. *Deep South.* Chicago: Univ. of Chicago Press, 1941.
182. Davis, A., and Havighurst, R. J. *Father of the man: How your child gets his personality.* Boston: Houghton Mifflin, 1947.
183. Davis, Clara. Self selection of diets: An experiment with infants. *The Trained Nurse and Hospital Review.*, 1931, *86:* 629-634.
184. Davis, D. R. Increase in strength of a secondary drive as a cause of disorganization. *Quart. J. Exp. Psychol.*, 1948, *1:* 22-28.
185. Davis, K. Final note on a case of extreme isolation. *Amer. J. Sociol.*, 1947, *52:* 432-437.
186. Dempsey, E. W. *Homeostasis.* In S. S. Stephens (ed.), *Handbook of experimental psychology.* New York: Wiley, 1951.
187. Despert, J. A method for the study of personality reactions in pre-school age children by means of analysis of their play. *J. Psychol.*, 1940, *9:* 17-29.
188. Dewey, E. *Behavior development of infants.* New York: Columbia Univ. Press, 1935.
189. Diehl, H. The ritual of science. *J. Psychol.*, 1941, *12:* 13-19.
190. Diethelm, O., and Jones, M. Influence of anxiety on attention, learning, retention and thinking. *Arch. Neurol. Psychiat.*, 1947, *58:* 325-336.
191. Diller, L. Conscious and unconscious self-attitudes after success and failure. *J. Pers.*, 1954, *23:* 1-12.
192. Dockeray, F. C., and Rice, G. Responses of newborn infants to pain stimulation. *Ohio State Univ. Stud.*, 1934, *12:* 82-93.
193. Dollard, J. *Criteria for the life history.* New Haven: Yale Univ. Press, 1935.
194. Dollard, J. *Frustration and Aggression.* New Haven: Yale Univ. Press, 1939.
195. Dorris, R. J., Levinson, D. J., and Hanfmann, Eugenia. Authoritarian personality studies by a new variation of the sentence completion technique. *J. Abnorm. Psychol.*, 1954, *49:* 99-108.
196. Driscoll, Gertrude. *How to study the behavior of children.* New York: Bureau of Publications, Teachers College, Columbia Univ., 1941, *8:* 1-84.
197. Dubois, Rachael-Davis. *Get together Americans.* New York: Harper, 1943.
198. Dunlap, K. *Habits: Their making and unmaking.* New York: Liveright, 1932.
199. Dymond, Rosalind. Personality and empathy. *J. Consult. Psychol.*, 1950, *14:* 343-350.
200. Dymond, Rosalind. A scale for the measure of empathic ability. *J. Consult. Psychol.*, 1949, *13:* 127-133.
201. Dymond, Rosalind. The relation of accuracy of perception of the spouse and marital happiness. *Amer. Psychol.*, 1953, *8:* 344.

202. Dymond, Rosalind, Hughes, Anne, and Raabe, Virginia. Measurable changes in empathy with age. *J. Consult. Psychol.*, 1952, *16:* 202-206.
203. Edwards, W. The theory of decision making. *Psychol. Bull.*, 1954, *51:* 380-417.
204. Eichler, R. Experimental stress and alleged Rorschach indices of anxiety. *J. Abnorm. Soc. Psychol.*, 1951, *46:* 344-355.
205 Elkin, F. Specialists interpret the case of Harold Holzer. *J. Abnorm. Soc. Psychol.*, 1947, *42:* 99-111.
206. Elkisch, P. Children's drawings in a projective technique. *Psychol. Monog.*, 1945, *58*, No. 1.
207. Engel, E. The role of content in binocular resolution. *Amer. J. Psychol.*, 1956, *69:* 87-91.
208. Engel, Mary. *The stability of the self concept in adolescence.* Unpublished doctoral dissertation, Peabody College, 1956.
209. Epstein, S. Unconscious self-evaluation in a normal and schizophrenic group. *J. Abnorm. Soc. Psychol.*, 1955, *50:* 65-70.
210. Eriksen, C. Defense against ego threat in memory and perception. *J. Abnorm. Soc. Psychol.*, 1952, *47:* 230-235.
211. Eriksen, C. Perceptual defense as a function of unacceptable needs. *J. Abnorm. Soc. Psychol.*, 1951, *46:* 557-564.
212. Eriksen, C. Psychological defenses and "ego strength" in the recall of completed and incompleted tasks. *J. Abnorm. Soc. Psychol.*, 1954, *49:* 45-50.
213. Eriksen, C., and Lazarus, R. Perceptual defense and projective tests. *J. Abnorm. Soc. Psychol.*, 1952, *47:* 302-308.
214. Evans, R. Personal values as factors in anti-Semitism. *J. Abnorm. Soc. Psychol.*, 1952, *47:* 749-756.
215. Evvard, J. Is the appetite of swine a reliable indication of physiological needs? *Proc. Iowa Acad. Sci.*, 1916, *22:* 375-411.
216. Farberow, N. L., and Sarbin, T. R. A clinical study of role and self in hypnotic age regression. *Amer. Psychologist*, 1950, *5:* 305.
217. Faw, V. A psychotherapeutic method of teaching psychology. *Amer. Psychologist*, 1949, *4:* 104-109.
218. Feingold, G. Q. Intelligence of the first generation of immigrant groups. *J. Educ. Psychol.*, 1924, *15:* 65-83.
219. Festinger, L., Pepitone, A., and Newcomb, T. Some consequences of de-individuation in a group. *J. Abnorm. Soc. Psychol.*, 1952, *47:* 382-389.
220. Fey, W. F. Acceptance by others and its relation to acceptance of self and others: A revaluation. *J. Abnorm. Soc. Psychol.*, 1955, *50:* 274-276.
221. Fiedler, F. E. A comparison of therapeutic relationships in psychoanalytic, nondirective and Adlerian therapy. *J. Consult. Psychol.*, 1950, *14:* 436-445.
222. Fiedler, F. E. The concept of an ideal therapeutic relationship. *J. Consult. Psychol.*, 1950, *14:* 239-245.
223. Fischer, R. P. Schilder's mind: Perception and thought and goals and desires of man. *Psychol. Bull.*, 1944, *41:* 30-40.

224. Fitts, W. H. *The role of the self-concept in social perception.* Unpublished doctoral dissertation, Vanderbilt Univ., 1954.
225. Flanders, N. A. Personal-social anxiety as a factor in experimental learning situations. *J. Educ. Res.*, 1951, *45:* 100-110.
226. Fleming, Louise, and Snyder, W. U. Social and personal changes following non-directive group play therapy. *Amer. J. Orthopsychiat.*, 1947, *17:* 101-116.
227. Fletcher, J. M. Homeostasis as an explanatory principle in psychology. *Psychol. Rev.*, 1942, *49:* 80-87.
228. Flowerman, S. H. The use of propaganda to reduce prejudice: A refutation. *Int. J. Opin. Attitude Res.*, 1949, *3:* 99-108.
229. Frank, L. K. The fundamental needs of the child. *Mental Hyg.*, 1938, *22:* 353-379.
230. Frank, L. K. *Projective methods.* Springfield, Ill.: C. C. Thomas, 1948.
231. Frank, L. K. Projective methods for the study of personality. *J. Psychol.*, 1939, *8:* 389-413.
232. Franklin, J. C., Schiele, B. C., Brozek, J., and Keys, A. Observations of human behavior in experimental semi-starvation and rehabilitation. *J. Clin. Psychol.*, 1948, *4:* 28-45.
233. Freeman, F. N., Holzinger, K. J., and Mitchell, B. C. The influence of environment on the intelligence, school achievement and conduct of foster children. *Yearb. Nat. Soc. Stud. Educ.*, 1928, *27:* Part I, 102-217.
234. Freeman, G. L. *The energetics of human behavior.* Ithaca, N. Y.: Cornell Univ. Press, 1948.
235. Frenkel-Brunswik, Else. Distortion of reality in perception and social outlook. *Amer. Psychologist*, 1949, *4:* 253.
236. Frenkel-Brunswik, Else. Mechanisms of self-deception. *J. Soc. Psychol.*, 1939, *10:* 409-420.
237. Frenkel-Brunswik, Else. A study of prejudice in children. *Hum. Relat.*, 1948, *1:* 295-306.
238. Freud, A. *Introduction to technic of child analysis.* Washington: Nervous and Mental Disease Pub. Co., 1928.
239. Freud, S. *A general introduction to psychoanalysis.* Garden City, N.Y.: Garden City Publishing Co., 1920.
240. Freud, S. *An outline of psychoanalysis.* New York: Norton, 1949.
241. Freud, S. *The problem of anxiety.* New York: Norton, 1936.
242. Friedenberg, E. Z., and Roth, J. A. *Self-perception in the university: A study of successful and unsuccessful graduate students.* Chicago: Univ. of Chicago Press, 1954.
243. Friedman, I. Phenomenal, ideal, and projected conceptions of self. *J. Abnorm. Soc. Psychol.*, 1955, *51:* 611-615.
244. Fromm, E. *The art of loving.* New York: Harper, 1956.
245. Fromm, E. *Psychoanalysis and religion.* New Haven: Yale Univ. Press, 1950.
246. Frymier, J. R. The relationship of certain behavioral characteristics to perception. Unpublished doctoral dissertation, Univ. of Florida, 1957.

247. Funkenstein, D. H. The physiology of fear and anger. *Sci. Amer.*, 1955, *192* (5): 74-80.
248. Gage, N. L. Accuracy of social perception and effectiveness in interpersonal relationships. *J. Personality,* 1953, *22:* 128-141.
249. Gage, N. L. Explorations in the understanding of others. *Educ. Psychol. Measmt.*, 1953, *13:* 14-26.
250. Gaier, E. L. Selected personality variables and the learning process. *Psychol. Monogr.*, 1952, *66,* No. 17 (whole No. 349).
251. Geig, A. C. Learning disability in intelligent children. *Med. Ann. Dist. Columbia, 6,* No. 9.
252. Gerard, R. W. *Unresting Cells.* New York: Harper, 1949.
253. Gesell, A., Ilg, F. L., Ames, L. B., and Bullis, G. E. *The child from five to ten.* New York: Harper, 1946.
254. Gesell, A., Thompson, H., and Amatruda, C. S. *The psychology of early growth.* New York: Macmillan, 1938.
255. Gibson, J. J., and Crooks, L. E. A. A theoretical field-analysis of automobile driving. *Amer. J. Psychol.*, 1938, *51:* 453-471.
256. Gilchrist, J. C., Ludeman, J. F., and Lysak, W. Values as determinants of word-recognition thresholds. *J. Abnorm. Soc. Psychol.*, 1954, *49:* 423-426.
257. Goldstein, K. *The organism.* New York: American Book Co., 1939.
258. Goodenough, Florence. *The measurement of intelligence by drawings.* Yonkers-on-Hudson, N. Y.: World Book, 1926.
259. Goodenough, Florence. Racial differences in the intelligence of school children. *J. Exp. Psychol.,* 1926, *9:* 388-397.
260. Goodman, H. Self-insight, empathy and perceptual distortion: A study of the relationships between measures of self-insight, empathy, and perceptual distortion as obtained from ratings made by individuals on themselves and others in their group. *Dissertation Abstr.*, 1953, *13:* 120.
261. Goodman, Mary E. *Race awareness in young children.* Cambridge, Mass.: Addison-Wesley Press, 1952.
262. Gordon, H. Mental and scholastic tests among retarded children. London: Bureau of Education, Educational Pamphlet No. 44, 1923.
263. Gordon, T. *Group-centered leadership: A way of releasing the creative power of groups.* Boston: Houghton Mifflin, 1955.
264. Gould, R. J. Some sociological determinants of goal striving. *J. Soc. Psychol.*, 1941, *13:* 461-473.
265. Greer, F. L., Galanter, E. H., and Nordie, P. G. Interpersonal knowledge and individual and group effectiveness. *J. Abnorm. Soc. Psychol.* 1954, *49:* 411-414.
266. Grossack, M. M. Some effects of cooperation and competition upon small group behavior. *J. Abnorm. Soc. Psychol.*, 1954, *49:* 341-348.
267. Grover, K. B. The use of English compositions to gain understandings of pupils. *Sch. Rev.*, 1946, *54:* 605-610.
268. Haigh, G. Defensive behavior in client-centered therapy. *J. Consult. Psychol.*, 1949, *13:* 181-189.

269. Haigh, G., and Fiske, D. W. Corroboration of personal values as selective factors in perception. *J. Abnorm. Soc. Psychol.*, 1952, *47:* 394-398.
270. Haimowitz, Natalie R., and Haimowitz, M. L. Personality changes in client-centered therapy. In W. Wolff and J. A. Precker (eds.), *Success in psychotherapy*. New York: Grune & Stratton, 1952, 63-93.
271. Haller, M. W. The reaction of infants to changes in raw intensity and pitch of pure tone. *J. Genet. Psychol.*, 1932, *40:* 162-180.
272. Hallowell, A. I. Cultural factors in the structuralization of perception. In J. H. Rohrer and M. Sherif (eds.), *Social psychology at the crossroads*. New York: Harper, 1951.
273. Halpern, H. M. Empathy, similarity and self-satisfaction. *J. Consult. Psychol.*, 1955, *19:* 449-452.
274. Halpin, A. W. James Clerk Maxwell on the dynamical and the statistical modes of thought about man. *J. Abnorm. Soc. Psychol.*, 1951, *46:* 257.
275. Hamilton, G. V. A study of perseverance reactions in primates and rodents. *Behav. Monogr.*, 1916, *3:* No. 13.
276. Hanlon, T. E., Hopstaetter, P. R., and Connor, J. P. Congruence of self and ideal self in relation to personality adjustment. *J. Consult. Psychol.*, 1954, *18:* 215-218.
277. Hartley, E. L. *Problems in prejudice*. New York: King's Crown Press, 1946.
278. Hartley, Margaret. Changes in the self-concept during psychotherapy. Unpublished doctoral dissertation, Univ. of Chicago, 1951.
279. Hartshorne, H., and May, M. A. *Studies in the nature of character*. I. Studies in Deceit. Book 1: General methods and results. Book 2: Statistical methods and results. New York: Macmillan, 1928.
280. Hastings, P. K. A relationship between visual perception and level of personal security. *J. Abnorm. Soc. Psychol.*, 1952, *47:* 552-560.
281. Hastorf, A. H., and Cantril, H. They saw a game: A case study. *J. Abnorm. Soc. Psychol.*, 1954, *49:* 129-134.
282. Havighurst, R. J., Robinson, Myra Z., and Dorr, Mildred. The development of the ideal self in childhood and adolescence. *J. Educ. Res.*, 1946, *40:* 241-257.
283. Hebb, D. O. *The organization of behavior: A neuropsychological theory*. New York: Wiley, 1949.
284. Henry, J., and Henry, Z. Doll play of Pilaga Indian children: An experimental and field analysis of the behavior of the Pilaga Indian children. *Res. Monogr. Amer. Orthopsychiat. Ass.*, 1944, 4.
285. Hildreth, G. *The child mind in evolution: A study of developmental sequences in drawing*. New York: King's Crown Press, 1941.
286. Hildreth, G. *Learning the three r's*. Philadelphia Educ. Pubs., 1936.
287. Hilgard, E. R. Human motives and the concept of self. *Amer. Psychologist*, 1949, *4:* 374-382.
288. Hilgard, E. R. *Theories of learning*. New York: Appleton-Century-Crofts, 1948.
289. Hinckley, E. D., and Rethlingshafer, Dorothy A. Value judgments of heights of men by college students. *J. Psychol.*, 1951, *31:* 257-262.

290. Hoffman, M. L. Some psychodynamic factors in compulsive conformity. *J. Abnorm. Soc. Psychol.*, 1953, *48:* 383-393.
291. Hogan, R. A. A theory of threat and defense. *J. Consult. Psychol.*, 1952, *16:* 417-424.
292. Hollander, E. P. Authoritarianism and leadership choice in a military setting. *J. Abnorm. Soc. Psychol.*, 1954, *49:* 365-370.
293. Hollingshead, A. B. *Elmtown's youth.* New York: J. Wiley, 1949.
294. Horney, Karen. *The neurotic personality of our time.* New York: W. W. Norton, 1937.
295. Horowitz, E. L. The development of attitude toward the negro. *Arch. Psychol.*, 1936, No. 194.
296. Horowitz, E. L. Some aspects of the development of patriotism in children. *Sociometry*, 1940, *3:* 329-341.
297. Horrocks, J. E. The relationship between knowledge of human development and ability to use such knowledge. *J. Appl. Psychol.*, 1946, *20:* 501-508.
298. Hovland, C. I., and Sherif, M. Judgmental phenomena and scales of attitude measurement: Item displacement in Thurstone scales. *J. Abnorm. Soc. Psychol.*, 1952, *47:* 822-832.
299. Howard, A. R., and Kelly, G. A. A theoretical approach to psychological movement. *J. Abnorm. Soc. Psychol.*, 1954, *49:* 399-404.
300. Hull, C. L. *Hypnosis and suggestibility.* New York: Appleton-Century, 1931.
301. Huntley, C. W. Judgments of self based upon records of expressive behavior. *J. Abnorm. Soc. Psychol.*, 1940, *35:* 398-427.
302. Husserl, E. *Ideas: General introduction to pure phenomenology.* London: Unwin, 1952.
303. Husserl, E. *Logische untersuchungen.* Halle, Germany: Niemeyer, 1921.
304. Immergluck, Ludwig. The role of set in perceptual judgment. *J. Psychol.*, 1952, *34:* 181-189.
305. Ittelson, W. H. *The Ames demonstrations in perception.* Princeton: Princeton Univ. Press, 1952.
306. Ittelson, W. H. The constancies in perceptual theory. *Psychol. Rev.*, 1951, *58:* 285-294.
307. Jahoda, G. Political attitudes and judgments of other people. *J. Abnorm. Soc. Psychol.*, 1954, *49:* 330-334.
308. James, W. *The principles of psychology.* New York: Henry Holt, 1890.
309. Janis, I. L., and Feshbach, S. Effects of fear-arousing communications. *J. Abnorm. Soc. Psychol.*, 1953, *48:* 78-92.
310. Jastak, J. A rigorous criterion of feeble-mindedness. *J. Abnorm. Soc. Psychol.*, 1949, *44:* 367-378.
311. Jenkins, Gladys G., Shacter, Helen, and Bauer, W. W. *These are your children: How they develop and how to guide them.* Chicago: Scott, Foresman, 1949.
312. Jensen, M. B. Mental deterioration following carbon monoxide poisoning. *J. Abnorm. Soc. Psychol.*, 1950, *45:* 146-153.

313. Jersild, A. T. *Child psychology.* New York: Prentice-Hall, 1954.
314. Jersild, A. T., and Tasch, Ruth. *Children's interests and what they suggest for education.* New York: Bureau of Publications, Teachers College, Columbia Univ., 1949.
315. Johnson, D. M., and Smith, H. C. Democratic leadership in the college classroom. *Psychol. Monogr.,* 1953, *67* (No. 361).
316. Johnson, T. F. Conceptions of parents held by adolescents. *J. Abnorm. Soc. Psychol.,* 1952, *47:* 783-789.
317. Kanner, Leo. *Child psychiatry.* (3rd ed.) Springfield, Ill.: Thomas, 1957.
318. Kardiner, A. *The individual and his society.* New York: Columbia Univ. Press, 1939.
319. Kates, S. L. Subjects' evaluations of annoying situations after being described as well adjusted and poorly adjusted. *J. Consult. Psychol.,* 1952, *16:* 429-434.
320. Katz, D., and Braley, K. Racial sterotypes of one hundred college students. *J. Abnorm. Soc. Psychol.,* 1933, *28:* 280-290.
321. Katz, D., Maccoby, N., and Morse, Nancy C. *Productivity, supervision, and morale in an office situation.* Part I. Ann Arbor: Institute for Social Research, Univ. of Michigan, 1950.
322. Katz, I. Emotional expression in failure: A new hypothesis. *J. Abnorm. Soc. Psychol.,* 1950, *45:* 329-349.
323. Keister, M. E. The behavior of young children in failure. *Univ. Iowa Stud. Child Welf.,* 1938, *14:* 27-82.
324. Keister, M. E., and Updegraff, R. A study of children's reactions to failure and an experimental attempt to modify them. *Child Develop.,* 1937, *8:* 241-248.
325. Kelley, E. C. *Education for what is real.* New York: Harper, 1947.
326. Kilpatrick, W. H., and Van Til, W. *Intercultural attitudes in the making; parents, youth leaders, and teachers at work.* New York: Harper, 1947.
327. Kimball, Barbara. The sentence-completion technique in a study of scholastic underachievement. *J. Consult. Psychol.,* 1952, *16:* 353-358.
328. Kinsey, A. C., Pomeroy, W. B., and Martin, C. E. *Sexual behavior in the human male.* Philadelphia: Saunders, 1948.
329. Klein, G. S. The personal world through perception. In R. R. Blake, and G. V. Ramsey, *Perception.* New York: Ronald Press, 1951, 328-355.
330. Klein, G. S., Schlesinger, H. J., and Meister, D. E. The effect of personal values on perception: An experimental critique. *Psychol. Rev.,* 1951, *58:* 96-112.
331. Kluckhohn, C., and Leighton, D. *The Navaho.* Cambridge: Harvard Univ. Press, 1946.
332. Koffka, K. Perception: An introduction to the gestalt-theorie. *Psychol. Bull.,* 1922, *19:* 531-585.
333. Koffka, K. *Principles of Gestalt psychology.* New York: Harcourt, Brace, 1935.
334. Köhler, W. *Dynamics in psychology.* New York: Liveright, 1940.

335. Köhler, W. Psychological remarks on some questions of anthropology. *Amer. J. Psychol.*, 1937, *50:* 271-288.
336. Korchin, S. J., and Basowitz, H. Perceptual adequacy in a life stress. *J. Psychol.*, 1954, *38:* 495-502.
337. Krall, Vita. Personality characteristics of accident repeating children. *J. Abnorm. Soc. Psychol.*, 1953, *48:* 99-107.
338. Krasnogorski, N. I. The conditioned reflex and children's neuroses. *Amer. J. of Diseases of Child.*, 1925, *30:* 753-768.
339. Krech, D. The challenge and the promise. *J. Soc. Issues,* 1946, *2:* 34-46.
340. Kutner, B., Wilkens, Carol, and Yarrow, Penny. Verbal attitudes and overt behavior involving racial prejudice. *J. Abnorm. Soc. Psychol.*, 1952, *47:* 649-652.
341. Landsman, T. Four phenomenologies. *J. Ind. Psychol.*, 1958, *14:* 29-37.
342. Laffal, J. The learning and retention of words with association disturbances. *J. Abnorm. Soc. Psychol.*, 1952, *47:* 454-462.
343. Lange, C. G., and James, W. *The emotions.* Baltimore: Williams & Wilkins, 1922.
344. Lantz, Beatrice. Some dynamic aspects of success and failure. *Psychol. Monogr.*, 1945, *59:* No. 1.
345. Lanzetta, J. T., Haefner, D., Langham, P., and Axelrod, H. Some effects of situational threat on group behavior. *J. Abnorm. Soc. Psychol.*, 1954, *49:* 445-453.
346. Lashley, K. S. Nervous mechanisms in learning. In C. Murchison (ed.), *A handbook of general experimental psychology.* Worcester, Mass.: Clark Univ. Press, 1934, 456-496.
347. Lazarus, R. S., and Longo, N. The consistency of psychological defenses against threat. *J. Abnorm. Soc. Psychol.*, 1953, *48:* 495-499.
348. Lazarus, R. S., and McCleary, R. A. Autonomic discrimination with awareness: A study of subception. *Psychol. Rev.*, 1951, *58:* 113-122.
349. Lazarsfeld, P. F., Berelson, B., and Gaudet, H. *The people's choice.* New York: Duell, Sloan & Pearce, 1944.
350. Lecky, P. *Self-consistency: A theory of personality.* New York: Island Press, 1945.
351. Lee, Dorothy. Notes on the conception of the self among the Wintu Indians. *J. Abnorm. Soc. Psychol.*, 1950, *45:* 538-543.
352. Leeper, R. A study of a neglected portion of the field of learning—The development of sensory organization. *J. Genet. Psychol.*, 1935, *46:* 41-75.
353. LePage, W. R., and Lett, R. P. A study of teaching methods in engineering. *J. Eng. Educ.*, 1954, *44:* 317-324.
354. Leuba, C., and Lucas, C. The effects of attitudes on descriptions of pictures. *J. Exp. Psychol.*, 1945, *35:* 517-524.
355. Levanway, R. W. The effect of stress on expressed attitude toward self and others. *J. Abnorm. Soc. Psychol.*, 1955, *50:* 225-226.
356. Levine, J. M., and Murphy, G. The learning and forgetting of controversial material. *J. Abnorm. Soc. Psychol.*, 1943, *38:* 507-517.
357. Levine, R., Chein, I., and Murphy, G. The relation of the intensity of

the need to the amount of perceptual distortion: A preliminary report. *J. Psychol.*, 1942, *13:* 283-293.

358. Levy, D. M. *Maternal over-protection.* New York: Columbia Univ. Press, 1943.
359. Levy, D. M. Studies in sibling rivalry. *Res. Monogr. Amer. Orthopsychiat. Ass.*, 1937, No. 2.
360. Levy, L. H. Sexual symbolism: A validity study. *J. Consult. Psychol.*, 1954, *18:* 43-46.
361. Lewin, K. The conflict between Aristotelian and Galilean modes of thought in contemporary psychology. *J. Genet. Psychol.*, 1931, *5:* 141-177.
362. Lewin, K. Defining the "field at a given time." *Psychol. Rev.*, 1943, *50:* 292-310.
363. Lewin, K. *A dynamic theory of personality.* New York: McGraw-Hill, 1935.
364. Lewin, K. *Field theory in social science.* (Ed. by D. Cartwright.) New York: Harper, 1951.
365. Lewin, K. Group decision and social change. In G. E. Swanson, T. M. Newcomb, and E. L. Hartley (eds.), *Readings in social psychology.* (2nd ed.) New York: Henry Holt, 1952, 459-473.
366. Lewin, K. *Principles of topological science.* New York: McGraw-Hill, 1936.
367. Lewin, K., Dembo, T., Festinger, L., and Sears, P. S. Level of aspiration. In J. McV. Hunt (ed.), *Personality and the behavior disorders.* New York: Ronald Press, 1944.
368. Lewin, K., Lippitt, R., and White, R. K. Patterns of aggressive behavior in experimentally created "social climates." *J. Soc. Psychol.*, 1939, *10:* 271-299.
369. Lewis, Claudia. Children of the Cumberland. New York: Columbia Univ. Press, 1946.
370. Liddell, H. S. Conditioned reflex method and experimental neurosis. In J. McV. Hunt (ed.), *Personality and the behavior disorders.* New York: Ronald Press, 1944.
371. Lifton, W. M. A study of the changes in self concept and content knowledge in students taking a course in counseling techniques. *Microfilm Abstr.*, 1951, *11* (1): 55-56.
372. Lindgren, H. C., and Robinson, Jacqueline. An evaluation of Dymond's Test of Insight and Empathy. *J. Consult. Psychol.*, 1953, *17:* 172-176.
373. Lindzey, G., and Rogalsky, S. Prejudice and identification of minority group membership. *J. Abnorm. Soc. Psychol.*, 1950, *45:* 37-53.
374. Linton, R. (ed.) *Acculturation in seven American Indian tribes.* New York: Appleton-Century, 1940.
375. Linton, R. *The cultural background of personality.* New York: Appleton-Century, 1945.
376. Linton, R., Fisher, Mary, and Ryan, W. *Culture and personality.* Washington, D. C.: American Council on Education, 1941.
377. Lippitt, R., and White, R. K. An experimental study of leadership and group life. In G. E. Swanson, T. M. Newcomb, and E. L. Hartley (eds.), *Readings in social psychology.* (Rev. ed.) New York: Henry Holt, 1952.

378. Maas, H. S. Personal and group factors in leaders' social perception. *J. Abnorm. Soc. Psychol.*, 1950, *45:* 54-63.
379. MacLeod, R. B. The phenomenological approach to social psychology. *Psychol. Rev.*, 1947, *54:* 193-210.
380. Maier, N. R. F. Reasoning and learning. *Psychol. Rev.*, 1931, *38:* 332-346.
381. Maier, N. R. F. Reasoning in children. *J. Comp. Psychol.*, 1936, *21:* 357-366.
382. Maier, N. R. F. Reasoning in humans, I. *J. Comp. Psychol.*, 1930, *10:* 115-143.
383. Maier, N. R. F. Reasoning in humans, II. The solution of a problem and its appearance in consciousness. *J. Comp. Psychol.*, 1931, *12:* 181-194.
384. Maier, N. R. F. *Studies of abnormal behavior in the rat.* New York: Harper, 1939.
385. Marks, E. S. Skin color judgments of Negro college students. *J. Abnorm. Psychol.*, 1943, *38:* 370-376.
386. Martin, W. E., Gross, N., and Darley, J. G. Studies of group behavior: leaders, followers, and isolates in small organized groups. *J. Abnorm. Soc. Psychol.*, 1952, *47:* 838-842.
387. Maslow, A. H. Dynamics of personality organization. *Psychol. Rev.*, 1943, *50:* 514-539.
388. Maslow, A. H. *Motivation and personality.* New York: Harper, 1954.
389. Maslow, A. H. Self-actualizing people: A study of psychological health. *Personality,* 1950, Symposium No. 1, 11-34.
390. Maslow, A. H., and Mittleman, B. *Principles of abnormal psychology.* New York: Harper, 1941.
391. Masserman, J. H., and Balken, E. R. The clinical application of phantasy studies. *J. Psychol.*, 1938, *6:* 81-88.
392. Mausner, B., and Siegel, A. The effect of variation in "value" on perceptual thresholds. *J. Abnorm. Soc. Psychol.*, 1950, *45:* 760-763.
393. Mayo, E. *The human problems of an industrial civilization.* Boston: Harvard Univ. Graduate School of Business Administration, 1946.
394. McCarthy, Dorothea. Personality and learning. *Amer. Coun. Educ. Stud.*, 1949, *13* (35): 93-96.
395. McClelland, D. C., and Atkinson, J. W. The projective expression of needs: I. The effect of different intensities of the hunger drive on perception. *J. Psychol.*, 1948, *25:* 205-222.
396. McConnell, J. Abstract behavior among the Tepehuan. *J. Abnorm. Soc. Psychol.*, 1954, *49:* 109-110.
397. McGinnies, E. Emotionality and perceptual defense. *Psychol. Rev.*, 1949, *56:* 244-251.
398. McGinnies, E. Personal values as determinants of word association. *J. Abnorm. Soc. Psychol.*, 1950, *45:* 28-36.
399. McGinnies, E., and Adornetto, J. Perceptual defense in normal and schizophrenic observers. *J. Abnorm. Soc. Psychol.*, 1952, *47:* 833-837.
400. McGinnies, E., and Bowles, W. Personal values as determinants of perceptual fixation. *J. Personality,* 1949, *18:* 224-235.

401. McGranahan, D. V. The psychology of language, *Psychol. Bull.*, 1936, *33:* 178-216.
402. McIntyre, C. J. Acceptance by others and its relation to acceptance of self and others. *J. Abnorm. Soc. Psychol.*, 1952, *47:* 624-625.
403. McKellar, P. Provocation to anger and the development of attitudes of hostility. *Brit. J. Psychol.*, 1950, *40:* 104-114.
404. McQuitty, L. L. A measure of personality integration in relation to the concept of self. *J. Personality*, 1950, *18:* 461-482.
405. Mead, G. H. *Mind, self and society from the standpoint of a social behaviorist.* Chicago: Univ. of Chicago Press, 1934.
406. Mead, M. (ed.) *Cultural patterns and technical change.* Paris: UNESCO, 1953.
407. Mead, M. *From the south seas.* New York: Morrow, 1939.
408. Mercer, Margaret, and Hecker, O. The use of Tolserol (myanesin) in psychological testing. *J. Clin. Psychol.*, 1951, *7:* 263-266.
409. Merker, F. *Die Masai.* Berlin, 1904.
410. Miller, J. G. Discrimination without awareness. *Amer. J. Psychol.*, 1939, *52:* 562-578.
411. Mittelmann, B., and Wolff, H. G. Emotion and skin temperature observations on patients during psychotherapeutic (psychoanalysis) interviews. *Psychosom. Med.*, 1943, *5:* 211-231.
412. Monroe, Ruth L. Diagnosis of learning disabilities through a projective technique. *J. Consult. Psychol.*, 1949, *13:* 390-395.
413. Moreno, J. L. Psychodrama and society. In A. A. Roback (ed.), *Present-day psychology.* New York: Philosophical Library, 1955, 679-686.
414. Morgan, C. D., and Murray, H. A. A method for investigating phantasies: The thematic apperception test. *Arch. Neurol. Psychiat.*, Chicago, 1935, *34:* 289-306.
415. Morse, Nancy C., and Allport, F. H. The causation of anti-Semitism: An investigation of seven hypotheses. *J. Psychol.*, 1952, *34:* 197-233.
416. Moustakas, C. E. *Children in play therapy.* New York: McGraw-Hill, 1953.
417. Moustakas, C. E. *The teacher and the child.* New York: McGraw-Hill, 1956.
418. Mowrer, O. H., and Kluckhohn, C. Dynamic theory of personality. In J. McV. Hunt (ed.), *Personality and the behavior disorders.* New York: Ronald Press, 1944, 69-135.
419. Murphy, G. *Personality: A biosocial approach to origin and structure.* New York: Harper, 1947.
420. Murphy, G., Murphy, Lois, and Newcomb, T. M. *Experimental social psychology.* (2nd ed.) New York: Harper, 1937.
421. Murray, H. A. The effect of fear upon estimates of the maliciousness of other personalities. *J. Soc. Psychol.*, 1933, *4:* 310-329.
422. Murray, H. A. *Explorations in personality.* New York: Oxford Univ. Press, 1938.
423. Mussen, P. H. Differences between the TAT responses of Negro and white boys. *J. Consult. Psychol.*, 1953. *17:* 373-376.

424. Mussen, P. H. Some personality and social factors related to changes in children's attitudes toward Negroes. *J. Abnorm. Soc. Psychol.*, 1950, *45:* 423-441.
425. Mussen, P. H., and Jones, Mary. Self-conception motivations, and interpersonal attitudes of late-and-early-maturing boys. *Child Develop.*, 1957, *28:* 243-256.
426. Neilon, Patricia. Shirley's babies after fifteen years: A personality study. *J. Genet. Psychol.*, 1948, *73:* 175-186.
427. Norman, R. D., and Ainsworth, Patricia. The relationships among projection, empathy, reality and adjustment, operationally defined. *J. Consult. Psychol.*, 1954, *18:* 53-58.
428. O'Connor, Patricia. Ethnocentrism, "intolerance of ambiguity," and abstract reasoning ability. *J. Abnorm. Soc. Psychol.*, 1952, *47:* 526-530.
429. Olson, W. C. *Child development.* Boston: D. C. Heath, 1949.
430. Olson, W. C. Self-selection as a principle of curriculum and method. *Educ. Digest*, 1945, *10:* 17-19.
431. Omwake, Katherine T. The relation between acceptance of self and acceptance of others shown by three personality inventories. *J. Consult. Psychol.*, 1954, *18:* 443-446.
432. Ort, R. S. A study of role-conflicts as related to happiness in marriage. *J. Abnorm. Soc. Psychol.*, 1950, *45:* 691-699.
433. Osgood, C. E. *Method and theory in experimental psychology.* New York: Oxford Univ. Press, 1953.
434. Pavlov, I. P. *Lectures on conditioned reflexes.* Vol. II. Conditioned reflexes and psychiatry. (Trans. & ed. by W. H. Gantt.) New York: International Publishers, 1941.
435. Pearl, D. Ethnocentrism and the self concept. *J. Soc. Psychol.*, 1954, *40:* 137-147.
436. Perrin, F. A. C. An experimental and introspective study of the human learning process in the maze. *Psychol. Monogr.*, 1914, *16*, No. 4.
437. Peterson, R. C., and Thurstone, L. L. *Motion pictures and the social attitudes of children.* New York: Macmillan, 1933.
438. Phillips, E. L. Attitudes toward self and others: A brief questionnaire report. *J. Consult. Psychol.*, 1951, *15:* 79-81.
439. Piaget, J. *The child's conception of the world.* New York: Harcourt Brace, 1929.
440. Piaget, J. *Judgment and reasoning in the child.* New York: Harcourt Brace, 1928.
441. Piaget, J. Principal factors determining intellectual evolution from childhood to adult life. In E. D. Adrian, and others, *Factors determining human behavior.* Cambridge, Mass.: Harvard Univ. Press, 1937, 32-48.
442. Pintler, M. H. Doll play as a function of the experimenter–child interaction and initial organization of materials. *Child Develop.*, 1945, *16:* 145-166.
443. Plant, J. S. *The envelope: A study of the impact of the world upon the child.* New York: Commonwealth Fund, 1950.

444. Plant, J. S. *Personality and the cultural pattern.* New York: Commonwealth Fund, 1937.
445. Pomeroy, D. S. Ameliorative effects of "counseling" upon maze peformance following experimentally induced stress. *Amer. Psychol.*, 1950, *5:* 327.
446. Porter, E. H., Jr. The development and evaluation of a measure of counseling interview procedures. *Educ. Psychol. Measmt.*, 1943, *3:* 106-126.
447. Porter, E. H., Jr. The development and evaluation of a measure of counseling interview procedures. *Educ. Psychol. Measmt.*, 1943, *3:* 215-238.
448. Postman, L., Bronson, Wanda C., and Gropper, G. L. Is there a mechanism of perceptual defense? *J. Abnorm. Soc. Psychol.*, 1953, *48:* 215-244.
449. Postman, L., and Bruner, J. S. Multiplicity of set as a determinant of perceptual behavior. *J. Exp. Psychol.*, 1949, *39:* 369-377.
450. Postman, L., and Bruner, J. S. Perception under stress. *Psychol. Rev.*, 1948, *55:* 314-323.
451. Postman, L., Bruner, J. S., and Walk, R. D. The perception of error. *Brit. J. Psychol.*, 1951, *42:* 1-10.
452. Postman, L., Bruner, J. S., and McGinnies, E. Personal values as selective factors in perception. *J. Abnorm. Soc. Psychol.*, 1948, *43:* 142-154.
453. Postman, L., and Schneider, B. H. Personal values, visual recognition, and recall. *Psychol. Rev.*, 1951, *58:* 271-284.
454. Potter, Muriel. The use of limits in reading therapy. *J. Consult. Psychol.*, 1950, *14:* 250-255.
455. Pottle, H. *An analysis of errors made in arithmetic addition.* Unpublished doctoral dissertation, Univ. of Toronto, 1937.
456. Poull, Louise. The effect of improvement in nutrition on the mental capacity of young children. *Child Develop.*, 1938, *9:* 123-126.
457. Pratt, K. C., Nelson, A. K., and Sun, K. H. The behavior of the newborn infant. *Ohio State Univ. Stud. Contr. Psychol.*, 1930, No. 10.
458. Precker, J. A. Similarity of valuings as a factor in selection of peers and near-authority figures. *J. Abnorm. Soc. Psychol.*, 1952, *47:* 406-414.
459. Prescott, D. A. *Emotion and the educative process.* Washington: Amer. Council on Educ., 1938.
460. Preston, M. S., and Heintz, R. K. Effects of participatory vs. supervisory leadership on group judgment. *J. Abnorm. Soc. Psychol.*, 1949, *44:* 345-355.
461. Prince, M. *Clinical and experimental studies in personality.* Cambridge, Mass.: Sci-Art Publishers, 1939.
462. Prince, W. F. The Doris case of multiple personality. *Proc. Amer. Soc. Psychol.*, res., 1915, *9:* 1916, *10.*
463. Proshansky, H. A projective method for the study of attitudes. *J. Abnorm. Soc. Psychol.*, 1943, *38:* 393-395.
464. Proshansky, H., and Murphy, G. The effects of reward and punishment on perception. *J. Psychol.*, 1942, *13:* 295-305.
465. Pugh, R. W. A specific relapse phenomenon during the course of electric convulsive therapy. *J. Consult. Psychol.*, 1953, *17:* 87-91.
466. Pullen, M. S., and Stagner, R. Rigidity and shock therapy of psychotics: An experimental study. *J. Consult. Psychol.*, 1953, *17:* 79-86.

467. Raimy, V. C. The self-concept as a factor in counseling and personality organization. Unpublished doctoral dissertation, Ohio State Univ., 1943.
468. Raimy, V. C. Self reference in counseling interviews. *J. Consult. Psychol.*, 1948, *12:* 153-163.
469. Rapaport, D., Gill, M., and Schafer, R. *Diagnostic psychological testing.* (2 vols.) Chicago: Year Book Publishers, 1945-46.
470. Raymaker, H. *Relationships between the self concept, self ideal concept and maladjustment.* Unpublished doctoral dissertation, Vanderbilt Univ., 1956.
471. Reeves, J. M., and Goldman, L. Social class perceptions and school maladjustment. *Personnel & Guidance J.*, 1957, *35:* 414-419.
472. Ribble, Margaret A. Infantile experience in relation to personality development. In J. McV. Hunt (ed.), *Personality and the behavior disorders.* New York: Ronald Press, 1944, 621-651.
473. Ribble, Margaret A. *The rights of infants: Early psychological needs and their satisfaction.* New York: Columbia Univ. Press, 1943.
474. Richter, C. P. Biology of drives. *Psychosom. Med.*, 1941, *3:* 105-110.
475. Riesen, A. H. Arrested vision. *Scientific Amer.*, 1950, *183:* 16-19.
476. Rivers, W. H. R. *The Todas.* New York: Macmillan, 1906.
477. Roethlisberger, F. J. *Management and morale.* Cambridge, Mass.: Harvard Univ. Press, 1941.
478. Roethlisberger, F. J., and Dickson, W. J. *Management and the worker.* Cambridge: Harvard Univ. Press, 1939.
479. Roethlisberger, F. J. *Management and morale.* Cambridge, Mass.: Harvard Univ. Press, 1941.
480. Rogers, C. R. The attitude and orientation of the counselor in client-centered therapy. *J. Consult. Psychol.*, 1949, *13:* 82-94.
481. Rogers, C. R. *Becoming a person.* (Pamphlet.) Hogg Fdn. for Mental Hygiene, Univ. of Texas, 1956.
482. Rogers, C. R. *Client-centered therapy.* Boston: Houghton Mifflin, 1951.
483. Rogers, C. R. *The clinical treatment of the problem child.* Boston, Houghton Mifflin, 1939.
484. Rogers, C. R. The concept of the fully functioning person. (Mimeographed statement.) Univ. of Chicago, 1957.
485. Rogers, C. R. *Counseling and psychotherapy.* Boston: Houghton Mifflin, 1942.
486. Rogers, C. R. Significant aspects of client-centered therapy. *Amer. Psychologist*, 1946, *1:* 415-422.
487. Rogers, C. R. Some observations on the organization of personality. *Amer. Psychologist*, 1947, *2:* 358-368.
488. Rogers, C. R., and Dymond, Rosalind F. *Psychotherapy and personality change.* Chicago: Univ. of Chicago Press, 1954.
489. Rogers, C. R., and Skinner, B. F. Some issues concerning the control of behavior. *Science*, 1956, *124:* 1057-1066.
490. Rohde, A. R. Explorations in personality by the sentence completion method. *J. Appl. Psychol.*, 1946, *30:* 169-181.

491. Rokeach, M. Attitude as a determinant of distortions in recall. *J. Abnorm. Soc. Psychol.*, 1952, *47:* 482-488.
492. Rokeach, M. The effect of perception time upon rigidity and concreteness of thinking. *J. Exp. Psychol.*, 1950, *40:* 206-216.
493. Rorschach, H. *Psychodiagnostik.* New York: Grune & Stratton, 1942.
494. Roseborough, Mary E. Experimental studies of small groups. *Psychol. Bull.* 1953, *50:* 275-303.
495. Rosenstock, I. M. Perceptual aspects of repression. *J. Abnorm. Soc. Psychol.*, 1951, *46:* 304-315.
496. Rosenzweig, S. An outline of frustration theory. In J. McV. Hunt (ed.), *Personality and the behavior disorders.* New York: Ronald Press, 1944, 379-388.
497. Rotter, J. B. The nature and treatment of stuttering: A clinical approach. *J. Abnorm. Soc. Psychol.*, 1944, *39:* 150-173.
498. Sanford, R. N. The effects of abstinence from food from imaginal processes: A preliminary experiment. *J. Psychol.*, 1936, *2:* 129-136.
499. Sanford, R. N. The effects of abstinence from food upon imaginal processes: A further experiment. *J. Psychol.*, 1937, *3:* 145-159.
500. Sarbin, T. R. The logic of prediction in psychology. *Psychol. Rev.*, 1944, *51:* 210-228.
501. Schafer, R., and Murphy, G. The role of autism in figure-ground relationship. *J. Exp. Psychol.*, 1943, *32:* 335-343.
502. Schein, E. The effect of group interaction on judgment of physical stimuli. Unpublished master's thesis, Stanford Univ., 1949.
503. Schmidt, B. Changes in personal, social, and intellectual behavior of children originally classified as feeble-minded. *Psychol. Monogr.*, 1946, *60,* No. 5.
504. Schneirla, T. C. The nature of ant learning. II. *J. Comp. Psychol.*, 1943, *35:* 149-176.
505. Schneirla, T. C. Studies in the nature of ant learning. I. *J. Comp. Psychol.*, 1941, *32:* 41-82.
506. Schrodinger, E. *What is life?* New York: Macmillan, 1945.
507. Schwebel, M., and Asch, M. J. Research possibilities in nondirective teaching. *J. Educ. Psychol.*, 1948, *39:* 359-369.
508. Scodel, A., and Mussen, P. Social perceptions of authoritarians and non-authoritarians. *J. Abnorm. Soc. Psychol.*, 1953, *48:* 181-184.
509. Sears, R. R. Experimental studies of projection: I. Attribution of traits. *J. Soc. Psychol.*, 1936, *7:* 151-163.
510. Seeman, J. A study of the process of non-directive therapy. *J. Consult. Psychol.*, 1949, *13:* 157-168.
511. Selye, H. *The physiology and pathology of exposure to stress.* Montreal: Acta, Inc., 1950.
512. Selye, H., and Fortier, C. Adaptive reactions to stress. *Res. Publ. Ass. Nerv. Ment. Dis.*, 1950, *29:* 3-18.
513. Selye, H., and Fortier, C. Adaptive reactions to stress. *Psychosom. Med.*, 1950, *12:* 149-157.

514. Seymour, A. H., and Whitaker, J. E. J. An experiment on nutrition. *Occup. Psychol.*, 1938, *12:* 215-223.
515. Shaffer, L. F. *The psychology of adjustment.* Boston: Houghton Mifflin, 1936.
516. Shaw. C. R. *The Jack-Roller.* Chicago: Univ. of Chicago Press, 1930.
517. Shaw, C. R., and Moore, M. E. *The natural history of a delinquent career.* Chicago: Univ. of Chicago Press, 1931.
518. Sheerer, Elizabeth T. An analysis of the relationship between acceptance of and respect for self and acceptance of and respect for others in ten counseling cases. *J. Consult. Psychol.*, 1949, *13:* 169-175.
519. Sheldon, W. D., and Landsman, T. An investigation of non-directive group therapy with students in academic difficulty. *J. Consult. Psychol.*, 1950, *14:* 210-215.
520. Sherif, M. An experimental approach to the study of attitudes. *Sociometry*, 1937, *1:* 90-98.
521. Sherif, M. A preliminary study of intergroup relations, in J. S. Rohrer and M. Sherif, *Social psychology at the crossroads.* New York: Harper, 1951, 388-424.
522. Sherif, M. *The psychology of social norms.* New York: Harper, 1936.
523. Sherif, M. A study of some social factors in perception. *Arch. Psychol.*, New York, 1935, No. 187.
524. Sherif, M., and Cantril, H. *The psychology of ego involvements.* New York: Wiley, 1947.
525. Sherif, M., and Sherif, Carolyn. *Groups in harmony and tension.* New York: Harper, 1953.
526. Sherif, M., and Sherif, Carolyn. *An outline of social psychology.* New York: Harper, 1956.
527. Sherif, M., White, B. J., and Harvey, O. J. Status in experimentally produced groups. *Amer. J. Sociol.*, 1955, *60:* 370-379.
528. Sherman, M., and Henry, T. R. *Hollow folk.* New York: Crowell, 1933.
529. Shirley, Mary. *The first two years.* Minneapolis: Univ. of Minnesota Press, 1933, Vol. 3.
530. Siipola, E. M. A group study of some effects of preparatory set. *Psychol. Monogr.*, 1935, *46*, No. 210.
531. Skeels, H. M., and Fillmore, E. A. The mental development of children from underprivileged homes. *J. Genet. Psychol.*, 1937, *50:* 427-439.
532. Slotkin, J. S. Social psychiatry of a Menomini community. *J. Abnorm. Psychol.*, 1953, *48:* 10-16.
533. Small, L. Personality determinants of vocational choice. *Psychol. Monogr.* 1953, *67* (1), (No. 351).
534. Smith, A. *An inquiry into the nature and causes of the wealth of nations.* London: Strahan and Cadell, 1796.
535. Smith, M. B. The phenomenological approach in personality theory: Some critical remarks. *J. Abnorm. Soc. Psychol.*, 1950, *45:* 516-522.
536. Smith, S. Language and non-verbal test performance of racial groups in

Honolulu before and after a fourteen-year interval. *J. Gen. Psychol.*, 1942, *26:* 51-93.
537. Smith, W. M. Past experience and the perception of visual size. *Amer. J. Psychol.*, 1952, *65:* 389-403.
538. Smock, C. D. The influence of psychological stress on the intolerance of ambiguity. *J. Abnorm. Soc. Psychol.*, 1955, *50:* 177-182.
539. Snyder, U. An investigation of the nature of non-directive psychotherapy. *J. Gen. Psychol.*, 1945, *33:* 192-224.
540. Snyder, W. U. *Casebook of non-directive counseling.* Boston: Houghton Mifflin, 1947.
541. Snygg, D. Configurational aspects of tachistoscopic observation. Unpublished doctoral dissertation, Univ. of Iowa, 1931.
542. Snygg, D. Maze learning as perception. *J. Genet. Psychol.*, 1936, *49:* 231-239.
543. Snygg, D. Mazes in which rats take the longer path to food. *J. Psychol.*, 1935–1936, *1:* 153-166.
544. Snygg, D. The need for a phenomenological system of psychology. *Psychol. Rev.*, 1941, *48:* 404-424.
545. Snygg, D. The psychological basis of human values. In D. Ward (ed.), *Goals of economic life.* New York: Hopkins Bros., 1953, 5-57.
546. Snygg, D. The relative difficulty of mechanically equivalent tasks: I. Human learning. *J. Genet. Psychol.*, 1935, *47:* 299-320.
547. Snygg, D. The relative difficulty of mechanically equivalent tasks: II. Animal learning. *J. Genet. Psychol.*, 1935, *47:* 321-336.
548. Snygg, D., and Combs, A. W. The phenomenological approach and the problems of "unconscious" behavior. *J. Abnorm. Soc. Psychol.*, 1950, *45:* 523-528.
549. Society for the Psychological Study of Social Issues. *Soc. Psychol. Stud. Soc. Issues Newsletter,* Nov., 1956.
550. Solomon, R. L., and Howes, D. G. Word frequency, personal values and visual duration thresholds. *Psychol. Rev.*, 1951, *58:* 256-270.
551. Soper, D. W., and Combs, A. W. Planning future research in education. *Educ. Leadership,* 1957, *14:* 315-318.
552. Sorokin, P. A., and Berger, C. F. *Time-budgets of human behavior.* Cambridge: Harvard Univ. Press, 1939.
553. Spitz, R. A. Hospitalism. In A. Freud, and others, *The psychoanalytic study of the child.* New York: International Univ. Press, 1945.
554. Spock, B. *The common sense book of baby and child care.* New York: Duell, Sloan & Pearce, 1946.
555. Stagner, R. Stereotypes of workers and executives among college men. *J. Abnorm. Soc. Psychol.*, 1950, *45:* 743-748.
556. Stern, W. M. Cloud pictures. *Charact. & Pers.*, 1937, *6:* 132-146.
557. Stephenson, W. A. A statistical approach to typology: the study of trait-universes. *J. Clin. Psychol.*, 1950, *6:* 26-37.
558. Stevenson, I. Language and non-verbal test performances of racial groups

in Honolulu before and after a fourteen-year interval. *J. Gen. Psychol.*, 1942, *26:* 51-93.
559. Stewart, Naomi. A.G.C.T. scores of Army personnel grouped by occupation. *Occupations,* 1947, *26:* 5-41.
560. Stock, D. An investigation into the interrelations between the self-concept and feelings directed toward other persons and groups. *J. Consult. Psychol.*, 1949, *13:* 176-180.
561. Sullivan, H. S. *Conceptions of modern psychiatry.* Washington, D. C.: William Alanson White Psychiatric Foundation, 1947.
562. Symonds, P. N. Criteria for the selection of pictures for the investigation of adolescent phantasies. *Psychol. Bull.*, 1938, *35:* 641.
563. Tagiuri, R., Blake, R. R., and Bruner, J. S. Some determinants of the perception of positive and negative feelings in others. *J. Abnorm. Soc. Psychol.*, 1953, *48*· 585-592.
564. Taylor, C., and Combs, A. W. Self-acceptance and adjustment. *J. Consult. Psychol.*, 1952, *16:* 89-91.
565. Taylor, D. M. Consistency of the self-concept. Unpublished doctoral dissertation, Vanderbilt Univ., 1953.
566. Tentative social studies program, Campus Elementary School, Oswego State Teachers College, Oswego, New York, 1945.
567. Terman, L. M. *Genetic studies of genius.* Stanford, Calif.: Stanford Univ. Press, 1925.
568. Thetford, W. N. An objective measure of frustration tolerance in evaluating psychotherapy. In W. Wolff and J. A. Precker (eds.), *Success in psychotherapy.* New York: Grune & Stratton, 1952.
569. Thibaut, J. W., and Coules, J. The role of communication in the reduction of interpersonal hostility. *J. Abnorm. Soc. Psychol.*, 1952, *47:* 770-777.
570. Thigpen, C. H., and Cleckley, H. A case of multiple personality. *J. Abnorm. Soc. Psychol.*, 1954, *49:* 135-151.
571. Thistlethwaite, D. Attitude and structure as factors in the distortion of reasoning. *J. Abnorm. Soc. Psychol.*, 1950, *45:* 442-458.
572. Thompson, G. G. The social and emotional development of preschool children under two types of educational program. *Psychol. Monogr.*, 1944, *56:* No. 5.
573. Thompson, Laura. Perception patterns in three Indian tribes. *Psychiatry,* 1951, *14:* 255-263.
574. Thrasher, F. M. *The gang.* Chicago: Univ. of Chicago Press, 1927.
575. Tolor, A. Teachers' judgments of the popularity of children from their human figure drawings. *J. Clin. Psychol.*, 1955, *11:* 158-162.
576. Tomkins, S. S. Experimental study of anxiety. *J. Psychol.*, 1943, *15:* 307-313.
577. Tomkins, S. S. *The Thematic Apperception Test: The theory and technique of interpretation.* New York: Grune & Stratton, 1947.
578. Torrance, P. The phenomenon of resistance in learning. *J. Abnorm. Soc. Psychol.*, 1950, *45:* 592-597.

579. Torrance, P. Rationalizations about test performance as a function of self-concepts. *J. Soc. Psychol.*, 1954, *39:* 211-217.
580. Toynbee, A. J. *A study of history*. London: Oxford Univ. Press, 1935–1939.
581. Tresselt, M. E. The influence of amount of practice upon the formation of a scale of judgement. *J. Exp. Psychol.*, 1947, *37:* 251-260.
582. Twersky, V. On the physical basis of the perception of obstacles by the blind. *Amer. J. Psychol.*, 1951, *64:* 409-416.
583. Ugurel-Semin, Refia. Moral behavior and moral judgment of children. *J. Abnorm. Soc. Psychol.*, 1952, *47:* 463-474.
584. U. S. Federal Security Agency. Children's Bureau. *Infant care*. Washington: U. S. Government Printing Office, 1945.
585. Vargas, M. J. Changes in self-awareness during client-centered therapy. In C. R. Rogers and R. Dymond (eds.), *Psychotherapy and personality change*. Chicago: Univ. of Chicago Press, 1954.
586. Walsh, Ann M. *Self concepts of bright boys with learning difficulties.* New York: Bureau of Publications, Teachers College, Columbia Univ., 1956.
587. Wapner, S., and Witkin, H. A. The role of visual factors in the maintenance of body-balance. *Amer. J. Psychol.*, 1950, *63:* 385-408.
588. Warner, W. L., and Lunt, P. S. *The social life of a modern community.* New Haven: Yale Univ. Press, 1941.
589. Watson, J. B. *Psychology*. Philadelphia: Lippincott, 1919.
590. Watson, J. B. *Psychology: From the standpoint of a behaviorist.* (3rd ed.) Philadelphia: Lippincott, 1929.
591. Wechsler, D. *The measurement of adult intelligence.* (3rd ed.) Baltimore: Williams and Wilkins, 1944.
592. Wechsler, D., and Hartogs, R. The clinical measurement of anxiety. *Psychiat. Quart.*, 1945, *19:* 618-635.
593. Wees, W. R., and Line, W. The influence of the form of a presentation upon reproduction: The principle of determination. *Brit. J. Psychol.*, 1937, *28:* 167-189.
594. Weingarten, Erica M. A study of selective perception in clinical judgment. *J. Pers.*, 1949, *17:* 369-406.
595. Wellman, B. L. The effect of pre-school attendance upon the I.Q. *J. Exp. Educ.*, 1933, *1:* 48-69.
596. Wellman, B. L. Growth in intelligence under differing school environments. *J. Exp. Educ.*, 1934, *3:* 59-83.
597. Wells, F. L., and Ruesch, J. (eds.). *Mental examiners' handbook.* New York: Psychological Corporation, 1942.
598. Werner, H., Wapner, S., and Chandler, K. A. Experiments on sensory-tonic field theory of perception: II. Effect of supported and unsupported tilt of the body on the visual perception of verticality. *J. Exp. Psychol.*, 1951, *42:* 346-350.
599. Wertheimer, M. Laws of perceptual form. In W. O. Ellis (ed.), *A source book of gestalt psychology*. New York: Harcourt, Brace, 1939.

600. Wever, E. G., and Zener, K. E. The method of absolute judgment in psychophysics. *Psychol. Rev.*, 1928, *35:* 466-493.
601. Wheeler, L. R. A comparative study of the intelligence of East Tennessee mountain children. *J. Educ. Psychol.*, 1942, *33:* 321-334.
602. Whorf, B. Science and linguistics, *Technology Rev.*, 1940, *42*(6): 229-231 and 247-248.
603. Whyte, W. F. *Street corner society.* Chicago: Univ. of Chicago Press, 1943.
604. Wieder, G. S. Group procedures modifying attitudes of prejudice in the college classroom. *J. Educ. Psychol.*, 1954, *45:* 332-344.
605. Williams, H. D. An experiment on self-directed education. *Sch. Soc.*, 1930, *31:* 715-718.
606. Wispe, L. G. Evaluating section teaching methods in the introductory course. *J. Educ. Res.*, 1951, *45:* 161-186.
607. Wispe, L. G. Teaching methods research. *Amer. Psychologist,* 1953, *8:* 147-149.
608. Wittreich, W. J. The honiphenomenon. *J. Abnorm. Soc. Psychol.*, 1952, *47:* 705-712.
609. Wolfenstein, Martha. The emergence of fun morality. *J. Soc. Issues,* 1951, *7*(4): 15-25.
610. Woodrow, H. The problem of general quantitative laws in psychology. *Psychol. Bull.*, 1942, *39:* 1-27.
611. Worchel, P., and Berry, J. H. The perception of obstacles by the deaf. *J. Exp. Psychol.*, 1952, *43:* 187-194.
612. Young, K. *Personality and problems of adjustment.* New York: Crofts, 1940.
613. Young, P. T. Studies of food preference, appetite and dietary habit. VI. Habit, palatability and diet as factors regulating the selection of food by the rat. *J. Comp. Psychol.*, 1946, *39:* 139-176.
614. Young, P. T. Studies of food preference, appetite and dietary habit. V. Technique for testing food preference and the significance of results obtained with different methods. *Comp. Psychol. Monogr.*, 1945, *19:* No. 1.
615. Young, P. T. The experimental analysis of appetite. *Psychol. Bull.*, 1941, *38:* 129-164.
616. Zander, A. T. A study of experimental frustration. *Psychol. Monogr.*, 1944, *56,* No. 3.
617. Zimet, C. N., and Fine, H. J. Personality changes with a group therapeutic experience in a human relations seminar. *J. Abnorm. Soc. Psychol.*, 1955, *51:* 68-73.
618. Zimet, C. N., and Fine, H. J. A quantitative method of scoring picture story tests. *J. Clin. Psychol.*, 1955, *11:* 24-28.
619. Zorbaugh, H. W. *Gold coast and slum.* Chicago: Univ. of Chicago Press, 1929.

Index

SPECIAL NOTE: *All authors whose work was consulted in developing this frame of reference have been listed in this index whether such authors are specifically named in the text or not. Where the author's work is not specifically indicated in the text, the reader may find the work referred to by consulting the proper page number in the References (pages 466-479).*

Combs, Arthur Wright.

Individual behavior; a perceptual approach to behavior. Rev. ed. New York, Harper [1959]

522 p. illus. 25 cm.

First ed., by Donald Snygg and A. W. Combs, published under title: Individual behavior; a new frame of reference for psychology.
Includes bibliography.

1. Individuality. I. Snygg, Donald, 1904– Individual behavior; a new frame of reference for psychology. II. Title.

BF697.C57 1959 137 58–13962 ‡

Library of Congress

LEARNING RESOURCE
S0-EAJ-314
COMMUNITY COLLEGE

THE THERAPEUTIC SELF

Psychotherapy Series

The Initial Interview in Psychotherapy
Argelander, H., M.D.

Children and Their Parents in Brief Therapy
Barten, H.H., M.D. and Barten, S.S., M.D. (Eds.)

Brief Therapies
Barten, H.H., M.D. (Ed.)

The Art of Empathy
Bullmer, K., Ed.D.

Basic Psychological Therapies
Fix, A.J., Ph.D., and Haffke, E.A., M.D.

Assert Yourself!
Galassi, M.D., Ed.D., and Galassi, J.P., Ph.D.

Psychodrama
Greenberg, I.A., Ph.D. (Ed.)

The Group as Agent of Change
Jacobs, A., Ph.D. and Spradlin, W., M.D. (Eds.)

The Narcissistic Condition
Nelson, M.C. (Ed.)

Emotional Flooding
Olsen, P.T., Ph.D. (Ed.)

The Couch
Stern, H., Ph.D.

Psychotherapy and the Role of the Environment
Voth, H.M., M.D. and Orth, M.H., M.S.W.

The Therapeutic Self
Watkins, J.G., Ph.D.

Clinical Child Psychology
Williams, G.J., Ph.D. and Gordon, S., Ph.D. (Eds.)

Family Therapy
Zuk, G.H., Ph.D.

THE THERAPEUTIC SELF

Developing Resonance—Key to Effective Relationships

John G. Watkins, Ph.D.

Professor of Psychology

University of Montana,
Missoula, Montana

HUMAN SCIENCES PRESS
72 Fifth Avenue, NEW YORK, New York 10011 / 3 Henrietta Street, LONDON, WC2E 8LU England

Library of Congress Catalog Number 77-27633

ISBN: 0-87705-306-5

72 Fifth Avenue, New York, New York 10011

Printed in the United States of America
89 987654321

Library of Congress Cataloging in Publication Data

Watkins, John Goodrich, 1913-
The therapeutic self.

Bibliography: p. 495
Includes indexes.
1. Psychotherapy. 2. Psychotherapist and Patient.
3. Self. 4. Psychology–Philosophy. I. Title.
RC480.5.W28 616.8'914 77-27633
ISBN 0-87705-306-5

To Helyanthe,
A living therapeutic self
Who, like the sun for whom she was named,
Bestows a radiance of warmth and being
On all who are near.

CONTENTS

PART V. THE THEORY OF THE THERAPEUTIC SELF

PART VI. EXPERIMENTAL FINDINGS

PART VII. CLINICAL STUDIES

PART VIII. SUMMARY AND IMPLICATIONS

PREFACE

> Myself when young did eagerly frequent
> Doctor and Saint, and heard great Argument
> About it and about: but evermore
> Came out by the same Door as in I went.
> —The Rubaiyat

Four decades ago a young student at the University of Idaho sat enthralled while a genial and dynamic professor, Dr. Joseph Wesley Barton, began unfolding the mysteries of psychology. It was so simple and clear in those days. Human behavior could be accurately understood and controlled. A given stimulus produced a specific response. We need but discover which stimulus brought the desired result, and the worries of an adolescent, the inappropriate behaviors of a criminal, the pains of a neurotic and the delusions of a psychotic would vanish as the night at dawn. The age of science had been reached. No more need mortals wallow in a swamp of vagaries. A bright new discipline, armed with the precise tools of mathematics, had arisen. Scientific control of behavior would now take the place of those introspections that had so wasted the time of soft-thinking philosophers in the past.

Could any youth but be inspired by such a challenge. And so from the fires enkindled by a brilliant instructor in the imagination of a 17-year-old begins a long journey that, many experiences later, many hopes later, many frustrations later, brings forth the modest contribution offered in this work.

Somehow *the* solution never came. Each new answer raised several more questions, and the roads to certainty seemed to multiply with every passing year (Watkins, 1960). The few personality theories of that day could be numbered on one hand. There were the old and tired theories of functionalism, structuralism, and the false theory of psychoanalysis (or so my wise mentor affirmed); and there was the brave new world of behaviorism, which promised the control so eagerly sought. A young psychologist, armed then with a new and exciting theory, was willing to challenge all others—just as many young psychologists, fitted with new versions of this behavioristic theory today, disdainfully dismiss as invalid and unscientific the wisdom of those other searchers for the truth who discovered it not in the laboratory and under the brave battle flag of science. Somehow greater confidence is placed in the tools created by men's brains than in the brains that created the tools. The research design and the computer are respectable while the "mind" languishes in unhonored neglect.

As theories multiplied, and as the questions grew ever more numerous, the findings supplied from the laboratories seemed to offer pitifully small answers—tiny replies to such significant questions. We could reinforce a "response" but we knew so little about how to bring meaning to a purposeless existence. We could punish a "behavior," but we could not rehabilitate a psychopath. We could trace an axone or a dendrite, but we did not understand at all what was involved in a "thought." We could chart the motivation of the thirst drive in an albino rat, but we did not comprehend the meaning of "hope" in a human life. We knew nothing about what happens in a man when he develops a "value," a "curiosity," or a "love." How sad that we had so many tiny answers for so many petty questions, those that could be adapted to some statistical design—the one and two dollar questions of human living. But on the sixty-four dollar problems of man's existence we were babes in the woods, and our much-vaunted psychological science like tiny pebbles in an ocean of human need.

What is the essence of psychotherapy? Why is it that two people can interact, and after a period of time the one who has been most disturbed, most unhappy, most ineffective in living seems to improve? His depression subsides, his behavior becomes more efficient, and his relationships with others constructive. Many investigators today are attacking this question with sophisticated research designs, trying to tease out from a great mass of interactions the truly efficacious factors. In this work, also, efforts at empirical control will be utilized in several objective studies to be described. However, this report is primarily observational and theoretical. It is like the notes of the explorer, tracing paths here, indicating high mountains there, offering description and hypotheses. At times it adheres to well-validated experimentation. Occasionally it may indulge in flights of speculative feeling, philosophical—even poetical. For it is the nature of man with which this book deals, man as viewed both from the standpoint of science and of the humanities.

From observations on the behavior of healing arts personnel, I have been convinced that there is such an entity as a therapeutic self, a person whose impact on others is consistently beneficial—over and beyond his technical knowledge. We shall examine this concept from many different theoretical points of view. Before trying to explain such an individual we must give some thought to the very nature of the term "self." How does one acquire a self, and then a "therapeutic" self? What are the conditions in the treating situation that implement its operation?

A theory will be brought forth suggesting an effective way by which a psychotherapist and patient can interact. Several corollaries will then be drawn that bear on the selection and training of psychotherapists. Recorded case examples of the therapeutic self in action are presented and attempts to study this entity through objective evaluation. Our quest includes such questions as, "Can we develop therapeutic selves in young healing arts personnel, in parents, teachers, or in statesmen and diplomats?" Could we then have a significant constructive impact on this world of crime, injustice, and war?

The human brain, as well as the heart, has been known to play tricks. So we must move from heart to brain, from feeling to thinking, from intuition to validation—and back again. There is room for both men of words and men of numbers. This will be primarily an offering of words.

However, it is not our thesis here to abandon science, to eliminate objectivity, to be governed only by our passions. Rather the main contention will be that in the integration of the subjective with the objective, and the feeling with the thought, comes man's highest achievement and his greatest potential for growth.

To move back and forth between two ways of being, two ways of doing, is indeed a difficult task. The objectivists and the subjectivists so often plod each their separate paths. At a recent meeting of the American Psychological Association, I journeyed between two hotels where a series of discussions and presentations were being held. At one, the stalwarts of "science" presented lengthy papers, well documented by analyses of variance. They proved beyond a shadow of a doubt (at least beyond 95 per cent of a shadow of a doubt) that the proper and timely application of reinforcements brought constructive change. One heard such terms as "significant," "schedule," and "operant." At the other hotel, people felt together and touched each other. They sought for true meaning in man's existence, eschewed mathematics, and let their emotions be their guide. They used such words as "phenomenal," "humanism," and "existential." Although I visited each hotel several times, I rarely saw a person at one who appeared later at the other. A few years ago I tried to put together some concepts I had heard from one hotel with some from the other. The small contribution was entitled "Operant approaches to existential therapy" (Watkins, 1967 c). My paper pleased nobody. It would have been rejected in both hotels.

Nature seems to start with the simple, moves to the complex, and then returns to the simple. Evolution begins with cells and fashions species. Ultimately life ceases on a planet, and it reverts back to the inorganic. So it is with the single human existence. It too starts with a cell, divides, differentiates, and builds ever more stately mansions until the magnificence of a mature adult is achieved. Then slowly at first, but irresistably with time, this masterpiece of complexity disintegrates and is reduced back to the simple, to the inorganicity of molecules and atoms. We speak then of "death." Something of this must have been on Freud's and his associates' minds as they described the principles of Eros and Thanatos. The first brings people together for cooperation, for relationship, for procreation. Life builds gladly, and the wondering peaks of human beingness are achieved. The second, like the ebb of life's tide, carries man (often painfully) back to the sources from whence he came. Over and over again this eternal variation is repeated.

This work will start with a few simple observations

and questions. From these we shall spin more complex theoretical structures and bring to bear some objective scientific evidence. It is an integrative effort, one that aims at bridging communication gaps between different conceptions of man. Concepts developed within one brand of psychology will often be redefined in the language of another. The house of psychology has become like a tower of Babel. We speak, but we do not hear each other. It is to be hoped that this endeavor, before it returns back to its simple origins, might reduce the separation existing between the many different students of human behavior. For if psychologists cannot talk to one another, how then can we expect other men to do so.

It is truly in man's separation from his fellow men that the tragedies of hate and conflict arise, the experimentalist from the clinician, the young from the old, the criminal from his victim, the Americans from the Russians. And it will be through the integration of such differences that we can move from destructiveness to constructiveness. For therapy of the human species involves the breaking down of walls, walls that block communication, relationships, and that kind of resonance for one another that might bind humanity into some common bond of identity. What is wise for all men can be wise for each of us, for he who best keeps his neighbor, best keeps himself.

ACKNOWLEDGMENTS

I was once told that the original person is he who borrows from the widest number of sources. If so, this is an original work; because I am, indeed, beholden to so many people for its completion.

There are those who contributed directly by generously sharing their ideas with me, stimulating the concepts, criticizing the theories, critiquing the manuscript, and aiding in its revisions. Still other sections are the products of inspiration I received from interaction with friends, acquaintances, and other significant individuals in my life. The influence of parents and early teachers has shaped many a phrase, not only because of what they once said to me, but also because they have been incorporated in the form of permanent introjects within my self, internalized states that have guided and modified my thinking.

This work is also a creation from many sources, because a person is a confederation of different ego states.

The self is not unitary but a composite of several people, each of whom is activated, becomes executive for a period of time and is replaced by another. The differing contributions of changing ego states within my own being will be evident as one procedes from chapter to chapter; for the tone, the manner, the style, and the form often vary from one to the next.

The voice of the scientist, the scholar, the clinician, the therapist, the poet, the logician, the teller of stories can be heard—yes, and the exhibitionist, the compulsive one, the loose thinker, the behaviorist, the humanist, and the psychoanalyst. You the reader will perhaps recognize many of them as you peruse these pages; and even though the tenor of this work is a striving toward integration, the frequent failures to achieve such a goal will be obvious. One is often left puzzling at the unresolved confrontation of inconsistencies.

The wise therapeutic handling of different ego states requires that we try as far as possible to meet the needs of each. Accordingly, there is within an intent to give recognition to the origins from which each of my self states was derived. While it is not possible to credit fully every source, every influence, I must surely indicate the debt of gratitude owed those who played a major role in the development of this self and its product—this writing.

To a father and a master teacher, John Thomas Watkins, I owe an enormous debt for the unquenchable thirst to know and understand, the love of learning and the eager curiosity to discover. He did, indeed, reinforce my every achievement with words of wisdom and reward. As his only child, I was taught to revel in challenging the mysteries of nature. Thus was born the scientist and the scholar.

From a mother, Ethel Goodrich Watkins, English teacher par excellence, I learned the discipline of hard work, the striving for accuracy, the joy of a well-put phrase, the artistic pleasure of painting with words, and the importance of accurate communication.

A brilliant Latin teacher, Aileen Caskey, planted in my adolescent mind the idea that perhaps I could write. She also inculcated a sense of majestic awe for the wisdom of the ancients as derived through centuries of history. She inspired all her students with a vision of how the past lives on in the now.

And then there was Elford C. Preston, professor at the College of Idaho, who allowed me, a high school student, to act as an assistant to his class in astronomy, to lecture and to demonstrate with my telescope the joys of viewing the mountains on the moon and the rings of Saturn. He shared my dreams of the time when mankind would explore these far-off worlds, but he did not live to see them come true.

Dr. William Judson Boone, then president of the College of Idaho and a distinguished botanist, patiently listened to my youthful idealism. With mature wisdom and dignity, he nurtured still further the concept that life can be most meaningful if spent in trying to uncover the secrets of nature either by empirical research or by rational analysis.

Dr. Joseph Wesley Barton, professor of psychology at the University of Idaho and a sturdy behaviorist, thundered forth the inevitable connections between cause and effect, between stimulus and response. Alas, I have departed from many of his most sacred axioms, but the fire of enthusiasm he enkindled for understanding the behavior of a human organism has never been quenched. I hope it never will be. From the moment of contact with him, all other careers, which at times had caught my fancy, faded: chemist, physicist, astronomer, musician. All that was now important was to find out what went on in the "little black box," that mysterious entity within a human that determines how the stimuli of environment is translated into behavior. Only within the science and profession of psychology could fulfillment be found.

There were so many others from whom bits and pieces were incorporated, influences that have seeped into these pages: Mr. Tucker, stimulating high school science teacher, Dr. Frederick Church, eloquent professor of history, not to mention that brilliant array of scholars under whom it was my good fortune to study as a graduate student at Columbia University: John Dewey, Edward Lee Thorndike, Gardner Murphy, James L. Mursell, Irving Lorge, Helen Walker, George Counts, and Arthur Jersild. From one for whom I had the privilege of serving as an assistant, Carter Alexander, I learned about the many keys that would unlock the library storehouses of information.

It was due to no wisdom of choice that an unsophisticated Idaho boy was at Teachers College during its Golden Age. The occasional lecture from world traveler, philosopher, and politician, Nicholas Murray Butler, came to the ears of this naïve graduate student only because chance circumstances had sent him into this neorenaissance of time and place. Unplanned though they were, the impacts received there were never to be forgotten. Nor can I say just what in which pages herewith I owe to each. Nevertheless, it is here, passed on to the best of my ability as it was given by these to me. I cannot take the credit for creating it.

On the couch of that wise old student of Freud and analysand of Federn, Dr. Edoardo Weiss, I was introduced to secrets deeply buried within my being of which I was not very proud, and whose unearthing caused much stress. I sweated, I struggled, and I fought back—but I grew. And in that growing, I came to appreciate the vast inner world of unconscious process, which many people are never permitted to view.

Freud, Federn, Skinner, Rogers, Reik, Reich, Stekel,

Watson, Dostoyevsky, Darwin, Shakespeare, Churchill, Byron, Hardy, Burns, Rank, Aristotle, Plato, Shopenhauer, Kierkegaard, Jefferson, Lincoln, Buddha, Jesus, and many more; I read and read and read. Somewhere in the following pages one can find much that was first conceptualized by these, but their contributions are here so woven into other fabrics that I no longer know how to align the proper credit with signatures. If I have failed to give due recognition, it was with no malice aforethought or wish to deceive. Their words, like life's energies at death, have simply flowed back into a universal ocean of knowledge from which I dipped, seeking new samples of wisdom.

The years of commuting between clinic and campus were loaded with the rich stimulation of many interesting people: students, patients, colleagues; incorporating, modifying, summarizing, theorizing, comparing, questioning, and arguing. Out of all this milieu emerged many ideas and feelings, words and numbers, statistics, travels, proofs, intuitions, and incantations. There was science, magic, and a big, rich, impacting world that brought sadness, happiness, and pain. These, not I, have written this work. They have been registered in engrams, organized into ego states, and respectively activated to accomplish these words.

Among those who most closely existed in my social milieu, I owe debts of gratitude to many immediate colleagues, Drs. Richard Ball, John Means, Janet Wollersheim, Al Walters, and James Walsh, for reviewing parts of this manuscript and providing professional feedback. Marianne Andersen, Dr. Erika Fromm, and the students in my psychotherapy classes at the University of Montana and the International Graduate University read through early versions of this work, recorded their reactions, and initiated changes. Their suggestions are highly appreciated. The manuscript was largely typed in its many drafts by Camille Blanchette and Charlene Hapeman. I am also grateful to Dr. Lewis R. Wolberg, distinguished psychiatrist and author, who so kindly consented to write the introduction.

One learns much from those whose lives have been closely and intimately bound with one's own. As a father, I made many errors; but growth comes as well from mistakes reconsidered as from successes. I am, therefore, both proud and humble to have shared in the development of John Dean, Jonette Alison, Richard Douglas, Gregory Keith, and Rodney Philip from the moment of their birth through their unfolding as young men and women. As their father, I taught them much; but perhaps, as my children, they taught me even more. Two gracious ladies, Evelyn and Doris, mothered these offspring and shared my earlier homes. From them I learned that close relationships, although sometimes happy and sometimes painful, are meaningful and can be sources of self-growth and understanding. They, too, are a part of this work.

With two newer children, Karen and Marvin Huth, but recently acquired, I have been finding out how to relate to family members whose early childhood I did not share. In challenges such as these, the concept of resonance finds a true test; and they have taught me that it works.

Finally, from their mother and my wife, Helen Huth Watkins, I acquired the purpose for putting it all together. Companion, colleague, and sweetheart, she, as a psychologist and superlative therapist in her own right, has contributed most directly to this book by sharing some of her most significant treatment experiences in Chapter 22. But over and beyond all that, she has, in her own life and work, provided an inspiration that embodies the very basic thesis of this work. For she has taught me, as well as her many patients, students, and associates, what love is really all about.

J. G. W.

INTRODUCTION

Lewis R. Wolberg, M.D.

Behavior change may be brought about by a variety of measures other than formal psychotherapy. A fortunate friendship, an enlightened educational experience, an exciting emotional adventure are among the incidents that may initiate a different life orientation. Influenced are not only selected parameters of complaints and symptoms but also the personality structure itself, which may serendipitously undergo transformation resulting in better interpersonal relationships and a more wholesome self-esteem.

Psychotherapy approaches behavior change in a less capricious way. It studies the variables that require alteration, the circumstances that brought symptoms about, the forces that support illness, the resistances that obstruct progress. It then, within a medium of a professional encounter, sets about to help the individual order faulty behavioral and feeling patterns. The communicative instrumentality for this task are techniques and interventions, parcels of the therapist's training and experience.

Contemporary systems psychotherapy offer the practicing therapist a rich menu of available techniques with which to approach the multiform patterns of emotional illness. Illustrating the great varieties of treatment methods is a recent book containing such chapters as Assertion-Structured Therapy; Verbal Behavior Therapy; Implosive Therapy; Conditioned Reflex Therapy; Therapy #52—The Truth (Operant Group Psychotherapy); Attitude Therapy; Assumption-Centered Psychotherapy; Rational-Emotive Therapy; Confrontation Problem-Solving Therapy; Transactional Analysis; Fixed Role Therapy; Gestalt Therapy; Some Powerful Tools and Techniques for Positive Psychotherapy; The Illumination Method; Problem-Centered Guidance; Integrity Groups Today; Reality Therapy; and Christian Psychotherapy. There are many other types of therapy not mentioned, the listing of which would probably occupy a small monograph. This is not to derogate any of the proposed methods. Many of them are undoubtedly effective. Our question is why?

It is to be expected that in practice each therapist, no matter how bound to a system he imagines himself to be, if he is flexible and experienced, will make whatever modifications of method are required by the existing needs of an individual patient and by the exigencies of the prevailing reality situation. Thus variations will occur in session frequency, the degree of activity and support, the content of the interview focus, and the conjoint employment of adjunctive measures, such as drugs and other somatic therapies, as well as group therapy. His theoretical orientation will still operate as a guide to explain ensuing reactions and developments. Whether such explanations are factual and could survive the sunlight of scientific inquiry is another matter and apparently not pertinent to pragmatic results. For if both therapist and patient believe in the validity of a theory, however flabby it may be, it can serve as anchorage for successful therapeutic interventions.

This fact is particularly disturbing to those who seek to evaluate the true virtues of a theory. No less distressing is the finding substantiated over and over again that treatment methods, as diverse as they are, in the hands of effective therapists achieve satisfactory results. A search for common elements among the contrasting psychotherapies brings us face to face with varying opinions as to what constitutes the most important factor in therapy. For example, if we look through the literature or talk to therapists in active practice in order to inquire as to what constitutes for them the essence of the psychotherapeutic process, we find the following areas of focus stressed by different therapists:

1. The relationship that develops between patient and therapist. Here there may be emphasis on special aspects, as: (a) the degree to which the relationship supports the patient's failing defenses and unpropitiated needs; (b) the degree to which the relationship permits of a factual understanding of the patient's problem (insight); and (c) the degree to which the relationship serves as a corrective emotional experience for the patient enabling him to live through and to master in a more favorable setting frightening, frustrating, retarding, and destructive relationships with authority.
2. The innate, spontaneous constructive forces of mental health operating within the patient that will require nurturing and liberation, while neutralizing or eliminating retarding elements.
3. The system of psychodynamics of the therapist considered to be responsible for the neurotic process.
4. Intercurrent, nonspecific agencies operative in all

helping relationships, such as the placebo influence, emotional catharsis, suggestion, protective solace provided by the new idealized therapeutic authority, and dyadic group dynamics.

5. The special techniques and methods employed by the therapist, such as: (a) interviewing methods with the ability to select aspects from the verbalizations for purposes of focus that seem pertinent to the prevailing goals; (b) accuracy of interpretations; (c) the degree to which resistances are recognized and resolved; (d) the degree of mobilization and working through of transference; (e) the appreciation and meeting of the emotional needs of the patient with changing of one's techniques to meet his needs; (f) the active extension toward the patient of advice, support, and direction in gearing him toward new constructive experiences; and (g) the reinforcement of positive and adaptive and unreinforcement of negative, maladaptive behavioral tendencies through positive and negative reinforcers actively manipulated by the therapist.

Undoubtedly most or all of these variables operate during the process of psychotherapy. But since treatment is implemented in the medium of an interpersonal relationship what seems to be most significant is its *manner* of execution. This obviously hinges on the qualities and characteristics of the administering agency—the psychotherapist himself. Thoughtful observers have noted that irrespective of the kind of techniques employed, effective therapists are potentially capable of enabling their patients to make constructive use of the relationship that helps to release strangulated energies for effective living. Out of the creative interaction of therapist and patient, step by step, there is a challenging of burdensome patterns and a reformulation of outmoded values.

If we attempt to investigate how the alchemy of these changes evolve, we are confronted with alternative approaches. Proponents of a clinical view of psychotherapy have attempted to examine the therapeutic interaction in global terms that are highly impressionistic, metaphorical, and elusive. On the other hand, those with empirical pretensions have attempted to work with variables that can be manipulated or to study models, designs, and patterns of behavior while attempting to remain scientifically aloof from the observational data. The results of both these stratagems have not been too impressive in the few studies that are available for study. Most of the ideas concerning the nature of the effective psychotherapist are speculative explanations rather than inferences drawn from the testing of hypotheses.

The present volume is an attempt to deal with some of these shortcomings. It is essentially an effort to delineate through ego psychology the factors that enter into the organization of the therapeutic self. Watkins describes the therapeutic self as a complex of related behaviors that have a constructive effect on the responses of others.

The individual with a therapeutic self is behavioral, since he has learned to reinforce adaptive and not to reward less adaptive behavior. He constantly provides a model of adaptive responses. He is psychoanalytic by perceiving his own inner problems and conflicts to avoid contaminating the data received from the patient and to prevent himself from utilizing the therapeutic relationship for his own emotional needs. He also is existential-humanistic in that he relates himself as a human being to another.

Exploring the self necessitates concepts beyond the penumbra of science into the murky field of philosophy. It is here that Watkins scores a triumph because he capably transcends the ambiguous language characteristic of those who boldly plunge into the never-never lands of metaphysics, epistemology, ethics, logic, and aesthetics; it is a journey considered by many to have a long history and no future. Introduction of existential principles are fruitfully employed by Watkins in probing this area. The impact between the experiencer and the "other" (that which is being experienced) constitutes the essence of existence. With the object-subject dichotomy and their interrelationship as a base, one may, instead of looking at the self as a unity, regard it as a dynamic system of interrelated elements constantly changing its organization to both itself and the outside world. Employing Paul Federn's idea of the ego as a unifying, integrating energy, Watkins introduces modifications of Federn's views that, though complex and theoretical, drawing terms from classical Freudian metapsychology, provides him with a platform for a unique approach to existence. More fanciful are what Watkins terms "flights into outer space" in which he considers ego energy as moving in a time dimension. His delineating of ego states is a helpful and original excursion into an extremely complex zone, which has important implications for therapeutic process.

Employing ego psychological theories, Watkins explicitly and clearly delineates what goes into the making of a good psychotherapist. To validate his ideas there are presented the beginnings of a controlled study including a proposed scale for resonance, which is the empathic quality essential for a good therapist. But most interesting is the description of experiments on training to acquire this elusive and essential quality that permits functioning effectively in a therapeutic situation. Can one "learn" how to be empathic, and if so, are there some types of candidates who are more readily disposed to its acquisition than others? Around these questions, if they can be answered positively, lie many answers to the future of training in psychotherapy, including who to train and the preferred content of training.

Unique approaches are always of great interest since they challenge conventional thinking and force a review of sacrosanct and entrenched credenda. Their virtue will of course be proved in how valuable the ideas and methods show themselves to be in professional operations. The therapist who seeks to develop his skills may very well benefit from the infusion of new, even anomalous, tactics, some of which are contained in the chapters on ego-state therapy.

Freud once remarked that one of the most fundamental measures of maturity in man is his capacity to tolerate uncertainty. If this be the case, the field of psychotherapy is a fertile gauge since our ideas of how people become emotionally ill and get well again are continually undergoing challenge and change. We are confronted with a staggering array of treatment methods, complicated by lack of agreement regarding their virtues. The facts are that all systems of psychotherapy in the hands of effective professionals seem to work. The techniques employed appear to act as communicative vehicles for the unique relationship that develops between patient and therapist. This provides potential power for the release of strangulated energies in the patient, which can lead to the discarding of burdensome patterns and reformulation of outmoded values. But to secure such results requires possession by the therapist of a therapeutic self, the dimensions of which Watkins has so skillfully and imaginatively given us in this volume.

Part I

ORIGINS

The concept of the therapeutic self has evolved over a period of some 22 years. Bits and pieces have been drawn together that originated in the writer's clinical practice, personal analysis, theoretical study, and research. It has been (and still is) a constantly expanding formulation. In this first chapter some of the early milestones marking its development will be described, and we will try to set the stage for its delineation within the integration of diverse points of view.

Chapter 1

THE INCUBATION OF A CONCEPT

The gaunt young woman lying in the bed was pale and unsmiling as she looked up. A nurse's aide hurriedly entered, excused herself, and scurried away carrying the tray of uneaten food. Looking at me questioningly, the little patient spoke in a flat and listless voice.

"I guess you know I'm going to die, don't you, doctor?" She looked so fragile, so tired and motionless beneath the stark white sheets. Silently I cursed.

"How in the devil does she know that? Everybody had strict orders not to tell her. Only her closest relatives had been informed. Did somebody talk?"

Looking at the spot where her feet should be I managed a casual remark.

"What makes you think that?"

"Nobody has told me I am going to die, but I know it is so. I can even tell just when they diagnosed my case as terminal. Ever since that time, my doctor doesn't stay long in the room."

Her lips quivered a bit, and there was the trace of a tear in her eye.

"And—and the nurse looks the other way."

Of course I knew she was terminal. Her ward doctor had informed me of that at the time he referred her for psychotherapeutic treatment.

"Just try to keep her calm and not depressed," he had remarked as he passed rapidly on to the patient in the next room.

It came as a great shock to realize that our staff had been unsuccessful in concealing from this girl the knowledge of her impending death. Through cues of which we were unaware, we had unconsciously told her that she would die, that we were not able to save her, and that we felt guilty at our inability to rescue her from this imminent disaster. Not a word about death had been spoken to her, but she knew. This information had been transmitted through many tiny postural and gestural movements that so eloquently expressed what our sealed mouths had aimed to withhold. We had been talking in a universal language that can be sensed by all, regardless of from what part of this globe they come.

If we cannot even mask from our patients our feelings and knowledge, then how great indeed is our responsibility to be authentic. For we cannot successfully hide a wish to be rid of our commitments to their needs simply by the pose of a therapeutic manner. It is not just what we "say and do" that counts. It is how we "be" toward them that makes the difference.

The patient inwardly knows our attitudes toward him. He discovers, in spite of our subterfuges, whether we like him, whether we care, or whether we have written him off. True "caring", as described in that beautiful little contribution by Mayeroff (1971), constitutes "the worth I experience in the other" as "something over and above any value it may have for me because of its ability to satisfy my own needs." Phony caring may appear superficially the same as true caring, but in the deeper levels at which humans communicate, we know—we know. For the true reality of our motivations in relation to our patient's needs is registered at some realm in his being in spite of our smiling face, our casual remark, our hearty reassurance, or any other aspect of that front we call the persona.

The yellow brick walls of the hospital towered high above the dark green countryside. From the windows on this floor, one could gaze across the beautiful city nestling in the evening shadows below and sprinkling a thousand lights over the dwellings of its inhabitants. This ancient building was a place to suffer and to heal, to live or to die. Over the past few decades, many hundreds of those who had served on their country's battlefields had come here to do just that.

Still further up the hill, huddled into its humps and folds, crouched the many impressive buildings of the medical school. There, numerous workers toiled to find the secrets of man's ills and to transmit them to the initiated. From this fount of wisdom came many visitors: consultants, researchers, attending and resident physicians. These doctors were rotated at three-month intervals through the various medical and surgical services: cardiovascular, gastrointestinal, orthopedic, urological, etc. Eager and dedicated came these young physicians seeking the experience that would qualify them for the challenges of independent practice.

The Psychology Service consisted of several clinical psychologists available on consultation when called by the ward doctors to study cases of behavioral problems or suspected psychogenicity. Our job was to evaluate and advise, to recommend transfer to psychiatric institutions in cases of severe mental abnormalities, and to provide brief, intensive psychotherapy to selected patients. Accordingly, we had the opportunity to observe closely the reactions of many different patients to many different physicians.

During their therapy sessions, the patients often talked about their doctors and nurses. At one time, several patients on the urological ward would complain about the treatment and manner of Dr. X, his brusqueness, his arrogance, his impatience, his irritability. During the same period, we might be hearing from several patients on the gastrointestinal ward about their great regard and affection for Dr. Y, a young resident who was the same in age and medical experience as Dr. X.

Three months passed. The young physicians rotated assignments. And now from the gastrointestinal ward came increased requests for emergency consultations. Irritations rose, anxieties mounted, ward problems increased, and ulcers flared. Dr. X was in charge. On the urological ward, to which Dr. Y had been transferred, all was tranquil. The patients complained less about their illnesses. The requests for pain medication diminished, and there was a lack of behavior problems.

Why did the patients of Dr. Y do so much better than those of Dr. X when both of these physicians graduated with comparable standing from the same medical school? Both completed their internships in the same institution, and now both are taking residency training in internal medicine at the same hospital and working with the same kinds of patients. Why does the disturbance that marked Dr. X's administration on the urological ward follow him to the gastrointestinal ward? And why does the presence of Dr. Y seem to mobilize the constructive processes of psyche and soma in his patients?

On another ward in this same hospital, a young man suffering from porphyria[1] lay in an almost continual state of coma. Occasionally hallucinating, he seemed to be rapidly approaching death. The ward doctor shrugged his shoulders.

"There's not much we can do for him. His condition is terminal."

As a psychologist who was ignorant of the destined eventualities in such a disease, I naively asked, "If there is nothing which can be done, would you object if we tried some massed suggestion on him to see what might happen?"

The young resident doctor scratched his chin thoughtfully for a moment and then replied, "Go ahead. You can't do him any harm."

It was early spring. Just outside the room's window, a large camellia bush had started to shed its petals. The fading blossom clusters seemed almost to symbolize and predict the passing of this youth so early, even before he could enjoy the summer of his life. Must we simply wait for the inevitable?

During the next six weeks, the patient was hypnotized four times a day, and for about fifteen minutes each session there was fed into him a continuous barrage of suggestions telling him that we, the staff, had much confidence in him, that we felt he could mobilize himself and get well, that we cared.

At first nothing happened, but gradually he showed signs of improvement. Psychotic thought processes subsided. Periods of alertness lengthened. Finally, one day he got out of bed and began acting like a normal man. By midsummer he left the hospital, and in September he returned to a large West Coast university to resume his studies.

We have no follow-up. Perhaps now he is alive. Perhaps not. Maybe he got well because of the massed suggestions, maybe in spite of them. This is but a single case. No scientific controls were employed, and no conclusions from this incident can be made. Yet the possibility remains that somehow in this case of a generally incurable disease a kind of constructive or reintegrative principle might have been mobilized. We cannot dismiss the experience as simple coincidence.

Selye (1956) has pointed out the deteriorative effects of stress on the function of many physiological systems within man.[2] And the opposite effect of recovery has been so frequently noted (Alexander & French, 1948) when successful resolution of inner neurotic tension has resulted in the halting of organ disintegration and a resurgence of normal functioning.

The physician treats all illness by intervening in the organism, physically, surgically, pharmacologically, or psychologically (educationally). He introduces into the human something new that serves to mobilize constructive forces. This "something" may be a chemical or an idea. But it changes the balance within and tips processes from disintegration to reintegration.

There are many bits of evidence pointing to the operation of an interpersonal factor in the development of illness or health. A hospital study noted that certain institutions had a much higher recovery rate than others. This occurred when no relationship could be shown to the care with which the surgery was scrubbed or asepsis practiced throughout the hospital. Again, something other than normal technical medical factors was having its effect. In certain hospitals, patients got well. In others, they didn't.

The same variability occurred in the frequency of malpractice suits. Some surgeons seemed to be prone to malpractice suits. Others, with no better medical training, might leave a sponge in a patient and still be forgiven. In fact, the majority of malpractice suits have been initiated against only a small minority of doctors. It would appear that those doctors who were the frequent target of such suits must generally have had a poor interpersonal relationship with their patients.

One final note, recorded by the French pharmacist Émile Coué comes to mind. Whenever he received a prescription from a physician he liked he would say to the patient, "This is excellent medicine, Madame B. It greatly helped Madame A." When he was given a prescription from a doctor he disliked he would remark to the patient as he handed it over, "Huh! Did he give you this stuff?" He would then record in his book of prescriptions exactly what was said to each patient. Coué concluded that the recovery of many of his patients was related more to what he said than to the ingredients of the prescriptions.

The concept that relationship is an effective, if not *the* effective, ingredient in psychotherapy is certainly not new. Many writers, Fromm-Reichman (1950), Gendlin (1962), Jourard (1971), Rank (1950), Rogers (1961), Truax and Carkhuff (1967), to mention but a few, have stressed this factor. Even the more conservative psychoanalytic writers, including Freud (1935), Fenichel (1941), and Glover (1955), have charted the effect of relationship on the course of therapy, although they referred to it as transference and tended to perceive it in negative terms as a resistance that impeded treatment (Freud, 1953 a). The handling of this transference was primarily a matter of control by the analyst of his own feelings and accurate understanding and interpretation of it when discovered in his patient. In general, the analytic writers failed to consider this relationship between therapist and patient as a positive, vital force for cure. Rather it was an artifact to be controlled or resolved by interpretation and working through. The dynamics of the cure inhered in the interpretative skill of the analyst, not his being as a person. In this respect, the cognitive rather than the affective aspects were emphasized.

Not all analysts adhered to this point of view. Reich (1949) stressed the liberation of bound emotion as the "character armor" was broken down, while Alexander and French (1946) and their colleagues in the "active" Chicago School emphasized the release of feeling by skillful "manipulation of the transference." However, the basic analytic approach was to picture the therapist as treating the patient like an object—albeit an interesting object—and to minimize his own role *as a person* within the therapy. We do not find among these writers the idea of the self of the therapist as possessing therapeutic properties in its own right, over, above, and beyond the technical skill of the treating one. Therapeutic failures were viewed as resulting from an inadequate grasp of analytic theory, mistakes in technique, or inadequate personal analysis that had failed to remove emotional blocks and countertransferences within the analyst.

This book is about human relationship and some of the subtleties that occur in the interactions between two people—between me and thee. There are many things happening *between* people, as well as going on *within* people that little lend themselves to a simple stimulus-response description. We are forced to use higher-level terms to describe clusters of responses and response-potentials. One such term is "self." It is a thesis here that this self, this bundle of consonant behavior potentials within an individual, can have a therapeutic or a pathological effect on others, and that these effects are a matter for our serious consideration if we would discover how to help people most effectively.

That some people are bad medicine for others is well known. Many studies (Arieti, 1960; Lidz & Fleck, 1960; Mark, 1953; McGhie, 1961; Reichard & Tilman, 1950.) show the impact of "bad" parents on children.

Little work, however, has been done to evaluate the converse of this problem, namely to examine the people who are just "naturally" beneficial to others, those who are "good medicine" to all who contact them. Psychiatrists and psychologists have too long concerned themselves primarily with the study of the pathological. It is time we busied ourselves more assiduously with the evaluation and cultivation of positive, life-enhancing tendencies within those upon whose shoulders fall the burden of helping the disturbed.

From a reflection on all these observations there emerged the concept of the therapeutic self, an entity that seems to exist to some degree in all effective practitioners of the healing arts. It appears to exert an influence on patient behavior and recovery that is over, above, and beyond the practitioner's knowledge, experience, or technical skills.

If there exists such a self, how does it come into being?[3] Is it inherited, learned as a child, acquired in later life? What are the factors governing its development? If it is an important essence of good treatment, how can we teach it to the young practitioner or cultivate it in ourselves? It certainly is not now the subject of any consistent attention in our medical schools, our dental schools, our university departments of psychology, or our schools of nursing.

Science starts with validated observation, with findings that can be shared between people. And through science, we have made great strides in bettering the lot of mankind. But science is not the only method by which man has learned and developed. Through thought, philosophy, feeling, and intuition he has discovered much which has proved useful, although the connections between cause and effect, between stimulus and response, have not been established.

This treatise is an earnest inquiry into the apparent

existence of a therapeutic self in some people. Theoretical formulations will be offered as to its nature, followed by corollaries that can be logically drawn as consequences. Experimental studies and case material will be presented in support of the concept. Finally, suggestions will be presented as to how it can be developed in all of us.

In pursuing these goals, we shall endeavor to draw from behavioral science as much empirically validated data as possible. Facts and probabilities experimentally derived or clinically observed will be integrated into our proof whenever possible. However, we shall not hesitate to use feelings as well as intellectual mechanisms in our quest. For truth can often be felt and experienced as well as proved. And the way to it has been approached by men with such different backgrounds as Aristotle, Shakespeare, Darwin, Einstein, Freud, Edison, Buddha and Jesus—each searching for the essence of reality with his own unique tools: empirical, rational, and experiential.

Part II

DIFFERENT PERSPECTIVES

The reservoir of therapeutic systems is overflowing today as creative wells from hundreds of contributors are deluging the books and journals with innumerable new theories, approaches and techniques. The therapist of today feels overwhelmed in trying to keep abreast of this plethora of research articles, case studies, and theoretical proposals even in any one of the major streams of psychotherapy.

Some of these are new and original contributions. Others are old wine in newly labeled bottles. High is the competition for innovative titles designed to capture the eye of those readers who seek the latest wisdom in how to understand man and treat his ills. Each new system develops its corps of disciples and its unique terminology. Thus we have transactional analysis, gestalt therapy, primal scream, reality therapy, implosive therapy, and hypnodrama, to name but a few. Accordingly, it is with both misgivings and hesitation that in these pages we launch still another term and another system of treatment. Mankind, however, never stands still in its restless search for truth and the better life. So there shall be no apologies. If this contribution only muddies the waters further then let it so be until such time as valid research and integrative thinkers in the future can cull the wheat from the chaff and consolidate or reject our concepts in a new and more comprehensive approach.

While each new system or technique has its unique aspects, almost every one of them can be subsumed under one of a few major headings. There are three major streams in the therapies of today: the psychoanalytic channel, the behavioral channel, and the existential-humanistic channel.

Psychoanalytic therapy is the oldest and a well-developed approach. It is replete with a coherent theory and many well-studied techniques. It holds close to the medical model and considers mental pathology as due primarily to faulty maturation. Its aim is to remove unconscious blocks to maturity through a corrected understanding called "insight." It is rationalistic and emphasizes man's need for knowledge and self-control. There are many variations in both theory and tactics.

Behavioral therapy has been a great stimulus to experimental research in the past decade. Its centers of development are in the university departments of psychology. It holds that behavior disturbances are due to faulty learning. The treatment is to modify such unadaptive behavior through application of tested principles of learning. It relies on empirical validation and aims to show how deviant behavior in man can be controlled and predicted.

Existential-humanistic therapy[1] has many proponents among private practitioners of both group and individual therapy. It considers that pathology is due to faulty perception, perception of one's own self and of others. It aims to increase life's meaningfulness through improved self-awareness and more realistic interpersonal relationships. It emphasizes inner experience and holds that man should learn how to liberate his self from controls to achieve true freedom.

Some people are healers; others are not. Let us belabor this point no further. We have chosen here to call that personal ingredient that characterizes the effective therapist the therapeutic self. How can this concept be presented so that it can be translated by the behaviorist, the humanist, or the psychoanalyst into his own idiom and hence be meaningful to each? By the very use of the word "self" I have employed a term that makes little sense in the terminology of one of these. So if this work is to have value to different practitioners of treatment (behavior therapy or psychotherapy as one prefers) then it is important to define the therapeutic self in terms clear to each. Later, the author will present his case in his own terminology.

In many of the treatises on new approaches to

therapy one sees a tendency to magnify the differences between that being advocated and some earlier therapeutic system. The earlier method is often described with its assets minimized and its deficiencies exaggerated. This is then contrasted with the author's "new" and "innovative" system, which is presented as the utopia in theory and methodology and one that all therapists should espouse. Case reports, glowing with success achieved in much less time, are compared with the "older", "unscientific," and "ineffective" methods of the past.

Thus, the behavior therapists have written countless passages disparaging the contributions of psychoanalysis and extolling their own techniques. Many humanists have done likewise in comparing their approaches to those of the behaviorists. The fact is that every method has had its successes and its failures. One impression stands out—namely, that the enthusiasm and commitment of the therapist to his own technique is an important factor in its success.

During the next few chapters we shall try to present the concept of the therapeutic self as it might be viewed from the vantage point of each of the three major streams of therapy: behaviorism, psychoanalysis, and humanism. In the thumbnail descriptions of these major streams we cannot hope to be thorough enough to satisfy those who have made intensive study and identification with each. But we shall endeavor to portray each as fairly and honestly as possible without minimizing or denigrating its contribution. For the theoretical system and treatment techniques to be proposed in this work have borrowed from all three streams. It is heavily indebted to many behavioristic, psychoanalytic, and humanistic therapists whose contributions we shall endeavor properly to credit.

A long time ago, when the writer was a small boy,

he read many fables, many stories. One in particular impressed itself on his mind. It was that of the blind men and the elephant. Like the blind men in the parable, each of us also has a grasp on part, but not all, of the truth; and a complete "elephant" of personality theory has yet to be assembled.

FOOTNOTES

Part 1

1. An uncommon metabolic disorder characterized by excessive porphyrins in the urine. It was regarded at that time as being incurable.
2. Throughout this work the terms "man" and "mankind" are used to represent the entire human race, including women and children. They are used solely for convenience; no brief is held for concepts of masculine superiority, and the strivings of women for full economic and political equality have our utmost support.
3. Some writers on therapy avoid the word "self" entirely. Sullivan (1954) tended to use it more as an adjective, referring to the "self system" or "self dynamism." The modern behaviorists Krasner and Ullmann (1965), Wolpe (1958) and most others of this persuasion, apparently regard the word "self" as unscientific and rarely mention it.

Part 2

1. Throughout this book we shall usually refer to it simply as "humanistic."

Chapter 2

THERAPEUTIC SELF FROM THE VIEWPOINT OF BEHAVIORISTIC PSYCHOLOGY

The middle-aged man sat relaxed in his chair. For the moment, gasping and coughing had subsided: the problem, emphysema, and a doctor's strict warning that he must relinquish his long-established habit of smoking on pain of prematurely losing his life. For 30 years, whenever he felt tense, he had been accustomed to reach for a smoke instead of a sweet" (as suggested in an old Lucky Strike advertisement). The practices of a lifetime are not easily terminated. Often he had achieved a high resolve to stop, and each time for several days he had sweated and cursed. All to no avail. Wisdom said, "You must stop." But feeling screamed, "I want! I need!"—and feeling proved the stronger.

His features looked peaceful. The deep hypnotic relaxation, patiently induced by his therapist, enveloped him, and for the moment his fears subsided. Earnestly the treating one (Watkins, H. H., 1976) began pouring into him suggestions of well-being, suggestions specifically determined by prior study of his needs, suggestions aimed to reinforce nonsmoking behavior.

"You tell me you want to feel a sense of victory over your smoking habit—a sense of willpower and self-control—a feeling of winning over this vice. You can have this feeling by doing the following: Every time you pick up a pack of cigarettes and then put that pack down again without removing one, this feeling of victory will come over you. You will feel good and strong. It's like winning one battle after another, until the final victory when you win the war—the victory over your smoking habit." A feeling of victory and strength was being made contingent on putting down the pack without extracting a cigarette. The intense, hypnotic relationship was being utilized to potentiate this suggestion. He would receive a reward of good feeling each time the impulse to smoke was followed by a cigarette-rejecting response. His therapist was combining here two approaches to treatment: hypnotherapy and behavior modification. No expectation was held that this tactic alone would do the job and eliminate all smoking behavior, but it was one element in a treatment plan that used a significant and well-validated learning principle. The therapist was pitting her knowledge of her patient, her sensitivity to his needs, her skill in communication, and her very self against the clutches of smoking, for him a life-destroying habitual response.

A behavior therapist would probably take immediate exception to the use of the term "self." For him, the only concrete phenomenon available to scientific inquiry is "behavior," that which can be manipulated. So let us for the moment consider self merely as *a cluster of behaviors* that hang together, that are capable of description and measurement, and that have certain predictable consequences.

The total of these responses, called the "self," is

characteristic of a given individual, and it is in the perception of these behaviors within his own functioning by which the person establishes his sense of identity. He observes his own responses, notes their consistency and predictability, perceives their continuity, and then engages in the verbal behavior of stating "This is my self."

While the behaviorist tends to be distrustful of the validity of self-observation and prefers that behavior be evaluated by outside observers who can consensually validate each other's perception, he cannot always obtain such conditions. Accordingly, many studies in behavior therapy rely on "self report" or introspection. The behaviorist must therefore accept and deal with the word "self" even though he would prefer otherwise.

Since we have no other term that adequately describes that cohering cluster of behaviors by which an individual senses and identifies himself, we shall continue to use it even while thinking like a behaviorist. A psychologist need not hypothesize the self as some mysterious inner entity. He can consider it only as a useful construct to represent a set of responses, just as the behaviorist may use the term "neurosis" even though he does not accept it as a disease entity underlying and causative of external behaviors termed "symptoms." He perceives the symptoms as the disease itself. They are behaviors and should be dealt with directly in their own right.

For the moment, let us consider "self" as a useful, descriptive term representing a group of related behaviors. Then what constitutes therapeutic self? As previously outlined, there is considerable evidence that some individuals do possess a complex of related behaviors that have constructive impact on the responses of others, such as patients or clients.

From the behavioral standpoint, we might state that any individual who constantly modifies the behavior of others with whom he interacts in constructive and adaptive ways can be said to possess a therapeutic self. This term implies a somewhat different direction of emphasis from the focus of most early studies in behavior modification.

Behavior therapists, starting from principles of learning discovered in the experimental laboratory, have aimed at developing a technology of reinforcement application. A reinforcement was originally considered to be specific and, like a drug prescription, discrete and constant in its effect on a subject regardless of who administered it. But behavior modifiers have come increasingly to the realization that the potency of a reinforcement is determined also by who administers it and in what setting it is administered (Paul, 1969). In the first case (who administers it) they are moving toward the very thesis of this book, the concept of a therapeutic self. And in the second (in what setting it is administered) they seem to be reverting again toward a field theory conception of human personality functioning (Lewin, 1951), just as earlier psychologists did. The history of psychology repeats itself as the whole person and his "life space" become once more important concepts in the application of a scientific, laboratory-validated, behavior technology.

But how can the responses of one individual constructively modify the behavior of another? Since we are here considering mental illness only as maladaptive behavior, and since behaviors are learned, we can unlearn such behaviors or relearn better ones. From the studies of learning theorists (Hilgard & Bower, 1975) and from the many recent investigations demonstrating the employment of established learning principles in modifying maladaptive responses (Bandura, 1969) we know that behavior, both adaptive and maladaptive, is developed, modified, and maintained by its consequences. These are termed "reinforcement contingencies." In its simplest form, any behavior, whining for example, if followed by a positive reinforcement (reward) such as a nickel, will tend to be strengthened, and we can expect it to be repeated. Reinforcements might also include food, candy, praise, and affection. It is by such reinforcements that the symptoms (behaviors) representing a neurosis are acquired. The process by which this is accomplished has been termed "operant" learning, because the consequences of the behavior operate to increase its incidence. All this is very elementary to those who practice in the field of behavior therapy, but it is presented here for the benefit of readers who may be unfamiliar with this orientation.

The same conditions that brought about the original learning of maladaptive responses can be manipulated to extinguish the behavior or to replace it with more adaptive reactions. Hence, rewards (reinforcements) might be administered to the whining child at various intervals during which he has refrained from whining. This should operate to reduce the frequency of such behavior.

Studies have clearly shown that the attempt to extinguish behavior, such as whining, through the administration of aversive stimuli (punishment) does not fare as well as might be thought. While rewards seem to have a powerful effect toward building in behaviors, punishments do not have as clear an opposite result, sometimes extinguishing, sometimes reinforcing and sometimes having little or no effect (Holz, Azrin, & Ulrich, 1963). Perhaps this is why our correctional system of prisons and reformatories, built as it is on the concept of attempting permanent change through punishment, has been such a notorious failure in achieving its goal.[1]

However, in the behavioral approach, maladaptive responses are extinguished by ensuring that they are not reinforced. Thus, the parent who refused to attend to the whining behavior or to reward it in any way would increase the likelihood of its being extinguished. If the child then emitted more constructive behavior, such as offering to perform a chore, the parent, by rewarding the offer, would be helping to replace the neurotic response with one that would be more constructive and acceptable in our society. Hence, behavior can be changed by the application of appropriate reinforcements and can be extinguished by the refusal to so reinforce it.

Another behavioral approach especially effective in the reduction of fears was first described by Jones (1924). It was later developed by Wolpe (1958) and termed "systematic desensitization." The principle here is essentially that of presenting to the anxious subject a fear-inducing stimulus, either in a weakened form, or simultaneously in the presence of strong, nonfear-provoking stimuli; for example, suggestions of calmness and relaxation. The subject tends to become desensitized, and the original stimulus loses its ability to initiate fear. A hierarchy of fear-inducing situations, programmed about a single topic, may be presented to such a degree as to be inadequate to overcome the relaxed behavior and feelings of the subject. The desensitization of the fear-inducing stimulus situation then proceeds by small steps until the original stimulus in its full intensity is no longer capable of eliciting an anxiety response.

For example, a fear of snakes may be systematically desensitized by presenting a hierarchy of imagined snake situations to a patient who is completely relaxed and secure. After he has achieved the deeply relaxed state, he might be first instructed to imagine that there was a snake in a field a mile away. If he does not signal to the therapist that this evokes anxiety in him, he is next asked to visualize a situation in which the snake is a hundred yards up the road. If no fear response is evoked, the image is changed to one of seeing the snake still closer. If at any time he signals, perhaps by lifting a finger, that he is becoming tense, the therapist returns to an earlier and safer visualization and gradually works forward again until the closer image can be tolerated. Ultimately, the subject no longer responds with fear behavior to the snake stimulus. He has become desensitized to it.

Another behavior treatment involves that of modeling or social reinforcement (Bandura, 1965; Lovaas, Freitas, Nelson, & Whalen, 1967; Kanfer & Marston, 1963). It is an approach that focuses on inducing a subject to imitate a constructive behavior so that it can be positively reinforced. If the model first demonstrates a mature reaction to a situation, the subject (client, patient), especially if young, is more likely to attempt a similar response than if it is left purely to chance for him to try a new, constructive behavior. The technique of modeling may often be only the first significant element in a reinforcement approach.

Recently behaviorists have shown an increasing interest in cognition (Mahoney, 1974; Meichenbaum, 1973) and in imaginal or covert processes (Cautella, 1967, 1970, 1971). In these latter, covert reinforcements or extinction are applied to fantasied situations rather than to behavior *in vivo*. Except for the absence of a formal hypnotic induction, the procedures are similar to those practiced earlier by hypnotherapists (Erickson, M. H., 1944, 1948; Watkins, 1952).

We have defined the term "self" behaviorally as simply a cohering cluster of responses in an individual by which he senses his own identity. As a behaviorist, how might we define and explain the term "therapeutic self"? From this theoretical viewpoint, the individual who possesses a therapeutic self is one who has learned to apply the principles of behavior change consistently in his everyday, social interaction. For example, he is first a person who is sensitive to evidences of mature behavior and potential constructive responses in others. These elicit in him positively reinforcing responses. He does this with little cognitive activity as a precursor. Rather, his positive reinforcing behaviors occur almost automatically as part of his natural responding activities in a social situation. By natural, we do not mean uncaused; only that the eliciting stimuli have come from within the organism or are so transmitted into behavior through mediating variables that we cannot discern an immediate relationship to the environment. Perhaps as a child he happened on such a response once by chance and then was himself reinforced by positive responses of affection from others. Thus, he was fortunate in living and growing within a mutually positive, reinforcing social system called his "family."

It is difficult sometimes to know who is reinforcing whom. Patterson (1969) concluded on the basis of his own studies and on data provided by Ray (1965) and Jones (1965) that "the chronic non-responsiveness of the autistic child produces the 'refrigerator parent' described by Kanner (1944)." Kanner had claimed that it was the refrigerator parent that had produced the autistic child. One individual behaves. His behavior is followed by a reinforcing or punishing response from another person. That one, in turn, reacts back. Both parties are influencing the behaviors of the other by the contingencies inhering in their respective interactions. A reinforcing individual thus is developed in a reinforcing social climate. That person in turn, reinforces others within this setting. An adaptive climate operates beneficially for all within that situation.

So the individual who has the therapeutic self has learned within a social reinforcing system the behavioral habits of positively responding to the more adaptive behaviors of others and of refusing to reinforce their less adaptive responses. From the standpoint of the desensitization techniques, he may well have acquired habits of responding to fear and hate responses in others with relaxing and accepting behaviors that permit these others to release such emotions and systematically desensitize themselves. Again, the behaviors of the helpful one are not planned but occur naturally or covertly. Thus, people who interact with a therapeutic self are being continuously desensitized; they feel calmed, more at peace, and a general sense of release from strong fear and hate behaviors.

Finally, from the standpoint of social reinforcement, the therapeutic self is constantly providing a model of adaptive behavior. Being relatively mature, well-adjusted himself and lacking in severe anxieties, such an individual consistently displays before those with whom he interacts an array of constructive, mature, and adaptive responses. These may be specific responses to discrete social situations, or they may represent the stimulus generalizations called attitudes. At any rate, by his general behavior, he elicits in others a greater number of adaptive responses than do most people. Then by his consistent provision of positive reinforcements to these more adaptive behaviors (which have been elicited by him), and by his relative ignoring of the more maladaptive responses of others, he again naturally helps them to extinguish neurotic behaviors and replace them with a more constructive repertory. Such a person is continually desensitizing the fears of others, partly because in his relationship with them he does not threaten. He arranges the conditions of his interaction so as to provide them with anxiety-inducing stimuli only when he also accepts and reinforces them so strongly that the total situation is nonthreatening. His therapeutic self is continuously operating like that of a master diplomat.

Obviously, there are people who continually and almost automatically arrange behavior contingencies for others so as to reduce fears and extinguish maladaptive behaviors. They elicit constructive responses by their own modeling and by positively reinforcing adaptive tendencies. Such a person was Dr. Y, whom we met in the first chapter.

Perhaps Dr. Y was only a natural master behavior modifier. He took no courses in theories of learning. He knew not consciously, and with scientific planning how to establish a schedule of reinforcement. He made no staged efforts to model a healthy role for his patients. He did not record and chart maladaptive responses so that he could extinguish them by ignoring. He did all of these things unwittingly, easily and naturally because that was the way he was reared. It came without effort or thought for him to identify a well remark of his patient and to respond with the reinforcing smile. Somehow, he automatically ignored neurotic whining or irrational complaining. Yet he consistently responded to the genuine grievance, thus reinforcing the patient's right to mature self-expression. He rewarded with his attention the healthy release of pent-up anger and reassured when the patient verbalized unrealistic guilt.

These social skills did not come from research or study. They were acquired because he had learned them firsthand. His early, authoritative family figures (or later equivalents) modeled these examples. They transmitted to him through behavior modification their own therapeutic selves. And now, in addition to all of the medical technology he had learned, he treated and constructively modified his patients by teaching more adaptive ways of living. For them, he had become a healer, a doctor in the original sense of the Latin word *docere* meaning "to teach."

Our behavioral colleague might remark now, "Why,

you've only described a good behavior modifier." And perhaps, indeed, that is all we have done. But the few and fortunate people who constantly engage in such reinforcing behaviors have not necessarily acquired these skills by formal training in the laboratory or classroom. This consistent application of reinforcing behaviors, and this provision of constructive role models to others, may often have been acquired through early social learning. The ability to reinforce others positively is like a gift, passed down from one generation to the next.

If treatment is a form of learning, then the acquiring of a therapeutic self is also a form of learning. Perhaps what we know about the reinforcement of adaptive behaviors in the ineffective person can be used to train therapeutic selves, since all we mean at this point by this term is a systematic matrix of reinforcing behaviors that influence others constructively. There is one difference, though, from the usual goal of behavior modification. In behavior therapy we aim to alter the responses from the "sick," or maladaptive, to the "well," or adjusted. Here, we are suggesting the shaping of the behavior of therapists to make *them* respond more consistently in therapeutic ways.

The implication so far in this chapter has been that the fortunate few who possess this attribute acquired it as a consequence of contingencies that occurred in their early family situations. The behavioristic psychologist is not content to leave behavior change to chance reinforcements but seeks to modify responses by planning and control. How can we develop by training a therapeutic person so that he consistently reinforces constructive behaviors in his patients? What learning programs can be initiated in the development of young physicians, psychologists, psychiatrists, social workers, counselors, and nurses that would systematically develop their response abilities in this direction? This need has been recognized by behavior therapists. Thus Krasner (1962) points out that there is reason to believe that traditional interviewing procedures could become a more effective base for changing deviant behavior if the therapist were more carefully programmed in the way in which he dispenses social reinforcers. And Patterson (1969, p. 354) states, "The characteristics of the social agent dispensing the social reinforcers determine a significant portion of the variance associated with behavioral change."

Obviously, we should expect a modeling effect to obtain as we observe treatment sessions, movies, and video tapes and as we listen to audio recordings that demonstrate reinforcing behaviors as actually practiced on patients by outstanding, experienced therapists. However, more specific techniques need to be devised that would provide immediate reinforcement to the young therapist's own behavior in the treatment situation when it successfully imitates such models.

One device that has been tried is the "bug-in-the-ear" (Korner & Brown, 1952). It has been used in the supervision of more traditional therapy approaches. The young therapist treats his patient and is observed by his supervisor through a one-way vision screen. At times, the supervisor makes remarks or suggestions on the course of the treatment, which are transmitted to the therapist by a hearing aid device. The beginning therapist can then modify his tactics accordingly since he is receiving directions while they are in process.

This device could be used to provide systematic and immediate reinforcement of those responses (made by the young therapist) that have been deemed reinforcing to the patient by the observing supervisor. Thus a "good" or "nice job" transmitted to the ear of the therapist immediately after he has emitted a reinforcing response to his patient should tend to increase his incidence of such behavior. Consistent application of this teaching device might be expected to improve his therapeutic abilities considerably. Experienced researchers in this area could devise other ways by which the reinforcing ability of the trainee therapist might itself be reinforced. The net result of such training should in time develop an individual who consistently demonstrates toward others those clusters of behavior we have termed therapeutic self.

The behaviors continually practiced by therapeutic selves can be explained and accounted for by the same learning principles that develop other aspects of personality functioning. And apparently these same principles of operant conditioning, desensitization, and modeling could be applied by teachers of therapy on developing therapists to shape their therapeutic behavior. However, not all psychologists are willing to explain deviant behavior in these terms, to think in this terminology, or to treat with the methods of behavior technology. There are many who approach their patients from the positions of developmental or perceptual psychology, who derive their understanding of the etiology of such conditions from a different frame of reference and who speak in a different language. Accordingly, let us turn next to an entirely different theoretical orientation to explore further the phenomenon termed therapeutic self.

FOOTNOTES

1. It should be noted that treatment by punishment (aversive procedures) has not had a good trial since conditions that govern effective behavior change through punishment contingencies seldom obtain in our present correctional system (Rachman & Teasdale, 1969).

Chapter 3

THERAPEUTIC SELF FROM THE VIEWPOINT OF PSYCHOANALYTIC PSYCHOLOGY

". . .and I remember when I was about four years old. I was supposed to come home from kindergarten at noon. But instead I walked down the railroad tracks and got so interested in the engines in the roundhouse that it was about two hours later before I got home. My father had been out looking for me and he was very angry. He gave me a severe licking with the razor strap. I didn't think I was so bad, but all of a sudden, I felt, 'Daddy doesn't love me, or why would he beat me so?' I guess after that I always felt a little bit afraid of him."

The patient on the couch twitched anxiously, fighting back tears. Why would the father he loved be so cruel?

The wise old man sitting behind the couch cleared his throat. "The coward," he muttered.

"The coward! What do you mean, the coward? My father was always a very brave man. What's that got to do with his beating me?"

In a firm but gentle voice the old analyst replied, "He was afraid, very much afraid. That's why he beat you."

"I don't understand. Why would he beat me if he was afraid?"

"He was afraid because you endangered the life of his only son, the son he loved so much."

Now the tears erupted into a flood as the man on the couch came face to face with the realization that his father had truly loved him; but he was human, had reacted impulsively out of fear and had administered the severe punishment to protect his son from future hazards. A new understanding, another step in the long road toward maturity.

The measure of a man's impact on the world must surely be related to the number of times his name is mentioned by others. Tyrants, kings, and dictators, who were known to millions, have arisen in history. But their lasting effect is usually established only after their death. Do men of future generations still play their music, admire their paintings, or quote their thoughts? One hears little now concerning Attila the Hun, and even the name Hitler is fading in the memories of humanity.

But the teachings of Jesus, the music of Beethoven, the paintings of Michelangelo, and the plays of Shakespeare live on. They continue to influence the thoughts and feelings of countless newcomers to the human race. In the fields of science, great debts of gratitude are owed to such contributors as Aristotle, Newton, and Darwin, the intellectual giants of their time.

Judged by the criterion of being quoted or attacked, the name of Sigmund Freud ranks high among those who have been students of man. He has been slavishly quoted as gospel by some—and bitterly attacked by others as unscientific or anathema; but he has seldom been ignored. Modern-day psychology has found fault with many of his theories, and in some behavioral circles he is scornfully dismissed. Behaviorists consider themselves as scientists, and hence they are highly critical of the uncontrolled data extracted from verbalizations by patients on the couch that served as the basis for Freud's theories. However, these "scientists" seem to ignore the many well-controlled, empirical research studies that have validated a great deal of Freud's views (See Kline, P., 1972).

Even though there are strong academic prejudices today against psychoanalysis, these learned psychologists have felt the need to mention Freud and to quote him. So it is not surprising that in many introductory textbooks in psychology the name of Freud is mentioned more often than that of any other psychologist.

One may quarrel with his theories of psychosexual development and minimize the efficiency of his treatment procedures, but one cannot escape the fact that Freud, like Columbus, discovered a whole new unknown world, a universe of inner unconscious processes within man himself. Since the concept of the therapeutic self is closely related to unconscious processes (covert behaviors) in the healer, we must recognize the great debt of gratitude we owe him and the many of his concepts we have borrowed in pursuing this thesis.

This is not a book on psychoanalysis, and we shall spend little time attempting to outline its complex theory structure and intricacies of therapeutic technique. These have already been done much better elsewhere (Fenichel, 1945; Freud, 1935; Menninger, K., 1958). However, in the development of the therapeutic self concept we shall attempt to draw from many psychoanalytic ideas and procedures. This can best be done by describing psychoanalytic training.

The learning of the psychoanalyst involves first a personal analysis in depth whereby he becomes acquainted with his own unconscious motivations and "works through" internal conflicts, "blind spots," and emotional blocks that might interfere with his clear perception of his patients' problems and his appropriate therapeutic behavior in the treatment situation. This personal, or "didactic," analysis as it is called, is then followed by the analyzing of patients under supervision (known as "controls"). During the same period he is taking formal courses and seminars at the psychoanalytic institute. The entire process may require five to eight years. Thus, the learning of the young analyst-to-be is of three types: becoming aware of his own unconscious processes, intellectually mastering psychoanalytic theory and technique, and supervised practice.

Psychoanalytic theory states that neurotic behaviors are the result of conflicts between repressed impulses and social demands. Healing takes place when such repressions are lifted through the process of understanding them. This is called insight. Insight, to be effective, must be deep and thorough and represent emotionally experienced understanding as well as intellectual knowledge. The learning within the analysis is implemented by the use of three primary methods: free association, dream interpretation, and analysis of the transference. In the first, it is hypothesized that if the patient lets his thoughts roam at will without censorship or attempted direction, they will in time make increasing sweeps into forgotten and repressed areas. The analyst may intervene from time to time by an interpretation in which he points out to the patient some underlying implication to the associations that have just been made. Properly timed, such interpretations can break through a resistance and help the patient achieve a new perspective to his behavior.

Since Freud (1938) considered the dream to be the royal road to the unconscious, many analysts place great emphasis on the interpretation of dream material for revealing inner, repressed thoughts. The following is an example of a significant and revealing dream: One of my depressed patients reported during the second hour of treatment she had dreamed that, "Ivy vines were growing over my house." In her associations to the dream, she mentioned that she had attended the movie *Ivy* the day before. She was asked, "What thoughts do you have about this movie?" She replied that at the beginning of the movie there was a symbol of a vase with ivy vines growing over it. Then, "Oh, yes, at the end of the movie the same symbol was brought back, only this time the vase was shaped like a skull."

When asked about the plot of the movie *Ivy* she was quite resistant and appeared to have forgotten most of it. The therapist had attended the movie himself and knew that it was the story of an unhappy wife who had murdered her husband. The patient had revealed her marital dissatisfaction and perhaps her death wishes toward her own husband. In the dream, ivy vines were growing over *her* house. It was decided at this early stage to pursue the dream no further since she was not prepared yet to recognize and assume responsibility for such death wishes.

The third, and most important, technique involves the achieving of insightful understanding through the recognition of transference feelings projected on the person of the analyst (French, 1946). These are attitudes acquired in relation to earlier significant people in the life of the patient that are now attributed to the analyst. Thus, if the patient always felt rejected by his father and had tried to deal with this rejection by extreme politeness towards him, he may, in the course of the treatment, begin to feel that he is being rejected by the analyst. Perhaps he reveals this by becoming extremely (and unrealistically) polite. Since the analyst has been sitting out of sight from the couch and has said or done very little, he can point out to the patient that he, the analyst, has done nothing to warrant the conclusion that he is rejecting the patient. Thus, the unrealistic nature of the patient's attitude and behavior is demonstrated. The patient becomes aware of his false perceptions concerning the analyst and also of other significant father symbols in his life. He can then lose his unrealistic fear of authority figures, such as his boss, his supervisor, or the policeman, and respond toward them more realistically.

It is obvious that an analysis is a self-learning experience and that the analyst is cast in the role of a teacher of unconscious processes. This he does by skillfully guiding the thoughts of the patient until he discovers these. Hence he learns for himself—a learning that results in genuine conviction and change. The analyst in training goes through this process of self-education personally. It is considered a vital and necessary part of his preparation if he is to be therapeutic in his own treatment of others (Balint, 1948).

Psychoanalysis does develop a therapeutic self in its practitioners, although the term itself is not generally used. There are, however, a number of distinct differences in the way this is conceptualized here and in traditional psychoanalytic training. In psychoanalysis the emphasis would be placed, not so much on the analyst's *being,* as on his *doing,* the conscious, planned and technically skillful interventions he makes with his patients. Although he is supposed to represent a model of mature thought, his patients are carefully kept from social contact with him. They will know him only from what he *says* in the office, not from what he *does* in his outside life. His personal life remains a secret to them. Freud believed that the analyst should represent a screen onto which the patient would project his fantasies; if the patient knew him as a real person, this would serve to nullify the process of transference. The analyst, then, provides a model of mature *thought* but not necessarily of mature *behavior,* since his own actions outside the therapeutic hour are not revealed to the patient.

Words are stimulus cues and presumably initiate behavior, but verbalization alone is not necessarily synonymous or congruent with other behavior. Accordingly, analyses sometimes become quite wordy. The patient does not utilize the words as cues for genuine growth. We then speak of him as having only "intellectual insight." His apparent understandings do not get translated into significant personality change. The benefit of encouraging transference reactions derived by the analyst's neutral and impersonal behavior toward his patient may be offset by the treatment's absence of a *behavioral* role model and its overemphasis on word cues. It may resemble the situation in an old-time revival meeting where the preacher enjoined his parishioners to, "Do as I says! Don't do as I does!"

Cognitive processes are important. As Freud said, "The voice of the intellect is soft, but it is persistent." However, man lives not by thought alone, and the neglect within traditional psychoanalysis of "being" and other behavioral processes may partially account for the long time required in the typical treatment.

Within psychoanalysis the self would be most closely equated with the term "ego," that province of the person governed by the reality principle. It is the ego's function to reconcile the varying, and often opposing, demands coming from the environment, from the id, and from the superego. The id was hypothesized by Freud (1947) to represent a reservoir of primitive, undifferentiated impulses, childlike in nature, which are governed by the pleasure principle. It is the source of behavior potentials that stem from heredity and early infantile conditioning.

Unacceptable thoughts and feelings are repressed by the ego to make behavior consistent with reality and with the demands of the superego. The superego exemplifies the social controls we have learned from parents, church, school, and law. It is governed by the duty principle and is closely related to what is commonly called the conscience.

There is a difference between the psychoanalytic term "ego" and our use of the term "self" here, although there is some overlap. Symonds (1951) distinguishes between ego and self as follows: "Ego refers to the self as object—the self which perceives, thinks and acts—and which would be described by an outside observer. The self, on the other hand, is the subjective self as it is perceived, conceived, valued and responded to by the individual himself. The self includes one's view of himself and his awareness of his own existence; it is not always governed by the reality principle." However, if we were to use the term "therapeutic ego" in order to relate our concept to the psychoanalytic terminology, we would arrive at a similar position. We would be talking about that part of one that is governed by the reality principle and is therapeutic to others.

Undoubtedly training does hope to build a true therapeutic ego within its practitioners. The emphasis, though, is in removing the blocks, the blind spots, hence eliminating negative factors within the therapist. It is assumed if his perception is not clouded with unconscious distortions, and his behavior toward his patient not contaminated with immature, countertransference reactions, that his reactions in the treatment situation will be realistic.

This position is cast in the medical model in which normality (the desirable goal of functioning) is the absence of pathology. Both the behavioristic and psychoanalytic models aim at the removal of symptoms, the first directly, the second indirectly. As envisioned in this book, the therapeutic self is not merely the absence of distortion; it actively promotes the enhancement of living, the increase of meaning, and the facilitation of rewarding behavior in its clients (and in its practitioners). In this respect, it is closer to the humanistic-existential model (to be described in the next chapter).

Psychology and psychiatry have long concerned themselves with the pathological, the abnormal, the sick. At least equal attention should be applied to the tendencies of a patient toward more mature and integrative behavior. Here is one of the great contributions that the field of behavior modification has brought to the problems of treatment. This basic concept has not received among psychoanalytic and humanistic therapists the credit it deserves.

Some years ago this writer, when teaching a course in Rorschach[1] interpretation, gave the following instructions to his class: "First, analyze the protocol in terms of potential pathology. Note well the signs of F minus, the poor integration of color and form, the appearance of contaminations and confabulations. Write these down and consider them. Now, re-examine the entire protocol from a very different point of view. Find out everything you can that is *right* with the patient. Where are the efforts toward good form integration, where the patterns of consistency in the relations of whole and detail responses, where the attempts to bring constructive human movement into the picture, etc. When you finally bring together that which discloses your patient's liabilities with that which depicts his assets, write your report in such a way that it will enhance and emphasize his constructive tendencies. Without sacrificing objectivity state your findings so that if they are shown to your patient he might say: 'Now there's someone who really understands me.' He would then feel good about your evaluation.

Because of your reinforcements he would develop further his mature points and as a by-product lessen his pathological ones."

It would be our thesis that the effective therapist is not merely free of neurotic perceptions and behavior, but that he adds something distinctly positive to the therapeutic interaction. He is not just neutral toward his patients but a definite, active, constructive influence. He does not rely only on the belief that if a patient fully understands his problems—even in the genuine insight sense—he can, and will, take the positive action necessary to change himself and his behavior. Putting it in the words of a popular song of a few years back, it is not sufficient merely to "eliminate the negative." One must also actively "accentuate the positive."

During psychoanalytic treatment, the analyst attempts to maintain a state of free-floating attention in order to sort out from his patient's comments those that are truly objective from those that are subjectively contaminated. It is his function then to direct his patient's attention to the subjectively biased remark by interpretation of the resistance or of the transference. The aim is to secure increased objectivity in the patient's perceptions and interpersonal relationships.

As to the goal we have no quarrel. However, it was pointed out in the last chapter that research has demonstrated we learn most when behavior is positively reinforced and that the punishment of unconstructive behavior is not so effective. Yet the analyst seldom interprets the correct, objective behavior of his patient. Usually, the objective, constructive responses of his patient are simply accepted, not reinforced, while the behavior or statement contaminated with subjective defense becomes the center of attention. Since attention is itself a reinforcement, and since this reward is so often administered when the patient reports immature behavior, there is a constant enhancing of the wrong aspect in the one being treated. There are immense rewards in behaving in an infantile way and in reporting such behavior to one's therapist. It is to such that he pays the most attention.

Furthermore, by constantly interpreting the negative we stimulate what Rank (1950) called the "will," a force that seeks to maintain the integrity of the patient and helps him to avoid cognitive dissonance. By challenging the patient in this way we mobilize resistance. What we then must "work through" is, not only the natural defenses of our patient, but a much greater amount of resistance that we ourselves have created. One might speculate what would be the outcome of an analysis in which most of the interpretations offered reinforced growth potentials rather than directed attention toward the patient's infantile liabilities.

Since it is conceded that psychoanalytic training does seek to develop practitioners whose interaction with their patients results in benefit and healthy growth to them, let us briefly consider the various aspects of the education designed to enhance that goal. During his personal analysis, the analyst-in-training not only removes blocks to his realistic perception of a situation, but he also resolves inner conflicts that might impel him to "act out" with his patients. For example, if he were not aware that for him women are perceived as symbolic mothers, that he is unconsciously seeking the lost love of his childhood, he could easily begin to view a female patient in this role. He might then respond to her with affection, seeking the gratification of his own needs, rather than solving her problems. His therapy could degenerate into a love affair instead of a treatment (Freud, 1953c). His awareness and control of such countertransferences enables him to remain realistic and truly therapeutic in his interaction with his patient.

Since he has learned to become attuned to slight manifestations of inner drives within himself—verbal, gestural, and postural—he more readily acquires the ability to perceive these in others. He develops a sensitivity to unconscious processes in his patients, or as Theodore Reik (1948) put it, a third ear. This sensitivity and understanding of others is the very core of what is meant by therapeutic self.

One of the traits cultivated in psychoanalytic training is the ability to be objective, to avoid contaminating the data received from a patient with one's own emotional needs. This is very valuable. In our development of the therapeutic self it will be stressed as a most significant aspect of the therapist's diagnostic acumen. But here also there will be a difference. This objectivity need not be exclusive. In fact, if it is, a rich source of understanding is neglected. There is a way of using the personal aspects of self without distorting reality through interfering countertransferences—but that is another story, which must be dealt with later.

In conclusion, the psychoanalytic model does not specifically aim at developing a therapeutic self, where one's being, as distinct from one's conscious doing, is enlisted into the therapeutic process. However, psychoanalytic training provides many features for approaching this goal. One cannot but applaud the principle that says to the therapist, "Know thyself" first. The personal analysis can be a very valuable experience for all healing arts personnel, and for some it is a necessity. The removal of blind spots in perception, the development of emotional maturity, the increase of sensitivity, the understanding and realistic control of one's own behavior, all these are essential and significant growth experiences for the would-be analyst. Such personal therapy removes from the doctor many impediments that could prevent him from being truly helpful. In fact, with them he might well initiate more pathology than he resolves. And lacking this personal growth there are so-called therapists today who are beaters, rather than treaters, of men.

For the discovery of unconscious processes, the building of a significant personality theory, and the development of sensitive therapeutic techniques for the changing of pathologic processes, we are deeply indebted to Sigmund Freud, his associates, and, his followers. Through their understanding of the human in depth, the hundreds of analysts have, over the past 70 years, brought much help to thousands of sufferers. Approaching the problems of their patients from the first comprehensive theoretical view of human personality functioning, these sincere and objective practitioners have developed a way of treating characterized by intellectual honesty, one that each acquired through rigorous self-examination first. They bring to those in need an accepting manner that is nonmoralistic, noncondemning, and ever the ally of the mature strivings in their patients' egos. These traits, combined with a trained sensitivity to subtle communications from mental areas of which the subject had been unaware, have enabled these practitioners to develop a close approximation to what is implied here by the term "therapeutic self."

It should also be noted that the very rigid classical form of psychoanalysis is not typical of that employed by most present-day analysts, and that psychoanalytic treatment has become much more flexible in practice than it was originally in theory.

Although psychoanalysis has often been criticized as being too verbal and too intellectual, its deeper significance was so well dramatized during its early years by an act of great meaning. It was customary at the end of an analysis, after the irrational transferences had been resolved, (especially during the training, or didactic, analyses) for the analyst to invite the analysand to a dinner at his house. This signified the change from a doctor-patient relationship to a friend-friend relationship between two equals. Today, this beautiful symbolic act is rarely practiced since our increased understanding of the complexity of the human psyche does not permit us to determine just when further analytic work is unnecessary. Accordingly, analysands of today *take* analysis rather than *complete* an analysis. This charming human gesture of an earlier day expressed most eloquently that the original analysts perceived the goal of their endeavors as a liberation of their patient from the prison of neurosis and a return to normal living. As the treating and the treated one sat down to eat together it demonstrated that now *both* were capable of giving and receiving affection. Here, we also see a reenactment of the ancient rite where the fatted calf, a symbol of immaturity, is killed, and the reunited family celebrates the return of the prodigal child to a world of meaning and love. The analysand is no longer a neurotic. He has rejoined the family of "normal" mankind.

FOOTNOTE

1. For those who are unacquainted with this psychological test, it is a method of personality evaluation based upon the subject's perception of ink blots.

Chapter 4

THERAPEUTIC SELF FROM THE STANDPOINT OF HUMANISTIC PSYCHOLOGY

"Doctor! I can feel that pencil. I'm really feeling it now." Tears swept down the cheeks of the excited woman. "For the first time in 30 years, I'm feeling something real." This intelligent woman, although skilled in her profession, had been existing for a long time in a schizoid fog of being. Her adjustment to others was adequate, but it was mechanical. She had a continuous feeling of depersonalization within herself and estrangement from the outside world. Life was empty, devoid of meaning. To herself, she seemed like a robot, and the objects she contacted, whether by sight, sound, or touch were like dream materials—ethereal, unreal.

The *Umwelt* of things in her world, the *Mitwelt* of social interactions with others, and the *Eigenwelt* of self-perceptions (May, 1958: Watkins, 1967a): She was certain that all of these existed. Yet somehow, this existence was like the knowledge any of us has about a foreign country to which we have never been. We have read books about it, have seen pictures of it, and have heard others describe it. We could recognize this country if we were suddenly transported there. But we have never truly experienced it firsthand. The land has never contacted the core of our living self. So it had been with this patient. And now, like a blind person who is glimpsing a flash of light for the first time, she was both stunned and delighted. Where this would lead in our treatment only time could tell—but for the moment she "really felt" a pencil.

A small light bulb throws out a dim illumination at night. Its rays, scattering in all directions, are so soon enfeebled that one can barely make out the gross form of large objects like trees. The veins in the leaves and the corrugations in the bark reflect light stimuli that are below the threshold of perception in the eye. So is it when the sense organs that serve as boundaries for the ego, those that divide the self from the not-self, are too lightly energized. They cannot pick up the reality of objects in the world. We speak then of a weak ego, and we say our patient has feelings of estrangement. He is like one who has too few rods and cones in his retina to record fine differentiations of light and shadow.

The focusing lens of a flashlight gathers the rays of the small bulb within and projects them onto a single spot. Now, at the point where the flashlight's rays fixate, the beholder can really see the veins in the tree's leaves and the indentations of its bark. In a similar way a wise military commander knows the ineffectiveness of spreading his forces too thinly. He concentrates his men and matériel on a limited sector when attacking and thus registers a powerful impact at that point.

The skilled therapist knows that he must often be content with making real to his patient a small bit of insight at a time. Should he attempt to interpret an entire neurotic structure at one stroke he might well find that his reserve of credibility in the acceptance of his patient was not equal to his demands for such drastic change in the latter's personality structure. He has attacked on too large a front and suffers a therapeutic Waterloo.

A few minutes before being handed the pencil, our patient, who was suffering from estrangement, had been hypnotized and told, "All your energies, all your resources, will be concentrated at one point in the boundary between you and the world—your finger tips. All your feelings of selfhood will exist for the moment in these fingers, and you will feel, you will really feel, this pencil."

She took the pencil. She touched it. Lovingly she caressed its fluted sides with her fingertips as tears of surprise and happiness flooded forth. No matter that for three long decades life had been gray. No matter that heretofore existence had achieved neither a hell nor a heaven, only a neutral "blah." For the moment, in the here and now, even though only in the small area of impact between her fingertips and this pencil, there was life, meaning, and reality. In such a brief encounter the validity of her own being was affirmed. It was. She was.

We still knew no more than before why her self had become so enfeebled, why she had deserted the universe of people and things, what had been done to her so that she had turned from life as the burnt child from the fire. Why were the normal rewards, the positive reinforcements, which so motivate learning and growth in others, ineffective in her case? They had often been transmitted to her, but she received them not. Like a radio with dead batteries she failed to record the signals emitted by the outside world. By such a therapeutic maneuver we had achieved no analytic breakthrough, no insight, no desensitization; but in that brief minute a tiny flame of being had flared up. There was a moment of living, perhaps a promise of more. Hope returned.

All workers in the fields of psychotherapy devote their energies and abilities toward helping their fellowmen. But there is a great difference in their views of the therapeutic goals. Here lies a major issue, which separated those in the two hotels at the American Psychological Association convention mentioned in the preface to this work. There are those who seek the causes of human misery in the traumas of the past, the psychoanalysts; and there are those who attempt to change the behavior of their patients through reinforcements in the present, the behavior modifiers. The latter perceive their job primarily as eliminating the crippling symptoms or destructive behaviors, which are like boulders in the immediate path that besets the life traveler.

The existential-humanists have their eyes on the distant hills. What is the journey all about? Where are we going and why? Their goals are long-range, their aspirations high. Pain, dysfunction, behavior problems, and all other symptoms are perceived only as events in the *Weltanschauung* (worldview) of the patient. Teach him genuine meaning to his life, and he will eliminate or ignore suffering. He will react realistically with his neighbor. His life will become worthwhile. The humanists, like the psychoanalysts, see the neurotic symptoms and behaviors as the result of pathology within, while the behaviorists consider these symptoms as themselves the pathology to be treated directly. However, unlike the psychoanalysts, the humanists look to the future, toward becoming, rather than toward the past, for the answers to their questions.

Since the enhancement of self, of becoming, is the focus of our thesis here, then the concept of therapeutic self, although not hostile to other theoretical orientations, finds truly a home in the framework of this approach. Therapeutic self is a humanistic concept, and it is within this position that we now pursue its meaning and development.

The current humanistic approaches to psychotherapy have stemmed from the fusion of two basic streams of thought: existential philosophy and phenomenological psychology. Existential philosophy was initially formulated some 120 years ago in the writings of Kierkegaard (1954) although elements can be traced as far back as Plato (1930-35). More recent significant contributions include those by Buber (1955); Heidegger (1949); Jaspers (1952); Marcel (1948); May (1958); Sartre (1953), and Tillich (1952). In the Orient similar thinking has characterized the practice of Zen Buddhism (Suzuki, 1950; Watts, 1957).

It will be recalled that Immanuel Kant (1934) confronting the dilemma of materialism versus idealism challenged the very tool (reason) through which man had arrived at a skepticism (Hume, 1963) that apparently by rational explanation could prove the nonexistence of both mind and matter. Here we see a searching inquiry into the nature of man's self and the reality of his existence. Central to existentialism is the concept of being-in-the-world, a fusion of self and nonself. As Gendlin (1970) puts it, "For existentialism there is no 'subject' within separate from the 'object' outside." All of these existential writers were deeply concerned with meaning, becoming, and the experiential world of a human.

Attention to such aspects of human nature developed as a protest to the dehumanization of man that accompanied the Industrial Revolution. Great materialistic gains had been made during the 18th century; during that period man learned about gravitation, electricity, and took giant strides forward in the physical sciences. This increase in technology continued in the 19th and 20th centuries and increased man's material possessions a thousand-fold greatly enhancing his abilities to cope with the physical world.

Somehow though, as man acquired great physical satisfactions he began to lose himself. His awareness and certainty of identity became unclear. Even the more tangible neuroses, such as the hysterical conversion reactions (often limb paralyses) that characterized the patients of Freud, and the breakdowns of World War I, tended to diminish. Instead, "existential" neuroses, where life became meaningless, were seen with increased frequency in the offices of therapists. This loss in zest for living afflicted both old and young. Many, especially in the white-collar executive class, sought through compulsive achievement (as described so well by Whyte, 1956) to throw themselves into the quest for more money and status; often they lost it all at retirement. The cessation of such striving disclosed to these men the true emptiness of their selves. With no worlds left to conquer they became nobodies, developed depressions, and often died within a year or so.

Still others, especially the young, sought meaning to their existence by an aversion to materialistic striving and the abandonment of the values espoused by their forefathers. Through an ever-increasing withdrawal into the pleasures of sex and drugs, external reality was denied. And as their world shrank so also did the "being-in" it diminish, for the two go hand in hand. Desperately they sought to revive existence through increased intake of psychedelic or narcotic drugs. Finally, if mental death (psychosis) did not come first, physical death often overtook them, by suicide, by an excess of drugs, or by the ravages of disease to their neglected bodies.

The search for self and for the meaning of existence became more frenzied as many people developed "future shock" (Toffler, 1970) at the almost impossible task of keeping up with a world whose values, laws, customs, morals, and demands were changing faster than the nervous systems of men could integrate.

Human need has a way, as Eric Hoffer (1951) put it, of stimulating "men of action" to put into effect the ideas of the "men of words." Accordingly, it is not surprising to find that a number of existential clinicians, such as Binswanger (1958) Straus (1958), Sonneman (1954), and Laing (1969) began translating these philosophical concepts into therapeutic approaches with their patients. The inspiration was here, the needs of the suffering ones delineated, the goals of treatment defined. These men knew what needed to be done and each strove to accomplish his therapeutic objectives through his own techniques, analytic or otherwise. What was lacking were approaches that could be taught to students: a body of specific treatment techniques and skills and the methodologies required for changing the state of affairs.

This movement was not one-way, since others who were originally therapists, such as Erikson (1968) and Frankl (1972), drew on their clinical experience to define more specifically the identity crises of our time and to formulate further philosophical positions. But theory was now ahead of practice, and the need was to proceed from the general to the specific. Philosophy could formulate the "whither to"; scientific experimentation and clinical experience must answer the "how." Some fertilization from a new point of origin was required.

This second source, which was to unite with existential philosophy to form the present humanistic therapy movement, may have originated in the break which Rank, the optimist, made with Freud, the pessimist. Rank (1952), in a personal trauma of birth, cut his own umbilical ties of dependency to "Mother" Freud and struck out for the concept of man's freedom as opposed to his determination by unconscious forces outside of his control, the view maintained by classical psychoanalysis. This thesis of the inherent dignity of the individual who could will for himself, who was not merely the product of a determined past, excited such disciples as Taft (1936) and Allen (1942). These in turn stimulated the creative mind of Carl Rogers (1942, 1951) whose client-centered therapy, backed by a phenomenological psychology, brought the next great advance toward a treatment of selves by selves.

Rogers drew from the idealism of Rank the theoretical background for a new type of counseling in which the self of the client was both the object of change and the controlling agent toward that change; it was a type of counseling in which the person of the therapist was the catalyst, not the director of the process. In the work of Rogers one sees also the influence of John Dewey (1916), that apostle of permissive growth in children, whose teachings so permeated the setting of Teachers College, Columbia University, at the time that Rogers took his doctorate there. The client-centered therapists translated the idealism of Rank and Dewey into a technique for treatment, a way of doing toward clients, which gradually became a way of being. Rogers first called this "non-directive" therapy.

Perhaps the essential elements in the phenomenological psychology (which is a psychology of perception) promulgated by Rogers were the theses that "Every individual exists in a continually changing world of experience of which he is the center." He "reacts to the field as it is experienced and perceived." "This perceptual field is, for the individual, 'reality.' " Accordingly, "the best vantage point for understanding behavior is from the internal frame of reference of the individual himself."

This represented a major break with the behavioristic position that the best (and for some behaviorists, only) vantage point for correctly understanding behavior lies in controlled, objective observation by another who evaluates it from an external position. This had been in the tradition of the early behaviorists (Watson, 1929) who completely disavowed introspection as an acceptable tool of science.

In his early rejection of the manipulative approaches of directive psychology, such as had been advocated in the writings of Thorne (1950), Rogers (1942) abandoned entirely the leading role of the therapist and proposed a completely listening and following approach. It was hypothesized that the client had within himself the resources for his own growth, and that if these were encouraged by the acceptance of the counselor, pathology would be replaced by self-understanding, an understanding that the client had arrived at by himself. The job of the treating one was to listen and to reflect back after each client comment the essential feeling aspect conveyed to him. The therapist was cast in the role of a kind of mirror. Through the responses of the counselor the client would realistically see himself and make the necessary changes.

This formulation proved inadequate as treatment often deteriorated into a mechanical repetition of the client's words preceded only by a "You feel that. . . ." During the second stage in the development of his current approach Rogers (1951) and his associates undertook many objective research studies designed to investigate the nature of the therapist-client interaction. Much attention was given to the self-concept and its full development within the client. Both process studies (Cartwright, 1957; Rogers, 1959) aimed at determining the nature of the therapeutic movement, and outcome studies (Rogers & Dymond, 1954) designed to evaluate the success of the treatments were undertaken. In fact, his investigations, which clearly demonstrated the effectiveness of his treatment approach, became a prototype for much of the outcome research performed by the behavior modifiers a decade later.

During this period Rogers apparently would have defined a therapeutic self as one who provided for the client a "permissive atmosphere," placed the responsibility for the treatment "genuinely" with the individual being treated, and showed a "basic respect for the capacity" of that person. This appeared for him at that time to be the necessary and sufficient conditions for therapy.

It remained to the third step in the evolution of Rogers's thinking (1961, 1967) for the achievement of a fuller and more adequate formulation of his earlier principles. Here Rogers proposed three basic ingredients he considered essential in the treatment process, and by inference essential to the ability of a therapeutic person. He did not use the term "therapeutic self ", but he described three conditions as necessary for such:

1. Accurate empathy.
2. Unconditional positive regard.
3. Congruence.

With the development of these concepts Rogers's client-centered approach was now termed experiential therapy.

By accurate empathy Rogers meant the ability of the therapist to understand the responses of the client fully and correctly, especially the feelings implied in them. If one is content to accept Rogers's view as equating accurate empathy with correct understanding, then our psychoanalytic colleagues could argue that what he is describing is only what is done in their own therapy when a correct understanding of the patient is reflected back to him by an analytic interpretation. However, Rogers was more concerned with the emotional tone and implications of each response than with the unconscious origins of a sequence of behavior.

There is a question as to whether or not Rogers requires that this understanding be based on a similar feeling, which the therapist is actually sensing at that moment. At one time Rogers (1951) wrote, "The experiencing with the client, the living of his attitudes, is not in terms of emotional identification on the counselor's part, but rather an empathic identification, where the counselor is perceiving the hates and hopes and fears of the client through immersion in an empathic process, but without himself, as counselor, experiencing those hates and hopes and fears."

In a more recent statement, Rogers (See Shlien, 1961, p. 304) defines empathy as follows: "This means that he senses and comprehends the client's immediate awareness of his own private world—it means not only recognizing those aspects of experience which the client has already been able to verbalize, but also those unsymbolized aspects of his experience which have somehow been comprehended through subtle non-verbal cues by the delicate psychological radar of the therapist. The skillful therapist senses the client's world—as if it were his own but without ever losing the as if quality." He states (See Koch, 1959) that "if this 'as if' quality is lost then the state is one of 'identification.'" Rogers apparently holds that once it has become identification then the counselor would no longer be able to understand fully, since to do so would require that he retain his objectivity.

Some of the client-centered writers seem to be advocating just such a state of identification. Thus Raskin (See Rogers, 1951, p. 29) states that "The counselor. . .tries to get within and to live the attitudes expressed instead of observing them. . .If he is attempting to live the attitudes of the other, he cannot be diagnosing them." Still others of Rogers's followers (Tomlinson & Whitney, 1970) maintain that the therapist experiences the client's feelings "as if they were his own." This point will be crucial in our later development of "resonance", a term central to the concept of the therapeutic self, which will be compared with Rogers's "accurate empathy."

The second factor Rogers holds as significant in the effective therapist is one he terms "unconditional positive regard." Others have called it simply "acceptance." Thus, Van der Veen (1970) defines "acceptance" as "valuing or prizing all aspects of the client, including the parts that are hateful to himself or appear wrong in the eyes of society." He notes that the therapist does not manipulate the client into behaving in a way that the therapist values.

This statement that the therapist accepts even those parts of the client that are "hateful" seems to be rather extreme. The behaviorists would suggest that in doing this the treating one is actually reinforcing destructive responses. Perhaps a more defensible position would be that the therapist shows unconditional positive regard for the *self* of the client, although not necessarily always for his *behavior*. This implies, of course, a distinction between the client's being and his doing, a distinction behaviorists probably would not accept.

Finally Rogers has posited the factor of congruence. Simply put, it means that the therapist tries to adhere to that old maxim, "To thine own self be true." He is continually authentic. He behaves and speaks as he feels. He does not conceal or mislead by saying one thing to the client when actually he feels something different. If he feels angry at the client he does not pretend to feel kindly toward him. Congruence is not merely an honest act put on by the therapist; it is a constant way of being, which he manifests toward his clients at all times because that is the way he lives. He has learned to be congruent toward all people. By being true to himself he provides the client with a genuine relationship different from the phony facades we so often present to each other. The patient in such an authentic atmosphere is truly free to grow and to become authentic himself. Accurate empathy and congruence are considered the most significant of these three factors, and in the Rogerian humanistic position a sine qua non for effective treatment.

Burton (1972) adds still another factor when he calls attention to the point that many therapists, even though authentic, need constant new stimulation. Otherwise, they tend to cease growing, to settle into one type of therapy, one way of being, toward their clients. He summarizes this with the statement that "Improvisation is the fount of creativity every therapist needs," and he suggests a number of activities whereby the therapist can continue to develop and keep from becoming dull. The failure to change has caused many therapists to give up active treatment during the latter part of their careers.

One can hardly be surprised to find the gradual coming together of Rogers and his disciples with such existential thinkers as Rollo May (1961), himself an analyst. The marriage of phenomenological psychology and existential philosophy has brought forth as offspring many forms of humanistic therapy such as one finds in the writings of Bugental (1967), Satir (1967), Burton (1972), Shostrom (1967), not to mention those like Horney (1950), Moreno (1946) and Perls (1973), who moved from the psychoanalytic position in the humanistic direction.

It is not our purpose here to mention more than a few of the contributors to humanistic-existential therapy. The variation and innovations are many, but the general tenor of their approaches all accent optimistic and idealistic values. They are deeply concerned with self, with self and being as distinguished from behavior and doing. Behavior, especially in interpersonal relationships, is still a focus of attention in the work of many of these, such as Bach (1954); Bach and Wyden (1969); and Berne (1961). Yet unlike the behaviorists, they regard the self, however it is defined, as a worthy object of study, development, and treatment.

The idea that the goal for both client and therapist is the achievement of genuineness, of consistency in behavior, has been described in different ways by different writers. Jourard (1971) speaks of the "transparent self," the individual who is sufficiently free of deceptions, games, and blockings to be willing to disclose himself fully and honestly to others. Jourard would probably hold that to be a therapeutic self one must first be willing to be a transparent self. Thus he states that "Psychotherapy is the art of promoting self-disclosure and authentic being in patients who withhold their real selves from expression." By being authentic himself, the treating one is truly a therapist for "the person who reads or listens to the hitherto concealed authentic experience of another is enriched by it." For Jourard the transparent self achieves the goal of authenticity of which Bugental (1965) speaks.

Both Jourard and Shostrom consider manipulation as the antithesis of authentic therapy, but the latter speaks of "actualizing behavior" as an optimal, or "creative," form of manipulation, since we are all manipulators at best.

It is apparent that the various existential-humanistic writers have chosen different aspects to emphasize, and each contributor has built his system around a somewhat different term. But many of these terms are synonymous or at least highly overlapping. And all the humanistic therapists tend to agree about the general, basic characteristics they would ascribe to a therapeutic personality.

Summarizing, we might say that from the humanistic position the good therapist is concerned with genuine meaning in existence, that he regards humans as growing or becoming, and that the therapeutic goal is to become authentic, genuine, transparent, nonmanipulative, and congruent in one's relations with others. They would hold that this can be achieved within the therapy or counseling situation as the therapist himself exemplifies these traits. They would hold further that this process will occur as the therapist shows great positive regard for the client by accepting him for what he is without trying to impose the therapist's values on him. They would feel that the therapist can do this only if he has a very accurate empathy for his client by fully understanding the client's world and by reflecting back to the client that understanding. Such an understanding to be complete must be emotional and experiential, not merely intellectual.

If the therapist can "be" toward his client in these ways, if he can exemplify such qualities in his own life, then he will help the other to grow, to discover his own true self, and to develop genuine meaning in his own existence. Such a therapist as a facilitator of authenticity would truly be a therapeutic self. The essence of this position has been stated most beautifully by Tillich as follows:

> "The other person cannot be controlled like a natural object. Every human being is an absolute limit, an unpierceable wall of resistance against any attempts to make him into an object. He who breaks this resistance by external force destroys his own humanity; he never can become a mature person."
>
> "This interdependence of man and man in the process of becoming human is a judgment against a

psychotherapeutic method in which the patient is a mere object for the analyst as a subject. The inevitable reaction then is that the patient tries in return to make the analyst into an object for himself as subject. This kind of acting and reacting has a depersonalizing effect on both the analyst and the patient. The transference phenomenon should be reconsidered in the light of a 'philosophy of encounter' in which existentialist and essentialist elements are united."

—Paul Tillich (1960)

PART III

THE SELF

Probably the first questions formulated by living organisms as soon as they achieved the ability to differentiate themselves from the rest of the world was "What am I?", or "Who am I?" From the earliest historical times man has tried to define himself. The highest mental endeavors of our great philosophers have wrestled with this issue, and we might assume that even the Neanderthal must have felt the pressure of need to understand himself, albeit with primitive and undeveloped language. At what point in the evolutionary scale of life this concept was first manifested we will probably never know. But since the first task of every organism is to differentiate itself from that which is object, we can infer that life begins coping with this enigma very early, both ontogenetically within each individual and phylogenetically within the evolution of life forms.

During the next four chapters we too shall struggle a bit with the problem. If we are to develop a concept called the therapeutic self, we must first try to define what we mean merely by the self, the genus before the species. Accordingly, let us pursue the concept of self back into the realms of human speculation, the region from whence artists draw their inspirations, and into the region of philosophy, that mother of sciences, which through the ages of man has ever spawned new vistas concerning the meaning of life. For the therapeutic self, concerned as it is with the enhancement of the human being, cannot develop or exist as a separate entity from the great questions of man's existence. Since the self can only be experienced by each of us within our own selves, our explorations must of necessity be speculative, but we can endeavor to be as rational as possible. There is little hope at this point to validate with empirical evidence.

Chapter 5

SUBJECT-OBJECT

I live in the land of my self. Within this land there are many territories that I own. They include my thoughts, my wishes, my feelings, my impulses, my dreams, my body. I am aware of all these. Some of my kingdom is very beautiful: my happy feelings, my loves, the values I prize. There are parts though that I wish were not here: my pains, my worries, my anxieties, the clashes in conflict between two or more of my principalities. And there are slum areas in my self that I would like to avoid perceiving: my inconsistencies, my evil thoughts, my shameful lusts, my ignoble behaviors. There are also many other lands that do not belong to me: all you other people, the plants, the animals, the rocks and sky and all the things that make their presence known by impinging on the boundaries of my territory.

My world of self started with an infinitesimal speck and has grown over the many years. Its boundaries have expanded and vast areas are now included within my domain. As I came to know about the great outside world, I built within myself replicas of what I perceived and gradually expanded to become the mighty nation of me that now exists.

At first I was totally immersed in an ocean of warmth, a universal fluid that met all my needs. Then, the workings of my bodily self unfolded and built ever greater structures as if directed by an ancient plan designed eons ago by a master architect. At that time I had little intelligence of all this activity. It just happened, or perhaps it would be better to say that *I happened.*

I developed many different body parts, a head, arms, legs, hands. I moved, I kicked, and I found that something around me inhibited the magnitude of my kick. I had much liberty, but there were limits to that freedom. As I reached out, there was a soft, yielding wall that contained all of me, and I could travel but little. As time passed, and as I grew larger, my home gently expanded. However, my need for movement and freedom enormously increased. There came a time when the house in which I resided was no longer large enough to include all the boundless me, which sought to feel, to touch, to reach out, to do.

With a mighty surge I squeezed out the door and found myself in a vast world beyond comprehension. Strange sensations came over me. Many new and weird objects contacted my boundary. Some made me feel very good; others hurt. Furthermore, needs that before seemed always to have been met were not now gratified immediately. I would often ache with a gnawing sensation, which I discovered might be satisfied by the outside forces if I made great protest.

All this time the artisans of my self were very busy. I was constantly reaching out and expanding into new lands. Within, I was busily engaged in examining, ordering, cataloging, storing, and assigning to some place in my realm of being all the new objects of my conquests. For most of these I established deeds of ownership, and they became truly mine. But some of the things I had seized did not fit readily into my society of being. Although I kept them within the walls of my own cities they were like visiting aliens. I never truly experienced them as mine. Often I felt as if they were dangerous strangers, potential saboteurs from the outer world, who might do me harm. However, others were there in whom I placed considerable confidence. In fact, I came to rely on them to fulfill my needs. They stroked me in loving ways and made me feel much pleasure.

My life seemed to be completely engrossed in three functions: acquiring, having, and keeping. For it was not enough simply to get. Once one has them it is important to protect one's possessions if one is to retain them. At first I was very busy in acquiring and enjoying the having thereof. Accordingly, it came to me as a great shock to find that there were others who would deny my acquiring. In fact, they tried to take from me that which I already had. This was almost unbelievable. A great deal of my resources had to be devoted to the national defense of my territory. I was required to guard my self from hostile incursion abroad and to engage in certain policing activities within so as to assure that antisocial elements, internal traitors to my own integrity, would not precipitate civil war and disrupt the consonance of my living. But if I must spend much energy-money in protecting my stability from external aggressors and from internal dissidents then little would be left to procure for me the abundance of a rich and enjoyable existence. How complex my life had now become.

You know, I never thought that you on the outside might be having similar problems. I was so busy acquiring I did not realize that those from whom I took might feel the same sense of dismay that came over me when I lost one of my possessions to another. I was concerned only in directly enhancing my own existence. It only occurred to me much later, after I had developed tremendous complexity, that my own welfare was bound up so intimately with yours. Nor did I discover that I could gain from you if I would cease to treat you as an object to be seized and digested. I was so concerned with differentiating my self from you, declaring my own independence, building my own economy and establishing my own government that I was unable to perceive my self and the world from your vantage point. In not being able to do so I missed something of value.

The concept of the self, the "I" as distinguished from "not-self," has preoccupied philosophical and psychological thought for centuries. Thus many of the differences that separated the approaches of Plato and Aristotle toward the world revolved around this conflict. The later conflict between Locke (1963), Berkeley (1929), and Hume (1963) and the attempted resolution by Kant (1934) also centered about man's great enigma and his attempt to prove his own existence. Many other writers, both philosophers and psychologists such as Buber (1970), Freud (1947), and Fairbairn (1944; see also Guntrip, 1952) have made yeoman efforts to explain the phenomena of subject-object. Psychotherapies tend to divide themselves between those concerned with object relations and those whose focus of attention is the self. It is the inability to discriminate between what is self and what is nonself that constitutes the heart of that mental illness called schizophrenia. The psychotic perceives some of his own thoughts objectively as perceptions. We term these hallucinations. It is with the greatest of difficulties that therapists can help him to correct this situation. Drugs, electroshock, surgery, recreation, activities, human relationship, and talk have all been utilized in the attempt to teach the patient to test reality, to allocate to the world of *it* that which belongs there and to the world of *me* that which emerges from self. By reality we mean that which is consensually validated, that to which a number of outside observers (at least the majority) would agree.

A patient in a mental hospital was once asked by a young psychiatrist, "Tell me, my good man, why are you here?" To which the other replied, "Because, sir, there are more people in the world like you than like me."

However, it is not only psychotics in which the confusion between subject and object occurs. Much of the misunderstanding between theoreticians, therapists, and just plain people inheres in the failure of all of us to label clearly an objective item from a subjective one in our interactions.

The practice of law is much concerned with the problem of objectivity. Attorneys are trained to ask questions during the taking of testimony aimed at determining with the highest degree of precision just exactly what it was that the witness directly observed and what he inferred. The good trial lawyer is one whose abilities are highly trained to discriminate between that which is object and that which is subject, and to make proper objection to the latter. His is the task of determining the world of fact contaminated as minimally as possible from the subjective world of speculation. And where the subjective needs of the respective parties are such as to clash with that objectivity, a judge (who is presumed to be objective and impartial) is provided in the court of law to mediate and to decide what is the true objective reality and what is not. The mere fact that some judges are known to be tough on criminals and some easy shows that objectivity in the human is relative, not absolute. A good attorney will endeavor to bring his client before a judge known to be subjectively favorable to the issues represented by that client, and psychologists are being called upon today (Schulman, Shaver, Colman, Emrich & Christie, 1973) to assist lawyers in picking jurors whose attitudes would more likely be favorable toward their client or position. Man strives for objectivity; he never completely achieves it. Something of his own self colors his every thought, his every judgment, his every behavior.

Scientific methodology is engaged in a constant struggle to increase objectivity and minimize subjectivity. Sources of contaminating biases in data, operator variables (Rosenthal, 1966; Orne, 1962) and errors in perception are guarded against as if man does not truly trust his own self. Actually, most men do trust very much their *own* selves. Try and argue with a paranoid that his delusional beliefs are based on false reality testing. See what little success you have! He will maintain the objectivity of his reality testing regardless of all evidence to the contrary. Nor need we restrict this observation to the mentally ill. The couplet, "The man convinced against his will is of the same opinion still," is based on the common knowledge that when we have committed ourself to a belief, to a position, we are not willing to accept observations that are opposed. To do so involves us in an inner inconsistency, in "cognitive dissonance" (Festinger, 1957). All our being, with all skills available to it—selective perception, repression, denial, and all the other defensive mechanisms we have learned—will be employed to defend and maintain that position to which we have committed ourselves.

Even the supposedly objective scientist when confronted with experimental evidence contradicting his theoretical position seldom abandons the position. How often do we find a researcher in the literature publishing a statement such as, "In the light of the findings of Dr. K., I see that my previous position was incorrect, and accordingly, I renounce it." What is more likely to happen is that Dr. J. will now redouble his efforts to secure experimental findings that reinforce his original position and tend to discredit that of Dr. K.

No, it is seldom that a man doubts his own self or his own objectivity. It is that of others he distrusts. And it is because of this doubt that he erects complicated systems of jurisprudence in the field of government and sophisticated mathematical research designs in the field of science.

Most of us have a tendency to trust our own selves and resent having to submit our veracity to objective controls established by others. However, we simultaneously are suspicious of subjective statements by others and feel greater security when we can impose objective evaluations on *them.* It is precisely the problem, objectivity versus subjectivity that is the focus of this book. How can we balance these two factors both in our own selves and in others?

To achieve such a harmonious balance it is necessary that we be able to delineate clearly just what is subject and what object. It is precisely this lack of clear distinction that we find lacking in so many therapeutic writings, both psychoanalytic and humanistic. The behaviorist simply ignores the problem by refusing to accept the subjective as a legitimate source of data.

Psychoanalytic therapists talk about libidinal cathexis as it affects an interpersonal relationship, and humanistic writers discuss empathizing with a client without specifically pointing out in the situation just what is an objective item and what a subjective one. There is a vague flooding through of boundaries. For example, if one is enjoined to be kind, who is one to be kind to, one's self or to others? If one understands the feelings of another, is it as an outside observer who knows what such feelings are like and is perceiving in the other the kind of behavior associated with them? Or is the therapist actually experiencing within his own person the same feelings? Are his own adrenal glands working; is his own blood pressure increasing, etc.? Such terms as "empathize," "understand," and "relate to" do not distinguish the objective from the subjective aspects of the processes being labeled.

Yet the interrelationship between one's own self and that of others, the breaking down of the subject-object dichotomy, is the theme of much of the world's romantic writings. Breathes there a lover who did not equate himself so closely with his beloved that harm to the other was felt painfully on his own self? For we separate ourselves from our mother and the rest of the world to establish our own unique identity only to seek the loss of that separateness by a return to that which had been made object. The most meaningful lives include identification with others. And the greatest triumphs of meaningful living seem to be reached only for those who, having established their hard-won independence, are willing to lose it again in a fusion with other people or with causes.

> No man is an Iland, intire of it selfe; every man is a peece of the Continent, a part of the maine; if a Clod bee washed away by the Sea, Europe is the lesse, as well as if a Promontorie were, as well as if a Mannor of thy friends or of thine owne were; any man's death diminishes me, because I am involved in Mankinde; And therefore never send to know for whom the bell tolls; It tolls for thee.
>
> —John Donne (1623)

Chapter 6

EXISTENCE AS IMPACT

Just I—A Soliloquy of Self

In the beginning there was just I, but I didn't know me, not until you and I touched—I mean all you out there, you things and people that are not me. So I guess there had to be a you for there to be a me.

As time went on there became more of me. That's because some of you joined up and became me. So now there's a lot of me, most of which I know, and some of which I don't know. I usually know when something is me. That means a part of me is touching another part. Sometimes, however, I meet a bit of me that I don't recognize. Maybe that's because I don't feel very proud of that part. So I bury it in a dark corner of myself or pretend that it's you out there and not me. But if I do that then there's less of me, and I get smaller.

I often wonder what there was before me. That's ridiculous, because in the beginning there was just I. That must be why the same single mark that stands for "I" is also the number "1."

What's it going to be like when I am gone? That's equally stupid. I have always been; I will always be. You out there simply don't exist unless you impact me. You owe your being to the fact that I am. To think otherwise is impossible. So not only in the beginning was there just I, but in the ending there will also be—just I.

In an earlier paper this writer (Watkins, 1967a) wrote as follows: "The question as to whether there is such a thing as a sound if a tree falls in a forest containing no listener has often been discussed in philosophical circles. The scientist or objectivist would argue that the presence or absence of a listener in no way changed the reality of the existence of those physical vibrations which constitute sound. The subjective-minded philosopher, however, would answer that sound is an experience, not a vibration, that it is generally (although not necessarily always) initiated by a physical vibration, but that, being an experience, it cannot exist without an experiencer.

"Such a line of thought leads us into consideration of just what constitutes 'an experiencer'; what is the nature of being, of existence? We are baffled as to its essence. We can describe manifestations of being; we can communicate to each other in reasonable equated symbols, called words, our own unique experience of being, but existence, like hypnosis, lends itself better to description and observation than to precise definition."

In that paper the thesis was proposed that "it is the impact between two entities—one, an experiencer, and the other, that which is being experienced—which constitutes the essence of existence."

This point of view differs from that held by many others concerned with the development of existential thinking and its Oriental counterpart, Zen psychology. Rollo May has written (1958, p. 19), "Eastern thought never suffered the radical split between subject and object that has characterized Western thought, and this dichotomy is exactly what existentialism seeks to overcome." Again May notes (1958, p. 14) that "Kierkegaard and the existential thinkers appealed to a reality underlying both subjectivity and objectivity." The Zen Buddhist searches for a state of true existence. He may call it satori or, in other sects, nirvana, but primarily it means the loss of an individuated self through its identification and total merging with the universe.[1] Likewise, existentialism seeks to find a true state of being more fundamental than object-subject, one that avoids, and hence solves, the many problems and dilemmas created by this dichotomy.

The search for original states of being has not had a history of great success. We may recall that when matter was broken down to what was considered its ultimate particle, this turned out to be arrangements of energy. It seems that our search for original states, whether they are states of consciousness, states of hypnosis, or states of being, may well resolve into process—into something that can be better described by a verb than by a noun.

In certain studies,[2] normal subjects were isolated in rooms from which light, sound, smell, and other possible sensory stimulations had been eliminated. In other words, they were removed from contact with the outer world and the world of human relationships (*Umwelt* and *Mitwelt*). Existence did not cease for these subjects. They soon created for themselves an inner world *(Eigenwelt)* in the form of hallucinations. The experimental subjects reported that, like dreams, these hallucinations were sensed and responded to as if real. Similar findings have been verified when subjects have undergone extended sleep deprivation (Kleitman, 1963; West, 1967).

It would seem that the real essence of being does not lie in some hypothetical underlying state that eliminates the differences between subject and object; rather it lies in the energy impact between subject and object as separate, distinct, and different entities. It is this impact between two different entities that constitutes real existence, real being; I, for one, would echo the proverbial French comment made to a different but similar situation, *"Vive la différence!"*

The reality of a subject-object dichotomy seems to be one of the most significant and verifiable of all psychological facts. Why must we try so hard to lose ourselves in a fluid identification with everything? Our unique and individual existence, as opposed to that which is not our own self, is one of the most precious values we have, one that has been laboriously acquired through maturation and learning as we came to differentiate ourselves from our mothers and from the rest of the world. The unhappiest people seem to be those who have either lost, or have never acquired, this ability to differentiate themselves from others and who consequently can develop no healthy object relationships with others. It is through our impact on others that the reality and meaningfulness of our own existence is validated.

Beginnings seem to be characterized by the coming together of two—two elements, forces, things, or people. Molecules begin with the union of at least two atoms, relationships are between two different people, individual human life by the contact first of two people, then of two cells. Even the Bible speaks in Genesis of the earth being created by the impact of God on the void.

The two elements coming together are not identical; they are always different from each other (e.g., hydrogen-oxygen or man-woman). Wars begin with the contact of two different political entities on each other—and it is precisely the fact that they are different that brings on that which is new, the conflict. Newness involves change, and it is change that is the essence of life and existence. The history of the existences of men is the saga of their impacts on each other and on the elements of nature.

As previously mentioned, existential theory has considered three fields of impact: The *Umwelt,* or environmental world around us; the *Mitwelt,* or "withness" between people as they interact socially with each other; and the *Eigenwelt,* the relations with one's own self. Various psychotherapies have dealt with these three areas of interaction. However, some treatment systems have been more concerned with one than with the others. For example, while not denying the existence of a self system, interpersonal relationship therapies, such as the so-called Washington school developed by Sullivan (1954), have emphasized the disturbances that occur to the individual when there is conflict in his social interactions, how he gets along with people. Are his impacts with others constructive or destructive; and if the latter, how might they be improved?

The "self" therapies, those described as existential or humanistic, while not neglecting the field of interpersonal relationships, tend to concentrate on intrapersonal relationships *(Eigenwelt),* one's transactions within one's self.

Regardless of their differential emphases all of the therapists are dealing with contacts between the individual and his world, himself and others, or between different aspects of himself. In fact, the transactions between counselor and client, between therapist and patient, are themselves impacts designed to alter existence by initiating change, new beginnings, new becomings. The fundamental principle is the same; only the field of concentration differs.

It is our contention, therefore, that the greatest values of life are achieved when there is the clearest delineation between me and thee, followed by the most rewarding interaction between us. Buber (1970) puts it, "Egos appear by setting themselves apart from other egos. Persons appear by entering into relation to other persons." In other words, the experience of being occurs when there is first a differentiation of self followed by an impact between the self and other selves (or nonself objects). Let the sharpest possible distinctions be drawn between subject and object, for it is not in their fusion, but in their impingement on each other that true existence and being are realized. We approach others, not to lose our differences by a flowing together, but in order that we may increase our impact on each other by minimizing as much as possible the spatial, temporal, and psychological distances by which we are separated. The smaller the distance between two bodies, the more powerful their impact on each other. The greater the magnitude of their touching, the greater the awareness of existence, the more meaningful the life of each.

In the deepest and the broadest dimensions, it is your impact on me that makes me intensely aware that *I am* and *you are.* Likewise, I do the same to you. By maintaining our differences and reducing our separation we exert on each other a maximum of force for change, for beginnings, for happenings—for existence. It is this closeness of two humans wherein true living is experienced, two beings who touch but do *not* fuse.

Neutrinos are particles whose existence was hypothesized in 1930 by Wolfgang Pauli. They have no mass, no charge, no magnetic field, no physical properties, and can pass through the earth in a fraction of a second. Since they possess no mass they could not impact other particles. Accordingly, their existence remained only a speculation until their discovery much later (Reines & Cowan, 1956) during the rare occurrence when one neutrino impacts another. The discovery of neutrinos teaches us that there may well be other forms of energy about which we are entirely unaware. This leaves as an open question the hypothesis that life, or more specifically self, is an energy. Some scientists would argue that we have no objective evidence of an energy that is self. One answer to that is that I (my self) have very definitely made an impact on others. I do many things that influence others in the same way that energy influences a galvanometer. If I merely turn the hands of a watch, I am altering by my "self" action a scientific measuring instrument. What is lacking in my turning is a constant and predictable action as in a certain quantum of electricity. Behavioristic psychology has aimed to make such action (behavior) constant and predictable. To date it has not succeeded.

The theory that existence is impact would hold only in *this* universe when matter strikes matter (or energy strikes contraenergy). Quantum physicists (Dirac, 1930) hypothesized the existence of particles of antimatter, or negative matter. Such a hypothesis seemed ridiculous at the time. But a year later Anderson (1932) verified the existence of such an antimatter particle. Koestler (1972) reports that we have now discovered the existence of some 50 different antimatter particles. It is interesting to note that the impact of a particle on an antiparticle results in the nonexistence of both. Some have speculated that an antiuniverse exists that equals and matches the universe as we know it; if so, then if the boundaries between these two universes were to break down, and they impacted each other, there would be total nonexistence.

It also seems strange to equate existence in this universe with impact and then note that if the impact is between particles of matter and antimatter (e.g., from the negative universe) the result is nonexistence. However, this is only another example of the observation by Gestalt psychologists many years ago that the response elicited by a stimulus depends on the field within which the stimulus operates. We so often forget that the human being is not like an inert stone, which when bumped moves according to the early formulations of energy and mass. The stimulus that impacts the human and brings about existence is interpreted by him through a highly complex filtering and integrating system. When identical stimuli impact different organisms, the behavior that comes out may be very different in each case.

Three men, who were standing beside each other and doing the same kind of work, were once asked the same stimulus question, "What are you doing?" The first replied, "I'm piling bricks." The second muttered, "I'm making twenty-five dollars a day." The third looked up slowly, and with a sense of awe exclaimed, "I'm helping to build a new cathedral." In the following chapters we shall aim to do more than merely pile bricks or earn twenty-five dollars a day.

FOOTNOTES

1. One of the Zen koans, or paradoxes, asks the question, "What is the sound of the clap of one hand?" (e.g., what is the experience of an essence without an impact on another?)
2. For surveys of these see Solomon, Kubansky, Leiderman, Mendelson, Trumbull, & Wexler, 1961; See also Jackson & Ellis, 1971.

Chapter 7

THE LOCUS OF SELF

The psychologist Edward Lee Thorndike once wrote that if something exists it must exist in some quantity. And if it exists in some quantity it can be measured.[1] A similar axiom might be that if something exists, it exists in some place. If that is so where lies the self? Where do *I* reside: my body, inside my skin, in my heart, or in my brain? The philosopher Descartes believed that the soul was seated in midbrain within the pineal gland. On the other hand, since the word "heart" is used to represent the center, and since the heart is so vital to living function, there are those who would place the self as lying within that organ. When asked, "Where are *you* located?" some subjects will point between the eyes just above the bridge of the nose. The tendency in scientific circles to equate the "mind" with neurological functioning would probably induce some to place self within the central nervous system.

A number of years ago a young man who was a patient of mine exhibited the behavior of Don Juanism. His success in the conquest of the female was truly outstanding. It undoubtedly would have been the envy of many males. However, he was miserable. He felt that he, his person, his self, was only "a big penis." He complained that he neither felt like a person nor was he treated like one by others. It was as if his selfness existed only in his genital organ.

The classical psychoanalytic explanation of Don Juanism is that the weak male, plagued by fears of latent homosexuality, seeks to prove his masculinity through the frequent seduction of women. Each time he secures only temporary reassurance. In fact, after the expenditure of his masculine energies during the act, the voice of the feminine component within him becomes that much stronger and his doubts are reactivated.

It would appear that in this case my patient repetitiously sought not so much to establish his masculinity as to prove his being; but in so behaving he verified only the existence of his genital organ. That was the only part of him that received validating feedback from others in his world. The panic he felt could be better described as existential dread than as castration anxiety. Such dread is a more fundamental and serious conflict. Unlike many other more typical cases of Don Juanism this man did not need to prove that he was a man, that he had a penis. He desperately needed to know that he was not *merely* a penis, that he was also a person. This is similar to the problem that, according to Reik (1957), confronts each woman. Her greatest fear is that she will be taken as only a vagina by men, not as a unique person in her own right. This fear lies at the base of the women's liberation movement today, where the struggle is against the woman being regarded as a "sex object."

The ability of the child to establish a sexual identification by differentiating its own self as male or female is a basic problem. Failure to do so may result in a neurosis. However, an even more fundamental challenge is to separate one's self from one's environment (as for example, the mother's breast). Failure to achieve a solution to this problem can result in psychosis.

The psychotic is continually confusing subject and object. Ideas and feelings from within are projected onto the outside world and experienced as hallucinations and delusions (Arieti, 1955). Boundaries between the self and not-self are fluid, with each occuping more territory at one time and less at another. The locus of self may constantly change. Although for "normal" people the self may expand and contract, there is a certain consistency as to what it is and where it is placed. The "heart" of the self is experienced as being within one's body and reasonably stable. It is this lack of a home port that brings such confusion and fear to the psychotic, as well as to the borderline psychotic. Before having the courage to solve other problems of life I must first know what I am and where I am.

There are those who would equate self with the entire body. "My self is my body and its functioning." Very few, except perhaps some with a more mystical bent, would regard their self as other than inside their body. Thus, if one tries to picture his teeth, he is more likely to think of them as if he were inside the mouth looking at them as they curve around him rather than visualize them as if he were standing outside his body and perceiving them as he would in a mirror.

In an informal experiment 50 subects were given the following instructions: "Close your eyes. Now perceive and experience your teeth!" After a five-second pause each subject was asked, "Did you experience them (the teeth) as if you were looking at them in a mirror, or did you experience them as if you were inside your mouth and they were wrapped around you?" Twelve experienced the teeth as if looking at them in a mirror; 38 experienced them as if being observed from inside the mouth. Hence, 12 of them experienced the situation as if the self (subject) was located outside the body and looking at the teeth (as objects). The 38 majority experienced the locus of their self as being within their mouth. They perceived the teeth from the inside.

The word "experience" is more commonly used when we wish to describe the perception of some feeling within our own self. The word "perceive" may also represent that, but it is generally used to imply the perception by our own self of some object outside (e.g., not-self). Considering the possibility that by use of the word "experience" we had stacked the responses in favor of an internal point of view, the study was repeated with another 50 subjects who were asked, "Did you *perceive* them (the teeth) as if you were looking at them in a mirror or did you *perceive* them as if you were inside your mouth and they were wrapped around you?"

In this second study, which replicated the first with change only of one word, 14 reported the external, or "mirror," perception, while 35 reported the internal point of view. One stated that he viewed his teeth "like a dentist's x-ray"—also an external reference point. It is apparent that there was very little difference between the two studies. Both of them demonstrated to a significant degree[2] that in such a situation more people locate their observing or experiencing self as within the body rather than outside it.

However, if someone attacks a loved one of mine I will react as if it were an attack on my own self. It is as if I have included the loved one within my self. In this sense the self has transcended the boundaries of the skin. I may also be willing to fight (and even die) for *my* cause, *my* beliefs, or *my* country—as have innumerable humans before me. In other words, I act as if my selfness inheres in many other places than merely within my own skin. Impacts on these other places by outside forces initiate in me responses similar to those I make when it is my own self that is being assaulted.

While there is little or no *scientifically accepted* evidence (The British Society for Psychical Research to the contrary)[3] to the effect that one's self can exist outside of one's body[4] it is interesting to note the inconsistency which many people who espouse "hard-nosed" science evidence. Many a biologist, physicist, or psychologist of scientific repute would refuse even to consider as tenable the hypothesis that self can exist outside one's body. Such an idea would be scornfully dismissed in his laboratory or academic classroom as either nonsense or mystical, mystical being that which is not subject to the controlled observation of the scientific method. Yet this same man may attend a church on another day of the week, pray to a God, recite creeds and beliefs to the effect that there is a life hereafter, hold with his neighbors that one's self (soul, being, existence) will continue after one's body has been destroyed, and on his own deathbed find solace in such faith. In fact, the Christian view that one's self will continue to live and exist in a heaven filled with much pleasure (or a hell of pain if one has been bad) has won millions of converts.

At one level of his being, the scientist accepts as real only that which can be objectively studied, while at another level he also accepts phenomena as real that are not subject to objective study. These two sets of contradictory beliefs are carefully kept from each other within different "ego states" so as not to produce anxiety and cognitive dissonance. The left hand knows not what the right hand is doing. Mysticisms are either rejected *in toto* without serious study by scientifically minded men—or are accepted *in toto* also without any serious study by the same men. The difference seems to lie in whether or not the mysticism is tied in to a system of religious belief. What is important about all this is that many men who will have nothing to do with concepts that are unamenable to the usual tools of scientific investigation will blindly accept similar concepts if they are presented within religious beliefs that they have been taught to accept on faith. We are here neither advocating nor denying the concept of a self that transcends (or is capable of transcending) the physical boundaries of body. We are only suggesting that the courage to be consistent is not universally held among all scientific researchers.

There is an intermediate position regarding whether one's self can exist outside one's body. If self is to be considered as a form of energy, and if it appears to be located (at least primarily) within the physical body, it might be thought of as an energy field. Physicists concerned with the structure of the atom have both hypothesized and demonstrated the existence of such fields in which matter particles, such as electrons, are inbedded and which extend their influence out into the motion of such particles (Gamow, 1966). The self acts at times like just such a field. Accordingly, we might compare it to a magnetic field that has a rather constant location (within the body) but that also extends from its primary fixation point to influence nearby phenomena—and nearness may be measured along the fourth dimension of physics, time, not merely along the three dimensions of space. Since development of the theories on relativity (Einstein, 1955) Newtonian concepts of space, time, energy, and matter that originated from earlier common sense observations are no longer considered as valid by physicists (the ultimate in hard-nosed scientists). Many psychologists today still think along Newtonian lines in their compulsive investigations of stimulus-response paradigms. But it may be the study of more "taboo" topics (Farberow, 1963) that will reawaken this science of human behavior.

Over the centuries the scientific method was developed as man's most valuable tool for the study of natural phenomena. However, let us not define a phenomenon as real only if it is suited to manipulation by our tool. The tool should always be in the service of understanding the event, not the other way around. Signorelli (1974) makes this point in a critical examination of that tool of which psychologists are most fond, namely, statistics.

An interesting experience in the apparent change of the self's locus occurs in one of the more sophisticated hypnotic induction techniques (Watkins, 1963a, p. 381).

"For example, we ask our subject to imagine that he is driving his car to our office. We picture to him the passing scene, the road, the other cars, the stores, the houses. He parks his car near our office. He turns off the key, opens the door and gets out of the car. In all of this he feels himself as the focus of the activity, the hero of the dream. There is no doubt as to where the *I* is. It is that to whom all these things are happening, and who is reacting.

"Next, we suggest that he see himself close the car door. He is standing behind 'that man' getting out of the car, the man who looks like him and who is dressed like him, the man whose features resemble what he sees when he looks into the mirror. This 'man' proceeds along the walk and enters the waiting room. Soon he is called into the consultation room by the practitioner.

" 'You watch him as he sits down in the easy chair, that man who looks like you. You notice his eyes becoming heavy. You watch them close. You see his hand becoming lighter and approaching the man's face. You know that he is entering a deep and profound state.' "

Here we have a manipulation of subject-object. The

observing ego is detached from the body ego. The body is de-egotized and becomes object, or *it.* In this type of induction the patient may become quite insensitive to painful stimuli since the 'outside' observing ego cannot feel what 'that man over there' is experiencing.

In a situation like this, the location of the ego becomes an intriguing question because the body, which is normally equated with it, or considered as its "home," is deegotized. The body has become object and no longer seems to the subject to be housing his self. A similar condition inheres in the ordinary dream where the dreaming ego, or self, seems to be no longer connected to the body.

The hypnotic modality has often been used to manipulate subject and object, hence to move the self from one place to another. Hypnoanesthesia (Marmer, 1959) involves the suggestive removal of selfness from a part or all of a subject's body while he is under a state of hypnosis. For example, under a hypnotic trance an obstetric patient can be told to "sit down in that chair over there and watch that woman on the delivery table have her baby." The lifting of repressions in hypnoanalysis (Schneck, 1965; Wolberg, 1945), the breaking through of amnesias (Watkins, 1949; Stross, 1966) and the hypnotic activating of various ego states in multiple personalities (Prince, 1906) all involve changing the locus of self.

In cases of multiple personalities (of which almost a hundred have been studied according to reports in the literature), the self seems to move its locus from one set of behaviors and attitudes to a different one, perhaps alternating among as many as five or more. This is like an occupying force that moves from one land to another when it is not strong or large enough to occupy all the different lands simultaneously.

A useful psychotherapeutic procedure, called the

empty chair technique (Watkins & Watkins, 1975), involves dividing the ego of the patient into different "states," which are attached to different chairs. Variations of the technique are used both in transactional analysis (Berne, 1961) and Gestalt therapy (Perls, 1969, 1973). In the transactional frame of reference the "child" might be seated in one chair, the "parent" in another, and the "adult" in still a third. The patient is induced to engage in dialogues between these three as he activates one of these at a time by sitting in the designated chair. In this way, he makes one such state subject for the moment while treating the other two as objects. This is like changing the locus of his self (or what will be referred to in a later chapter as the executive ego state) from one internal point of reference to another. By sitting in one chair his self enters a matrix of child behaviors, and we speak of him now as being his child self. Later, he moves the locus of his self to another internal position as symbolized (or initiated) by his physical movement to another chair, and his adult or parent self becomes operative. There is thus created temporarily, and for therapeutic purposes, an experimental multiple personality in which the different states can interact with each other for the purpose of their better cooperation and integration into an effectively functioning individual.

An interesting experiment in altering the geographical perspective of one's self is to imagine first, that you are in New York preparing to travel to some West Coast city, say San Francisco. With your eyes shut, and in your mind, visualize the terrain over which you will journey. Look at San Francisco as if you were approaching it from the east. Now assume that you have arrived and turn yourself to look eastward toward New York from where you came. Notice that there is a distinctly different feeling that takes place as you visualize this change from the new geographical reference point at which you have now stationed your self. On arriving in San Francisco, as you turn to face east, you can sense the movements of your eyes under the closed lids.

Viewing one's self objectively is not easy, but it has been the goal of many a therapeutic endeavor and often leads to a reorganization of self-perception and new maturity. As the Scottish poet Robert Burns put it, "Oh wad some Power the giftie gie us/To see oursels as ithers see us!" "This means developing the ability to move the locus of the observing self out of what had been the experiencing self and to look at this latter as would an outsider. It might be termed a "self skill." Most people acquire it only with the greatest of difficulty.

At the beginning of this chapter we asked the question, "Where do *I* reside?" We have done much speculating about this problem, but it is obvious we have not arrived at any definitive answer. However, the locus of self seems to change from person to person, from time to time, and from experience to experience. Moreover, it is subject to manipulation. Perhaps it can transcend the physical body. Whatever this self is, it does not seem to be very amenable to study by the usual objective techniques of the scientific method. It has, however, been the subject of much philosophic inquiry by rational processes based on personal and reported experience.

The self is man's most priceless possession, the lack of which would render of no value to him everything else that he can know or do. Elusive as the concept is, it is worthy of our most thoughtful quest; for we may be able through better understanding of this phenomenon to increase greatly our joy and being in this world.

FOOTNOTES

1. We shall not pursue the interesting possibility that if *self* exists, it exists in some quantity and that such quantity presumably can be measured. Existentialism is much concerned with the quantity of existence, the amount of being or meaning possessed by a person, but as yet we have not delineated it in such a way as to make it capable of objective measurement. At this point it would seem almost amusing to think of a time when we might say, "George has 72 units of self, but John has only a 56 self." However, if Thorndike is right, then perhaps some day man will devise such a measure.
2. In the first experiment chi-square was 11.52, which indicates statistical significance at the .001 level (that is, there is less than one possibility out of a thousand that chance alone could have accounted for the finding that more people select the internal point of self-reference than the external).

   In the second experiment chi-square was 8.00. This is still significant at the .01 level (e.g., there is less than one possibility out of a hundred that chance alone could have caused more people to select the internal self-reference point).
3. This organization numbers many highly reputable investigators among its members. As presidents it has included ten fellows of the Royal Society, three Nobel laureates, one prime minister, and a number of professors, including physicists and philosophers. It may not yet have proved its main theses to the scientific world, but its studies cannot be dismissed without serious consideration.
4. During the 1972 Conference of the American Academy of Psychotherapists Robert A. Monroe (1971), a Virginia businessman, reported his experiences in "out of body travel." His

evidence, though not convincing to many of the skeptical scientists in attendance, was of sufficient interest to have brought about his invitation to make such a presentation at this meeting of a reputable scientific society. Reactions to his paper were mixed. However, a few years ago such a presentation would have been unthinkable at a scientific meeting. Psychologists, like quantum physicists (Hoffmann, 1959), are beginning to think the unthinkable.

Chapter 8

THE COMING AND THE GOING

When one considers the world of change he is struck by the fact that movements occur along a dimension with two directions. There is up and down, forward and backward, hotter and colder, greater and lesser, good and evil. Tides come in and go out. Time can be measured either toward the future or toward the past. Bodies are attracted to each other or repelled by each other. Magnetic forces are positive or minus. The orbits of the planets are governed by a combination of centrifugal and centripetal forces. Through fusion, atoms and molecules are created and through fission they return again to the simple. Civilizations rise and fall.

It seems as though the universe is governed by the interaction of two great basic principles, an integrative one and a disintegrative one. We speak of life and death, the first of which is eagerly sought, the second bitterly avoided. No matter how successful we are in embracing the first, we ultimately must face the second.

In his beautiful paper on "The theme of the three caskets," Freud (1953e) most eloquently illuminates for us an ancient wisdom concerning maturity and the joy of living, which has come down through the myths of many lands. It is a principle that can be extended through the entire field of psychotherapy. In *The Merchant of Venice,* Bassanio chooses the plain lead casket instead of the gold and silver ones, a selection that wins for him the hand of the fair Portia. Freud traces this choice to one between three women of whom the third, although apparently the ugliest, is the real possessor of beauty and happiness. Freud relates these women to the three fates, or Norns: Clotho, "the fateful tendencies each one of us brings into the world"; Lachesis, "the accidental within the decrees of destiny"; and Atropos, "the inevitable," hence Death.

These three can be equated simply with birth, life, and death. Freud personifies these into mothers: "The mother herself, the beloved who is chosen after her pattern, and finally Mother Earth who receives him again." He notes man's struggle against the third, exemplified, for example, in the drama of King Lear who rejects his third daughter, Cordelia, the dumb (dead) one, and demands love from the first two. Freud concludes with the statement, "But it is in vain that the old man yearns after the love of woman as once he had it from his mother; the third of the Fates alone, the silent goddess of Death, will take him into her arms."

If we modify this statement to read, "But it is in vain that man yearns after the love of woman as once he had it from his mother or wife. . ." we arrive at a basic principle of maturity as sought in psychotherapeutic education. It might be summarized as follows: The greatest joy and freedom in living comes when one is willing, however unpleasant the choice, to elect consonance with that part of one's destiny appropriate for his time of life. Thus, it is the neurotic who, although physically grown up, continually seeks the love of the original mother, the one who gave him birth, when it is time for him to live with the second, "the beloved who is chosen after her (the mother's) pattern." Also, in later years when Death comes closer, many people chase vainly after their youth. Through cosmetics, youth pills, and forced romances, they, like King David on his deathbed,[1] desperately run in fear from Mother Earth. In each case, where man refuses to accept the destiny of his chronological position in life, the joy and meaningfulness of present living is sacrificed to futile efforts at regaining a lost past. Man becomes a slave to his destiny and loses the true beauty of a harmonious existence. By choosing the third—hence, accepting the inevitability of death—man frees himself for meaningful being in his remaining years. The fear is gone, and by his choice he has reaffirmed his integrity.

The middle-aged neurotic who finds new freedom, happiness, and peace of mind after successful analytic resolution of his oedipal conflict, and who relinquishes his dependent ties to his mother and finds life and potency with a new love, is matched by the elderly man who fears not his impending demise. It has often been noted that the psychotic depressive who had decided on death shows a rapid recovery. For a few days he evidences great happiness before terminating his existence by suicide. Hospital staffs have learned through sad experience not to confuse this condition with true recovery.

All this could be simplified into the maxim, "Be your age." For there is a time in every person's life to be an infant, an adolescent, a lover, a parent, and an elderly one. There is a time for birth, for love, and for death; and happy is he who chooses to govern his life in harmony with natural law, for he who does so is truly mature.

It is this wisdom that the ancient myths as analyzed by Freud teach us in "The theme of the three caskets." This contribution shows Freud at his philosophic best; it is also a literary jewel.

In his "Beyond the pleasure principle", Freud (1922) grappled with the concepts of integration and disintegration. The first he termed "Eros." It was Eros who brought people together, created the conditions of love, initiated the pleasurable, and made life worthwhile. It represented the forces of creation and growth. Under the influence of such a principle, Freud experimented, treated, discovered, and developed the new complex understandings of man's mental life that have so influenced the studies of human behavior. Eros is the creative principle.

Freud, himself, must have unconsciously sensed his impending destruction by forces that were probably already operative. Within a year after publication of "Beyond the pleasure principle," the first symptoms of his mouth cancer appeared. Subsequently he endured many painful operations to exist. In that contribution he described the death instinct and termed its energy "mortido." Even as Eros built more complexities, Thanatos,[2] the death instinct, reduced these back to the simple.

The Oriental philosophies, product of ancient cultures, wrestled maturely with the basic problems of life when the Western world was still in its infancy. They also emphasized acceptance of the inevitable, and the willingness to treat these two principles equally. During World War II, the fanaticism that permitted many Japanese soldiers and pilots to attack heedless of personal danger derived from Shinto and samurai traditions, which taught that death in the service of a high value equaled great life. Thus, personal destruction in the service of the emperor was often eagerly sought. There is no doubt that many individuals who have lead meaningless lives have in the moment of sacrificing that life achieved a validation of their existence, which made it worthwhile. Sydney Carton, the ne'er-do-well in Dickens's *A tale of two cities,* who permitted himself to be offered up to the guillotine as a substitute for the friend he loved, exemplifies this principle most poignantly. In his farewell speech he says, "It is a far, far better thing that I do, than I have ever done; it is a far, far better rest that I go to, than I have ever known." In his final moment he yields himself to Thanatos in the service of Eros and thus achieved that genuine being and meaningful relationship with a personally significant other, which is so clearly depicted by Buber in *I and thou* (1970).

The Western world is, perhaps, in its adolescence as compared to the ancient Oriental cultures, and the adolescent is one who is thriving midstream in the integrative principle of Eros. He grows; he loves; he seeks eagerly to acquire the new and make it part of himself. Little thinks he during those hours of his existence about that other side of the equation, about a time when he must return to the womb of nature. So it is that we today seek to build, to acquire, to enjoy pleasure; and we seek to avoid pain, age, and a lessening of our developing self. This is good. For it should be so.

Our culture, with all its faults, has not yet reached that period in its development that marked the demise of the ancient Egyptian, Greek, Roman, Moorish, or Aztec civilizations. A fundamental tenet of the Judeo-Christian tradition is the belief in life after death:

> When that which drew from out the boundless deep
> Turns again home.
>
> —Tennyson

At first glance this appears to be only wishful thinking. Man cannot tolerate the thought of his own nonexistence, so he accepts death only by creating for himself the reassuring concept of a heaven, a life after death. Undoubtedly, for many people the view of a post-mortem corporeal existence where they shall "sit by the right hand of God" enables them to overcome the terrors of an existential anxiety that would be overwhelming if they were fully confronted with the possibility that at death they would lose self-awareness. Witness the struggles reported in various cases of multiple personalities (Prince, 1906; Thigpen & Cleckley, 1957; Watkins & Watkins, 1973) where the minor self fights vehemently to avoid being absorbed into a more dominant personality. The awareness of a unique and independent being is a most priceless possession to most individuals, especially in countries that stress the rights of individual existence and competition rather than socialistic values.

But a belief in life after death has more obvious validity if one is willing to relinquish the necessity of its being so individualized. After all, science teaches us that neither matter nor energy is destructible, and if life is a form of energy (which in the next chapter will be more forcefully argued) then it can only be changed, not eliminated.

The religious injunction to accept God before one dies "to be saved" is simply another way of saying, "Identify with the great integrative principle of the universe, triumph over Thanatos by a willing return to the simple beginnings of Creation for 'In the beginning, God. . .' " From that point there can be no movement but upward again toward the complexities of structure and function that we call living. "Yea, though I walk through the valley of the shadow of death, I will fear no evil: for thou art with me" (Psalms 23.4). Perhaps this might have been said (though with less poetic beauty) "I am with Thee. I join myself in a complete identification with the principle of Eros and prepare for new beginnings, new becomings."

It is like telling ourselves that when the river of our life reaches its outlet, we do not seek vainly to swim upstream but accept that the droplets of our self will merge with a universal ocean. It is from this ocean that the energy of the sun will lift the tiny molecules of moisture for precipitation on the hills to begin once again a new life journey, from spring to brook and down river to still another Nirvana.

> Humanity is a crystalline river, singing, in a rippling rush, and carrying the secrets of the mountains to the depths of the sea.
>
> —Kahlil Gibran

We may then think of existence as mutable if not terminable. However, there are distinct differences between the phase of man's being during that period we call his lifetime and that part during which he has no awareness of an individualized self. The first exists in time, measurable time, and it has boundaries. The second apparently is timeless and has no boundaries. Thus the person is unique, and he becomes aware of his uniqueness through feedback from a physically tangible world. It is this uniqueness that man strives to actualize and that he must accomplish within the boundaries of the time allotted to him. I have used the word "allotted" not in the sense that it is bestowed by a whimsical, unpredictable God, but rather that the course of each "river of life" from spring to delta passes through rather ordered and predictable stages, which will be determined by its own energy of movement and the impact of external terrain upon it.

Man lives subjectively in time, which is measured chronologically, objectively, and experientially. Through health and medically preservative measures we seek to prolong its chronological duration as measured objectively. In existential therapy we seek to increase its meaning and thereby incrėase its experiential time. Some people (Mozart, for example) lived more in three decades than others did in a century. It is a shame that so many humans turn their years of chronological time into only minutes of experiential existence. They waste the substance of their being in futile self-conflicts and through exhausting efforts to swim upstream in the river of their life. Thye are so constantly spending energy in unnecessary efforts to defend themselves against themselves or against imagined threats from abroad that there is little left for the enrichment of daily living. Their world is an austere region of threat, of fear, and of hate. They tie their existence to Thanatos and die soon, experientially if not chronologically.

To rescue them from such a futile life plan, whether it is called neurosis or psychosis, becomes our aim as therapists; and it is in the better implementation of this goal that we seek to develop the therapeutic self within our own persons.

The purpose of Eros is to develop, to build, and to grow; its culmination is not death but the ripeness of maturity. As long as we are approaching maturity our life forces are in the ascendancy. Like infinity, we can only draw closer to this wise objective. It is not to be reached and grasped. For life growth is a movement *toward* not an achieved status. Viewed in this way a therapeutic self becomes only an extension of our integrative strivings, a closer approximation to maturity, in which the possessor mobilizes his Eros, not merely for personal well-being, but beyond that for the furtherance of such development in others. The therapeutic self extends himself beyond the bounds of his individual existence to identify with the strivings of others and to become their ally. In such constructive impact with these others, he more completely validates his personal selfness. His own life becomes ever richer and more meaningful. Through apparent selflessness he achieves the aim of complete selfishness. True therapeutic selves cannot be other than happy. Since the therapeutic self includes others within his own boundaries, their enhancement cannot but magnify his own being. Accordingly, the more he helps them, the more he helps himself.

At the beginning of this treatise, observations were presented that brought us to speculate on the existence of a therapeutic self. We then explored the meaning of such a term from the behavioral and psychoanalytic positions. During the last few chapters we have examined this concept of the self from an existential-humanist point of view.

It is time now to draw from a relatively unknown psychoanalytic theorist a more specific theory of the self and from the implications of his concepts describe the functioning of a very specialized self, the therapeutic self.

FOOTNOTE

1. It will be recalled that a virgin was brought into the bed of the dying David in the hopes that it would rejuvenate him (1 Kings 1.1–4).

Part IV

EGO ENERGIES AND STATES

In Chapters 9 through 14 the ego psychology theories of Paul Federn (and his disciple, Edoardo Weiss) are explained. With modifications they offer some possible rational answers to the questions on the nature of self, which were raised in Part III. In this section, also, a structural view of the human personality is proposed on which the main thesis of this work is based: namely, the concept of the therapeutic self and how it functions in the clinical situation.

Many writers in talking about the self treat it as a unity. In the formulation presented here, it is viewed as an extremely complex pattern of energy interactions, differentiated into many separate states that vary greatly in size, content, and relative strength. These entities can be consonant or dissonant with each other, and they are continually changing in their relationships to each other and to the outer world. The self thus becomes a dynamic system of equilibrium that cannot be treated as one but must be considered as a group of interacting forces. By attention to its different facets, many problems in psychotherapeutic treatment that seemed incomprehensible become more readily subject to rational understanding and handling.

Chapter 9

THE EGO PSYCHOLOGY OF PAUL FEDERN

Paul Federn was one of the earliest and most faithful disciples of Freud. He is described (Weiss, 1966) as having great breadth in both scientific and literary background. He was also romantic and mild in manner. It was his intervention that moderated many of the quarrels between ambitious associates of Freud in the frequent vehement theoretical debates that beset the Vienna Psychoanalytic Society. His scientific understanding was balanced by emotional resonance with his patients. He was subject to depressive moods and the persistent idea that he would eventually end his own life—which he did after falling victim to an untreatable cancer.

He was always very close to Freud and was one of the few early colleagues who outlived him and remained faithful to him throughout Freud's life. However, Federn was also one of the least known in both analytic and lay circles. His contributions to ego psychology were neither well understood nor well received by his fellow analysts. Federn's theoretical views of the ego differed significantly from those of other psychoanalytic contributors, such as Hartmann (1951), Kris (1951) and Rapaport (1958). His conceptions of the ego, as well as those concerning the libido, also were quite different from Freud's, but Federn felt it necessary to minimize such differences. Apparently, he himself did not become fully aware of the extent to which he had broken new ground until near his death. Unlike other early associates of Freud, such as Adler, Jung, Stekel, and Rank, he remained very loyal to Freud and did not strike out independently on his own. He went to the United States in 1938 at the time of the Nazi takeover in Austria and lived in New York until his death in 1950. His major contributions have been compiled by his analysand, friend, and disciple, Edoardo Weiss (Federn, 1952; Weiss, 1960).

It is often difficult to explain another man's theories within the few pages of a single chapter, especially since the original author spent a lifetime writing over 90 papers to develop his concepts. However, we must try because the theory of the therapeutic self to be presented in this book builds a great deal on Federn's contributions. A general familiarity with his views will be necessary if the reader is to proceed further.

Federn's ideas have not received in the psychological and psychiatric realms the full credit they merit. This is because, first, his theoretical conceptions are very difficult to grasp. Second, he thought and wrote in the German scientific idiom, which renders understanding for the English-speaking reader difficult, even when translated. Finally, we must recall that the bulk of his contributions were made during the same period when Freud's were attracting much attention. His were overshadowed.

Freud had coined the term "libido" to represent a kind of sexual energy with which we might cathect or invest our perceptions of objects. By cathect Freud meant to attach or to allocate a quantity of energy for the accomplishment of some psychological process. Thus, as we cathect our perceptions of outside objects, primarily other individuals, they become more important to us—for example, loved ones. In Chapter 5 an "object" was defined as the perception of something from outside our own self, hence a mental item that is not-self. "Subject" refers to something, the stimulus for which originates within ourself, like an idea. When I *see* an apple, the image of that apple, which has been sensed, first by the impingement of a stimulus from without on the retina and then transmitted into my mind, is called an "object." However, if I *think* about an apple, the image of that apple, which is raised in my mind by the idea of an apple, would be considered as subject, not object. The apple stimulus has arisen from within. I know that I am aware of it, not because I *see* it but because I am *thinking* of it. In the second case (subject) the apple is *my* idea of an apple, not a perception of an object that exists outside my self. When we cathect a perception with object energy (invest it with object cathexis) we heighten our interest, attention, or "love" for it. This object cathexis might be compared to the beam from a flashlight, which, if focused on an object in the room, would brightly illuminate that object and bring out for our fullest attention all its details. In a similar way, if I allocate or direct a certain quantity of electricity toward a motor, I can activate that motor, that is, provide it with the energy to make its processes go. This is what Freud meant when he spoke of cathecting an object with libido. By such libidinal (or object) cathexis we *activate* the psychological process of perceiving it.

In his theories on narcissism, or self-love, Freud

(1953d) discussed the directing of this libido by the ego reflexively back onto its own self. He then used the term "ego-libido." Federn decided that this ego-libido was qualitatively different from libido or object cathexis. For Federn, ego-libido was the representative of one's own existence, one's selfness. He equated the ego with the "actual sensation of one's own ego," the ego feeling. He considered this ego as a unifying, integrating energy that gives us the "feeling of unity, continuity, contiguity and causality" in our experiences. In other words, we sense our self as being a oneness (a "unity"). We do not feel our self as being many. We think of this self as having always existed, (a "continuity") as being indestructible. By "contiguity" Federn meant that all the elements of the self were in close proximity, touching, and in communication with each other, so that a stimulus to one part is simultaneously transmitted throughout the entire self. Finally, by "causality" Federn implied that we view our self as being rational and subject to the normal laws of cause and effect. It is not considered as esoteric, strange, or mysterious. We sense it as "familiar." Federn defined "experience" as being an "investment of continuously changing contents with the unifying, coherent ego feeling."

Perhaps the following analogy might be suggested. As we think our own thoughts and experience our own feelings, these thoughts and feelings might be compared to pictures on the film in a movie projector. They, like lighted movie film, come to life (are activated) as they are invested (cathected) with the energy that passes through them. We invest happenings with selfness. They are then experienced as *our* thoughts, *our* emotions, etc. We inject our selfness into a mental or bodily item, and it becomes part of *us*, of our own being.

Federn described two different kinds of such energy, an object cathexis and an ego cathexis. If the representation of a thought within our mind is invested with libido, with object cathexis (it-energy), we experience it as a perception, something that exists outside ourselves that we have seen (read) or heard. However, if this same idea is invested with ego cathexis (I-energy) it is experienced as one's own thought. Federn often referred to this energy as ego-libido. The feeling of "I-ness," of an item being part of me, is directly related to the amount of such ego cathexis with which it is invested. To Federn, the ego was an *experience* which he described as the "sensation and knowledge of the individual of the lasting or recurrent continuity, in time, space and causality of his bodily and mental life."

Thus, a *perception* of another person would be a mental item invested with object cathexis. An *idea* would be a mental item invested with ego cathexis. Throughout the rest of this treatise we will use the term "cathexis" to mean a quantity of energy that (like the beam of light)[1] is attached to or directed at a particular psychological item to activate it, to bring it to existence. When the item is a thought or feeling that is being experienced as "mine," the energy that activates it will be ego cathexis, a kind of energy that is the bearer of selfness, or self feeling. When the item is a perception derived from the awareness of stimuli originating in an object outside the self, the kind of energy that activates the process of awareness of it is an object cathexis, or it-energy. Considering it in the converse an item of psychological awareness which is invested only with object cathexis, one that contains no ego cathexis, will be experienced by the person as an object. It is a not-I, and will be felt as originating outside of my self, as having an existence in outside reality.

The members of one's body are normally invested with body ego cathexis and hence are experienced as part of one's own self. However, in the case of a hysterical paralysis, when a limb is devoid of feeling and the ability to move, the ego cathexis has been withdrawn. The limb is experienced as "it," hence as existing in the outer world and not within one's own self. The lifting of the paralysis and restoration of normal self feeling would be accomplished when that part of the body had been reenergized with ego cathexis.

Federn held that the ego, as subject, was experienced in various modes. The *active* ego cathexis was experienced during planning, thinking, and acting, in fact any time when attending. The *passive* ego cathexis determined the need to receive stimuli. The *reflexive* ego cathexis operated during self-love or self-hate. He believed that originally the ego cathexis existed in a kind of "middle voice," that is, in a neutral form. He spoke of the *objectless* or *medial* cathexis. This was represented by such activities as "I live," "I prosper," "I develop," and—in its destructive component—by "I age" and "I die." Federn affirmed that this medial cathexis was the manifestation of *primary narcissism,* that with which we are born. He believed that we normally feel this ego cathexis as a "pleasantly familiar" one, and in this way we sense our own existence.

Freud had described the life instinct, termed it "sexual," named it Eros, and called its energy "libido." He had also hypothesized the existence of a death instinct (Freud, 1922). However, it remained for Federn to explore this concept further. He delineated two types of cathexis: an integrative or life energy, which he called "libido," and a disintegrative or death energy, which he termed "mortido." Weiss, Federn's disciple, collaborator, and the editor of his writings, preferred to call this second energy "destrudo" (Weiss, 1935). However, the term "mortido" has been used by other analytic writers more generally and will be employed here.

This mortido, as the opposition energy to libido, was

considered to draw elements apart, to reduce objects back to the simple, even as death reduces the organism to the single atoms from which it was constructed. Ego-libido was experienced as pleasantly familiar; ego-mortido was experienced as pain, mental or physical. When it was mortido *object* cathexis (not ego cathexis) with which an item was invested, the individual experienced it as the perception of some object (person or nonperson) outside himself that he hated.

Another major contribution of Federn was his structural view of the mind. Like Freud he accepted the tripartite division of id, ego, and superego. However, Federn was much more specific about the nature of the ego's boundaries, those that separated the ego from the id and from the outside world. Although most people equate their selves with their bodies, Federn pointed out that "the ego boundary does not always coincide with the body boundaries. . .it may either not fill them up or extend beyond them. The latter situation is well illustrated by the driving motorist who always extends his bodily ego to the fenders of his car." (Federn, 1952, p. 331). He also hypothesized the existence of a number of ego "states" with boundaries separating each other.

His structure of the ego might be compared to that of a country like the United States. All items within the ego are egotized (ego-cathected) to some degree and hence, like all Americans, hold citizenship—are experienced as self. However, an ego state includes contents that are usually experienced together and have more in common. These ego state contents would be comparable to the citizens of a single state, such as Montana or New York.

Normally no ego state is entirely devoid of cathexis (investment with self-energy). However, at any given time one is usually much more highly cathected than the others. That one, then, holds *executive* power and is felt as the self. The term "executive" is used to represent the specific ego state that is experiencing in the here and now. It is subject and at the moment preponderant over other (currently unactivated) states.[2] Figure 1 presents a diagrammatic representation of personality structure as conceived at this point.

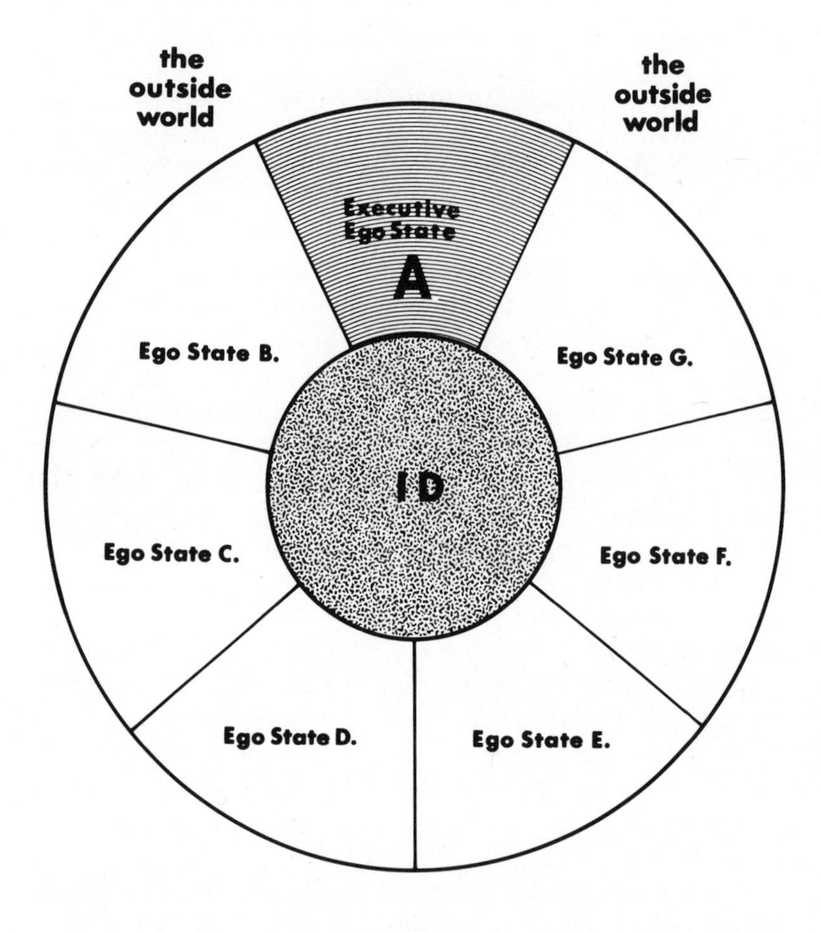

Figure 1. THE STRUCTURE OF PERSONALITY AS CONCEIVED IN FEDERN'S THEORETICAL SYSTEM.

The executive Ego State A is represented as the one most highly cathected, hence with the greatest energy. It is thus activated and its contents represent the present experience of the person. For example, Ego State A might include those contents that are experienced while a student is in a classroom. These could include his thoughts and feelings relevant to this particular class. Ego State B, on the other hand, might include those thoughts and feelings that are experienced at a social gathering of his friends. When he leaves the classroom and goes to the party, Ego State A becomes deactivated. The cathexis flows into Ego State B, which then becomes executive. The student then experiences his friends, the drinks, the jokes, the party games. The thoughts that were foremost in his mind at class when Ego State A was executive, have now sunk into unawareness. They are either quite forgotten, or at most only experienced dimly on the borders of consciousness. He now experiences himself (and often behaves) differently. It is almost as if he were a different person at the party than in the classroom. However, if the boundary between the two different ego states is not too rigid, some energy will permeate the boundary, and his ego state at the social gathering will be aware that the one that was executive in class was also his own self. He will perceive himself as one person and experience that "feeling of unity, continuity, contiguity and causality" of which Federn speaks.

When an element that has originated in an adjoining nonself, hence lightly cathected ego state, impacts the boundary of the one holding this executive power (the self-ego state), the executive ego state recognizes it as coming from within the organism, and it is experienced as one's own thought or feeling. Federn (1952, p. 225) states as follows: "To speak of inner ego boundaries means no more than the fact that the ego senses itself, not only as an indiscriminate whole, but also as having a thousand different 'shades' of feeling, depending on which aspect or state or sector of the ego comes uppermost in influencing the others. The quality of the cathexis is also involved."

If the boundaries between two states are so tight that the flow of cathexis (selfness) from the one to the other is completely prevented, then one self will disown another self. Only in multiple personalities and cases of amnesia does this condition exist. We usually recognize that the previous state was part of our self and one to which we may return during another occasion.

This common energy (ego cathexis) invests all ego states, though to different degrees. Accordingly, any such ego state, when it impacts the internal boundary of the executive state, is experienced as lying within the organism and not outside. This is analogous to the fact that although an individual may be a resident of Montana, he is accepted as an American citizen when he crosses the Idaho border. However, a citizen of a foreign country, like Mexico, is perceived as alien regardless of which state border he contacts. Similarly, the ego treats as alien (not-me) any object from the outside that impacts its external boundary. The ego boundary, like the national one, is where we distinguish "us" from "them."

Federn notes that former or repressed ego states can be awakened by hypnosis, a procedure often used in the treatment of dissociated personalities (Prince, 1906; Thigpen & Cleckley, 1957). An ego state was determined by the specific contents within it at a given time. The ego boundaries were viewed as flexible so that an item could exist within a number of ego states simultaneously, and items could move from one ego state to another. This was represented as the extension of an ego state over the item or withdrawal from it by movement of the ego state's boundary. Ego states could overlap (and indeed necessarily would have to) to some degree if we did not have a multiple personality situation. An ego state might "contain" a perception, an object representation (that is, an item only object-cathected), but of course that object would not be experienced as a part of the self. According to Federn, objects were not considered as being included within ego state boundaries.

Federn noted that the ego can be both subject and object. For example, if *I* pinch *my arm,* the ego state that includes the bodily contents of the arm experiences the situation the same as if it were pinched by another person. The ego state that includes the pinching fingers is sensed as an object by the arm ego state that is experiencing the pain. Also, as the ego state that includes the fingers feels the texture of the skin it is pinching, it experiences the arm as an object and itself as subject. The integration of the two impressions by my total being enables me to recognize that the pinching of *my* arm is by *my* action. This may involve some kind of rapid alteration between the two states, each taking its turn at being executive.

An entire ego state could be subject to repression as well as a single item if its ego cathexis were withdrawn. For example, sleep would be a condition in which the ego cathexis is withdrawn from the body. As long as mental life still was partly egotized the individual would experience dreams. Complete or dreamless sleep would result when the ego cathexis was withdrawn from all mental as well as bodily activities.

According to Federn, reality testing was distinguished from the *sensing of reality.* Any object-cathected item that contacted an ego boundary would be sensed as real, hence existing outside the person. In most cases this would be the stimulus (visual, auditory, etc.) that impinged on the person's sense organs. However, if the internal ego boundary became very weak (decathected) a repressed item might penetrate such a boundary and enter mental life before it was detected as being object-cathected (not ego-cathected). This item would then be experienced by the person as a perception and reported by the individual as "real." Others would say that he was having a hallucination. In this case, the individual would be sensing as real an item that did not come from without.

Reality testing consists of turning the head and eyes and observing that a real object would change its relative position in space. A pseudoreal object, hence object from within that was sensed as real (like an id-originated thought), would not make such movements in space. The psychotic is one who has suspended the reality testing of external movement and relies on the sensing of his weakened ego boundaries that cannot now, because of their inadequate energizing, distinguish between the perception of external reality and repressed ideation.

Federn notes that any increase or decrease in cathexis of the ego boundary is felt by the subject—more ego cathexis and one feels wide awake; less ego cathexis and one feels drowsy. A deficiency of such cathexis in the external ego boundary makes it difficult to sense reality in an item impinging from the outside, and the person's experience may be one of *estrangement.* For example, if there were very few border guards between the countries of the United States and Mexico, individuals could slip across the boundary without verification of their credentials. A Mexican national might be perceived as an American citizen and vice versa. The sensing of reality at the ego's boundary is analogous to citizenship verification at a nation's border. It tells us what is ourself and what not ourself.

The phenomenon of *depersonalization,* according to Federn, stemmed from a deficiency of cathexis in the core, or heart, of the ego. An individual faced with such a situation may panic with true (existential) anxiety as he cannot ascertain whether or not he actually exists. Estrangement, the incomplete sensing of outside objects, and depersonalization, the incomplete sensing of one's own self, are common experiences of the pre-psychotic or borderline psychotic. They represent in this theory an ego energy deficiency, in the first case of the boundary, and in the second of the core of the ego.[3]

Federn held that psychotic individuals sense the contents of their delusions and hallucinations as real because they originate from repressed mental stimuli that have entered consciousness without obtaining ego cathexis, not because of faulty reality testing. Federn did not equate consciousness with egotization, although it is probable he considered that to be conscious an item had to be more highly cathected.

An interesting explanation of the mechanism of *identification* can be derived from Federn's theories. The individual through perceptions builds within himself a replication of another person. He then withdraws the object cathexis from this and invests it with ego cathexis. The individual then thinks and acts like the other person. At least he thinks and acts like those items from his perceptions of the other person that were included in the internal replica of him. As an example, consider the case of a boy who observes his father walking along the street swinging his arms. The young fellow mimics or copies his dad and tries to walk along swinging his arms in the same way. This is because he wants to become like the father. After awhile, the arm swinging becomes automatic. This behavior is now ego-cathected. It is no longer merely acted. The youth "be's" the parent's behavior naturally. In this respect he has now identified with his father. The neighbors who observe him and his father walking together and swinging their arms similarly may remark, "Isn't he a chip off the old block?"

Perhaps Federn's greatest contribution was his extension of this theory to the treatment of psychoses. According to him schizophrenia occurs when there is a weakness of the ego, hence an inadequate supply of cathexis to its boundary or core; or in other words, there is an energy crisis. Accordingly, the psychotic patient would have difficulty distinguishing between self and not-self experiences, between what is his "me" and his "not-me." Treatment should involve a better economic management of this energy. The psychotic must have his life simplified as much as possible. Few demands should be made. He should not be analyzed in the sense that the therapist strives to lift repressions. The problem is that already too much repressed material has emerged into the ego without being first egotized. So the treating one must try to reestablish repressions, to conserve ego energy and to help the sick one restore adequate cathexis to those ego boundaries that have been weakened.

Federn noted that a deficiency of cathexis did not necessarily occur uniformly over all ego functions. An individual might perform very well at work yet exhibit paranoid delusions in relationships with a given person. Accordingly, therapeutic strategy requires that the ego be strengthened specifically in those areas where it is weak. In other areas of behavior and perception, the individual might function quite normally.

An ingenious therapeutic technique developed by Federn for the treatment of psychotics involves teaching them to distinguish between stimuli that enter the ego from its external boundary and those that penetrate through an internal one. Usually, therapists will not reinforce the patient's claim that his hallucinations are real. Federn, however, would tell his patient that the hallucinations are real, but that there are two kinds of reality. Reality A represents those perceptions that all people have and that can be shared with others—such as seeing the image of the therapist and hearing his voice. Reality B, on the other hand, is a personal and private experience that can not be shared by the patient with others—such as the accusatory voices persecuting him. Federn reported that psychotic patients, when asked whether any experience they described was Reality A or Reality B, could always differentiate between the two. Even though both were perceived as objects, there was apparently some difference experienced when an object had entered into the ego space from the outside world through the external boundary rather than through an internal one. By calling attention to this difference, (reinforcing the differentiation) Federn would improve reality testing. He would then tell his psychotic patients that if they would never mention Reality B to others they could leave the hospital and go home. One's first reaction is that he merely taught them to conceal their psychotic condition. However, he found that the continuous exercising of the differentiating function by the ego boundaries tended to strengthen them—hence increased their egotization, and that in time the hallucinations were actually re-repressed. The patient no longer experienced Reality B. This procedure is consistent with current behavioral reinforcement theory.

Federn advocated a supportive, reassuring manner, an avoidance of inquiry into psychotic fantasies or dreams, and the assistance of a mother figure therapist. In this approach Gertrude Schwing (1954) collaborated with him and provided a nurturing mother substitute. Federn held that it was the lack of such nurturing early in life that resulted in the inadequate ego cathexis later.

We shall not proceed here in further detail concerning his treatment of psychotics, but he obviously was very aware of the therapeutic self interaction that a mother figure could provide. Whether one wishes to account for the efficacy of such a benevolent intervention within this theory or in other ways, there seems to be little doubt concerning its effectiveness.

In the Virgin Mary, Christianity has created a nurturing mother figure to whom sufferers in all ages have repaired when they felt the need for support—the need to receive reassurance and to strengthen their egos. Mary, who is almost deified by some believers, represents for many a religious symbol of the therapeutic self. Such historical figures as Clara Barton and Florence Nightingale, as well as the entire nursing profession, also wear the mantle of this tradition. A reverence for the compassionate woman who can renew health and life, because she originally gave us our life, is imbedded deep in man's unconscious. It is, therefore, not surprising that the great Renaissance artists, such as Michelangelo and Raphael, drew their inspiration from the depths of their own unconscious as they created the sculptures of the Pieta and their paintings of Madonna and child.

FOOTNOTES

1. The author is indebted to Erika Fromm (1965) for this analogy, which she employed to explain awareness and consciousness.
2. Federn was fully cognizant that one state could be dominant ("aroused") while others were repressed, but he did not specifically use the word "executive." Accordingly, the concept of the "executive state" is given more emphasis here than in the writings of Federn. This is because it becomes a central concern in the development of therapeutic self theory.
3. A similar phenomenon may be based on an inadequate energizing of an internal boundary where one ego state contacts another. Federn mentions this possibility, but calls it a special form of estrangement. This might better be termed depersonalization since it involves the sensing of another part of the self as strange.

Chapter 10

MODIFICATIONS AND EXTENSIONS OF FEDERN'S THEORIES

As scientific observation and experimentation increase our knowledge, older theories are altered or replaced. Not that the older theories are necessarily wrong, but rather that all theories tend to be incomplete. When viewed in the light of more recent evidence, changes, greater or lesser in magnitude, are usually suggested. Federn's theories present one model of the human self that fits many observations made about behavior. They offer a rationale for the psychotherapeutic treatment of psychoses. And they propose a number of alterations in classical psychoanalytic theory.

At this point in the development of the therapeutic self concept, we can tentatively accept many of Federn's views. Still, several reservations and points of disagreement and modification come to mind. Accordingly, we shall consider in further detail a number of his ideas and offer modifications, realizing that others later, with additional validated facts available, will develop even better and more comprehensive understandings. Furthermore, the terminology that must be used is not quite satisfactory to one whose early training in psychology was in a strict behavioristic framework. However, we deal here with inner experience more than with external behavior, and the language of behaviorism is not suited to the description of such phenomena.

In the last chapter it was noted that Federn equated the self with the "actual sensation of one's own ego," and that he considered this ego sensation as an integrative energy that gives us the "feeling of unity, in continuity, contiguity and causality" in our experience. To him, this ego energy was itself the experience and feeling of selfness. He seemed to consider it as an original essence, and that by merely *being* this essence sensed its own existence. In fact, Federn specifically stated, "Ego feeling, therefore, is the simplest and yet the most comprehensive psychic state which is produced in the personality by the fact of its own existence, even in the absence of external or internal stimuli" (1952, p. 63).

In Chapter 6 we defined existence as impact—a contact between subject and an object. This existence, or awareness of self, required a contact with something that was not-self. It is obvious that a fundamental difference exists here between our concept of existence, which requires impact, and the statement by Federn that the ego cathexis represents a "feeling" merely by the fact of its own being and in the absence of any stimuli. The necessity that both subject and object must exist for an experience to be registered was apparently recognized by Federn. However, he attempted to resolve this by maintaining that the ego energy had both qualities simultaneously. Thus he wrote, "The ego is the bearer of consciousness; yet by a unique paradox the individual is conscious of the ego. Therefore the ego differs from all other existing phenomena. In spite of all rules of grammar, and disregarding the apparent paradox, the ego is at once subject and object."

Difficult as it is to understand how an essence could be aware of its own self—hence be both the "feeler" and the "feelee"—there is some recent experimental evidence that supports this position. Sherman (1971) studied individuals under very deep hypnosis. Subjects at "extremely profound depths" described their experience as "being everything, feeling oneness with everything, loss of knowledge of individual identity, no 'self,' absolute mental quiet, no thoughts or images." Sherman concluded that "the subject has passed beyond all those cognitive patterns that define him as a specific person and separate him from other people and his environment. What is left is undifferentiated awareness—the awareness of purely 'being' through which the person is identical to everything in the universe." The state he has depicted appears to be very like the state of satori in which, through meditation, a student of Zen Buddhism aims to achieve oneness with the universe.

Hypnosis has been described as a modality that permits the direction or control of cathexis, for example, removing feeling from an arm by hypnotically anesthetizing it (Watkins, 1967a). It would appear that in deep hypnosis the ego state boundaries have been decathected so that the phenomenon of impact does not exist. But in the absence of impact there is still a primary awareness that Federn is describing when he states that "The ego is at once subject and object." However, this primary awareness as set forth by Sherman's subjects did not include "knowledge of individual identity." Accordingly, we must assume that such individual identification requires there to be both subject and object energies and boundaries between them that can be impacted.

This undifferentiated state of primary awareness is also similar to the state of life after death that was hypothesized in Chapter 8. It was argued there that if ego cathexis (being) is an energy, then we know from the study of physics that energy is not destructible, only changeable in form, and that which is lost at death is "the awareness of a *unique and independent* existence." In death the "droplets of our self will merge with a universal ocean." Sherman's subjects emerged from the deep hypnosis to describe specifically their "loss of the knowledge of individual identity" and their "undifferentiated awareness."

Sherman also found that "at extremely profound depth—the amplitude of the electroencephalogram, from both vertex and occipital electrode loci, showed periods of drastic decrease," and that "these periods of marked amplitude diminution were easily distinguishable" from the electroencephalographic patterns immediately preceding and following the deep hypnotic state. The pattern of brain energies thus approached complete cessation, a state that would mark a condition of death.[1] No one to our verified knowledge has returned from complete death to describe a postmortem state of awareness. It may be that the two are similar; but if so the experience of death, unlike that of the deep hypnosis, is not reversible and we are left only with conjecture and not objective reports. However, in the light of this possibility our original thesis that "existence is impact" (Chapter 6) should now be modified to hold that that kind of existence (which might be termed secondary existence), characterized by knowledge of one's independent identity, is contingent on an impact between subject and object. This leaves the possibility that primary existence or undifferentiated awareness can continue after death.

By ascribing to the same essence (the ego cathexis) both the characteristics of subject and object, Federn has answered the question of how one knows his own self only to open up a Pandora's box of confusions and inconsistencies as one tries to understand other aspects of human perception and behavior. How can the simplest psychic state, defined as a unitary energy, act in such contradictory ways and assume opposite roles? Under what conditions is it subject; under what conditions is it object; and how can it change from one to the other?

This confusion seems to have stemmed from Freud's early speculations. Thus, he used the term "libido" to represent an object energy, an integrative energy, and a sexual energy that activated the principle of Eros, or love. Freud then coined the term "ego-libido" during his deliberations on the condition of narcissism (1953d). This ego-libido was called a "narcissistic cathexis" and represented a turning back of the libido to the ego; hence one came to love one's own self. Federn used the same terms "ego-libido" and "narcissistic cathexis" but then described this as a subject energy, the essence of selfness manifested by an ego "feeling."

By the time we bring in the concept of a mortido cathexis, a death energy, which in opposition to libido is disintegrative; we become really confused. The problem appears to lie in the attempt by both Freud and Federn to make the same term carry many different connotations. At the risk of taking too much liberty with terms devised by others let us try to simplify this situation by redefinitions as follows:

cathexis, An attached or allocated charge of energy that activates a psychological process.

ego cathexis, a kind or quality of energy that is the bearer of the essence of selfness. It is a *living* energy and is subject. Any element invested with it is experienced as "I" or "my"; hence, belonging to "me" as a part of my self.

object cathexis, a kind or quality of energy that bears no essence of selfness. It is a *nonliving* energy and is object. Any element invested with it is experienced as "it" or "not me"; hence, belonging to something outside my self. However, my awareness of it occurs only after it has impacted my ego.

libido, An energy direction that approaches or attracts. An element invested with libidinal energy (whether ego or object in nature) draws other elements closer. It is integrative and tends to bind elements together into more complex entities. It activates the principle of Eros. It is similar to centripetal force. Its characteristic is to move *toward* something else.

mortido, An energy direction that withdraws or repels. An element invested with mortidinal energy (whether ego or object in nature) pushes away other elements. It is disintegrative and tends to separate complex entities into simpler elements. It activates the principle of Thanatos. It is similar to centrifugal force. Its characteristic is to move *away from* something else.

We have now defined two different kinds of energy, one a self or subject energy and the other, an object or not-self energy. We have also indicated two different directions of movement that either of these energies may manifest, a toward, or integrative direction (libido), and an away-from, or disintegrative direction (mortido). By such a redefinition and differentiation we hope to avoid the confusion between subject-object that characterized so much of psychological (and specifically, psychoanalytic) writing.

At this point we encounter another conflictual meaning. It involves the term "introject." This has been defined as an internal object. So far, so good! But once the object has been introjected, and is within, we now find writers treating it as if it were subject and a part of self. Thus Guntrip (1952) in describing Fairbairn's theory of schizoid reactions states, "The child is emotionally identified with his objects, and when he mentally incorporates them he remains identified with them and they become part and parcel of the very psychic structure of his personality."

If an introject is to be defined as an object (even though within) then after the individual has identified with it (Federn would say ego-cathected the item) it becomes subject and is no longer object. In this case, the person no longer experiences it as not-self. Rather, he perceives the rest of the world as this introject-no-longer-object does, hence through the "eyes" of this introject.

For example, a child takes into himself the introject of a cruel parent. He identifies with that introject and infuses the item with selfness (ego cathexis). Now, he no longer deals with it as if he were its victim. He *becomes* the cruel parent and treats others with cruelty. The defense mechanism of identification often involves a protection of the self by becoming one with an aggressor. An old political saying is to the effect that "If you can't lick 'em, join 'em." Thus, the safest thing for a Jew to do in Germany before World War II was to carry out the aims of the Nazis. Certain individuals did precisely that and became the most cruel guards of all at such concentration camps as Treblinka.

Some years ago I had occasion to treat a young woman in a veterans hospital who was referred from the orthopedic ward because of "stinging pains in the lower back region for which no organic pathology could be found." She noted that as an adolescent she lived with a very hostile and punitive grandmother. The therapist's "third ear" pricked up on hearing that this grandmother was prone to beating the girl on the back with a switch (stinging pains). Later in the therapy the patient described her own marital problems. She would frequently get into a fight with her husband. She would then banish him from the house and lock the door. A few days later he would return and they would be reconciled. She once mentioned that her grandmother, too, fought a great deal with her husband and also would throw him out of the house.

Since the patient's bouts with stinging back pains occurred intermittently, she was asked to record the specific days when she suffered these symptoms. A record was also kept of the days when she had fights with her husband. As one might have expected, the pains occurred on days when her relationship with her husband was good. When she was fighting with her husband, she did not experience any such pains.

This alternation of back pains and marital quarrels can be explained by a repetitive identification and deidentification with the grandmother. Let us consider that first she introjected the image of the grandmother. This grandmother introject now operated within her like an object and repeated within what happened to her when she was a teenager. The "grandmother" inside beats her now just as the real grandmother beat her then. She experiences conversional pains in the back. The grandmother introject is at this time object to her.

After awhile, she solves this problem by the process of identification. She can no longer cope with the punitive grandparent, so she "joins" her. She identifies by the process of infusing the grandmother introject with selfness (ego cathexis). The grandmother introject no longer beats her, and she ceases to have back pains. But now she *is* the grandmother, so she must think and act like her. She *does* what the grandmother did; she fights with her husband and throws him out of the house. This continues until she feels lonely for the relationship with her husband, or perhaps we should say until her feelings of loneliness for her spouse are greater than her fears of her grandmother. The balance changes, and she reconciles with her husband. She de-identifies with the grandmother, withdrawing the ego energies from that entity and reconstituting the internal grandmother image once more as introject, as object. The beating from this object now resumes, and her back pains return. Only by a clear understanding of what is object and what subject in this case can we explain satisfactorily the alternation of back pains with marital quarrels.

The word "introject" becomes confusing if we speak of it as an internal object (since objects have *not-self* characteristics) and then continue to use the same designation when we mean an entity that is no longer object, but has been egotized, infused with selfness, and has now become part of the "I." The term "identification" is commonly used in this situation, but it has been employed indiscriminately to represent both a process and the product of that process, hence "an identification."

It seems desirable, therefore, in order to avoid confusion, to create a new term to designate the entity that, once introjected, has now become subject through egotization—and leave the word "identification" to represent only the process. In this book we shall term the product of the identification process an "identofact."[2] The symptom alternation in this woman then occurs because of an alternation of identification and de-identification, an egotization and de-egotization of the internalized grandmother image. Thus, the introject changes to identofact and vice versa. We now have a terminology that enables us to distinguish clearly whether we are referring to subject or object, a most necessary distinction in the establishment of one's identity.

At this point it would seem desirable to give a number of examples from treatment situations where we can differentiate object from subject, introjects from identofacts:

1. A patient reports the following memory:
   "My father beat me when I was a small boy."
   The patient is presenting a memory of an incident at which time the father (an external object) impacted on his sense organs and caused pain. His self (subject) directly experienced his father (object) visually and tactually.
2. The patient reports the following fantasy:
   "It was like a dream. I saw my father. He was beating a small boy who looked like me when I was little."
   The father is now an introject and perceived as an object. His own child ego state, the "boy," has been decathected and is also viewed as an object. The two "objects" are perceived by the self as impacting each other. The ego, accordingly, experiences no pain.
3. The patient reports the following fantasy:
   "It was like a dream. I was a small boy. My father was beating me, and it hurt like hell."
   The father, still an introject, continues to be perceived as an object. However, the child state, the "boy," is ego-cathected. It is now subject and experienced as self. It *feels* the pain inflicted upon it by the father object.
4. The same patient reports the following experience:

> "My son told me a lie. Children must be taught honesty and discipline, so I gave him a licking."
> The father, originally internalized as an introject (object), has been changed through identification to an identofact (subject); that is, the internalized father entity has been invested with ego cathexis. The father state is now subject and is experienced as self. The patient has so identified with the views and attitudes of the father that they are advanced as his own. The individual's child state is no longer ego-cathected but has been invested with only object energy. It has been projected onto the patient's son; that is, it has become congruent with the introject of that son. The patient has now *become* his own father, and his own child self (as projected on his own son) has become the object of the punishing father.

The process of identification whereby we change introjects into identofacts is the basic way in which the ego grows. That which enters us first as object from the outside is assimilated by the ego and becomes the thought or feeling we activate and experience later. Just as we take in food and metabolize it into body structure, we take in objects and egotize them into self-structure.

By changing an introject into an identofact through its investment with ego cathexis, the individual brings it into the realm of self-control. Self determination can now become operative because control of it by the self also means assumption of responsibility for its behavior. The action of an introject, since it is an object, can be self influenced but is not under self control. In this respect it is like the behavior of external objects (such as other people) who can be influenced but not controlled by one's self. As long as the entity is only object-cathected the neurotic's claim that he cannot control it is theoretically correct. He cannot.

During psychoanalysis the process of insight involves the egotization of what was previously object—like Freud's statement that "Where there was Id there shall be Ego." By inducing the investment of an introject with self energy we change the patient's perception of a situation from "It is being done to me. I am the victim of forces not under my control," to "I am doing this. I am responsible for it and can control it." Both psychoanalysis and reality therapy (Glasser, 1965) stress the achieving of this goal.

The essence of neurosis is the abdication of responsibility for his own behavior on the part of the patient. Thus, the essence of therapy is to reverse this situation. Through self-cathexis of his internalized objects the individual takes responsibility for his actions and assumes control of them in the future. True insight (as opposed to intellectualization) has been characterized in some psychology texts as the "Ah-hah!" experience. In analysis, it is more likely to be the "Oh-no!" experience. When insight is genuine, and not pseudo, it involves a reorganization of self structure as the ego extends its control over areas that were previously object (Erikson, 1964).

If we now return to our basic concept that differentiated existence is impact, a contact between two entities different from each other, such as a subject and an object, how does it become possible for us to sense or experience our own individual self? By our definition of existence we rule out the possibility of an impact of one subject on another subject. Since the introject is invested with object cathexis it would, of course, always be possible for the self to perceive it (although some introjects remain below thresholds of consciousness and are repressed or unconscious to the individual). But what about the identofact? If it is invested only with ego cathexis, then it should be incapable of being sensed by the self, since the *difference* necessary for the experience of existence is not there. Ego cathexis cannot impact ego cathexis; it can only fuse with ego cathexis. The object energy makes it possible to be sensed by the self; the ego energy infuses it with "me-ness." Accordingly, to experience my child as an identofact means that the perceptions and image of my child have been invested with both types of cathexis. The object cathexis permits me to experience an image of the child; the ego cathexis establishes that it is *my* thought and *my* child rather than visualization of a "not-self" object in space. The two together provide both impact and recognition of the experience as coming from within my self. I then say, "*I* am thinking of *my* child."

Perhaps the degree of selfness or objectness experienced is determined by the relative amounts of ego or object energies with which the identofact is cathected. Thus, the concept of "my child" is invested with a relatively much larger ego component than is the concept merely of "my car." Selfness, according to this view, is a relative matter and can inhere with varying degrees of strength within an array of behavioral contents.

Not only are internalized objects changed into identofacts through the cathexis of self energy, but also the opposite often takes place. Items of self are decathected and experienced as objects, especially in psychosis and in dreams. For example, a patient who was normally a friendly man once dreamed that he saw a large sleeping bear. As he walked away from it the bear awakened and approached him. It was huge, like a Kodiak or giant grizzly and reared up on its hind legs. When it was finally standing directly in front of him he reached out his hand and stroked it gently. It seemed to smile and act friendly. Unexpectedly, in a violent rage, it thrust grinding jaws at him. In great fright he awakened. His ego, suddenly aware of the enormous power of his own repressed and potential viciousness (the sleeping bear), immediately recathected itself, awakened, and its executive state broke off contact with the sleeping bear concept.

In our dreams, it is customary that repressed elements within us will be represented as objects. The dreaming executive ego state (in Stage 1 sleep) has been considerably deegotized, and its boundaries are therefore considerably weakened. We might hypothsize that the *self* field of force that centers in the executive state normally extends out with some ego energizing to other adjacent states. During sleep this field of force becomes dormant, contracts, and thus removes any "my-ness" in the elements of these other nonexecutive states. Accordingly, these elements now retain only their object cathexis. On impacting the weakened boundaries of the sleeping executive ego they break through, are objectified, and are experienced as "it." The dreamer does not sense the impulse as "my rage" but as "that angry bear." The impact is therefore felt as an external threat. The self in alarm awakens by instant reegotization. Like a sleeping army attacked at night by a small enemy patrol it immediately mobilizes its full strength and repels (re-represses) the invader. By waking, ego control is reestablished and fear subsides.

Impacts between separate entities must be experienced by the contact of their boundaries. Two people, two nations, two different entities of any kind must experience their existence in relation to each other at that point (line, area) in space-time that divides one from the other. It is there where impact occurs. Accordingly, they must have boundaries. And if one part of the ego is to experience another part there must be some boundary between the two parts to permit impact. We know that there are millions of different objects, separated from each other by boundaries. It would therefore make no sense to hypothesize a single, unified, and undifferentiated ego structure with one boundary separating it from the outer world. Such a self could perceive outer objects that contacted that boundary, but it could achieve no apprehension of its own self. And we do feel the existence of our own self. Accordingly, we must hypothesize that the self structure is divided into segments, parts, or states. As meaningful beingness is more greatly experienced when the individual matures, the self has become ever more complex and subdivided into innumerable states separated from each other by boundaries, probably flexible and permeable rather than rigid. This brings us to another whole area of consideration, which shall be reserved for a later chapter.

Federn failed to explain clearly the implications of his theory of ego cathexis to the phenomenon of consciousness. He, like Freud, did not continue to equate the ego only with consciousness. However, by using his concepts of ego and object cathexis and relating them to the theory that existence is impact we may be able to provide a rationale for consciousness.

It is well known that a certain quantum of stimulus energy is required to set off the discharge of a neuron. There are also many other examples in physics where a minimal amount of energy is required to trigger a reaction. If existence (experience) is related to impact, then it might be inferred that the impact must be of sufficient magnitude to precipitate the reaction of consciousness. An event must be at least of a certain size to secure our attention. According to this view, the phenomenon of consciousness becomes an economic problem within the theory of ego psychology. The two contacting elements (subject and object) must each be endowed with a certain minimal amount of cathexis for the impact to be sufficiently strong as to evoke a conscious experience.

A highly cathected self would be able to perceive

lightly cathected objects, while the individual whose ego is invested with only a small amount of ego cathexis would require an impact from a highly cathected object in order to become aware of it. Big Ben Clocks used to advertise, "First he whispers, then he shouts" to indicate that the alarm bell would ring softly first. If the sleeper did not then stir the clock shortly afterward would give forth a loud, raucous jangle to force him to awaken. The individual who was sleeping only lightly, hence whose self was more egotized at the moment, would hear the soft bell and respond to it. The one whose ego cathexis had been largely withdrawn into a deep sleep would require a much more highly energized object for the impact between it and his sleeping ego to be strong enough to arouse him to consciousness.

It follows that the person whose ego is well endowed with large quantities of ego cathexis, both in its core and in its boundaries, is capable of a much higher degree of consciousness toward both himself and stimulating objects. He is extremely sensitive to subtle interpersonal relationships. As a therapist his third ear is finely tuned to communications that are unconscious to others—and even to the communicator from whom they originated. Tiny feelings of others, which arrive at his sensory system but lightly object-cathected, are sensed and experienced by him consciously because of the high degree of energizing of his ego boundaries. He is like the "sleeper" who is very much awake and who would hear even the slightest whisper of the elarm clock. In the cognitive field such an individual can interpret the finest nuances of differentiation within thoughts and words. Such men as Aristotle, Freud, and Einstein must have been fortunate in possessing highly cathected egos.

Let us consider the experience of unconscious as well as conscious from the viewpoint of this ego psychology. Unconsciousness might well be of two kinds: 1.

normal forgetting because the items have now lost too much of their object cathexis (They no longer impact the individual's ego with a sufficient wallop as to evoke conscious awareness); and 2. the process of repression where, for dynamic reasons, the ego (perhaps through the employment of mortidinal energies) forces the item away from impact with its boundary.

The withdrawal of cathexis from unwelcome objects (or the withdrawal of ego cathexis from the boundaries facing them) has been called repression. It is viewed as an active process initiated by the individual's need for consistency, for cognitive consonance. As such, dynamic reasons are usually considered as the impetus for such a maneuver by the ego.

Forgetting, even of the repressive nature, may be dictated primarily by economic considerations, however. If to be conscious, a certain minimal quantity of object and ego cathexis must be employed, then there are limitations on one's energy pocketbook. The individual can no more afford to be consciously aware of all that he "knows" than can a furniture store display all its wares when limited space in the showroom requires that many pieces must be stored in the warehouse. It might even be hypothesized that the attempt to have too much continually in consciousness would so weaken the ego as to precipitate a psychosis. It is well known that sleeplessness often precedes a schizophrenic break. The ego needs the respite from continuous consciousness to recoup its energies. That is why sleep is so necessary to everybody. It has been found that when sleep is not permitted or is continually interrupted hallucinations begin to appear. It must be concluded, therefore, that unconsciousness, like consciousness, serves a definite need of the organism, and that the most efficient existence requires a balance between the two.

The economics of energy distribution may throw

some light on why one individual is introjected by a person and another is not. It seems logical that any external object is sensed by an internal replication of it that is object-cathected by the ego, much as vision requires that an image of that which is to be seen is focused on the retina. However, certain objects, such as important people in our lives, are introjected, hence formed into permanent internalizations, some of which may later be changed into identofacts by the process of identification. We might propose that that which distinguishes a temporary object or perception from an introject, or more permanent structure, is dependent upon the quantum of object energy with which it is cathected. If a warm iron is placed on my wrist it will be sensed, but upon its withdrawal it will have no future impact on my psychological economy. However, if it is very hot (highly cathected) it will leave a permanent image or brand on my wrist that will continue to act as a stimulating influence long after the iron has been withdrawn. So may it well be with our perception of significant objects. Those that excite such strong feelings in us as rage, fear, or love leave their "brand" within an ego state that, like the introject of the feared grandmother, continue to impact the ego long after the original stimulus is gone. Somehow, the highly cathected object effects a permanent alteration within self structure.

In Chapter 9, we have tried to present the key concepts in Federn's ego psychology. In this chapter certain modifications and extensions have been offered. Perhaps it should be concluded by summarizing the essential differences that are here formulated.

Federn holds that the ego can serve both as subject and object. He states (Federn, 1952, p. 106) that "The 'ego' as subject feels this 'ego' as object." He then modifies this (ibid., p. 216) as follows: ". . .it is not exact to say that the ego feels itself; it would be better to say that the ego *is* the feeling of itself." At still another point (ibid., p. 62) he writes, "Ego feeling, then, is the totality of feeling which one has of one's own living person. It is the residual experience which persists after the subtraction of all ideational contents."

In Chapter 6 we have proposed that existence is impact, impact between subject and object, between self and non-self. Federn talks of the contact by which one ego state senses another, but he does not seem to make this a prerequisite for "being." We do not rule out the possibility of a "primary narcissism" that inheres within ego cathexis, but we lay much more emphasis on the need for impact to validate the uniqueness of one's existence—even as we verify the existence of another person when his sound waves impact our ear drums, his light waves impact our retinas, or his skin impacts our organs of touch.

Second, Federn (ibid., p. 290) declared that object cathexis and ego cathexis were the antithesis of each other; "the first term indicated that the object, and the second that the ego, is that which is cathected by the libido."

The position taken here is that object cathexis and ego cathexis are *two different* kinds or qualities of energy. The first is a nonliving or "it" energy; the second is an organic, living, or "self" energy. An item becomes object or subject depending on which of these two energies cathects it. If its object cathexis is withdrawn and replaced with ego cathexis, the item ceases to be an object and becomes incorporated into the ego, and vice versa.

The term "libido," as used by Freud is confusing since it may mean a sexual energy, an integrative life energy, or an object energy. Federn adds to this confusion by using the term "libido" to refer to an object energy and "ego libido" (and sometimes merely "libido") to refer to an ego energy. Accordingly, we here consider libido as a *directionality,* hence a characteristic of either energy that attracts items so invested toward other items. Both libidinal object cathexis and libidinal ego cathexis are characterized by a tendency to draw items together when one or both of them are so energized. When the directionality of either energy is disintegrative such that the items so cathected repel others, we term this cathexis as mortidinal in nature.

Finally, the concept of the executive ego state holds a much more central position in the theoretical formulations being advanced in this work than it did in Federn's writings.

In the preface to his brilliant discussion on *Identity: Youth and Crisis* Erikson (1968) wrote as follows.

"One of my teachers in the Vienna Psychoanalytic Institute in the late twenties was Dr. Paul Federn, a fascinating man equally inventive in new concepts and in slips of the tongue. At the time, his concept of 'ego boundaries' was much discussed as important but opaque. We students, in some desperation, asked him to give us as many seminars in succession as he deemed necessary to explain it to us. For three long evenings he held forth; and on concluding the last one he folded up his papers with the air of one who has finally made himself understood, and asked, *"Nun—hab ich mich verstanden?"* ("Now—have I understood myself?") Perhaps it is time at the end of the last two chapters for this writer to ask the same question, *"Nun—hab ich mich verstanden?"*[3]

FOOTNOTES CHAPTER 10

1. It is interesting to speculate on whether the energy flows recorded on the electroencephalograph are in fact cathexis movements. It would also be of significance to know whether the encephalograms of dying patients resembled those of Sherman's subjects.
2. In psychoanalytic theory the introject is, of course, invested with object cathexis. We are calling it an "identofact" when it is ego-cathected. This is not to imply that the object cathexis has been entirely removed and replaced with ego cathexis, only that ego cathexis has been added. The complete removal of all object energy raises other questions about self-experience that will be discussed later.
3. The implication of Erikson's observation was that Federn was so confused (and confusing) that he was doubting whether he even understood himself. One might conjecture, however, that Federn was a man who was constantly reliving and rethinking his theories even while he was lecturing. In his lecture he was talking to himself. By that we mean one ego state (as teacher) was talking to another ego state (as pupil) in the effort to make clear to the second the conceptions of the first. Whether or not he had succeeded in clarifying his position to his psychoanalytic students, Federn must have felt at that time that it was most important for him to understand his own theories both from the subjective viewpoint (that of the teacher ego state) and from the objective one (that of the pupil ego state). In this remark he showed that he was more concerned with convincing himself than his pupils.

Chapter 11

FLIGHTS INTO OUTER SPACE

It is time that the science of psychology cease to be so atomistic and become more relativistic. If it must take physics as its model, let it do so with some awareness of that science's departure from Newtonian models into the areas of relativity and quantum mechanics. We shall now take a brief and relativistic flight into space and time to seek implications for the further understanding of human behavior.

Mankind has recently taken "one giant step" in reaching the moon. He now explores geographical and theoretical areas that a generation ago were mentioned only in *Amazing Stories* magazine. In this chapter we will indulge in some far-reaching speculations with possibilities considered that extend much beyond presently available evidence. Occasional flights beyond the stratosphere ought to be excused. The potential for new understandings exceeds the likelihood of damage.

Existence is always in what we call the now. It is that

point in the dimension of time that we call the present. We have described selfness as being composed of an energy. Let us think of ego energy as moving in a time dimension. This would be comparable to light energy traveling through our universe. As a light corpuscle impacts upon an object that object is illuminated for the moment; that is, it becomes visible (and for us, exists). A series of objects stretched continuously along a space dimension would be progressively illuminated as the light corpuscle passed through them.

Now think of a number of events (or happenings) arranged along a continuum of time. As a unit of ego or self energy impacted an event, that event would happen or come to existence in our experience. As the cathexis passed on immediately afterward to the event adjacent to it on the time dimension, the first happening would return to nonexistence, hence become a part of the past. The second event would now exist, etc. The array of events stretching from the past into the future would come into being for that self as its cathexis, traveling along the time dimension, contacted each in turn. The location of the ego energy unit as it impacts each objective event is always in the now. The future represents all events that precede the now, while in the past are all events through which the now (existence) has passed in its movement along the time dimension. The total of these experienced (ego-illuminated) events we would call our "life." A television program entitled *This is your life* held its viewers by portraying (or describing) a series of events in the life of some prominent person beginning with his birth and tracing them up to the time of the program.

All events in the future are nonexistent until they have been activated in the now by the cathecting self energy. Afterwards, they become again nonexistent as they are decathected by the self that has moved its "now" into events that were previously future. Existence for the self thus becomes as Federn defined it, ". . .an investment of continuously changing contents with the unifying, coherent ego feeling."

One might speculate that if this unit of ego energy follows a predetermined path from which it could not deviate without the intervention (impact) of outside forces then it will encounter only a very specific set of events. It would not have been possible for it to have encountered any other set of events. We would say that the individual self that particular unit of ego cathexis represented was following his "destiny." We are now thrown back upon the same old controversy of determinism or free will, which has plagued man for centuries.

Freedom of choice becomes possible apparently only if the self has the ability itself, without outside interference, to modify either its directionality or its magnitude. As we consider directionality, perhaps the unit of ego cathexis can expand energy (like a space ship) so as to alter its direction of movement, thus directing its pathway away from the location of previous sets of events into different sets. Maybe it could speed up or slow down its passage along the time dimension. Experiential time, as we well know, may be correlated with chronological time but not to a high degree. However, it is hard to conceive of ego cathexis as having such self-determining abilities. Whether or not it can also regulate its intensity along the path so as to increase or decrease the magnitude of its investments is a moot question. But if it could, then the self would be able to determine its own destiny and to choose those events it wishes to exist in its life experience. Let us conclude this discussion by an exerpt from an earlier contribution on this question (Watkins, 1967a):

> Consider the case of a man riding in a railroad car and observing the passing countryside through a view window. There are certain times when the sun brilliantly illuminates the entire landscape. Sometimes, the pattern of

sun and cloud make various objects clearly visible while obscuring others. Occasionally, the dimness of dusk makes difficult all or most of the passing scene. Finally, periods of night occur during which nothing outside can be seen. These differences in illumination might be compared to variations in object cathexis. The objects which are brightly lighted command the traveler's interest and attention. He tends to ignore those which are dimly illuminated. They have little impact on his retina. If, by chance, the sun shines brightly during the times when a beautiful area of meadow, forest or other scenic region is being traversed, he is happy. He enjoys that part of his existence. If the illumination is most clear when the train is passing through slums, ugly industrial sites, deserts or waste areas, then the viewer finds his existence boring or painful. Two different travelers journeying through the same region on different days might arrive at totally different conclusions about its beauty and worthwhileness. The first had the opportunity of well-illuminated vision during the more charming vicinities. The light failed as his train passed through the regions of ugliness so that he withdrew his attention. At those times, he engaged in conversation with others or read to himself. This man would affirm that the trip from X to Y was a wonderful and beautiful experience.

A second man who traversed the route on a different day in which the various differentiations of light and shadow were reversed would arrive at the exact opposite conclusion. He would proclaim that he was never so miserable, that he experienced only ugliness during the trip between X and Y. Thus, two different people may pass through certain common experiences in life, but because of the different cathexis of the objects with which they must interact, one finds life rich and rewarding, the other only painful and meaningless.

So far we have been considering only "that which is being experienced," the object, and by its illumination, the cathexis of that object. *Being* comes from impact between object and subject. The subject is quite capable of altering attention, cathecting and de-cathecting various ego boundaries such that at times the energized boundary is the one presented toward viewing through the window. At another time, the energy is withdrawn from this boundary and invested instead into one which is sensitized toward conversation with a companion. At still another time, all ego energy may be invested in receiving the impacts from a magazine. Accordingly, it is not only the varying illumination outside the train that determines the impacts of experience, but also the selectivity of the experiencer. Sometimes he may doze, paying little attention to a brightly lighted pleasant or ugly countryside. At other times he may even go to sleep, withdrawing all cathexis from the outside world. If he were to sleep throughout the day, remaining awake only at night, he would not experience the scenery between X and Y at all, since he would have no ego boundary cathected to receive impact from the outside cathected object. When his own ego boundaries were so energized (at night), there would be no outside cathected object available. Such a person would not live in the *Umwelt,* the outer world. His being would be concentrated only in the self-world of inner preoccupation (the *Eigenwelt*) and perhaps in nocturnal conversation and interpersonal relationship with his neighbor (the *Mitwelt*).

It now becomes obvious that two travelers might ride the same train the same day, but because of changes in their own inner ego states and the differences in dispositions of their ego cathexis, each might arrive at an entirely different picture of the trip from X to Y. This differential disposition of object and ego energies could account for the tremendously different experiences of "being" for different people—why some are happy, lead meaningful, integrative and joyous lives, while others spend an existence filled with pain, boredom and misery.

How different might the trip of the unhappy voyager be if there could have been beside him a guide informed about the route, who could suggest the times when it might be fruitful to look out the window, or direct his attention to the picture magazine as the train passed the most unpleasant areas. Such a guide would suggest when sleep was the most worthwhile activity, when one should don one's dark glasses to avoid the pain of too bright sunlight, and when to take them off in order to perceive a particularly beautiful, though dimly illuminated, scene. It is not usually given to us to have such a guide, nor is there anyone who has previously traversed the same route, since we pass this way but once. However, it is possible for some people during the trip to acquire the help of one who is relatively sophisticated about the route and who can teach better techniques for making the journey rich and meaningful. It is valuable to receive help in knowing when to sleep and when to remain awake, when to read, when to converse, when and what to observe. Such guidance may immeasurably assist one to complete a life journey with greater enjoyment.

Those of us who are psychotherapists are manipulators of cathexis whether we realize it or not. When, through suggestion, we restore feeling and movement to a hysterically paralyzed leg we are investing that part with ego cathexis and including it once again within the boundaries of the body ego. When we analytically lift a repression and bring to consciousness mental material once amnesic we are ego-cathecting that thought. Full egotization may ensue when the insight has surpassed intellectual boundaries and has involved all organs of bodily and mental meaning within the self. When we apply a positive reinforcement to an adaptive response, we are energizing it with greater "selfness."

We use our therapeutic skill to enhance the being of our patient, he who is traveling the train of life. When we hypnotically induce an anesthesia for a painful operation, we are removing an ugliness from the passing scene. As we help our traveler to ignore it, he de-cathects that ego boundary on which the painful stimulus must impinge. Just as there is no sound, in the experiential sense, when there is no listener present, so also is there no pain when the experience is absent. We direct his cathexis away from the boundary of impact. The pain, like the sound in the forest, strikes, but there is no one there to feel it. For the moment there is no "being" at the point of contact. Later, when the pain has lost its object cathexis, we restore energy to the patient's ego boundary, even as we direct his attention to the new and beauteous scene that follows the moment of passing ugliness.

Through suggestion and interpretation we direct his gaze outward when the relationship next to him becomes unrewarding and inward to his own meditation when there is nothing worthwhile in the immediate *Umwelt.* When frightening fantasy from his disturbed *Eigenwelt* threatens to engulf him in psychotic terror, we turn the cathexis into the boundaries which are adjacent to the constructive relationship (the *Mitwelt*) with ourselves or integrative others within his social world. By the intelligent displacement of cathexis utilizing interpersonal communcation, and employing a wide variety of technical devices for altering such displacements as suggestion, construction, interpretation, working-through, reinforcements, etc., we assist him to "be." He comes to exist in a world of impacts which are integrative, and which make his existential journey through life more meaningful and satisfying. We call this experience "psychotherapy."

Chapter 12

ENERGIES AND THEIR DIRECTIONALITY

In earlier chapters we have been considering in some detail the nature of subject and object energies, termed ego and object cathexis. We also defined libido and mortido as directions in which those energies move: the first, toward, and the second, away from. Let us now extend their theoretical nature further in regard to these latter characteristics. Perhaps another way of viewing these two forces is to consider them as acting to accomplish two major functions of living creatures, integration and differentiation.

The human self develops by perceiving similarities and differences. Entities that have similar elements are classified together and grouped into generalizations called concepts. As the child grows into an adult, his thinking, which is originally very concrete, becomes more abstract. Both the child and the schizophrenic (as well as the brain damaged) often demonstrate this concrete type of thinking (Kasanin, 1944). Thus, a child once drew a picure of a wagon, placing a large circle on its box. When asked what the circle represented he replied, "Why, that's the sunshine." In concrete thinking an element (in this case the sun's roundness) is used to represent an entire object—the sunshine. The whole is identified by a part of it and is equated with another if they have one part in common. This leads to false generalizations. Thus, if all men are mortal, and Socrates is mortal, it does not necessarily follow that because of this Socrates is a man.

Just as it is necessary that similarities be perceived, and that elements be classified together or integrated when they are the same, so also is it essential that the organism learn to distinguish differences clearly, to differentiate, to separate unlike elements by placing boundaries between them. We have already noted earlier that psychosis results when an individual cannot differentiate subject from object, his perceptions from his thoughts. But even finer differentiations are required. Within the object field and within the subject field differences between elements occur that require separation, hence placing them in separate "boxes." A country like the United States requires finer political divisions than merely states. There are counties, townships, cities and towns, precincts, paving districts, etc. Within the politically integrated whole there are many differentiated subdivisions. Sometimes these different principalities are completely separate from each other. In other cases they overlap so that an individual element might be a citizen simultaneously of two or more different jurisdictions. Furthermore, from time to time the various areas and boundaries may undergo change. So also is it within the ego.

These two processes, integration and differentiation, are achieved by the interaction of the two energy directions, libido and mortido. The first draws elements together, hence integrates. The second pushes them apart, hence differentiates. The mature, successfully functioning individual is one vast complex of elements bound together and separated, integrated and differentiated, by the disposition of libidinal and mortidinal energies.

Let us return for the moment to the Freudian concept of the ego as being separated internally from the id by a boundary and externally from the environment by another boundary. A boundary, like the fence around a plot of land, is designed to keep out those who are alien and so do not belong. It has a repelling function in both directions. In a similar manner, the guards on the prison walls keep the inmates in and other citizens out. But this pushing away is precisely the function that characterizes mortido. Accordingly, we must hypothesize that ego boundaries, either between the ego and id, the ego and the world, or between different ego states must be manned by (cathected with) mortidinal energy. Elements in the core of the ego would probably be more highly egotized with libido—that is, ego libido. This binds together within a common boundary those elements that are similar. It establishes within an ego boundary a unified state, giving us that feeling of "unity, continuity and contiguity" that Federn describes. We feel our self as one. We sense as object those elements that are differentiated and outside the boundary.

If we are to think of two different kinds of energy, ego cathexis and object cathexis, and two different directions that can characterize either, libido-toward mortido-away-from, then we need certain symbols by which we can designate each in a diagram. There is something about object cathexis, whether libidinal or mortidinal, that is active and moving. It is like an energy of motion, either toward or away from. It is comparable to an electrical current or a *kinetic* energy. On the other hand, the nature of ego cathexis is like a fixed charge, an allocation, a *Besetzen*—hence an occupation. It is more comparable to static electricity and represents a *potential* energy or energy field. As the representation of self it is more a "being" energy than a "doing" energy.[1] Let us therefore use the following symbols to represent each:

Object Cathexis

Object libido	•——>	An object energy that attracts.
Object mortido	•——|	An object energy that repels.

Ego Cathexis

Ego libido	<—Ⓢ—>	A subject or ego energy that attracts.
Ego mortido	|—Ⓢ—|	A subject or ego energy that repels.

Using these symbols the kind and directionality of energy actions in certain interpersonal relationship situations might be portrayed as in Figure 2.

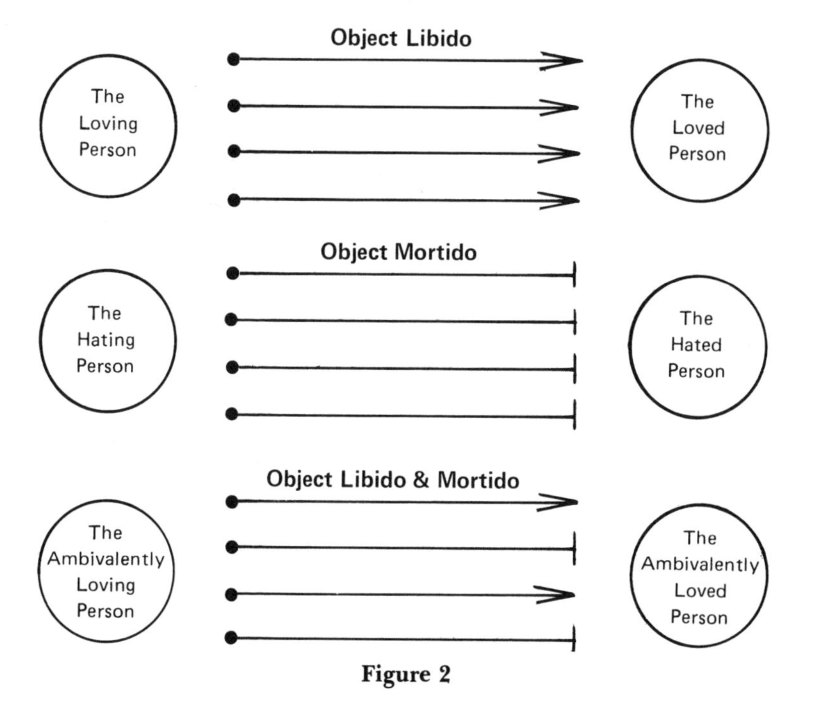

Figure 2

Let us theorize further about the nature of object and ego cathexes. Our tools of inquiry at this point must be almost entirely rationalistic, since we have very little empirically either to support or to invalidate such speculation. If we are to think of object cathexis as an "it," or nonliving, energy, then we have no difficulty in maintaining that its magnitude and directionality is determined, like that of any other physical force, by the laws of cause and effect or in the realm of psychology by the factors of stimulus and response. The investment or divestment of object energies are established entirely by the action of other forces upon them.

However, we have hypothesized the ego cathexis as a living, being, or self energy. The self is thus the total of all elements and processes within an organism that are invested with such energy. There must be something essentially different in the basic quality or nature of ego cathexis that distinguishes it from object or nonliving energy. Wherein lies this difference? We are at once placed again in that eternal dilemma of choosing the frying pan of free will or the fire of determinism. For if all processes are part of a cause and effect continuum then what started the first cause, and what will be the result of the last effect? To cope with such questions we must at some point abandon a science based wholly on strict determinism and entertain the possibility of partial determinism or the operation occasionally of a principle of indeterminancy.

The ancients simply said, "In the beginning God—." He was hypothesized as the original cause, the source of creation, not determined Himself, but determining all that came after Him. He was assumed to be self-created and self-determined. These same writers also held that "God created man in his own image," hence that He endowed humans with some of His own original cause—thus giving them free will.

Without accepting or rejecting this thesis, let us for the moment pursue some of the consequences of a position that holds that ego cathexis (as an energy that activates living process—probably within all living organisms) is distinguished from object cathexis by the fact that it is capable of self-initiating behavior, that it is determining, that it has inhering within it the essence of first cause and that, therefore, its actions are not necessarily determined by influences from without. We need not insist that it is uninfluenced by the impact of other forces, only that it retains certain prerogatives of self-direction, and that its operations cannot be determined or predicted on a strict cause and effect basis.

Such a hypothesis is harmonious with man's view of himself, with his beliefs, his feelings, his practices, and his laws. It is a theory that *feels* more right to most men than one of strict determinism. And who is to say whether man's *feeling* or his *cognition* has in this situation most grasped the truth.[2]

If one aspect in the functioning of a human organism, the ego energy, is not bound by the same rules as that of inorganic energy then we have returned to a dualistic position. A corollary of this is that psychology as the study of behavior can never be an exact science, since the tools of science can account for only part of its processes. We will always be confronted with a science of possibilities and probabilities. From a statistical point of view we are faced with the likelihood that a piece of the variance will always be unaccounted for. This may be most disconcerting to those who seek perfect control, but if our empirical tools, based on a cause and effect principle, can only approximate perfection, not because of their crudeness, but because the basic principle under which they operate is not universal, then so what? If psychological truth can be approached by our scientific methodologies but never be completely grasped, if certain energy systems can never be completely described and controlled, if cause and effect operate most (but not necessarily all) of the time, then so what?

All that is lost is our own dream of omniscience and omnipotence. We can still learn much about our behavior, our experience, our motivations, our perceptions, and we can still find how to live our lives more harmoniously. Our tools of science need not be discarded because they can never answer all the questions we might ask. The scientific method is still the best method we have for the discovery of new truth. It need not be abandoned simply because it is not capable of dealing with all truth.

And even if the subject aspect of our own selves will not always follow the same principles as nonliving objects, it is that very subject essence, the functioning of that very ego cathexis within our own selves, which is part and parcel of the rational processes whereby we as thinking beings study the rest of the universe. It is through the operation of such ego energies that we engage in scientific experimentation, the development and testing of hypotheses, the weighing of data, and the determination of validity. That unpredictable essence, the unknown element in the behavioral equations, is itself a part of all the processes of science by which man comes to know his world. And the influence of such forces within our studies should operate to bring us closer to correct understandings, albeit we may often have to utilize ego-cathected thought processes to transcend the limits of objective observation.

Let us pursue our considerations further by accepting that ego cathexis, unlike object cathexis, can operate as a self-determining agent. It would then appear that within the organism the self (the ego-cathected elements and processes) has the power of disposing or of directing the object cathexes. The object cathexes become, therefore, like a possession of the self to be used as it, the self, sees fit.

The self in reaching out to contact the world by impacting its objects in order to exist might be compared to a man in a dark forest who explores his environment equipped with a flashlight and a pair of eyes. As he focuses the beam on a tree, hence investing it with light, the energy is reflected back to impact the man's retina, and vision takes place. As the self directs a bit of object energy upon an internalized image of something in the outer world that has entered the organism through its sense organs, that energy is reflected back by the object and impacts a state of the ego at its boundary. Experience then takes place. This achieves the condition we have described as necessary for existence, the impact of object on subject, of not-self on self, of "it" on me.

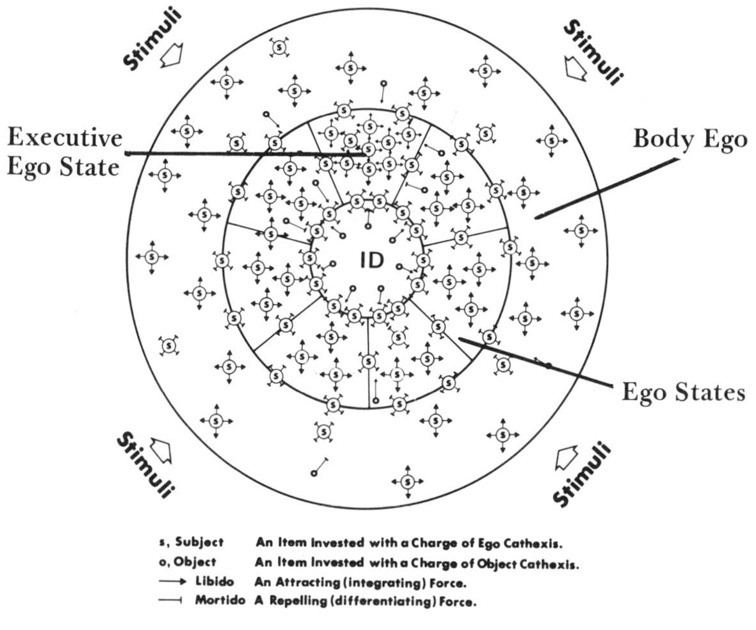

Figure 3 **OUTSIDE WORLD ENVIRONMENT**

In Figure 3, a possible diagram of the organism is depicted using the symbols for ego and object cathexes and for libido and mortido directions. The entity of the id, which is hypothesized in psychoanalytic theory, is retained although its existence as a single unit containing only object energies operating according to basic instincts seems questionable. There is no doubt that we have within us repressed objects, and that these can have an unconscious influence on our feelings and behavior. Furthermore, depth therapies such as psychoanalysis often elicit such phenomena, but it is quite possible that id elements represent various isolated, object-cathected states that are simply so cognitively dissonant with the ego that they must be deeply repressed. Such object-elements may also be imbedded throughout various ego states and need not necessarily have a common area. Furthermore, the whole question of what is instinctual is highly controversial, and there is inadequate empirical evidence to support Freud's theory of instincts.

Nevertheless (although with considerable misgivings), the concept of the id is temporarily retained and placed within our diagram. It is pictured as a reservoir of object libido and mortido as represented by the corresponding symbols. The ego is depicted as divided into various "states," the nature of which will be discussed further in the next chapter. The gray area represents the executive, or primary ego, state of the moment. It is more highly energized with ego cathexis than the others. The boundaries that separate ego from id, ego from environment, mental ego from body ego, and that differentiate one ego state from another are portrayed as being invested with ego mortido.

Since the function of a boundary, like a fence or like border guards, is to separate, hence to repel elements in both directions, it is obvious that this function requires that a boundary be invested with mortidinal energy. The core of the ego state includes elements that can be cathected with either ego libido or ego mortido; if the organism is healthy and growing, however, it would probably represent more of the former.

The body must be cathected primarily with ego energies, also more libidinal in its early and growing stages. In Figure 3 the amounts and dispositions of cathexes are drawn to represent a comparatively young, healthy, and untraumatized individual. The quantities of ego and object libidio exceed those of ego and object mortido. The person is in the process of growing and integrating. The body ego is highly energized with ego cathexis of a libidinal type. The ego states are also innervated largely with libindinal energy, and the person feels himself as a coherent whole. The charges of mortidinal energy that man this person's ego boundaries are adequate to establish impact with all objects that contact them and sufficient to differentiate into different states those elements that need some separation. The mortidinally cathected elements in the core of the ego states are few and greatly outnumbered by those invested with ego libido. The few introjects (represented by—➤or—|) are primarily cathected with object libido, thus representing constructive or loving individuals in the person's world. Only a few of such internalized objects (—|) are destructive, hence cathected with mortido.

We must hypothesize that as the organism ages the proportion of mortidinal energies increases. This would be evidenced by a greater rigidity of the ego state boundaries. The individual becomes more fixed in his attitudes. New elements cannot enter an ego state, either from the outside environment or from another adjacent state, as the boundary becomes less flexible, less permeable because of its investment with ever larger quantities of ego mortido. We say that it is more difficult for older people to change and learn ("You can't teach an old dog new tricks.") The more time passes, the more aging occurs. Finally the proportion of ego mortido to ego libido becomes very great. The repulsion between many elements that are strongly cathected with mortido tear the boundaries apart.

No longer energizing constructive differentiation the excessive mortido cathexes now simply destroy integration. Boundaries between id, ego states, the body, and the world break down; and all energies, undifferentiated and unintegrated, flow back into the outside world. The organism has been reduced to its simplest elements. We say that death has taken place. The individual has ceased to exist as an independent and bounded self. His energies, like the waters of a river, have rejoined the universal ocean.

> No farther seek his merits to disclose
> Or draw his frailties from their dread abode.
> (There they alike in trembling hope repose,)
> The bosom of his Father and his God.
>
> —Thomas Gray (1751)

FOOTNOTES

1. One is reminded here of the biological view of masculinity as being active and moving (the sperm) and femininity as passive and receptive (the egg). Even as the contact between sperm and egg creates life so also does the impact between object and subject create existence.
2. This concept of the self as an original cause is currently entertained by other scientific contributors. Thus, Thorne (1973), who strongly insists that all psychotherapy must be based on validated science, quotes a personal communication from T. H. Krawiec to the effect that "I am the cause of my own effects," which Thorne holds "describes the conscious Self capable of modifying its own outcomes."

Chapter 13

EGO STATES

That most people are fairly consistent in their behavior is well known. That they often display inconsistent patterns is also obvious. And that a given pattern frequently has an internal consistency and is consistently elicited under the same circumstances is also common. It seems that certain behaviors and experiences "hang together." Thus the man who is almost always quiet when seated at the dinner table may be almost always noisy and vociferous when attending a baseball game. His behavior at the game is inconsistent with his behavior at dinner, but it always appears at each game. It is as if he were a different person at home when dining than when watching his favorite sport. The studious, hardworking scholar who seems so logical, so rational during the five days a week when he lectures at the college becomes a swinger at Saturday night parties. Most of us know of individuals whose personality seems to change drastically when they are under the influence of alcohol. There is the shy swain who, after a few drinks, makes passes at every woman; the pleasant, peaceful fellow who, after a few martinis, belligerently demands to fight all comers; and the hail-fellow-well-met salesman, normally so sociable and laughing, who retires depressed to a corner table in the bar and sulks over his Scotch on the rocks.

What brings about these remarkable changes in behavior patterns? What activates configurations of perceiving, thinking, and feeling so that the same body seems to be inhabited by different selves? These transformations require the hypothesizing of different ego states, different states of consciousness, to account for their variability.

An ego state compares in some respects to a geographical state like Idaho or California. It has an area that includes many individuals or elements, and it is surrounded by a boundary that distinguishes it from other states. Also, ego states can be very large or very small. Some may contain only a few elements; others may be so large that they encompass the entire living activities of an individual through extended periods of his life.

However, unlike geographical states they cannot be adequately represented on a two-dimensional surface. They contact each other, interlap, and extend in many different dimensions. A single mental element may be a citizen of many different states. Furthermore, the boundaries of states, although showing resistance to change, are permeable, flexible, and subject to many alterations. A single state may enlarge to include elements that previously only belonged to other states. Or it may contract and relinquish items that were once included within its boundaries. This structure of the ego as composed of many states is continually changing. The ego as a whole is a dynamic system of equilibrium; and like other such systems, for example the sun, a flame, or the atmosphere, it is constantly adjusting its energies to maintain its integrity in the face of constant fluctuations of stimulus input from the outside and its own output of behavior, thought, feeling, or other psychological movement. It is a microcosm of a complex society that includes both cooperative and antagonistic elements.

Just as a person may belong to a church, a professional society, the male or female sex, live in a certain town, be included in a certain income bracket, be of a certain age range, and identify himself with a certain occupation, so also can a given mental item belong to many different ego states. Whenever any state that includes it is activated, the item itself is so activated that it becomes within the immediate range of experience and behavior of the individual.

For example, in demonstrations of hypnotic phenomena it is common that the subject will be regressed back to some earlier age level in his life, perhaps that which existed when he was six years old and in the first grade. By the activation of that particular state elements, both subject and object, included within it are now available to consciousness and report. The regressed individual may display feelings and opinions he had at that time—hence subject elements. Also activated may be old introjects, such as his teacher or parents of that period. They once more become immediate influences on his behavior.

If this state has been reactivated as a means for hypnoanalytic therapy, the therapist may, through questioning or association, explore the entire living space of his patient at that time, eliciting reports on feelings, events, significant relationships, emotional conflicts, symptoms, etc., which existed then, but which do not exist directly in the ego states of the present. The psychoanalyst achieves a similar effect by reactivating this earlier state in the transference relationship. There are many similarities between the state of hypnotic trance (which is a kind of regression) and the ego state initiated by a transference reaction, also a regression (Watkins, 1963a). Furthermore, there were undoubtedly many different ego states that existed during that period, some that were active when the individual was in school, others when he was with his family, and still others that existed only transitionally in response to temporary thoughts or feelings. Each, however, includes a finite number of experience elements, and each has some kind of boundary that distinguishes it from a different state. Federn would have described the elements within a state as having a common cathexis.

Since all items within the boundaries of an ego state are held together by a state cathexis, yet all states within the normal self are also invested with a common (national) ego energy, each ego state must of necessity experience itself as both an "I-ness" and a "we-ness." This might be compared to the resident of a geographical commonwealth, such as Pennsylvania. As a citizen of that state, he is a Pennsylvanian, but as a citizen of the United States, he is also an American.

In the normal individual, the "I-ness" and the "we-ness" can usually be reconciled. However, there are situations where an experiential item finds itself in conflict between its identification within a state and its role as an element within the entire ego body of the individual.

A similar conflict must have been experienced by Robert E. Lee at the beginning of the Civil War. It will be recalled that he was offered command of the Union armies by President Lincoln, but that he decided to remain with his native state, Virginia, which had seceded. Here his loyalty to his home state (I-ness) transcended his commitment to the Union (we-ness).

In capitalist nations, the rights of individuals, hence "I-ness," are stressed. In socialist countries, the emphasis is on responsibility to the state (we-ness).

As will be seen in clinical examples to be presented (in Chapter 22), internal conflict occurs within a person when the desires of an ego state are in opposition to the needs of his entire self community. Unless these are reconciled, the person suffers from continual anxiety or psychosomatic symptoms.

It will be noted here that the term ego state is used to include a living region or area. It covers all subject- and object-cathected items belonging within that region. In the strict sense, as Federn employed the term, an *ego* state included only subject items, hence those cathected with ego energies. It is more useful at this point to use the term to include both subject and object items that exist or interact with each other within a common experience.

The Executive Ego State

In the diagram of the ego (see Figure 1, Chapter 9), one state was designated as "executive." By executive is meant that state most highly cathected and so energized that it is considered to be the one activated at that moment. It is the "self" of the "now." As it exhausts its cathexes another state is more highly energized and becomes executive, thus the difference in behavior between our individual at a party and at work. Such transitions account for the changes in mood that characterize most people. In its most discrete form, the executive ego state of one moment may be completely unaware of the executive state of another time, and we have a multiple personality. Somehow, the two states do not have common areas that they share or boundaries that are permeable. The deactivated state is completely objectified with only the executive state retaining ego cathexis. "Eve White" becomes aware of "Eve Black" only as object, if at all (Thigpen & Cleckely, 1957). The executive ego state being highly cathected is a ferment of experiential activity—like a beehive. Many impacts take place within it. Thus it is the center of being. As the various items included within it that are subject- or object-cathected impact each other and/or the internal boundary of the state, they are experienced by the self. Existence takes place. The importance of the executive state can be compared to that of a metropolitan capital in an essentially rural country. It is where the primary awareness is located, where the action is, and where decisions regarding the individual's policies and behavior are consciously determined.

Impacts between elements and boundaries in other (noncathected) ego states are minimal. Because of the lesser energy there is little activity, and experiences in these tend to be ancillary to the main nucleus of self, which resides in the executive state. Because of the lower frequency and intensity of impacts in these other states such experiences as occur may well be below the threshold of awareness, hence unconscious. Thus, events do happen to a person within nonexecutive ego states, but they tend to have and to result from lesser impact.

However, when a change of ego states occurs a new state becomes executive. It is charged with cathexis and, so to speak, comes to life. The center of self activity has now moved to it. It has received the charges of energy that have been withdrawn from the previous ego state. The new state with its experiential items, its happenings, its introjects, and its identofacts becomes the administrative center of the self. The former executive state, now decathected and deactivated, takes its place along with other dormant states. In fact, it may become completely repressed. It must await its turn for activation again until other environmental impacts or internal changes of energy equilibrium once more bring it to the fore.

The various defense mechanisms play a significant

role in the dynamic interplay of ego states as well as in the behavior mediated by a particular state. For example, some individuals are subject to the situation where behavioral and experiential items are disowned by the executive ego state and imputed to other people. We call the mechanism projection. The difference between such activities within the normal person and the paranoid is one of degree. In the paranoid the ego boundaries are rigid, inflexible. There is no egotized communication channel between the executive state and the material projected in delusional form. The individual experiences large areas of himself only as "it."

A paranoid schizophrenic patient I once treated specifically referred to the gang that persecuted him as "the damned Its." The "Its" made life miserable for him, calling him homosexual names and plotting his downfall. Since "Its" are perceptions or images that come from external stimuli, his ego sensed them as originating from the outside environment. Thus his own hatreds were felt as coming from outside himself because their ego cathexes had been withdrawn. Such thoughts contained only object energy and were experienced as, "They hate me."

Transitions from one ego state to another occur along the pathway of some common element. Thus, if Ego State A and Ego State C have an element, B, in common, and if Ego State A is executive at the moment, by directing attention to item B the cathexis can be withdrawn from A and moved to C. B serves as a bridge between the two states. In the free association method of psychoanalysis, cognitive trains of thought move along the interlocking chains of ideas that take the patient from his present experiential state back to some other experience in the past, and an earlier ego state is activated.

Gestalt psychology and field theory (Lewin, 1951)

teaches that a figure cannot be evaluated independent of the ground in which it is imbedded, or an item independent of the field surrounding it. Thus, the fact that a descriptive term may be common to two different ego states does not necessarily mean that the cathexis will flow over it from the first to activate the second if the item is immersed in a different field in each. A commonness in meaning would be required if such an item were to serve as a bridge between the two states.

For example, a young man might describe his sister as being "a pretty girl." At another time, he might state that he is turned on sexually by "a pretty girl" and that such a one stimulates his desire to go to bed with her. However, it is doubtful that his associating of the concept "pretty girl" in relation to his sister will act as a bridge that permits him then to activate a state of sexual striving. "Pretty girl" in the field of sister is simply not the same thing as "pretty girl" in the field of sex. In this case, the same verbal term has two very different meanings, depending on the setting within which it occurs.

A therapeutic technique called the "affect bridge" by this author (Watkins, 1971) has employed a procedure to activate older ego states by focusing on a common feeling rather than a common idea as follows: A young woman was referred for hypnotherapy in order to lose weight. She had gained some 40 pounds during pregnancy and had not lost them since the birth of her child. She reported that she was given to craving cakes and cookies at different times. She described a recent incident when she was taking care of her child. The craving arose, and she rushed into the kitchen to gratify it.

She was regressed under hypnosis to the ego state of being in the nursery and caring for her child. As part of this state, the experience of craving arose. She was then told, "You are forgetting where you are, how old you are. All you can experience is craving, craving, craving." In other words, all aspects of the state were obliterated and all cathexis was directed toward the item of "craving." She was next told, "You are now going back through time and space as if on a road consisting only of craving, back to some early period in your life where you experienced this same craving. Where are you? What is happening?" She replied, "I am in bed. There are slats up the side of the bed, and I want to suck my thumb. But Mommy has put a cloth with bad black medicine on it." She was told, "Take off the cloth! Now, go ahead and suck your thumb!" She "took off the cloth" and engaged for the next few minutes in sucking and slobbering on her thumb. After a while she removed the thumb and said with a smile, "I feel so yummy." The ego state she experienced when taking care of her baby in the nursery had included the item of "craving." All except the "craving" in that state had been hypnotically ablated, and she had been directed to move back to some earlier ego state that also included the same feeling. In other words, the affect of "craving" had become the bridge to move from the first ego state to another, to deactivate a present ego state and reactivate an earlier one. The ego cathexis had flowed from the one to the other over the common affect of "craving." The earlier ego state was now activated and described, hence the crib scene. The craving affect was permitted to satisfy itself (exhaust its cathexis), and it was replaced by the patient with a different affect, "yumminess."

She was next instructed as follows: "You are forgetting all about the crib, the slats, the bad black cloth. All you can feel is yumminess. You feel yummy. The world is yummy. You are now going back to some earlier time when you first felt yummy." The patient then placed her two hands in front of her mouth as if grasping something large and began suckling. Another affect bridge, this time of yumminess, was used to move her from the crib ego state back to an earlier state characterized by nursing at the mother's breast.

After a while she was asked, "Do you know where you are and what is happening?" The transfer to an earlier ego state under hypnosis is never so complete that we are not in communication with the patient. She replied, "Yes." She was then asked whether she would be willing to return to the present and to bring back with her the memory and experience both of the black cloth and the meaning of yumminess. Again she replied, "Yes." She was counted back out of the regression and out of hypnosis. She emerged laughing. "Now I know why I crave cakes and cookies. I don't want to *have* a baby I want to *be* a baby." Her craving ceased, and within the next few weeks she lost most of her excess poundage.

This brings us to the concept that movements of the executive from one ego state to another must occur along some common bridge. This bridging element can be an idea, an affect, an image, or some common memory. It is probable that the changing of ego states occurs in this way whether naturally or by therapeutic manipulation.

While the number of different ego states of which a given individual is capable seems to be almost infinite, actually a comparatively few account for most of his behavior. However, we do seem to respond with a characteristic state that is almost identical when impacted by the same stimuli or a similar situation. Thus, husbands and wives learn to respond to each other in characteristic ways. Dominant and submissive patterns once established tend to perpetuate themselves. An individual may appear to be passive by nature, yet when faced with an entirely different situation he may show a surprising change in personality.

In the play *The Admirable Crichton,* James M. Barrie

(1918) depicts a family consisting of a father, mother, daughter, son, and Crichton, the family butler. Crichton was always a most obedient and loyal servant. The entire family was shipwrecked on a desert island, and only Crichton showed the abilities needed to organize their new life. He took all the initiative and in short time assumed almost the role of king. It was arranged for him to marry the daughter, and the marriage was about to be consummated when a British ship appeared on the horizon. The family was rescued and returned to England, whereupon all of them, including Crichton, resumed the roles that had characterized their behavior before the shipwreck. Crichton's newly found dominant ego state ceased to be executive, was repressed, and his earlier state, which was marked by loyal, subservient behavior, once again became executive.

There are increasing indications today that perhaps states rather than traits are the primary elements of personality which should be studied (Thorne, 1973). In a recent publication, the Hilgards (1975) summarized the result of a number of investigations on the hypnotic relief of pain. Subjects were asked to place their arms into extremely cold water, and their pain was reduced by hypnotic suggestion. Many of them responded by showing no signs of pain and by indicating that they did not feel pain. Yet later under hypnosis they reported experiencing the pain. It was as if the pain was felt by a repressed ego state or at least by one that was not executive at the moment. When the other state was activated under hypnosis it was found that the individual had indeed experienced it. The Hilgards held that these studies indicated the need for a new look at theories of dissociation that have "been out of style for many years." The Hilgards first called this phenomenon "the hidden observer" but then termed it more formally as a "cognitive control structure." In an earlier paper E. R. Hilgard

(1973) had noted, "The fact that we can direct attention from one system to another suggests that the hierarchical status of any one system can be changed, from total inactivation at one extreme to dominating awareness and behavior at the other." Thus repression need not be a pushing down into unconsciousness, but a removal from awareness of material by the decathecting of it in an adjacent or co-level ego state. Hilgard, without placing this in an ego state terminology, held that "A theory of substructures in control of human behavior, with varying degrees of awareness, is implied in neo-dissociation theory."

Since his hidden observers, or cognitive control structures, appeared to represent the same phenomena as Federn's ego states we (Watkins, J. G., & Watkins, H. H.) 1977 in a previously unpublished study activated these in ten good hypnotic subjects and interviewed them in depth. In each case they described themselves as having identity ("I" as opposed to "him" or "her" when referring to other states or to the entire subject), discussed their function in the psychological economy of the entire subject, and sometimes dated their origin from a specific (often traumatic) event. In other words, the hidden observer, cognitive control structure, or ego state functioned like a part-person or covert multiple personality.

In a second study reported at the same time, several patients treated by "ego-state therapy" (see Chapter 22) in which various ego states were known (identified and named over a year earlier) were used as experimental subjects. Their "hidden observers" were activated, first following hypnotically induced deafness, and second after the initiation of hypnotic anesthesia in their right hands. These entities were then interviewed in depth. They also proved to be underlying ego states. Furthermore, the ego state which claimed to hear during the hypnotic deafness part of the study were not necessarily the same ones which reported sensing the unconscious pain. Our conclusions were that the "hidden observers" of the Hilgards represented the same phenomena as Federn's "ego states", hence, covert multiple personalities, or underlying "part-persons."

One of the more vital streams of psychotherapy today is that of transactional analysis. It is based on a psychology of ego states. Originally formulated by Berne (1961) this system has developed a model of the self that somewhat parallels the Freudian structure of id, ego, and superego but simplifies them and equates them with "child," "adult," and "parent." These three are termed ego states, and Berne, who acknowledges his debt to Federn, used many of Federn's concepts in explaining the interaction of these states. A recent popularized version of transactional analysis, *I'm OK, you're OK,* (Harris, 1969), which became a best seller among nonfiction books, makes no mention, however, of the contributions of the man to whom it owes the greatest debt for its theoretical base—Paul Federn.

A transactional analytic therapy session is often like an hour of psychodrama (Moreno, 1946) except that the actors are internal, hence the three hypothesized ego states: parent, child, and adult. For example, a young woman being treated for obesity, after having received explanations of her parent-child-adult ego structure was asked to objectify and subjectify each in turn and to have them engage in dialogues with each other. The therapist said, "Mary, here are three chairs facing each other. In this one over here is seated your child self, the one which wants to eat. I want you to sit down in that chair and let your child self come out. Let it be, speak and tell us of what it wants."

Mary sat in the child chair and began to talk, "I like

to eat. It feels so good. I don't care what Mother says. She's always trying to shame me out of eating, but when I don't eat I feel unhappy."

Mary was next instructed to sit in the mother chair and let her parent self speak. We then heard something like, "Mary! You're always making a pig out of yourself. You are getting to be so fat that people are making fun of you. Do you want to grow up and never marry because the boys will find you ugly? Why don't you listen to your mother?"

It will be noticed that first the child self was made subject. The individual was asked to identify with it, to establish it as executive, and to let it express its own needs. Then the patient was asked, through a symbolic move to the other chair, to decathect the child self. The parent self was egotized, became executive, and spoke to the child self as object. By such an alternation, a dialogue between the child and the parent was stimulated with the object of acquainting each with the viewpoint and reasoning of the other. For example, the child was asked, "Why do you eat so much?" To which it replied, "Because Mother doesn't love me, and I feel so bad. Only when I eat do I feel better." The child was then instructed to tell this directly to the mother. "Mother, you don't really love me. You are always scolding me." The patient was next asked to move to the parent seat, and unbidden, she spoke as follows: "Why, Mary, of course I love you. I only correct you when you do wrong because I want you to grow up and be happy and successful." And so the dialogue went. At times the patient was asked to sit in the adult chair and activate the part of her, neither parent nor child, that was capable of a mature and objective appraisal of the situation. The therapeutic goal was to increase the role of the adult in the determination of the patient's eating behavior. In other words, the transactional therapist tries to make the adult ego state more frequently executive so that the individual can become less controlled by impulsive infantile desires or by a tyrannical, unreasonable, parent-derived conscience. This is the same goal that psychoanalysis undertakes but from a different theoretical position.

Other ego-state therapists may use a similar internal psychodrama technique but do not necessarily assume that the self is composed only of the three states, parent, child, and adult. While it may be argued that these three represent major influences in everyone's life, states may obviously be organized around many other different principles or elements. These can be determined projectively by letting the patient respond to whatever "voices" arise in him rather than instructing him in the parent-child-adult self structure and requiring him to respond accordingly (See Chapter 22).

One therapist (Helen H. Watkins) in treating a patient found five different ego states manifesting themselves. The first three corresponded reasonably well with the traditional parent-child-adult trilogy. The fourth represented a destructive trend in the psychic economy, but the fifth was very puzzling. The patient reported that as he looked at the fifth chair the figure he could visualize seated there was blurred. He was asked to concentrate on that figure and squint his eyes to see if he could identify it. He did so, and shouted in amazement, "My God! It's the devil!" This led into an area in his life in late adolescence when he had rejected God as the symbol of a benevolent father authority and had introjected the devil. This concept had maintained a significant influence in his later life. A full understanding of the role of this state brought significant relief from anxiety. It is of interest that long after this episode in his life had been forgotten and repressed he, as a teacher, had enjoyed most of all the presentation of Goethe's *Faust* to his classes.

The concept of different ego states and their influence on behavior, although known by Freud and developed by Federn has been inadequately represented in classical psychoanalysis. The better understanding of the role of such psychological units in both their objective and subjective aspects adds a great deal to case understanding. For the analytic therapist it enables him to activate and deal with larger units of behavior and experience than often appears in detailed and piecemeal analysis. Even the behavior modifier can benefit from the incorporation of this concept into his therapeutic strategies.

A recent presentation (Watkins & Watkins, 1973) was made involving the attempt to get a patient to accept a female therapist toward whom he felt considerable anxiety. Under hypnoanalysis it became obvious that a small boy state, approximately four years old, had split off from the rest of the self during an incident involving his mother. He had been refused permission to go out and play and cursed his mother who was in the kitchen peeling potatoes. She turned toward him with the knife in her hands and threatened him. With a scream the frightened child self split off leaving a rather bland, schizoid, and unfeeling shell of a person behind. It was this underlying child self who so feared the female therapist.

The child state was hypnotically activated and a procedure of systematic desensitization undertaken along the lines of Wolpe's approach (1961). The male therapist gave reassurance and held the hand of the patient while the child self was made executive. The female therapist was brought progressively closer starting at some 30 feet away. A number of sessions over several days were required before the child self could tolerate the close presence of the female therapist. Finally, he not only came to tolerate her but to care for her. He could then accept her as his therapist during a three-month absence of the male therapist and was able to work with her in the solution of a number of mother-child problems.

Behavior modification methods of desensitization and reinforcement have proved to be effective, but they must be applied to the person requiring them. If the "person" whose behavior needs modifying is a repressed ego state, such techniques will be ineffective. One gains no constructive therapeutic effect by treating "the little man who isn't there." A reinforcement to be effective must be applied to the one whose behavior needs change. If that "one" is an underlying ego state, it should first be activated before attempting to modify it.

Perhaps the failure of many educational and therapeutic techniques to achieve effective change occurs because we simply haven't been applying them to the right party. A human being is an extremely complex society of interlocking states, or coherent behavior patterns. One can no more assure that punishments or rewards applied to a "family of self" will selectively correct the inappropriate behavior of one of its member ego states than a similar procedure applied to a human family for the transgressions of one of its children.

There is a general assumption that the self and the body are the same. Researchers test an individual, apply an experimental procedure, and then retest him, blithely assuming that the person who takes the second test is the same as he who took the first one. Judges apply punishment to the individual in front of them in court on the assumption that he is the same one who committed the crime. Such assumptions are by no means always valid (See a reanalysis of the Patty Hearst case from an ego state point of view by Watkins, 1976).

When a person imbibes an alcoholic beverage, his self obviously undergoes a number of changes. The first aspect of him to disappear is usually the conscience, the super ego, or that state concerned with duty and responsibility. Next the ego, that subsystem concerned with reality testing, gets decathected leaving the id, or child, as executive. Pleasure and irresponsibility reign. Upon further alcoholic input, this too is anesthetized and the individual sinks into a coma. By the time only the child state is left, most people realize the futility of appealing to the person to modify his behavior through duty or reality perception. We recognize that we are not now dealing with the same individual as before. Ego states, however, do not necessarily need drugs in order to change. Both external stimuli and internal alterations in dynamic equilibrium may initiate activation or decathecting.

When the ego is completely decathected we know quite well that the self is no longer there. Thus, in the days when corrective punishments were by physical beating, these were usually ceased when the culprit "passed out." It was obvious that no corrective relearning would take place merely by beating the inert body.

At one level we equate the physical presence of the body with the simultaneous presence of the self; at another we know that this is not so. What we fail to recognize is that the self is not entirely here or entirely gone, that it is composed of many states or subsections, and that at different times different ones of these may be activated and present. Thus, the experimenter may think he is evaluating the effect of his procedures on the same person, yet his results can be quite invalid because the initial test was given to ego state John Parent, the procedures applied to ego state John Adult, and it was ego state John Child who showed up the following week to take the final test. The behavior therapist who applies his reinforcements to an individual without considering whether the responses he hopes to modify lie within the ego state currently activated may be like a lawyer trying to give advice to a sleeping client. It is not surprising that psychological research studies generally have such a large amount of unaccounted for variance.

Chapter 14

THE HYPNOTIC ACTIVATION OF EGO STATES

"Mary, just relax now and sit back in your chair. That's it. Let go. Your eyes are getting heavier and heavier. Now they're closing. A deep sense of relaxation is pouring through every fiber of your body." Etc., etc., for five minutes, by which time Mary appears to be in a profound hypnotic state. The therapist-patient interaction proceeds as follows:

T: Deep sleep, deep sleep, deep sleep, deep sleep, deep sleep, deep sleep.
Hello.
P: Hello.
T: Who are you?
P: Hideaway.
T: Hideaway?
P: Mh-hm.
T: Hideaway, our girl seems to be rather disturbed today.

P: Yeah, she is sort of disturbed about that yesterday and I guess it's bothering her and, uh, I guess she's afraid Bill's mad and everything.
T: Oh? She said she didn't care what he thought.
P: Yeah, she does though, you know, I can feel most of her feelings down deep.
T: Oh.
P: I can feel that she's quite upset about it.
T: I see. Uh, you mentioned to me that she didn't, uh, want to go in the tavern, I think it was, and yet somehow she did, something made her go and uh . . .
P: Yeah, she didn't want to go in there. She didn't want to go in there Wednesday night, she didn't want to go in there Tuesday afternoon, you see, but she went in there. Well, it was like that, someone or something, don't ask me what it is 'cause I don't know.
T: Oh?
P: Something was pulling her in.
T: You don't know?
P: No.
T: Somebody else was pulling her in?
P: Yeah. It wasn't me. I was telling her to stay out of there.
T: Yeah.
P: She would go in anyway.
T: Well, is there anybody else who could be doing this pulling?
P: Maybe Medusa's back again.
T: Medusa?
P: Yeah.
T: You think so?
P: Well, I don't know.
T: Have you seen anything of Medusa lately?
P: Well, Mary got kind of mad at Bill today and she got

nasty with him but Medusa wasn't there; it was just her. Medusa wasn't there.

T: Let's go back to the time where she is standing outside the tavern debating whether to go in or not. Can you go back to that time?

P: That was when she, that was the afternoon.

T: Yeah. She's standing there and she's thinking that she doesn't want to go in. This means Mary doesn't want to go in?

P: Yeah.

T: Uh-huh. And now something's been telling her to go in and we're going to hear from that somebody now!

P: Ah, go on in. Be an optimist; go on in; go on in; go on in.

T: Who are you? What's your name?

P: Me?

T: Yeah.

P: (Laughs) Why do you want to know my name?

T: Haven't you ever told me your name?

P: Huh-uh. Not going to either.

T: You're not going to?

P: Huh-uh.

T: Why not?

P: 'Cause I don't want to.

T: You don't like me.

P: What?

T: You don't like me.

P: Oh.

T: Huh?

P: Oh, kind of, but I don't want to tell you my name.

T: Why? Would I be surprised or hurt if you tell me?

P: Uh, you'd be a little bit surprised I suppose.

T: Are you anybody I've known before?

P: No.

T: No?

P: Huh-uh.

T: You're a new person.
P: Mh-hm.
T: And I've never known you before.
P: Huh-uh. You keep goin' in though. I told her to go in.
T: You told her to go in?
P: Yeah, Hideaway can go to hell, but I'm telling you I'm the one that told her to go in.
T: Well, where have you been all these weeks?
P: Well, you just never called upon me before.
T: I never called on you before?
P: Huh-uh. See, I'm below Hideaway but I'm above Love.
T: You're below Hideaway but you're above Love?
P: Uh-huh. Love, I don't know, she's kind of a fairy.
T: Yeah, what do you think of Love?
P: I don't like her. I don't particularly care for Hideaway either.
T: You don't care for Hideaway?
P: No.
T: What about you, are you Medusa?
P: No, I'm not.
T: Oh, you're not?
P: Huh-uh, Medusa isn't around.
T: You know about Medusa then?
P: Oh sure.
T: But you . . .
P: I don't particularly care for her either.
T: You're below Hideaway but above Love, and I've never called for you before.
P: Hm-mh.
T: How long have you been around?
P: Oh, let's see. I haven't been for long. I haven't been around, oh, I think I've been around since about the 18th of July.
T: Well, that happened the 18th of July?

P: Well, don't you know?
T: No.
P: Mary came back.
T: Oh, Mary came back home.
P: Mh-hm.
T: And then you started in?
P: Mh-hm.
T: And what makes you different from Mary?
P: Oh, I kind of tell her to do things that she doesn't particularly want to do, you know, you see, but I tell her to go ahead and tell her to do it anyway.
T: What kinds of things?
P: Oh, like going into taverns when she knows she should stay out of 'em because of the temptation of going . . .
T: Do you think you're going to succeed?
P: I don't know. That's why she's, that's why she's in such a conflict you know.
T: Oh, she's in this conflict because you, you're interfering with her and that makes her upset and depressed.
P: Yeah.
T: I see. How do you feel? Yourself?
P: I feel pretty good.
T: You do?
P: Mh-hm.
T: What do you want?
P: Oh, uh, just, I just wanna have a good time; that's all.
T: Did you ever exist before July 18th?
P: Nope.
T: No. You just started then.
P: Mh-hm.
T: Well, why didn't you ever talk to me before? I've seen you; I've seen your family here several times since July 18th.

P: I didn't feel like coming out.
T: You didn't feel like coming out.
P: Mh-hm.
T: I see.
P: Because you didn't say; you didn't say; I didn't have the opportunity to come out see, until today.
T: Until today.
P: No.
T: Uh-huh. How do you like being out?
P: Oh, it's fun.
T: You do?
P: Mh-hm. I'm glad you got me out of there 'cause I wanted to talk to you.
T: You did?
P: Uh-huh.
T: Well then, why don't you tell me your name so we can get acquainted?
P: Oh.
T: You know I'm Dr. Watkins.
P: Yeah.
T: Yeah?
P: Oh, I'm Marge.
T: You're Marge, huh?
P: Mh-hm.
T: Uh-huh. Why are you Marge?
P: I don't know, that's just my name.
T: I see. That's your name. Well, tell me a little bit, in what way are you different from the other girls?
P: Well, uh, you know Love and then there's Hideaway and there was Medusa and there's Mary, you know . . .
T: Well, uh, what kind of a person are you, Marge?
P: Oh, I'm just, uh, well, I don't know, I'm not wild exactly, uh, but I like to go out and have a good time, and have a few drinks and be friendly with everybody but not too friendly.

T: You've been getting around more lately then?
P: Yeah.
T: Mh-hm.
P: You bet ya.
T: And uh, can you tell me what other ways you're different from Mary?
P: Well, uh, I think I'm more easy going than she is. I'm not as high-strung. Uh, she's kind of jumpy, you know, most of the time.
T: Mh-hm.
P: And uh, of course, me being in here like this, she doesn't like it I suppose 'cause I—she doesn't want to go into places, and I go ahead and tell her, ah, go in and have a good time.
T: She doesn't seem to know about you.
P: I guess she doesn't. I don't know, I don't think she knows about me.
T: Well, uh, apparently even Hideaway doesn't know about you.
P: No. Nobody does I guess.
T: Nobody?
P: No.
T: Love doesn't know about you?
P: Huh-uh.
T: How do you manage to keep yourself sort of hidden from Hideaway and Love? They don't seem to know about you, yet you seem to know about them.
P: Well, it's kind of difficult, but I did it.
T: You did it.
P: Mh-hm.
T: What do you think of Hideaway?
P: Yea, I kind of like her a little bit, not too much. I don't particularly, I don't like Love at all, and I didn't care at all for Medusa. Mary is OK; she's kind of like Hideaway a little bit, but not much.
T: What do you like about Hideaway?

P: She's got some spice.
T: Well, what don't you like about her?
P: Oh, I don't know, she's kind of a holy, holy, you know. She's always telling me not to do this, and not to do that and shut up and lay down and be quiet and everything and not uh, let Mary take care of herself, you know, and let her do the deciding and let her, Hideaway herself make the decisions instead of me and I don't like that.
T: I see. You don't like that.
P: You know, Hideaway's trying to be holier than thou, you know.
T: Uh-huh. Well, uh, who wins out, you or Hideaway when you . . .
P: Oh, uh, it splits about half.
T: I see.
P: But I'm beginning to do a little bit more than splitting in half here. I'm taking over a bit more than that.
T: Oh, uh, I was wondering something; Hideaway never opened her eyes, can you open your eyes?
P: Gee, I don't know.
T: If you want to you can, I don't object.
(Pause 10 seconds then opens eyes)
T: Can you see?
P: Mh-hm.
T: Uh, Hideaway was always afraid to open her eyes. Are you afraid?
P: No, not now that I've got them open.
T: Now that you've got them open.
P: Mh-hm.
T: Do things look strange or do they look . . .?
P: Oh, kind of, I was scared when I first opened them.
T: Why?
P: Oh, all those books and all, and the furniture, it's kind of crowded.

T: Yeah. You've never been here before?
P: No.
T: I see. Well, you must have known about me.
P: Well, yeah, I knew about you when I was uh—'cause I was inside her—at least I heard when she'd come in here and see you and talk to you, and, uh, Love talked to you a couple times too. She came out and talked to you a couple times?
T: Yeah.
P: Well, that's all I've been around. You didn't call on me, didn't have the opportunity to, didn't have the opportunity to call on me so that's why I didn't come out.
T: Well, I never knew about you.
P: Oh?
T: I wouldn't have known you existed if you hadn't pulled Mary into the tavern.
P: No?
T: It was just when Mary was telling me—well, Hideaway was too—about how Mary had something inside of her pulling her into the tavern against her own will. I knew that there must be somebody else doing it, and when I asked Hideaway she said she didn't do it and there was no Medusa around, so I called on the one that did it, and here you came. OK. Well, uh, why don't you go back to sleep again, Marge, I'll talk to you again. I'd like to talk to Hideaway. I'd like to talk to Hideaway. Is Hideaway there now?
P: Mh-hm. Hello.
T: Hello. Where have you been, Hideaway?
P: I've been sleeping.
T: You've been sleeping.
P: I heard everything Marge said, though.
T: Oh, you mean you know about Marge?
P: I heard her, yeah. Now I know about her. I don't think she knows me. She knows, she does know that

I exist though, doesn't she?

T: Oh, yeah, she knew about you, but you never ever said anything about her.

P: Well, I heard her talking.

T: Oh. But you didn't know before?

P: Huh-uh.

T: Well, you didn't know any more than I did.

P: I didn't know she was there until she started talking.

T: Oh, you could hear her talk?

P: Mh-hm.

T: What do you think of her?

P: She's quite a gal.

T: Yeah.

P: Not so wild though, really; she's a gal that would like to have fun.

T: Oh, a gal that would like to have fun. Do you think she's gonna be an asset or a liability to the family?

P: A little bit of both.

T: I see.

P: I think that we all are.

T: Uh-huh. What do you think of her ideas?

P: Well, that's a pretty good idea about us getting together someday, but I don't know.

T: You want to wait a while?

P: Mh-hm.

T: Mh-hm. OK, Hideaway, will you go back to sleep again and I'd like to go way down and talk a bit with Love. I want to talk to Love. Is Love there? Love, are you there?

P: Mh-hm. Hello.

T: Hello. Tell me about yourself.

P: I'm not growing. (Faintly)

T: What?

P: I'm not growing.

T: You're not, you're not growing?

P: Hm-hm.

T: You said once that you were growing.
P: I'm not anymore.
T: Are you getting smaller?
P: Hm-mh. I'm staying the way I am.
T: What do you think about all this?
P: Well, she surprised me. I didn't know she was there.
T: Who?
P: Marge.
T: Oh, you heard Marge, too?
P: Mh-hm.
T: But you didn't know anything about her?
P: No. Not until she talked to you today.
T: Oh. But, uh, but what about, uh, what about Marge, what do you think of her?
P: Oh, uh, she's kind of reckless and I don't think she's gonna help Mary.
P: Huh-uh.
T: What do you think about your future.
P: I'm kind of worried about it.
T: Why?
P: 'Cause I want to grow.
T: What could help you to grow?
P: If Mary would settle down a little bit more and she wouldn't be running around all the time.
T: Well, Marge, doesn't want to settle down very well.
P: Huh-uh.
T: Do you think of Marge as being your friend or not your friend?
P: Huh-uh. No.
T: Oh, she isn't?
P: No.
T: You mean you're gonna be fighting with her.
P: Mh-hm.
T: How do you feel it's going to come out?
P: I hope I win.
T: How do you feel?

P: 'Cause I'm not as big as she is.
T: You're not as big as Marge?
P: Huh-uh.
T: I see. OK. You can go down. Go to sleep. All the girls can go down and go to sleep. Going down, going down, down.

The foregoing case material represents exerpts from a recorded therapeutic session with a patient with a multiple personality, the dynamics of which shall not be pursued further at this time. Our concern here is with the interaction of such ego states especially as manifested under a state of hypnosis. These various personalities are states so dissociated from one another that not only do they treat each other as objects but any one of them (like Marge) may remain hidden below the threshold of awareness of the others.

Multiple personalities should be viewed as only the extreme on a continuum of dissociation that extends from the minor changes of moods that characterize all people. While most individuals probably have many different states within them, it is only in the true multiple or dissociated personality that they can be observed in such a pure form. Even here one can influence the behavior of another and yet not be conscious of that other. Obviously, the ego boundaries between the states are not completely impenetrable.

The subject of ego states in general, and multiple personalities specifically, is indeed a fascinating one, but at this point we are interested in the facility with which they can be activated and manipulated within the condition of hypnosis.

Marge, a previously inactivated state, became executive when cathexis (attention) was directed her way by the therapist. He had been alerted to her existence by the apparently unegotized influence she had on Mary's behavior in entering the tavern—an action against Mary's wishes. However, this flow of energy during the therapeutic manipulation (from Hideaway) to the Marge state was achieved only by suggestion administered under hypnosis. It was as if the hypnotic condition permitted this maneuver to be successful. Accordingly, let us give consideration to the nature of hypnosis itself.

The phenomena of hypnosis—we almost have to refer to hypnosis in the plural—have been subjected to much study. Two nationally recognized societies and one international organization[1] are composed of scientists and practitioners in the area. These are affiliated with such societies as The American Association for the Advancement of Science and the World Federation for Mental Health. The American Psychological Association also has a division devoted to the study of hypnosis. A number of major universities have well-supported research laboratories devoting full time to the better understanding of hypnotic phenomena, and the number of published scientific contributions in the literature in this area is becoming extremely large (Fromm & Shor, 1972).

Although there is considerable validated information concerning alterations in behavior and perception that are possible under hypnosis, an agreed definition of the condition eludes workers in the field. It has been called a state of hypersuggestibility (Braid, 1899; Liebeault, 1866; Bernheim, 1895); a form of sleep (Hull, 1933); a conditioned reflex (Pavlov, 1957; Salter, 1944); a goal-direct striving (White, 1964); role playing (Sarbin & Lim, 1963); a form of dissociation (Janet, 1907; Charcot, 1890); a state of decreased criticalness (Kline, 1958); a form of transference (Ferenczi, 1926; Watkins, 1954, 1963b); a kind of relationship (Watkins, 1967a); a loss of ego boundaries (Kubie & Margolin, 1944); a state of contemplative meditation (Naruse, 1962); a regression in the service of the ego (Gill & Brenman, 1959); an atavistic regression (Meares, 1961); and a primitive psychophysiological functioning (Schneck, 1962). No one of these seems to be fully adequate. Shor (1962) depicted hypnosis as having three dimensions: role playing, trance, and archaic involvement, the last term being comparable to the regression theories.

In spite of such wide divergences of opinion concerning its "true" nature, hypnosis possesses a number of characteristics about which there is much concurrence. Although one prominent investigator and his associates (Barber, 1969) hold otherwise, most workers in the field believe that when certain processes of communication (called induction) occur between a hypnotic operator and his subject, the subject enters an altered state of consciousness within which unusual changes in behavior and personality functioning become possible. This altered state, like sleep and drug-induced narcosis, operates to modify the normal responses of the subject so that he becomes less critical and more suggestible. He may experience hypermnesia (Watkins, 1949), a heightened recall of earlier experiences; or under regression (Reiff & Scheerer, 1959; Kline, 1963) he may actually behave in ways similar to those in which he engaged earlier in life, perhaps back in childhood. It is known that under hypnosis the hypnotist (operator, hypnotherapist) may intervene in the subject's dream and fantasy life (Moss, 1970; Sacerdote, 1967) and in general stimulate more obvious manifestations of underlying primitive and unconscious process (Gruenewald, Fromm, & Oberlander, 1972; Hodge & Wagner, 1969).

In Chapter 11, the analogy has been employed of comparing life to a journey on a train. The existential concepts of the *Umwelt,* or external world, the *Mitwelt,* or world of relationship and interaction between individuals, and the *Eigenwelt,* or inner world of self were described there. A summarizing thought in that passage indicated that the meaningful change from one to another through the direction of a "guide" or counselor constituted the essence of psychotherapy. Now that Federn's concepts of ego and object cathexis have been developed (Chapters 9 and 10) we might return to that analogy with an additional thought—one that was mentioned in the earlier paper (Watkins, 1967a); namely that hypnosis may be considered as a modality for the facilitation of such movements of cathexis, both ego and object.

When we hypnotize a person and anesthetize his arm, we are withdrawing ego cathexis or selfness from that member. When we lift a repression hypnotically and bring into consciousness that of which the subject had previously been unaware, we are adding to its object cathexis if it is an introject or to its ego cathexis if it is an identofact. Through the medium of suggestions transmitted within hypnosis we are transferring energy, hence making possible the activation or deactivation of various elements. We often accomplish this by simple suggestions administered when the subject has not been hypnotized, but somehow the prior induction of hypnosis seems greatly to facilitate this process.

In psychotherapy the state of hypnosis is induced by an intensive interpersonal relationship; once induced it seems to enhance and potentiate such relationship. It thus behaves as if it were a special kind of relationship. Since other aspects of hypnosis are more like those characteristic of a state of consciousness, we here prefer to call it a "state-relationship." When employed in psychotherapy, both factors are operative to some degree and cannot be separated from one another, as is often attempted in the experimental laboratory.

There is something about the malleability, the flexibility of the human personality in a state of hypnosis that might be compared to that of a block of marble that has been placed in a softening fluid by a sculptor prior to carving it into more agreeable form. However, from the case examples to be presented it appears that the hypnotized individual does not, as Anna Freud had maintained (1946), *lose* his ego or all his defensive controls. He just becomes less rigidly bound by them.

Hypnosis is thus not a kind of therapy; it is a special sort of state-relationship in which any form of treatment, psychoanalytic, client-centered, or behavioral may be practiced, often with greater facility and improved therapeutic leverage. Now that the nature of ego states has been more fully developed, let us extend further the concept of hypnosis as a modality for the manipulation of cathexis.

Entire ego states become activated or deactivated depending upon the amount of cathexis they possess. Items become conscious or unconscious depending on the size of their impact on each other or on ego boundaries. Accordingly, the quantum of existence at any one moment in one's life depends on the amounts of ego and object energy active at that point. In psychotherapy, through suggestion, interpretation, and reinforcement we are directing and focusing energies. If these can be more efficiently accomplished in the state-relationship of hypnosis, then hypnotic intervention becomes a powerful tool of the therapist to make certain ego states executive while deactivating others. In other words, we have in hypnosis a significant and potent modality for the constructive modification of behavior and personality functioning. This is true whether the specific procedures we are employing in this state-relationship are suggestion, interpretation, or reinforcement.

Psychoanalytic therapists denied themselves this powerful therapeutic help under the mistaken impression that changes in personality made under hypnosis "bypassed the ego" and would not be permanent. They constantly repeated Freud's beliefs on this matter, (1953a) written by him long before all the clinical and experimental evidence to the contrary, which has now been amassed, was available (Gill & Brenman, 1959; Hilgard, 1965; Kline, 1958; Schneck, 1965). We have much evidence now to indicate that permanent alterations in personality functioning may result from either the suggestive interventions of a hypnomanipulative therapy or the interpretative resolutions of a hypnoanalytic treatment.[2] Field and Palmer (1969) have also shown that there is a definite factor of "depth" within the hypnotic state. The state-relationship of hypnosis only adds a further dimension to the therapeutic armamentarium of the treating one; be it that he directs, nondirects, reinforces—or interprets transference reactions.

This book is not about hypnotherapy. There are many excellent treatises on the subject (Kroger, 1963; Marcuse, 1971; Meares, 1961; Wolberg, 1972; Crasilneck & Hall, 1975). It is brought in now to point out that such a unique state-relationship as hypnosis can be employed to potentiate the functioning of a therapeutic self, that phenomenon of which we are primarily concerned here. During the case chapters, (21, 22, and 23) this should be apparent by the intensity of the therapist-patient interactions depicted and the facility in which significant "character" changes were accomplished.

FOOTNOTES

1. The Society for Clinical and Experimental Hypnosis, The American Society of Clinical Hypnosis, and the International Society of Hypnosis.
2. The issues of the American Journal of Clinical Hypnosis and the International Journal of Clinical and Experimental Hypnosis are filled with many articles reporting the effects of hypnosis on a variety of disorders. A number of these have involved careful controls and long-term follow-up.

Part V

THE THEORY OF THE THERAPEUTIC SELF

In Chapters 15, 16, and 17 we try to put it all together. Resonance, a key tool of the effective therapist, is pictured in detail together with its relationship to the more objective aspects of therapeutic intervention. From the basic theories developed thus far, many corollaries are proposed that help a treating one to provide both a rationale and a methodology, which we believe can add greatly to the effectiveness of any therapist, be he an analyst, a behaviorist, or a humanist.

Part V represents the heart of this work. It attempts to integrate all that has come before and to outline a way of being, a way of treatment, that is not only effective in psychotherapy but which could also be applied to a much broader range of human problems.

Chapter 15

THE CONCEPT OF RESONANCE

If the A key on a piano is held down, and the same note on another piano nearby is struck, the A string on the first piano will begin vibrating sympathetically. This can be shown by recording instruments, but it can also be verified simply by stopping the sound from the second piano. The vibrating A string in the first piano will be clearly heard although in lesser volume than the original sound. This phenomenon is known as resonance.

If all the keys on the first piano were depressed, leaving the strings free to vibrate, a Beethoven sonata played on the second would be simultaneously and faithfully reproduced by the first. If only some of the keys are held down, the sonata will be incompletely rendered in its resonant reproduction. While if fingers are busy at the same time on the keyboard of the first, sounds will emerge that will be a mixture of those the instrument is receiving by direct stimulation of its keys and those initiated through resonance.

A human being, like a piano, is also a responding and reproducing instrument. He too is capable of emitting behavior resulting both directly from stimuli impinging on him from without and also indrectly through resonance with another human. This latter process has been described in Chapter 9 under the term "identification." The only difference is that identification is considered to bring a more permanent change in the individual, while resonance should be viewed as simply a temporary identification, activated for the moment and not necessarily resulting in any permanent alterations of personality structure.

Psychological *resonance* is an experience of which all people are capable, although some more than others. Since we are concerned here with the psychotherapeutic situation let us define it as *that inner experience within the therapist during which he co-feels, (co-enjoys, co-suffers) and co-understands with his patient, though in mini-form.* He does this by replicating within his own ego as close a facsimile of the other's experiential world as he possibly can considering the limits of the communications offered him by the patient (verbal, postural, gestural) and his own sensitivities in reception and interpretation of these. He builds this replication within one state of his own ego (the experienced ego) and senses it by its impact on another, an observing part (the experiencing ego, or "self"), also called the executive ego state.

Since resonance is an inner experience it may be observed directly only through introspection. Its presence in an individual, however, may be indirectly inferred by observation of his behavior. Such external manifestations of resonance are termed "resonant behavior." Resonant behavior can be objectively scored (See Chapter 19).

Considered from the modified position of Federn's ego psychology (as described in Chapter 10) we can explain resonance as follows: During resonance, a part, or state, of the self incorporates the impressions that come from an external object (such as another person) and infuses these with selfness (ego cathexis). They then become a part of the experienced ego. When these contents impact on the experiencing or observing ego state, they are interpreted as one's own thoughts and feelings. Accordingly, the therapist's self at the moment is capable of experiencing a patient in two different ways. As an original object the patient is sensed directly through the stimuli received from him that impacts the external boundary of the therapists's executive ego state. In Figure 4 this is represented by the impact of Object O on the Executive Ego State A's external boundary a at Point 1. A experiences O objectively as a perception. (I see, hear, touch, smell him.)

Simultaneously or alternately a patient may be experienced through a facsimile of him, when first replicated within the therapist's experienced ego state, as it impacts the executive ego state at their common boundary. In Figure 4, this is represented by the formation of introject o as a facsimile of Object O within nonexecutive ego state F.

After this introject has been invested with ego cathexis (self energy) we call it an identofact to distinguish it from its original unegotized condition. It may also be considered as a semiobject since the fact that it has received some ego cathexis does not mean that it has lost all of its object energy. The difference in quality that makes it possible for an identofact to have an impact on the boundary of the executive ego state requires that it retain at least a minimal quantum of such object energy. Only qualitatively different items can have an impact on each other.

When this identofact, or semiobject, then contacts executive Ego State A's internal boundary fa at point 2, A experiences O as self, that is O's feelings, behavior, and thoughts are felt as one's own. Therefore, its retention of some object cathexis makes it possible to be

Figure 4 Terms and Concepts

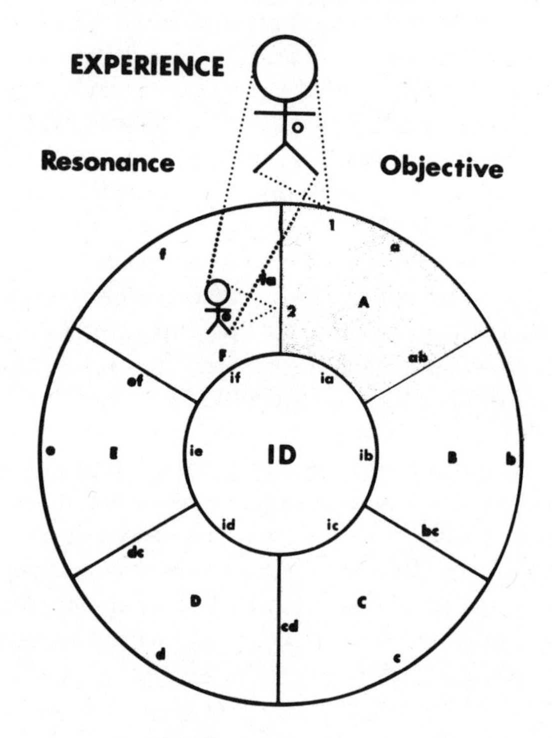

A Highly cathected (executive) ego state (self).

B,C,D,E,F Lightly cathected, (nonexecutive) ego states.

O External object (person).

o Introject (replica) of external object (O).

After it has been invested with some ego cathexis it might be re-termed an identofact since it is no longer purely object but has, by the process of identification, become Subject F. At such time as this element now impacts the boundary of executive ego state (A), (Point 2), it will be experienced as a self feeling or thought and not as a perception.

1	Objective experience (perception).
2	Resonant experience (thought, feeling).
a,b,c,d,e,f	Boundaries between the various ego states and the outside world.
ab,bc,cd,de,ef,fa	Boundaries between various ego states.
ia,ib,ic,id,ie,if	Boundaries between the id and the various ego states. Id is a nonego state and invested only with object cathexis.

sensed by the executive state, but the fact that it is also invested with ego cathexis ensures that it will be recognized as originating from within the individual and experienced as "my thought," not as "my perception." This process is termed "resonance." It may be either cognitive, affective, or both.

The self now is capable of comparing the data it receives about O from two different sources: The direct, sensory impressions of the individual (objectivity), and the apprehended inner replication of him (resonance).

Most people understand others by some combination of these two processes. On first contact with strangers we view them largely objectively. Resonance tends to develop as we see in others aspects similar to our selves and hence have more points for identification. One might say that, at least up to a certain point, resonance increases as the intensity of an interpersonal relationship grows. It is much easier to resonate with people who are more like ourselves in sex, race, age, or manner. This is quite logical since to build replicas of others who are very different from ourselves within our own egos and then to cathect them with self energy would create dissonance and conflict. Because it is normal to minimize self disturbance, and in fact all the defensive reactions are designed specifically for that purpose, it becomes quite understandable why this is so.

This tendency is so universal that jokes with a jolting impact have been built about examples where the resonance was contrary to normal expectations. For example, one has been told about a small child who was crying while watching the scene in the movie *Ben Hur* in which Christians were being devoured in the Coliseum by wild beasts. When asked why he was crying, he replied, "Because that little lion isn't getting his share."

During movies most of us tend to resonate with the hero or heroine. When they are threatened, our adrenals are working; when they are unjustly put upon, we are angered; when they are involved in a gentle love scene, we feel tender; and when they are behaving with lust, we are sexually stimulated. Actually, resonance is only describing from an experiential point of view the same principle that inheres in the behaviorist's term "modeling."

While many people can sensitively resonate with others, it is also obvious that there are those who are quite incapable of such feelings. Thus, the criminal who callously injures or kills his victim is treating that one purely as object, otherwise he would hurt himself when he hurt the other. The greatest lack today seems to be the scarcity of resonating abilities in so many people.

Everyone wishes to be loved, yet so few seem capable of giving it. Girls are seduced with but little thought for *their* feelings. Wives complain that they are "used," hence treated as objects by their husbands, rather than loved. People make cruel jokes about others with apparent complete insensitivity to internal reactions of those others. It is obvious that love, and in fact all human relationship, is based to some extent upon resonance.

Novelists and other storytellers build our identifications into various characters in their stories. They are described with the same human needs, assets, and weaknesses we perceive in ourselves. We can even resonate with animals, especially when they are depicted as humanlike. Witness the many children's storybooks about Winnie the Pooh, Peter Rabbit, etc. Walt Disney built a fortune by providing animals with whom we can resonate. This should be so obvious to the hunter who is confronted with his crying child, "Daddy, you aren't going to shoot Bambi, are you?" Raising rabbits for food can be a profitable business for small fry—unless the rabbits are given names. Who is there so hardhearted as to eat dear old "Stubby-tail" for dinner?

While not so common, nor so easy, resonance can extend to inanimate objects as well as to humans and animals. Many a collector of prize coins, jewels, or automobiles has treated them as if they were a part of his own self. An aggression, attack, or criticism directed against them is reacted to as if it were an attack on the person of the owner.

My self, whether through longer-term identification or by the more immediate resonance, includes so much more than what is encompassed by my skin. I may fight and die for "my" country, "my" children, "my" loved one, etc., as if for my own self. The boundaries of the self have been enlarged to include identofacts of all these, all of which entered originally as introjects.

How anemiated is the self that has never learned to resonate. It is filled only with objects devoted to its own immediate survival and firsthand pleasure. Its stimulation comes almost entirely from without, and it is the pawn of its environment. Such people, devoid of a rich inner existence, were the first to collapse and die in the concentration camps of the Nazis (Frankl, 1972). But those who had developed inner richness, inner values, and inner meanings survived. They could shut off some of the harsh stimuli on the outer boundaries of their self and open the inside ones to meaningful life from other, previously enriched ego states. Through resonance they had built an internal existence that gave them something to live for, something to strive for—or something to die for. Their lives ended not in a tragic zero. Their history of internalizing constructive impacts with others bore fruit in the dignity and nobleness with which they either died or survived in that hell.

And it was precisely the lack of the ability to resonate in Hitler and his associates that not only initiated the sadism of that period, but which in the end brought to nothing the Third Reich, which was to endure for a thousand years. Yes, this phenomenon of resonance represents something basic in the ability of men to surmount their environments, to establish relationships with each other, to love, to live meaningfully, to build societies, and through their impacts on those who follow, to continue to exist in the actions and feelings of others long after their bodies have ceased to move.

In explaining the concept of resonance to others I have often been asked, "But isn't this just the same as the term 'accurate empathy' advanced by Carl Rogers?" Indeed, there is much in common between the two, but there also appears to be a distinct difference. Rogers says that empathy means the *understanding* (italics mine) of the feelings of another. He holds that the therapist does not necessarily himself experience the feelings. If he did, according to Rogers, that would be identification, and this is not the same as empathy.

Resonance *is* a type of identification which is temporary. Unlike identification, it is not designed to make permanent alterations in the character structure of the resonating one. However, it is considered true resonance only if the resonating one is himself actually experiencing inwardly the same feelings of the other, even though in mini-form. Like empathy it seeks to achieve understanding of the other. That understanding is not based on previous memory, knowledge of concomitant behavior, etc., but on an actual replication of the inner affective or cognitive experience happening at that time to the other. It is a temporary and partial identification in a common feeling state and an understanding derived by participation in such a state.

Resonance should also not be confused with countertransference. They are very different dynamic processes, even though on the surface there is some similarity. True, both involve the arousal of feelings in the therapist and behaviors that result from those feelings. However, in countertransference the patient is an *object* to the therapist; in resonance he is *subject*. Countertransference is an "againstness" between therapist and patient; resonance is a "withness" between them. Thus, in countertransference the counselor has feelings *toward* the client; in resonance the feelings are *with* him and directed toward some person or aspect of life significant to the treated one. In countertransference the patient acts as a stimulus that releases in the therapist a preestablished and permanent feeling that was originally developed many years before by the therapist toward some earlier person in his own life; in resonance the therapist takes over a feeling state from the patient temporarily and internalizes it for the purpose of understanding by experiencing it personally within his own self.

For example, consider an analytic situation in which the patient is angry at his therapist because he sees in him a dominating father figure. This is transference. If anger is now stimulated in the analyst because the accusations of his patient reactivate in him the feelings of resentment he once held toward a younger brother, that is countertransference. If the analyst temporarily identifies with the anger of his patient and feels this as being directed *against the patient's father,* that is resonance. The resonating analyst experiences anger, but he knows that he is merely echoing the patient's rage toward the dominating father, and that he himself has not permitted this therapeutic situation to reinvoke his own conflict with his brother.

However, there certainly could be countertransference elements in a resonating situation if the conflict and the accompanying feeling state that has been aroused in the patient is similar to one in the therapist's life, especially if the therapist's was repressed and had not been resolved. It is easier to resonate to a situation we have already experienced.

This ability to co-feel, co-suffer, and co-enjoy in a common moment of "withness" is a trait possessed today by all too few people. Therefore, the tracing of this force, its origin, what it can do, and how it can be developed in people are questions of the first order, the sixty-four dollar ones that constitute the truly worthwhile challenges to the behavioral sciences. For the survival of man depends as much on answers to these questions as it does on those regarding pollution, overpopulation, and atom bombs.[1]

Objectivity is a highly desirable trait in a scientist, but our failures when we are psychotherapists are often because we have been only objective; we have failed to resonate with our patient. We have observed and evaluated him only from the external point of view or from the perspective of our own needs, not his. We have failed to establish that alliedship, that "withness" that both enhances our own understanding of him and transmits to him a feeling that he is cared for, that he is not alone in his struggle with disintegrative forces. The "experiencing" of the patient instead of merely "observing" him on the part of the psychotherapist was to Rollo May (1961) a crucial issue in differentiating the existential therapist from those clinicians who practiced from a purely "objective" point of view.

Many years ago the secretary of the psychiatric service in a hospital where I served developed a breast carcinoma. Lillian was a middle-aged woman who was widely known and respected throughout the institution for her cheerful disposition, her conscientious devotion to her responsibilities, and the constructive relationships she established in the role of receptionist with the many patients referred to our service for evaluation.

Her condition deteriorated rapidly. By the time surgery was performed, the cancer had metastasized and spread throughout her body. It was diagnosed as terminal, the fact of which she was quite aware.

On numerous earlier occasions, cases of intractable pain had been referred to me from the various medical and surgical services for treatment by hypnosis, and Lillian had typed my clinical reports. She asked if I would be willing to help her if her pain became too great, to which request I readily agreed. There came the time when she asked her physician to call me as a consultant to see if I could relieve the pain hypnotically. I drove out to her house that afternoon in high hopes that my hypnotherapeutic techniques would be successful.

For an hour Lillian and I worked together. I tried many different approaches; eye fixation, relaxation, fantasy, hand levitation, and other technical maneuvers that had often been effective in inducing a hypnotic state. None was successful. Lillian was discouraged, and I left depressed and with a dull headache. Why had I failed?

That night I had two dreams. In the first, a "university man" said to me, "You are insufferable." In the second, I was killing a very ugly looking man.

That wise old man on whose couch I had labored and sweated for so many, many hours had taught me what to do. I reclined, closed my eyes to shut out the stimuli of the present, regressed back to the ego state that had included him, and reactivated his introject.

With Lillian I had failed as a therapist and teacher. I must go back to school, to be treated myself and learn anew.

"And what comes to mind when you think of 'university man' "? asked the introject.

"Well, he is a professor, a man of learning. I would respect such a person." I lapsed into a period of silence.

"Perhaps you have more thoughts about this," suggested the kindly introject.

"Maybe he was like my father, who was a high school teacher. He taught me a great deal, and his opinions were almost always right."

"But you said that the man in the dream was a 'university' man. Why university?"

"The hospital where I work is a teaching hospital affiliated with the medical school of a university. Maybe the dreams are related to my inability to help Lillian, who also works at this hospital."

The introject was thoughtfully silent, perhaps a murmured "Hmm." He didn't speak it, but I could almost read his mind, and what he was silently thinking was what I, too, would have thought had I been sitting in his chair.

"Of course, you stupe. Why do you think you had those dreams on the night after your failure to help Lillian?"

The gentle but firm and persistent voice of the other spoke once more. "I was wondering. Just after you received the news that Lillian had requested a consultation from you, and you knew you were being called into the case, what were you thinking about?"

With a slight sense of dismay my executive ego state replied, "Well, I drove right out to her house because I wanted to be of help. I remember thinking along the way, 'Here's my chance to prove to doctors at the hospital, those skeptics, that hypnosis is a valuable treatment.

Will they be surprised if I can remove Lillian's pain. It'll sure be a feather in my cap.' "

There was another long silence, and I felt uncomfortable.

"You weren't thinking much of Lillian, her needs, her pains, were you? You didn't suffer; you didn't care. You were 'insufferable.' Isn't that what the university man said?"

My introjected analyst was behind the couch. But if I could have seen his face then I am certain it would have had a disapproving expression—just like when I dropped the cat out of the second story window, and Dad said sorrowfully, "You weren't thinking much of the feelings of the cat, were you, son?"

"I guess that was pretty ugly of me, to be so selfish and uncaring for Lillian."

"Ugly? Did you say ugly? Then what must you do about it?"

That one puzzled me for a few moments. "How do I know what I must do?"

"You told yourself in the second dream what to do. You must kill the ugly man, that is, the ugliness within your own self. You must give up dreams of impressing the members of the medical staff at the hospital and think only of how you can help Lillian."

A wave of painful realization swept through my entire self. Of course, I knew what had to be done. Now, warm light began to creep through my internal world. But just before I became fully alert, there rapidly crossed my mind that it was late in the year, that Christmas would soon be here, and there was a fleeting thought concerning Charles Dickens. Oh yes, he had written about another man who in the self-analysis of three dreams had faced his own ugliness. The point was clear. I sat bolt upright on the davenport.

That evening Lillian and I had another session. All

the way to her house I was growling at myself, "To hell with what the doctors at the hospital might think. What kind of a goddamn psychologist are you, anyway? Your job is to help Lillian, not show off before Daddy. Yoo hoo, Daddy, look what a smart boy I am. It's about time you started to be a man," etc.

Therapeutic hypnosis is not merely an altered state of consciousness in which we can manipulate a subject. It is also an intensive interpersonal relationship experience in which we communicate at deeper and more sensitive levels. That evening Lillian got a different message. She was no longer being regarded merely as an interesting object whose behavior changes might be used for the benefit of another. I was now resonating with *her* needs. In a relatively short time her eyes closed, and her breathing slowed. She entered a deep hypnotic state. No scintillating variety of induction techniques labeled eye fixation, hand levitation, etc., were required.

It was possible now to say to her, "Lillian, you need not pay attention to any unpleasant sensations coming from below your shoulders. You can simply ignore them. Instead, you will be able to enjoy books, music, friends, good conversation, radio, and television. These will fill your thoughts and feelings. Life will seem vibrant and worthwhile. It will be good to feel happy again."

She emerged from the hypnotic state, smiled, and said simply, "It doesn't hurt."

It "didn't hurt" for the next three or four days. Then the effects of the hypnotic suggestions wore off. Pain returned. The relationship needed renewing, and we held another session. The results were the same. Each time she emerged from the hypnotic condition, calm, relaxed, and smiling. This procedure was continued at twice-a-week intervals. She expired five weeks later.

All of us who are associated with the healing professions should recognize that we can never prevent our patients from dying. Everyone dies; only the date is unknown. But sometimes if we understand, if we resonate, if we practice our clinical skills in a therapeutic relationship that treats the patient as more than an object to be manipulated, we may be able to rescue for him a bit of "life stuff," a piece of meaningful existence, which in experiential time cannot be measured by five weeks, five minutes, or five years.

FOOTNOTES

1. It might be noted by the reader that the first part of Chapter 5 was written in the *resonant* rather than the *objective* mode. The writer temporarily identified with the concept of a developing self. He described the self as he felt *it* would have experienced *its* world. This passage could have been written in the objective mode. In which case the phraseology for the first sentence might have been: "Existence inheres in that phenomenon called the self," instead of, "I live in the land of my self." That which followed would then also have been written similarly as the "object" rather than "subject." Most of this book is written in the objective mode, but at times the writer has chosen specifically to express his thoughts about something subjectively and in attempted identification with that something. At that time the writing style might be characterized as being in the resonant mode.

Chapter 16

THE FUNCTIONING OF THE THERAPEUTIC SELF

A commander waging a military battle, such as an attack on a fortress, may well succeed or fail depending on the completeness of his military intelligence. He can observe the enemy, evaluate his strength, and estimate the disposition of his forces by patrols or by observing him through a telescope. He knows his own resources and the tactics available to himself. But how much more effective might it be if he also had an observer or spy within the fortress who could report on how the enemy thought, felt, and reacted to his maneuvers.

In some respects psychotherapy is like military combat except that it is not the patient, but the pathology within, that is our enemy. It seems axiomatic that the better a therapist can understand his client, the more complete and precise his diagnosis or psychological evaluation, the better he can plan his therapeutic strategy, and the more effective will his procedures be.

Since the patient, like any human, is a constantly

changing and dynamic system of equilibrium, this understanding is not one to be acquired only at the beginning of treatment. No case histories, psychiatric interviews, or psychological tests, regardless of how skillfully performed or regardless of the degree of their depth, can ever take the place of a constantly revised apprehension concerning the feelings and reactions of the patient. In fact, classical psychoanalysis, one of the most thorough and intensive probes into the human psyche, relies very little on initial tests and interviews. The small amount of information known about the treated one at the beginning of therapy pales into insignificance as compared to the new perspectives of his functioning that emerge during the many months of treatment. Therefore, one of the marks of a truly therapeutic person is that he has the wherewithal to upgrade his understanding continually so that through successive approximations to the truth he can constructively intervene for the enhancement of integrative forces. The therapeutic self is, accordingly, not only a manner of being; at the cognitive level it is also a series of personal skills that can be learned or developed in the healing one. It, like the third ear, is a way of securing more intelligence about a patient and the nature of his problems. It is a complex diagnostic technique in which the healing one has learned to use the feeling and emotional aspects of his self, as well as his intellect, for the better comprehension of his therapeutic task. At this evaluative or diagnostic level, the doctor with a well developed therapeutic self is able to mobilize far more comprehensive and sensitive techniques for gathering data about his patient than the therapist who employs only his sense organs and cognitive processes.

At still another level the therapist with such a self is, not only a better diagnostician, but his therapeutic interventions, whether analytic or behavioral, carry far greater weight with the suffering one because they draw upon one of the most widely used and successful healing principles known to man: the constructive impact of one self upon another. It has been estimated, if one considered all methods of treatment ever used by all healing arts persons in all ages and throughout all societies in the world, that more people have been treated by one interpersonal technique alone, suggestion, than by all other approaches, physical, surgical, or pharmacological. This attests to the immense power that human relationship has in altering physiological and psychological processes.

The self is not only an effective diagnostic instrument; it is also a powerful medicine. The therapeutic self helps to mobilize constructive tendencies in others because of its own personal integrative nature. However, its ability to do this is enhanced because of the increased evaluative sensitivities that it also possesses. So let us consider first the therapeutic self's diagnostic strengths.

It seems a truism to affirm that the more sources of data, the more different perspectives we can gather about another, the better we are likely to understand him. Many people rely primarily on one source for gathering knowledge about others, namely observation and perception. The other is treated as an object, and as an interesting object he is scrutinized with the highest degree of concentration. The therapist who is very devoted to his mission of helping watches his patient most intently and listens to his every utterance. He observes every nuance of postural and gestural change in the other. He is highly sensitive to slight inflections of voice, to changes in the character of his associations. He listens with a highly tuned third ear to the unconscious implications underlying the overt statements. The skilled music lover is aware of the voice of the cello, the obligato of the bassoon, and the rhythm of the violas as well as the melody of the violins in an orchestral rendition. Likewise, the sensitive therapist is intently listening to all the voices of the other's self. He records the tinges of anxiety, the insinuations of hostility, and the subtle denials of stated belief; for a human self, like a symphony orchestra expresses many themes simultaneously, some consonant with the others, some dissonant.

The patient who is treated by such a therapist soon becomes aware that he is the object of intense interest and dedication. He appreciates this and likes the doctor who is willing to devote this effort in his behalf. Such a therapist is often very effective. These qualities should be possessed by every counselor. Nor can we say that this is insufficient. Countless sufferers have benefited by the ministrations of sincere healing arts people who diagnose and treat in this way. Whenever the patient is viewed as an interesting object worthy of one's best efforts, the therapy is more likely to be constructive than destructive.

However, such a doctor, one who treats his patient *only* as object, has not fully mobilized his own therapeutic abilities. His therapeutic self is only half activated, for there is another entire perspective available to him that will provide much more information about the other, one that will enormously increase his diagnostic skills.[1]

Let us take the example of an internist palpating a patient's abdomen for evidences of physical pathology. The doctor relies on the verbalizations and exclamations of his patient and the feel in his own fingertips to locate potential trouble spots. Now consider the situation where the internist is palpating his own abdomen. Just as in the first case he gathers data about possible hard masses from the feel in his own finger tips. But in addition, he is aware of the sensations in his belly as the tissues respond to being impacted by his fingertips. In other words, the internist who is feeling the body of another is gathering information from one point of view, that of objective perception. The doctor who is exploring his own abdomen is securing data from two different perspectives, the external or objective sensations in his fingertips *and* the internal or subjective experience from his guts. One must conclude that when information input comes from two different sources, the objective *and* the subjective, the knowledge of the condition should be more complete than when it comes from one source alone, the objective. The internist in the second situation should be able to arrive at a better diagnostic evaluation than in the first by reason of having superior intelligence concerning the problem.

The true therapeutic self might be compared to the internist in the second example. He, like all other therapists, gathers the greatest amount of data concerning his patient's condition by intense concentration and by sensing the other as an interesting object to whose welfare he is devoted. But in addition, he also internalizes the other, first as a temporary introject, which he then changes to identofact through an investment of ego cathexis. He establishes a temporary identification infusing the internalized replica of the other with his own selfness. He can then "feel" the other as he would feel his own self. He extends the boundary of an ego state over the internalized object of the other and makes it for the moment a part of his own being. This permits him to co-suffer, co-enjoy, and co-experience the feeling and understanding states of the other.

As these identofacts of the other impact his own executive ego state he senses them in the same way he senses the impact of palpating fingers on his own abdomen. As the patient is hurt, frightened, gladdened, or angered, he too is hurt, frightened, gladdened, and angered. He is resonating with his client. Like the second piano described in Chapter 15, in his own inner being he is performing the same self-orchestration that the patient is living as he reexperiences his life story within the therapeutic interchange.

Much is made in many therapeutic systems of understanding the client. But there are *two* kinds of understanding, objective understanding and subjective understanding. One is external, derived through perception. This is the way we apprehend objects in the outside world. The other is internal and derived normally through insight. We come to understand a facet of our own self when the ego state of which it is a part impacts the executive ego state and thus comes to experiential existence.

These two different forms of understanding need to be clearly differentiated one from the other because they afford us different sets of data derived from different perspectives. The understanding secured objectively through external perception does not necessarily yield us the same knowledge or conclusion about our patient as the understanding secured through the temporary identification of resonance. They are like reports on a situation by two different observers, each looking from a different vantage point. These two reports may coincide, making it easy for us to arrive at a valid evaluation; or they may clash, thus requiring further testing before arriving at decisions. At any rate, the therapist who receives both reports will be better informed about his therapeutic task than the one who receives only the objective data.

A therapist is listening *objectively* to an inmate in a correctional institution give his life history. He may receive the following impressions: "This man is a menace to others. He cannot control his violent emotions. He seems to be very depressed since he arrived here. He is also quite immature. He has always reacted toward authority figures with hostility. He should probably be diagnosed as a passive-aggressive personality with strong sociopathic trends. He has little ego strength and does not relate well to the other inmates. His fight the other day with the correctional officer demonstrates this extreme sensitivity to criticism and his lack of emotional control."

Let this same therapist now adopt a *resonant* mode while listening to the inmate, and he may receive the following different impressions: "It is very tough to be committed to a prison. One gets to feeling so lonely; it's hard not to be sad and depressed. I don't seem to find much in common with the other inmates. It makes me so mad when I get picked on. Why did that guard have to yell at me to hurry up when I was going as fast as I could? And the judge that sent me here, he didn't like me any more than my father did. I try to behave right and please people, but they just won't let me alone. They're always bugging me."

Is the first or the second set of impressions a correct picture of this man's "being in his world?" The answer of course is, "Both." The two of them together enable the counselor to understand this inmate better than either of them alone. This more comprehensive evaluation permits the therapist to do a much better job of planning a strategy aimed at reconciling this man with society.

The person receiving two sources of data about the same situation must be prepared to cope with more complex input. It takes a bit of egodoing to handle, integrate, and act on this increased information. Either one deals with each source through only a part of his self, or one must somehow alternate in his attention to each. Studies in which a message is piped to one ear while a different one is transmitted to the other (Hillyard, Hink, Schwent, & Picton, 1973) show that one is listened to while the other is inhibited. Conscious awareness is focused on one while the other is ignored. In Gestalt terms one side is figure while the other is ground and vice versa, as in such illusions as the Necker cube, the profile vase, and the reversible staircase (see Dember & Jenkins, 1970, pp. 220-221). This same alternation may occur as two different ego states take turns being executive.

The question of what the individual does with sets of data concerning the same external object when these are received through two different perceptual modalities is a most intriguing one. Of course, when they are complementary and not conflictual with each other (such as watching another person while he is talking) the two sets are integrated into a more inclusive and realistic understanding of the stimulus source. Even when they enter through two channels of the same sense, such as two eyes or two ears, the differences are reconciled into a unitary apprehension. In fact, we know that the slight differences in angle of vision between the right and left eyes are not only fused into a single image, but that the two together enable us to understand more about the stimulus object (such as its distance from us). The slight differences in volume and synchronization between the sounds entering the two ears permit us to localize their source. Thus, the integration of two perspectives result in greater knowledge of their source than when only one of them is available—at least, when they do not differ significantly from one another.

But what might be the case if the objective perception of a patient by a therapist differs greatly from the resonant experience of him? Would these two be integrated, or would they be more clearly differentiated so that the therapist would settle on one, or alternate between the two?

Some data from early studies in perception may have a bearing on these questions. Stratton (1897) reported his experiences with a lens arrangement that reversed and inverted the visual field. The wearer of these inverting glasses perceived the world upside down and reversed from left to right. For example, when an object appeared to the left, the sound it emitted actually came from the right and vice versa. The individual was now receiving contradictory impressions. His vision told him one thing and his hearing another about the stimulus source. Likewise, when he reached out to touch an object he perceived (albeit inverted) in his visual field it was not there. Not only audition and vision, but also touch and vision contradicted each other. Stratton found that the *visualized* object initially took precedence over its touch or sound in localizing it. After several days the data coming from the two different senses (vision and touch) were integrated by the individual into a harmonious perception. Stratton stated, however, that "the results show that the harmony comes only after a tedious course of adjustment to the new conditions."

Young (1928, 1937) undertook a similar experiment, which involved reversing the hearing from the two ears by a "pseudophone." This instrument consisted of two semicircular trumpets placed in the ears so that the bell that gathered the sound on the right side was transmitted to the left ear and vice versa. When the eyes were closed, sounds were heard in reverse localization. Cars moving from right to left were experienced by the subject as traveling from left to right. However, when the eyes were open, and the cars could be seen, the data from the pseudophone was apparently suppressed, and the individual experienced normal sound localization. Again, vision was dominant over audition. At times, especially in the early stages of the experiment, there was an alternation when suddenly the sound (even though both visual and auditory senses were functioning) would reverse its localization. Gradually with habituation the sound was heard where the eyes said it was. Apparently, the memory or knowledge of its true source was also able to overcome the auditory reverse localization even when the eyes were closed.

Willey, Inglis, and Pearce (1937) repeated Young's experiment with somewhat contradictory results in that habituation did not resolve the conflict. A comment by Stewart (1914) adds an intriguing thought if applied to the concept of the therapeutic self. He stated that "the pseudophonistic techniques provides a simple means of discriminating between those conditions which reside in the stimulus and those which reside in the organism." If this were so perhaps the therapist who is observing his patient from the two perceptual modalities (objective and resonant) would be able to distinguish more clearly than the purely objective counselor between what constituted the reality of the patient and what his own countertransferences placed on that one.

The fact that a message from one source is for the moment outside the center of conscious attention does not mean that it is being ignored, that its communication is forever lost to the self. Even though the therapist may not be consciously aware of all the data being received simultaneously from both objective perception and resonance, he may continue to record and integrate. His information retrieval processes may, many therapeutic sessions later, pull out significant matter bearing on his patients' problems, information he received and filed in ego states that were consciously inactive at the time of the input. These emerge later to his apprehension as his own insights, which he discovers in the course of the therapy. To the extent to which a therapist utilizes both objective perception and resonant processes, he makes of his self a most sensitive receiving, recording, learning, and understanding instrument. May (1961) credits Albert Wellek with describing this as "an ability to experience critically." We interpret "experience" in this definition as meaning to resonate, and "critically" as the simultaneous retention of objectivity, the two being integrated. He understands his patient far better, and whether he treats as an analyst, a humanistic therapist, or a behavior modifier his interventions can be more realistic, valid, and therapeutic. He has become a superior diagnostician and evaluator.

We have been considering the diagnostic functioning of a therapeutic self and have hypothesized that by evaluating from both the objective and the resonant modes it affords a superior understanding. It is concluded also that superior understanding facilitates superior therapy. However, the greatest leverage such a flexible self can exert in treatment comes because of its actual therapeutic operation within the doctor-patient relationship.

"Do unto others as you would have others do unto you." So runs the Golden Rule. In the therapeutic self, this maxim is enforced since through resonance the other *is* you. Through this temporary identification the patient's hopes, fears, strivings, and conflicts have become yours. Whatever you do unto him you are doing to yourself. You must and will treat him as you would your own self. If he is successful, you will feel happy. If he is filled with fear, you will feel afraid. If he is hurt, you will suffer. Even though the resonant side of your self operates through only part of you (or all of you part of the time), and even though you may experience his feelings in lesser intensity, in mini-form, you will still sense them. Your self will be imbedded in them. If the therapy is successful, you will be enhanced; if it is a failure, you will be lessened. You have committed part of your self to the therapeutic enterprise; you have invested your "being money" in the firm. No longer can you sit back smugly and reflect to the client a "You feel hurt when. . .," or think, "If you feel hurt, that's your problem. I don't feel hurt. I will go home from the office and your hurt won't bother me. I will get my salary or fee whether or not you get over your hurt." If you are a resonating therapist and your patient hurts, then you will hurt. It will be painful, and you will seek with all the resources at your command to eliminate your own hurt, his hurt—our hurt.

If you are a wise therapeutic self, you will not let his hurts take over your whole life. You will distance yourself from them during other hours of the day and other days when you do not see him. You will do this, not only for your own protection, but because you must also resonate to the hurts of others. We seldom devote our professional life to the treatment of only one patient. As a therapeutic self you will be a good therapist—or you will not survive. For if you fail more often than you succeed in your treatment efforts, if more of your patients are harmed than helped, you too will go down the drain with them. For better or for worse you have joined up with them. You and they are in the same boat.

How much better most of us do when we are doing for our own selves. How much more intensely do we concentrate on our own problems that require solution. How much more gently and kindly do we treat our own selves than others. How much more energy do we put into activities that directly benefit our own fortunes. How much more alert are we when a mistake is costly to our own selves. It is that added measure of personal interest that the therapeutic self brings to his clinical task. It is that selfish, personal need for his own happy beingness that the therapeutic self activates on behalf of his client—and that is lacking in the purely objective therapist. Through resonance you have become a stockholder in the firm of "we-ness," not merely an employee.

If the study of human motivation in psychology teaches us anything—whether it is the motivation of achievement or learning—it is that the highly motivated person is much more successful and effective than the unmotivated one. In the therapeutic self, we need no longer appeal to idealistic altruism to induce the healing arts person to address himself to the needs of others. He does so out of his own personal, selfish needs. His patients must *be* in order that he can *be*. They must *become* in order that he can *become*. In the interest of the therapeutic venture we enlist the most powerful drives possible. The therapeutic self is a true capitalist. The more effective he is, the more he succeeds in helping others. The more he helps others, the more self reinforcements he himself receives. Here it can but be hinted what a world society of "self capitalists" would be like where "being money" was the reward instead of dollars, and where the payoff came from helping others. There are many people who have discovered this secret but not enough. They are the happiest of persons, but they have not large bank accounts as measured by the dollar economics of the day. They are simultaneously both the most selfish and the most unselfish of people. By serving their own best interests they constantly enhance those of others.

We cannot lose sight of the fact, though, that *both* objectivity and resonance are required. If we are completely objective toward our patients, we have mobilized only part of our resources for understanding and helping them. They will sense this limited commitment—and they will make limited progress. On the other hand, if we are only resonating and never objective toward them, then there is a *fólie à deux* created. Two people are sick together.

The therapist within his own self must form a kind of bridge. One foot is placed squarely in reality, in objectivity, in the world as it is. The other foot of his self is extended into the patient's pathology, resonating with it, living it. A bridge has two legs and a connection in between. All the therapist's skills and knowledges are then mobilized to help the patient move from the position of pathology, of immaturity, of sickness to the position of health, of reality, of strength.

For a period of time the therapist accepts into his own self a replica of the patient's world and offers to the patient a replica of his own. If his own be not better than the patient's, then it is the patient who should be the therapist. No one has all the good—or all the bad, so that in the exchange the patient will bring to the therapist some of his own assets that will have a constructive change upon the treating one. The bargain will not be only one-way.

The therapist who is resonating with the pathology of the patient has now internalized some of the sickness and unhappiness of the other. Furthermore, there will be cognitive dissonance within his self as his own values and those of the patient clash. Cognitive dissonance creates anxiety, and the therapist will not feel at peace with himself. This very self-dissonance, which he has now assumed, will serve as a motivating force for the mobilization of all his intellectual and emotional resources toward the resolution of the patient's conflict within the therapeutic "we-ness."

From the patient's point of view, a new and constructive force has entered his world. "We" can now do what "I" alone could not. As he senses the therapist's fuller commitment to their joint endeavor, he is encouraged to allocate more of his own meager self-resources to the same process. A winning team atmosphere takes over from a losing self-concept. Daddy (or Mother) and I can do what I am not strong enough to do all by myself. He receives through resonance a "self loan," which will help him to overcome his personal bankruptcy and make the business of his self once more solvent and earning profits.

The key seems to be one of balance. A therapeutic self views the patient with objectivity part of the time and experiences him through resonance another part of the time. We might hypothesize that the optimum balance is one where at least half of the time is devoted to objectivity.[2]

Resonating with half the self does not mean half resonating with all the self. There is a great difference whether, with part of his own ego, the therapist is receiving fairly complete data about his patient's needs, although in mini-form (hence diluted), or whether he is getting incomplete information through his entire self.

For example, suppose one's patient is transmitting at subtle levels, "I have a passive homosexual need, but I am not ready to face this fact yet." If the therapist's third ear is sufficiently sensitive to pick up the first part of that communication but not the second, he may blunder ahead with a deep interpretation, prematurely delivered. The patient rejects it, and because his weak ego is now alarmed, he raises his level of resistance. The therapist has lost ground instead of gaining it. He has created the very resistance that he must now work through.

This is a common mistake in the inexperienced analyst. His therapeutic zeal exceeds his wisdom. Putting it in therapeutic self terms he has resonated to the passive homoesexuality in his patient, but he has not resonated to the present strong defenses in that one against becoming aware of such a need. Had the young analyst resonated more completely he could not have delivered the unacceptable interpretation. Being more fully identified with his patient he would have hurt and frightened himself to have so spoken. If the resonance is "complete," he would anticipate in advance the impact such an interpretation would make on his patient. For the moment he *is* the patient; hence, he, the analyst, could not deliver what he, the patient, could not accept. It has been truly said that a little bit of knowledge can be a dangerous thing.

There is a strong similarity here in the two facets of therapeutic self interaction—resonance and objectivity—to an approach described by French and Fromm (1964) for the interpretation of dreams. In the analysis of a dream structure, they first employ "empathic understanding." This is then followed by a direct, objective technique that they term "conceptual analysis." It is hypothesized here that the therapeutic self employs these two processes simultaneously in all interactions between therapist and patient.

We have taken a long time to build up this concept of the therapeutic self. Ways of viewing it from the behavioral, the psychoanalytic, and the humanistic standpoints have been presented. We have considered complex energy theories on the nature of self. But over and beyond all such psychological concepts as libido, reinforcements, Thanatos, introjects, identofacts, ego states, and resonance we can once again reduce all this to the simple. The therapeutic self embodies no more nor less than certain fundamental principles that have been known to man for generations.

The two great developmental functions in man's interaction with his world and other humans are differentiation and integration. In the first, he defines his self by separating it from the rest of the world. It is this separateness that is emphasized by the process of objective perception in the therapist. In the second, he rejoins others and unites himself with his fellow man. This integration is the essential ingredient in the second therapeutic self process, that of resonance. We must balance the needs of our own self and that of others.

In the concept of resonance, we have only clothed in new garb an old bit of human wisdom, an inherent principle in every religion that also underlies every form of civilized government. We must be "our brother's keeper" and practice the Golden Rule, because it is the most enlightened form of selfishness. Our own being and our very survival is intimately bound with that of others. We must either "hang together, or assuredly we shall all hang separately."

> "When you want to recognize and understand what takes place in the minds of others, you have first to look into yourself. Such a searching is only possible when a division of yourself has preceded the observation."
>
> —Theordore Reik (1956)

FOOTNOTES

1. "Diagnosis" is used here as meaning a continuously changing personality evaluation, not merely the assigning of a static label to a hypothesized clinical syndrome.
2. It should be noted that here is where therapeutic self differs from Rogerian client-centered theory. In the latter, the condition of accurate empathy (which is the closest approximation to resonance) is considered to be so desirable that the more the therapist employs it the better.

Chapter 17

OF TRADES AND LOANS AND RISKS

Then of the THEE in ME who works behind
The Veil, I lifted up my hands to find
A Lamp amid the Darkness; and I heard,
As from Without—"THE ME WITHIN THEE BLIND!"
—*The Rubaiyat*

The Exchange of Egos Concept

When the therapist internalizes the patient, first as object and then changes him through identification into an identofact, the patient is induced to do likewise. If the counselor is willing to accept into himself some of the pain, the conflict, the pathology that plagues the client, then that one senses the "we-ness" that is so created. He becomes more willing to accept within his own self the values, attitudes, and interpretations stemming from his doctor. An exchange of egos takes place within the therapeutic relationship. The channels of communication are opened up. As the input of data that communicates to the therapist the world view of the treated one is increased, the acceptance of counselor feedback of reflections, suggestions, and interpretations by the client is also increased. Resistance and defense between the two becomes lowered. They grow ever closer together. There is a *quid pro quo* reciprocity. If I give unto you, you are willing to give unto me. If I share with you, you can better share with me. A new unit of therapeutic "one-to-oneness" is created between the two participants, and the process of unfolding, of learning, and of growth is facilitated.

This developmental movement was designed for the primary benefit of the patient, but in the therapeutic self mutual resonance is also new growth for the therapist. If the problems of the client that are solved represent previous personal conflicts the therapist had resolved in himself, the therapy of the patient becomes mental hygiene for the doctor. He has once again the opportunity to review and relive insights of maturity and wise decisions for responsible behavior. Both benefit from this process. When the problems that arise for solution in the therapy represent conflicts new to the therapist, their resolution will provide the doctor with an ever greater understanding, which may serve him well in his confrontation with other clients or in possible future amelioration of his own problems. Furthermore, the reinforcement of success in dealing with them will sharpen the therapist's coping mechanisms and his very self skills in future interactions with others.

The Investment Concept

Another way of looking at the function of the therapeutic self is to compare it with an investment firm. It provides loans of cathexis to patients whose ego banks are depleted, who on their own have not been able to cope with the demands of life because they have learned unwise self-monetary policies and are now nearly bankrupt. Through his acceptance, his willingness to relate, to resonate, to assume some responsibility for the overwhelming problems of his client, the counselor creates a therapeutic "we-ness"—and "we" together are always stronger than "I" alone. Like a "have" nation extending an international loan to a "have-not" country, the counselor provides some of the self-capital that permits the patient to reorganize his psychic economy and put it on a paying basis. It is a kind of individual Marshall Plan for the rehabilitation of a devastated personal country.

But it is a loan, not a gift. The identification of resonance is temporary. If it becomes a welfare payment for the continual relief of self-poverty then the therapy settles down into a long stalemate in which the patient becomes ever more dependent. The therapist supplies continual ego reinforcements (strokes) to the impoverished self for the sheer maintenance of its present level of existence. None of this is plowed into capital goods, whereby the economy of the individual is rebuilt. So many cases degenerate into this blind alley when the counselor becomes only a source of immediate gratification. Helplessness is reinforced, and constructive change does not take place. The exchange of egos did not occur. There is only a giver and a receiver. After all, the purpose of therapy is for the therapist to put himself out of a job.

As the doctor spends ever greater cathexis capital in the unprofitable therapeutic venture, he becomes weaker himself. Failure and frustration overcome him; he may give up the case, and if personal exhaustion is too great he may even stop being a therapist. Not that he necessarily quits practicing, only that he becomes a disillusioned therapeutic robot, one who accepts patients and their fees, who goes through the motions of treating, but who achieves meager results. We have all too many such mechanical nontreating therapists whose degrees still permit them to put out their shingles. They have become like the old analytic joke in which a man asks his psychoanalyst acquaintance, "How do you stand to listen to so many people all day?" The analyst replies, "Who listens?" A therapist can be dead long before his heart stops beating.

The Economy of the Therapist

A few years ago I was sharing a coffee break with a young medical resident. "Jack," he said, "I'm no damned good as a doctor. All my patients are dying." He was spending a three-month rotation as the head physician in a monstrosity, a terminal tumor ward of that hospital. Here were sent all the old people who were dying of cancer. The atmosphere exuded death. The young doctor was systematically being destroyed (under the pretense of getting experience). He could choose to ignore the suffering about him. He could treat all his patients as objects, as things, the loss of which was not important to his life. They could die alone, unloved, uncared for, and never understood. For at the deepest levels, to be loved is to be understood and vice versa. To our patients understanding is love. When we give them understanding, they equate it with love. They sense the empathy with which another has revalidated their right to be.

Yes, this young physician, like so many other healing arts robots, could have protected himself by keeping them as objects. But he was a good doctor; he had discovered the secret of healing by relationship, and he wanted to help his patients.

When we resonate with another we invest his internalized replica with ego cathexis, we pour our selfness into it and change it into identofact. The identofact is a part of our own self. So when that other dies, a piece of our own being disintegrates. Bit by bit, patient by patient, identofact by identofact, the self of this young physician was being destroyed. He could only cry in anguish, "I am no damned good as a doctor. All my patients are dying."

It is sad that (like the young woman in Chapter 1) so many of us must die alone. Yet it is not that people are cruel and uncaring. There are too few who can afford to invest in losing enterprises. For their own protection, humans withdraw cathexis from their identofacts and return them to impersonal objects. We can then let them die painlessly. They are no longer a part of our own selves; they have become things. Let us not condemn such individuals. It is a matter of economics. Only the rich can afford a number of bad investments. Most of us possess only enough ego strength to keep solvent when confronted with the normal problems of life. When a loved one dies, a bit of our own self dies with him. But when all of a doctor's patients die, then a resonating therapeutic self is devastated and dies also.

A therapist becomes increasingly successful as his patients get well. He is reinforced. When his patients die, he is lessened as a person and as a doctor. How does one deal with a dying patient? How can we accept him, resonate with him, understand him, and love him without being drained of our own beingness when he leaves?

Perhaps there is no clear solution to this problem, but one that this therapist has found most helpful is as follows: Let us think of *living time* as experiential, weighed by its *quality* of meaning, rather than by its *quantity* measured chronologically. One is then a successful therapist if he has been able to rescue any amount whatsoever of meaningful existence for his patient. Since all of our patients will die sometime, the only question is when. If through one's understanding a suffering fellowman has been able to experience a few days, a few hours, a few minutes of worthwhile existence, one has not been a failure as a doctor. He has rescued a bit of life stuff. His efforts have had reward. He is reinforced instead of lessened. When we can validate our worth as therapists we do not go down the drain with the patient who has left us either through death or psychosis.

It becomes obvious now that the building and maintenance of a therapeutic self is also an economic problem. We must be concerned with the how-muchness of our ego cathexis reserves. If we invest in a patient, if we resonate with him, then we have made a self commitment to his recovery. If he gets well or even improves, we receive our investment back with interest. If his internalized identofact, constantly changing as the patient grows, no longer clashes in cognitive dissonance with our own values or our own systems of maturity, then cathexis energy is released. We no longer need to struggle with ourselves to achieve a congruence. We become self-consonant, since of course the identofact of the patient is a part of our own self. The demands he makes upon us lessen or cease. Now, the reinforcements our ego receives through being successful in accomplishing our therapeutic goal add to our own self reserves. When the "cured" patient terminates treatment, he normally leaves behind only such a remnant of his replica within us (introject or identofact) as can be easily assimilated into our ego. The little energy required for its integration is much less than the return of our cathexis capital plus success interest. We are a more complex person than before but with a greater personal strength, a greater reserve of ego cathexis. Through successful encounter with this patient, we have added a bit more of well differentiated and integrated ego to the preexisting body of our self. The relationship now is one between two "normals" rather than between a neurotic and a therapist.

A normal relationship is one involving two individuals in which the cathexis investment each makes in the other is matched by a similar energy return from the other. As each gives to the other, neither puts out considerably more than he receives. Both profit from the reinforcement and satisfactions found in a pleasant relationship between two mutually supporting friends. Such should be the finale of a successful therapy. Perhaps this ideal goal is seldom fully reached, but the end result is usually one of benefit to both client and therapist.

As viewed economically, the number of therapeutic relationships a given counselor can assume is directly related to his ego capital. If you have lots of self money in the bank you can afford many more investments than if your cathexis reserves are meager. What you have will depend on what you received through inheritance plus the early savings deposited in your account by good parents and kindly significant others in your childhood—teachers, friends, your successes, etc. From this store must be subtracted the energies required to bind and maintain defenses in dealing with pathological others, first as they impact from the environment without, and later as they have been internalized within. In addition, your happiness in work and love will determine what you have available for therapeutic loans. If you must live in a difficult marital situation, then cathexis energy will be consumed in coping with this problem. There will be less to invest in your patients. No wonder personal therapy is desirable for the doctor. If successful, it frees energy resources for their employment in treating.[1]

The jealousy that patients often feel toward each other need not be based only on the Freudian concept of sibling rivalry. After all, the therapist has a limited amount of ego energy to invest. If he gives more to one, there will be that much less for another. He may choose to treat a few patients with great intensity, great commitment and a high cathexis investment in each. Or he can assume a heavy case load and divide his self into many smaller pieces spread over a larger number of clients.

Subject-Object Love Relationships

Psychoanalysis has stressed the forming of an "object relationship" as the model of mature love. It seems to us that the most mature love should, like the functioning of the therapeutic self, be of a "subject-object" nature. Consider the man-woman interaction.

Humans are bisexual in nature. That is, males have a feminine component and females a masculine component. However, in most men masculinity is the major component and femininity their minor component. In females, the reverse holds. From an ego state viewpoint we would say that masculinity is the executive sexual ego state for men and that femininity is the executive sexual ego state for women. Traditionally, masculinity has been associated with aggressiveness, competitiveness, and destructiveness. Femininity, with nurturance, conservation, and gentleness. Women's liberation movements today challenge these as socially induced stereotypes that have been forced on women to permit men to be the more privileged sex. Whether or not these roles are biological or social in origin, and aside from the question of equal challenges and equal economic rewards, it is the sperm that is more active, the egg that is more passive. It is the male genital (phallus) that is named after a spear, and it is the female who nurtures and preserves the developing infant first within her body and then generally without. Time and social change may modify these roles. However, let us first establish a model of male-female interaction along the traditional lines. If women become more aggressive and men less so, this model can be adapted to such changes.

In Figure 5 we have depicted a heterosexual object relationship between the masculinity (M components) and femininity (F components) in each. We are assuming that masculinity and femininity (although both elements exist in both sexes) are complementary. They fit together and complete each other as do the male and female genitals. It should not be surprising if men's and women's psychological sexual structures are complementary like their physiological structures.

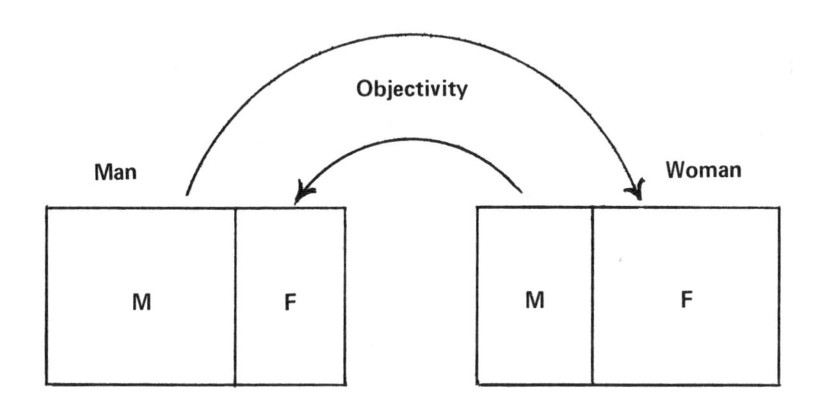

Figure 5 Heterosexual Object Relationship

In the man, his M component (masculinity) is the executive ego state. His F component (femininity) is present as a nonexecutive state. In the woman, her F component is the major state and is normally executive, her masculinity or M component usually more repressed. The direction of the arrows proceed from M components to F components and depict the more aggressive and manipulative aspects of masculinity. The above interaction represents the greater activity of the normal male and hence the greater object of aggression and manipulation that the woman often perceives herself as being. It is purely sexual interaction and exemplifies the treatment of the woman as a sex object, such as is characterized by feminists as chauvinistic. The partners above do not love one another, but they can "screw." As men become more passive, their M component becomes less executive, and as women become more active, theirs becomes more executive. But the interaction pattern remains much the same. It is obvious that if women's M component becomes their major state, they will seek males whose F component complements that—and then men will feel themselves as being the sex objects of aggressive females.

In Figure 6 the same objectivity holds between the M and F components of the respective partners, but something different in the form of a *mutually resonant* relationship has been added. The F component of the male resonates, hence partially identifies, with the major femininity component of his mate. Accordingly, his aggressive seizing of her as a sex object is tempered by his need to please her, and thus through resonance his own F state. She, likewise, perceives her man not simply as an object whom she wants to pleasure her directly. As her M component resonates with his M executive state she will strive to do that which makes him happier, since in so doing she, through her M state, adds to her own satisfaction. The purely object relationship depicted in Figure 5 may typify a rape interaction. The model in Figure 6 represents a mature love in which the partners meet each other's needs in both their major and minor components (in their sexual executive and nonexecutive states). The balance here between objectivity and resonance is similar to the functioning of the therapeutic self in an optimal treatment relationship. It is, therefore, more rewarding and integrative to both.

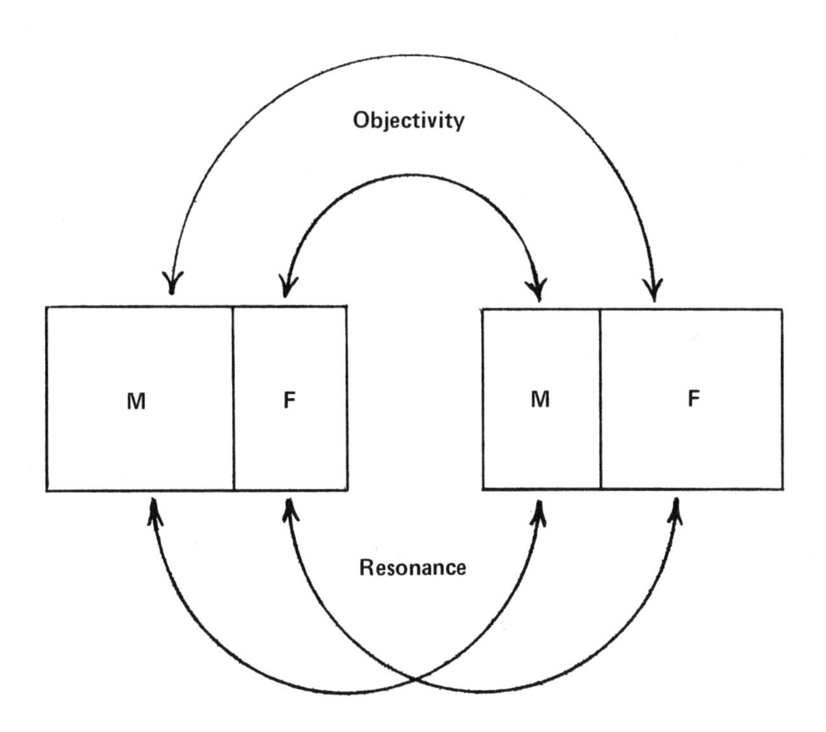

Figure 6. Heterosexual Subject-Object (Love) Relationship

The Relative Validity of Objective and Resonant Impressions.

A question that may arise to the thoughtful reader is the following: The total stimuli, auditory, visual, tactual, etc., from another person that impact our sense organs as object are the same stimuli used in the formation of first an introject and then an identofact; so where is there any difference in the data received? If objectivity and resonance present the same material, why should one differ from the other?

That which is broadcast from a sender is not necessarily that which is recorded by a receiver. All perceptual systems are selective. They screen the stimuli impacting them, rejecting certain items, accepting others, amplifying still others, and interperting differently. Psychoanalysts often speak of an "analytic scotoma," or therapeutic blind spot. This refers to the therapist who is unable to see in a patient certain problems. Because of his own countertransference needs, he has screened them out of his apprehension. He simply ignores, let us say, communications from his patient related to a brother jealousy because he, the therapist, still suffers from a jealousy of his own brother. He defends his equanimity by refusing to react to the patient's associations. This would activate his own problem, so he simply doesn't hear what the patient is saying.

Of equal importance, but less emphasized in psychoanalytic ranks, is the concept of an "analytic fovea"; that is, an area which the analyst sees only too well because he is unduly sensitized to it. A young staff psychiatrist, who had recently completed an analysis, was observed at a diagnostic case conference in a mental hygiene clinic. When the first patient was presented he scratched his head thoughtfully and then said, "I think this man is suffering from castration anxiety." As he was asked his diagnostic opinion on the second patient to come before the professional panel he remarked, "It seems to me that we have here a case of castration anxiety." When the third patient was presented the young psychiatrist exploded convincingly, "Now there's an example of castration anxiety if ever I saw one." He may have been correct in all three cases, but we might suspect that he was still close to the analytic working through of his own problem. Castration anxiety constituted for him an analytic fovea.

Whenever anything is invested with self, with "meness," it is viewed differently than when it is not. *My* children are better than those of others. *My* country is noble; others are unfair. The fact that an item is invested with *my* self will cause me to select for attention its more favorable elements and ignore those I do not like. We are all aware of the personal interest that most people have when judgment is being made about their own family or a loved one. We would not allow a husband to sit on a jury judging his wife. We say he could not be "objective." The assumption here is that if selfness is invested in the item judged, then the evaluation will not be objective, correct, valid.

However, the mere fact that an object remains free from investment of selfness does not ensure that perception and evaluation of it is necessarily correct, only that it is probably different. Our evaluative scotomas and foveas operate in both cases. An alien may be more harshly judged than he should be simply because he is not one of us. Racial prejudice is based on the fact that those with whom we cannot identify because of color or some other distinguishing characteristic are met with a selective perception that overemphasizes their faults and underperceives their virtues.

Accordingly, even though the stimuli that strike the sense organs and are transmitted through objectivity directly toward impingement on an ego boundary are the same as those that through resonance arrive at contact with the executive boundary only after having been invested with self, the final impact is not the same. A set of stimuli that is object cathected passes through a different perceptual filtering system before impacting the executive state than when it is ego-cathected. Experientially the two sets of data will not be equal. One may include perceptions ignored by the other, and vice versa. That is why objectivity and resonance do not yield the same impressions, and why an integration of the two of them provide us with a more complete understanding of another person than either alone.

Here is a specific example where the feelings initiated in a therapist from a patient will be very different if received objectively than if received through resonance. Consider the case of an attractive young female patient being treated by a male therapist. She is describing a situation in her life in which she was raped. If he is feeling sexy toward her as he listens to the relating of this incident, if he wishes that he had done the raping, then he is listening only objectively. If he had been listening with resonance, his feeling would not have been lust, but outrage. He would have permitted his feminine or minority component to respond, and he would have experienced the situation the way a woman would, with indignation and outrage.

This is a difficult therapeutic task for a young male therapist since it requires that he be very safe and sure in his basic masculine identification. If he has some inner fears that he might not be completely a man, if he has some latent homosexual tendencies that he has been repressing, then he would not dare to let that feminine component state become executive. He would be too frightened to permit himself to resonate with his patient's outraged femininity. He would remain objective, and his feelings would be those of sexual lust toward her. However, if his therapeutic self is perceiving her both objectively and through resonance, then he would either simultaneously experience both lust and indignation, or he would alternate in his feelings between the two.

How difficult it is for a therapist to resonate with a sadist, a child molester, a murderer, a schizophrenic, etc. If he fears tendencies within himself that he thinks might become activated into similar behavior, then his resonating abilities will be excluded in these directions, and he must treat that patient only as would an objective therapist. The experienced, mature, and flexible therapist is not afraid to let himself *be* that which is his patient. He knows that his investment of self capital into the enterprise of the other is only a loan, that the identofact so created is only for purposes of understanding and therapy, that his own basic identity is securely anchored, and that he will safely return to it on termination of the treatment.

During World War II a battalion surgeon was referred to the special treatment company in our army hospital with a tremor of the right hand, which he himself had falsely diagnosed as Parkinson's disease. During the initial interview he mentioned the unfair treatment he had received from his commanding officer at the hospital where he had been stationed in France. Becoming more angry as he described the injustices inflicted on him by this man he concluded with, "What I wouldn't do with him if I could get him on my operating table." It was decided to let him release this rage by "giving" him the offending man on "his operating table."

He was hypnotized, and the operating room revivified. He was told that the door was locked, and only he and I were present. The hallucinated "officer" (a pillow) was laid on the table before him, and an imaginary scalpel was placed in his right hand. For the next twenty minutes the two of us sweated and cursed. He stabbed and tore at the pillow, while the therapist shouted, "Give it to the son of a bitch. He deserves it", etc. When the reaction slowed, it was stopped and repeated. The tape, so to speak, was rewound and run again. Over and over the abreaction was reenacted, three times, four times, five times. Finally, through sheer physical and psychological exhaustion he could do no more.[2]

We had completed his need to murder. It was possible to achieve a closure in his conflict. He could now accept interpretations that he was transferring a repressed anger originally aimed at a cruel father onto the commanding officer. The violent release of this anger in a fantasied murder had exhausted the energies that had manned its repression. Insight and personality reorganization were now possible. He emerged from the hypnotic state, smiled, and lifted his hand. There was no trace left of a tremor.

Sometimes as therapists, if we would resonate with that which our patient experiences, we must risk our self and be willing to descend with him into the inferno of his pathology. But like Orpheus of old, who went into the underworld seeking his dead wife, we need to be secure in the assurance that we know the path to return to our own land, to our own identity. Then we are not afraid. We can open up the gates of our resonating abilities and let in the floods of feeling. We descend with our patient into the maw of his pathology without fear, in the confidence that we will return, and in the hope that we can also bring him with us out of "the jaws of death, back from the mouth of hell" (Tennyson's "The Charge of the Light Brigade").

FOOTNOTES

1. There are tremendous implications here in the training of young healing arts personnel, since the interaction with their academic parents, not only sets the model of constructive doctor-patient relationships, but provides the novice with either more or less cathexis capital. Students cannot be made into therapists by supervisors who demand from their young charges more than they give to them. Treaters of men cannot be developed by teachers who themselves are beaters of men. However, we shall reserve the training and development of therapeutic selves to a later chapter.
2. Behavior therapists now practice a similar technique, which they call flooding, or implosive therapy (See Stampfl, 1967).

Part VI

EXPERIMENTAL FINDINGS

If a theory is to be taken seriously, it must provide not only a rationale that accounts for phenomena, but it should also be capable of study and validation through empirical evidence. In Chapters 18, 19, and 20 a start is made in this area. Much more needs to be done, for each tiny finding raised several new questions. However, the evidence presented here indicates that the concept of resonance can be objectively and reliably rated, and that the ability to evaluate it is teachable. This makes it possible to devise experimental studies that could empirically test the theoretical concepts of the therapeutic self.

Chapter 18

INFORMAL STUDIES

During the academic years of 1967 through 1970, a small group of graduate students in psychology met with the author in an attempt to bring some objective evaluation into the concept of the therapeutic self.[1] The first and most basic consideration to undergo our attention was the distinction between subject and object. This problem, of course, has plagued psychologists and philosophers for many centuries; nor has it ever been solved, since it involves the most significant questions possible about self and existence. It seemed to us that difficult as the concepts are to define scientifically, introspectively people make very clear, continuous distinctions between what is self and what not-self. We have always purified the consonance of our egos by allocating to not-self, to the object world, those items that are dissonant with our self image. We admit to owning the good; the bad belongs to others.

Furthermore, all that we know of dissociation, of

repression, of the establishment of hysterical symptoms, of hypnotic phenomena, and of the mechanisms of introjection and projection confirms that the organism is capable of turning objective phenomena into subjective and vice versa. The criminal eliminates guilt by disowning his crimes; the individual who seeks marital counseling almost invariably perceives the spouse as the aggressor and the self as the victim. Getting items changed from objective to subjective status and vice versa in the interest of reality orienting becomes the goal of most therapies. The resistances thrown up to such changes by the patient in therapy is eloquent testimony to the universal need to support the status quo, to continue neurotic equilibrium.

These defense maneuvers are aimed at maintaining the present disposition of subject and object energies in the interest of anxiety reduction. The resistance to change, therefore, is highly motivated for the protection of neurotic needs. But, we might ask, can changes in subject-object be accomplished, perhaps at will, when there is not a conflict involved? Can individuals reverse subject and object energies by conscious purpose when they are not defending themselves?

This small therapeutic self study group first tried a number of informal investigations to explore tentatively such questions. In one of these, each individual thrust his right hand into a basin of hot water and simultaneously his left hand into one of cold water. After a period of time to allow for accommodation, the two hands were removed and placed against each other. The question asked now of the individual was, "Do you feel heat, or do you feel cold?" Then, "Can you locate your self in the left hand, make it subject, and experience the hotness of the right hand as object?" Next, "Can you move the self over into the right hand and then experience the coldness in the left hand as object?"

We were concerned whether it was possible to manipulate subject-object, and if so, could it be done by anybody, or by only a few? Were some individuals resistant to make such changes? If we were to expect a therapeutic self counselor to change his sensing of a client from subjective-resonance to objective-perception, then he should have a "flexible" ego that would permit him to "choose" to make such alterations. Perhaps a subject-object manipulation of simple physical perceptions, such as temperature sensing, would be indicative of a flexible person who could best operate as a therapeutic self.

It soon became obvious to us that to conduct a controlled study, we would need to know much more about the psychophysics of temperature perception, to measure temperature differentials above and below normal skin temperature so as to acquire equal balance. Otherwise, the physical stimulus intensity value of the hotness might be much more or less than that for coldness; if so, it might not permit an alternation to the other side, or it might be possible only with the expenditure of much energy.

We decided that the study could be performed, but that the job of undertaking the project should be left to others with more sophistication in the psychology of perception. However, we did find considerable variability among the five of us. Only one individual claimed to be unable to reverse the subject-object experience. Some could do so quite rapidly, others with difficulty.

We next decided to try to change subject-object identifications while watching athletic contests. We would select a football game shown on television, neither of which team carried any degree of commitment for us, from cities that commanded no loyalties from us. We would then attempt to watch the game and switch identifications each quarter. Thus, during the first quarter the team in dark jerseys would be ours. We would try to involve ourselves most intensively in loyalty for it. If it made yardage or scored we would cheer. We would temporarily adopt that team and see if we could experience dismay at every loss by it. Then, during the second quarter, we would attempt to switch our identifications to the team with the light jerseys and experience our loyalties accordingly. The opponents of the first quarter had now become our team, and those with whom we had previously identified would now become enemy objects. We found this was possible when we did not start with any strong pregame loyalties already established.

Next, we tried to see if the identifications could be switched more often. For example, we would always cheer for the offensive team or always for the defensive team. This, too, we could do, except, as might have been expected, some of us found it easier to identify with the defensive team rather than the offensive one and vice versa. It is obvious that such internal personal dynamic needs have much to do in determining with which patients we are able to resonate, as well as the respective balance between resonance and objectivity for such patients. For example, some of us naturally tend to identify with underdogs.

Maintaining a therapeutic self with clients who represent different types, races, attitudes, dress, dispositions, and values so as to establish a balance between resonance and objectivity is obviously a very difficult and complex task. Probably, a therapist would find some clients with whom it was easy to overresonate, to overidentify, while others would evoke little natural feelings of resonance. At best, one could only be as objective as possible and minimize bias.

We next tried to transfer this experience of altering identifications from the athletic game to the treatment hour. The group would observe or listen to a counselor dealing with a client. Each student would be instructed, for example, to identify first with the therapist, to listen to the patient as if he were sitting in the therapist's chair and to determine whether he could experience the patient in the same way as the therapist who was currently interviewing him.

We would then try to identify with the patient, resonate with his needs, anticipate his responses, and view the therapist as might the treated one. Again our findings were incomplete and incapable of generalization, except that each member of the group began to get some subjective awareness of how he himself might operate in the therapeutic situation and to get some awareness of the ease or difficulty he might experience in trying to operate according to the theory of the therapeutic self.

From these preliminary studies, the greatest need that began to manifest itself was for some objective scale by which resonance could be evaluated. Some criteria were needed that would provide a reliable rating before we could engage in any controlled studies of therapeutic self or of resonance, its most significant component.

With such a scale available, a number of fascinating investigations could be opened up. If resonance truly involved the ability to co-feel, co-sweat, co-enjoy, and co-suffer with another, then we should be able to determine whether the adrenals of the therapist are secreting when the patient is experiencing emotions. Perhaps even brain wave studies would show similarity in patterns between the client and his resonating counselor.

If the theory was sound, optimal balance should involve almost half resonance and half objectivity in the treating one. Many other questions also came to mind: Does resonance tend to be established early in a therapeutic hour, in the middle, or toward the end? Are there typical changes in the resonance-objectivity balance in good sessions versus unproductive ones? What is to be expected in the relative balance between the two during the early sessions in a course of therapy, the median ones, and the later ones? What happens in the relationship of couples in love with each other? Do they resonate more?

Gradually the attention of the group began to focus increasingly on the degree to which the two factors of resonance and objectivity could be rated in the therapist-patient interaction. Neither process nor outcomes studies could be undertaken in the absence of objective criteria for the measurement of these two factors. We had all experienced our own introspections and could report whether we "felt" we were resonating to the various football teams and to the individuals in recorded therapeutic hours, but the important question was whether we could observe the behavior (and listen to the responses of clients) and judge whether or not they were reacting with resonance or with objectivity. It was also essential that we establish such criteria for judgment as would afford a reasonably high reliability with independent raters.

If we could reliably (and validly) rate these two factors then, not only could the theoretical tenets of the therapeutic self theory be tested, but also we might have an instrument that would predict therapeutic talent in candidates for training and would afford some evaluation of competence after education. Furthermore, we could then approach such problems as whether resonance is a trainable ability and what procedures might be employed for developing it in healing arts practitioners.

Accordingly, the cooperative efforts of the first research group, as well as that of two following teams, became increasingly devoted to the exclusive problem of defining the nature of resonance, of contrasting it with objectivity, of determining criteria for its rating, of establishing units within the therapeutic sessions to be evaluated, and, finally, of breaking down resonance into different types and degrees.

We had hoped before now not only to have validated our scale for the measurement of resonance, but also to have completed a number of the studies proposed above. However, the amount of theory development that had been undertaken, and the need to report our studies to date has impelled the publication of this book before these objectives have been completed. The scale that will now be described has, however, had sufficient use as to warrant the hope that both we and others will experiment further with it and that the concepts presented here will be subjected to further validation. For in the final analysis, a theory is limited when supported by rational processes alone; empirical studies can verify or disqualify its proposals. Such future studies must tell how much of therapeutic self theory is valid and applicable.

FOOTNOTES

1. The initial research team (1967-68) consisted of Richard Fuhrer, Elizabeth Lundberg, Edward Shubat, and Nancy Shubat. In later years Edward Bitter, Mason Dikeman, Frank Eisle, James Farnes, Daniel Moritz, James Shulman, Michael de Stefano, and Kenneth Welt were involved. The writer is indebted to each of these former graduate students for contributing to the studies described here.

Chapter 19

THE SCORING OF RESONANCE

Resonance is an inner experience. As such, how does one arrive at a measure of it? Perhaps subjectively? Through introspection? "I feel that I was resonating with the patient at that time?" No! Resonance cannot be reliably evaluated unless independent observers can perceive a therapist in action and agree that he was resonating. Our first step, then, was to try and objectify resonant behavior, those overt responses by the therapist that can be agreed upon by raters as indicating such an inner experience within him. They obviously would represent verbal reactions, which include intonation and emphasis as well as content, plus postural and gestural movements. To try to observe and rate all these factors simultaneously would present the observer with an extremely difficult task. We decided, therefore, to concentrate on verbalizations.

At first, we simply listened to a number of therapy sessions, observed through one-way vision screens, and played tape recordings. Several observers would monitor a session at the same time and then give their independent subjective reports as to whether they thought the therapist was or was not resonating with his client. It soon became obvious that the therapy hour must be divided into segments and that the presence of resonance would have to be determined for each segment. We noticed that a therapist might be responding in a purely objective manner during a portion of the interview, that he might suddenly show evidences of resonant behavior for a while, and then return to objectivity afterwards. Except for noting that the earlier parts of a therapeutic hour appeared to be characterized by less resonance than later segments, we found no typical patterns in these early observations.

Our first division into units was along a time dimension. A therapy hour was recorded, transcribed, and played back; the transcription was then divided into one minute segments, numbered consecutively. Judges were asked to listen to the recording while following the typed script of the hour and at the end of each minute to record whether or not they detected evidence of resonance on the part of the therapist within that time interval. It was quickly apparent that resonance would come and go, often several times, within the one minute segment, although sometimes the therapist seemed to "be with it" and would appear to be continuously resonating over a number of minutes.

Accordingly, the therapeutic hour transcription was divided into 30-second intervals and judges were asked to indicate the presence or absence of resonance within each such segment. The thinking here was in line with that employed by the author (Watkins, 1942) in a previous study on the evaluation of sight reading in instrumental music. At that time the musical measure was the unit and was scored right or wrong. It was scored as wrong if a mistake (carefully defined in terms of pitch, time, notation, etc.) was made by the musician within that measure.

The more we worked with time intervals, the greater the difficulty became. Supposing almost all the therapist's responses within such a half-minute segment were objective, but one comment alone showed resonance. How could we compare this with a 30-second interval during which the therapist seemed to be largely resonating. Or supposing there were no therapist responses during a 30-second segment, all the verbalizing being done by the client. What then?

The entire concept of judging time intervals appeared to be unworkable and was abandoned. Instead we decided to try a unit consisting of a single client verbalization followed by a therapist response. This introduced great variability into the length of these segments. At times the patient might verbalize for five or ten minutes before the therapist replied. Sometimes the unit consisted only of a single exclamation by the client and a mere "Uh-huh" by the counselor, but units defined in this way proved to be scorable. A typical therapeutic hour might range from 80 to 150 such units, but we found that it was possible to make a specific judgment on the presence or lack of resonance within each unit, hence after each single, unified therapist response.

We decided to score R for *resonance* if the judge, while simultaneously listening to and reading a patient-therapist response unit, decided that there was evidence of resonant behavior on the part of the therapist. If not, the unit would be scored O for *objective*. The protocols on several therapeutic hours were divided into segments, which were numbered consecutively. Boxes were placed at the end of each segment where the judges would record an R or O after simultaneously hearing and reading that therapist-patient response unit. Thus such units might be as follows:

Unit No.		*Scored*
25	P No matter how hard I try I can't seem to get a passing grade in the course. T You feel desperate and hopeless in the situation.	R
26	P There doesn't seem to be anything to do but quit school. T You realize, of course, how much you will lose by dropping out.	O

The judges were instructed to score R if the therapist seemed to feel *affects* being experienced by the patient or if the therapist showed a *cognitive* (intellectual) understanding of events reported by the patient that appeared to be the same as the patient's cognitive understanding of the same events. If the therapist showed that he was *objectively perceiving,* that is, sensing the patient as an external object to himself, then the unit was to be scored O. The unit was scored R if the primary meaning or predominant tone of the therapist's response was judged to be resonant and O if it was largely objective. No attempt at this time was made to evaluate the relative weight of R and O within a single response unit.

It did not take long for us to find that a number of responses, which might best be described as *facilitative,* could not be scored either R or O. Thus a therapist's "Uh-huh" or "Tell me more" would tell us little about the therapist's feelings except to indicate that he was encouraging the client to continue talking. Accordingly, these facilitative responses were scored F.

It was found that almost all of the patient-therapist

response units could be scored as R, O, or F. However, occasionally one appeared that seemed to result from some train of thought in the therapist that was facetious or irrelevant and that may have followed a period during which the therapist was simply not listening to his client. These were scored I for *irrelevant.* Finally, a very few responses were noted that did not seem to fall into any of the above categories and those we simply agreed to score N for *nonscorable.*

The research group, consisting at that time of five individuals, now proceeded to evaluate a number of therapy hours that had been recorded by the instructor and the students, and also tapes and protocols published by the American Academy of Psychotherapists Tape Library. These included hours recorded by Carl Rogers, Franz Alexander, Albert Ellis, and Norman Cameron. Each typescript was divided into therapist-patient response units, which were numbered consecutively. The research team would then listen to the recording while reading the protocol and score together.

A number of problems immediately became manifest. Sometimes the units were short and would follow each other so rapidly that a judge had a hard time making and recording his evaluation of such a unit without losing his needed attention to the next one. If we only played one unit at a time, then the continuity was often lost.

Accordingly, we practiced scoring together by listening and judging some ten consecutive units. We would then stop and compare ratings. Whenever there was disagreement on a score we would argue and discuss it together, each member of the group presenting the rationale by which he chose to score it as he did. This would be continued until we arrived at unanimity or at least a four to one consensus.

As we judged and practiced our scoring together in

this way over a number of hours, we found our disagreements shrinking and our times of agreement increasing. Whether or not our judgments were valid, at least they were becoming increasingly reliable. More and more we were paying attention to the same aspects of each response unit and tending increasingly to judge on the same criteria.

It will be noted that we had defined resonance as either cognitive (i.e., understanding like the patient) or affective (i.e., feeling like the patient). The more we practiced scoring resonance, the more important this difference seemed to become. Finally, we decided that instead of scoring R we would score A for *affective resonance* and C for *cognitive resonance.* The scoring system now permitted the assigning to a patient-therapist response unit any one of six different scores: A, C, O, F, I, or N.

Some finalization had now been achieved in the types of different scores. Definitions and samples of each had been recorded, and we had spent many hours practicing and comparing ratings until we could largely agree. It was time for some controlled data on the reliability with which protocols could be so scored. Accordingly, a single therapeutic hour, which had been recorded by the author several months before, was transcribed and divided into response units. Without a pause, the first 100 patient-therapist response units were rated simultaneously by the five judges, and comparisons were made of their evaluations. Table 1 shows the number of scores assigned by each judge to the various categories: A, C, O, F, I, and N.

From Table 1 it is obvious that there was not a high amount of agreement (in terms of numbers of scores) in the differentiation of affective (A) from cognitive (C) resonance, but that three of the judges (JW, BL, and FI) agreed very closely in the number of responses they considered resonant (R). We often found considerable difficulty in deciding whether a response was A or C even though we agreed that it was resonant. Two of the judges assigned only a few O scores, one an intermediate number, and two a large number. With the exception of one judge (BL), there was considerable agreement as to the number of facilitative (F) responses. The I and N scores were infrequent, a fact all judges agreed upon. Table 2 shows the percentage of agreement in scoring between each rater and each of the other judges when A and C were scored separately.

TABLE 1

(Scorer)	JW	NS	BL	FI	FN
A	17	27	5	6	6
C	22	28	33	35	19
R (A plus C)	39	55	38	41	25
O	31	11	11	25	39
F	29	31	49	32	32
I		1	1		2
N	1	1	1	2	2
	100	100	100	100	100

TABLE 2

	NS	BL	FI	RF
JW	56	42	56	47
NS		44	59	48
BL			55	50
FI				68

A, C, O, F, I, N
Average agreement: 52.5 per cent

Table 3 shows the percentage of agreement in scoring between each rater and each of the other judges when A and C are combined into R.

TABLE 3

	NS	BL	FI	RF
JW	68	62	59	60
NS		65	79	62
BL			60	53
FI				71

(R, O, F, I, N)
Average agreement: 63.9 per cent

It is obvious that the percentage of agreement between raters is considerably increased when they simply score resonance (R) without trying to differentiate as to whether it is affective (A) or cognitive (C). It was our conclusion that for us to reliably rate A and C with a high amount of agreement, we would need to spend much more time in practice scoring and training together to ensure common differentiating criteria.

We next assumed that the modal rating on a response unit would be considered as its "correct" evaluation. For example, if three of the raters scored it C, one of them A, and one of them O, the correct score was assumed to be C. A correct scoring was then secured for the entire protocol and the ratings of each judge compared with it. The percentages of overlap in this validity study for the various judges are presented in Table 4.

TABLE 4 Per Cent of Agreement by Each Judge with the "Correct" Scoring.

A and C scored separately		*A and C combined into R*	
JW	73	JW	88
NS	68	NS	80
BL	68	BL	70
FI	87	FI	89
RF	77	RF	79
Average: 74.6 per cent		Average: 81.2 per cent	

Since the above data represents only five judges the validity score is based on internal consistency, one-fifth of it being determined by each judge. Accordingly, the percentages above are more closely representative of reliability than of validity. However, they are sufficiently high to justify the conclusion that resonance is a ratable trait and that resonance and objectivity, the two chief factors in the theory of the therapeutic self, are capable of objective and reliable measurement. It is also clear that even though the two forms of resonance, affective and cognitive, are capable of differentiation, at this stage of the study this distinction needs more careful definition and investigation. The most reliable ratings (average 81.2 per cent) are secured simply by scoring R, O, F, I, and N.

During the 1968-69 academic year, a further refinement was agreed upon by the research group. It involved the definition of four different *levels* of resonant behavior, either affective or cognitive. These were based on the level at which the therapist was *apparently* resonating with his client. They might have descriptively been called: 1. The conscious level; 2. the preconscious level; 3. the unconscious level; and 4. the pseudoresonance level. Since these would be either affective or cognitive, resonance ratings could be defined even more precisely into A-1, A-2, A-3, A-4, C-1, C-2, C-3, and C-4 scores.

In view of the fact that the differentiation of resonance into A and C scores had not been reliably established, it might seem premature, if not foolish, to define even finer differentiations. We must admit that as yet we have no actual data concerning the four different levels of resonance. However, after a great deal of qualitative examination of response units, and mindful that the publishing of a scoring system would make possible the initiation of such studies by others as well as by ourselves, we decided to define these levels as carefully as possible, with examples taken from actual protocols, and to leave to future investigation the validation of this refinement in the scoring. Accordingly, the Therapeutic Self Scoring System as we finally established it was as follows:

The Therapeutic Self Scoring System

Resonance (R)

Resonance is that process by which an individual (therapist) attempts to replicate within his own self a close facsimile of another's experiential world. The presence of this resonance in the individual (therapist) may be inferred by the observation of his behavior in the relationships. This includes such nuances as intonation, posture, and gestures, as well as verbal content.

Score A (Affective Resonance) if the therapist's behavior indicates that he *feels,* or is *attempting to feel,* the *affect* being experienced by the patient.

Score A-1* if this resonance corresponds to the affect that the patient is currently experiencing at the fully conscious level. This therapist response does not directly stimulate any new insight.

Example: P He was cruel to me.
T He really was cruel, wasn't he? (Scored A-1)
P Yes.

Score A-2 if this resonance corresponds to an affect at a level of awareness that is not yet fully conscious to the patient (i.e., preconscious), but becomes conscious as a consequence of the therapist's response.

*To judge level of response, hence 1, 2, 3, or 4, therapist's statement must be compared with the patient verbalization that both precedes it and follows it.

This is evidenced by an immediate confirmation by the patient. (This response is assumed to facilitate new insight.)

Example: P And when he did come in to talk to me, he was civil, if only on a social basis. I just had nothing to do with him.

T You had a kind of elated feeling, kind of like you'd gotten one up on him a bit. (Scored A-2)

P That's it. I was overjoyed. I've been laughing about it ever since.

A-3 and A-4 represent attempts to resonate on the part of the therapist that are ineffective, or fail, for the following reasons:

Score A-3 if the therapist is experiencing an affect that is unconscious to the patient who consequently rejects an interpretation of its presence.

Example: P I have a tendency to start running from people when they start acting a little bit decently toward me.

T You mean you're afraid they're going to hurt you in some way? (Scored A-3)

P Well, I don't know whether it's that, or whether it's something else.

Score A-4† if the therapist is attempting to resonate but apparently is experiencing an affect that does not correspond to any feeling the patient is having at that time at any level, and that the patient consequently rejects.

Example: P He was jealous. And see now, this is not a figment of my imagination because he absolutely came out verbally and said this before.

†A-4 (as well as C-4) responses, although included under R, are not true resonance. The therapist may be attempting to resonate but he has failed at all levels. Frequent appearance of such responses probably represent countertransference needs on his part.

T Uh-huh. Maybe in some ways you'd like him to be jealous? (Scored A-4)

P No. I'm only sorry he's so jealous. You must have misunderstood me.

Score C (Cognitive Resonance) if the therapist's behavior indicates that he has, or is attempting to have, a *cognitive (intellectual) understanding* of events that appear to be the same as the patients current understanding of the same events.

Score C-1 if this resonance corresponds to the cognitive understanding that the patient is currently experiencing at the fully conscious level. This therapist response does not directly stimulate any new patient insight.

Example: P I don't get a chance to be myself. They always act for me.

T I hear you saying, "Everybody's all ready to be me for me, even before I get the chance." (Scored C-1)

P Yeah. Just like they all got part of me, and I got none of myself.

Score C-2 if this resonance corresponds to a cognitive understanding at a level of awareness that is not yet fully conscious to the patient (i.e., preconscious), but which becomes conscious as a consequence of the therapist's response. This is evidenced by an immediate confirmation by the patient. (This response is assumed to facilitate new insight.)

Example: P But I always wonder what to say—what to do.

T You're uncertain about how others will react to you. (Scored C-2)

P Well, uh, yeah. I hadn't thought of it that way before.

C-3 and C-4 represent attempts to resonate on the part of the therapist that are ineffectual, or fail, for the following reasons:

Score C-3 if the therapist is experiencing a cognitive understanding that is so unconscious to the patient that he consequently rejects an interpretation of its presence.

Example: P That night I had this dream about Mother. This is what shocks me about it. I've never been able to turn this emotional commitment, so to say, on and off, just like that. But the next day, I did.

T Because of the dream about your mother, you could turn it on and off? (Scored C-3)

P No! Not because of the dream. It was kind of a gradual thing that has taken place over the last—well, ever since then.

Score C-4 if the therapist is apparently attempting to resonate but actually is experiencing a cognitive understanding that does not correspond to any cognitive understanding the patient is having at that time at any level, and that the patient consequently rejects. (See also footnote under A-4).

Example: P They've got a few more facts in there and, therefore, they're beginning to figure what the crux of the situation is.

T You're saying now they're ignorant. (Scored C-4)

P No! No! I'm saying they aren't ignorant.

Objective (O)

Score O if the therapist is not resonating, but instead is *objectively perceiving* the patient. He is sensing the patient as an external object to himself.

Example: There may not be enough room to put my sister's girl in a room by herself.

T She has two children? (Scored O)
P She has a boy of seven and a girl of four and a half.

Facilitate (F)

Score F if the response of the therapist is *primarily facilitative:* hence, is intended to encourage the patient to continue communicating. This would include such reactions as "Uh-huh"; Tell me more"; "What do you think?"; "How does it seem to you?"; etc. A reaction calling for a specific response, rather than merely encouraging continued communication should be scored Objective (O) rather than Facilitative (F).

Example: P There may not be enough room to put my sister's girl in a room by herself.
T Uh-huh. (Scored F)

Irrelevant (I)

Score I if the response of the therapist seems to be *facetious or irrelevant.* In this case, unlike A-4 and C-4, the therapist is obviously not even attempting to resonate.

Example: P I haven't been working lately because I seem to have so much difficulty getting along with people.
T Well, you can't win 'em all, ha ha! (Scored I).

Nonscorable (N)

Score N if the therapist's response appears to be *nonscorable* in terms of the above categories. Such a score should occur rarely.

When two different elements (such as resonance and objectivity) both seem to be part of a response two scores may be assigned, the primary one first, e.g., O,C or A,O. In the final tabulations, we usually considered only the primary score—although a part-score weighting system might be used assigning two-thirds of a point to the primary score and one-third to the secondary one.

To illustrate the varying categories of responses, a set of possible therapist reactions to a patient statement would be scored as follows:

P I'm having a beast of a time in school. I'm fed up, ready to quit, and I don't want to go on.
T You feel desperate and hopeless (Scored A, affective resonance).
T It doesn't seem worthwhile continuing in the present situation. (Scored C, cognitive resonance).
T You realize, of course, how much you will lose by quitting school. (Scored O, objective).
T Uh-hum! How so? (Scored F, facilitative).
T If you feel that way, forget it. You'll never make it. (Scored I, irrelevant).

After development and experience with the foregoing scoring system, our research group concluded that therapeutic self is not only an idealized, abstract concept, but that its components are subject to objective definition and evaluation. Such a rating system now made it possible to move from the stage of armchair theorizing toward controlled studies concerning its process and efficacy.

Chapter 20

TRAINING FOR RESONANCE

Many years ago when this writer entered Columbia University in search of a doctoral degree, he was given a bit of counsel by another graduate student (name unfortunately forgotten), to whom he owes an immeasurable debt of gratitude. This young friend imparted to him the following bit of wisdom: "Take people. Don't take courses." This was a strange idea to one who had always depended on the course descriptions in the college catalog to make such decisions. But with some trepidation I decided to try his advice.

For several hours I stood in the registration line to get to the academic adviser, Dr. Arthur I. Gates, whom I had hoped would be willing to skipper my fragile scholarly craft through the dangerous shoals of academia. He was only a name to me then, but I was well aware of his distinguished contributions in the fields of educational psychology and reading. Just before closing time I managed to reach him and, expecting a rebuff, timidly put my vita and educational credentials before him. He scarcely glanced at them before asking, "With whom have you studied?"—not, "What have you studied?" but, "With whom have you studied?" My record was not outstanding, nor had I graduated from a celebrated university. Moreover, we could only discover one professor among my instructors with whose work he was familiar.

His smile was a bit more reassuring as he asked, "And what do you want to take this semester?" Feeling most uncomfortably my limitations as a small-town school teacher from a Western state not known for illustrious institutions, I finally dared to respond, "Who are your strong professors, and what are they offering this term?"

He proceeded to reel off a who's who in the psychological world of that day: "Let's see. Dr. Thorndike will be teaching learning. Dr. Gardner Murphy offers his course in social psychology. Dr. Arthur Jersild is presenting an advanced seminar in child psychology. And, oh yes, Dr. John Dewey is breaking his retirement and coming back to offer a course in the philosophy of education."

Overwhelmed and stunned, I was barely able to mutter, "Just sign me up for whatever they're offering." With a kindly smile, the distinguished mentor filled out my registration card, and then signed his name as major professor. I staggered away in a fog of ecstasy.

This was my puberty rite of initiation into the understanding that one learns more from people than from things or books. People should be more important than things, even though we learn much from the products of people—their writings, their paintings, their sculpture, their compositions. All library materials, books, articles, outlines, etc., are the creations of people. In advising me to "take people, not courses" my student friend was suggesting that I contact the original sources of understanding. Perhaps it is because so many students take courses instead of people that the universities have become a place where one acquires knowledge—not wisdom.

Long before Bandura's excellent studies on modeling were published (1965), I found myself trying to apply his principle as a modality for self growth. At the beginning of each class, a line was drawn down the middle of the first page in my notebook with a plus on the right-hand side and a minus on the left. I would then write down for each instructor specifically those traits and characteristics that I wanted to copy and those I would hope to eliminate. Could I but have the sincere earnestness in classroom attitude exemplified by Dr. A? Would I ever be able to acquire the smooth and graceful use of language that characterized the lectures of Dr. B? And was it possible to avoid the dull, monotonous voice in which Professor C always made his presentations?

During my early interest in psychoanalysis, training in that discipline was not open to psychologists; but one could find models and, by resonating with their writings, introject some of their wisdom and through identification incorporate these into identofacts of self growth. I acquired a rather complete set of the books by Wilhelm Stekel (1939a, 1939b, 1940, 1943a, 1943b, 1943c, 1949). This analyst was not always regarded highly by Freud (See McGuire, 1974), perhaps because he was more interested in clinical work than theoretical positions, perhaps because he tended to ignore ego functions in his pursuit of the id, or perhaps because he showed considerable jealousy of Freud and finally parted from him. However, even my more conservative analytic friends conceded that Stekel was considered very sensitive as an interpreter of dreams.

In describing many cases he had analyzed, Stekel would present the case history background and then give one dream after another. Following each dream he would offer his "intuitive" interpretation of its meaning. In the hopes of acquiring some of his sensitivity, I would read each case and the dream. Then closing the book I would write down my efforts at interpreting the dream and compare it with his. After a period of time I found that I would respond in a similar way to the dream elements, and my written interpretation would be very much like his. Whether this dream approach was valid or not, I was being trained to respond to the same cues in a similar manner. This learning procedure obviously involved both modeling and operant conditioning.

At the present time, there is a great surge of interest in programmed learning. Manuals are devised that offer students an opportunity to model their behavior and to secure feedback in the form of checking their responses immediately afterward. When it is correct, the right responses receive the positive reinforcements of being validated. Hence, they learn and increase the correctness of their behavior.

Since the ability to resonate with others appears to be such a worthwhile trait in anyone, and is especially necessary in the psychotherapist, could we use these behavioral principles of modeling and positive reinforcement to develop resonance in budding psychologists and psychiatrists?

During the early stages in developing a scoring system (as described in Chapter 19), the student members of our research group were impressed with the benefits they derived as therapists from the study and scoring of individual responses, both from protocols of others and from their own treatment cases. Although they had undertaken this project for research purposes, they noted that their own ability to resonate in the clinical situation seemed to improve as they gave careful attention to recorded patient-therapist response units.

Accordingly, we next decided to see if resonance is a trainable trait. We also wanted to determine whether psychology students "naturally" possess it, and if so, do they have this ability to a higher degree than students from other scholarly disciplines.

Study 1

From our file of recorded treatment sessions*, five were selected representing therapists of very different theoretical persuasions as follows:

Tape No. 1. "Loretta" by Albert Ellis (rational-emotive therapy)
Tape No. 2. "The case of Laura" by John G. Watkins (hypnoanalytic therapy)
Tape No. 3. "The case of Harry" by John Cameron (eclectic-insight therapy)
Tape No. 4. "An interview with P. S." by Carl Rogers (client-centered therapy)
Tape No. 5. "Psychoanalytic therapy" by Franz Alexander

It will be recalled that the original research team (Chapters 18 and 19) that developed the scoring system consisted of the instructor and four graduate students. Over many weeks these five had been rating numerous protocols, comparing responses, and reaching ever closer agreement on their independent scorings of various sessions. Since their abilities to score had evolved gradually and included the establishing of the defined criteria in

*Tapes 1, 2, 3, and 4 are published by the American Academy of Psychotherapists Tape Library, 1040 Woodcock Road, Orlando, Florida, 32803. Tape No. 5 is published as part of a series entitled *Six modern therapies*, Glenview, Illinois: Scott-Foresman, (Stewart B. Shapiro, Editor, Western Psychological Center).

the scoring system, there was no base line with which their present reliability could be compared. However, there was usually overwhelming agreement on the score to be assigned to each response, and little difficulty arose over establishing a "correct" set of ratings for each session as, for example, in the case of Laura (See Chapter 21). Rarely was there more than one member of the group who did not agree with the others as to the correct score for any response.

We decided to compare the ratings of a "naïve" group of scorers on the protocol with the consensus of the experienced group to see how much the experienced group might have progressed in reliability and validity. The naïve group consisted of seven other graduate students in psychology who had received no specific training in distinguishing between resonance and objectivity, and had little (if any) familiarity with therapeutic self theory at that time.

This naïve group was asked to read through the Scoring System (as published in Chapter 19). They then scored the tape of a treatment session entitled "Loretta," Albert Ellis as the therapist, listening to it while reading the transcript of the session. No attempt was made in this study to ask the naïve group to distinguish between affective and cognitive resonance. Accordingly, the directions they read included a definition of resonance and examples of R responses. The approved (correct) scoring of this session, as based on agreement of the research team, showed the first one hundred responses of this session to be composed as follows:

R	16
O	76
F	8
	100

The comparison of the scoring by this naïve group of raters (who had only read the scoring instructions once) with the correct scoring as agreed upon by our experienced team was most discouraging—at least as to the prospect of judges being effective without extended training. The percentages of agreement by our naïve raters with the correct scoring was as follows:

Rater No.	*% Correct*
1.	28
2.	58
3.	49
4.	53
5.	52
6.	57
7.	42
Average	48.4

In other words, our best naïve judge agreed with the correct scores only 58 per cent of the time, and our worst, 28 per cent. Since there were 100 possible scores and three possible ways of rating (R, O, and F), our poorest judge did less well than chance. Obviously, simply reading through the scoring instructions, even by graduate students in psychology, ill prepares one to be an effective judge of resonance. This was highly unsatisfactory. Accordingly, we undertook further studies to see whether subjects could be trained to be reliable and valid judges of resonance.

Study 2

A second group of naïve judges was chosen randomly from a number of volunteers in the introductory psychology class. They were undergraduate students whose ages and major fields were as follows.

Student	*Age*	*Major Field*
T. A.	25	Sociology
B. F.	22	Accounting
J. L.	20	Geography
J. M.	20	Art
W. P.	20	Speech
G. T.	21	Physical Education

The exclusion of psychology students from this group was deliberate. As in Study 1, the subjects were asked to read through the scoring instructions. They then listened to each of the five tapes and scored accordingly. It should be noted that in both studies the judges were presented with a much more difficult scoring task in that they listened to each tape (100 therapist responses each) without any break. Each unit had to be scored immediately after hearing it. The correct scoring keys, on the other hand, had been arrived at by the consensus of a group of "experts," who were given as much time as necessary to listen to, read, and consider every response.

The group scored one tape each day for five days in succession as follows:

Monday	Tape No. 5	Alexander
Tuesday	Tape No. 2	Watkins
Wednesday	Tape No. 4	Rogers
Thursday	Tape No. 1	Ellis
Friday	Tape No. 3	Cameron

No feedback was given to the subjects as to their successes or failures.

The results in this second study were very similar to those in the first. The naïve group of undergraduate students who served as raters did as well as the psychology graduate students, in fact slightly better. The percentage of correct scores of this second group of naïve raters ranged as follows:

Tape 1"Loretta", Albert Ellis, therapist
Mean 42.8 per cent
Range 26-50 per cent

Tape 2 "The case of Laura," John G. Watkins, therapist
Mean 50.2 per cent
Range 26-49 per cent

Tape 3"The case of Harry," John Cameron, therapist
Mean 48.4 per cent
Range 28-54 per cent

Tape 4"An interview with P. S.," Carl Rogers, therapist
Mean 73 per cent
Range 25-87 per cent

Tape 5"Psychoanalytic therapy," Franz Alexander, therapist
Mean 55.6 per cent
Range 26-59 per cent

Results in four of these cases are similar. Only the Rogers tape seemed to be rated much more accurately. The question of why this was so is an intriguing one. Is the client-centered approach easier to score? Is it due to the fact that there were more resonant responses in this session? The experience of the original research team had been to the effect that resonant responses are more difficult, not easier, to score than objective or facilitative ones.

It is interesting to note the actual proportion of R, O, and F responses for each of these therapists as rated by the original group of experienced judges (and accordingly considered as the correct responses). In Table 5. these are set forth as follows:[1]

Table 5

Therapist	*1. Ellis*	*2. Watkins*	*3. Cameron*	*4. Rogers*	*5. Alexander*
R	16	19	18	56	43
O	76	44	55	11	23
F	8	37	26	33	8
			1 (N)		
Total:	100	100	100	100	100

The inference that the much higher validity of scoring for the Rogers tape was due to the high frequency of resonant responses by this therapist was not confirmed in the Alexander tape, which also had a much higher frequency of such responses than the other three. The difficulty in scoring the Alexander tape, however, may have been related to the fact that the therapist spoke in a rather pronounced German accent that was not always easy to understand.

There was one distinguishing characteristic that separated the Rogers session from all the others. This lay in the nature of the communications. The Rogers hour was characterized by rather long passages of client communication followed by brief reflections of feeling from the therapist. By far the greatest amount of time was used in client verbalizations. The other four therapists tended to react more often, sometimes verbalizing more than the client. A sentence or two of client talk would be followed immediately by a therapist reaction, which may well have been almost as long. Accordingly, the Rogers tape of 100 responses required a much longer period of listening than 100 responses from the other therapists. This meant that the rater had to make his judgments more rapidly during the Ellis, Watkins, Cameron, and Alexander hours. Each Rogers response was followed by a rather lengthy next communication from the client, which enabled the judge to take more time in recording his rating. It would appear that it requires a few moments of thought to render a correct judgment. The necessity of making rapid differentiations apparently operates to lower very significantly the validity of such judgments. This position was strengthened by the fact that several of the raters complained about the rapidity with which they were forced to make ratings on the Ellis, Watkins, Cameron, and Alexander tapes.

A third study was now undertaken involving a more controlled experimental design to see if naïve judges could be taught to use the Scoring System effectively.

Study 3

LEARNING TO SCORE RESONANCE by John G. Watkins and Karen Huth Eiblmayr

Thirty volunteers were secured from introductory psychology classes and divided randomly into five groups of six subjects each. Each group scored R, O, and F on 100 patient-therapist response units from a session by each of five different therapists. The therapists and cases* were as follows:

No. 1. Watkins, The case of Laura.
No. 2. Alexander, Psychoanalytic therapy.
No. 3. Ellis, The case of John Jones.
No. 4. Rogers, An interview with P. S.
No. 5. Greenwald, The case of Marnie.

As in the previous studies a correct scoring for each protocol was first secured by consensus of the inves-

*Numbers 3 and 5 were published by the American Academy of Psychotherapists Tape Library. The others published as previously noted.

tigators. This involved long and careful consideration of each response and final agreement by those who were thoroughly experienced in using the scoring system. This correctly scored protocol then constituted the criterion with which the subjects' ratings were compared. A subject's correctness score then represented the percentage of ratings he made that were the same as those on the criterion.

The purpose of this study was to determine whether the ability of a subject to score correctly would significantly improve over a series of five protocols with continual reexplanation of the scoring system, instruction in its use, and comparison of his responses with the criterion.

Each scoring session required about an hour, and two were held each week for each group. Hence, the entire training experience required two and a half weeks for each group to complete consideration of the five therapy sessions. Since the therapy sessions being scored differed in difficulty from one another it was necessary to rotate the order of presentation in order to rule out this factor. Accordingly, Group I scored protocols in the following order: Watkins, Alexander, Ellis, Rogers, and Greenwald. Group II scored Alexander, Ellis, Rogers, Greenwald, and Watkins in that order. Group III rated Ellis, Rogers, Greenwald, Watkins, and Alexander in order, etc. This meant that each session was rated first by one group of six judges, second by one group, third by one group, fourth by one group, and last by one group. The primary hypothesis, then, was that there would be a significant improvement in scoring within each group between the first and last sessions as a result of the training and experience acquired during the evaluation of the five sessions. In other words, we hypothesized that the ability to recognize and score resonance could be learned.

Procedure

At the beginning of each session with each group the experimenter (K. H. E.) read the scoring system and answered all questions by members of the group. Explanations of the various scores and examples were given. Following this, the first tape was played, which consisted of 100 patient-therapist response units. The group of judges listened to the recording and simultaneously followed the session by reading the protocol. They recorded their scores on the protocol after each patient-therapist response unit.

They then exchanged papers while the experimenter read off the correct scoring. Wrong answers were circled, and the correct score written beside them. The corrected protocols were then returned to their original raters and all questions answered. This permitted each judge to ask for clarification on any response that he had incorrectly scored and permitted the experimenter to reexplain the rationale behind the correct scoring of that item. Papers were not graded, e.g., the number of correct or incorrect scores were not totaled as it was not desired that judges make comparisons with each other. The fact that we were primarily interested in the improved scoring of each rater in relation to his own first judgments was constantly emphasized. Thus, judges were continually informed that they were competing with themselves in improving their rating skill, not with each other.

This procedure—reading of the scoring system, questions on scoring criteria, scoring, exchanging papers and correcting, return of scored protocols to the original raters, and explanation of the rationales for the correct scoring of items mistakenly judged—was followed for each group at each of the five scoring sessions.

Findings

The data were analyzed by a one-way analysis of variance with repeated measures.* The basic hypothesis was strongly supported. In other words the ability to score resonance according to this rating scale is a teachable trait and can be significantly improved in naïve judges by explanation, repetition, and comparison of results with a correct protocol.

It is interesting to note that this improvement did not follow a straight line; it developed stepwise almost as if each session in which an advance had been made was followed by a required consolidation of that progress in the next session. There was no significant effect for the

*Statistical Note:
Factor A (order of tapes)

1st.	*2nd.*	*3rd.*	*4th.*	*5th.*
70.3667	68.9667	64.0667	70.1667	70.8000

Sum of squares 921.827 (No significance)
Factor J (Particular session)

1st.	*2nd.*	*3rd.*	*4th.*	*5th.*
64.7000	67.8333	67.8000	72.0000	72.0333

Difference between 1st. and 5th. learning session significant at .00341 level. Significant gains made stepwise during alternate sessions, hence, between 1st. and 2nd. sessions and between 3rd. and 4th. sessions.
Sources of Variance

	Sum of squares	*Mean square*	*DF*	*Error DF*	*F ratio*	*Probability*
A	921.8227	230.457	4	25	0.697	.60345
J	1182.36	295.590	4	100	4.281	.00341†
AJ	2064.6	1287.79	16	100	18.652	.00000†

†Significant

different orders taken as a whole. However, certain sequences paid off at a much better rate. Thus, further studies might find that learning would be maximally facilitated when the protocols of certain therapists were scored in practice before those of others.

Another study (Lennon, 1974) investigated the relationship between Rogers's "accurate empathy" and our concept of "resonance" and attempted to increase empathy in counselors. The initial session tapes of two groups of counselors were rated on the Truax Accurate Empathy Scale (Truax, 1961) by five experienced and trained judges. The groups consisted of 15 counselors each. After the initial rating of their sessions, both groups were given training in transactional analysis. However, the experimental group received also a course in Counselor Effectiveness Training (Gordon, 1970). Tapes of later sessions rated by the judges showed that all counselors had significantly increased their empathy, but that there was no differential increase between the experimental group that had received the CET training and the comparison group that had not.

The same tapes were also rated for both cognitive resonance and affective resonance according to the Therapeutic Self Scoring System. There were significant correlations between the scores for resonance and the accurate empathy scores. There were also increases in resonance after the training, the greatest being in affective resonance.

The results from this study tend to confirm what has already been hypothesized; namely, that accurate empathy and resonance are closely related, even though there are theoretical differences. It should be noted that in the five tapes rated in our studies reported here, the sessions recorded by Dr. Rogers showed the highest R component (56 per cent R consisting of 29 per cent A and 27 per cent C).

While only a start has been made, it would appear that the concept of therapeutic self is capable of objective study. Further work might investigate its effect on outcome of therapy, its evaluation in prospective therapists, and its significance in the selection and training of psychologists and psychiatrists.

Conclusions

1. A clinician's therapeutic self is hypothesized to operate maximally when there is a balance between objectivity and resonance.
2. A rating scale is proposed for the evaluation of objectivity and resonance in therapists' responses.
3. The scale can be scored reliably, and independent judges experienced in its use can arrive at comparable evaluations.
4. The ability to score resonance is a teachable trait, and naïve judges can be trained to use the scale.
5. The scoring of therapy protocols on the factors of objectivity and resonance can constitute a significant learning experience for the student therapist in evaluating both his own treatment efforts and those of others.

FOOTNOTE

1. No conclusions should be drawn from this table that the relative frequency of R, O, and F responses are characteristic of these therapists, since only the first 100 patient-therapist units within one session for each was scored.

Part VII

CLINICAL STUDIES

Science studies its data by two different approaches, nomothetic and idiographic. In Part VI the first was employed. It involved evaluating the responses of a number of judges on various single factors to discover trends or principles. In Chapters 21, 22, and 23 we use the second approach. We are interested here in the way a number of variables interact within a single individual. Much of what we know about psychopathology, psychodynamics, and psychotherapy, including psychoanalysis, has been discovered in the treatment office by this method through intensive scrutiny of the reactions between doctor and patient.

Chapter 21 illustrates a hypnoanalytic approach employing resonance. It is scored according to the standards presented in Chapter 19 to demonstrate how objective ratings can tell a great deal about just what is happening within a therapeutic hour. Chapter 22 ("Ego-state therapy," by Helen H. Watkins) presents some of the unusual results possible as one contacts and works with a number of such states. It illustrates the wide variety of common elements, both physical and psychological, about which states can be organized. In Chapter 23, a rather dramatic therapeutic battle over a harmful introject ensues. The case was treated by cotherapists assuming the two parental roles. The interactions involve ego state manipulation, abreactions, resonance, and analysis of transference in an extremely disturbed, schizoid individual who was both suicidally and homicidally inclined. In these chapters the concepts of resonance, objectivity, ego states, libido and mortido, introjects, and identofacts emerge from theory and reveal themselves as facets of real living, struggling human beings.

Chapter 21

The Case of Laura

This young woman, Laura[1], had been suffering from recurring headaches and a schizoidlike detachment, which came over her at times. It was similar to estrangement but not so severe as the kind often found in the borderline psychotic. An excerpt from one of the more significant hypoanalytic treatment hours is reproduced verbatim here.

On the left hand side of the page are presented the communications between therapist and client. On the right side are associations and reactions of the therapist, which he experienced at the time of the session. Included also are some after-interpretations concerning his alternations from objectivity to resonance, and the changing ego states within the patient.

At the end of each response by W (the therapist) there is a letter in parenthesis, (A), (C), (O), (I), or (N). These represent, respectively, "affective resonance," "cognitive resonance," "objective," "facilitative," "irrelevant," and "nonscorable" responses. In Chapter 19, this rating system was described in detail together with the research on which it was based.

THE CASE OF LAURA[2]

	The Therapeutic Hour	Therapist Associations and Reactions
1. L:	You've been gone all day. I've been trying to call you to tell you that I had to work a second shift.	1. She's scolding me. "You should be available at any time I call. Why are you neglecting your responsibilities?"
W:	Oh, well, that's all right. Well now . . . What's been happening to you? (O)	Therapist, taken a bit aback, makes weak reassurances then decides to demonstrate concern for patient by question.
2. L:	Oh, I ended up with a good headache and got rid of it yesterday. It was a real nice one. Oh, you would have liked it.	2. Look what a dilly of a symptom I had, Daddy. And I conquered it without your help, too.
W:	Um-hum . . .What happened? (F)	
3. L:	It started, oh, I don't know, sometime . . . sometime Monday morning. I just got over it last night sometime.	
W:	Um-hum. (F)	
4. L:	It went up one (?) and that was it. It was a hard one. I didn't like it.	4. When in doubt, be nondirective.
W:	That's the worse you've had for some time. (A_2)	
5. L:	Um-hum . . . it was pretty bad.	5. Maybe we can find out dynamic reasons for the symptom by carefully studying the time and conditions of its precipitation.
W:	What were you doing; What . . . what can you remember about what you were doing or before the headache? (O)	

[2] Therapist: John G. Watkins

6. L: I was getting up getting ready to go to work.

W: I see. (F)

7. L: That was it.

W: How's the work been going? (O)

> 7. Maybe the headache's related to "work." Let's talk more about work.

8. L: Well, the hours are long and it's hard, but other than that it's fine.

> 8. Perhaps she throws a headache to avoid the "work"?

W: Gets tiresome? (A_1)

9. L: Yeah, I'm just thankful I like people. They're the only thing that keeps me going down there at times.

> 9. Does she really "like people?"

Responses 10 to 32 are concerned only with routine discussion about certain other people who were not significantly involved in Laura's problem. We resume the hour with response 32 W.

32. W: Are you happy or not happy? (O)

> 32. Let's see if she likes this symptom or not.

33. L: I can't tell.

W: I see. (F)

34. L: Just . . . um . . . I can't, just I can't decide . . . I don't know if I'm too decided or what.

> 34. She won't give a clear answer. Let's try again.

W: Do you find life, uh, difficult or unbearable or miserable or unhappy? (O)

35. L: No . . .

W: Maybe you don't have a problem. (O)

> 35. This is a forcing play. It's forcing her to be more specific and creating some anxiety.

36. L: Well, if you go . . . I don't know, when . . . use this for example, it's the only one I can think of right now. When you have about . . . three drinks of uh fair potency.

W: Yes? (F)

37. L: Not enough to make you . . . uh . . . happy or to intoxicate you actually, just enough to give you a feeling that . . . what you are seeing through your eyes for instance, your, your mind is somewhere else. It's out behind you just kind of watching in.	37. Now she's indicating a dissociative defense and perhaps an existential problem.
W: Yes? (F)	
38. L: You're, you're just observing . . . what's going on. That . . . uh . . . you go through the motions of something . . . but you're adopting it.	38. This reminds me of the multiple personality case of three years ago. Could it be . . .?
W: You say when you have a few drinks, then you . . . (O)	
39. L: This is the only way I can explain the feeling . . . that you would understand it.	
W: Yeah? (F)	
40. L: That . . . you get to a point where you almost feel that your body is just a puppet. You're going through motions you don't really know if your mind is even here . . . or if it's this mind that you were thinking of somewhere else.	40. The deegotizing defense is getting clearer.
W: I see. (F,C_1)	
41. L: That . . . that you're just kind of split . . . and many, many times I'll feel this. I'll feel that I'm going . . . through the motions, and I'm doing them properly, but I don't know where my mind is, if it's, if it's watching or if I'm just seeing it through my eyes like a movie screen.	41. Uh-uh. Multiple . . . ? Therapist interest in the hour is now picking up. However, he's still relating to the patient as an interesting object—not with resonance yet. But he's trying hard to understand her.
W: Um-hum. You mean it doesn't feel like in *you* that it's behaving in your body and	

moving about and looking and so on? (A_2)

42. L: Uh-huh. I don't feel like I'm —I'm part of myself.

W: You're not a participant in the life. You're sort of observing while your body is going through the living. (C_2)

43. L: Um-hum.

W: Is this a . . . a bad feeling, an unhappy feeling, a bad state, or how do you feel? (O)

43. Is this dissociative defense working? Is it self rewarding?

44. L: Oh, it isn't a . . . a bad feeling. It's just kind of a strange feeling.

W: Um-hum. (F)

45. L: And I can feel it right now to an extent.

W: You can? (F)

45. Perhaps I'm threatening her right now by this probing, and she's reacting with the deegotizing defense—estrangement, e.g., "I'm feeling it right now."

46. L: Um-hum.

W: Now, but you say you . . . that there are times when you do feel part of yourself? (O)

47. L: Um-hum.

W: What kind of times are those? What are they like? (O)

47. Let's get more information about the ways she uses this defense.

48. L: Oh, I really . . . I can't say when . . . all of a sudden I just split, and then I'm back together again. . .

W: Can you think of some recent times in which you've had a feeling of full participation in your actions? (O)

48. And when can she accept a full egotizing of herself?

49. L: . . . I did this morning when I woke up.

49. When rested? (Ego cathexis is restored by sleep. Schizoid

feelings more likely to appear when tired.)

W: Yes? (F)

50. L: When I went to work.

W: Yes? (F)

51. L: I don't know, I guess . . . somewhere during the morning or afternoon I did the split.

51. Use her word "split" in refring to it.

W: Somewhere during the morning or the afternoon you started this split sort of thing, you say? (F)

52. L: Um-hum, and when I was walking across the field over to here, I had no feeling . . .

W: Yes? (F)

53. L: Of this. So I must . . . have gone back together again. I . . . I can feel the split now.

W: You can feel the split now? (F)

54. L: Um-hum.

W: Strongly split now? (O)

55. L: Not really. I . . . I really can't . . . give it any strength or any degree.

55. Trying to resonate to her *feel* of the experience.

W: Would you say that acts in a sense that . . . uh . . . you kind of feel like it isn't you now that's talking to me? Is that how you mean it? (A_2)

56. L: Um-hum, and yet I am. Somewhere along the line something's . . . far away.

56. Is this experience validly described by the point that we can differentiate between "it" and "you" in discussing it with her without distorting the real situation? If the split is there, let's recognize it out, let's not suggest or create an artifact.

W: This something that's far away, is it . . . uh . . . can you tell where it is? What is it thinking? In what way is it different than you that's talking to me? (O)

57. L: It . . . it's just a . . . a feeling. I can feel it especially with

my eyes . . . that . . . somehow what's . . . what's receiving what my eyes are seeing.

W: Yes? (F)

58. L: It's somewhere else. That it's a greater distance than right behind them.

58. Therapist beginning to resonate more.

W: A sort of feeling of detachment from the present situation. (A_2)

59. L: Um-hum. It'll be . . . well, just the same as when you go to a movie.

W: Um-hum. (F)

60. L: And you're watching everything through the camera's eye. It's seeing it through its eye directly, but then again you're . . .you're seeing it quite a ways away from it.

60. Clear-cut subject versus object. "I" observe "me" (Federn says the ego is the only thing that can be both subject and object. One ego state "senses" another.)

W: I see. (F)

61. L: Especially in a . . . a very good movie where you feel that you're a part of the situation yet you know you're watching it.

W: Is it more when you're with people or when you're away from people that you feel this way? (O)

62. L: Both.

W: Does it make any difference . . . what people you're with? (O)

63. L: Um . . . no.

63. She indicates this is a self problem, not directly and and immediately related to the interpersonal relationship present. Does husband cause this defense?

W: How do you feel when you're with your husband? Do you feel you're a part of the situation, or away from it? (O)

64. L: Sometimes one and sometimes the other.

64. Guess not.

W: I see. Then you don't know when one starts and the other one . . . (C_2)

65. L: No.

W: Nor why. (C_2)

66. L: It's just as though . . . all of a sudden I become aware of it. It might be it's going on, I might have split an hour ago. All of a sudden I'll just . . . I'll realize it.

66. Executive ego state suddenly alerted to deegotization of adjacent state.

W: Yeah . . . how do you feel when you realize it? Does it bother you? (O)

67. L: Very, very strange. I don't know, I feel very detached. I feel like I . . . I'm, I'm a puppet.

67. Hmmm. "puppet". She doesn't use this term as a paranoid would. I don't feel a sense of alarm.

W: And what . . . is pulling the strings? (O)

Should I have said "and who" instead of "and what"?

68. L: My mind . . . but . . . I don't know where this . . . this mind . . . this . . . thinking part of the mind is . . .

W: Um-hum (F)

69. L: Whatever is controlling the strings. . . . .

69. I think we've got enough of a picture of the experience now. Let's try some hypnosis to explore etiology deeper.

W: Would you like to relax a little and explore this . . . further perhaps? (O)

70. L: I'll try.

W: All right . . . make yourself comfortable. (O)

Response 71 W is a hypnotic induction followed by deepening (scored 0). It required about ten minutes. We resume the hour with response 72 W.

72. W: I want to see if you can do something. I want you to withdraw yourself from your

72. Let's hypnotically create her symptom by suggesting a deegotization of the body.

body and your actions and your thoughts such . . . that you will be, as you have described it, the kind of situation when you are . . . not part of yourself . . . And when you have been able to do that, so that you are not at all a part of yourself, *the hand* will come up in the air to indicate that this has happened.	
Take all of yourself away from yourself, so that it is as if you weren't in contact with your	And test to see when we've succeeded.
self . . . And when that has happened, *the hand* will lift up into the air to indicate that this situation has happened clearly and distinctly . . . I shan't say anything for . . . a little bit . . . while you achieve that state . . . Go ahead. Achieve that state . . . Remove yourself . . . from yourself . . . (Silence)	We structure the situation so that the patient perceives the hypnotic state as an achievement, not as something she has been forced to do.
W: Tell me what things are like now, Laura. Describe how you experience yourself in the world right now. (O)	Create the dissociated state and encourage her to describe it while she is experiencing it.
73. L: Like . . . uh . . . far away from this earth? . . .	
W: Yes. (F)	
74. L: And I'm just an observer.	
W: Yes . . . (F)	
75. L: But my . . . my mind . . . controls it from a distance of watching.	75. The ego at a distance?
W: Um-hum. But not participa-ing? (C_2)	
76. L: No.	76. Let's test the hypnosis behaviorally. If she responds we'll know she has reached a somnambulistic stage. We temporarily split "mental
W: Laura, could you let your mind stay where it is right now, in the chair, observing,	

but not participating, while your body at a distance got up, walked over to the window and looked out the window a moment and then came back and sat down? (O)

ego" state from "body ego."

77. L: Um-hum.

77. We don't need to deepen more. She's ready to work in the hypnotic state now.

W: Let that happen.

(It happens. She goes to window, returns, and sits down.)

W: What was your experience? (O)

78. L: That thing up?

78. "That thing", object—not part of self.

W: That thing up. How did it make you feel? Did you like it or not like it? . . . (O)

79. L: I don't know.

W: Does that part of you . . . that's your mind, is yourself, *off*? Can it tell me anything about that, Laura? . . . that might have some bearing upon the situation? . . . (O)

80. L: It's . . . part of something (indistinct) that's watching the puppet.

W: Yes. (F)

81. L: Who enjoys . . . confusing her? (F)

W: Enjoys confusing her? (F)

81. Tell us more. One state de-egotized) referred to as "it." Another state also deegotized referred to as "her." Neither called "I" or "me," hence "self" removed from both. Executive ego state passive observer of both.

82. L: Um-hum.

W: Why? (O)

83. L: Because it's a reason . . . it's a reason to . . . to watch her without being a part of her.

W: Yes. (F)

84. L: It's very enjoyable.

W: It's very enjoyable. Why is it enjoyable?

84. The pleasure reinforcement of this defense becomes more clear. She enjoys dissociating. It furnishes relief from anxiety.

85. L: Because it's in control of . . . at a distance.

W: How do you mean, in control at a distance? (O)

86. L: It controls, but it's not involved.

W: It doesn't have to take the responsibility then for her actions? (C_1)

86. Reduction in "cognitive dissonance."

87. L: Um-hum.

W: At least not as far as the world is concerned, hum? (C_2)

88. L: Um-hum. At least not as far as it's concerned.

W: I see. And so it's enjoyable then? (A_2)

89. L: Um-hum.

W: When Laura has a headache, who is having a headache . . . Is *it* having a headache or are *you* having a headache? I mean it, the puppet, or you? (O)

89. Case reports of multiple personalities often report that when "it," e.g. another personality, is trying to become manifest, the struggle to to overcome and replace the present ego state is perceived as a headache, sometimes described as a migraine headache.

90. L: Both

W: Both. Is there a time where . . . one is having a headache and the other isn't? (O)

90. Such a differentiation is not clear in this case.

91. L: Not very often.

W: Not very often . . . the one that's off in the background, does that have a name any different from Laura? (O)

92. L: No.

W: No . . . both the puppet is called Laura then, and the part that is back there controlling? (C_1)

92. Hypothesis not validated. Doesn't look like this is a real case of multiple personality.

93. L: Um-hum.

W: Is the puppet always completely under the control of that Laura or does it sometimes . . . do things by itself when it is not under the control? (O)

94. L: It's always under control.

94. Hm. "I can turn it on or off as I wish."

W: It's always under control . . . (C_1)

95. L: Sometimes part of the puppet, other times just the controlled puppet.

W: How do you mean? (F)

95. Just how much is this symptom under conscious control or not? She is *now* in a hypnotic state, not a conscious state. So her report on her "control" cannot be taken as an indication of fully "conscious" control.

96. L: Sometimes . . . it's within the puppet. Other times it isn't.

W: Is it outside now? (O, C_1)

97. L: Um-hum.

97. Let's try to achieve an integration by hypnotic suggestion. Can the "it" object be egotized?

W: Now, Laura, can you pull yourself together, and the and the puppet, and the part that's back, so that they're one and the same? And its feelings are your feelings, its thoughts are your thoughts. Its actions are your actions. They are together, very much together. And when . . . you have achieved that, then you

"*you* lift *your* hand." We want the hand egotized now, not dissociated, hence "your" hand, not "*the* hand."

lift your hand up to indicate . . . that has been achieved. (O)

98. L: I can't.

W: You can't? (F)

98. Too much resistance. Deegotizaion defense necessary. Anybody who thinks the patient becomes an automaton under hypnosis (relinquishes ego functioning) and can be pushed around by the hypnotist as he wishes is wrong. There are limits. Defenses may be softened by hypnosis; they are not eliminated.

99. L: It doesn't want to.

W: *It* doesn't want to? (F)

100. L: No.

W: That which is back . . . doesn't want to, or the puppet doesn't want to? (O)

101. L: It.

W: It? (F)

102. L: It, the puppet.

W: Why doesn't it want to? (O)

103. L: It don't. Just doesn't. It's not ready to.

103. Let's try a projective hypnoanalytic technique.

W: Could you see . . . a kind of a large movie screen as if you were sitting in a theater? Could you bring that up so that you could see that? (O)

104. L: Um-hum.

W: What's it look like? (O)

105. L: Like anything I see through the eyes.

105. Defensive resistance manifests itself even when using a projective technique, aimed at bypassing it.

W: Now, maybe if you watch

that movie screen, a picture will start on it. And maybe that will have something to do with *why it* doesn't want to join the puppet. To be at one with the puppet. Maybe something will appear on that screen. Watch it, and tell me what you see on the screen. (O)

	Transcript	Commentary
106. L:	There's nothing.	106. Keep on though. Maybe we'll work through this resistance and get at significant, underlying material yet.
W:	The lights in the theatre are slowly dimming now. Can you see them get more dim? (O)	
107. L:	Yes.	
W:	Now there's a bright light that appears on the screen. And it's going to some kind of a picture. A movie is starting. Just tell me whatever you see. What's happening on the screen? . . . (O)	
108. L:	There's a little girl.	108. We're getting somewhere.
W:	A little girl. What's she doing? Where is she? (O)	And you know who the little girl is.
109. L:	Sleeping, Big house. Back yard.	109. Hypnosis helps in reducing such defenses as criticality. It encourages the emergence of significant memories and fantasies. (When the ego's away, the fantasies play.)
W:	Big house. Back yard. (F)	
110. L:	She's playing with herself.	
W:	She's playing with herself? (F, C_1)	
111. L:	There's no one else around, but her.	111. Therapeutic technique here is to encourage continued associations simply by repeating patient's responses. This is not true resonance. As yet the therapist is not actually "experiencing" them.
W:	There's no one else around but her? (F, C1)	

112. L: And yet she has many, many friends there.

W: And yet she has many, many friends there. How do you mean? (F, O)

113. L: You can't see them.

W: You can't see them? (O)

114. L: No, they're . . . imaginary friends.

W: They're imaginary friends, yes? (C_1)

115. L: She must be so lonely. She must have other friends . . . make them up.

Gradually these repeating responses begin to be resonant. The purely facilitative element in them lessens and the resonant element increases.

W: She must be so lonely . . . (C_1, F)

116. L: That she makes up her friends.

W: That she makes up her friends? (C_1, F)

117. L: Yeah.

W: Is she a very lonely little girl? (A_2)

117. Therapist beginning to resonate.

118. L: Yes (whispered).

W: How does she feel? (A_1, O)

119. L: Oh.

W: Could you let yourself feel like she feels? (O)

119. Let's quit playing roles now and *be* your role. Let *you* no longer be a *role* but *be you*. Egotize "her" feelings.

120. L: I do.

120. She can.

W: You do . . . No friends. (A_1)

121. L: She's climbing up . . . There's a fountain in the corner . . .

W: Yes. (F)

122. L: She's climbing up it to the wall, a great big wall in the

122. She's moving in toward an existence in this role, but

yard. There's some children playing on the other side.

the third person is safest to use. Therapist goes along with it.

W: Yeah. (F)

123. L: She wants to go and play with them.

W: She wants to go and play with them. (C_1, F)

124. L: But she can't.

W: Why not? (O)

124. Is this situation a real memory? A screen memory? A fantasy? If it's *psychologically* real, her recalled perception, then it's real as related to her problem. We'll treat it as valid.

125. L: Her mother won't let her.

W: Why won't her mother let her? . . . (O)

126. L: I don't know. (tears)

W: She is so unhappy . . . she wants to cry. (A_2)

126. Tears are a gift—to both patient and therapist. They tend to validate the experience. Let's encourage them.

127. L: She is . . .

W: She is crying. (A_1)

127. Release.

128. L: Imaginary friends are comforting her.

W: Imaginary friends are comforting her. (A_1)

128. A little girl's dissociation and defense.

129. L: Saying that when she gets over it she'll make her own friends.

W: Says that when she gets over she'll have grown friends? (C_4)

129. So many unhappy little people console themselves with imaginary friends.

Therapist didn't hear clearly.

130. L: She'll make her *own*.

W: She'll make her own friends. (C_1)

130. My mistake.

131. L: She's taking a trip now.

W: Yes, she's taking a trip now. (C_1)

131. The memory-fantasy continues.

132. L: They must be moving.

W: They must be moving. (C_1, F)

132. Keep the flow coming as nondirectively as possible, using the stimulus reaction of simple, identical repetition.

133. L: Yes, they're arriving in a different town.

W: They're arriving in a different town. (C_1, F)

134. L: She hopes she can make friends here.

W: She hopes she can make friends here. (C_1, F)

135. L: She's going to school.

W: She's going to school. (C_1, F)

136. L: She has no friends.

W: She has no friends. She's just as lonely as ever. (A_3, F)

137. L: Um, they live in an apartment house.

W: They live in an apartment house. (C_1, F)

138. L: She can't have friends over because they're too noisy.

W: She can't have friends over because they're too noisy. (C_1, F)

139. L: She can't go to others' houses.

W: She can't go to others' houses. (C_1, F)

140. L: 'Cause her mother doesn't want her to play indoors.

W: Her mother doesn't want her

136. I, your therapist, must now resonate, identify, be as you. I echo verbatim because I must strive to reproduce the identity of you within my own self. For the moment there is only one of us and that one is lonely, can't play with the other children, can't have friends. That one (we) experiences in a joint co-feeling all that it must be like to exist in this lonely child world as you are describing it. It is a painful world, which hurts us. And if I can but be with you within it, discarding objectivity, a separate existence, and the role of observer then perhaps I can transmit to you the feeling of a joint strength as you share your world with me and I share my ego strength with you and we are both enriched thereby. There will come a time later when I must

to play indoors . . . doesn't . . . ? It hurts too badly for her to stay in herself and try to meet . . . real, live friends, and there aren't any, and mother won't let them come. And it doesn't hurt so much if she crawls back *out* of herself and can imagine her friends. Hum? (A_2, C_2)

partially de-identify with you, reestablish my separate existence as your therapist, make objective comments on your reactions and interpret to you. That will come later, but not now. We both use the third person "she", but the feelings welling up now in the patient and simultaneously through resonance in the therapist indicate clearly "we" have now invested ourselves in "her." The patient continues to use the third person but identifies herself with that "her." The therapist has changed his perception of the "her" to an identofact and also feels like "her."

141. L: Um-hum.

W: It doesn't hurt so much . . . 'cause then she has some friends that play with her and do as she wants, and she's not hurt. (A_2, C_2)

142. L: True.

W: She feels so sad . . . unhappy. (A_2)

143. L: Very shy.

143. "We" feel like crying.

W: And very shy. She's an unhappy little girl . . . and she's so lonely and she feels like crying cause she has no friends . . . nobody knows . . . how she feels . . . (A_2)

144. L: She has pride.

W: Yes, that's why she doesn't tell people, doesn't, isn't it? (C_2)

145. L: Um-hum.

W: She keeps it to herself . . . but she maybe wants to have friends, and she wants to have playmates who like her and love her . . . she is so miserable and unhappy . . . (A_2)

146. L: What should she have done?

146. A little girl is blocked—no way out.

W: What should she have done? It doesn't seem as if . . .

there's much she could have done, does it? (C_2, O)

(Tears) (Therapist opens desk, gets tissue box, and hands to patient.)

More affective release. Good. Can I resonate, unstand, and transmit to her that I do understand. Tears subside. The energy discharged in the affective release is that which prevously manned the defense. Now I return from participant to observer role. The resistance against insight is now low. Now, and not before, comes a time for interpretation. Let's interpret first while she's still under hypnosis.

147. L: What can she do now?

W: Do you see why . . . she withdrew her from herself? Because to be herself *hurt*. And to withdraw from herself, protects her. It is pleasant, because she can rearrange her world with people who are friends and playmates who like her and love her, even though they're imaginary. And when she's in herself, for real . . . and together, that's the time that she's, she gets hurt. By withdrawing from herself she protects herself from being hurt, Laura. (C_2)

147. Interpretation must be kindly—oh, so gentle and kindly. oh, so gentle and kindly. Let's not hurt the little girl more. She's most available to understanding and most vulnerable to hurt right now. The estrangement barrier between the "I" and the "it," the self and the puppet, has temporarily lost its strength through the affective discharge. Now's the time to make our "Brownie points" in therapeutic process.

148. L: What does she do now? Is she still the same? Different now?

W: Laura, if a person finds that the world is hostile around them, and people will hurt them, and if they build a house with a great big high *wall* all around it, they will keep out the people that hurt, won't they? And they'll also keep their friends out, won't they? And they'll be all alone . . . (C_2)

149\. L: Where does she start?

W: She got the view of the world . . . the way it was when she was a little girl. Her mother wouldn't let playmates come, and there was a fence up around and a wall around her. And this is the way the world was when she was a little girl *then* in *that family, there*. Maybe the world today isn't *really* that way. But maybe she's still living as *if* it were that way. (C_2)

149\. How shall I tell her without being directive, without being "preachy"? She's ready, and it's my job to make it clear.

150\. L: How does she break through? (Tears) I'm, don't like this business.

W: I know . . . I know. She already made a start . . . when she cried. (C_2)

150\. More tears. Good, I hope she keeps them up until the well is dry.

151\. L: Careful, there's going to be a flood-out.

W: That's OK. (indistinct) They're for real. (Therapist blows nose, gets up and closes window) I have plenty more of these (tissues). (A_1)

151\. Returning objectivity in therapist. He's a bit embarrassed about his tears so displaces "crying" to nasal passages. We can "cry" with our noses as well as our eyes.

152\. L: I'm glad you're prepared . . . How do these connect with the headaches? Is it just this, the clash, one me against the other?

W: I don't know, maybe. What do you think happens when one tries to go two ways at the same time? (O)

152\. She seeks now to understand her symptoms.

153\. L: Well, it causes a normal tension.

153\. The therapist is vacillating between his identification with the patient (participant) and his role as objective interpreter (observer). Part of the time he uses "I" and part of the time "you." He's also dramatizing the "it" and the "puppet."

W: And suppose there was a great big grownup, Laura, that said I want to be part of this world. I want to be close to people. I want to have friends. I want to be loved and liked and I want to interact. And I want to be myself. And then suppose that there's a little girl, Laura, who says uh-uh, don't do it! You're going to get hurt. You're going to get humiliated. You're going to be told to stay away and there'll be no friends for you. You're just putting your heart on your sleeve, and it's going to get struck down again if you do. Let's go the other way. And if one tries to run *toward* something and run *away* from something at the same time, what might happen to a person? (C_2, O)

154. L: Cause tension?

W: It could, couldn't it? And how do you think that tension might show itself? (C_2)

155. L: It could make a party have headaches.

155. "By Gad, she's got it." (said in *Pygmalion*.)

W: Or something like that? (C_2)

156. L: Or sick.

W: One's trying . . . One has two values. One's trying to go toward something and one's trying to go away from something at the same time. One wants to be part of this world, and one wants to live, and love, and enjoy life, but one is afraid to . . . because one is afraid that one will be hurt, and rejected, and isolated, and humiliated, and made alone. (C_2)

157. L: I've hated those words ever since I've remembered. (more tears)

W: Yes. (F)

175. Fictional third person discarded. Now it's "I." The "it" and "her" are fully egotized.

158. L: Then there were so many times I found it easier just to be the clown and to be laughed at.

W: Yes. (C_1, F)

159. L: So much easier.

W: Um-hum. And so then you could just sort of sit back and say, "That's the clown out there. They're not laughing at me. They are laughing at the body out there that's performing. They're laughing at the puppet . . . not me." Huh? And then it didn't hurt. (A_2, C_3)

160. L: Oh, it did, when it had to come into the body again.

160. When the ego returned.

W: Sometimes. (C_1)

161. L: It was (indistinct) . . .

161. The hypnosis is lightening all this time. Spontaneously.

W: But each time it did, it got *hurt* again. And by getting out of the body it avoided being hurt. It let people laugh at the puppet. It let the *puppet* be the one . . . that sort of took the rap when friends couldn't come around, and all this sort of thing. And it could imagine life in the world the way it wanted to. It could build its own friends, its own satisfactions. Why shouldn't it want to live that way? (C_2)

162. L: It shouldn't . . . You really can't blame it.

W: No, you can't, can you. But Laura, that way of life was built on a perception . . . of a life that was *real* . . . and the way the world was *at that time*, then . . . is it possible that *now* being grownup, the world really isn't that way? Maybe there aren't any fences around to stop you. Maybe there aren't any mothers around to say, "No . . . you can't have friends over." (C_2)

163. L: Are there any kind of a mother?

W: What? (F)

164. L: What if they're that kind of a mother? (indistinct) . . .

W: But maybe, Laura, you're still behaving as if it were the little girl thinking. Do you see what I mean? You have the same fears as the little girl had, and so . . . you're afraid . . . kind of as we say . . . the idea of wearing your heart on your sleeve, so it gets

164. (Afterthought of therapist) Too much interpretation? Am I being overinvolved here, reiterating what has already been said, trying to drive home the insights with too much repetition. Repetition. Repetition is essential in learning—it can also drive away and cause boredom. Perhaps the therapist should return more to the objective role here. He is

hurt. You're afraid to be genuine and real. And so, you come back . . . and you . . . let the puppet be out in front of the people. And you don't take the chance of committing *your real self*. And you said to me a little ago, "What should she do?" Don't you think that when she cried, and the tears came, that she was really putting herself together at the moment (indistinct) all along the line? The tears came . . . because *she* and the *puppet* were together and the same. There wasn't any puppet any more. This was really Laura crying. And what she felt was genuine and real, and *it hurt*. And so one doesn't run away from hurt. One says to one's self, "So, it might hurt. So I might get humiliated. So I might get laughed at; but I'm still going to *be*, and I'm still going to be myself with people and interact with them *even if it does hurt*." Does this give you any idea of what she should do when you say, "What should she do?" (C_2)

trying to move too far, too fast. Steady as it goes. We can't do it all today. She needs time to work through and integrate all this.

165. L: (Indistinct) question . . .

W: Um-hum. And be prepared to take some hurt, and keep on going. (C_2)

165. I don't think we've over-interpreted yet.

166. L: And yet to . . . to be yourself, to be myself, I'm afraid that I'm going to hurt someone else.

W: You are a little angry . . . at all that's happened. (A_2)

167\. L: Yet, the first on the list would be my parents, and I don't want to hurt them, they've had enough from me.

W: Well? (F)

167\. She's translating the implications of her new insights into the realities of the present. They can create problems.

168\. L. This is where I think this, this split came in.

W: Um-hum . . . but you're not *with* your parents right now. (C_2)

169\. L: No, but I shall be this weekend. We're going up there.

W: Yeah . . . and you are afraid that if you are really yourself, and put yourself together, then you'll hurt your parents, hum? (A_2)

170\. L: I probably will.

W: Maybe . . . um . . . you know, there's something that, uh, becomes to a to a person who decides . . . that she's never going to hate. Do you know what happens to her, and what the price is that she pays for deciding that she's never going to hate because it might hurt somebody? She's never going to love, either . . . If she can't give one side of the coin, she can't give the other side. She's *just* a neutral *blah*, a *puppet* . . . not a person. (C_2, A_2)

170\. This a long "teaching" interpretation. It is the time it should be delivered. The only question is whether it is too much. Next session she will close over again some. Two steps forward, one backward, but perhaps we can estimate just how much yardage we did or did not make today.

171\. L: The house without a heart.

W: Right. If she's going to be a *person*, and a *loving* person, she has to take the chance of also being a

171\. Good, she's still taking it.

She is spontaneously, slowly emerging out of hypnosis. This is as it should be. More hating person, too. Because . . . it takes both sides to make one person . . . And so . . . your decision is *not* whether you're going to hurt somebody or not, whether you're going to hate or not, whether you're going to be angry or not, the decision is: Are you going to be a real person or a puppet? That's the decision. Because a real person is capable of both love and anger, but sometimes when there's a lot of anger there first, it has to come out before the love side gets to come out. Do you see what I mean? (C_2, C_3)

and more of ego is contacting the emerged feelings.

172. L: Um-hum, I think it's going to take a while.

172. She's saying, "Enough. Don't push more."

W: It's going to take some practice, and it's going to take *not being afraid to* take a chance, and *not running back to* a little girl who lives her life in fantasy. But to be, to decide, to really live and be a big girl, and live in the world the way it is, pluses and minuses, and that maybe the world today doesn't have as many minuses in it . . . as the little girl's world. Because you do have control, you know you can climb that fence, and you can contact people. (Indistinct) And Mother isn't here to tell you, "no". (C_3)

(afterreaction) Therapist—shut up. You've said enough. It's time to quit.

173. L. Well, wish me luck. It's going to take it.

W: I wish you all the luck in the world, Laura. And I

will be . . . cheering on your team. (C_1)

174. L: Oh, that's a (indistinct) . . .

Eyes opening

174. Hypnosis almost gone.

W: Well, would you like to come back next Wednesday, and let's see what's happened this week? (O)

175. L: Yeah.

W: OK. (C_1)

176. L: OK.

W: Are you wide awake now? (O)

177. L: Yeah, I'm wide awake.

177. Hypnosis completely gone.

W: You are? Good girl. (O)

178. L: Fighting yourself is sure a strange battle. Both sides have to win, and yet the other can lose.

178. Therapist can't resist one parting "preachment."

W: You know really *both sides can win*. The only thing that can lose is just a plain waste of life. (C_3)

179. L: Good afternoon.

(whispered)

179. She's not angry, nor hurt.

W: Bye now. (O)

180. L: Bye-bye.

180. "We" are tired, but we do feel better.

LAURA SESSION

Tabulation of Scores

A_1	6		
A_2	17		
A_3	2		
A_4	0		
Total A	25	35 per cent of R	
C_1	22		
C_2	22		
C_3	2		
C_4	1		
Total C	47	65 per cent of R	
Total R (A plus C)	72		40.2 per cent of Total
O	60		33.5 per cent of Total
F	47		26.3 per cent of Total
I	0		
N	0		
Total responses	179		

Scoring: Resonant, Objective, Facilitative

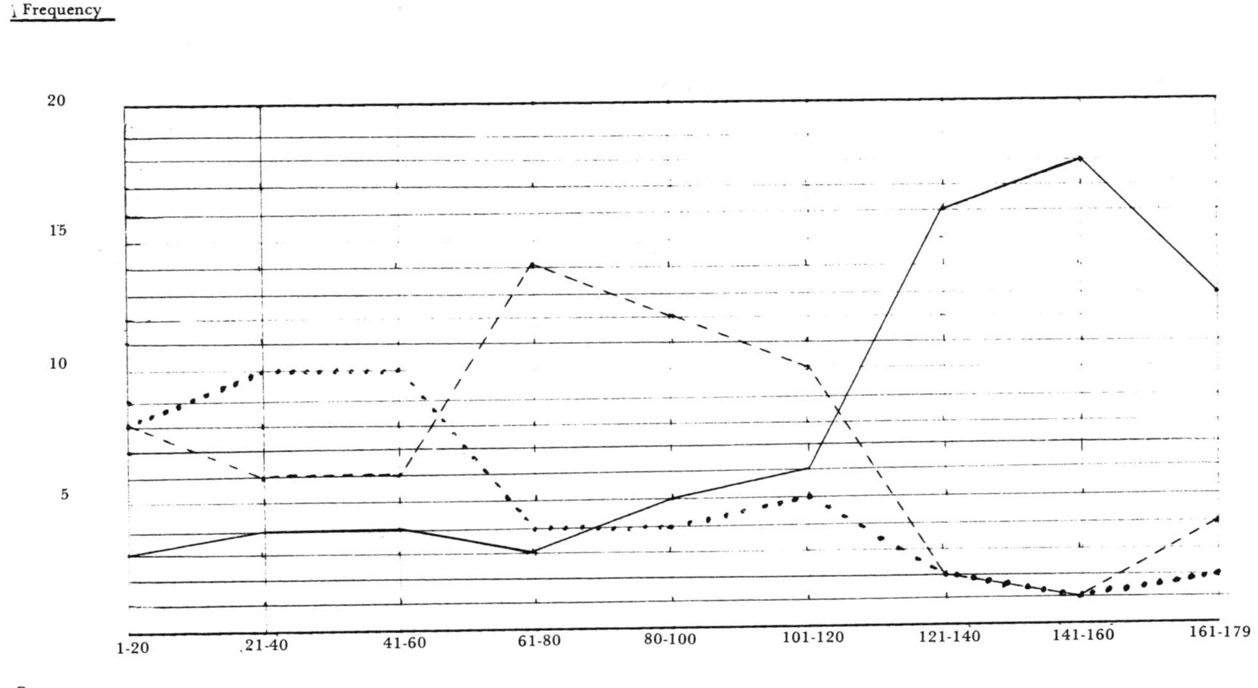

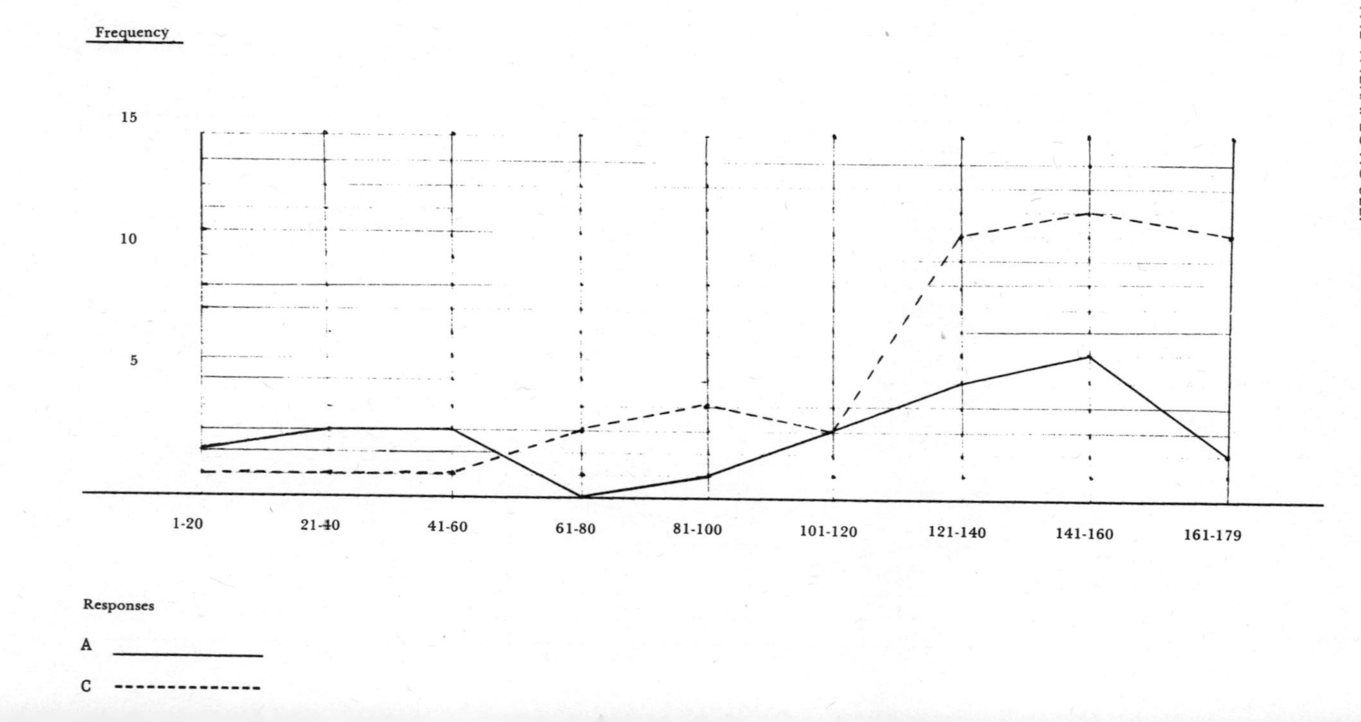
THE CASE OF LAURA
Scoring: Affective (A) and Cognitive (C) Resonance
Frequency
15
10
5
1-20
21-40
41-60
61-80
81-100
101-120
121-140
141-160
161-179
Responses
A
C

FOOTNOTE

1. The name is fictional. A tape recording of this session (No. 33, Laura) is available for purchase by professional therapists from the American Academy of Psychotherapists Tape Library, 1040 Woodcock Road, Orlando, Florida 32803. Students have reported that when they listened to the recordings while following the scripts and therapist notes they received a much greater understanding of the concepts of resonance and ego states than when merely reading the scripts alone.

Chapter 22

EGO-STATE THERAPY

Helen H. Watkins

In the early development of group therapy, techniques were first used that were adaptations of those employed in individual treatment. Some were effective, but group therapy developed an entire methodology that was unique to the social situation (Kaplan & Sadock, 1971). In ego-state therapy we borrow from many of the techniques used in group and family therapy. They have been effective in the group situation to reconcile *interpersonal* conflicts between individual members of a group or family. Similar procedures are here used to reconcile *intrapersonal* clashes between the various ego states that constitute a "family of self."

Ego-state therapy differs from transactional analysis (Berne, 1961) in that it does not postulate in advance three specific states, such as Parent, Child, and Adult. It allows the patient to define the boundaries and contents of his own ego states and give them appropriate names. The units of self are those the patient himself has so differentiated and not ones assigned to him through preconceptualized theory; Parent, Child, and Adult states often do appear, but not universally nor exclusively.

Accordingly, ego-state therapy does not limit itself to three entities, but accepts and deals with all those that manifest themselves as units within the ego economy and are pertinent to the adjustments of the patient. As one is activated and becomes subject, the others (if the individual is aware of them) are regarded by that state as object. A therapist employing the therapeutic self approach, would endeavor to resonate with each state whenever it is executive. The activation and deactivation of different ego states is much easier to control when working in the hypnotic modality, and a therapist can call up these different self components for communication and relationship when so indicated.

In the case of Joan, exerpts of which are presented here, the therapist and writer of this chapter, does precisely this. She activates various ego states along different dimensions by calling upon them under hypnosis. She then deals with each activated state as subject; that is, for the moment it is treated as if *it* were the patient. Even though these different states are at times in conflict and opposing each other, each is treated with warmth and respect.

The Case of Joan[1]

Joan was a 30-year-old college student, very schizoid in manner, who often suffered from temporary dissociations and hallucinations. She was considerably overweight (originally over 200 pounds), and in the past had sought, unsuccessfully, to reduce. At the time of the sessions reported here, she had been in therapy about a year on once-a-week sessions. Striking changes had already been achieved. She had lost some 70 pounds of weight, had begun to socialize with others, had become active in various student activities, and now seldom dissociated. However, those problems that were still unresolved occasionally manifested themselves in the form of anxiety and psychosomatic symtoms. The sessions whose exerpts are presented here were crucial in their therapeutic effect and helped Joan to achieve a new level of adjustment.

A COMPROMISE WITH THE DARK ONE

Therapist-Patient Interaction	Therapist Reactions and Theoretical Notes
H[2]: Feel yourself go down. And when you have gone down as far as you can possibly go, then your right index finger will rise up to let me know you're there.	Brief hypnotic induction not recorded.
And now, I want you to tell me how you're feeling right now. What's been going on with you?	
J: I've just walked around . . . kinda numb. And my head . . . I'm worried, but I'm turning things off.	
H: You're turning things off. You say you're worried?	
J: My stomach's worried.	
H: Your stomach's worried.	Repetition used so that patient knows she has been heard correctly by the therapist. It also gives the therapist time to decide on a response.
J: I can't see why.	
H: Concentrate on your stomach.	
J: And the muscles.	

[2] Therapist: Helen H. Watkins

H: The muscles are kind of tight. Is that it? Is that how it feels? Keep on concentrating on your stomach right now. And the stomach will let you know . . .

J: My head.

H: What?

J: My head's tight.

H: Your head's tight?

J: I don't understand it.

H: Concentrate on the stomach right now . . . and keep on concentrating . . . keep on concentrating on your stomach . . . and in a moment I'm going to ask your stomach to talk . . . to talk what it's worried about. Stomach, I want to hear from you. What are you worried about?

The whole body seems to be involved, but one ego state must become executive in order to speak for itself.

J: I'm the visceral region. I'm the muscles.

H: You're the muscles. What are you so worried about? How come you're so tight?

J: Things aren't right.

H: Things aren't right. What things?

Any physical or mental component of the person that can be distinguished from the rest of the organism by some apparent boundary, physical or ego, is treated by the therapist as if it were a self in its own right. It is addressed and asked to communicate like a separate person. The entire individual is viewed like a society of such component parts.

J: Nothing should be the way it is. I can't let anything happen.

H: Can you explain why?

Therapist talking to Muscles.

J: She has to be tense.

H: She has to be tense. Why does she have to be tense?

J: To support the mind.

Muscles treats the patient's "self" as an object or "it" ("she") For the moment, Muscles is subject and communicates in the first person.

H: To support the mind. Can you explain that more?

J: The mind is tense, so the muscles . . . tense up.

H: Are you saying that you're just kind of taking directions from the mind?

J: Yes.

H: OK., in that case, I want to talk to the mind. Mind, why do you have to be tense?

Therapist searching for the source.

Pause

J: Readiness to fight.

Mind now activiated as subject by therapist's request. Muscles no longer executive.

H: Readiness to fight. Fight what?

J: There's fighting . . . it's . . . it just seems right. The internal and external . . . aren't right.

H: Can you explain that to me a little more?

J: There's a massive indecision inside. We can't go on either path, we have to *stop* . . . just stop.

Mind reports on the interal civil war going on.

H: Stop what?

J: Just stop everything until we make a decision. Stop.

H: What's the decision to make? What's the decision to be made?

J: There's too much confusion inside. We have to stop and settle it before we go any further.

Mind refers to all parts of Joan as "We."

H: OK.

J: But we can't stop.

H: You can't stop. Do you know what the problem is?

J:	*I* merely suspect . . . but this one doesn't really know the problem.	
H:	What do you suspect?	
J:	She doesn't want to change. But she has to. She *wants* to change so badly, yet at the same time she doesn't want to change so badly.	Mind also treats patient's self as object, "She".
H:	How do you mean that?	
J:	She wants to lose weight; it's more real than anything.	Content of struggle coming through.
H:	What's stopping her?	
J:	She doesn't know . . . she is real as she is now. She doesn't know what she'll be like, if she'll be real. She is losing already. Already she's lost what was real to her. There's more. Every day she loses more. More of what she thinks is real.	
H.	She's losing every day, more of what she thinks is real. Can you tell me what those things are?	According to Mind, She, the patient, considers her bodily flesh as "real." Hence, the loss in weight represents to her a loss in her reality.
J:	Things she thinks are true. Ah . . . they're scattered. They're jerking around.	
H:	For example.	
J:	She decided she must be alone, yet now she seeks company. She . . . she never wanted to feel anything for men. If she starts to feel, this upsets her, upsets her much. She's afraid of what she's feeling. This causes me to tense up. This, the most, she doesn't know what she feels. She doesn't *want* to feel.	Because She (Joan) now seeks male company, I (Mind) becomes tense.

	Dialogue	Commentary
H:	She's afraid that she sees changes now. She has always thought of herself as being alone, and isolated, and being different from others. She had always perceived herself as never getting married, and now all of a sudden, there's changes, and she associates the changes with losing weight. She's becoming more friendly, and she kind of sees herself as being interested in men and socializing more, and she's kind of scared, isn't she?	The loss in weight and the new abilities to socialize, including the interest in men, threatens her previous style of life. These gains, which have resulted from her therapy thus far, are cognitively dissonant with her accustomed defenses. Accordingly, anxiety is arising.
J:	She's afraid of what she's starting to feel. She doesn't want it so bad. She doesn't want it.	Mind is reporting what She feels.
H:	I wonder in terms of She, if you can give her a name and how old she is.	Therapist needs to clarify who She really is.
J:	She . . . (pause)	
H:	How old is She? (another pause) I think you know, Mind, because you're wise, and you know these things, and you can see.	Not a ploy, but the therapist's real feelings.
J:	The mind is the last one to know.	
H:	Am I talking to the mind, or who am I talking to?	Therapist is getting the impression that not Mind but some other ego state is talking.
J:	You're talking . . . to one deeper than the mind.	
H:	One deeper than the mind. What's her name? Or what do you want to call her?	Therapist impression confirmed.
J:	There is no age. I can't see a person, nor a name. There is no person.	
H:	It's just a She.	

J:	A He.	This is a real surprise, although the therapist had met "him" before in previous sessions.
H:	A *He*? Are you the He?	
J:	Yes.	
H:	Oh, you are the He, and you have no name.	
J:	No.	
H:	When were you born?	
J:	Seventeen years ago.	
H:	Seventeen years ago? How old were you then? About four?	Therapist suspects that He came into existence at the time when patient was molested at three or four years of age. In multiple personalities, it is common to find that there was a split at the time of a great trauma.
J:	Three.	
H:	Three. How did you get to be born? How did it happen?	
J:	I was born between light and dark.	
H:	Between light and dark? What happened when you were born?	The experience happened at dusk, or she may be referring to the moments prior to fainting.
J:	I saw eyes.	
H:	You saw eyes? . . . What else? . . . What was going on when you were born? What was happening?	The memory of molestation trauma was recovered during an earlier session. Apparently, a large man entered the house while the patient, a little girl of three, was alone. He pressed his mouth against hers, his body weight down upon her and touched her genitals. She was too frightened to communicate this experience to her parents and had never told anybody about it.
J:	There was tension, tension between inside and outside. Pressure . . . pressure . . . gray between light and dark . . . pressure, a wall. . . that presses flat.	
H:	I see. Why were you born?	
J:	Because of the pressure.	
H:	Because of the pressure. To protect yourself against the pressure?	An ego state dissociated (was created) to act as a protector for the little girl.
J:	Yes, to press back. Use my hands and press back.	

H: And you had to be a *boy* to do that.

J: Maleness is strength. There is no real gender. Just anything with strength. It's male. Females have no strength.

Only males are strong enough to be protectors. The new dissociated ego state had to be created masculine.

H: Females have no strength. Men do. So I'm talking to He. A He. To protect the girl that was molested, that's who I'm talking to. You were born when she was molested, and the strange man came, and you felt the pressure, the weight of his body on you. And you were born at that moment. Is that right?

J: Yes.

H: Are you still trying to protect her?

He, the protector, has existed as an autonomous entity ever since.

J: Yes.

H: Now you were talking about She, a little while ago. Are you talking about the same little girl?

J: Yes. She mutates, She . . . She's older but She's . . . I think of her now . . . the older one. *I* am the same.

The patient is no longer a three-year-old girl and has grown up. She has changed (mutates). But He has remained the same, in structure and in purpose.

H: You are the same. And what is your function now?

J: To stop her.

H: From what?

Present reality must come to an anachronistic ego state.

J: To protect her.

H: From what?

J: From the outside, from pressure.

H: Are you the same one that

The Dark One, once considered

we used to talk about as the Dark One?

by both patient and therapist as the Evil One because of its resistance to constructive change is now seen as blindly protecting Joan according to its view of itself and its originally created purpose for existing.

J: Yes.

H: You're still there. You're still trying to protect her. You're still saying, "No, you can't meet men, because they will hurt you; and you can't socialize, because people will hurt you. And I must protect you from this." Is that right?

J: Yes.

H: Well, she has a real problem.

J: I can feel her hurting.

H: But you're the one who's hurting her. She doesn't need your protection anymore. And you are keeping her away from the world, and she can handle the world now. You don't need to protect her anymore.

Therapist directly interprets to Dark One its now misguided protection.

J: She herself has said she doesn't want it.

He tries to rationalize his actions.

H: Are you sure it was her or was it the voice of you speaking to her? It's important that you become honest now, for her sake.

Therapist demands He (Dark One) be authentic and show that he is really concerned with Joan's welfare. He admits but hedges (like any other normal person).

J: I influenced her to say it. She accepted it.

H: You influenced her to say it, but she accepted it because she believed you, right? (Nods assent) Well, Dark One, it was a wonderful thing for you to protect her when she was very young and when she had the experience of being molested. And you were born out of desperation to protect her. And that was a good thing. And there were other times, too, you came out, other incidents that occurred to her that were somewhat similar in which you protected her. But now, she is in a real struggle because of your voice . . . because of your voice that she listens to all the time, and you make her afraid. You make her afraid to lose weight. But she wants to because the part of her that is grown up and that is a woman, she really needs to do these things. She needs to experience her world as a woman, and I'm trying to help her do that. And what I'm wondering about at this point is how you feel, Dark One, about me and about what I have been doing with her. I guess what I want to know from you, do you trust me?

Therapist does not challenge "He." She resonates to the aspirations of this ego state, gives him credit for his past protective behavior, and asks that he now relinquish that control, which is preventing Joan from becoming a mature woman.

Does Dark One perceive therapist as an enemy?

Therapist tests relationship to determine how much therapeutic leverage she may have with the Dark One.

J: I hide from you.

H: Do you trust me? Do you trust me to do good things and protective things for her?

Dark One is wary. Therapist may be good for Joan, but is she good for the Dark One?

J: I believe you are right. I won't use the word trust.

H: What I'm wondering about is, would you be willing to kind of hand over your influence and to kind of trust me to use it. And what I'm talking about when I say influence I'm talking about would you be will-

Therapist thinking through a strategy—making a request to which she anticipates a "no" with the hope of gaining a "yes" to a lesser request.

	ing to hand over the reins, I think that's what I want to say, of what you have been doing with her? The kind of reins that control. And hand me those reins, but I'm not going to control them. I'm going to help her to grow and be safe, and I need your cooperation. I need you to let go of the reins, of what you have been doing to her. I will do what I feel is best for her growth. And that's the reason I'm wondering if you could trust me to take over now and you can kind of . . . if you would be willing to go away . . . How do you feel about that?	Therapist has almost asked the Dark One to die, to not exist ("go away").
J:	Not good.	He is upset.
H:	Why not?	
J:	I won't leave.	Even ego states have ego survival needs. He demands the right to exist: he will not go away. One cannot destroy an ego state, only decathect it. It can be deactivated by withdrawal of its energy but its structure remains.
H:	How come?	
J:	I have to stay. I'm the strength.	He justifies his being; he considers himself to be an asset in the society of Joan.
H:	What I was thinking about, that I wasn't asking you to leave in other areas, but only in this one. And what my thought was, that maybe you can give her strength which she needs in other areas of her life, but not to induce fear, but to give her strength, to accomplish, and to be, and to stand up for herself. That's the way that you can really help her, and you could really	Therapist accepts Dark One as an asset and asks only that he use his strength constructively.

use your strength to do that.

J: I could do that.

He agrees.

H: I'm not asking you to die; I'm asking you to change form, so that you could really help her. Do you think you could do that?

J: Yes.

By accepting Dark One's right to live and function within the economy of Joan's/therapist self, H. has turned a hostile, rigid, protective "character armor" into a useful contributor to Joan's mental equilibrium. He can now be friend and not enemy.

H: OK. I'm going to state then, maybe what you and I can do together to help her. You can be her strength, and standing up for herself, and becoming mature, and handling her world in a kind of forthright, strong manner, and being successful in whatever she chooses to do. You can operate in that area; and I will operate in the other area that you used to take over. I'll help her become a woman, because since you are a male element, you really can't help her become a woman. Does that make sense to you?

J: Yes.

H: OK. But I am a woman, and I will help her to become a woman, and socialize and deal with men so she won't be hurt, and lose weight. Let me take over that department, and you can take over the other department. How's that?

Therapist sets up a cooperative arrangement, a compromise with the Dark One, which allows both Dark One and therapist to work together for the good of Joan.

J: Yes.

H: Will you promise then to leave her alone in terms of the weight reduction and let her do what she wants to?

J: Yes.

H: Yes. I feel good about your compromise, and I really feel good about you, because you could do her so much help and you could be so important to her, in a very healthy, strong way. And I really feel very much touched and feel very good about you, that you're willing to do that, and that you would trust me enough that you would allow me to take over her growth as a woman. How do you feel?

Therapist's authentic feelings.

J: I feel . . . better that she is relaxing now. She is relaxed . . . I can feel her relaxing. I'll still watch. But I'll let her do it.

Joan no longer has to be a battleground between her therapist, who is working for her maturity as a woman, and Dark One, who must blindly protect a three-year-old girl from men. Of course, She is relaxing now.

H: OK. All right Joan. In a moment I'm going to count up to five, and when I count up to five, you'll be wide awake, fresh and alert, feeling relaxed, and the conflict resolved. Coming up now at the count of five. 1 . . . 2 . . . 3 . . . 4 . . . 5.

The next session reported here occured one week later as therapist expands her allyship with Dark One. Joan has shown considerable improvement but comes to this hour indicating some kind of setback, a disturbance causing anxiety and psychosomatic pains.

DARK ONE STIFLES THE TICKS

Therapist-Patient Interaction	Therapist Reactions and Theoretical Notes
H: OK, Joan. Now you've been telling me just a while ago that you've been really kind of tense and nervous, and we want to discover what this is	A hypnotic state has been induced and the therapy proper begins.

	all about right now, this feeling of tension and nervousness. What can you tell me about it?	
J:	Even now, I'm tense. I can feel it, just all my muscles are tense.	
H:	Do you feel the tension any place else?	
J:	Just in my head, basically.	
H:	OK. What I want you to do is just to kind of concentrate on your muscles and the tension in your muscles, and let those muscles kind of speak for you, so that the tension talks.	Therapist is asking Muscles ego-state to become executive.
	(Pause)	Muscles slow to respond.
J:	We just react to the tension she thinks, to the conflict.	But finally do. They do not perceive themselves as a cause but a result of Joan's conflict.
H:	What conflict?	
J:	She wants what she doesn't want. She . . . she wants to move, but she wants to stay.	
H:	You're talking about moving this fall, is that what you mean?	Therapist temporarily on wrong track.
J:	No. We only react to chemicals.	
H:	Oh.	
J:	Muscles can think a little bit but not . . . not . . . that much. We only do what the chemicals make us do.	Muscles can think "a little bit." Reminds of Cannon's (1932) "wisdom of the body."
H:	Could you explain to me a little bit more about the moving that you mentioned, I . . . I don't understand.	
J:	The changing of her thinking. The changing . . . she has to	

	change her thinking before she can change her body. Before she can change her environment, yet the thinking . . . the thinking deep inside, can't be changed . . . and she thinks to herself she wants to change, yet deep inside, there still isn't change.	
H:	Are you saying, Muscle, that you're getting two different signals?	Tension is always created in one's muscles when they are getting conflicting cues simultaneously.
J:	Yes . . . the chemicals clash. She thinks she wants to be calm; the chemicals say "run."	
H:	The chemicals say "run," but she's saying she wants to be calm . . . do you know what the chemicals represent, or who they represent?	Very literal, in tune with how she is thinking.
J:	The chemicals . . . the Mind creates the chemicals in times of fear . . . in times of fight or flight. The chemicals . . . adrenalin . . . the chemicals make us work more, make us tense, ready to fight, ready to strike out and hit. She has nothing to hit but the wall. She's burning herself out.	
H:	Then you're saying that it is the Mind that is controlling the chemicals and therefore the muscles that represent you, is that right?	
J:	Yes, the glands, the Mind.	
H:	Then perhaps the person or the part that we need to talk to is the Mind who is producing all these changes, which is producing the fear. Is that right?	
J:	Yes.	

H:	All right, Muscle, thank you for your information. Now the part that I would like to talk to is the Mind that is producing, sending out these signals for fear, for flight. Mind, I want to hear you talk. The part that is determining this.	Mind now called forth as subject.
J:	I am the physical part of the mind. I'm in the back of the head near the neck. I see danger, so I make the chemicals.	Mind answers and locates self.
H:	What danger do you see?	
J:	I see danger in the environment. She is afraid of these people. When I perceive fear, I make the chemicals.	Mind conditioned by previous fears. Transference?
H:	She is afraid of these people, and then when you perceive the fear, you make the chemicals.	
J:	Yes.	
H:	Do you happen to know anything about why she's afraid of what people.	
J:	It doesn't matter to me, I just see fear. I make the chemicals.	Mind not conscious of origin of fear. Reacts automatically and blindly.
H:	All right, Mind, thank you for your information. Now I want to talk to the part that perceives the fear, and creates the fear.	Something more original is cuing off Mind. Therapist seeks that something.
J:	There are parts of us that see it.	
H:	Who are you, Parts?	Therapist calls for "fear parts" ego state to become activated.
J:	We are scattered. No definite place. But we can't help it if . . . ah . . . we fight with the other parts that tell us there's nothing to fear. There must	

	be something to fear.	
H:	Why must there be something to fear?	
J:	Because there must be. It happened before. It can happen just using logic; we can use logic. It's too unstable, too unsafe.	"Our" fears are logical, because they have been justified in the past.
H:	What can happen that happened before?	
J:	She can get too close.	Closeness to others activates fear state.
H:	Too close to what?	
J:	We remember she was hurt before, and it can happen again. These are other bodies, just like that one. Some parts say no, but the body can hurt.	Components of fear state ("We") "remember" and react accordingly. (Transference—stimulus generalization).
H:	Do you have a name that we can identify you with?	Therapist wants a handle that can be used to address these fears.
J:	We are the Young Minds.	Joan gives name indicating early origin of fears.
H:	The Young Minds?	
J:	Yes.	
H:	What does that mean?	
J:	There are many of us, and we remember. We have a direct link.	There was more than one feared situation that happened to Joan's Young Mind.
H:	You remember what?	
J:	We just remember. We're on the surface, the Dark One is deep inside, but we're on the surface.	Young Minds place themselves in relation to the Dark One ego state.
H:	You're on the surface, and the Dark One is deep inside. How does the Dark One influence you?	
J:	He's stronger than us.	More highly cathected.
H:	What kind of messages do you	

	get from the Dark One?	
J:	None right now. We were always with her, and he was created.	Dark One keeping last week's promise. Dark One a later development than Young Minds.
H:	You were always with her, and he was created when you were about three and a half, is that right?	Dark One created as protective state at time Joan was molested.
J:	Yes. He has a shape and a form. We don't. We're just parts of the mind.	Dark One a better organized state.
H:	You are the fear parts of the mind, is that right?	
J:	Yes. We're afraid.	Young Minds' only function apparently is to express early fears.
H:	You're always afraid.	
J:	Yes.	
H:	Were you born at any time? When did you begin to exist?	
J:	Very young in the hospital.	At age one and one half, Joan was hospitalized. She was isolated and parents not permitted to contact her. Young Minds fear state apparently born at this time.
H:	In the hospital; why were you born there?	
J:	Because there was fear.	
H:	Why was there fear?	How can a regressed ego state talk about experiences which happened before the individual had acquired language? If an adult had come from a foreign land, say France, at the age of eleven, and only learned English after that age, he can still relate in English events which happened to him prior to eleven when he knew no English words. Apparently, experiences can be recorded before the advent of language and be described later when words have been associated with these meaningful experiences. We believe that infants (and even embryos) can experience and remember.
J:	It was unknown.	
H:	It was unknown. Can you tell me anything more about being born there. You were about a year and a half, is that right?	
J:	No concept.	
H:	No concept.	
J:	We can't . . . can't see that, we don't know numbers.	

H.	How can we help you be less afraid? How is this possible?	Therapist wants cue to therapeutic strategy.
J:	We don't know.	
H:	Would the Dark One have any influence upon you?	Therapist searching for an ally, for therapeutic leverage.
J:	We don't know. The Dark One could . . . think.	
H:	Would I be able to have any influence upon you?	
J:	We don't know.	
H:	In other words, you have been there so long, and always there, that it's kind of a constant state.	
J:	If you could see us, you would see there are three, maybe four of us, and we sit on the mind like ticks. Like a picture of ticks. We have roots that spread out and attach, and we are attached.	
H:	Well, what is your purpose in being there like ticks on the mind?	Therapist checking out if there is any therapeutic value to fear parts.
J:	We don't need a purpose; we only exist.	
H:	Then you don't know what your function is.	Fear no longer serves useful function. Should be extinguished.
J:	No.	
H:	All right. So you don't know, even suspect that maybe the Dark One might be able to reduce your energy. Do I understand that right?	Reduce energy—decathect state.
J:	Yes. We're a little afraid of him. We look with uneasiness, down at him. Down where he is. He hasn't touched us yet, but . . .	Each ego state claims existence in its own right. Perceives threat to reduce or kill it as would any individual. Defends right to existence.
H:	Has he ever touched you?	
J:	No.	

	Dialogue	Commentary
H:	All right. Now, I want you to relax even deeper, Joan, until I can talk to the Dark One, whom I consider to be my friend. And when you can . . . the Dark One can speak, let him say hello. (Pause)	Therapist calls once again on Dark One.
J:	Hello.	
H:	Hello, Dark One. I think that you and I both have a problem. You must have heard what the ticks, those parts of . . . the fear parts of the mind, as you heard them described as ticks. They're kind of looking down on you a little bit to see that you have power, and they keep Joan afraid all the time because they keep sending out messages to the mind to activate the muscles, and produce fear and send out chemicals. Uh, we need to do something about it. What do you think?	Therapist outlines problem to Dark One and seeks his cooperation.
J:	I've always known they were there. They always worked to my purposes before, so I didn't bother them.	Dark One ego state always aware of Young Minds, but since he, too, had been engaged in scaring Joan away from relationships he had perceived Young Minds as serving his purposes. Accordingly, he left them alone.
H:	I wonder, now that you and I understand each other, and you and I have made an agreement, and I trust you and I know that you have been leaving her alone this week, I wonder if you could stop their activity.	Therapist makes direct request of Dark One to use his strength in behalf of the therapeutic goal.
J:	I could.	
H:	Would you be willing?	
J:	I'd be willing to try.	Dark One acquiesces.

H: How could you do it?

J: It wouldn't be easy.

H: Do you have a way that you might be able to do it? I realize you haven't done it before, but I wonder how you could do it now.

Therapist is curious as to just how Dark One can accomplish this. Just how does one ego state remove cathexis from another?

J: I could take over. I could take over for now, and attack them, stifle them.

H: Why don't you do that right now? And tell me what's happening.

J: I would do it in action while she is going through the day.

Transfer of energy to be accomplished during the day when Joan is acting, not during sleep.

H: In other words, it's not a matter of just talking to them, it's a matter of just reacting and cutting down on their energy, is that right?

J: That's right. I would work while they worked. I would stop them as they start to work.

Can phobias be treated by creating a counterphobic ego state that could be activated when an individual sensed the onset of his fear?

H: By the way, do you have any way of getting rid of them permanently, or not? I'm just asking.

J: I don't believe so.

Ego states can be deenergized, but the contents are not destroyed.

H: OK. In other words, maybe sometimes she needs those chemicals. Is that right?

J: Yes.

H: OK. I wonder now, since she does not need to be afraid of anything, if you would help me out and take over, because I know you have a lot of power . . . and you're really a very important part of her, and I really need your cooperation. Would you be willing to do that?

J: Yes. I don't like fear. I have a pride for this body. I know I stifle too, but I have a pride for this body. I don't like those . . . those fearsome little things.

H: All right, why don't you start cutting down on their influence, on their energy right now, so that in a moment, when I wake her up, she will feel relaxed. Would you be willing to do that?

Therapist suggests immediate action.

J: Yes. I must make her strong.

(Pause)

Dark One sees his role now as a positive one, not the earlier sabotaging one.

H: I can see, Dark One, that you are working on this task. And when you feel that you are finished, then let me know.

J: I've located them, and I'll take over, but when I take over Joan won't be as nice as she was.

Dark One is tough, masculine, and undiplomatic. During the time that he is waging a battle to decathect the Young Minds, Joan may not be pleasant to be around.

H: How do you mean, she won't be as nice?

J: I know that I am harder than she is. I have to be . . . to kill these Young Minds.

H: In other words, in order for you to take over, she will . . . behave differently somehow in her world? Is that what you mean?

J: Yes.

H: How will this translate itself into behavior in her world?

J: She may be cold. Distant . . . other people will bother her.

H:	How long do you think it will take you to take over to reduce the influence of these fear elements?	
J:	Perhaps three days.	
H:	Well, for three days, I would imagine it would be worth it, and I trust you, and I know that Joan and I both need you to do this, and I know that you will do a good job. And then, in three days, after you have taken care of these fear elements, and reduced their influence, and cut off their energy, then will she be able to be just natural and free again?	Dark One contracts to do the job in three days.
J:	Yes, I believe so. She won't have the chemicals . . . the chemicals pumping through her, making her more afraid than she has to be.	
H:	All right, Dark One, it's a deal, and I trust you to take good care of the situation. And now you can go where you need to go. Now I want to talk to Joan. Joan, in a moment, I am going to count up to five, and when I count up to five, you'll be wide awake, fresh and alert. Coming up now at the count of five . . . 1 . . . 2 . . . 3 . . . 4 . . . 5. How do you feel?	Therapist and Dark One agree on deal.
J:	Fine. My head isn't tense. It's, uh . . . I feel relaxed. Much more relaxed.	Joan already feels better since influence of Young Minds is being reduced by Dark One, and Dark One is now a friendly ally, not an entity to be feared.
H:	What do you remember of what we just did?	
J:	The Dark One. The Dark One	

came out. He's here now. I can feel him right here.	
H: In your head?	
J: Um-hm.	
H: We can now trust the Dark One. Do you realize that?	
J: Yes.	
H: He's our friend.	On being brought out of the hypnotic state we find that Joan is aware of what has been going on and gives her agreement to the project.
J: Yes.	
H: Let him do what he needs to do. Do you understand what he needs to do, or how long it's going to take him?	
J: Yes, yeah.	
H: What do you understand?	
J: Um-m . . . In order to stop this fear . . . this, this uptightness I've been having, um-m, He's going to stifle some fear elements. Some . . . I don't know what they are. Something that I've been afraid of in my life.	
H: Do you know how long it's going to take?	
J: Three or four days.	
H: I just want you to know that so you're kind of prepared for it, and so, for the next three or four days, he's going to have to take over, and you may feel, as a result, kind of cool and distant, but don't let it worry you. When he's through with his work, then you'll be back to normal again. OK?	Therapist reminds Joan of possible unpleasant behavior during the next three or four days.
J: Sure. Fine.	What would have been the therapeutic situation if the therapist had followed classical character analysis and treated the Dark One
H: All right.	

as a resistance to be broken through? As Otto Rank has noted (1950) so often we mobilize the very resistances (the will) of the patient, which we then take many months to analyze and "work through".

THE DARK ONE AS COTHERAPIST

This session[3] was recorded approximately three months later, following a summer vacation during which few sessions were held. Joan had never had any kind of job, but during the summer she obtained employment in a job she liked and at which she functioned well. She moved out of her parental home for the first time in her life and shared an apartment with a girl friend. These behaviors were indicative of important progress and growth in her life.

The Dark One was obviously allowing her to expose herself to the world in ways he had never allowed before. At the previous session, the Dark One had agreed to continue a fear desensitization begun with the one-and-one-half-year-old Little One, the ego state that was hospitalized and encased in fear within the oxygen tent. At the beginning of the following session, the nonhypnotized Joan complained of tenseness, being irritable, wanting to hit people, and her hands hurting. She is now hypnotized.

[3]**Therapist Note:** When this tape was originally made, I found, to my dismay, that it had not recorded. I asked the patient to return the next day, stating that I wanted to repeat our session because of the lack of recording and because I thought repetition of an important session might be therapeutic and reinforcing for her. She agreed. The next day I regressed her to the previous day and repeated the session. To my delight, the results were almost identical. Repetition is a valuable learning tool, and repeating key sessions through a regression technique might make their impact more permanent. This technique would be particularly useful to induce repeated abreactions.

H: Now I'm going to put my hand on your shoulder and I want you to breathe in deeper than you are right now. Just as deeply as you can go. That's it. I'm putting my hand on your shoulder, way down, and when you have gone as deeply as you can go, your right index finger will rise to let me know that you are there . . . All right. Now I want to talk to the Dark One, and when he

Therapist hypnotizes Joan and and calls for the Dark One.

	is here, he can just say I'm here or say hello . . .. I want to talk to the Dark One. Are you there, Dark One? . . .	
J:	I'm here.	
H:	All right. I understand from Joan that she's been nervous and her hands have ached at times. I know that we made an agreement this week that you would help her look at the world and I just want to know from you what's happened this week.	Previously determined that aching hands represent pain of injections and intravenous feedings when in oxygen tent.
J:	I made her see. I made her feel.	Apparently Dark One has cooperated.
H:	How did you do that?	
J:	I exposed her, exposed her to the sensations. I removed her bandage . . . She had a bandage of fantasy and it hurts her when I remove it; that's why her hands hurt.	A somatic memory from hospitalization at age one and a half.
H:	How often did you do that this week?	
J:	Now and then. A minute or so at a time. Very briefly. It hurt her.	Dark One applies principles of gradual desensitization.
H:	In other words, you only did it for as long as she could handle it.	
J:	Yes. I could feel her. I was in her, I know. It hurts her. I only do it briefly, very briefly.	Dark One is both subject and object.
H:	That's a very wise thing to do, and I appreciate your sensitivity to not having her exposed to more than she can handle . . . How do you feel about doing this, this week?	Therapist resonates with Dark One and reinforces him for his therapeutic sensitivity.
J:	It's necessary. It has to be done. I don't like it, but it has to be done to strengthen her.	Dark One is resonating with Little One's pain but still can be objective.

H:	I can understand your need not to hurt her, and I appreciate however also your understanding that she must face this in order to be free of fear.	Therapist gives resonance and reinforcement.
J:	Yes. It hurts her. She cries.	
H:	What do you do when she cries?	
J:	What can I do? I let her retreat . . . I give her her bandage back. But only for a while. It distresses me but she can't hide . . . She's angry at me sometimes.	Dark One cares for Little One like a parent for a child and is thus willing to do an unpleasant task for her benefit. Little One can stand only so much pain at one time. This anger translates itself into irritable behavior.
H:	She wants her bandage back. Is that right?	
J:	Yes. She has no protection.	
H:	I'd like your opinion on something. Do you think it might help her if I contacted her directly right now and held her hand as I did last week?	Therapist treats Dark One, her cotherapist, as a colleague.
J:	I don't know.	
H:	Why is it that you don't know?	
J:	I can see her . . . She'll have to come out again now . . . I don't know if I want her to or not.	Dark One ambivalent. His desires to help the Little One are in conflict with his own need to remain executive. He likes being on stage as cotherapist.
H:	Is it all right with you if I try to reach her directly right now?	
J:	Yes.	
H:	All right, Dark One. Thank you. I'll talk to you later again, but right now I'd like you to step aside and let the Little Girl come out, and when the Little Girl is here, then that right finger, the index finger, will rise again to let me know that she is here . . . All right. That's a girl. I'm going	Little One was the name used by the therapist and Dark One in referring to this underlying ego state. In talking directly to this state, however, the therapist often called her "Little Girl."

to take your left hand again and if any time that you want to talk to me through your left hand, remember that the left index finger will rise if you want to say yes, the middle finger will rise if you want to say no, and the thumb will wiggle if you want to say I don't know or I don't want to say anything . . . I know that you've been having a hard time this week being frightened. I know that the Dark One has taken off your bandages so that you could see the world, and I feel for your fear and your pain. Would it be all right if I touched your hand right now?

Little Girl doesn't talk, so therapist must assume responsibility for communication and rely on nonverbal cues to understand Little Girl's replies. Therapist attempting to resonate with Little Girl's needs.

This ideomotor (finger) technique for hypnotically communicating with underlying, non-speaking entities has been developed by David B. Cheek (See Cheek & LeCron, 1968).

J: (Nods head)

H: I see that you're nodding your head. All right. I'm just going to take my hand and you can do with my hand whatever you wish. That's it. Just hold on to it . . . I have a feeling that you're in pain. Is that right?

Therapist gets this from stiffness in Joan's hand.

J: (Nods head)

H: That's what I thought. Is your pain in your right hand?

J: (Nods head)

H: I want you to just concentrate on that right hand, and as you concentrate on that right hand, you're going to feel a flow of energy coming from my hand into your hand. And as you feel this flow of energy, this flow of caring coming into your hand, the pain will les-

Is this suggestion or transfer of ego cathexis?

Therapist, however, actually vibrates her hand.

sen and the discomfort will go away. Pay attention to your hand and feel that flow of energy going to your hand. Can you feel it?

J: (Nods head)

H: Fine. Does it feel better?

J: (Nods head)

The nonverbal message provides powerful assurance that the world is not harmful.

H: Yes, I see . . . You understand now, Little One, that I represent, I belong, to the world. Do you understand that?

J: (Nods head)

H: Yes . . . And I want you to realize that right now you felt me, and I belong to the world, taking pain away from you, not giving you pain. Do you understand?

The aim here is to help Little Girl unlearn her fixed idea that the world is harmful.

J: (Nods head)

H: All right, I see you saying yes. I'm not going to bother you any more right now. I just want you to think about that, that the pain, that the world, does not have to hurt you. That the world is not the same as it was under the oxygen tent. That this is a different world which will not hurt you. . . And the Dark One has been helping me, helping me . . . help you look at your world by taking the bandages from your eyes and although it hurts you occasionally, he is very understanding of you. He doesn't leave those bandages off any more than you can handle it, and what he's trying to help you do is to reduce your fear and reduce your pain so you will not be afraid, so that you can

This explanation is designed to increase the Little One's confidence in the Dark One.

	come out into the world and become strong, so that you will no longer hurt. Do you understand that?	
J:	(Seems unsure)	
H:	I know that's hard to understand but trust him, OK? Even if it hurts for a little while, it will not hurt in the long run . . . Can you understand that?	
J:	(Nods head)	
H:	All right. Now I'm going to put your hand back again. That's the way. And the hand is all right now. The hand feels fine. And you can go to sleep again Little One . . . And now I'd like the Dark One to come back. And when the Dark One is here, then he can just say hello again.	Therapist felt change in Joan's grasp.
J:	I'm here.	
H:	All right . . . How is she now, and what do you think about what we just did?	Therapist wants to check out her perception with Dark One.
J:	It's all right.	
H:	How does she feel?	
J:	She's all right. She's safe.	
H:	I'd like to say something to you, Dark One. I really appreciate what you've been doing for her, for the Little One. I guess I kind of see you as my assistant or co-worker in what we're trying to do together to help her. And of course what we're trying to do is to help her be less fearful and to become strong . . . How do you feel about that?	Therapist accepts Dark One in the role of cotherapist.
J:	It has to be done . . .	
H:	How do you feel helping me	

out, being my co-worker so to speak, in this project, what we're trying to do together?

J: I do this because the unit has to survive. I was once the absolute monarch of this universe and I don't like giving up this monarchy, but I must survive within her fragile body and I must help her to survive.

He doesn't like giving up his absolute autonomy, but he is realistic and increasingly mature.
Dark One still thinks of Joan as being a little child. He was born when Joan was three because she was fragile and needed protection (the molestation).

H: I am touched by your willingness to step down from total control. I realize it must be hard to give up power, but I guess I believe that we are both here for the same purpose and our ultimate purpose together is to have the total personality become a happy, well integrated personality, so that she's really put together, functioning well and content in this world. Do you agree?

Therapist resonates and reinforces Dark One.

J: Yes. I appreciate your efforts to make her stronger. She must be made stronger. I appreciate the work you're doing to help us survive.

Dark One speaks like a colleague. He now resonates back. The *quid pro quo* reciprocity between therapist and patient (see Chapter 17).

H: Thank you, Dark One. That makes me feel good, too. Now, Dark One, I'm going to be gone for two weeks and I'd like you to take over and continue to help the Little One face the world. Use your judgment as to how much she can handle just as you've been doing before. Do whatever you feel is right for her and what will help her and not damage her. But as you and I both know she has to face a little pain in order to get over it. Are you willing to do that while I'm gone?

Therapist responds to Dark One's resonance with her.

Therapist shows confidence and trust in her cotherapist.

J: Yes.

H: And now Dark One, fine, thank you. I'd like you to go to sleep, and I want to talk to the total personality. I'm going to count up to 5 in a moment, and when I count up to 5 you'll be wide awake, fresh and alert. Coming up at the count of 5. 1 . . . 2 . . . 3 . . . 4 . . . 5. How do you feel?

J: Just fine.

H: What about the pain?

J: Nope. A little bit in my arms, but it, it's fine.

Note change from "her" to "my." Total personality feels Little Girl's pain.

H: Fine. All right. What do you remember?

J: Mmm, the little, the Little Girl and the Dark One.

H: Do you know what's happening between them?

J: Between them? He's bringing her out of hiding, he's pushing her out, making her see things.

After hearing Dark One and Little Girl interact, the nonhypnotized Joan understands what is happening to her.

H: That's right. What he's doing is to desensitize her to her fears by gradually exposing her a little bit more and more fear. That is, exposing her, taking the bandages off and exposing her a little bit more and more to the world and having her view the world as it is. She's been blinded by her fantasies, and therefore, it's going to hurt every once in awhile. You're going to experience this pain once in awhile. And sometimes you'll be angry because she gets angry at him when he takes the bandages

Therapist makes final summarizing interpretation to the integrated Joan.

off, but it will only be temporary and it will become less and less. Do you understand? Just so you know what's going on. OK? So you won't need to worry about it. OK?

J: Yeah.

How does an ego state regard its own self? If it has changed, how might it think of itself as "what I was" in relation to "what I am"? During the following brief exerpt from a later session, Dark One gives us a glimpse into his reactions on this point.

THE DEMON AND THE EXORCIST

H:	Just as deeply as you can go. Way, way down . . . that's it. Now I'm going to put my hand on your shoulder and I'll push you just a little bit more; that's it and down farther and farther . . . And now I'd like to talk to the Dark One, and when the Dark One is here with me he can just say I'm here . . .	Session starts, as usual, with the the recorded ending of a brief hypnotic induction.
J:	I'm here.	
H:	All right, Dark One. The last time that we talked together you said that you would continue the fear densensitization of the Little One while I was gone. What happened during the week?	Therapist seeking information from Dark One on his progress in desensitization of Little One's fears.
J:	She was raw. She was pushed by new sensations. She still doesn't know how to handle herself.	Dark One's report appears to be objective. He seems able to keep his evaluation from being influenced by his personal desires to succeed and impress therapist.
H:	What did you do during the week . . . ah . . . you said she was raw. I'm not sure	

	just what you mean.	
J:	I removed her shell, she doesn't even know she has it still. I removed it at odd times for longer and longer periods and it was very irritating to her, very rough on her . . .	Dark One is a good behavior modifier.
H:	How do you . . . how did you feel (I should say) . . . How did you feel about doing this?	
J:	It's a necessary thing to, to toughen her emotional skin. She has to go through a period of rawness.	Dark One is objective and tough but not sadistic.
H:	How is that effecting her in terms of her everyday life?	
J:	It's distressing to her but she's already getting stronger. She can tolerate it, she can tolerate it well.	Dark One demonstrates his therapy is effective.
H:	Sounds to me like you've done a pretty good job.	Therapist continues to reinforce her cotherapist.
J:	Yes, I have.	
H:	That's great. I . . . I really feel both grateful to you and I guess kind of proud of you and kind of amazed at what you were able to accomplish. I guess my feelings are one of admiration of you.	In theoretical terms the therapist is directing all the cathexis possible into a constructive tendency within the patient.
J:	Thank you.	Ego states enjoy praise just like whole persons
H:	By the way, and this is an aside, Joan was telling me that, all of you saw *The Exorcist* last night and she was telling me that you had a different reaction from the rest of her. Would you like to tell me what that was, felt like?	Therapist brings up a sensitive area indirectly.
J:	It was asinine! It's really . . . it wasn't . . . I had better things to do than	Joan reported being intrigued by the picture but not Dark One. For him, it hit too close to home.

	watch that. It was just silly.	
H:	How come you thought that?	
J:	Hmm, just the concept, the concept of the exorcism, of exorcising a demon . . . If demons exist, they can't be exorcised in such a way.	
H:	What can be done with demons?	. . . the therapist asks naively!
J:	If a demon exists within a human, the demon is a sprout of that human's mind and the human can defeat it.	Dark One shows some psychological sophistication.
H:	Is that what you are, a sprout of a human's mind?	Therapist decides to confront Dark One's sensitivity on this point directly.
J:	Yes.	
H:	In other words, you have experienced change within yourself . . . and I guess you can see that change in you has been possible, that you have changed form. That you're no longer the punitive and evil one, that you're really no longer what Joan considered you to be, a demon.	Therapist gives him reassurance of her present esteem for him, and at the same time reinforces his conversion to a constructive force in Joan's psychic economy.
J:	I might have been. I might be now, but the concept of that demon in the movie even if it is parasitic, it would not destroy its host. That made me angry. I would not destroy my host. I would not destroy this fragile body. Then we would all die.	Dark One shows righteous indignation at the movie's portrayal of a demon, however, the generalization is not universally true. He would not *now* destroy his own host, but if all destructive ego states in people could show as much insight and change there would be many fewer suicides.
H:	That's the point isn't it? If you destroy Joan you die too, and therefore it becomes important (and I guess I feel exactly the way you do) that we all work together so that all survive. In this	Therapist is now deeply resona-

	society of ego states I guess I don't see you as a demon, I see you as an ego state, I see you as a very essential part of her, who can be very constructive and very important. I guess we kind of see this whole situation very similarly, don't we?	ting with Dark One's needs to be regarded as a good and strong self, her therapeutic helper, and a necessary element in the "society of Joan."
J:	Yes.	
H:	Well, what about . . . what do you view as our next step in terms of the Little One?	They now get together on the next steps in therapeutic strategy.
J:	She's no longer as afraid as she was. She feels tremors of fear but she no longer panics. I can see her now, she's no longer afraid but she's naive. She, she has no care. She steps on things; she touches things she shouldn't.	Dark One reports progress but warns of the hazards of naivete.
H:	In other words she's just like a natural child who needs to learn what other people are feeling.	
J:	Yes.	
H:	She apparently doesn't really know what effect she has upon the world.	
J:	None. She has no concept of the world affecting her either. She doesn't know how to interact.	Little One needs to react realistically to a world of people. She is just coming out of her shell and needs socializing.
H:	Well, I guess our next step then is . . . I'm going to have to help her and teach her. Do you agree?	Therapist suggests that Little One now needs interpersonal relationship skills.
J:	Yes.	Dark One agrees.

It is not the purpose of this chapter to present Joan's case in detail. Rather, the objective is to present a sample of ego-state therapy technique. To describe ego-state therapy in detail, with or without hypnosis, will require another book. There were many sessions before and after those excerpted here that illustrated fascinating interactions between the therapist and Joan's various ego states. Suffice it to say that during the treatment she changed significantly. At the beginning of therapy, she was an antisocial and unattractively overweight young woman, who dissociated frequently and was often tortured by malevolent hallucinations. Her passive, withdrawn exterior belied the turmoil within, but by keeping this to herself she avoided hospitalization and presented an appearance to others sufficiently acceptable to enable her to remain in school.

During the therapy she changed into an attractive, charming person, who now forms friendly relationships that are mutually valued. At this writing she is not quite ready for dating relationships with men, but that is the direction the therapy is moving. She has become a leader in a campus club and is able to express her self-assertiveness and leadership qualities. She very rarely dissociates spontaneously now and does not hallucinate. The various ego states cooperate to form an integrated self. There are still some anxieties, some insecurities, and occasional psychosomatic symptoms, but these are not excessive, and Joan knows how to master them herself most of the time. The previous malevolent ego states have either been decathected or turned into constructive forces within her psychic economy.

The case excerpts have been presented to illustrate how a therapy can be handled using ego-state theoretical concepts and a balance of resonance with objectivity.

FOOTNOTE

[1]"Joan" is a pseudonym.

Chapter 23

A CHILD DIES

A Battle With An Introject

An introject is an internalized object. It is within us and yet not a part of our own self. Like a particle of food undigested within our stomach, it is a bit of the environment, inside, yet retaining the same characteristics as perceived when it was outside. In some respects the superego may be considered an introject. We internalize the attitudes and values of authority figures. If these remain as introjects then we follow their bidding. They impinge on our ego and require that it behave accordingly. When these introjects become egotized (e.g., invested with ego cathexis) they are changed into identofacts. The superego now is considered as part of our self. We apply its injunctions "naturally," not as if forced to do so, but as if they represented our own attitudes and values, which indeed they have then become.

The introjects a child takes into himself early in life have a very fixed character, much as if imprinted (Lorenz, 1935). That is, they tend to remain and exert influence throughout the life of the individual. If these introjects were loving, accepting parents, then the child goes through life feeling appreciated and wanted. He tends to develop a happy personality. It is as if the sun is always shining on him. He is continually receiving what is described by the transactional analysts as strokes (Harris, 1969; Holland, 1973). Such a fortunate person has few self doubts. His introjects continually reassure him that he is a "good" boy or a "good" girl, that what he does is worthy of praise, and that his person is welcome and appreciated.

On the other hand, if parent figures were perceived as nagging, dominating, rejecting, or cruel, and if he has internalized them as introjected objects, then he goes through life constantly hearing (unconsciously) the voice of the critical parent. If he has been painfully beaten, he may replicate such beatings in the form of psychosomatic pains and in the same parts of the body that had been recipients of the whipping stick. He leads a chronically depressed and unhappy life. If he is unable to throw out (extraject) such malevolent objects then he can escape from their tyranny only by identifying with them, that is, by infusing them with self energies and establishing them as identofacts. He then becomes cruel and rejecting toward his own children, but he does not suffer. To throw out these introjects means to withdraw object cathexis from them, to render them inactive by deenergizing. Like a car out of gas, they then cannot function. They cease to have impact on his self.

Just as the introjects of loved (and loving) parents are invested with object cathexis of the libidinal type and serve the principle of Eros by their integrating tendencies, the introjects of hated (and hating) parents must be invested with object energies that are primarily mortidinal in character. As we know, the effect of such energies is to push away, to separate, and to simplify an organism, hence to move it in the direction of death. Such is the consequence of introjecting hating persons.

But this withdrawl of object cathexis from the hate introject is not easy. Introjects that have been internalized early in childhood are very sticky; they have become deeply imbedded in the individual's entire fabric of behavior, values, and attitudes. They are an integral part of what Adler (1963) has called the "life style." To remove them is a major job in psychological surgery. Painful as they be, unhappy as they make the individual possessing them, he will cling to them like a drowning man to a straw. The therapist who attacks them can anticipate bottomless wells of resistance to their removal.

The process is dynamically similar to that which exists when a spouse engages in endless mourning at the loss of a loved one. Freud in his brilliant paper "Mourning and melancholia" (1925) has clearly described these mechanisms. In a popular contribution, Watkins (1967b) translated this dynamic formulation into terms more easily understandable to the layman. The situation may be briefly depicted as follows:

When John woos Mary and takes her on a date, there is a common experience accompanied by a pleasurable feeling. The behavioral principles of learning through positive reinforcement (Skinner, 1953) apply here. The commonness is enhanced and reinforced. Every such experience, the first kiss, each embrace, the marriage, sexual relations, the having of children, etc., constitutes another commonness behavior followed or accompanied by pleasurable reinforcement. The couple fall, or rather grow, in love. In terms of our personality model, the two establish introjects of each other that are increasingly built in by pleasurably reinforced ties. The internalized images are benevolent and provide mutually reinforcing strokes. They are "in love" with each other.

When the time comes many years later that one of them, say John, dies, the other, Mary, is left with an introjected image of him that has no existing counterpart now in real life. John has gone to the world of unreality, while she is forced to continue existence in this, the real, world. If her ego is too weak to tolerate this deprivation, if she has become too dependent upon him, then when confronted with the choice of giving him up and remaining in this world or continuing to hold on to him and following him into a world of unreality, she may choose the latter. She develops a psychosis. Shortly after his death, she informs her friends and other family members smilingly that John is with her again. He has returned; she sees him and speaks with him. We say she now has a hallucination. Unwilling to decathect John's introject to harmonize his demise with his absence in the real world, she decathects reality and remains with him in an internalized world of fantasy.

However, if her ego is built more sturdily, and if it seeks to continue its function of reconciling her to reality, then she must go through the painful operation known as mourning. This is really a relearning, a "falling out" of love, the reverse of those processes that occurred in the establishment of her relationship to John. Now she reviews in her mind, over and over again, each happy incident they experienced together but this time followed by the hurt of realization that he is gone. It is like repeating such experience of commonness but now accompanied by punishment rather than reward. The effect is to weaken and dissolve the ties that had bound them together. After each such painful reminiscence, a bit of object cathexis is gradually withdrawn, until finally the day comes when he is only a memory, no longer the necessary light of her life. Her libidinal cathexes have been withdrawn, and she is free to invest them in a new object. She can now love and live again.

This process is painful and takes time for its accomplishment. Freud (1925) spoke of it as "mourning work." If one does not do one's mourning work after the loss of a loved object, one may be forever bound to that person; one may never become free. Sometimes well-meaning friends who are distressed at Mary's weeping (perhaps because it reminds them of the potential loss of one of their own loved ones) may try to abort this process in her. "Come on now, Mary, you've got to snap out of this. Why not go to the movies with us tonight? It'll get your mind off his death." Such friends do Mary no service. Unless the mourning (like an abreaction) goes on to completion, there will be no closure in her relationship contract with the now departed John. She will remain forever in bondage to his image.

However, sometimes we do find cases where a spouse engages in interminable mourning. The sadness goes on for years as he or she continually affirms to the world the great loss suffered. Then people say, "She loved him so much that she has never gotten over his death." It is seldom realized that this continual mourning is not the result of an enormous love, but rather of an ambivalence. She *hates* John as well as loving him. Of course, the hatred is unconscious; it must be denied. But this unresolved hatred provides the "hook" that prevents a freeing of herself from attachment to his image. From a learning theory point of view, each time she reminisces about a commonness experience she, like the others, is simultaneously aware of John's death. But this recognition of his death brings an unconscious pleasure; she had previously wished his death since she was not happy in the relationship. Her superego and self image do not permit her to recognize this hostility toward him. And as long as she continues to repress this side of her ambivalence, then mourning with its verification of his death becomes an unconscious pleasure. It is positively reinforced by the subliminal knowledge that "the S.O.B. is now dead."[1]

Since Mary must repress the hatred side of her ambivalence toward John, it is obvious how difficult will be the task of that therapist who undertakes to rescue her from eternal mourning, who would free her for new life and new love. She will resist with every possible defense the recognition that she continually mourns, not because her love was so greater than others, but because it was mixed with hostility and wishes for his death.

If the introjects of love (or ambivalence) that are established late in life are clung to so tenaciously, how much more sticky are those which are imprinted on the small child during the first years. The rejecting parent may be hated by the child, but he is also the only source of nurturance, of food, of gratification, of life itself. If the child were to turn from the rejecting parent then he might be abandoned and die. The child must continue to grasp and cling to his malevolent introjects, to endure the pain, the deflation of ego, the self doubts and unhappiness if he is merely to survive.

Accordingly, just as the ambivalent spouse could not accept her unconscious hostility, the child who is tied to a hate-love parent, and who recognizes and verbalizes to the therapist his hatred of the parent, cannot accept that he also loved that person and was dependent on him. He "had" to love the parent. Otherwise he, the child, would die.[2] To admit that his feelings for the parent were ambivalent, that his rage was mingled with dependent need and love is just as intolerable to the "child" in analytic therapy as the acceptance of her own hostility was to Mary. Even as Mary goes on in continual mourning, this rejected child never ceases in his hatred of his parents and his rage at the world. Only after he can come to grips with his ambivalence can he detach himself from the hate-love introject to which he has been so completely chained. The therapist must help him to express the hostility directly at the introjected parent, perhaps in repeated abreactions. Following this, interpretations of his dependency and love toward that one become possible.

The love of the rejected child for his parent may also be forced by fear. The child dare *not* love the parent. If the child shows rejection of the parent in any way, that powerful one might annihilate the little fellow. The story has been told of the youthful leader of an East Side gang of subteenagers in New York who called his crew together and informed them: "Listen, you guys, you better like me, or you'll get a punch in the nose."

To undermine the power of a malevolent introject the therapist must do all possible to establish himself as a powerful, as well as accepting, ally of the patient. The therapist needs to appear both loving and strong. This can be done as he gives to the patient that love (understanding equals love) and acceptance that develop in the patient sufficient ego strength to confront and resolve his dilemma with the introjected parent. The therapist is gradually introjected, cathected with object energies, and replaces that of the parent. The introjected therapist now can provide strokes, ego strengthening and the support of "we-ness" needed by the patient so as to enable him to confront the powerful hated parent introject and overthrow him ("kill" him); that is, he removes cathexis from him and reduce him to an unpleasant memory, no longer a power in the life style of the patient. Of such was the case of M.

THE CASE OF M

M was a young man of schizoid personality whose entire existence revolved around the concept of hate.

His view of life was that of hating a world that he perceived as hating him. His thoughts and fantasies had been preoccupied with both suicide and murder. He reported frequent incidents of rejection and cruelty by his parents involving threats of castration and abandonment. Many months were required by the two cotherapists (the author and his wife, Helen H. Watkins) to establish even a tenuous working relationship. There had been a continuous working through, utilizing dream material, transference reactions, and hypnotic abreactions of many experiences from the present back to early incidents that had apparently occurred prior to the age of two. Throughout all this, however, the patient maintained that the therapists "didn't exist." They were a part of his schizoid world, which represented his defense against the threat of rage discharge from within. Such anger, if expressed, might result in the death of himself or others. The "freezing" of it in schizoid character armor (Reich, 1949) served to hold at bay those figures in the outside world whom he perceived as hating him.

He did not feel that his therapists hated him at the time of this session—although it had taken some doing to remove them from that category. However, he protected them from a transference of his hatred toward his parents by making them "unreal." Communication was on a schizoid basis and was not permitted to have a significant impact on his internal dynamic structure.

It was obvious that he suffered from enormous fear of his rejecting parents and that his self was like a small country that was prostrate under the heel of Hitlerlike introjects. His earlier anger had been expressed against the mother, but it was his father toward whom his greatest fear and rage was now directed. Accordingly, he was able to manage some relationship and communication better with the female therapist (H. H. W.). At this stage of the therapy he could talk to her more easily and could respond by entering a state of hypnosis better when she induced it.

In one sense he had introjected the therapists and did have constructive relationships with them. This was manifested by his feeling better when in their presence and after therapeutic sessions. This appeared theoretically to have been accomplished by his having constructed their introjects within an ego state separate from the one containing the introject of his parents. The ego state containing parent introjects was obviously the more powerful (the more highly cathected) since it occupied most of his time, thought, and experience. If he was not feeling depressed and hated, he was experiencing hate toward the world, alternating perhaps by a process of identifying and deidentifying with his parental introjects. His relationship with the therapists had previously never seemed strong enough to induce him to turn direct anger against the parent images and to enable him to emancipate himself from their tyranny.

Even when the therapists used their best therapeutic selves, the utmost of persuasion and support and the strongest motivation, together with continuous interpretation of the transference situation, the patient would quail when trying to verbalize hatred toward the parents, especially the father.

He was preoccupied with the delusion that he was the recipient of poison, which was equated with milk. His dreams and associations brought poison, hate, and milk into symbolic equivalence. Gradually he recalled that when his parents rejected him they would throw him back into his crib and shove a bottle into his mouth. Thus milk became directly associated with their hatred and rejection. Later when he learned that "poison kills," this concept was added. To him, his parents were going to kill him by forcing him to drink poisoned milk.

The efforts of the therapists had been to try to induce him to reject the "poisoned milk," to "talk back" to his introjected parents, and to tell them off, thereby demonstrating his independence of them. This could be a first step in replacing their introjects with those of the two therapists who, as loving and loved new parent figures, could then provide strokes.

It is a therapeutic truism that you cannot kill an enemy in his absence, and that harmful introjects, identofacts, attitudes, values, and conflicts cannot be dealt with unless they are first activated. This is done in traditional psychoanalysis within the transference relationship. Valuable as is this tool, we feel that the repressed states can often be more rapidly activated within a hypnoanalytic relationship than in the conscious condition.

Accordingly, since M responded best to the female therapist, sessions were usually initiated by her induction of a deep hypnotic state and regression of him back to the earliest levels. During a number of previous attempts, we had been unable to get him to confront the feared-hated parental introjects and talk back to them. His fear of death at their hands had been too great. However, it has always been our therapeutic strategy that when in doubt we work on the relationship. Accordingly, we had dedicated ourselves as completely as possible to resolving his problem and had given him almost unlimited time, two-hour to three-hour sessions twice a week. Analytic interpretations aimed at blocks or impairments in our relationship were accompanied by all the realistic strokes possible. As the weeks passed, it became clear that he dared move closer and closer to a realistic confrontation with the powerful parental introjects. Presented here are recorded excerpts of several significant three-hour sessions, during which the patient began to respond as if his therapists were real, as if within such a therapeutic allyship his ego felt sufficiently strong so that he could tell off his parental introjects, and begin a working-through process of decathecting them, and accept a benevolent "re-parenting."

By the time of this session, the understanding of the therapists and the intellectual insight of the patient concering the childhood events that had initiated his schizoid withdrawal from reality were somewhat as follows: Apparently from the earliest age (6 months to two years) whenever he experienced an erection his parents would turn on him violently, slap him, and threaten to cut off his "pee-pee." They would often throw him back into his crib, and to still his cries, shove a bottle into his mouth. Accordingly, milk meant hate and rejection to him. Later when he found that poisons were used to kill, he reinterpreted these experiences to mean that they were trying to kill him with poisoned milk. Often, after a severe beating he would black out, hence "die."

On one occasion, at age two, his father threatened to cut off his penis with a pair of scissors, which were displayed in front of him. At that time his mother laughed and urged the father to do so. The patient had equated his penis with his ability to "love," so this meant taking his "love" away. Somehow, he had fantasied that father would cut off his penis and that then mother would eat it. After this threatening session, his father had given him an enema. Accordingly, he interpreted this as meaning that following castration he would be a girl and that he might then "receive love" only by quieting down after the enema—translated later as accepting anal rape from father.

To escape from the intolerable situation of losing his penis he would black out. This eventually crystallized into a schizoid withdrawal from the world, so that his parents and others became unreal, "don't exist." His self entered a private world, a repressed ego state, leaving a schizoid shell of an ego state to interact with the environment. Under such circumstances, the therapists were not considered as real persons, and communications from them had no impact on his real (but internalized) self. The objective of the sessions, from which excerpts are reproduced, was to communicate under a hypnotic realtionship with his real, child self, to disposess the parent introjects and induce him to replace them with loving, accepting, therapeutic parents, and to secure a release of the enormous wells of repressed hatred that he could never express toward his parents, either their original persons, or their introjects.

We hoped that in this way we might allow him to "come out," to enter the real (our) world, to accept alliance with the two therapists, (hence, to take them in as benevolent introjects), gradually to decathect the original parental introjects, and to replace them with those of the therapists. This would permit mastering his fear of them.

His dilemma had been that he could retain his "love" (his penis) only by "not exist," leaving the real world and taking his "love" with him. The schizoid shell left to interact with the real world was now devoid of "love"—it could neither give nor receive love. The tremendous resistance to undoing this dynamic maneuver is obvious from the following excerpts of key sessions.

J:	Can you picture in your mind, can you picture my face?	Therapist J is rejected as "not real." The schizoid shell ego state which is on the surface interacts meaninglessly with the outside world.
M:	Uh, no.	
J:	Can you give me a description of it?	
M:	No . . . see, I . . . I don't feel that you have . . . ah . . . as a person . . . I feel it's on a different level.	
J:	But once you could view me	Therapist J offers closer relation-

	as another person then you would have a powerful ally, wouldn't you? Then you and I together would be much stronger.	ship.
M:	Ah, yeah, theoretically . . . yeah, it would work.	M's reaction intellectual.
H:	(Whispering) Your father would have to die. Your father would have to die. You could join forces with Jack. Your father would die.	Therapist H, adopting an alter ego role, continually whispers "suggestions," and tries to communicate with the underlying "child" ego state while the "shell" and J talk to each other.
J:	You would join forces with me. Your father would die.	
M:	Yes, I mean, the castration thing is there definitely . . . I mean you're going to have, you would have to work with that somehow.	Intellectually, the shell knows that his castration fear prevents him from real communication with J.
J:	Right now I think we'll work with you, just you as a person. All the *things* can be worked with much easier once you let me know you as a human being.	J ineffectually tries to become real to M.
M:	You're going to have to be something.	True. But how?
H:	(Whispering) Jack is not going to cut off your penis, like your father threatened to do. But Jack won't do that. Your father threatens to do that.	H tries to reassure the child state.
J:	I am not father. There is nothing in me at all like father. I am a very different person. I am a person willing to help you. I have strength, yes, but not strength against you.	J tries realistically contrasting his accepting behavior with the parenal rejection.
M:	There's . . . I . . . I don't know . . . it's just, like some sense of being overriding . . . I mean it goes to the past.	The fear is too "overriding." "I dare not oppose father and accept you, J."

J:	But that past has to be controlled by the present, until you can see that it doesn't apply to . . . I am not father. You can make me your father, yes, but I am not the person he was. I do not hold his views, his ideas, his values, share his relationships with you.	J argues "realistically." Was Freud right when he maintained that "the voice of the intellect is soft but persistent"?
M:	No, Jack, you have . . . it's like . . . talking that way doesn't help . . . uh . . . to you . . . separate . . . see, I have to be able to deal somehow . . . deal to you as a non . . . OK, you get rid of that, you know, completely destructive sense I have of you. That's . . . where I would be more valid. 'Cause, see, words don't mean anything at this level. Oh . . .	The shell reacts intellectually. No communication between J and the child. The transference fear is too strong.
J:	As long as I am . . .	
M:	No, look, it's almost in a . . . it goes to a pre . . . a sense what's . . . preverbal . . . see, to speak words don't have any meaning . . . But there's that sense of . . . you have to deal with that sense of a complete destructiveness (very haltingly) because I talk . . . you understand talking doesn't . . . it just would not . . . it doesn't have any reality . . . that overwhelmingness does seem real . . .	The child developed his fear and "ran away" at almost a preverbal age. J's words don't mean anything to him. The sense of destructiveness is both overriding and overwhelming. Potential love of J and H weaker than fear of father.
J:	We will have to communicate in some way, and what you have is not real.	
M:	Well, let's, I think, dwell on that overwhelmingness, see if I . . . *That* I think has value.	The shell suggests concentrating on (hence, experiencing the overwhelming fear)—an abreaction.
J:	Tell me about it.	
M:	I don't know, it's almost as if,	The fear is all-consuming.

	you know, I have an overwhelmingness out there, I mean, I know it's there . . . and, but, it isn't you know, I'm consumed by it.	
H:	(Whispering) The overwhelmingness is real. Reaching back to the real world. But *you* are the one that's running and does not face it.	The child says we aren't real. H accuses the child of abdicating reality and becoming himself unreal.
M:	NO!	Brings a violent denial from the child state.
H:	(Whispering) Yes it is. *You* are not real. You are running away. You left that little boy behind who's afraid of death. *You left him behind, you left him there.* Fear and suffering. YOU RAN OFF! You ran off and abandoned him!	
M:	No . . . !	Continued denials indicating that child state is activated enough to respond to H. This means making her real.
H:	(Whispering) Yes you did! You ran off! You let him lie there . . .	
M:	No . . . !	
H:	(Whispering) . . . there in fear.	
M:	No . . .	
H:	(Whispering) And now you try to tell me you're protecting yourself. You're not! You're not! You ran off! You don't exist. You don't exist. We exist.	Both therapists now addressing child state.
J:	I am Jack Watkins. My . . .	
M:	No, I . . .	
J:	. . . existence is real . . .	
H:	(Whispering) No. You don't exist. Jack exists. I exist. And	

	you know the world existed, then. But you're going to have to come back. You're going to have to stop running because you're in a false world. You're in the false world of images. Blackness. Nonreality. You're going to have to *come back*, and face the *real world*. Only the real world will not be . . . like it was. But you're going to have to come back to the new world. When you come back you will see Jack, and then you will see me. Then you'll be different. Then you will be part of . . . a real world.	
J:	You really wanted a father, didn't you? You wanted a good father?	J strikes a tender note in child. He resonates to that which child most wishes but must, through fear, deny.
M:	(Faintly) No . . .	
J:	Didn't you?	
M:	(Louder) No . . .	Child denies, but a tear coursing down cheek shows he's being reached.
J:	Yes. You wanted one who loved you and protected you, isn't that what you wanted? That was real. That's what you really wanted, wasn't it? You didn't have it. But you wanted it.	
M:	(Very faintly, and crying softly) No . . .	
J:	Yes. I think that you've searched now in yourself you can have the feeling that you would like very much to have one. You have that feeling, coming into . . .	Words of both J and H are penetrating schizoid shell, reaching repressed and fearing child state.
M:	No . . .	
J:	. . . your face, your eyes . . .	Trying to expand (by suggestion)

child cathexis over more of the body.

M: No . . .

J: . . . the realization that you really want to have a father.

M: No . . . !

J: You want a father.

M: No . . . !

J: And you want to have a mother.

M: No . . . !

J: And you would like to have both Helen and I . . .

M: No . . . !

J: . . . in these positions.

M: (Loud and desperate denial) NO!

J: Your words say, "No," but your heart says differently. That's reality.

In spite of his fear, child can't completely shut out therapists—make them unreal. He is responding because they are resonating to some of his deepest needs. Denials are ungenuine.

During the next hour (this session continued for over three hours) the "child" continued to express the facade of denial, while the therapists repetitiously, sometimes softly, sometimes vehemently, confronted him with that which he truly wanted, loving parents. As the hour wore on his denials became less, his strength greater. Signs of repressed anger at the parental introjects peep through the "overwhelming" fear. These are punctuated occasionally by returns of the shell, who intellectually describes the "split" that occurred and advises on therapeutic strategy. The shell ego state would emerge momentarily, calm, intellectual, and detached. Shortly afterward the emotional turmoil being experienced by the child state would return and the abreaction would continue.

M: I . . . I just . . . I don't . . . (hard breathing) I . . . just . . . split all the ego . . . I don't know, something there . . . I don't know . . . I don't . . .

"I . . . just split all the ego . . ." is a momentary surfacing of the intellectual shell through the "ocean" of emotion.

H:	Hold on to me.	H is holding M in her arms; J sitting beside her is holding M's hand. Therapists going all out to provide support, tangible contact, and protection to struggling child state.
M:	No . . . I . . . I lose contact . . .	
H:	I can be real to you, so hold on to me.	
M:	There's just one of those splits that . . . (chokes)	Shell state comes out for a moment. Can't stay. Emotion overriding.
H:	Hold on tight. HOLD ON TIGHT! HOLD ON! HOLD ON! And let go of that anger. Hold on tight and let loose of that anger. (M is breathing hard) Hold on, and receive something else besides hate. Receive love instead of hate. Receive love instead of hate; hold on tight. Come on! Receive love instead of hate.	
M:	(Breathing hard) I can't talk.	Shell state again.
H:	Feel that anger. Yes. That anger's coming *through*. That anger's getting through, you can feel it. You can feel it coming up through your chest and through your throat and through your eyes and through your mouth. You can feel it.	H working to initiate release of rage by abreactive technique. (Reich's "muscular armor.")
J:	You'd like to spit out that milk . . .	J turning to milk/poison/hate theme.
H:	You'd like to vomit it up.	
J:	Spit it out . . . and, and bite at her . . .	
H:	It makes you sick inside. All that milk and all that hate just make you sick inside.	
M:	Ssss . . . I . . . I . . . I . . . get	Part child, part shell.

ride . . . I . . . I don't . . . sss . . . it goes to her, as an object.

H: Angry. Mad.

M: No!

Denials not quite exhausted yet.

H: Mad at her! Yes you are! You're just enraged with her, angry at her, and the more you think about her, the madder you get! Just enraged and screaming inside; you can hear yourself screaming inside at her. Just feel those feelings coming up inside, just breaking loose, wanting to get at her, wanting to bite her, wanting to destroy her, wanting to get at her! Angry, angry hate! Anger at her! No love from her! Nothing but poison milk!

M: . . . No . . . you have to do . . . in taking of milk would be the inturning of the annngg . . . (chokes) . . . ger . . . instead of putting . . .

J: Turning the anger in and putting it inside you.

M: Yes . . . in just . . . to adjust . . . is to incorppp . . .

Shell with intellectual insight. Child wouldn't know word "incorporate."

J: To incorporate hate and anger inside yourself, isn't that it?

Therapist urging decathexis of mother introject.

H: (Whispering) You took her inside, you took her inside, you took her hate, you took her hate and her anger inside . . .

M: Nnno . . . part of it would be just to control ang . . . (with difficulty and crying sounds) It must be a . . . (breathes hard) to control angger . . .

H:	So it became the equivalent of anger, because it was used to control anger, because it *was* anger. It was hatred, it was hated milk. (M is breathing hard) And it was used to control anger.	
J:	And so this little boy survived on hatred. He learned that, only as he took in hatred could he survive.	
M:	I . . . just see . . . I'lll sssee if I can . . . get rid of the anger . . . it's just teeming inside . . .	
H:	Hold on tight. If you need, hold on tight. We'll be able to do it.	Therapists joining forces.
J:	We're with you.	
H:	Come on, we're with you, come on.	
M:	I . . . I'd like to just . . . on . . . the rage, into the milk . . . I really . . .	
H:	Right.	
J:	Just rage into that milk, go on.	
H:	You're swimming in it, swimming in it.	
J:	Pour it out at her.	
M:	I . . . it's . . . not drink . . . not incorporate milk . . . it has . . . in those themes of not . . .	
H:	I'm not going to drink it. I'm not going to drink it any more.	H phrases it in resonant terms.
J:	I don't have to have it, I don't have to have you anymore.	So also does J now.
H:	I don't need that poisoned milk. I have another source now. I don't need it.	

	Dialogue	Commentary
J:	I don't need *it*. I don't need *you*.	
M:	Nnnnot drink the milk . . . (breathing hard) It took in just . . . special milk . . .	"Not drink milk." First sign of child opposing parent.
J:	That's it, go ahead, you're fine.	
H:	Spit the milk out.	
M:	. . . It went to food later on . . . even eating food . . . spoonfed to . . . oh . . . not . . .	Shell returns momentarily and intellectualizes—part defense, part new understanding (at surface level)
H:	(Whispering) You want to kill her then, when you were spoonfed. You don't have to take that poison food. *You don't have to take that poison food.* (M is breathing very heavily)	H. pours it on emotionally.
M:	(Garbled) Do you all . . . that extreme dependency that's all there is . . .	Shell keeps intruding and thus holding off full emotional activation of child.
H:	Here you don't need her anymore, you can come to me.	
J:	You have somebody else.	Both therapists pour it on.
H:	You can come to us.	
J:	You have a new mother and father, you don't need her anymore.	
H:	You don't need her anymore. Kill, kill, kill, you don't need her anymore.	
J:	Spit it out.	
H:	Spit all that food out at her.	
M:	. . . Nnn . . . it goes . . . ddon't dddrink mmmilk . . .	Patient stuttered when a child. Stuttering replies come from child.
H:	Smash her. Kill her, kill her.	Incitations like these are continued for a good fifteen minutes

continually by therapists, building up child's emotions toward a genuine breakthrough.

* * *

J: Defy her, Defy her now.

H: (Whispering) Tell her you don't need her milk or her food. Defy her. Tell her you don't need it anymore.

M: (Very softly) Kill her . . .

H: (Whispering) That's it, that's it . . .

M: (Whispering) Kill . . .

H: Kill, come on.

J: Kill.

H: That's it, louder.

M: . . . Nnnnnot . . . I . . .

J: (Whispering) Kill her.

M: . . . Drink any milk . . .

H: That's right.

H: (Whispering loudly) Not drink any milk.

J: Yes, not drink any milk.

M: To drink mmmm . . .

J: Tell her you won't drink that milk anymore. Tell her, "No more milk." You're not going to drink any more of her milk.

M: . . . It's . . . oh . . . image . . . don't drink any mmmilk . . . kill her . . .

A tactic that the therapists employ here is one of attempting to resonate with a state not yet activated (the child) but which is close to, and pressing to, become executive. The verbalizations that such a state might be expected to make once it became operative are inferred by the therapists through resonance. These are then fed into the patient. Hence, continous suggestions are whispered (and shouted) at him, such as, "kill," "not die," etc. Sometimes he is specifically told to speak to the parental introject. "Tell her, 'not drink milk.' " The patient at first repeats these but only as words since they are representative of a still repressed state. However, they serve as a bridge over which cathexis flows from the present executive state into the repressed one. This latter becomes increasingly energized until it breaks through and occupies the executive position. The *role* now becomes *being*, and the patient violently experiences these repressed feelings.

Here comes the breakthough. Child now sufficiently supported by therapist and anger so highly activated that it comes out in spite of overwhelming fear. Release begins. Therapists don't let up.

H: (Whispering) Yes.

M: (Very faintly and breathing hard) Kill her . . . bitch . . .

H: (Whispering) *That's it.*

M: . . . Not drink any milk . . . goddamn *bitch* . . . — Loud and vehement.

H: That's it, come on.

M: . . . Mmmilk . . .

H: That's it. Good.

M: (Straining) Mmmmilk . . . not . . .

H: (Whispering) That's it, come on.

M: Drink mmmilk . . .

H: (Whispering) That's it, come on.

M: Not drink mmmmilk . . . not drink mmmilk . . .

H: That's it! Come on! That's it, tell her you're not going to drink any more milk! That's it! Tell her you're not going to drink any more of that milk or eat any more of that food! Tell her that! (Louder and louder) Come on, you're not going to drink any more of that hated milk, that poison milk!

M: Not drink milk . . . goddamn . . . nnno shshe kk . . . nno nno nnnot kill . . . mmmmake mmme ddrink mmmmilk . . . — Stuttering, angry child shouting rage at mother introject.

H: She's not going to make you drink any more of that milk! That's it, come on!

M: Nnnno . . . she cccan't . . .

H: *No*, she can't kill you any more, you kill her now.

M: (Shouting) But her poison . . . she cannot kkkill . . . not drink, not drink . . .

M:	Goddamn bitch . . .	Child has broken through. Now continues abreaction and rage release with little stimulation from therapists. H. urging on and J. temporarily out as anger is being directed against mother introject.
H:	That's it. That goddamn bitch. Come on.	
M:	Goddamn stinkin' bitch . . .	
H:	That's it! Come on, come on.	
M:	Kill the goddamn stinkin' bitch . . . not drink milk. . .	
H:	Come on.	
M:	I cannot kill her . . . kill sssself . . . (breathes hard)	
H:	Kill her, not kill self . . .	
M:	Not kill her . . . kill hhher . . .	Ambivalance. Kill "her" or kill "self"?
H:	Kill *her.* Kill *her.*	To "kill" mother means here to decathect her introject.
M:	Kill that goddamn bitch . . . goddamn . . .	
H:	That's it!	
M:	Not drink mmm . . .	
H:	That's it, don't drink the milk . . .	
M:	Kill that goddman stinkin' bitch . . .	
	(Ten minutes of similar verbalizations)	

* * * * * *

J:	Go on, she's getting smaller!	
H:	Come on, she's getting smaller and you're getting bigger!	
M:	Kill the goddamn stinkin' bitch!	
	The next quarter of an hour was	

devoted to a continuous "killing" of the mother introject. The reaction was carried to exhaustion, physical and emotional, of both M and the therapists.

EROS CONFRONTS THANATOS

Following this session a closer relationship developed with H as the new therapeutic mother. It was obvious that the original mother introject had much less influence and that H was being accepted as "real." A new and powerful mother-ally had joined with the "child," and a big therapeutic step had been taken in the treatment of this difficult and complex case.

Three weeks later the child was even more closely reached. As the following exerpt from that session begins, Therapist H is holding the patient in her arms. Throughout most of this session (three hours long) he is suckling her thumb. In this regressed state, he communicates the full extent of his needs to die.

An event occurred, apparently about the first month of life when, after repeated crying, the child attracted the attention of the mother. She came to the crib and tried to stifle his cries by putting her hand over his nose and choking him. After having been suffocated and strangled, he found no escape except to black out. This apparently was experienced as an overpowering need to regress back to where he came from, the womb. Later in his life this meant "death." Truly the mother who gave birth had been equated with mother earth to whom we all return. Freud's "Theme of the three caskets" (1953e) became meaningful to therapists and patients as he relived those understandings that impelled the Orientals to picture their mother goddesses as goddesses of both life and death—or, as the Bible states it, "For dust thou art, and unto dust shalt thou return."

Could the mother-therapist of now who promised life, conquer and replace the mother-introject of then, who represented death? Could she truly resonate to the needs of the infant ego state? Could the lifelong self-destruction compulsion in this patient be cancelled, and could the "destined" suicide toward which he had been programmed for so long be prevented?

NEXT SESSION

M: I don't . . . it's very . . . it has great importance that somehow that you will . . . OK, no, allright, it comes to a workthrough of the thing that

The session opened with M talking about his need for new parents, especially a mother, and his fear of investing himself in any relationships in which he might be somehow you will be a mother in a permanent sense.

disappointed. There are obvious limitations to the commitment therapeutic "parents" could make.

H: Mm-hm.

M: You know, a lot . . . hangs on that question, I don't know why. And I can't really, you know, break it down intellectually. Although I know it has to do with the permanence question, somehow, there's never been a sense of any permanence, everything's always been in a flow.

H: Mm-hm.

M: And something . . .

H: Maybe you'd like to hold on to something.

M: Ah, something, ah, right, there has to be a . . . continuing stable reality which you would represent, you know.

H: Mm-hm.

M: You know, like you being Mother, it's very much of a psychic thing. I mean, I'm not going to come over for my supper plate tomorrow, you know. (Laughter)

* * * *

H: (Softly) I'm reaching out, reaching out for you . . . reaching out.

M: It goes back to the nurturance thing.

H: Mm-hm.

H: And if I reach out for him he's going to stop crying?

H is referring to the four-week old baby.

M: Yeah . . .

H: Mm-hm. And now he wants to come to me.

M: Well, coming . . . he can't come.

H: Maybe I can reach for him.

M: Yeah, he has no sense of you . . .

H: I can reach out to him.

M: Then it goes, ah, to suffering.

* * * *

H: Come on, come on, little baby, come on, come to me . . . just suck on my thumb and I'll know you're there, and I know you've come to me. Then I know that I can take care of you. Come on. Just suck on my thumb. Then I know you are there. Come to me . . . come on, little baby. (Repeats this over and over) You don't have to cry anymore, you don't have to scream anymore . . . just keep sucking my thumb. That's it, that's the way. Then I'll know you're with me. Come on, I'll take care of you, just suck on my thumb and you can come to me. That's the way . . .

H has hypnotized M and regressed him to infancy. She is holding him in her lap and puts her thumb in his mouth. She continues in very soothing tones and words, as to a baby. Begins to hum a lullaby. M is crying slightly and occasionally.

M: (With thumb in mouth) . . . Strangling kind of smothering . . .

H: Smothering. Come on, hold your breath now. (Commanding) Keep on suckling and hold your breath. Come on, come on, keep on suckling. Keep on and hold your breath. Hold your breath and you can feel that smothering, you can feel her hand over your face. And you're smothering. You can feel the smothering. Just hold your breath. Keep on holding your breath, keep on

H attempts here to induce a reliving of the strangling incident.

holding it, that's it, come on. (M begins to gasp) Come on, come on, the baby can come to me. That's it, he's the one who's doing the suckling. He can come to me. You just pay attention now, pay attention to the smothering. Can't get your breath now, hold your breath, hold your breath, you can feel Mother's hand on your face. That's it, come on. That's it, just hold on, don't you leave now. I'll take care of you, stay with me, don't go away (M gasps). Come on, (Louder as M becomes agitated), stay with me now, come on, don't go away, come on little baby, keep on sucking. Don't go away now, stay with me.

M: You have to somehow . . . sssome type of decision to leave . . . to go . . . I don't know what the child . . . there was sssome decision mmmade.

The shell emerges momentarily and comments.

H: A decision to go away? To leave?

M: I don't know how . . .

H: I think he's coming back. Where is he now? Where is he now? Where is the baby now?

M: Oh . . . still close to him.

H: Mm-hm. I know that. I can feel him. I can feel him close to me. Stay with me now, don't go away. (M begins to cry.) Come on, that's it. You just stay with me, come on. I know you want to keep hold of my thumb, come on, I know you want to suckle on my thumb. Don't go away now, into limbo, into nowhere. Stay with me.

* * * *

The shell had reported after the child passed out ("died") at the time the mother put her hands over his nose and his throat, it, the child, went "into limbo"—a kind of "nowhere." It thus withdrew from the situation.

M: It becomes part of a greater movement.

H: Becomes part of a greater movement. (Repeats this phrase several times.) The child becomes part of a greater movement. You just see it, you can see it in front of you. The child becomes part of a greater movement.

M: (Breathing hard) No . . .

H: You can see it in front of you. The child becomes part of a greater movement. You can see it.

M: (Mumbles) Sssscre . . .

H: He's screaming?

M: Screaming . . .

H: He's screaming. (Repeats this several times.) Louder and louder. And you can hear it in your ears. Screaming, screaming, screaming.

* * * *

Several minutes of crying.

H: Where's he going? (M cries and sobs violently) Where's he going?

M: He's going to predea—life.

H: He's going to prelife. He's going back where he came from. He's going to go back to where he formed his existence. He's going back to the womb, and to the beginning of his time.

M: (Crying and sobbing) He's going to . . .

H: (Whispering) Where's he going to? Where's he going?

M: I don't see . . . I don't know . . . it's hard to describe . . . he's trying to blend back in.

The child seeks to regress back to its origins.

H: Blend back in.

M: It has no age, it has no time.

H: Has no age, has no time.

M: There's no . . . time does not exist.

H: Time does not exist. Where's he going back to? Where's he going now?

Whispered.

M: I don't . . . I don't know . . . he's searching.

H: He's searching, he's searching. What is he searching for?

M: He can't . . . he can't achieve it without me.

He, the child, can't achieve it without me (the shell).

H: He can't achieve it without you? Well, what is he searching for?

M: I somehow follow his . . . followed in some sense.

H: You followed. You followed him.

M: No, I did not follow . . . I became, was . . . his, of his return . . .

H: Of his return . . . you were cognizant of his return.

M: (Chokes and cries) Sssee, I can't communi . . .

H:	Go on. Go on.	
M:	Screaming search . . . desperate search . . .	
H:	Desperate search . . . desperate search. Desperate search for what?	
M:	He wants to integrate again? . . .	
H:	He wants to integrate again. He wants to come back to you.	With the shell?
M:	No!	No!
H:	He wants to integrate again.	
M:	Yes, he's going *back* to integrate.	To integrate with Mother.
H:	He's going back to integrate.	

* * * *

M:	(Hysterically) There's something chchch . . . there's something . . . I don't know!	
H:	It's all right, you'll be all right.	
M:	Just a black hole there.	Death, prebirth, and Mother equated.
H:	Just a black hole there. A black hole. It's when you fainted, it's when you fainted. That's the black hole. (M cries and gasps louder and louder.) Just hold onto me, that's it, hold onto me. A black hole. It's when you fainted. Into a black hole. All there is is this black hole when you fainted.	
M:	No!	
H:	Yes. No more breath, no more air.	
M:	No! (Cries and gasps)	
H:	Black hole. Black hole.	
M:	(Calmer) Black hole.	
H:	Black hole. A black hole.	

M:	I don't want to go to death.	The nonexistence of prelife is the same as the nonexistence of afterlife.
H:	Is the black hole death? (Louder) Is the black holde death? What is the black hole?	
M:	(Gasps) No . . . no . . .	Denials at first.
H:	What is the black hole? What is the black hole? What is the black hole? (M gasps suddenly and starts to cry again.) What is the black hole? Come on, look at it and tell me what it is.	
M:	No!	
H:	Look at it! I want you to look at it! What is it?	
M:	Blackness . . .	
H:	Blackness . . . What is the blackness? What is that blackness? (Long silence) What is that blackness?	
M:	Oh don't . . . no . . . no . . . no . . . I . . .	
H:	Let's go to the blackness together.	
M:	He goes . . .	
H:	Why don't you enter? Why don't you enter the blackness? Why not?	
M:	I was . . . sss (Whispered) stopped. I stopped.	
H:	You stopped.	At that time apparently the child, instead of dying, stopped and split instead, leaving the schizoid shell to continue existence and the child to go "into limbo."

* * * *

H:	We can go to the blackness together. Hold on tight. That's it. Just hold on tight. Let's	

go to the blackness together. Just tell me what you see. What's out there? We'll go together. We'll see it together.

M: (Begins to cry and gasp.) Helen, we can't go there . . .

H: We can go together.

M: No, Helen, I don't want you to go, I love you, I can't let you go there . . . (cries)

Love can conquer death. A loving Mother One, (See Chapter 8, discussion of Freud's "The three caskets.") the goddess of life, can rescue the child from Mother Three, the goddess of death.

H: I'm not afraid.

M: No, you can't . . . you must never go there.

H: Why not?

M: No, I can't let you go. (Whispered) You can't return.

H: You're going to come to me, then?

M: I c-c . . .

H: You're going to come to me? And leave the darkness behind?

M: (Cries and moans) No . . . noooooo . . .

H: No what?

M: No, Helen, no . . .

H: Do you have to go back to the darkness? Before you can come to me?

M: I don't know, there's just something there . . .

H: Let's see what's there. Let's see what's there together. You can take me. I'm not afraid.

M: No . . .

H: I'm not afraid. I'm not afraid to go. I'll protect you.

M: No! I can't let you go, Helen, you'll die.

H: Ah, the darkness is death.

M: No. But you can't return. I can't let you go. (Cries)

H: Then you'll have to come to me. You'll have to come to me. You'll have to leave the darkness behind, and come to me.

M: No . . . I can't . . . I c-c . . .

H: The darkness is death.

M: NO! — Vehement denial, overreactive.

H: THE DARKNESS IS DEATH. It beckons. But I'm going to take you away from death. And I'm going to go *with* you. I'm going to go with you because I'm going to take you away from death. I know death beckons. Death wants you to come. Death wants you to come there—that's what beckons is death, isn't it?

M: No . . .

H: The darkness is death, you tell me. I'm going to go with you.

M: No.

H: I'm going to go with you.

M: No, Helen, you can't go there.

H: I'm going to go with you.

M: No, Helen, you can't . . .

H: But I don't want you to go there.

M: I don't want you . . . I can't let you go . . .

H: Why can't you let me go with you?

M: (Crying) I love you, that's why.

H: Then you're going to come with me?

M: . . . You would be destroyed.

H: But I don't want you to go there. If you love me I want you to come to me. I want you to come to me, I don't want you to go to death. Then I want you to come to me.

M: No . . . no . . .

H: I want you to come to me. I don't want you to go to *death! I won't let death have you, do you hear me?* IF YOU LOVE ME I WON'T LET DEATH HAVE YOU! I WON'T LET DEATH HAVE YOU!

M: Oh . . . death . . . de . . . death . . . de . . . oh . . . (Crying)

H: (Softly) I won't let death have you. If you love me, I will *not* let death have you. I'll snatch you away from death. Death will not destroy you. The darkness will not destroy you. I will snatch you away. I will take you away from the darkness.

Eros can overcome Thanatos

M: It's peace . . .

H: Peace and love with me. There's love here, with me.

M: Something came from death . . . to help . . . to protect the . . . (Whispered) screaming child . . .

H: Something came from death to help protect the screaming child. The screaming child can come to me and I'll protect it.

M: Nnnno . . . it can come . . . came forth with all-powerful . . .	
H: What was all-powerful?	
M: (Whispered) I don't know . . . I don't know. . . it came . . .	
H: What was all-powerful?	
M: (Silent; then M begins to breathe heavily and cry again) . . . A form . . .	Death was experienced by the child as being taken over by a large "form."
H: A form! A *form.* A *form* was all-powerful, and had a form. What form? Was all-powerful and had a form. What kind of form?	
M: (Cries)	
H: We'll have to go back there and find out.	
M: . . . Just movement . . .	Death: a form and a movement.
H: Movement.	
M: . . . consume . . . the child screams . . . (Very softly) no longer hurt . . . the child screaming . . . ah, but i-i-it no longer hurts . . .	
H: The child could scream but then it no longer hurt . . . while it screamed? It didn't hurt?	The protective mantle of symbolic death initiates a remaining schizoid existence, but removes the hurt. It is experienced as a protective friend.
M: (Whispering, crying) I don't know . . .	
H: While the child screamed it could no longer be hurt.	
M: Nnnno, this thing . . . of . . . what, I don't know . . .	
H: This form, this thing, protected it, is that it?	
M: Nnno, it just, it came to it somehow . . .	
H: It came to it somehow. It came to it somehow. To help it, is that right?	

M: (Whispering) I think so . . . yeah . . .

H: Mm-hum? To protect it?

M: . . . What the child was looking for . . . screaming out of it . . . it felt some identity . . . *that* . . . or what thing, I don't know . . . all these things occur in, I don't know, floating sspace, there's a sense of space . . .

H: A sense of space, of floating space, a sense of floating space.

M: Like an ever-flowing point . . .

H: An ever-flowing point . . .

M: It's just imagery is all . . .

H: . . . Imagery . . .

M: I don't care for that world up there . . . let some . . . some aspect of me would have returned.

H: Some aspect of you returned . . .

M: I still want the child . . . want the child . . .

H: But the child will come to me. I can reach the child and you know that, don't you?

M: Something came to its . . . (Cries)

H: Something came to its rescue. Something came to its rescue.

M: It has no humanness, no form, really . . .

H: It has no form, no humanness, just a kind of energy . . . is that right?

Universal existence—an "ever-flowing point." Tart (1972) reports that subjects in the deepest states of hypnosis describe their sensations as: "blackness," "formless," "peacefulness," "no longer identified with body," "awareness of environment—zero," "feeling of oneness with—universe," "being in time no longer meaningful," etc. Noyes (1972) studied some 80 almost fatal encounters with sudden death. He describes three experiential stages through which the victim passes. In the third, there is a "sensation of profound tranquility" and " a peculiar split between body and mind"—a state that apparently permits him to "watch his own death with a feeling of detachment."

A feeling of beauty without grief, anxiety, or pain, with occasional visions of light, ecstasy, and the presence of "an outside force" was often experienced by Noye's subjects.

M: (Whispered) I don't, I don't know . . .

H: But I know I can reach it and you know that too, don't you?

M: You can reach the form . . . you can reach . . .

H: The child.

M: You can reach the child.

You (Mother) can reach the child and take it from the form. You can rescue it from death.

H: Yes, I can reach the form. But I can reach the child, and that's all that matters.

M: The form is loossse . . . too sss . . . it's everywhere . . . it's floating screaming child . . .

H: Floating, screaming child . . . floating screaming child. All around you. Float.

M: The child . . . I think . . . it had . . . some emotion was left empty. But it no longer hurt in some sense.

H: It no longer hurt. It no longer hurt with the form around it. With that form around it is no longer hurt. It no longer hurt with that form around it.

The "form" is death; it is "limbo"; it is what encased the child when it "died," leaving only the schizoid shell to continue living.

M: It wasn't around it, the form, I don't know . . . the form was just with it somehow.

In another sense the child lived but became frozen in the muscles and the posture. The shell is really the dead one—dead in the sense of not living meaningfully.

H: With it. The form was with it.

M: I don't have any . . . I don't like the form . . . I had no . . . I just . . . I don't . . . I don't really fear it either.

H: You just don't like it. You hate that form. What is it?

M: I don't know, Helen. I don't know. My preference is elsewhere . . . I don't like to deal in those realms.

H: You don't like to deal with it. You don't like to deal with that moving form.

M: I don't . . . I-I-I . . .

H: It frightens you?

M: I'm not really frightened, I just don't like it . . . there's nothing to fear of . . .

H: Mm-hm. What is it, then? Why are you shaking? Why don't you like it?

M: (Long silence) No . . . no . . . no . . .

H: What's going on? What's going on?

M: The form doesn't want to give the child up.

Resistance. Death is peaceful; it is protective. I don't want to leave it and return to the real world.

H: Why doesn't the form want to give the child up?

M: The child possesses something the . . .

H: The form wants?

The form (death) is personified and perceived as seeking the child.

M: He doesn't really have . . .

H: The child possesses something that the form doesn't have? Is that right?

M: The form will give it up, no . . .

H: The form *will* give it up.

M: It's . . . a . . . yeah . . . right, it has no . . . it isn't malicious . . .

H: No, it isn't malicious, its protective.

Death not to be feared.

M: No . . . i-i-it's inquisitive . . .

Why is death "inquisitive"?

H: Inquisitive . . .

M: Not really protective, it's just inquisitive . . . nn . . . withdraw . . .

H: It was wondering what it was all about and was drawn to the child. The form was drawn to the child, it was inquisitive. What did the form want to know?

Death is perceived as a passing stranger, curious, and drawn to the child by its cries. It "takes" the child into its protective custody like the "good Samaritan."

M: (Whispered) I don't know . . . just inquisitive . . .

H: It was curious about the child?

M: Somehow, yeah . . .

H: Mm-hm. Do you know what it wanted to know?

M: No, it has no knowledge. It has . . . just . . . being . . . I don't know, really (Becomes more excited and cries) I-I'm not sure, I don't know, really . . . it's just *there* . . . was there or something, I don't know . . .

H: But the form is, the form is a kind of *being*?

M: I don't know, maybe, I don't know . . .

H: But, the form will give the child up, won't it?

M: (Expending a breath) Yesss . . .

H: Yes.

M: Yesss . . .

H: Will he give the child to me?

M: Oh, it has no identity, the form.

H: I see, it's a kind of . . . existence.

M: Oh, yeah.

H: A fluid moving shape.

M: No, it's just . . . I-I-I don't know,

	Helen, it's hard to describe . . . I don't know . . . (Deep breath) the child would . . .	
H:	The child will come to me.	
M:	You are real.	
H:	I am real. I am real. And the child will come to me.	Prediction of things to come.
M:	Yes.	
H:	All right. And if the child will come to me, then what? Will he come to me?	
M:	Mmmm . . . nnn . . . it will come to you . . . I-I . . . how . . . I can't possess . . . I don't possess what it needs for what it p-p . . . for what it needs, it itself took . . . I-you possess what it needs.	
H:	I possess what it needs. (Long silence.) I possess what it needs. The child will come to me.	
M:	Yes.	M validates H's prediction.
H:	(Very softly) It will come to me. (Long silence) The child will come to me. I'm going to count to five, and when I count to five you will be wide awake, fresh and alert. One, two, three, four, five.	M emerges from hypnosis.

DEATH AND REBIRTH

The therapists decided that the only way to rescue the "dead" child and integrate it with the schizoid "shell" was to complete the psychological experience of the "death." The reunited child could then be reborn with new parents. In this next session the patient was hypnotized and regressed to the time just before the "death." During this reliving there is a simultaneous participation of both states. On the one hand, the feelings of the child are revived; yet, on the other, there is an awareness that this is being reexperienced in the presence of the therapists of today. We are close to fusion and integration.

The following excerpt begins about 40 minutes into the hour with the patient hypnotically regressed (or rather partially regressed, since both states are operative) to the crucial experience.

M: You and Jack are going . . . to kill me . . . you and Jack are going to kill me (Crying) . . . going to kill me . . . kill me . . . (With great difficulty) You want me to love you so you can kill me . . . kill me . . . kill . . . kill me . . . (Gasping) You want to kill me . . .	Child talking.

* * * *

M: (With difficulty) You want child to love you so you can kill . . . kill it . . . kill it . . . you want to kill child . . . (Breathes hard) Not let you kill child . . . not let you kill child . . .	Referring to "you and Jack" and "the child" as *it* indicates that it is not the child that is talking, but experiencing the fears in transference from the infant episode.

* * *

M: I have to go and ask her not to kill me, then I have to die when I realize there's not hope left . . .	The shell advises.
H: Where's the pain?	
M: No pain now, I have to deal with . . .	
H: Don't kill me. Say, "Don't kill me."	H resonates to probably unexpressed pleading by the child at that time. She urges child to address Mother.
M: (Slowly) Don't kill me, Mother.	
Together: Don't kill me, Mother.	
M: Ssss . . . make me go and make me realize that I am dead . . . I can . . . that's why it's all part of my existence . . . make me go into death.	
H: All right.	
M: Make me tell myself how I am, . . . dead, I guess.	The shell as therapeutic consultant.
H: All right. Say it.	
M: I . . . don't kill me, Mother. Don't kill me, Mother.	

H:	Breathe deeply.	
M:	(Louder) Don't kill me, Mother.	
H:	Say it louder!	
M:	Don't kill me, Mother. Don't kill me, Mother. Don't kill me, Mother.	
H:	Louder! Louder!	
M:	Don't kill me, Mother. (He repeats this over and over, ends crying) No, it has to go to the . . . she killed me.	Shell says, "She doesn't hear me. I speak only to myself."
H:	Say, "She kills me. She's killing me."	
M:	NO!	Denial from child state.
H:	She's killing me! She's killing me! Say, "She's killing me!" Say it, "She's killing me!" Say it!	
M:	(Whispered) I have to tell you she killed me . . .	
H:	Tell me. She's killing you. Tell me. (M is sobbing) (Whispered) She's killing you.	
M:	she . . . is killing me . . . (Cries)	
H:	Mother is killing you. Say, "Mother is killing me, Helen. Mother is killing me, Helen. Say that. "Mother is killing me."	
M:	No . . . no . . .	Child shrinks back.
H:	"Mother is killing me, Helen." Say that.	
M:	Would you hold me? I'm breaking my technique but . . . I'll see if I can face this.	The shell's "technique" of defense is dissociation, hence, not communicating or existing with child.
H:	OK. Hold me tight. (M cries violently)	

M:	. . . Have to make me say it . . .	Apparently *saying* it creates thinking it. Verbalization makes more "real." A cue toward effective therapeutic technique.
H:	Say it.	
M:	I've got to face the pain, I have to have you close . . .	
H:	You know that my love is real and that you want to come to me. I can offer that to you. And I can offer you Jack's love, our love is real, that's what you want. You're going to have to face her. You're going to have to die to reach us! You're going to have to let her kill you! She's killing you now!	
M:	Nnn . . . have . . . I gotta work on that concept . . . she's killing me . . .	Back to temporary intellectualizing again.
H:	Say it! "She's killing me. Mother is killing me." Say that.	
M:	(Whispered) Mother . . . is killing me . . .	
H:	Say it again. "Mother is killing me, Helen."	
M:	(Crying, with difficulty) Mother . . . is . . . killing . . . me . . . Helen . . .	Emotional involvement becoming progressively deeper.
H:	Say it louder.	
M:	Helen, Mother is killing me, Helen.	
H:	Hold on tight. We can face it together. Breathe deep. You're going to let go and say . . .	
M:	Mother . . . Mother is . . . Mother, Mother, Mother, Mother is killing me, Helen . . . killing me . . . don't kill me . . . don't kill me . . . I want your love . . . don't kill me (Cries)	M now shouting and crying in wavering voice.

H: I want your love.	
M: Mother, I am afraid you're killing me, Mother, I don't want to die . . .	
* * * *	Long silence.
M: You have killed me, Mother . . . you have killed me, Mother . . . you don't love me.	Wailed with deepest anguish.
H: You don't love me. You have killed me, Mother, you don't love me. Say that. "You have killed me, Mother. You don't love me."	
M: You . . . you have killed me, Mother, I don't love you . . .	
H: I don't love you. You have killed me, Mother, I don't love you.	
M: You have killed me, Mother, I don't love you.	
H: Say it louder.	
M: (Louder) You have killed me, Mother, I don't love you.	
H: Breathe deeply and say it.	
M: You have killed me, Mother, I don't love you . . . I don't love you!	
Together: (On "you," M screams) I don't LOVE YOU! (M cries)	
M: You have killed me . . . killed me . . . killed me . . . (He repeats this over and over) . . . you killed me, Mother, you killed me, Mother you killed me. (Repeats this over and over, becoming louder and crying) . . . you killed me, you killed, you killed me . . .	
* * * *	There is a long period of silence, perhaps fifteen minutes. The "child" has "died."

M:	Death . . . death . . . death, death wants me . . . death wants me . . .death wants me . . . (crying) death . . . (Long silence; then M repeats "death wants me" over and over at various volumes; he cries; then another long silence; he repeats the same again) I want to die . . . I want . . . death wants me . . . I want to die . . . death loves me . . . death wants me . . . it loves me, death loves me . . . it loves me . . .	"Mother Three" loves and wants me, even if "Mother One" doesn't.

* * * *

M:	. . . I think I'm dying . . . I don't know . . . there's a strong want, just to let everything go . . .	
H:	(Whispered) Let yourself die. Let yourself die. Let yourself die.	
M:	My heart quit for a moment . . . oh.	The shell thought it experienced a physical death when the child left.
M:	No. My heart quit beating . . . child floats all . . . (Long silence) leaves me . . . the child leaves me. Here! (Whispered) Here. Now! He left me here! (Normal voice) No . . . no you can't leave me, leave me, no, no you wouldn't . . . he left me! Can't find him . . . no, no . . . no . . . leave me here . . . (Cries) Why did he leave me here? (Long silence) Why did you leave me here? . . . no, no . . . he left me here . . . you bastard! . . . you bastard! . . . you bastard! . . . he left me here, he left me here, he left me, he left me . . he wouldn't leave me. He loved me, he wouldn't leave me . . . no, no . . . he loved, he loved me, he had to have loved me, he had to have	That which is left, that which returned to consciousness after the child has "died" and gone "into limbo" mourns the loss of this great area of self. The shell castigates the child for having abandoned it.

loved me . . . (Whispered) He had to have loved me, he had to have loved me . . . take mmme with him . . . he take me with him . . . why did he leave me . . . leave me . . . he did love me . . . he . . . he went to death and he wouldn't take me with him . . . why did he leave me . . . leave me . . . (Whispered) Wouldn't take me with him . . . he didn't love me . . . no . . . no . . . he left me . . . he left me . . . she doesn't love me . . . he left me and she doesn't love me . . . (Cries) Loved me . . . doesn't love me, doesn't love me . . .

* * * *

Another five minute silence.

J: When you open your eyes this time you're going to see two people who love you, here with you.

M: . . . He's gone.

J: We are here. We are here to love you. He will come back some day. When you are loved, he will come back. There is a place of love here. He can come back. When I have you open your eyes, will you come back to us and remember everything?

M: Mm-hm.

J: All right. At the count of five you open your eyes, and come back to Helen and Jack. And remember everything. Come back to people who care for you. One, two, three, four, five.

M removed from hypnosis.

M: (Long silence) Mmmm . . . not sure what left . . . some-

	thing definitely did, the images came back with meaning.	
J:	What left, left because there was no love, there was no place for it. Whatever left that was worthwhile will come back.	The psychological contents of the early child state are still within.
M:	No, it's gone forever. It went to death.	The child state, itself, was destroyed?
J:	What stands for it will return.	
M:	I definitely doubt it.	J and H are thinking of the components of the child state. M is talking about the state itself as an integrated entity.
J:	Yes.	
M:	It's the child I hear screaming.	
J:	Yes.	
M:	I think, I'm not sure, I think that's probably what it is. It chose, it chose death.	
J:	That's true.	
M:	It left it, it split.	
J:	That's true, that's true. That's what left, whatever was there, still inside your skin.	
M:	No I . . . you told me, Jack, it's something separate . . . I don't know why . . . something that was lost, that never can be . . . not . . . systems.	Perhaps a new child can be reborn. The old one is shattered and gone.
J:	Just provide a place of a little love and life here, and see what happens to you.	
M:	The only other alternative . . . I'm not that s . . . I'm not that certain, I'm just not that clear if it's nature . . . either that or it was death that came, then left again. I'm not . . .	Death did come—and is now gone.

J: But it will be clear. We can't get it all today, tonight, but in the coming . . .

M: I couldn't discern its nature, it either was part of I that left, or it was death that came, and was there for awhile.

J: Yes.

M: There's something extremely, you know, like barriers . . . it's hard for . . . like that can't be crossed . . . that it led to . . . it symbolized, in my symbolic world, as the baby crying, which is symbolic because . . . I don't know . . . it wasn't a baby crying that left, it was just something that . . .

J: That's all right. But you're not alone.

M: Mm-Hm.

J: Not now.

J: Maybe you don't need to search for it.

M: Well, there's been a definite search to want to go to death where he went.

There *has been* a definite search for death all M's life, a search to find and join again with the child.

H: Mm-hm. That's what the feeling is all about. To find the child. Maybe you don't need to search.

M: Theoretically.

H: No, that's real. (Jokingly, with laughter) That's not theoretical.

M is now relaxed and calm. At times he laughs lightly.

J: (Same) That's not symbolic either.

H: Kinda pooped out, aren't you?

M: No, not really.

H: Aren't you?

M:	Hm-mm.	
J:	How do you feel?	
M:	That wasn't a hypnotic trance, it was something different. I was very conscious of everything . . . different hypnotic trance, and they all qualify that . . . there was, yeah, great changes in ah, soma; there would be flooding, then just complete break with reality, oh, absolute everything, my complete physical body . . . then all at once I'd be back again with very intense . . .	There was a breaking down of the separateness between the child and the shell states—a flooding through ego boundaries.
J:	You were really living it then.	
M:	Like, the hand, I kept thinking you were touching me, finally you would call me out, it was my own . . . firing off. Yeah, right, it would fluctuate, in that sense. But, you know, everything was fairly conscious. Like the rational mind, was in the, like in the fog . . .	
J:	Consciousness was in the . . .	
M:	Was in the distance.	
J:	It was in that, in that experience.	
M:	The rational mind was there, but it was just an observer, in that sense, it took on that role.	Criticality had been suspended and M was experiencing. The rational self was observing.
J:	They were existing in that state.	
M:	Mm-hm.	
J:	You don't feel so bad right now.	
M:	Mmmm . . . no.	

J:	No. And you're not so tense either.	M is very relaxed.
M:	The real question is, what split off? That was the child . . . getting better. That's a fact. It was death that came and left, yeah, I'm just not sure.	
J:	It'll be kind of interesting to find out and see what it was, won't it?	
H:	You have to think of it in terms of what actually happened, the cutting off of the air would feel like death coming.	
M:	Well, this could've occurred in consciousness, I'm not sure when it occurred, but the mother, yeah, it could've. Yeah.	
H:	I mean, of course we're dragging out the time here. But that's when it happened, when the split took place, when you lost consciousness.	
J:	When you almost strangled.	
M:	I would guess it was probably then, yeah.	
H:	Sure. Whenever there's a loss of consciousness it's like death coming.	
M:	Mm-hm.	
H:	So, but then, she let *go* and then death went away.	
M:	If I was to say . . . I think it probably did occur while she was strangling but then this unconsciousness lingered on thing, this battle between this life and death force. Then there was resolution of it. No, it's something else just besides going unconscious,	

I think . . . because I've been unconscious . . . well, the type of similar unconsciousness has naturally . . . didn't bring back any remembrances of this.

J: I think we've talked about all the problem we can today.

H: Remember, you're only four weeks old!

(Laughter)

Many discovery and integration sessions occurred between M and the therapists, both before and after those reported here. But this was the crucial heart of the analysis. After this point H was accepted as real, a loving mother figure and a point of continual reference. During subsequent sessions the hatred and rejection of the father was worked through with J, who then became real. Following these sessions, despair, hatred and depression subsided, and M began actively planning for a return to his university studies. Today he can both give and receive love and is building a new life in a professional career.

In this case we see many different elements of therapy: support, reassurance, suggestion, desensitization, reinforcement, interpretations of transference, hypnodrama, and manipulation of ego states. The two therapists interacted with the patient in many different ways, both objective and resonant. But throughout, the principles of therapeutic self were employed, cast in the theoretical concept of ego states, and maneuvered in the hypnotic modality. The questions with which we struggled were the sixty-four dollar ones of life and death for this talented young man. His superior abilities will not now be lost to this world at so young an age.

FOOTNOTES

1. All obsessional thinking is probably maintained by the pleasurable reinforcements evoked by the repetitive thoughts. These could be either conscious or unconscious.
2. It should be recognized that this "love" in the small child for his rejecting parent is more in the nature of needing and being dependent upon than a true love. However, this is probably typical of the loves of most children within the first year or two of life.

Part VIII

SUMMARY AND IMPLICATIONS

Chapter 24, "The antitherapeutic (or pathologic) self," takes a brief look at the other side of the coin and presents a case illustration where such a state was temporarily created for purposes of observation.

Chapter 25 offers a summarizing review of the entire book, which probably would not be meaningful unless one had covered the preceding chapters.

A Therapists Credo attempts to formulate in resonant terms the beliefs and values that might be spoken by a therapeutic self to his patient, both as reassurance and as an affirmation by the therapist to his own self of what this interaction is all about.

Finally, the concept of resonance between human beings and the need for its development in balance with objectivity suggests too much of potential good for humanity in so many other spheres of human endeavor that we cannot stop without speculating in the last chapter about its broader implications.

Chapter 24

THE ANTI-THERAPEUTIC (OR PATHOLOGIC) SELF

The class sat expectantly while a psychodramatic demonstration of Rogerian client-centered therapy was enacted before them by the instructor and his graduate assistant.[1] They anticipated a typical example of the reflection of feeling and permissive atmosphere that had been described by Rogers (1951) during the second stage of his developing theories. Nancy was to be the therapist, and John would unfold to her a personal problem involving his disappointment and feeling of rejection at not receiving a reply from a former professor, whom he admired, and to whom he had recently written. The problem was partly real and partly compounded for the demonstration.

John began the interview by saying that he felt funny coming to "this clinic" for help inasmuch as it was on the campus, and that he, as a faculty member, felt somewhat embarrassed. With a smile on her face Nancy replied, "You come here for help even though you feel that perhaps you are too good to be seen here." There was a sharp, high-pitched tonality to her voice, and she displayed a rather rigid posture, which was maintained throughout the entire interview. At one point John made a direct request for help. Nancy rejoined with, "You want me to solve all your problems and you find it very difficult to solve your own problems." Somewhat later John commented that he felt very badly during this interview. Nancy reacted with, "You feel rotten."

Throughout the entire session Nancy followed all the rules of client-centered therapy and reflected feelings as reported by John. However, she continually selected elements that emphasized antitherapeutic aspects. The impact was powerful on all in that classroom. Even John, the "client," began to evince actual anxiety. Nancy had always been regarded as a warm and understanding therapist. Yet here the change in her therapeutic stance was so striking in character that the class became highly disturbed. One of them asked, "Nancy, what's happened to you today? You're not yourself." To which Nancy angrily replied, "I have not changed. What's the matter with you?" At this point the experimenter (J. G. W.) touched Nancy on the shoulder. A great transformation came over her, and somewhat anxious and flustered, she returned to her natural warm and empathic state of being. The class, after being asked how they could account for her behavior was then apprised of the therapeutic experiment that was being conducted.

A few days before, Dr. Means had approached the author with the suggestion that if a hostile set could be hypnotically implanted in a therapist then it would be possible to demonstrate to the class the effect of a negative countertransference reaction. In other words, could we create under hypnosis a temporary antitherapeutic self, and if so, how would it manifest itself in an actual interview?

Nancy, who was a good hypnotic subject, agreed to participate in a hypnotic experiment, the exact nature of which she was not informed, but with the assurance that no permanent, harmful effects would be created. Accordingly, she was hypnotized the day before the demonstration and given the suggestion that she was very angry with Dr. Means "because he had dealt unfairly with you on a previous examination." She was told that she would not be aware of this anger, but that it would continue until she was touched on the shoulder. On the morning of the interview she was hypnotized again and the suggestion reinforced.

After the antitherapeutic suggestion was removed from Nancy and the nature of the experiment explained to the entire class, Nancy described her own feelings about the incident to the group. She mentioned that the evening before, she had laid out one of her better dresses to wear at the demonstration before the class. The thought had occurred to her, "Why should I wear this for the S.O.B.?" and she changed to another dress. The class commented that during those portions of the interview in which she was being asked directly for help, her neck turned bright red.

Nancy remarked that while waiting for the class to start she had experienced rather strange thoughts, such as a strong impulse to pour coffee on Dr. Means as he ascended the stairs to the classroom. She also reported a feeling of nausea, which she felt was the result of having eaten some clam dip the evening before.

Seven years after the incident Nancy described her recollections to the author as follows:

"At the time, it was a very upsetting, emotional experience for me, not traumatizing, but simply unpleasant to recall. I had totally suppressed this—and only through difficulty (after reading my reminder to her) was I able to recall anything about it. This was textbook suppression, as if I were reading about a totally unfamiliar or unknown situation with vague hints of participation, and a very dreamlike quality.

"I recall the hypnosis explicitly. I had eaten some bad clam dip the night before and felt nausea and severe stomach cramping. When you brought me out of hypnosis, I was acutely discomforted by the severe cramping as opposed to the nausea. There was no time lag, it was instantaneous.

"On reflection of the situation, I am most impressed by the ability of a therapist with a negative set to do actual emotional or physical harm. I came closer to actually pouring scalding coffee on John Means than anyone realized. The negative set was stronger at that moment in time than realistic moral restrictions. As opposed to attempting to positively handle. . .my attitude toward John, I found myself consciously but subtly attempting to emotionally destroy him. Again, I was limited only by a need for self-preservation in that two of my major professors were involved, and a class of peers was viewing. Had I been alone with John there would have been no stops in, and I would have actively attempted, still through the Rogerian technique, to annihilate him. My reservations were based strictly on self-preservation, probably the strongest motivation of all. I had no guilt (at that time) regarding these extremely negative feelings nor about my attempts to harm John physically and emotionally. The amazing part of it all is how the mental attitude, in this case hypnotically induced but conceivably present in some therapists toward some of their patients without hypnosis, can override the socially approved moral structure of not harming another person. It was as if a very psychopathic set emerged, making guiltless bodily or emotional harm not only possible but, at that time, desirable."

This experimental incident demonstrates how an unconscious hostile or antitherapeutic attitude in a therapist can operate to bring about destructive rather than constructive results in a client.[2] In fact, such underlying attitudes may account for the fact that some psychotherapists have a high failure (and suicide) rate among their patients.

Therapists have long realized that it is very difficult, if not impossible, to treat a patient one dislikes. They have recognized the desirability in such cases of referring the patient to a colleague. But except for the personal analysis in the psychoanalytic trainee, little provision is made in most therapies to deal with the problem of a counselor who has deep-seated and extensive hostility to large classes of people. Such an individual, of course, should not be in any of the healing arts professions, and the various medical and graduate schools (and paraprofessional schools) should make strenuous efforts to diagnose this condition in prospective applicants and exclude them unless the hostility is successfully treated and resolved.

However, if the antitherapeutic attitude is limited to certain types of patients, then the therapist might function constructively by refusing to work with this type. This assumes that he is aware himself of his problem and willing to so limit himself.

Some years ago the author had occasion to treat a professional colleague who had a very severe interpersonal relationship problem including much repressed hostility. At the same time the author was also treating a young psychology trainee who had been previously treated by his colleague. Even though the colleague's pathology was more severe than that of the trainee, the trainee had benefitted from the previous counseling. This posed a theoretical problem. How could a patient be helped by a therapist who was more sick than the patient? Psychotherapy has been facetiously defined as a system of talk between two people, one of whom (the therapist) is less sick than the other. (One of my students on hearing this, rephrased it to "one of whom *thinks* he is less sick than the other.") A possible solution to the above problem might be that the colleague projected onto the trainee his own idealized self, and then devoted his efforts to realize, or actualize it, as Horney (1950) would say, that is, to achieve his own growth goals through the other.

If an ego state that interacts with others is filled with hatred—thus mortido cathected—then its effect would be destructive on these others, since such energy aims at reducing complex organisms to the simple. We have already taken note of those individuals who protect themselves by identification with their aggressors. The child who ceases to be a helpless object to a malevolent parent by changing the introject of that parent into identofact now enjoys relief from persecution; but he enjoys it at the cost of becoming himself harmful to others. Like Typhoid Mary he transmits his pathology to others but does not himself suffer. His mortidinal energies are engrossed in the destruction of others and no longer erode away his own self. Thus when a depression is lifted, the self-hate, is directed outwardly, and suicide can turn to murder. The eternal battle between Eros and Thanatos is waged both within individuals and between individuals.

The problem of what to do with hate is like that of a factory that must eliminate its pollution products. By dumping these into the air or nearby rivers it purges itself but at the expense of harm to others. Since this is a very hostile and angry society, there are millions of people who are loaded with such feelings; they are antitherapeutic selves who go about infecting others with their destructive pathology.

Sublimation, or the directing of emotional energies into constructive channels, seems to be one solution, although only a partial one. Most of the great civilizations—the Egyptians, the Greeks, the Romans, the Moors, the Aztecs, the Incas, and modern Western culture—have been aggressive ones. They gouged the earth to mine metals and chopped down trees for dwellings. In other words, by directing their aggressions against inanimate nature they partially sublimated their needs to kill each other. Civilizations have been built by angry people. Kindly, unaggressive cultures like the gentle Arapesh Indians (see Mead, 1937) enjoy life and each other but do not erect great buildings and develop sophisticated machines. There is little interest in fighting for territoriality (Esser, 1971), leadership, or prestige.

Another solution for society is the incarceration of pathologic individuals in prisons and mental hospitals. In fact, society has been doing precisely that as far back as history can record. Those people who are deemed harmful to the rest of a society are isolated in order that they not contaminate the social order or harm its members. The desirability of this depends, of course, on the values the society holds. Often it is not merely the rights of individuals but the cognitive consonance of a political entity that such isolation serves. Aleksandr Solzhenitsyn was banished from the Soviet Union, not because he was a menace to other citizens, but because his publications and teachings were deemed harmful to the organization of the Communist order. He was "spit out" by that nation as an amoeba spits out a particle of sand that needles its internal structure.

If society itself was basically composed of constructive elements and values, then perhaps the quarantine of cognitively dissonant individuals as pathologic or antitherapeutic would be one defensible procedure for the protection of others. But we start with a society, not all of whose administrative elements can be assured of operating for the general welfare of its members. Witness the Watergate scandal, which disclosed pathologic selves within the executive branch of the U. S. government. The popularity of a recent movie, *The exorcist,* is an example of the great human need to eliminate disrupting elements within the self. The pathology of a highly disturbed child is cast out (exorcised) by a priest, who himself then falls victim to the "devil." That a pathologic individual can make others "sick" has been well recognized in the stories of the werewolves, humans turned into wolves. In medieval folklore the bite of one in the full of the moon changes the bitten one himself into werewolf (Stewart, 1909). In the Middle Ages (and even later), men projected their internal pathologies (their devils) onto their less popular fellow creatures and burned them at the stake as witches. In this way they purged themselves of internal conflict. The expurgation of dissonant or malevolent elements by a society can range from the enforcement of "law and order" to the crucifixion of a Christ or the executions of an Inquisition. The desirability may vary, but the principle and mechanisms are the same.

In each case the projection of that which is bad within and its "killing" or banishment permits the remaining self to secure an untroubled existence. Thus, in *The picture of Dorian Gray,* Wilde (1909) describes a man who engages in all kinds of evil doing but retains his beauty of appearance. The evilness and its consequences, which would be expected to show upon the face of the profligate one, instead progressively appear on a portrait of the individual hidden in the attic. The bearer of the pathology is purged by their projection onto a picture, an external representation of his person. In his fantasies and stories man needs to assure the victory of good over evil. So, as Dorian finally dies, the evilness melts from the portrait back onto his face, leaving a shriveled and ugly corpse. In Stevenson's novel, *The strange case of Dr.*

Jekyll and Mr. Hyde (1961) the same struggle ensues between libidinal and mortidinal energies, and as in most tragedies the principle of the good survives by the sacrifice of the individual who is so tainted with the bad.

It does seem to be true that if destructive energies are contained they turn upon themselves and disintegrate. Thus, when the Nazi Third Reich, which was to endure for a thousand years, was encircled, it killed itself—as exemplified both actually and symbolically in the suicide of Hitler.[3]

If mankind is to survive, what must we do to blunt the destructive forces so threatening to our very existence? Man's hatred, his inner-self pathology, can now be implemented by atom bombs, unending streams of air and water pollution, destruction of the world's resources, and an insatiable increase in the number of hungry mouths for a constantly lessening supply of food.

Somehow, we must find ways of isolating pathology, whether within individuals, between individuals, whether within societies or between societies. Pathologic selves must either be treated or contained and their aggressions directed, perhaps through sublimation, toward nonhuman, nonliving elements. Let them seek to conquer physical nature, not other people. Let them dig and chop, grind and penetrate into the secrets of the universe, not destroy the selves of other men. We must blunt their impact by reducing contact or by minimizing effect. At the same time we must enhance the interpersonal interactions of those individuals who possess therapeutic selves. Perhaps in this way we can, over many generations, reduce the crime, insanity, and cruelty that so infect our present culture.

In Chapter 22 we saw where an originally malevolent force (the Evil One) was changed through resonance by a therapeutic self into a constructive influence in the life of the patient. It gives us hope that man's destructiveness can be reduced, not only by exorcism—a killing of part of the self—but also by its conversion into integrative behavior through the mediation of resonating others in the individual's world. The challenge to psychotherapists today is to help others, both in and out of the healing arts professions, to learn and practice such understanding skills. For if the antitherapeutic, the pathologic selves are permitted to grow in such number that they overwhelm the "good" in people, then our world society will ultimately turn and destroy itself like the cancer that spreads throughout an organism and itself dies only by killing its host.

FOOTNOTES

1. Dr. John Means and Nancy Shubat (now Dr. Nancy Shubat), referred to here as John and Nancy.
2. The question as to whether antisocial behavior can be elicited by hypnotic suggestion has been highly controversial among specialists in the field. This writer is one of those who feels quite certain that it can be (Watkins, 1947, 1951, 1972). However, many differences of opinion concerning this have been expressed by other workers in the area of hypnosis (See Conn, 1972; Kline, M.V., 1972; Orne, 1972; and Wolberg, 1972).
3. It is interesting to note that Hitler's final self-destructive response to being contained was almost predicted at the time of the Graf Spee incident (in 1939). This pocket battleship, after a bruising engagement with several British cruisers, had put into Montevideo harbor for repairs. These could not be completed in the time permitted by the Uruguay government, and a fleet of superior British and French naval power had assembled to intercept it if it tried to return to sea. Hitler instructed its skipper to scuttle the ship, which he did. Afterward, the captain committed suicide himself.

Chapter 25

REVIEW AND CONCLUSIONS

Theories are developed from observations. However, after being formally conceptualized they tend to get frozen into molds which no longer follow the input of new information. They then control by dictating the concepts and terminology within which such data must be interpreted and filed. Classical psychoanalysis—with its categories of ego, superego, id; with its oral, anal, oedipal, homosexual, and genital levels of development; and with its definition of instincts—has created a kind of psychological nosology into which the reactions of the patient on the couch are fitted, sometimes easily, and sometimes only through violence to their character. Even Freud had great difficulty justifying a continued belief in his death instinct theory (Fromm, Erich, 1973), a position he could never quite reconcile with other aspects of psychoanalysis—but which once formulated, he could also never quite relinquish.

In transactional analysis, a similar situation exists if

states must be conceptualized as either parent, child, or adult. In behavior modification there is little room to observe feelings and experience because they do not fit into the mold of theory. Furthermore, behavior to be learned or maintained must always be related to its reinforcements. The problem seems to be man's difficulty in determining what impression has come strictly from without, from observation (hence, what is object) and which impression has been placed upon the stimulus source from interpretative elements within (hence, what is subject). For just as early emotional experiences can alter the perception of new ones (transference), so also can our early theoretical concepts alter our interpretations of new observations—a kind of scientific transference reaction. Accordingly, our theoretical understanding of case material, like an early ego state, fights for the right of its own existence, even after it no longer serves a realistic function. Like the tics (Young Minds) of Chapter 22 our theories may react blindly and inappropriately to the perception of new data.

No doubt the terms "therapeutic self" theory and its associated "ego-state therapy" methodology, like all other conceptions of personality and its treatment, when once formulated, will begin the process of stratification. Nevertheless, it is hoped that the conceptualizations here voiced are sufficiently flexible so as to avoid this straightjacket as long as possible.

From a simple observation that the patients of Dr. Y did much better than those of Dr. X, an equally well-trained physician, we proceeded along many paths in our search for the "why" and the "how." Our quest has been for understanding this phenomenon, how it comes about, how we can acquire this precious ability, and how it can be transmitted to others. Since the need is for so-olution and application we care not one whit whether those who can contribute to our goal are classed as scientists, psychologists, psychiatrists, philosophers, anthropologists, sociologists, lawyers, statesmen, poets—or only warm people who possess this trait. Our aim has been practical, and we are quite content to beg, borrow, or steal concepts from behaviorists, psychoanalysts, humanists, physicists, mathemeticians, and artists if they can advance us closer to the truth. The trail has led through science, psychology, religion, law, philosophy, and literature. It has ranged from experimental studies to sheer speculation.

When a patient presents himself for treatment, the intensive study of his condition often develops into a comprehensive investigation of his entire life. So here, what started as a simple question has taken us into broad areas in the life of man, his origins, his development, his structure, his functioning, his relations with others, his future on this earth, and that ultimate question which has always gnawed at him: the meaning of his life and death.

Since we have borrowed from so many sources, perhaps there is nothing in this work that constitutes a genuinely new advance. Maybe it is only the reiteration of what has already been known. But if this discourse has served the principle of Eros, of life at all, it may be through integration, by drawing together different concepts and facts.

Many men have made discoveries and contributed thoughts but have had no communication with the discoveries and thoughts of others. In this age of specialization, not only do psychologists and historians seldom read each other, but even within the discipline of psychology, the behaviorists, the psychoanalysts, and the humanists interact but little. It has been our hope that we could contribute by crossing some of these lines, by building ties of communication between the various disciplinary ego states of humanity. For with all the differentiation that occurs between us from birth to death, we start the same and we end the same. Accordingly, let us review the major paths pursued in the work and see if we can end with some theoretical coherence.

There are many ways of viewing this entity, the therapeutic self, from the theoretical viewpoints current in present-day psychology. The behaviorist can well attribute such integrative behavior in human relationships to the skilled providing of appropriate reinforcements by the treating one to the treated one. The good doctor applies sound principles of learning for the modification of unadaptive responses in others, such as the methods of desensitization, operant conditioning, and modeling. Although some of this skill could be acquired through scientific study of human behavior, part may have been developed as the therapist himself was programmed by favorable family influences to respond in integrative ways to the behavior of others. We can develop more and better therapists if we will apply these same learning principles to the training of clinicians. From this perspective, behavior technology should be utilized for the extinction of unproductive responses in both the clients and the counselors.

From the psychoanalytic point of view, the building of a therapeutic self can be achieved when the doctor submits himself to a thorough personal analysis. As a therapist's own blocks, countertransferences, blind spots, and "foveas" are reduced, he can confront his patients with increasingly realistic understanding. Workers in the healing arts fail to be effective in their ministrations because their own neurotic tendencies, their own hangups, keep interfering with the clear apprehension that the treating one must bring to the clinical situation. A therapeutic self is of necessity a mature self. By undoing the developmental flaws that normally impair the vision and behavior of the therapist, we can build a corps of mental healers who are prepared to assist mankind in surmounting conflicts and immaturities.

The humanist-existentialist is much concerned with the concept of self and the true meaning of human being. Even as the behaviorists emphasize the role of learning and conditioning, and the psychoanalysts the effect of defective or incomplete development, the humanist sees the problems of man's condition inhering in a faulty perception of himself and his world. This can be changed through genuine and authentic interaction with mature others. The stress is on feeling, rather than cognition. To these therapists, the therapeutic self would be one who consistently practiced empathy, unconditional positive regard, and congruence in his treatment relationship. Equal, if not greater, emphasis is given to concepts of "being" rather than merely "doing." Both the therapist and the client are seen as growing or "becoming," the counselor being primarily a facilitator, a catalyst, rather than an initiator or manipulator. To the humanists the therapeutic self would be one who released potentials in others by his genuineness and freedom in the therapeutic encounters.

The heart of our theory here lies in the subject-object dichotomy and the clear distinction between what is "me" and what "not-me." Self cannot be equated with the contents of the skin, nor even with one's thoughts. But existence, or experience as a living being, is defined as the impact between subject and object, between me and not-me. It is hypothesized that without such impact, experienced being does not occur. Therapeutic self theory, although considering itself as existentialist, accordingly differs greatly from those forms of existentialism that define being as a state transcending the subject-object dichotomy. These other theories (as well as the Oriental existentialism called Zen) hold that man should strive to eliminate this dualism. Our theory here asserts that the sharper the difference between subject and object, the clearer the distinction between me and not-me, then the greater the "being" that results from their impact as two different entities.

An object is defined by its being a not-me, hence outside the boundaries of self. But where is the self located? This apparently is differently placed by different people, and by the same person at different times. Some identify their self primarily with their body or with a part of it. Others locate the heart of their identity within certain communities of thoughts and attitudes. This self may change qualitatively as it moves from one such constellation to another, or from one perspective to another. A few think of the self as being able to transcend the boundaries of the physical body. Multiple personalities represent different configurations of behavior in which the self alternately resides. It was postulated that self may be a kind of energy, or energy field.

Throughout the universe two principles seem to operate: a tendency for elements to come together to form more complex entities, and an opposing tendency for complex entities to be reduced back to their simple origins. In the first we see the union of atoms to form molecules, of molecules to form cells, of cells to form organs, of organs to form organisms, and of organisms to create new life. Individuals unite to form societies. All this has been called the principle of Eros. The term is used as a universal principle, not as Freud employed it to denote an "instinct" in man—although it would include the behavior subsumed under Freud's sexual instinct.[1]

As the opposing principle operates, societies disintegrate into unorganized individuals; people are reduced (through death) back to inorganic molecules and atoms. Complex entities are once more simplified. This is termed the principle of Thanatos. Freud called it the death instinct.

As elements come together (under the principle of

Eros), they impact and thus create being. By repelling each other, by flying apart, elements eliminate contact and thus destroy being. Hence, this death principle operates to terminate existence—in nations, in man, and in all organisms. Individual selves exist because of their integration and their uniqueness. They represent a *Verbindung*—a binding together—of a set of elements by the Eros principle, which is capable of experiencing this unity, this integration. When this self-entity through death is separated into its original elements, these flow back in undifferentiated form into the ocean of universal energies, even as the river joins the sea. The waters of the Mississippi are no longer differentiated from the waters of the Hudson. The self ceases to exist as a unique entity. Energies in the universe are changeable but not destructible. Hence the self does not die, but it loses its individual identity in a fusion with the energies of other selves that have also been reduced back to their simplest form. It becomes part of a universal reservoir of self energy from which will be drawn the cathexis needed to activate new organisms as they begin their integrative growth back toward complexity.

We have said that the self operates as if it were an energy. In the physical universe there are also many other forces, nonself and nonliving. Accordingly, to explain this difference, and to understand better the interactions between such different energies, we turned to the ego psychology theories of Paul Federn.

Freud had described a kind of energy, which he considered as sexual in nature. He termed it "libido." This energy was perceived as energizing (cathecting) various physical and mental entities so as to cause them to be strongly and erotically experienced by the individual. As such, libido was anobject energy, hence one that caused elements outside the "me" to impact the ego and be sensed by that entity. When this energy was turned back upon the self, Freud termed it "ego-libido."

Federn held that this ego-libido or ego cathexis was qualitatively different from ordinary libido or object cathexis. Ego cathexis contained the essence of living being. Any physical or mental item invested with it was experienced as being within, or part of, the self—as subject, hence as I, me, or my. If ego cathexis was withdrawn from a part of the body, that part was experienced as an object, an "it." For example, a paralyzed limb is devoid of feeling and feels as if it is an outside object. An idea or mental representation invested only with object cathexis would be experienced as if it were a perception and coming from outside the boundary of the self. Such an idea breaking out of repression through the internal ego boundary without being ego cathected would be experienced by the individual as a hallucination and would be attributed to something outside the person. Federn defined ego cathexis as "a unifying, integrating energy which gives us the feeling of unity, continuity, contiguity and causality in our experience." Experience, for him, constituted an investment of continually changing contents with such ego feeling.

In this book, the position is taken that two directionalities are possible for either of these energies. When the energy is integrative so that items invested with it attract each other, the cathexis is termed "libido" and considered as serving the principle of Eros. When the energy is disintegrative so that items invested with it tend to differentiate themselves from each other, to repel each other, it is termed "mortido." This directional energy serves the principle of Thanatos. The libidinal direction of integrating separate items operates to build more complex entities. Mortidinal energies reduce them back to their simple origins. The universe demonstrates a constantly fluctuating balance between these two principles as they operate in both living and nonliving entities.

Existence was defined here as the operation of the

"self" in the "now." The self, as an energy system was considered to be moving in a time dimension. As different events became cathected they happened, like unto the activation of changing scenes in a moving picture film as it rolls past the focusing light.

The psychological life of an individual is encompassed within the boundaries of a number of ego states. Each of these, like a geographical state, represents various contents surrounded by a boundary. These contents include mental and physical items, (behavior and experiences) which are object or ego cathected. They can impact each other because they are defined in a common region and included within a common boundary. For example, one ego state might represent one's self as it was experienced at a Saturday night party, another at work on Monday, another relates to experiences with Mother, and still another by that which happened during the first grade in school. There may be an almost infinite number of such ego states possible. However, most living experiences can probably be encompassed within a few major ones.

One ego state, the self in the now, represents those components most highly cathected at any given moment and is termed the "executive state." It constitutes the center of being. As ego energies flow from one state to another over some common element, different states take turns at being executive. This accounts for the varying behaviors of a person at different times. The phenomenon is demonstrated in its extreme form by multiple personalities, wherein the different ego states have no awareness of each other. The boundaries that separate them are impermeable.

Consciousness takes place when the impact between an object-cathected item and one invested with ego cathexis exceeds a certain minimum in magnitude. Impacts occurring at lesser levels of impact (more commonly found in nonexecutive ego states) are insufficient to evoke the experience of consciousness and are unconscious to the person. The ego state, rather than the trait, is probably the most significant psychological unit. From such a theoretical view of the structure and functioning of self the term "therapeutic self" was next developed.

The Therapeutic Self

Fundamental to this term is the concept of resonance, the experience that occurs when an individual temporarily identifies with another and experiences the other as his own self. The process involves building an inner replica of the other from the sensory impressions received about him. At this time it is an object. If permanently so internalized it becomes an introject. This object may then be changed into a part of the self through the process of identification or investing it with ego cathexis. The replica then becomes subject and is termed an "identofact." The feelings of the other are now experienced within one's self, and the ideas of the other felt as one's own thoughts. Temporarily, and with a part of one's own self, one has duplicated in mini-form the existential world of the other—even as a piano with its keys held down will replicate in string vibrations the pitches struck on another piano.

According to therapeutic self theory, there are two different ways of gathering data and understanding another person. Through objective observation and the employment of the senses, one can directly contact him as a separate entity, as an it that is part of the outside world. However, by building an inner replica from such observations, investing that replica with ego cathexis, and turning it into a part of one's own self, one can experience the other subjectively. Through such resonance one lives in the experiential world of the other. Experienced from the inside, the other is understood differently than when sensed from the outside. Both ways of knowing about another are valid. They are like surveying a situation from different vantage points. The two together are superior to either alone.

The therapeutic self is one who can understand his patient from *both* the objective and resonant points of view, either simultaneously or in alternation. Such an individual has greater sensitivity in diagnosis since his data his drawn from two different perspectives rather than one alone. If he were only objective he would not be able to understand the patient's world as it is experienced by the patient. If he resonates completely with all his self then he and the patient would be sick together. There would be a *folie à deux.* A balance between objectivity and resonance enables the therapist to understand and interact with his patient optimally. Because of this more complete understanding and partial 'being with' the patient, his therapeutic interventions should be more effective. Whatever he does to his patient he is now also doing to himself. If he is resonating with the treated one, a false interpretation or an inappropriate suggestion will be damaging to his own self.

By his willingness to commit his self to his patient's problem, to co-understand, co-suffer, and co-enjoy with the other, the therapeutic self establishes a "we-ness" that encourages the patient into a reciprocal *quid pro quo.* When the therapist understands and accepts the patient's pathology, the patient identifies (resonates) increasingly with the integrative self of the therapist as it is manifested in the therapeutic interventions. Resistances are lowered. Interpretations become more palatable, and insights are achieved sooner.

In the traditional analytic therapies we often create and reinforce the very defensive resistances that we must then work through and resolve. Treatment becomes much longer than necessary. What the objective therapist calls a resistance the patient experiences as a protection. By resonating to his patient the therapist, too, can experience it as a protection. By perceiving the patient's behavior from *both* the resistance and the protection points of view the therapeutic self can intervene in ways the patient can more easily accept.

The impact of the therapeutic self has been likened to a temporary loan of ego energies to the suffering, one that then stimulates a temporary exchange of egos. The strengths of the therapist, when fused with those of the patient, enable the patient to master the previously unsolvable conflicts and counter the formidable grasp of his pathology. All of this requires that we give considerable thought to the economy of the therapist, his acquisition, and utilization of ego energies. This problem becomes especially acute when he is confronted with treating the dying patient, one whose mortidinal energies are much greater than his libidinal ones.

In Chapters 18, 19, and 20, efforts to bring some scientific and objective studies to bear on the theory were described. A scoring system was devised for the rating of resonance and objectivity in therapist-patient interactions. This scale was demonstrated by applying it to recorded sessions of different therapists. Initial experiments were undertaken to determine whether the ability to resonate could be developed or trained.

In Chapters 21, 22, and 23, case examples were presented of treatment sessions that involved therapeutic self interactions with various patients and in which the concept of differing ego states became an integral part of the therapeutic strategies. These sessions depicted therapeutic self theory in action.

The concept of the therapeutic self would seem to have significance to many persons other than those who are engaged in the healing arts. Accordingly, in the following and final chapter, an effort will be made to relate the theories developed here to broader areas of human relationship, such as parent-child interactions, the impact of teachers on their pupils, the conflicts of labor and management, and the diplomatic interactions between nations.

However, before turning our eyes further afield, it is appropriate that we undertake to formulate some kind of credo based on therapeutic self principles, which might serve as a guide to those who are specifically engaged in the practice of psychotherapy. It is to the sincere and committed people in this area, the psychologists, the psychiatrists, the physicians, nurses, social workers, and counselors—those who fight in the front-line battles against human pathology, that this message is primarily directed. Perhaps some of them could resonate to the following thoughts as they might be transmitted to a patient.

A THERAPIST'S CREDO

As your therapist I shall try to come as near to you as I can, to touch you with every aspect of my being. I shall endeavor to experience you as you perceive yourself and your worlds, both without and within. But if I temporarily identify with you, take you into my inner world, treat you as myself, I do so only to achieve a greater understanding of you. For in the final analysis I shall retain me as me and perceive you as you. I shall neither totally submerge myself in you, nor lose my own selfness in a permanent fusion with yours. I shall achieve awareness of your existence to the best of my ability, and then I shall endeavor to transmit that awareness to you in order that we may both become ever greater in our beingness.

Existence is impact, and I shall aim to achieve with you the ultimate in closeness, the maximum of understanding, and thus to provide the greatest possible constructive impact between me and thee. For in this way you can achieve the ultimate in "knowing thyself"—even as this process shall also bring the greatest fertility in growth to my own self.

We undertake this mutual therapeutic endeavor because you have requested it, because you have indicated the greatest need, because you have sought me believing that I can help you. Therefore, I shall contract with you to strive to give you all that I know, all that I am, within the agreed limits of time and space. You have come to me because you believe that I can offer creative impact on you. And if I did not indeed have more constructive than destructive contact to present, then I would be most unworthy to contract for such a mutual endeavor.

It is understood that you offer me some type of authentic and legitimate recompense, perhaps monetary, provided either by yourself or others so that my time and energy will not go unrewarded. I undertake this compact with you discerning full well that you probably have more potential for destruction than have I. If it were not so, then it should be I who had sought you. But I also know that if our mutual endeavor is successful, you will recompense me far more than you now envisage, not with additional financial stipends, but with my own increased beingness.

Within our mutual transactions we shall pledge our selves to so maximize the forces of Eros, of love, of constructive integration, as to isolate the destructive elements of Thanatos and face them with a superior mobilization of life energies drawn from the reserves available to both me and thee.

It is understood that you have been fighting losing battles, or you would not be here. If I had not generally fought winning battles, I ought not to be here. We shall now form an alliance to refight *your* conflicts with *our* combined resources.

At first glance, it appears you might have the better of the contract. In return for some agreed stipend, I must be willing to accept and incorporate into myself, at least temporarily, some of your destructive forces. To do so may well facilitate my own destruction. For if I give you my assets, so laboriousty acquired, and take in return only your liabilities, then indeed would I have made a bad bargain.

However, I accept this risk because I believe that in our world, in this universe, in the here and now, Eros, the principle of life and love, the force of integration, is by at least some degree stronger than that of Thanatos. The existence of a universe of rationale and meaning, the existence of life in its ever more complex forms, up to and including the magnificent organic systems of equilibrium exemplified by such human beings as me and thee, require that I have faith in the greater strength of integration. For if the opposite were true, then how could all these have come into being in the first place? None could ever have developed above the zero point.

As we fight our therapeutic battles against the forces which would reduce you back toward nonbeing, we shall also confront such elements in my own self. No person has exclusive ownership of but one of these two principles. I too have lost battles, have suffered, have agonized, have pitted my best integrative energies against the same enemy. I have my personal "shadows." However, if I had never fought such engagements, then by what right should I assume here the role of counselor and guide?

As you win battles, so shall I. Hopefully may we emerge together from this undertaking the richer thereby. I shall have contacted in depth another human being, have accepted his challenges as my own, and have committed my self to his struggles. If these commitments are successful, *you* and *we* shall both be winners.

Accordingly, I undertake this engagement with you, not only because of the immediate recompense you offer me, but also because it is an opportunity for me to submit my own Eros to yet another examination, another trial of strength with my Thanatos. I know something of this enemy, having devoted a lifetime to the study of him as he has operated both within myself and in others. I have faced him often and have won more battles than I have lost. I fear not a new confrontation.

So let us about this contract. We shall come close. We shall impinge on one another, deeply and sensitively; we shall learn; we shall grow, and by our impacts shall live and *be* more richly. We do this in the conviction that we are allied with a life growth principle which mobilizes universal meaning, human living, and love. This force has been called many names by different people. Those of us who wish to be considered scientists might compare it with the physical force of gravitation (which draws bodies closer) or to that which binds cells together into increasingly complex species. Others of us, those with religious bent, may simply equate it with—Him.

A fire-mist and a planet,
    A crystal and a cell,
A jellyfish and a Saurian,
    And caves where the cavemen dwell;

Then a sense of law and beauty,
    And a face turned from the clod—
Some call it Evolution,
    And others call it God.

—W. H. Carruth

FOOTNOTE

1. The term "Eros" as used here is closer to the original Greek connotation, or to Jung's (1966) meaning than to Freud's "sexual" instinct.

Chapter 26

THERAPEUTIC SELF AND THE WORLD OF MAN

If experienced existence is determined by the impact between self and not-self, then a person's being can be defined by what he is for and what against. Translated into practical, basic needs men require a job, a friend, an enemy, a mate, and a home. Defined in process terms this means that one needs to do (a job), to be for (a friend), to be against (an enemy), to be with (a mate) and to be in (a home).

The first, by impact and achievement in the world, validates my existence. The friend brings me rewarding strokes and assurance that my world can be benevolent. Through an enemy my destructive needs are diverted away from my own self. My enemy, however, need not be another person. By pitting my will against war, injustice, poverty, cruelty, illness, and ignorance I can seek to destroy the enemies of all mankind and bind my self into a common integration with others. Through a loving mate I find a fulfillment and completeness that for most comes in no other way. Finally, in a home there is a place to restore the spent energies of the day and renew a sense of belonging. The lack of any of these leaves me with a sense of incompleteness. All else, including money and property, are subservient to these five.

Although the theory of the therapeutic self and its extension into ego-state therapy was developed as a contribution to the field of psychotherapy, its principles have broad implications throughout the entire world of man. Let us consider a few such possible applications.

During a dramatic production, the actors and actresses assume their roles with the aim of bringing to life the characters they are trying to represent. As previously described, the therapeutic self when resonating, constructs within itself a replica of another individual and then temporarily identifies with that object by investing it with ego energies. So likewise does the actor. He establishes within himself a replica of the character he is supposed to represent. This is built from all the information the playwright has furnished plus his own experience with similar people in the past. By resonating to this role he loses his own identity, and for the time lives that of the character in the play. In the movie spectacular, *Cleopatra,* at what point did Elizabeth Taylor cease being Elizabeth Taylor and become the queen of Egypt? How, when, and in what way did she momentarily lose her own self and live out the ill-fated existence of that ancient monarch?

Curious on this point, I asked several professional actors to describe their experiences on the stage. Did they lose their own identity and fuse with that of the part? I had expected them to answer "yes." To my surprise they reported that the "best actors" only partially lose their own identity. "We do become the characters in the play," they said, "but a part of us remains objective, is aware that this is a play, and that we are performing for an audience out there." Does the feedback from audience reaction require that an actor retain a certain amount of objectivity for him to please maximally in his role? If so, then even here a balance of resonance and objectivity is needed, just as in the case of the therapist.

We hear much today about the "generation gap," that break in communication between elder and child, especially between parent and adolescent child. Here we see the consequences of inadequate resonance between the respective parties. Children cannot experience their parents' needs, and parents have forgotten what it was like to be a child. So few adults seem willing to allow their own child ego states to be expressed freely and consciously. Either the child state is repressed, or it is acted out with lack of insight into its nature. If his child state is repressed by a parent, he will inhibit his own children when they try to express their childhood needs. On the other hand, the adult who acts out his child state unconsciously is soon in competition with his own children. In neither case can he take the role of a good parent, firm, objective, yet interacting with empathic understanding to the needs of his offspring.

If the parent does not resonate with his children, then they in turn cannot resonate with him. The *quid pro quo* of good interaction is never established. The children no longer identify with their parents; they take others as their models. The parents become resentful because the offspring of their own bodies reject them. No wonder that so many young people today depart from their parental homes and roam the highways or live incommunicado in the slum areas of cities, turning off reality in lives of crime or drug-initiated fantasies.

Many writers of child psychology books, such as Ginott (1965, 1969) and Gordon (1970) have endeavored to teach parents how to view their charges as these young ones perceive themselves. Training parents to resonate could pay great dividends in the happiness, adjustment, and family relationships of the coming generation.

From the age of six, children probably spend more time interacting with teachers than they do with parents. How many lost opportunities do teachers have who treat their pupils merely as objects, things to be manipulated so as to maximize the retention of memorized material? The resonating teacher like the resonating therapist (for a therapist is a teacher) understands, not only what the student needs to learn, but also what are his blocks to learning, and how the lessons should be presented to meet his specific capabilities. He becomes a good instructor because of the sensitivity of his own self, not because of the textbooks he has read on educational psychology.

Many years ago, when I was a young high school teacher, I perceived a boy in class cheating during an examination. With righteous indignation, I strode down the aisle, seized his paper, and tore it to shreds, making clear to the class in no uncertain terms that I would not tolerate cheating. This incident has been a matter of long and remembered sadness for me. The next day the boy did not come back to school. His academic education stopped at that point. By my unthinking and nonresonating act, a young man's development was significantly impaired. Cheating need not be tolerated. But the cheating behavior in the insecure student can be modified constructively by resonant understanding and a therapeutic intervention. As therapists we should always remember that the patient is never our enemy, only the pathology that afflicts him. So it is with the immaturity of a student. Teachers colleges would do well to develop the ability to resonate in the educators of tomorrow.

At periodic intervals the leaders of labor and the

captains of industry sit down to negotiate a contract. Frequently in bitterness they haggle over terms while stockholders lose money, workers cannot pay the rent, government dishes out millions in unemployment compensation, and the public suffers from a shortage of services or products. Each views the other as an "it" to be manipulated, an enemy to be conquered. Communications degenerate into shouting or sly games of maneuver. They resonate neither with each other nor with the public that is dependent on both.

Indeed it is true that the labor leader who resonated too strongly with company needs would soon feel the accusation of traitor from his union members. And the company president who too empathically accepted contracts based largely on the demands of his employees can expect his replacement by the board of directors. Such extreme cases represent the *folie à deux* that overcomes the therapist who does not match his resonance with substantial objectivity. Through a balance, the negotiators in a labor argument should soon be able to resolve their differences to the great benefit of all concerned: the workers, the company, the government, and the public. The demands that each made would be tempered with a feeling of what it is like to have such proposals made upon one's own self, and with a realization of what is possible and fair for both sides. Differences could still exist, but they would be minimal. The distances of compromise required of each side would not be so great as to prolong unnecessarily the industrial strife. When agreements were reached, the ability of the two parties to "feel with" each other would greatly reduce the bitterness that so often remains after an exhausting struggle. In Chapter 22, the interaction of the therapist with the Dark One showed clearly that much more can often be accomplished through resonance than through battle.

If such bargaining is to be successful for both, resonance must be practiced by both. The resonating negotiator is at a disadvantage against the purely objective opponent, at least temporarily. However, there is something about resonance that invites counterresonance. Such a mutual resonance might be expected to develop unless the immediate gains of the more unscrupulous and "it-minded" bargainer offset this tendency by reinforcing his adversary attitudes.

Rogers and Roethlisberger (1952) have suggested that controversies, such as are found in labor-management negotiations, can be best resolved if "each person is allowed to speak up for himself only *after* he has first restated the ideas and feelings of the previous speaker accurately and to that speaker's satisfaction." To do this would require that he attend and resonate to the communications of the other.

Headlines on newspapers today signal the tremendous problem of crime and of the great "law and order" efforts being made to cope with this crisis. Men in high places embezzle the funds of others that have been entrusted to their keeping. Adolescents from underprivileged communities mug and steal in the streets, often graduating from there to burglaries and holdups. Legion are the reports of individuals using and exploiting others for their own immediate personal gain with little consideration for the feelings and integrity of their victims.

Is it too much to suggest that the missing element here is resonance? If our theory is sound, then it would seem to be almost impossible for a person to hurt and exploit another if he resonates with that other. By making that other into a part of one's self, the pain one inflicted on the other would be felt within one's own being. The hand that would strike would be inhibited before it could even be raised.

Lest there be misunderstanding, it should be repeated again and again that we do not here advocate some selfless utopia in which everybody spends all his time and energies doing good for others. It will not happen; it should not. We seek no fusion with all others since that impact, which has been defined as the essence of existence, would be lacking. Healthy objectivity in defining one's own being as opposed to others, in safeguarding one's legitimate self-interests, in enhancing one's qualities of life within a common cathexis of general welfare is a good that has been prized by all who have sought freedom of the individual. It is a cornerstone of democracy, of the Magna Carta, of the Bill of Rights, and of the highest ethical concerns of many religions.

But it is in its excess that we now err. Could but a fraction of the money now being spent on law enforcement be somehow utilized to develop in large numbers of our citizens a concern for the existence of others, perhaps we might reverse the current trend of crime and human exploitation.

Although an appropriate balance between resonance and objectivity is significant in such diverse fields as the theatre, parent-child relationships, teacher-pupil interactions, labor-management negotiations, and law enforcement the very survival of mankind may well hinge on whether this principle can be applied to the vital fields of diplomacy and international relations.

The nuclear weapons of mass destruction can now eliminate man from this globe unless the nations come to understand each other's needs and reconcile their differences before the violent release of mortindinal energies reduces us all back to the simplest structures. Unless the Americans, the Russians, and the Chinese can resonate with each other the cataclysm could come at any time. A decade from now it may be the lack of resonance between Arab and Israeli that will spark the orgy of man's destruction.

The human self has been described here as composed of different ego states separated by boundaries. It has been likened to the structure of political principalities. From clinical observation we find that ego states can cooperate for mutual well-being, like allied nations against a common enemy. An ego state may become split, like East and West Germany, or fracture into many segments, like the Austro-Hungarian Empire. Ego states may become cognitively dissonant and hostile to each other, like Syria and Israel. In fact, the behavior of ego states within an individual is not unlike that between individuals, and between those groups of individuals called countries. Why should the behavior of human "stuff" not be substantially similar at all levels of its organizations? Identity no, but similarity, yes.

There will be some who point out that analogy is only a hypothesis, not necessarily factual, and that we have imposed a theory of mental structure artificially copied from the realities of political organization. Indeed this may be true. However, the evidence of self division into ego states is significant, and an equally tenable hypothesis might be that the states and boundaries of political entities have been imposed by men on each other because these represent an externalization of the internal divisions in their own selves. Is man's *Eigenwelt* the product of his *Mitwelt,* or vice versa?

If existence is truly the impact of subject with object, then certainly by that impact each must leave its mark of configuration on the other. So it is possible that the inner battle for dominance, for "executiveness" between the various ego states that constitute the individual self, may well mirror the outer battles for power and dominance between the political states composed of groups of men. We might thus consider whether the approaches that can bring peace within could help to bring peace without.

If there were more therapeutic selves among the world's diplomats and heads of state we could all feel safer. Foreign policies based on a balance of resonance and objectivity should be superior to those founded on self-interest alone because they are more truly realistic. By understanding the needs, the drives, and the positions of other countries, a nation would know what moves might be most successful in dealing with those countries. Nor should we fear such an approach. Resonance will permit a nation to understand the needs of another power, but objectivity will prevent it from sacrificing its own national interests. Sound policy demands a balance of both.

Trust and mutual security could replace the suspicions and hostility that so mark the interactions of nations today. Not that these are worse than in yesteryear, only that we now possess the weapons for humanity's total destruction. We can no longer chance the misunderstandings that have wreaked such frightful tolls in past wars, although never quite to the point of eliminating our species. Resonance today is not a luxury; it is a necessity for survival.

Is it too much to ask that candidates for the foreign service, that politicians, and all those who will determine the destinies of our people, have training in balancing objectivity with resonance? We even send ambassadors to other countries who are ignorant of the languages spoken in those regions, who are totally unversed in the history, the culture, and mores of those with whom they must deal. How can we expect such spokesmen for our country to understand these other peoples and represent our best interests before them? Why cannot we have men of vision in the White House who select their ambassadors on more vital criteria than the ability to contribute to the coffers of the party in power?

Unless man's psychological wisdom begins to approach his technical skills, we may soon be destroyed by the very elements over which for centuries we have so laboriously fashioned our controls. It is by the physical sciences that we have molded our present high standard of living. But if we choose to live by the physical sciences alone, by them alone will we be annihilated. We have tamed the atom, but we have not tamed the self-destructive elements in man's nature. A monumental effort in the social, behavioral, medical, and psychological sciences is now required if we are not to succumb to the principle of Thanatos. Perhaps such is the ultimate fate of all complex entities, but for us, need it be now?

What would this world be like if therapeutic selves could be developed in parents, in teachers, in industrialists and labor leaders, in administrators and public servants in all levels from mayors to presidents and prime ministers?

We harbor no delusions that such a hopeful state of affairs can easily or quickly come to pass. We cannot but feel, though, that a way of life based on objectivity balanced by resonance would provide for humans greater meaning and happiness than any system of control no matter how "scientific," such as proposed in *Walden two* (Skinner, 1948). The outcome of our struggle for survival may depend on whether men focus on their objects, their "its," or their values, their "selves."[1]

This work started with a few simple observations and questions. From these we spun more complex theoretical structures and brought to bear some objective evidence. It was an effort at integration, and as such an exercise in the extension of ego cathexis. From many sources—scientific research studies, clinical observations, art, poetry, the theoretical concepts of others, fiction, and drama—we have tried to put together some meaningful formulation on the nature of man, as he enters this world, develops, grows and dies, man as he exists within his self and with other selves.

Whether these attempts at integration have succeeded in penetrating any deeper into the mystery of existence only time and the judgment of others can say. But perhaps after this work is finished we can reduce it all back again to the beginning. Like that wise old analyst, Wilhelm Stekel, who on his deathbed is reported to have looked up as if to grasp the meaning of the hundreds of lives he had treated, we too shall whisper, "It's all a matter of love," roll over, and return to the simple sources from whence we came.

> And when Thyself with shining Foot shall pass
> Among the Guests Star-scatter'd on the Grass,
> And in thy joyous Errand reach the Spot
> Where I made one—turn down an empty Glass!
>
> *The Rubaiyat*

FOOTNOTE

1. The idea that men ruin themselves by attending to their immediate reinforcements rather than the long-term good is not new. Some 25 centuries ago Socrates tried unsuccessfully to convince the Athenians (prior to their downfall) that it is the great business of life to care for the soul before possessions or bodily pleasures, the soul being that which is most truly a man's self (Plato, 1952).

REFERENCES

Adler, A. *The practice and theory of individual psychology*. Totowa, N.J.: Littlefield, Adams, 1963.

Alexander, F., & French, T. M. *Psychoanalytic therapy*. New York: Ronald Press, 1946.

Alexander, F., & French, T. M. *Studies in psychosomatic medicine*. New York: Ronald Press, 1948.

Allen, F. H. *Psychotherapy with children*. New York: Norton, 1942.

Anderson, C. D. Energies of cosmic-ray particles. *Physical Review*, Aug. 15, 1932, *41*, 405-421.

Arieti, S. *Interpretation of schizophrenia*. New York: Brunner, 1955.

Arieti, S. Etiological considerations of schizophrenia. In S. C. Sher & H. R. Davis (Eds.), *The outpatient treatment of schizophrenia*. New York: Grune & Stratton, 1960.

Bach, G. R. *Intensive group psychotherapy*. New York: Ronald Press, 1954.

Bach, G. R., & Wyden, P. *The intimate enemy: How to fight fair in love and marriage*. New York: Morrow, 1969.

Balint, M. On the psychoanalytic training system. *International Journal of Psychoanalysis*, 1948, *17*, 206-216.

Bandura, A. Behavioral modification through modeling procedures. In L. Krasner & L. P. Ullmann, (Eds.), *Research in behavior modification*. New York: Holt, Rinehart & Winston, 1965.

Bandura, A. *Principles of behavior modification.* New York: Holt, Rinehart & Winston, 1969.

Barber, T. X. *Hypnosis: A scientific approach.* New York: Van Nostrand Reinhold, 1969.

Barrie, J. M. *The admirable Crichton; a comedy.* New York: Scribner, 1918.

Berkeley, G. *Essay, principles, dialogues.* (M. W. Calkins, Ed.), New York: Scribner, 1929.

Berne, E. *Transactional analysis in psychotherapy.* New York: Grove Press, 1961.

Bernheim, H. *Suggestive therapeutics.* (Translated by C. A. Herter), New York: Putnam, 1895.

Binswanger, L. The case of Ellen West. In R. May (Ed.), *Existence: A new dimension in psychiatry and psychology.* New York: Basic Books, 1958.

Braid, J. *Neurypnology: or, The rationale of nervous sleep, considered in relation with animal magnetism.* London: G. Redway, 1899.

Buber, M. *Between man and man.* Boston: Beacon Press, 1955.

Buber, M. *I and thou.* New York: Scribner, 1970.

Bugental, J. F. T. *The search for authenticity: An existential analytic approach to psychotherapy.* New York: Holt, Rinehart & Winston, 1965.

Bugental, J. F. T. (Ed.). *Challenges of humanistic psychology.* New York: Holt, Rinehart & Winston, 1967.

Burton, A. *Interpersonal psychotherapy.* Englewood Cliffs, N.J.: Prentice-Hall, 1972.

Cannon, W. B. *The wisdom of the body.* New York: Norton, 1932.

Cartwright, D. S. Annotated bibliography of research and theory construction in client-centered therapy. *Journal of Counseling Psychology,* 1957, *4,* 82-100.

Cautela, J. R. Covert sensitization. *Psychological Reports,* 1967, *20,* 459-568.

Cautela, J. R. Covert reinforcement. *Behavior Therapy,* 1970, *1,* 33-50.

Cautela, J. R. Covert extinction. *Behavior Therapy,* 1971, *2,* 192-200.

Charcot, J. M. Complete works (in French): *Metallotherapie et hpnotisme* (Tome IX). Paris, Fourneville & Brissand, 1890.

Cheek, D.B. & LeCron, L. M. *Clinical Hypnotherapy.* New York: Grune and Stratton, 1968.

Conn, J. H. Is hypnosis really dangerous? *International Journal of Clinical and Experimental Hypnosis,* April 1972, *20,* 61-79.

Crasilneck, H. B. & Hall, J. A. *Clinical Hypnosis: Principles and Applications.* New York: Grune & Stratton, 1975.

Dember, W. N., & Jenkins, J. J. *General psychology: Modeling behavior*

and experience. Englewood Cliffs, N.J.: Prentice-Hall, 1970.
Dewey, J. *Democracy and education.* New York: Macmillan, 1916.
Dirac, P. A. M. Electrons and protons. *Proceedings of the Royal Society,* Jan. 1, 1930, *126,* 360-365.
Einstein, A. *The meaning of relativity* (5th ed.) Princeton, N.J.: Princeton University Press, 1955.
Erickson, M. H. Unconscious mental activity in hypnosis—psychoanalytic implications. *Psychoanalytic Quarterly,* Jan. 1944, *13,* 60-78.
Erickson, M. H. Hypnotic psychotherapy. *The Medical Clinics of North America,* May 1948, New York Number, 571-583.
Erikson, E. H. *Insight and responsibility.* New York: Norton, 1964.
Erikson, E. H. *Identity: Youth and crisis.* New York: Norton, 1968.
Esser, A. H. (Ed.). *Behavior and environment: The use of space by animals and men.* New York: Plenum Press, 1971.
Fairbairn, W. R. D. Endopsychic structure considered in the light of object-relationships. *International Journal of Psycho-Analysis* 1944, *25,* 70.
Farberow, N. L. (Ed.). *Taboo topics.* New York: Atherton Press, 1963.
Federn, P. *Ego psychology and the psychoses.* (E. Weiss, Ed.), New York: Basic Books, 1952.
Fenichel, O. *Problems of psychoanalytic technique.* Albany, N.Y.: Psychoanalytic Quarterly Press, 1941.
Fenichel, O. *The Psychoanalytic theory of neurosis.* New York: Norton, 1945.
Ferenczi, S. *Further contributions to the theory and technique of psychoanalysis.* London: Hogarth Press, 1926.
Festinger, L. A. *A theory of cognitive dissonance.* Evanston, Ill.: Row, Peterson, 1957.
Field, P. B., & Palmer, R. D. Factor analysis: Hypnosis inventory. *International Journal of Clinical and Experimental Hypnosis,* 1969, *17,* 50-61.
Frankl, V. *Man's search for meaning.* New York: Pocket Books, 1972.
French, T. M. The transference phenomenon. In F. Alexander & T. M. French (Eds.), *Psychoanalytic therapy.* New York: Ronald Press, 1946.
French, T. M., & Fromm, Erika *Dream interpretation: A new approach.* New York: Basic Books, 1964.
Freud, A. *The ego and the mechanisms of defense.* New York: International Universities Press, 1946.
Freud, S. *Beyond the pleasure principle.* London and Vienna: The International Psycho-Analytical Press, 1922.
Freud, S. Mourning and melancholia. In *Collected Papers* (Vol. IV). London: Hogarth Press & The Institute of Psycho-Analysis, 1925.

Freud, S. *A general introduction to psychoanalysis.* New York: Liveright, 1935.

Freud S. *Basic writings. Book II, The interpretation of dreams.* New York: Modern Library, 1938.

Freud, S. *The ego and the id.* London: Hogarth Press, 1947. (Republished, New York: Norton, 1961.)

Freud, S. Freud's psycho-analytic method. In *Collected Papers* (Vol. I). London: Hogarth Press & The Institute of Psycho-Analysis, 1953a, pp. 264-271. (Originally published in 1904).

Freud, S. The dynamics of the transference. In *Collected Papers* (Vol. II). London: Hogarth Press & The Institute of Psycho-Analysis, 1953b, pp. 312-322.

Freud, S. Observations on transference love. In *Collected Papers* (Vol. II). London: Hogarth Press & The Institute of Psycho-Analysis, 1953c, pp. 377-391.

Freud, S. On narcissism: An introduction. In *Collected Papers* (Vol. IV). London: Hogarth Press & The Institute of Psycho-Analysis, 1953d, pp. 30-59.

Freud, S. The theme of the three caskets. In *Collected Papers (Vol. IV).* London: Hogarth Press & The Institute of Psycho-Analysis, 1953e, pp. 244-256.

Fromm, Erich, *The anatomy of human destructiveness.* New York: Holt, Rinehart & Winston, 1973.

Fromm, Erika. Awareness vs. consciousness. *Psychological Reports,* 1965, *16,* 7-12.

Fromm, Erika & Shor, R.E. (Eds.). *Hypnosis: Research developments and perspectives.* Chicago: Aldine-Atherton, 1972.

Fromm-Reichman, F. *Principles of intensive psychotherapy.* Chicago: University of Chicago Press, 1950.

Gamow, G. *Thirty years that shook physics.* Garden City, N.Y.: Doubleday, 1966.

Gendlin, E. T. *Experiencing and the creation of meaning.* New York: Free Press, 1962.

Gendlin, E. T. Existentialism and experiential psychotherapy. Chap. 5 in J. T. Hart & T. M. Tomlinson (Eds.). *New directions in client-centered therapy.* Boston: Houghton Mifflin, 1970.

Gill, M. M., & Brenman, M. *Hypnosis and related states.* New York: International Universities Press, 1959.

Ginott, H. G. *Between parent and child.* New York: Macmillan, 1965.

Ginott, H. G. *Between parent and teen-ager.* New York: Macmillan, 1969.

Glasser, W. *Reality therapy.* New York: Harper & Row, 1965.

Glover, E. *The technique of psychoanalysis.* New York: International Universities Press, 1955.

Gordon, T. *Parent effectiveness training.* New York: Peter H. Wyden, 1970.

Gruenewald, D., Fromm, Erika, & Oberlander, M. I. Hypnosis and adaptive regression: An ego-psychological inquiry. In Erika Fromm & R. E. Shor, (Eds.), *Hypnosis: Research developments and perspectives.* Chicago: Aldine-Atherton, 1972.

Guntrip, H. A study of Fairbairn's theory of schizoid reactions. *British Journal of Medical Psychology,* 1952, *25,* 86-103.

Harris, T. A. *I'm OK, you're OK.* New York: Harper & Row, 1969.

Hartmann, H. Technical implications of ego psychology. *Psychoanalytic Quarterly,* 1951, *20,* 31-43.

Heidegger, M. *Existence and being.* Chicago: Henry Regnery, 1949.

Hilgard, E. R. *Hypnotic susceptibility.* New York: Harcourt, Brace & World, 1965.

Hilgard, E. R. A neodissociation interpretation of pain reduction in hypnosis. *Psychological Review,* 1973, *80,* 403-419.

Hilgard, E. R., & Bower, G. H. *Theories of Learning* (4th ed.), Englewood Cliffs, N.J.: Prentice-Hall, 1975.

Hilgard, E. R., & Hilgard, J. R. *Hypnosis in the relief of pain.* Los Altos, Calif.: William Kaufmann, 1975.

Hillyard, S. A., Hink, R. F., Schwent, V. L., & Picton, T. W. Electrical signs of selective attention in the human brain. *Science,* Oct. 12, 1973, *182,* 177-180.

Hodge, J. R., & Wagner, E. E. The effect of trance depth on Rorschach responses. *American Journal of Clinical Hypnosis,* April 1969, *11,* 234-238.

Hoffer, E. *The true believer.* New York: Harper, 1951.

Hoffman, B. *The strange story of the quantum.* New York: Dover, 1959.

Holland, G. A. Transactional analysis. Chap. 10 in R. Corsini (Ed.), *Current psychotherapies.* Itasca, Ill.: Peacock, 1973.

Holz, W. C., Azrin, N. H., & Ulrich, R. E. Punishment of temporally spaced responding. *Journal of the Experimental Analysis of Behavior,* 1963, *6,* 115-122.

Horney, K. *Neurosis and human growth.* New York: Norton, 1950.

Hull, C. L. *Hypnosis and suggestibility.* New York: Appleton-Century-Crofts, 1933.

Hume, D. *The philosophy of David Hume,* (V. C. Chappel, Ed.), New York: Modern Library, 1963.

Jackson, C. W., & Ellis, R. Sensory deprivation as a field of study. *Nursing Research,* Jan. 1971, *20,* 46-54.

Janet, P. *The major symptoms of hysteria.* New York: Macmillan, 1907.

Jaspers, K. *Existentialism and humanism.* New York: Russell F. Moore, 1952.

Jones, M. C. The elimination of children's fears. *Journal of Experimen-*

tal Psychology, 1924, *7,* 383-390.

Jones, R. B. *Parent-child interaction in two cases of infantile autism.* Unpublished master's thesis, University of Oregon, 1965.

Jourard, S. *The transparent self.* New York: Van Nostrand Reinhold, 1971.

Jung, C. G. Chap. II, The eros theory. In *Two essays on analytical psychology.* New York: Pantheon, 1966.

Kanfer, F. H., & Marston, A. R. Conditioning of self-reinforcement responses: An analogue to self-confidence training. *Psychological Reports,* 1963, *13,* 63-70.

Kanner, L. Early infantile autism. *Journal of Pediatrics,* 1944, *25,* 211-217.

Kant, I. *Critique of pure reason.* New York: Dutton, 1934.

Kaplan, H. J., & Sadock, B. J. *Comprehensive group psychotherapy.* Baltimore: Williams & Wilkins, 1971.

Kasanin, J. S. (Ed.). *Language and thought in schizophrenia.* Berkeley and Los Angeles: University of California Press, 1944.

Kierkegaard, S. A. *Fear and trembling and the sickness unto death.* Garden City, N.Y.: Doubleday Anchor, 1954.

Kleitman, N. *Sleep and wakefulness* (2nd ed.). Chicago: University of Chicago Press, 1963.

Kline, M. V. *Freud and hypnosis.* New York: Julian Press & The Institute for Research in Hypnosis Publication Society, 1958.

Kline, M. V. Age regression and regressive procedures in hypnotherapy. Chap. 3, in M. V. Kline (Ed.), *Clinical correlations of experimental hypnosis.* Springfield, Ill.: Thomas, 1963.

Kline, M. V. The production of antisocial behavior through hypnosis: New clinical data. *International Journal of Clinical and Experimental Hypnosis,* April 1972, *20,* 80-94.

Kline, P. *Fact and fantasy in Freudian theory.* London: Methuen, 1972.

Koch, S. (Ed.). *Psychology: A study of science* (Vol. III) New York: McGraw-Hill, 1959.

Koestler, A. *The roots of coincidence.* New York: Random House, 1972.

Korner, I. N., & Brown, W. H. The mechanical third ear. *Journal of Consulting Psychology,* 1952, *16,* 81-84.

Krasner, L. The therapist as a social reinforcement machine. In H. H. Strupp & L. Luborsky (Eds.), *Research in psychotherapy* (Vol. II), Washington, D.C.: American Psychological Association, 1962, pp. 61-94.

Krasner, L., & Ullmann, L. P. *Research in behavior modification.* New York: Holt, Rinehart & Winston, 1965.

Kris, E. Ego psychology and interpretation in psychoanalytic therapy. *Psychoanalytic Quarterly,* 1951, *20,* 15-30.

Kroger, W. S. *Clinical and experimental hypnosis.* Philadelphia: Lippincott, 1963.

Kubie, L. S., & Margolin, D. The process of hypnotism and the nature of the hypnotic state. 1944, *American Journal of Psychiatry, 100,* 5.

Laing, R. D. *The divided self.* New York: Pantheon, 1969.

Lennon, J. W. *Counselor effectiveness: Empathy training.* Unpublished doctoral dissertation, University of Montana, 1974.

Lewin, K. *Field theory in social science.* New York: Harper, 1951.

Lidz, T., & Fleck, S. Schizophrenia, human integration and the role of the family. In D. D. Jackson (Ed.), *The etiology of schizophrenia.* New York: Basic Books, 1960.

Liebeault, A. *Du summeil et des états analogues considérés surtout au point de vue de l'action moral sur le physique.* Nancy and Paris: 1866.

Locke, J. *The works of John Locke.* Aalen, Germany: Scientia Verlag, 1963.

Lorenz, K. Der Kumpan in der Umwelt des Vogels. *J. für Ornithologie,* 1935, *83,* 137-213, 289-413.

Lovaas, O. I., Freitas, L., Nelson, K., & Whalen, C. The establishment of imitation and its use for the development of complex behavior in schizophrenic children. *Behaviour Research and Therapy,* 1967, *5,* 171-181.

Mahoney, M. J. *Cognition and behavior modification.* Cambridge, Mass.: Ballinger, 1974.

Marcel, G. *The philosophy of existence.* London: Harvill, 1948.

Marcuse, F. L. *Hypnosis: Fact and fiction.* Harmondsworth, England: Penguin Books, 1971.

Mark, J. C. The attitudes of the mothers of male schizophrenics toward child behavior. *Journal of Abnormal and Social Psychology,* 1953, *48,* 185-189.

Marmer, M. J. *Hypnosis in anesthesiology.* Springfield, Ill.: Thomas, 1959.

May, R. (Ed.), *Existence: A new dimension in psychiatry and psychology.* New York: Basic Books, 1958.

May, R. The emergence of existential psychology. In R. May (Ed.), *Existential Psychology.* New York: Random House, 1961.

Mayeroff, M. *On caring.* New York: Harper & Ros, 1971.

McGhie, A. A comparative study of the mother-child relationship in schizophrenia. *British Journal of Medical Psychology,* 1961, *34,* 195-221.

McGuire, W. (Editor). *The Freud/Jung Letters.* Princeton, N.J.: Princeton University Press, 1974.

Mead, M. (Ed.). *Cooperation and competition among primitive peoples.* New

York: McGraw-Hill, 1937.

Meares, A. *A system of medical hypnosis.* Philadelphia: Saunders, 1961.

Meichenbaum, D. Cognitive factors in behavior modification: Modifying what clients say to themselves. In C. M. Franks & G. T. Wilson (Eds.), *Annual review of behavior therapy, theory and practice* (Vol. 1). New York: Brunner/Mazel, 1973.

Menninger, K. *Theory of psychoanalytic technique.* New York: Basic Books, 1958.

Monroe, R. A. *Journeys out of the body.* Garden City, N.Y.: Doubleday, 1971.

Moreno, J. L. *Psychodrama* (Vol. 1). 2nd ed. New York: Beacon House, 1946.

Moss, C. S., *Dreams, images and fantasy: A semantic differential casebook.* Urbana, Ill.: University of Illinois Press, 1970.

Naruse, G. Hypnosis as a state of meditative concentration and its relationship to the perceptual process. In M. V. Kline (Ed.), *The nature of hypnosis* (Transactions of the 1961 International Congress on Hypnosis), New York: The Institute for Research in Hypnosis & The Postgraduate Center for Psychotherapy, 1962.

Noyes, R. The experience of dying. *Psychiatry,* May 1972, *35,* 174-184.

Orne, M. T. On the social psychology of the psychological experiment: With particular reference to demand characteristics and their implication. *The American Psychologist,* 1962, *17,* 776-783.

Orne, M. T. Can a hypnotized subject be compelled to carry out otherwise unacceptable behavior? *International Journal of Clinical and Experimental Hypnosis,* April 1972, *20,* 101-117.

Patterson, G. R. Behavioral techniques based upon social learning: An additional base for developing behavior modification technologies. In C. M. Franks (Ed.), *Behavior therapy: Appraisal and status,* New York: McGraw-Hill, 1969.

Paul, G. L. Behavior modification research: Design and tactics. In C. M. Franks (Ed.), *Behavior therapy: Appraisal and status,* New York: McGraw-Hill, 1969.

Pavlov, I. P. *Experimental psychology.* New York: Philosophical Library, 1957.

Perls, F. S. *Gestalt therapy verbatim.* Lafayette, Calif.: Real People Press, 1969.

Perls, F. *The gestalt approach and eye witness to therapy.* Lomand, Calif.: Science & Behavior Books, 1973.

Plato. *The Republic* (Translated by Paul Shorey). New York: Putnam, 1930-35.

Plato. Apology. In R. M. Hutchins (Ed.), *Great Books of the Western*

World. London: Encyclopedia Britannica, 1952.

Prince, M. *The dissociation of a personality.* New York: Longmans-Green, 1906.

Rachman, S. J., & Teasdale, J. Aversion therapy: an appraisal. In C. M. Franks (Ed.), *Behavior therapy: Appraisal and status,* New York: McGraw-Hill, 1969.

Rank, O. *Will therapy and truth and reality* (translated by J. J. Taft). New York: Knopf, 1950.

Rank, O. *The trauma of birth.* New York: Brunner, 1952.

Rapaport, D. The theory of ego autonomy: A generalization. *Bulletin of the Menninger Clinic,* 1958, *22,* 13-35.

Ray, R. *The training of mothers of atypical children in the use of behavior modification techniques.* Unpublished master's thesis, University of Oregon, 1965.

Reich, W. *Character analysis.* New York: Orgone Institute Press, 1949.

Reichard, S., & Tillman, C. Patterns of parent-child relationships in schizophrenia. *Psychiatry,* 1950, *13,* 247-257.

Reiff, R., & Scheerer, M. *Memory and hypnotic age regression.* New York: International Universities Press, 1959.

Reik, T. *Listening with the third ear.* New York: Farrar, 1948.

Reik, T. *The search within.* New York: Grove Press, 1956.

Reik, T. *Of love and lust.* New York: Farrar, Straus & Cudahy, 1957.

Reines, F., & Cowan, C. L., Jr. The neutrino. *Nature* (London), Sept. 1, 1956, *178,* 446-449.

Rogers, C. R. *Counseling and psychotherapy.* Boston: Houghton-Mifflin, 1942.

Rogers, C. R. *Client-centered therapy.* Boston: Houghton-Mifflin, 1951.

Rogers, C. R. A tentative scale for the measurement of process in psychotherapy. In E. A. Rubinstein & M. P. Parloff (Eds.), *Research in psychotherapy* (Vol. 1), Washington, D.C.: American Psychological Association, 1959.

Rogers, C. R. *On becoming a person: A client's view of psychotherapy.* Boston: Houghton-Mifflin, 1961.

Rogers, C. R. (Ed.). *The therapeutic relationship and its impact: A study of psychotherapy with schizophrenics* (with E. T. Gendlin, D. J. Kiesler, & C. Truax). Madison, Wis.: University of Wisconsin Press, 1967.

Rogers, C. R., & Dymond, R. F. (Eds.). *Psychotherapy and personality change.* Chicago: University of Chicago Press, 1954.

Rogers, C. R., & Roethlisberger, F. J. Barriers and gateways to communication. *Harvard Business Review,* 1952, *30,* 46-52.

Rosenthal, R. *Experimenter effects in behavioral research.* New York:

Appleton-Century-Crofts, 1966.

Sacerdote, P. *Induced dreams.* New York: Vantage Press, 1967.

Salter, A. *What is hypnosis?* New York: Richard R. Smith, 1944.

Sarbin, T. R., & Lim, D. T. Some evidence in support of the role taking hypothesis in hypnosis. *International Journal of Clinical and Experimental Hypnosis,* 1963, *11,* 90-103.

Sartre, J. *Existential psychoanalysis.* New York: Philosophical Library, 1953.

Satir, V. *Conjoint family therapy.* Palo Alto, Calif.: Science & Behavior Books, 1967.

Schneck, J. M. Discussion of 'An atavistic theory of hypnosis' by A. Meares. In M. V. Kline (Ed.), *The nature of hypnosis* (Transactions of the 1961 International Congress on Hypnosis). New York: The Postgraduate Center for Psychotherapy & The Institute for Research in Hypnosis, 1962.

Schneck, J. M. *Principles and practice of hynoanalysis.* Springfield, Ill.: Thomas, 1965.

Schulman, J., Shaver, P., Colman, R., Emrich, B., & Christie, R. Recipe for a jury. *Psychology Today.* May 1973, *6,* 37-44, 77-84.

Schwing, G. *A way to the soul of the mentally ill.* New York: International Universities Press, 1954.

Selye, H. *The stress of life.* New York: McGraw-Hill, 1956.

Sherman, S. E. *Very deep hypnosis: An experiential and electroencephalographic investigation.* Unpublished doctoral dissertation, Stanford University, August 1971.

Shlien, J. M. A client-centered approach to schizophrenia. In A. Burton (Ed.), *Psychotherapy of the psychoses,* New York: Basic Books, 1961.

Shor, R. Three dimensions of hypnotic depth. *International Journal of Clinical and Experimental Hypnosis,* Jan. 1962, *10,* 23-38.

Shostrom, E. *Man the manipulator.* Nashville, Tenn.: Abingdon Press, 1967.

Signorelli, A. Statistics: Tool or master of the psychologist? *American Psychologist,* Oct. 1974, *29,* 774-777.

Skinner, B. F. *Walden two.* New York: Macmillan, 1948.

Skinner, B. F. *Science and human behavior.* New York: Macmillan, 1953.

Solomon, P., Kubansky, P. E., Leiderman, P. H., Mendelson, J. H., Trumbull, R. & Wexler, D. (Eds.). *Sensory deprivation.* Cambridge, Mass.: Harvard University Press, 1961.

Sonnemann, U. *Existence and Therapy.* New York: Grune & Stratton, 1954.

Stampfl, T. G. Implosive therapy: The theory, the subhuman

analogue, the strategy, and the technique. Part I: The theory. In S. G. Armitage (Ed.), *Behavior modification techniques in the treatment of emotional disorders,* Battle Creek, Mich.: Veterans Administration Publication, 1967.

Stekel, W. *Sadism and Masochism* (Vols. 1 & 2). New York: Liveright, 1939a.

Stekel, W. *Impotence in the Male* (Vols. 1 & 2). New York: Liveright, 1939b.

Stekel, W. *Sexual aberrations* (Vols. 1 & 2). New York: Liveright, 1940.

Stekel, W. *The interpretation of dreams* (Vols. 1 & 2). New York: Liveright, 1943a.

Stekel, W. *Peculiarities of behavior* (Vols. 1 & 2). New York: Liveright, 1943b.

Stekel, W. *Frigidity in women* (Vols. 1 & 2). New York: Liveright, 1943c.

Stekel, W. *Compulsion and doubt* (Vols. 1 & 2). New York: Liveright, 1949.

Stevenson, R. L. *The strange case of Dr. Jekyll and Mr. Hyde and other famous tales.* New York: Dodd, Mead, 1961.

Stewart, C. T. *The origin of the werewolf superstition.* Columbia, Missouri: University of Missouri Studies, Vol. II, No. 3, 1909.

Stewart G. W. Phase relations in the acoustic shadow of a rigid sphere, phase difference of the ears. *Physical Review,* 1914, *4,* 252.

Stratton, G. M. Vision without inversion of the retinal image. *Psychological Review,* 1897, *July 4,* 341-360; *Sept. 4,* 463-481.

Straus, E. W. Anesthesiology and hallucinations. In R. May (Ed.), *Existence: A new dimension in psychiatry and psychology.* New York: Basic Books, 1958.

Stross, L. Impulse-defense implications in a case of amnesia. *International Journal of Clinical and Experimental Hypnosis,* April 1966, *14,* 89-103.

Sullivan, H. S. *Conceptions of modern psychiatry.* New York: Norton, 1954.

Suzuki, D. T. *Essays in Zen Buddhism.* London: Rider, 1950.

Symonds, P. M. *The ego and the self.* New York: Appleton-Century-Crofts, 1951.

Taft, J. *Dynamics of therapy in a controlled relationship.* New York: Macmillan, 1936.

Tart, C. Measuring the depth of an altered state of consciousness, with particular reference to self-report scales of depth. Chap. 14 in Erika Fromm & R. Shor (Eds.), *Hypnosis: Research developments and perspectives,* Chicago: Aldine-Atherton, 1972.

Thigpen, C. H., & Cleckley, H. M. *Three faces of Eve.* New York: McGraw-Hill, 1957.

Thorne, F. C. *Principles of personality counseling.* Brandon, Vermont: Journal of Clinical Psychology, 1950.

Thorne, F. C. Eclectic psychotherapy. Chap. 12 in R. Corsini (Ed.), *Current psychotherapies,* Itasca, Ill.: Peacock, 1973.

Tillich, P. *The courage to be.* New Haven: Yale University Press, 1952.

Tillich, P. Existentialism, psychotherapy and the nature of man. *Pastoral Psychology,* June 1960, *11,* 10-18.

Toffler, A. *Future shock.* New York: Random House, 1970.

Tomlinson, T. M., & Whitney, R. E. Values and strategy in client-centered therapy: A means to an end. In J. T. Hart & T. M. Tomlinson (Eds.), *New directions in client-centered therapy.* Boston: Houghton-Mifflin, 1970.

Truax, C. B. A scale for the measurement of accurate empathy. *Discussion Paper, No. 20.* Wisconsin Psychiatric Institute, University of Wisconsin, Sept. 26, 1961.

Truax, C., & Carkhuff, R. *Toward effective counseling and psychotherapy: Training and practice.* Chicago: Aldine Press, 1967.

Ullmann, L. P., & Krasner, L. *A psychological approach to abnormal behavior.* Englewood Cliffs, N.J.: Prentice-Hall, 1969.

Van der Veen, F. Client perception of therapist conditions as a factor in psychotherapy. In J. T. Hart & T. M. Tomlinson (Eds.), *New directions in client-centered therapy,* Boston: Houghton-Mifflin, 1970.

Watkins, H. H. Hypnosis and smoking. *International Journal of Clinical and Experimental Hypnosis,* Oct. 1976, *24,* 381-390.

Watkins, J. G. *Objective measurement of instrumental performance.* New York: Teachers College Bureau of Publications, Columbia University, 1942.

Watkins, J. G. Antisocial compulsions induced under hypnotic trance. *Journal of Abnormal and Social Psychology,* 1947, *42,* 256-259.

Watkins, J. G. *Hypnotherapy of war neuroses.* New York: Ronald Press, 1949.

Watkins, J. G. A case of hypnotic trance induced in a resistant subject in spite of active opposition. *British Journal of Medical Hypnotism,* 1951, *2,* 26-31.

Watkins, J. G. Projective hypnoanalysis. Chap. 19 in L. M. LeCron (Ed.), *Experimental Hypnosis.* New York: Macmillan, 1952.

Watkins, J. G. Trance and transference. *Journal of Clinical and Experimental Hypnosis,* 1954, *2,* 284-290.

Watkins, J. G. *General psychotherapy.* Springfield, Ill.: Charles C. Thomas, 1960.

Watkins, J. G. Psychodynamics of hypnotic induction and termination. Chap. 11 in J. M. Schneck (Ed.), *Hypnosis in modern medicine,* Springfield, Ill.: Charles C. Thomas, 1963a.

Watkins, J. G. Transference aspects of the hypnotic relationship. Chap. 1 in M. V. Kline (Ed.), *Clinical correlations of experimental hypnosis.* Springfield, Ill.: Charles C. Thomas, 1963b.

Watkins, J. G. Hypnosis and consciousness. Chap. III in M. V. Kline (Ed.), *Psychodynamics and hypnosis,* Springfield, Ill.: Charles C. Thomas, 1967a.

Watkins, J. G. The continuity of life: What to do when a loved one dies. *The Spokesman-Review Magazine,* Nov. 5, 1967b, pp. 6-7.

Watkins, J. G. Operant approaches to existential therapy. Unpublished paper. Presented July 14, 1967, at the International Congress for Psychosomatic Medicine and Hypnosis, Kyoto, Japan). 1967c.

Watkins, J. G. The affect bridge: A hypnoanalytic technique. *International Journal of Clinical and Experimental Hypnosis,* Jan. 1971, *19,* 21-27.

Watkins, J. G. Antisocial behavior under hypnosis: possible or impossible? *International Journal of Clinical and Experimental Hypnosis,* April 1972, *20,* 95-100.

Watkins, J.G. Ego states and the problem of responsibility: A psychological analysis of the Patty Hearst case. *Psychiatry and Law,* Winter 1976, pp. 471—489.

Watkins, J. G., & Watkins, H. H. *Multiple techniques by multiple therapists in the hypnoanalytic treatment of a multiple personality.* (Unpublished paper presented at the Society for Clinical and Experimental Hypnosis, Newport Beach, Calif.: Nov. 1973).

Watkins, J. G., & Watkins, H. H. *Making friends with enemy ego-states* (Demonstration clinic). Presented at the American Society for Clinical Hypnosis, Seattle, Wash., Oct. 16, 1975.

Watkins, J. G. & Watkins, H. H. Ego states and "hidden observers": Neo-dissociation theory applied to hypnoanalytic therapy. (Presented at the October meetings of the Society for Clinical and Experimental Hypnosis in Los Angeles), 1977.

Watson, J. B. *Psychology from the standpoint of a behaviorist.* Philadelphia: Lippincott, 1929.

Watts, A. W. *The way of Zen.* New York: Pantheon, 1957.

Weiss, E. Todestrieb und Masochismus. *Imago,* 1935, *21,* 393-411.

Weiss, E. *The structure and dynamics of the human mind.* New York: Grune & Stratton, 1960.

Weiss, E. Paul Federn, 1871-1950: The theory of the psychoses. In F. Alexander, S. Eisenstein, & M. Grotjahn (Eds.), *Psychoanalytic Pioneers,* New York: Basic Books, 1966.

West, L. J. Psychopathology produced by sleep deprivation. In S. S. Kety, E. V. Evarts, and H. L. Williams (Eds.), *Sleep and altered states of consciousness,* Baltimore: Williams & Wilkins, 1967.

White, R. W. *The abnormal personality* (3rd ed.). New York: Ronald Press, 1964.

Whyte, W. H. *The organization man.* New York: Simon & Schuster, 1956.

Wilde, O. *The picture of Dorian Gray.* New York: Putnam, 1909.

Willey, C. F., Inglis, E., & Pearce, C. H. Reversal of auditory localization. *Journal of Experimental Psychology,* 1937, *20,* 114-130.

Wolberg, L. R. *Hypnoanalysis.* New York: Grune & Stratton, 1945.

Wolberg, L. R. *Hypnosis: Is it for you?* New York: Harcourt Brace Jovanovich, 1972.

Wolpe, J. *Psychotherapy by reciprocal inhibition.* Stanford, Calif.: Stanford University Press, 1958.

Wolpe, J. The systematic desensitization treatment of neuroses. *Journal of Nervous and Mental Disease,* 1961, *132,* 189-203.

Young, P. T. Auditory localization with acoustical transposition of ears. *Journal of Experimental Psychology,* 1928, *11,* 399-429.

Young, P. T. Reversal of auditory localization. *Psychological Review,* 1937, *44,* 505-520.

A Glossary of Technical and Professional Terms

abreaction, the release of bound emotion through reliving (often violently) the experience originally connected with that feeling.
act out, to translate repressed drives into behavior as a way of avoiding insight into them. A defense mechanism commonly employed by a patient in psychoanalytic therapy.
actualizing behavior, actions designed to promote self-integration and to assist an individual in realizing the greatest possible functioning of his "being" potentials.
affect, a feeling, an emotion.
affect bridge, a therapeutic technique in which a common affect is used as a bridge to move an individual experientially from a present or recent experience to one in the past during which the same feeling was felt.
affective resonance, a temporary identification with another based upon coexperiencing with him the emotion he is currently feeling. (See also **cognitive resonance.**)

ambivalence, the condition of an individual who is impelled simultaneously by two opposing impulses, such as the desire both to do and not to do something at the same time.
analysand, the patient in a psychoanalysis.
analysis of variance, a statistical method of determining whether observed variations in a set of measures that has been exposed to the possible influence of another factor can be explained on the basis of chance alone.
analytic fovea, an area in the perception of an individual to which he is extremely sensitive and to which he is more reactive than normal.
analytic scotoma or analytic blind spot, an area in the perception of an individual to which he is extremely insensitive and to which he is less reactive than normal.
antimatter, a hypothesized substance composed of the counterparts, or opposite elements, of ordinary matter. When matter and antimatter contact each other, they are both eliminated, leaving only a radiation.
archaic involvement, the preoccupation of a subject with figures and concepts internalized very early in his childhood development and with behavior based on the projection of these upon individuals in his present-day life.
artifact, a psychological entity, artificially created by definition, that does not naturally occur in the personality of the individual.
atavistic regression, Meares has proposed that hypnosis is characterized by a regression of behavior and experience to that which was typical of aboriginal and prehistoric man. He termed this "atavistic."
aversive stimuli, stimuli that evoke feelings of unpleasantness and avoidance behavior in an organism.
behaviorism, a system of psychology which holds that behavior is the proper province of study for this discipline—as opposed to mind, consciousness, experience, or other mentalistic concepts.

behavior modification, a methodology for changing behavior based on laboratory discovered learning principles.
behavior modifier, one who undertakes to change behavior on the basis of principles of behavior modification.
behavior therapist, one who utilizes principles of behavior modification in the treatment of maladjustments.
being-in-the-world, an existential term that emphasizes the inseparability of an individual and his environment in defining his existence.
castration anxiety, a kind of anxiety postulated by psychoanalytic theory that occurs when a male child's oedipal affection for his mother (usually at three to five years old) stimulates a fear of castration by the father.
cathect, to attach or allocate a unit of energy.
character analysis, a type of psychoanalysis formulated by Wilhelm Reich. It holds that the ego is encased in rigid psychological patterns characterized by unyielding attitudes and behaviors that must be analyzed to release their energies in the analysand.
character armor, rigid patterns of thought and action that bind the ego. (See also **character analysis**).
chi-square, a statistical test to determine whether the results of an experiment are due to chance.
client, an alternate term to "patient," hence one who is being treated by a psychotherapist or counselor.
client-centered therapy, a type of treatment formulated by Carl Rogers. It is based on the concept that the client and not the therapist should be the center of their mutual endeavor and should take the initiative and responsibility for the verbal interactions.
cognitive consonance, intellectual harmony. Being "in tune" with the ideas of another; ideas within an individual that are consistent with one another.
cognitive dissonance, intellectual clash. Being "out of

tune" with ideas of another; ideas within an individual that are inconsistent with each other.

cognitive resonance, a temporary identification with another based upon coexperiencing with him the intellectual understanding he currently holds. (See also **affective resonance**).

cognitive structural system, a term used by Hilgard to designate an underlying awareness to hypnotically inhibited perception (such as induced deafness or analgesia).

concrete thinking, a type of thinking found in children, psychotics, and the brain damaged. It is characterized by an equating of two objects because of a similar characteristic. *Example:* "I hate John who has blonde hair. Therefore, I hate George who also has blonde hair."

conditioned reflex, a reflex that can be evoked by a secondary stimulus which has been associated with that which originally evoked it. (See also **reflex.**)

confabulation, the representing of fantasy as truth; the tendency (often found in psychotics) of generalizing an attribute of a part to a whole.

congruence, according to Carl Rogers, the ability of a therapist to understand his own inner experience and to transmit this authentically to his client.

contamination, a type of concrete thinking in which the perception of an individual or object is colored by some non-significant factor. (See also **concrete thinking.**)

contingency, the probability that a second event will occur when preceded by a specific prior event.

countertransference, a transference experienced by a therapist about his patient. (See also **transference.**)

covert, underlying, not obvious.

death instinct, a concept developed by Freud to describe a person's tendency to move toward destruction. Freud considered this to be innate. Some of his followers called the death instinct "Thantos." The concept is controversial among psychoanalysts.

deegotize, to remove from the ego. To decathect. To take away ego cathexis.
defense mechanism, a process by which reality is distorted to some extent to evade unpleasant confrontations and to reduce anxiety.
delusions, a false belief characteristic of psychotic thought, such as a delusion of persecution.
depersonalization, a lack of feeling the existence of self.
desensitization, to make less sensitive; a behavioral technique employed to reduce a fear.
didactic analysis, the personal analysis of one who is a psychoanalyst-in-training during which he is both being analyzed and being taught how to analyze.
differentiation, the perceptual recognition of differences and discrimination between two different objects.
dissociated personality, two or more different personality structures within the same individual that are independent (and often unaware) of each other, such as a multiple personality.
dissociation, the separation of two related psychological entities so that they are experienced independently of each other. For example, describing a frightening episode without experiencing fear. The fear and the memory are dissociated from one another.
dynamics. See **psychodynamics.**
ego, the psychoanalytic term for the "I" or self; also the center of a person to which all experienced data are referred.
ego boundary, the "wall" between the ego and the outer world, the ego and the id, or between different ego states.
ego cathexis, a term employed by Federn to denote "self" energy. It is considered here to be organic. Psychological and physiological items, such as thoughts or parts of the body, when invested or cathected with it are experienced as being within my self.

ego feeling, the feeling of selfness. When it is lacking the individual experiences depersonalization.
ego-libido, a term used by Federn as equivalent to ego cathexis.
ego-mortido, an ego cathexis characterized by a tendency to repel other psychological entities, thereby reducing complex structures toward their simplest elements.
ego state, a body of psychological elements, both object and subject, organized around a single principle and differentiated from other such states by a boundary. Federn included only items that were subject or ego cathected.
egotization, the process of investing with ego cathexis.
Eigenwelt, man's inner, subjective world of experience. (See also **Mitwelt** and **Umwelt**).
electroencephalograph, an instrument for recording brain waves.
empathy, the act of "feeling with" another person; emotional understanding.
emphysema, a disease of the lungs in which there is distention of the air sacs leading to shortness of breath, coughing, and other signs of respiratory discomfort.
empirical, an approach to knowledge that values facts and the direct observation of them rather than speculation or analysis by rational thinking.
Eros, a principle of attraction between two individuals, e.g., love.
essentialist, a philosophical theory concerned with the essence of things as contrasted with their existence.
estrangement, the inability to sense external objects as real.
executive ego state, that condition in which the experience of existence is currently felt. The "self" in the "now." That ego state which is most highly cathected.
existential, referring to the nature of being, of life.

exorcism, the throwing out of malignant entities from the self.
facilitative response, a response in the Therapeutic Self Scoring System, the only purpose of which is to encourage the client or patient to continue to communicate. Examples are "Uh-huh" or "Tell me more."
field theory, a point of view that emphasizes that the properties of things are derived from, or dependent upon, the field in which they are imbedded.
flooding, a therapeutic technique in which strong emotions are stimulated and permitted to "flood" through an individual for the purpose of desensitizing him to them. Similar to abreaction.
folie à deux, an illness or maladjustment common to two individuals. They copy each other.
fovea, analytic, See **analytic fovea.**
functionalism, a school of psychology associated with James, Angell, and Dewey that emphasized the study of the entire individual, including behavior, perception, and consciousness.
Gestalt psychology, a theoretical position in psychology that emphasizes that the response to a stimulus will be modified or determined by the configuration (Gestalt) or field in which it is a part.
Gestalt therapy, a system of therapy that perceives disturbing behavior as the result of a painful polarization between two discordant elements. Treatment involves bringing these elements into a here-and-now confrontation.
hallucination, the perception of something that is not real, hence something that does not exist outside the individual. Hallucinations often occur in psychotic individuals.
hidden observer, a term used by Hilgard to designate an underlying perceptual awareness to hypnotically initiated deafness and pain. (See also **cognitive structual system.**)

hierarchy, an order of stimuli arranged from low to high. Used in the systematic desensitization of a phobia.
hypermnesia, superior memory.
hypnoanalysis, treatment procedures involving the integration of psychoanalysis and hypnosis.
hypnoanesthesia, an anesthesia hypnotically created.
hypnodrama, a treatment technique involving acting procedures under hypnosis.
humanism, devotion to human welfare. Interest in, or concern for, man.
id, a psychoanalytic term used to refer to the hypothesized mental region that includes primitive, instinctual, and unsocialized tendencies of an individual. Forces in this area are presumed to be governed by the pleasure principle.
identification, the psychological process whereby one behaves and experiences himself similar to another individual whom he has copied. The process of investing the replicated image of another with ego cathexis.
identofact, the product of the process of identification. An ego-cathected replica of another individual or of a part "borrowed" from him.
implosive therapy, a behavioral therapy involving the violent release of emotion. Similar to flooding and abreaction.
imprinting, a process whereby an early experience acquires a very determining effect on the later behavior of an individual. This is apparently due to the exact time in the development of the individual at which it happens.
induction, techniques for initiating an hypnotic state.
insight, a global understanding involving both cognition and affect, thought and feeling. In psychoanalytic theory, insights are thought to be a prerequisite to personality reorganization.
integration, the bringing together of two or more ele-

ments so that they are consonant or can interact constructively with each other.

intellectualization, an incomplete insight that may involve some cognitive understanding without deep feeling and genuine conviction.

interpersonal relationships, relationships between two or more people.

intrapersonal relationships, relationships between two or more psychological entities (such as different ego states) within a single individual.

introject, the replica of another individual or part of an individual that has been internalized and invested with object cathexis. An internal object.

introspection, the observation of one's own inner experiences.

latent homosexuality, a condition in which an individual has tendencies toward homosexuality or homosexual impulses that are not conscious and not acted upon.

libido, a term used by Freud for a sexual energy; also a life energy.

life style, a term used by Adler to represent the typical manner of behavior and defenses employed by a given individual.

metastasize, the formation of new centers of disease that have been transferred from one organ to another not directly connected with it; as for example, the spreading of a cancer throughout the body.

Mitwelt, the experiential world of relationship between people. (See also **Eigenwelt, Umwelt.**)

modeling, imitating; the copying by one individual of the behavior of another.

mortido, a death energy. A repelling energy that tends to break complex structures down into their simple elements. In this book, a directionality of either ego or object energies.

multiple personality. See **dissociated personality.**
muscular armor, that part of the character armor described by Wilhelm Reich which is frozen into characteristic postures; the organic component of character armor.
narcissism, self-love.
narcosis, a state of profound unconsciousness produced by a drug.
neo-dissociation theory, a new and revitalized form of dissociation theory proposed by Ernest Hilgard.
neurosis, a psychological disturbance without an organic cause manifested by painful or incapacitating symptoms or maladaptive behavior. Less severe than a psychosis.
neurotic, an individual who has a neurosis; symptoms or behaviors not organically caused.
neutrino, a very small and uncharged particle. It is without mass.
nirvana, the Buddhist goal of life in which all desires are extinguished and individuality is merged with the universe.
nondirective therapy, an early form of client-centered therapy proposed by Carl Rogers in which the counselor's role is limited to reflection of the client's feeling.
object, something external to the self. A psychological element inside an individual that is not cathected with ego energy is experienced as an object.
object cathexis, a nonliving "it" energy which activates psychological processes that are not egotized. Term has been used as the equivalent of "libido."
objective, a therapist response (scored O in the Therapeutic Self Rating System) which is nonresonant; a psychological item outside the self; an observation of an external reality not distorted by self feelings.
obsession, a recurring thought that apparently cannot be eliminated by conscious choice.

ontogenetic, the biological development of a single individual as distinguished from phylogenetic, the biological development of an entire race (phylum).
operant, a response whose future occurrence is influenced by its consequences.
paradigm, a model or pattern that exhibits all the variable forms of something.
paranoid, a type of behavior characterized by extreme and unrealistic suspiciousness.
paraprofessional, an individual trained to use professional techniques in a limited way and usually under the supervision of a fully-trained professional, such as a medical technician or licensed practical nurse.
pharmacological, pertaining to drugs.
phenomenological, pertaining to a view that behavior is determined by experience rather than by external, objective reality.
phylogenetic, the biological development of an entire race (phylum).
porphyria or porphuria, a disease of the metabolism.
primal scream, an abreactive-type therapy which holds that maladjustment is based on unrelieved mental pain stemming from the earliest life experiences. These need to be "screamed out."
primary awareness, the awareness of existence that may inhere in "self energy" independent of any impact by objects.
programmed learning, a sequence of learning events arranged in order of presentation designed to maximize retention.
projection, a defense mechanism involving imputing to others unacceptable aspects of one's own self.
projective technique, a psychological testing procedure in which responses to unstructured stimuli (such as ink blots) are analyzed to evaluate personality functioning.

pseudophone, an instrument in which the sound collected by a trumpet over one ear is carried to the other. Thus, the right ear hears the sounds that normally enter the left ear and vice versa.
psychedelic, referring to drugs that influence or interfere with normal perception.
psychodynamics, the study of psychological processes (normally unconscious) that intervene between stimulus and behavior. The study of defense mechanisms.
psychopathology, the study of psychological maladjustment or mental illness.
psychophysics, the study of the relation between the physical characteristics of a stimulus and the magnitude of the sensation produced by it.
psychosis, a severe mental illness characterized by delusions, hallucinations, and/or such inappropriate affects as mania or depression. Psychotics are usually considered not responsible for their behavior. "Insanity" is the legal equivalent term.
psychosomatic, bodily conditions that are the product of both psychological and physiological factors. Many illnesses, such as peptic ulcer, migraine headaches, and arthritis are often psychosomatic.
psychotherapy, treatment by psychological (re-educative) procedures.
psychotic, pertaining to a psychosis.
quantum physics or quantum mechanics, the branch of mathematical physics dealing with the motion of such subatomic particles as electrons, protons, and neutrons.
quid pro quo, something given in exchange for something else. A *quid pro quo* reciprocity exists between two individuals, for example, when a friendly gesture by one evokes a similar friendly gesture by the other.
reliability, the consistency of a test wherein two independent measures of the same phenomenon by the test yields two equal or comparable scores.

reality therapy, a form of therapy, devised by William Glasser, which holds that maladjustment is caused by failure to confront reality. Treatment involves making the individual face up to reality and to his responsibilities.
reflex, a response automatically evoked by a certain stimulus. Both the stimulus and the response are usually quite specific. The reaction is not generally under conscious control.
regression, the return by an individual to earlier forms of behavior that were characteristic of him at a younger age.
reinforcement, the influencing of a behavior by applying to it something that will increase its likelihood of occurring (often a reward) or not occurring (a punishment); more commonly referring to a reward.
relativity, theory of, a theory formulated by Albert Einstein that asserts the equivalence of mass and energy and relates the size of mass to its velocity in motion.
repression, the unconscious effortful exclusion by an individual of material from awareness that is unacceptable or dissonant to his self concept.
resonance, that inner experience within the therapist during which he co-experiences, hence, co-feels, co-suffers, co-enjoys, and co-understands with his patient though in mini-form.
Rogerian technique, the techniques of client-centered therapy, named after Carl Rogers.
Rorschach, a projective personality test using responses to ink blots to evaluate functioning.
satori, a state of consciousness characterized by total enlightenment and infinite peace. It is the spiritual goal of Zen Buddhism and is to be attained by meditation.
schedule of reinforcement, a systematic procedure for rewarding or punishing behaviors in order to influence them in a prescribed way.
schizoid, a condition in which the individual appears

withdrawn and is not very responsive to interpersonal relationships or other external stimuli.

schizophrenia, a type of psychosis characterized by withdrawnness, delusions, and hallucinations.

scotoma, analytic. See **analytic scotoma.**

screen memory, a more pleasant memory retained to cover up an underlying, repressed, and painful experience.

shadow, a Jungian concept. That antisocial aspect of self that has been repressed in the interest of adjusting to others. It is characterized by anger, brooding, aggressiveness, and at times self-destructiveness. It may appear symbolically to an individual during nightmare-type dreams.

statistical significance, the probability that an observed measure could not have occurred by chance alone.

stimulus, something whose impingement on an organism initiates a response from that organism.

stimulus generalization, a process whereby a response is set off by a secondary stimulus that is similar to the original stimulus or condition that evoked it.

strokes, a term used in transactional analysis referring to compliments, rewards, or other positive reinforcements which are given to an individual and that are pleasant to him.

structuralism, a system of psychology that attempted to analyze mental states or contents into their simplest components by introspection.

subjective, referring to phenomena that are egotized, that is, part of the self as opposed to "objective," nonself phenomena.

sublimation, the indirect expression of emotional needs in socially acceptable ways when their direct expression would elicit disapproval.

superego, that region of mental life, according to Freud, which is governed by the duty principle. It represents the attitudes of responsibility that have been built in an individual by authority figures, such as parents, during his early life.

systematic desensitization, a technique of behavior therapy, devised by Joseph Wolpe for the treatment of phobias. It involves submitting the patient to the feared stimuli, but in weakened form at first and gradually increasing their strength until he can cope with them in full intensity.

terminal, a term used by physicians to a disease that will result only in death to the person suffering from it.

Thanatos, the term used by some of Freud's followers to refer to the death instinct. In this book it is used to refer to a principle, activated by mortido, that differentiates structures from the complex back to their simple origins, hence death.

third ear, a term used by Theoder Reik to refer to a level of sensitivity toward unconscious processes within a patient by a therapist acutely attuned to the slightest nuances of expression by which they are revealed.

transactional analysis, a theory of personality structure and accompanying system of therapy, first formulated by Erik Berne. It hypothesizes that behavior, both constructive and destructive, stem from the "transactions" between three basic ego states: child, parent, and adult.

transference, the psychological mechanism manifested when an individual reacts toward contemporary figures as if they were earlier significant people in his life, such as parents. This psychoanalytic term is similar to the behavioristic term, "stimulus generalization."

Umwelt, the individual's experience of the environmental world around him. (See also **Eigenwelt** and **Mitwelt.**)

unconditional positive regard, a basic condition for therapy according to Carl Rogers. This involves an attitude of total caring devoid of criticism.

unconscious, processes that are below the threshold of awareness.

validity, the characteristic of a test that determines the extent to which it actually measures that which it purports to measure.

variance, a measure of the extent to which individual scores in a set differ from each other.

working through, a psychoanalytic term referring to the process of rediscovery, repetition, and integration of material that has been lifted from repression.

Zen Buddhism, a school of Buddhism that teaches self-discipline, deep meditation, and the attainment of enlightenment by direct intuitive insight.

Author Index

Subject Index